2008 CHILDREN'S WRITER'S & ILLUSTRATOR'S MARKET KEY TO SYMBOLS

 market new to this edition

 Canadian market

 listing outside of the U.S. and Canada

 publisher producing educational material

 online opportunity

 book packager/producer

 publisher accepts agented submissions only

 award-winning publisher

ms, mss manuscript(s)

SCBWI Society of Children's Book Writers and Illustrators

SAE self-addressed envelope

SASE self-addressed, stamped envelope

IRC International Reply Coupon

b&w black & white

(For definitions of unfamiliar words and expressions relating to writing, illustration and publishing, see the Glossary.)

TEAR ALONG PERFORATION

CWIM08

2008 Children's Writer's & Illustrator's Market

Alice Pope, Editor

WRITER'S DIGEST BOOKS
CINCINNATI, OH

Editorial Director, Writer's Digest Books: Jane Friedman
Managing Editor, Writer's Digest Market Books: Alice Pope

Children's Writer's & Illustrator's Market Web page: wwww.cwim.com
Writer's Market Web site: www.writersmarket.com
Writer's Digest Web site: www.writersdigest.com
F+W Publications Bookstore: http://fwbookstore.com

Distributed in Canada by Fraser Direct
100 Armstrong Ave.
Georgetown, ON, Canada L7G 5S4
Tel: (905) 877-4411

Distributed in the U.K. and Europe by David & Charles
Brunel House, Newton Abbot, Devon, TQ12 4PU, England
Tel: (+44) 1626 323200, Fax: (+44) 1626 323319
E-mail: postmaster@davidandcharles.co.uk

Distributed in Australia by Capricorn Link
P.O. Box 704, Windsor, NSW 2756, Australia
Tel: (02) 4577-3555

Distributed in New Zealand by David Bateman Ltd.
P.O. Box 100-242, N.S.M.C., Auckland 1330, New Zealand
Tel: (09) 415-7664, Fax: (09) 415-8892

Distributed in South Africa by Real Books
P.O. Box 1040, Auckland Park 2006, Johannesburg, South Africa
Tel: (011) 837-0643, Fax: (011) 837-0645
E-mail: realbook@global.co.za

ISSN: 0897-9790
ISBN-13: 978-1-58297-504-7
ISBN-10: 1-58297-504-3

Cover design and illustration by Josh Roflow
Interior design by Clare Finney
Production coordinated by Kristen Heller and Greg Nock

Attention Booksellers: This is an annual directory of F+W Publications. Return deadline for this edition is December 31, 2008.

F+W PUBLICATIONS, INC.

Contents

© Laurent Linn. Reprinted with permission.

art by MATT PHELAN

The New

© 2006 Matt Phelan

THE MARKETS

RESOURCES

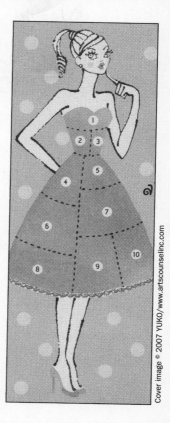

INDEXES

From the Editor

The other day I was scrounging around in my basement getting ready for a garage sale when I unearthed a box of journals from my tween/teen years. They are four fat spiral notebooks entitled "My Journal of Younger & Adolescent Days." (Title credit goes to my best friend Lisa. Our journals shared the same name and we always shared them with each other.)

I was almost afraid to open them, but once I cracked the first one, they were hard to put down, these daily chronicles of the angsty moments of my youth. Most of my entries fit into one of four categories: Who I Saw at the Mall, What I Ate at the Mall, No One Understands Me, and No One Is Ever Going to Love Me. (Not sure how to categorize my tremendously bad poem about my first hangover.)

People journal for all sorts of reasons. For me, MJYAD was a 99¢ therapist, someone to talk to who never judged me. Writers use journals to jot down ideas or for freewriting or as means to write every day.

For author/illustrator Ruth McNally Barshaw, her sketch journal is like a part of her, an ever-present accessory. It's also the means by which she got her first book contract for *Ellie McDoodle: Have Pen, Will Travel* (Bloomsbury). Ruth posted sketch journal entries on her Web site, which created buzz and caught the attention of her agent. (Visit Ruth's site at www.ruthexpress.com and read more in First Books on page 119.)

Ruth's story serves as a great lesson in getting yourself out there. Today aspiring authors can't expect to pick an editor's name out of *Children's Writer's & Illustrator's Market*, get discovered from the slush pile, and become a bestseller. As illustrator Matt Phalen advises in his Insider Report on page 150: "You never know what's going to work, so try everything." (For further inspiration, see the Insider Reports with Deborah Ruddell, page 310, and Jo Knowles, page 352).

Ruth's story also underscores that golden rule of writing: *write what you know*. After deciding to create a sketchbook novel, it was an essay that Ruth had written about camping in Michigan as a kid that became the basis for her book and helped her really dig into the process. "My agent and editor have both declared that I am Ellie," she says.

Ruth continues journaling, but these days I do not (My Journal of Almost 40 Chasing a Toddler & Doing Laundry Days, anyone?). But (yeah!) I have a blog (http://cwim.blogspot.com)—my outlet to share my not-quite-daily news and musings on children's books and publishing; my space to write what I know; my journal that someone besides Lisa gets to read (with only an occasional mention of goings-on at the mall).

Alice Pope
cwim@fwpubs.com
http://cwim.blogspot.com
www.myspace.com/alice_cwim

How to Use This Book

As a writer, illustrator, or photographer first picking up *Children's Writer's & Illustrator's Market*, you may not know quite how to start using the book. Your impulse may be to flip through the book and quickly make a mailing list, then submit to everyone in hopes that someone will take interest in your work. Well, there's more to it. Finding the right market takes time and research. The more you know about a company that interests you, the better chance you have of getting work accepted.

We've made your job a little easier by putting a wealth of information at your fingertips. Besides providing listings, this directory includes a number of tools to help you determine which markets are the best ones for your work. By using these tools, as well as researching on your own, you raise your odds of being published.

USING THE INDEXES

This book lists hundreds of potential buyers of freelance material. To learn which companies want the type of material you're interested in submitting, start with the indexes.

Names Index

This index lists book and magazine editors and art directors as well as agents and art reps, indicating the companies they work for. Use this index to find company and contact information for individual publishing professionals.

Age-Level Index

Age groups are broken down into these categories in the Age-Level Index:

- **Picture books or picture-oriented material** are written and illustrated for preschoolers to 8-year-olds.
- **Young readers** are for 5- to 8-year-olds.
- **Middle readers** are for 9- to 11-year-olds.
- **Young adults** is for ages 12 and up.

Age breakdowns may vary slightly from publisher to publisher, but using them as general guidelines will help you target appropriate markets. For example, if you've written an article about trends in teen fashion, check the Magazines Age-Level Index under the Young Adult subheading. Using this list, you'll quickly find the listings for young adult magazines.

Subject Index

But let's narrow the search further. Take your list of young adult magazines, turn to the Subject Index, and find the Fashion subheading. Then highlight the names that appear on

Find a handy pull-out bookmark, a quick reference to the icons used in this book, right inside the front cover.

both lists (Young Adult and Fashion). Now you have a smaller list of all the magazines that would be interested in your teen fashion article. Read through those listings and decide which ones sound best for your work.

Illustrators and photographers can use the Subject Index as well. If you specialize in painting animals, for instance, consider sending samples to book and magazine publishers listed under Animals and, perhaps, Nature/Environment. Since illustrators can simply send general examples of their style to art directors to keep on file, the indexes may be more helpful to artists sending manuscripts/illustration packages who need to search for a specific subject. Always read the listings for the potential markets to see the type of work art directors prefer and what type of samples they'll keep on file, and obtain art or photo guidelines if they're available through the mail or online.

Photography Index

In this index you'll find lists of book and magazine publishers that buy photos from freelancers. Refer to the list and read the listings for companies' specific photography needs. Obtain photo guidelines if they're offered through the mail or online.

USING THE LISTINGS

Many listings begin with one or more symbols. Refer to the inside covers of the book for quick reference and find a handy pull-out bookmark (shown at left) right inside the front cover.

Many listings indicate whether submission guidelines are available. If a publisher you're interested in offers guidelines, get them and read them. The same is true with catalogs. Sending for and reading catalogs or browsing them online gives you a better idea of whether your work would fit in with the books a publisher produces. (You should also look at a few of the books in the catalog at a library or bookstore to get a feel for the publisher's material.)

Especially for artists & photographers

Along with information for writers, listings provide information for illustrators and photographers. Illustrators will find numerous markets that maintain files of samples for possible future assignments. If you're both a writer and an illustrator, look for markets that accept manuscript/illustration packages and read the information offered under the **Illustration** subhead within the listings.

If you're a photographer, after consulting the Photography Index, read the information under the **Photography** subhead within listings to see what format buyers prefer. For example, some want 35mm color transparencies, others want black and white prints. Note the type of photos a buyer wants to purchase and the procedures for submitting. It's not uncommon for a market to want a résumé and promotional literature, as well as tearsheets from previous work. Listings also note whether model releases and/or captions are required.

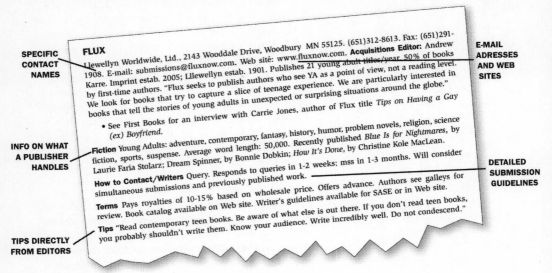

SPECIFIC CONTACT NAMES

E-MAIL ADDRESSES AND WEB SITES

INFO ON WHAT A PUBLISHER HANDLES

DETAILED SUBMISSION GUIDELINES

TIPS DIRECTLY FROM EDITORS

FLUX
Llewellyn Worldwide, Ltd., 2143 Wooddale Drive, Woodbury MN 55125. (651)312-8613. Fax: (651)291-1908. E-mail: submissions@fluxnow.com. Web site: www.fluxnow.com. **Acquisitions Editor:** Andrew Karre. Imprint estab. 2005; Llewellyn estab. 1901. Publishes 21 young adult titles/year. 50% of books by first-time authors. "Flux seeks to publish authors who see YA as a point of view, not a reading level. We look for books that try to capture a slice of teenage experience. We are particularly interested in books that tell the stories of young adults in unexpected or surprising situations around the globe."
  • See First Books for an interview with Carrie Jones, author of Flux title *Tips on Having a Gay (ex) Boyfriend.*
Fiction Young Adults: adventure, contemporary, fantasy, history, humor, problem novels, religion, science fiction, sports, suspense. Average word length: 50,000. Recently published *Blue Is for Nightmares*, by Laurie Faria Stolarz; *Dream Spinner*, by Bonnie Dobkin; *How It's Done*, by Christine Kole MacLean.
How to Contact/Writers Query. Responds to queries in 1-2 weeks; mss in 1-3 months. Will consider simultaneous submissions and previously published work.
Terms Pays royalties of 10-15% based on wholesale price. Offers advance. Authors see galleys for review. Book catalog available on Web site. Writer's guidelines available for SASE or in Web site.
Tips "Read contemporary teen books. Be aware of what else is out there. If you don't read teen books, you probably shouldn't write them. Know your audience. Write incredibly well. Do not condescend."

Especially for young writers

If you're a parent, teacher, or student, you may be interested in Young Writer's & Illustrator's Markets. The listings in this section encourage submissions from young writers and artists. Some may require a written statement from a teacher or parent noting the work is original. Also watch for age limits.

Young people should also check Contests & Awards for contests that accept work by young writers and artists. Some of the contests listed are especially for students; others accept both student and adult work. These listings contain the phrase **open to students** in bold. Some listings in Clubs & Organizations and Conferences & Workshops may also be of interest to students. Organizations and conferences which are open to or are especially for students also include **open to students**.

Quick Tips for Writers & Illustrators

I f you're new to the world of children's publishing, buying *Children's Writer's & Illustrator's Market* may have been one of the first steps in your journey to publication. What follows is a list of suggestions and resources that can help make that journey a smooth and swift one:

1. Make the most of *Children's Writer's & Illustrator's Market*. Be sure to read How to Use This Book on page 2 for tips on reading the listings and using the indexes. Also be sure to take advantage of the articles and interviews in the book. The insights of the authors, illustrators, editors, and agents we've interviewed will inform and inspire you.

2. Join the Society of Children's Books Writers and Illustrators. SCBWI, more than 19,000 members strong, is an organization for both beginners and professionals interested in writing and illustrating for children. They offer members a slew of information and support through publications, a Web site, and a host of Regional Advisors overseeing chapters in almost every state in the U.S. and in a growing number of locations around the globe (including France, Canada, Japan, and Australia). SCBWI puts on a number of conferences, workshops, and events on the regional and national levels (many listed in the Conferences & Workshops section of this book). For more information, contact SCBWI, 8271 Beverly Blvd., Los Angeles CA 90048, (323)782-1010, or visit their Web site: www.scbwi.org.

3. Read newsletters. Newsletters, such as *Children's Book Insider*, *Children's Writer*, and the *SCBWI Bulletin*, offer updates and new information about publishers on a timely basis and are relatively inexpensive. Many local chapters of SCBWI offer regional newsletters as well. (See Helpful Books & Publications on page 364 for contact information on the newsletters listed above and others. For information on regional SCBWI newsletters, visit www.scbwi.org and click on "Publications.")

4. Read trade and review publications. Magazines like *Publishers Weekly* (which offers two special issues each year devoted to children's publishing and is available on newsstands), *The Horn Book*, and *Booklinks* offer news, articles, reviews of newly-published titles, and ads featuring upcoming and current releases. Referring to them will help you get a feel for what's happening in children's publishing.

5. Read guidelines. Most publishers and magazines offer writer's and artist's guidelines that provide detailed information on needs and submission requirements, and some magazines offer theme lists for upcoming issues. Many publishers and magazines state the availability of guidelines within their listings. Send a self-addressed, stamped envelope (SASE) to publishers who offer guidelines. You'll often find submission information on publishers' and magazines' Web sites.

6. Look at publishers' catalogs. Perusing publishers' catalogs can give you a feel for their line of books and help you decide where your work might fit in. If catalogs are available (often stated within listings), send for them with a SASE. Visit publishers' Web sites, which often contain their full catalogs. You can also ask librarians to look at catalogs they have on hand. You can even search Amazon.com by publisher and year. (Click on "book search" then "publisher, date" and plug in, for example, "Lee & Low" under "publisher" and "2006" under year. You'll get a list of Lee & Low titles published in 2006, which you can peruse.)

7. Visit bookstores. It's not only informative to spend time in bookstores—it's fun, too! Frequently visit the children's section of your local bookstore (whether a chain or an independent) to see the latest from a variety of publishers and the most current issues of children's magazines. Look for books in the genre you're writing or with illustrations similar in style to yours, and spend some time studying them. It's also wise to get to know your local booksellers; they can tell you what's new in the store and provide insight into what kids and adults are buying.

8. Read, read, read! While you're at that bookstore, pick up a few things, or keep a list of the books that interest you and check them out of your library. Read and study the latest releases, the award winners, and the classics. You'll learn from other writers, get ideas, and get a feel for what's being published. Think about what works and doesn't work in a story. Pay attention to how plots are constructed and how characters are developed or the rhythm and pacing of picture book text. It's certainly enjoyable research!

9. Take advantage of Internet resources. There are innumerable sources of information available on the Internet about writing for children (and anything else you could possibly think of). It's also a great resource for getting (and staying) in touch with other writers and illustrators through listservs, blogs, social networking sites and e-mail, and it can serve as a vehicle for self-promotion. (Visit some authors' and illustrators' sites for ideas. See Useful Online Resources on page 367 for a list of Web sites.)

10. Consider attending a conference. If time and finances allow, attending a conference is a great way to meet peers and network with professionals in the field of children's publishing. As mentioned above, SCBWI offers conferences in various locations year round. (See www.scbwi.org and click on "Events" for a full conference calendar.) General writers' conferences often offer specialized sessions just for those interested in children's writing. Many conferences offer optional manuscript and portfolio critiques as well, giving you a chance for feedback from seasoned professionals. See the Conferences & Awards section for information on SCBWI and other conferences. The section features a Conferences & Workshops Calendar to help you plan your travel.

11. Network, network, network! Don't work in a vacuum. You can meet other writers and illustrators through a number of the things listed above—SCBWI, conferences, online. Attend local meetings for writers and illustrators whenever you can. Befriend other writers in your area (SCBWI offers members a roster broken down by state)—share guidelines, share subscriptions, be conference buddies and roommates, join a critique group or writing group, exchange information, and offer support. Get online—sign on to listservs, post on message boards and blogs, visit social networking sites and chatrooms. (The Institute of Children's Literature offers regularly scheduled live chats and open forums. Visit www.institutechildren slit.com and click on Scheduled Events. Also, visit author Verla Kay's Web site, www.verlaka y.com, for information on workshops. See Useful Online Resources on page 367 for more information.) Exchange addresses, phone numbers, and e-mail addresses with writers or illustrators you meet at events. And at conferences, don't be afraid to talk to people, ask strangers to join you for lunch, approach speakers and introduce yourself, or chat in elevators and hallways.

12. Perfect your craft and don't submit until your work is its best. It's often been said that a writer should try to write every day. Great manuscripts don't happen overnight;

there's time, research, and revision involved. As you visit bookstores and study what others have written and illustrated, really step back and look at your own work and ask yourself—honestly—*How does my work measure up? Is it ready for editors or art directors to see?* If it's not, keep working. Join a critique group or get a professional manuscript or portfolio critique.

13. Be patient, learn from rejection, and don't give up! Thousands of manuscripts land on editors' desks; thousands of illustration samples line art directors' file drawers. There are so many factors that come into play when evaluating submissions. Keep in mind that you might not hear back from publishers promptly. Persistence and patience are important qualities in writers and illustrators working toward publication. Keep at it—it will come. It can take a while, but when you get that first book contract or first assignment, you'll know it was worth the wait. (For proof, read First Books on page 119.)

Before Your First Sale

If you're just beginning to pursue your career as a children's book writer or illustrator, it's important to learn the proper procedures, formats, and protocol for the publishing industry. This article outlines the basics you need to know before you head to the post office with your submissions.

FINDING THE BEST MARKETS FOR YOUR WORK

Researching publishers thoroughly is a basic element of submitting your work successfully. Editors and art directors hate to receive inappropriate submissions; handling them wastes a lot of their time, not to mention your time and money, and they are the main reason some publishers have chosen not to accept material over the transom. By randomly sending out material without knowing a company's needs, you're sure to meet with rejection.

If you're interested in submitting to a particular magazine, write to request a sample copy or see if it's available in your local library or bookstore. For a book publisher, obtain a book catalog and check a library or bookstore for titles produced by that publisher. Most publishers and magazines have Web sites that include catalogs or sample articles (Web sites are given within the listings). Studying such materials carefully will better acquaint you with a publisher's or magazine's writing, illustration, and photography styles and formats.

Most of the book publishers and magazines listed in this book offer some sort of writer's, artist's, or photographer's guidelines for a self-addressed, stamped envelope (SASE). Guidelines are also often found on publishers' Web sites. It's important to read and study guidelines before submitting work. You'll get a better understanding of what a particular publisher wants. You may even decide, after reading the submission guidelines, that your work isn't right for a company you considered.

SUBMITTING YOUR WORK

Throughout the listings, you'll read requests for particular elements to include when contacting markets. Here are explanations of some of these important submission components.

Queries, cover letters, & proposals

A query letter is a no-more-than-one-page, well-written piece meant to arouse an editor's interest in your work. Many query letters start with leads similar to those of actual manuscripts. In the rest of the letter, briefly outline the work you're proposing and include facts, anecdotes, interviews, or other pertinent information that give the editor a feel for the manuscript's premise—entice her to want to know more. End your letter with a straightforward request to write or submit the work, and include information on its approximate length, date it could be completed, and whether accompanying photos or artwork are available.

In a query letter, think about presenting your book as a publisher's catalog would present it. Read through a good catalog and examine how the publishers give enticing summaries of their books in a spare amount of words. It's also important that query letters give editors a taste of your writing style. For good advice and samples of queries, cover letters, and other correspondence, consult *Formatting & Submitting Your Manuscript*, Second Edition, by Cynthia Laufenberg and the editors of *Writer's Market* and *How to Write Attention-Grabbing Query & Cover Letters*, by John Wood (both Writer's Digest Books).

For More Info

• **Query letters for nonfiction.** Queries are usually required when submitting nonfiction material to a publisher. The goal of a nonfiction query is to convince the editor your idea is perfect for her readership and that you're qualified to do the job. Note any previous writing experience and include published samples to prove your credentials, especially samples related to the subject matter you're querying about.

• **Query letters for fiction.** More and more, queries are being requested for fiction manuscripts. For a fiction query, explain the story's plot, main characters, conflict, and resolution. Just as in nonfiction queries, make the editor eager to see more.

• **Cover letters for writers.** Some editors prefer to review complete manuscripts, especially for picture books or fiction. In such cases, the cover letter (which should be no longer than one page) serves as your introduction, establishes your credentials as a writer, and gives the editor an overview of the manuscript. If the editor asked for the manuscript because of a query, note this in your cover letter.

• **Cover letters for illustrators and photographers.** For an illustrator or photographer, the cover letter serves as an introduction to the art director and establishes professional credentials when submitting samples. Explain what services you can provide as well as what type of follow-up contact you plan to make, if any. Be sure to include the URL of your online portfolio if you have one.

• **Résumés.** Often writers, illustrators, and photographers are asked to submit résumés with cover letters and samples. They can be created in a variety of formats, from a single page listing information to color brochures featuring your work. Keep your résumé brief, and focus on your achievements, including your clients and the work you've done for them, as well as your educational background and any awards you've received. Do not use the same résumé you'd use for a typical job application.

• **Book proposals.** Throughout the listings in the Book Publishers section, publishers refer to submitting a synopsis, outline, and sample chapters. Depending on an editor's preference, some or all of these components, along with a cover letter, make up a book proposal.

A *synopsis* summarizes the book, covering the basic plot (including the ending). It should be easy to read and flow well.

An *outline* covers your book chapter by chapter and provides highlights of each. If you're developing an outline for fiction, include major characters, plots and subplots, and book length.

Sample chapters give a more comprehensive idea of your writing skill. Some editors may request the first two or three chapters to determine if she's interested in seeing the whole book.

Manuscript formats

When submitting a complete manuscript, follow some basic guidelines. In the upper-left corner of your title page, type your legal name (not pseudonym), address, and phone number. In the upper-right corner, type the approximate word count. All material in the upper corners should be single-spaced. Then type the title (centered) almost halfway down that page, the word ''by'' two spaces under that, and your name or pseudonym two spaces under ''by.''

The first page should also include the title (centered) one-third of the way down. Two spaces under that type ''by'' and your name or pseudonym. To begin the body of your manuscript, drop down two double spaces and indent five spaces for each new paragraph. There should be one-inch margins around all sides of a full typewritten page. (Manuscripts with wide margins are more readable and easier to edit.)

Set your computer to double-space for the manuscript body. From page two to the end of the manuscript, include your last name followed by a comma and the title (or key words of the title) in the upper-left corner. The page number should go in the top right corner. Drop down two double spaces to begin the body of each page. If you're submitting a novel, type each chapter title one-third of the way down the page. For more information on manuscript formats, read *Formatting & Submitting Your Manuscript*, by Cynthia Laufenberg and the editors of *Writer's Market* (Writer's Digest Books). SCBWI members and nonmembers can refer to their publication *From Keyboard to Printed Page: Facts You Need to Know*. Visit their Web site www.scbwi.org and click on "Publications."

For More Info

Picture book formats

The majority of editors prefer to see complete manuscripts for picture books. When typing the text of a picture book, don't indicate page breaks and don't type each page of text on a new sheet of paper. And unless you are an illustrator, don't worry about supplying art. Editors will find their own illustrators for picture books. Most of the time, a writer and an illustrator who work on the same book never meet or interact. The editor acts as a go-between and works with the writer and illustrator throughout the publishing process. *How to Write and Sell Children's Picture Books*, by Jean E. Karl (Writer's Digest Books), offers advice on preparing text and marketing your work.

If you're an illustrator who has written your own book, consider creating a dummy or storyboard containing both art and text, and then submit it along with your complete manuscript and sample pieces of final art (color photocopies or computer printouts—never originals). Publishers interested in picture books specify in their listings what should be submitted. For tips on creating a dummy, refer to *How to Write and Illustrate Children's Books and Get Them Published*, edited by Treld Pelkey Bicknell and Felicity Trotman (North Light Books), or Frieda Gates' book, *How to Write, Illustrate, and Design Children's Books* (Lloyd-Simone Publishing Company).

For More Info

Writers may also want to learn the art of dummy making to help them through their writing process with things like pacing, rhythm, and length. For a great explanation and helpful hints, see *You Can Write Children's Books*, by Tracey E. Dils (Writer's Digest Books).

Mailing submissions

Your main concern when packaging material is to be sure it arrives undamaged. If your manuscript is less than six pages, simply fold it in thirds and send it in a #10 (business-size) envelope. For a SASE, either fold another #10 envelope in thirds or insert a #9 (reply) envelope which fits in a #10 neatly without folding.

Another option is folding your manuscript in half in a 6×9 envelope, with a #9 or #10 SASE enclosed. For larger manuscripts, use a 9×12 envelope both for mailing the submission and as a SASE (which can be folded in half). Book manuscripts require sturdy packaging for mailing. Include a self-addressed mailing label and return postage.

If asked to send artwork and photographs, remember they require a bit more care in packaging to guarantee they arrive in good condition. Sandwich illustrations and photos between heavy cardboard that is slightly larger than the work. The cardboard can be secured by rubber bands or with tape. If you tape the cardboard together, check that the artwork doesn't stick to the tape. Be sure your name and address appear on the back of each piece of art or each photo in case the material becomes separated. For the packaging, use either a manila envelope, a foam-padded envelope, brown paper, or a mailer lined with plastic air bubbles. Bind nonjoined edges with reinforced mailing tape and affix a typed mailing label or clearly write your address.

Mailing material first class ensures quick delivery. Also, first-class mail is forwarded for one year if the addressee has moved, and it can be returned if undeliverable. If you're concerned about your original material safely reaching its destination, consider other mailing options, such as UPS or certified mail. If material needs to reach your editor or art director quickly, use overnight delivery services.

Remember, companies outside your own country can't use your country's postage when returning a manuscript to you. When mailing a submission to another country, include a self-addressed envelope and International Reply Coupons, or IRCs. (You'll see this term in many listings in the Canadian & International Book Publishers section.) Your postmaster can tell you, based on a package's weight, the correct number of IRCs to include to ensure its return.

If it's not necessary for an editor to return your work (such as with photocopies), don't include return postage. You may want to track the status of your submission by enclosing a postage-paid reply postcard with options for the editor to check, such as "Yes, I am interested," "I'll keep the material on file," or "No, the material is not appropriate for my needs at this time."

Some writers elect to include a deadline date. If you don't hear from the editor by the specified date, your manuscript is automatically withdrawn from consideration. Because many publishing houses and companies are overstocked with material, a minimum deadline should be at least three months.

Unless requested, it's never a good idea to use a company's fax number or e-mail address to send manuscript submissions. This can disrupt a company's internal business. Some publishers and magazines, however, may be open to e-mail submissions. Study the listings for specifics and visit publishers' and publications' Web sites for more information.

Keeping submission records

It's important to keep track of the material you submit. When recording each submission, include the date it was sent, the business and contact name, and any enclosures (such as samples of writing, artwork, or photography). You can create a record-keeping system of your own or look for record-keeping software in your area computer store.

Keep copies of articles or manuscripts you send together with related correspondence to make follow-up easier. When you sell rights to a manuscript, artwork, or photos, you can "close" your file on a particular submission by noting the date the material was accepted, what rights were purchased, the publication date, and payment.

Often writers, illustrators, and photographers fail to follow up on overdue responses. If you don't hear from a publisher within their stated response time, wait another month or so and follow up with a note asking about the status of your submission. Include the title or description, date sent, and a SASE for response. Ask the contact person when she anticipates making a decision. You may refresh the memory of a buyer who temporarily forgot about your submission. At the very least, you'll receive a definite "no" and free yourself to send the material to another publisher.

Simultaneous submissions

If you opt for simultaneous (also called "multiple") submissions—sending the same material to several publishers at the same time—be sure to inform each editor to whom you submit that your work is being considered elsewhere. Many editors are reluctant to receive simultaneous submissions but understand that for hopeful writers and illustrators, waiting several months for a response can be frustrating. In some cases, an editor may actually be more inclined to read your manuscript sooner if she knows it's being considered by another publisher. The

Society of Children's Book Writers and Illustrators cautions writers against simultaneous submissions. They recommend simultaneously submitting to publishers who state in their submission guidelines that they accept multiple submissions. In such cases, always specify in your cover letter that you've submitted to more than one editor.

It's especially important to keep track of simultaneous submissions, so if you get an offer on a manuscript sent to more than one publisher, you can instruct other publishers to withdraw your work from consideration.

AGENTS & ART REPS

Most children's writers, illustrators, and photographers, especially those just beginning, are confused about whether to enlist the services of an agent or representative. The decision is strictly one that each writer, illustrator, or photographer must make for herself. Some are confident with their own negotiation skills and believe acquiring an agent or rep is not in their best interest. Others feel uncomfortable in the business arena or are not willing to sacrifice valuable creative time for marketing.

About half of children's publishers accept unagented work, so it's possible to break into children's publishing without an agent. Some agents avoid working with children's books because traditionally low advances and trickling royalty payments over long periods of time make children's books less lucrative. Writers targeting magazine markets don't need the services of an agent. In fact, it's practically impossible to find an agent interested in marketing articles and short stories—there simply isn't enough financial incentive.

One benefit of having an agent, though, is it may speed up the process of getting your work reviewed, especially by publishers who don't accept unagented submissions. If an agent has a good reputation and submits your manuscript to an editor, that manuscript will likely bypass the first-read stage (which is generally done by editorial assistants and junior editors) and end up on the editor's desk sooner.

When agreeing to have a reputable agent represent you, remember that she should be familiar with the needs of the current market and evaluate your manuscript/artwork/photos accordingly. She should also determine the quality of your piece and whether it is saleable. When your manuscript sells, your agent should negotiate a favorable contract and clear up any questions you have about payments.

Keep in mind that however reputable the agent or rep is, she has limitations. Representation does not guarantee sale of your work. It just means an agent or rep sees potential in your writing, art, or photos. Though an agent or rep may offer criticism or advice on how to improve your work, she cannot make you a better writer, artist, or photographer.

Literary agents typically charge a 15 percent commission from the sale of writing; art and photo representatives usually charge a 25 to 30 percent commission. Such fees are taken from advances and royalty earnings. If your agent sells foreign rights to your work, she will deduct a higher percentage because she will most likely be dealing with an overseas agent with whom she must split the fee.

Be advised that not every agent is open to representing a writer, artist, or photographer who lacks an established track record. Just as when approaching a publisher, the manuscript, artwork, or photos and query or cover letter you submit to a potential agent must be attractive and professional looking. Your first impression must be as an organized, articulate person.

For listings of agents and reps, turn to the Agents & Art Reps section. For additional listings of art reps, consult *Artist's & Graphic Designer's Market*; for photo reps, see *Photographer's Market*; for more information and additional listings of agents see *Guide to Literary Agents* (all Writer's Digest Books).

Running Your Business

The Basics for Writers & Illustrators

A career in children's publishing involves more than just writing skills or artistic talent. Successful authors and illustrators must be able to hold their own in negotiations, keep records, understand contract language, grasp copyright law, pay taxes, and take care of a number of other business concerns. Although agents and reps, accountants and lawyers, and writers' organizations offer help in sorting out such business issues, it's wise to have a basic understanding of them going in. This article offers just that—basic information. For a more in-depth look at the subjects covered here, check your library or bookstore for books and magazines to help you. We also tell you how to get information on issues like taxes and copyright from the federal government.

CONTRACTS & NEGOTIATION

Before you see your work in print or begin working with an editor or art director on a project, there is negotiation. And whether negotiating a book contract, a magazine article assignment, or an illustration or photo assignment, there are a few things to keep in mind. First, if you find any clauses vague or confusing in a contract, get legal advice. The time and money invested in counseling up front could protect you from problems later. If you have an agent or rep, she will review any contract.

Sources for Contract Help

Writers organizations offer a wealth of information to members, including contract advice:

Society of Children's Book Writers and Illustrators members can find information in the SCBWI publication Answers to Some Questions About Contracts. Contact SCBWI at 8271 Beverly Blvd., Los Angeles CA 90048, (323)782-1010, or visit their Web site: www.scbwi.org.

The Authors Guild also offers contract tips. Visit their Web site, www.authorsguild.org. (Members of the guild can receive a 75-point contract review from the guild's legal staff.) See the Web site for membership information and application form, or contact The Authors Guild at 31 E. 28th St., 10th Floor, New York NY 10016, (212)563-5904. Fax: (212)564-5363. E-mail: staff@authorsguild.org. Web site: www.authorsguild.org.

A contract is an agreement between two or more parties that specifies the fees to be paid, services rendered, deadlines, rights purchased, and for artists and photographers, whether original work is returned. Most companies have standard contracts for writers, illustrators, and photographers. The specifics (such as royalty rates, advances, delivery dates, etc.) are typed in after negotiations.

Though it's okay to conduct negotiations over the phone, get a written contract once both parties have agreed on terms. Never depend on oral stipulations; written contracts protect both parties from misunderstandings. Watch for clauses that may not be in your best interest, such as "work-for-hire." When you do work-for-hire, you give up all rights to your creations.

When negotiating a book deal, find out whether your contract contains an option clause. This clause requires the author to give the publisher a first look at her next work before offering it to other publishers. Though it's editorial etiquette to give the publisher the first chance at publishing your next work, be wary of statements in the contract that could trap you. Don't allow the publisher to consider the next project for more than 30 days and be specific about what type of work should actually be considered "next work." (For example, if the book under contract is a young adult novel, specify that the publisher will receive an exclusive look at only your next young adult novel.)

For More Info

(For more information about SCBWI, The Authors Guild, and other organizations, turn to the Clubs & Organizations section and read the listings for the organizations that interest you.)

Book publishers' payment methods

Book publishers pay authors and artists in royalties, a percentage of either the wholesale or retail price of each book sold. From large publishing houses, the author usually receives an advance issued against future royalties before the book is published. Half of the advance amount is issued upon signing the book contract; the other half is issued when the book is finished. For illustrations, one-third of the advance should be collected upon signing the contract; one-third upon delivery of sketches; and one-third upon delivery of finished art.

After your book has sold enough copies to earn back your advance, you'll start to get royalty checks. Some publishers hold a reserve against returns, which means a percentage of royalties is held back in case books are returned from bookstores. If you have a reserve clause in your contract, find out the exact percentage of total sales that will be withheld and the time period the publisher will hold this money. You should be reimbursed this amount after a reasonable time period, such as a year. Royalty percentages vary with each publisher, but there are standard ranges.

Book publishers' rates

According to figures from the Society of Children's Book Writers and Illustrators, first-time picture book authors can expect advances of $2,000-3,000; first-time picture book illustrators' advances range from $5,000-7,000; text and illustration packages for first-timers can score $6,000-8,000. Rates go up for subsequent books: $3,500-5,000 for picture book text; $7,000-10,000 for picture book illustration; $8,000-10,000 for text and illustration. Experienced authors can expect higher advances. Royalties for picture books are generally about five percent (split between the author and illustrator) but can go as high as ten percent. Those who both write and illustrate a book, of course, receive the full royalty.

Advances for hardcover novels and nonfiction can fetch authors advances of $4,000-6,000 and 10 percent royalties; paperbacks bring in slightly lower advances of $3,000-5,000 and royalties of 6-8 percent.

As you might expect, advance and royalty figures vary from house to house and are affected by the time of year, the state of the economy, and other factors. Some smaller houses may not even pay royalties, just flat fees. Educational houses may not offer advances or offer smaller amounts. Religious publishers tend to offer smaller advances than trade publishers. First-time writers and illustrators generally start on the low end of the scale, while established and high-profile writers are paid more. For more information SCBWI members can request or download SCBWI publication "Answer to Some Questions About Contracts." (Visit www.scbwi.org.)

Pay rates for magazines

For writers, fee structures for magazines are based on a per-word rate or range for a specific article length. Artists and photographers have a few more variables to contend with before contracting their services.

Payment for illustrations and photos can be set by such factors as whether the piece(s) will be black and white or four-color, how many are to be purchased, where the work appears (cover or inside), circulation, and the artist's or photographer's prior experience.

Remaindering

When a book goes out of print, a publisher will sell any existing copies to a wholesaler who, in turn, sells the copies to stores at a discount. When the books are "remaindered" to a wholesaler, they are usually sold at a price just above the cost of printing. When negotiating a contract with a publisher, you may want to discuss the possibility of purchasing the remaindered copies before they are sold to a wholesaler, then you can market the copies you purchased and still make a profit.

KNOW YOUR RIGHTS

A copyright is a form of protection provided to creators of original works, published or unpublished. In general, copyright protection ensures the writer, illustrator, or photographer the power to decide how her work is used and allows her to receive payment for each use.

Essentially, copyright also encourages the creation of new works by guaranteeing the creator power to sell rights to the work in the marketplace. The copyright holder can print, reprint, or copy her work; sell or distribute copies of her work; or prepare derivative works such as plays, collages, or recordings. The Copyright Law is designed to protect work (created on or after January 1, 1978) for her lifetime plus 70 years.

If you collaborate with someone else on a written or artistic project, the copyright will last for the lifetime of the last survivor plus 70 years. The creators' heirs may hold a copyright for an additional 70 years. After that, the work becomes public domain. Works created anonymously or under a pseudonym are protected for 120 years, or 95 years after publication. Under work-for-hire agreements, you relinquish your copyright to your "employer."

Copyright notice & registration

Some feel a copyright notice should be included on all work, registered or not. Others feel it is not necessary and a copyright notice will only confuse publishers about whether the material is registered (acquiring rights to previously registered material is a more complicated process).

Although it's not necessary to include a copyright notice on unregistered work, if you don't feel your work is safe without the notice, it is your right to include one. Including a copyright notice—© (year of work, your name)—should help safeguard against plagiarism.

Registration is a legal formality intended to make copyright public record, and it can help you win more money in a court case. By registering work within three months of publication or before an infringement occurs, you are eligible to collect statutory damages and attorney's fees. If you register later than three months after publication, you will qualify only for actual damages and profits.

Ideas and concepts are not copyrightable, only expressions of those ideas and concepts. A character type or basic plot outline, for example, is not subject to a copyright infringement lawsuit. Also, titles, names, short phrases or slogans, and lists of contents are not subject to copyright protection, though titles and names may be protected through the Trademark Office.

You can register a group of articles, illustrations, or photos if it meets these criteria:

- the group is assembled in order, such as in a notebook
- the works bear a single title, such as "Works by (your name)"
- it is the work of one writer, artist, or photographer
- the material is the subject of a single claim to copyright

It's a publisher's responsibility to register your book for copyright. If you've previously registered the same material, you must inform your editor and supply the previous copyright information, otherwise, the publisher can't register the book in its published form.

For More Info

For more information about the proper way to register works and to order the correct forms, contact the U.S. Copyright Office, (202)707-3000. The forms available are TX for writing (books, articles, etc.); VA for pictures (photographs, illustrations); and PA for plays and music. For information about how to use the copyright forms, request a copy of Circular I on Copyright Basics. All of the forms and circulars are free. Send the completed registration form along with the stated fee and a copy of the work to the Copyright Office.

For specific answers to questions about copyright (but not legal advice), call the Copyright Public Information Office at (202)707-3000 weekdays between 8:30 a.m. and 5 p.m. EST. Forms can also be downloaded from the Library of Congress Web site: www.copyright.gov. The site also includes a list of frequently asked questions, tips on filling out forms, general copyright information, and links to other sites related to copyright issues. For members of SCBWI, information about copyrights and the law is available in their publication: Copyright Facts for Writers.

The rights publishers buy

The copyright law specifies that a writer, illustrator, or photographer generally sells one-time rights to her work unless she and the buyer agree otherwise in writing. Many publications will want more exclusive rights to your work than just one-time usage; some will even require you to sell all rights. Be sure you are monetarily compensated for the additional rights you relinquish. If you must give up all rights to a work, carefully consider the price you're being offered to determine whether you'll be compensated for the loss of other potential sales.

Writers who only give up limited rights to their work can then sell reprint rights to other publications, foreign rights to international publications, or even movie rights, should the opportunity arise. Artists and photographers can sell their work to other markets such as paper product companies who may use an image on a calendar, greeting card, or mug. Illustrators and photographers may even sell original work after it has been published. And there are a number of galleries throughout the U.S. that display and sell the original work of children's illustrators.

Rights acquired through the sale of a book manuscript are explained in each publisher's contract. Take time to read relevant clauses to be sure you understand what rights each contract is specifying before signing. Be sure your contract contains a clause allowing all rights to revert back to you in the event the publisher goes out of business. (You may even want to have the contract reviewed by an agent or an attorney specializing in publishing law.)

The following are the rights you'll most often sell to publishers, periodicals, and producers in the marketplace:

First rights. The buyer purchases the rights to use the work for the first time in any medium. All other rights remain with the creator. When material is excerpted from a soon-to-be-published book for use in a newspaper or periodical, first serial rights are also purchased.

One-time rights. The buyer has no guarantee that she is the first to use a piece. One-time permission to run written work, illustrations, or photos is acquired, then the rights revert back to the creator.

First North American serial rights. This is similar to first rights, except that companies who distribute both in the U.S. and Canada will stipulate these rights to ensure that another North American company won't come out with simultaneous usage of the same work.

Second serial (reprint) rights. In this case, newspapers and magazines are granted the right to reproduce a work that has already appeared in another publication. These rights are also purchased by a newspaper or magazine editor who wants to publish part of a book after the book has been published. The proceeds from reprint rights for a book are often split evenly between the author and his publishing company.

Simultaneous rights. More than one publication buys one-time rights to the same work at the same time. Use of such rights occurs among magazines with circulations that don't overlap, such as many religious publications.

All rights. Just as it sounds, the writer, illustrator, or photographer relinquishes all rights to a piece—she no longer has any say in who acquires rights to use it. All rights are purchased by publishers who pay premium usage fees, have an exclusive format, or have other book or magazine interests from which the purchased work can generate more mileage. If a company insists on acquiring all rights to your work, see if you can negotiate for the rights to revert back to you after a reasonable period of time. If they agree to such a proposal, get it in writing.

Note: Writers, illustrators, and photographers should be wary of "work-for-hire" arrangements. If you sign an agreement stipulating that your work will be done as work-for-hire, you will not control the copyrights of the completed work—the company that hired you will be the copyright owner.

Foreign serial rights. Be sure before you market to foreign publications that you have sold only North American—not worldwide—serial rights to previous markets. If so, you are free to market to publications that may be interested in material that's appeared in a North American-based periodical.

Syndication rights. This is a division of serial rights. For example, if a syndicate prints portions of a book in installments in its newspapers, it would be syndicating second serial rights. The syndicate would receive a commission and leave the remainder to be split between the author and publisher.

Subsidiary rights. These include serial rights, dramatic rights, book club rights, or translation rights. The contract should specify what percentage of profits from sales of these rights go to the author and publisher.

Dramatic, television, and motion picture rights. During a specified time, the interested party tries to sell a story to a producer or director. Many times options are renewed because the selling process can be lengthy.

Display rights or electronic publishing rights. They're also known as "Data, Storage, and Retrieval." Usually listed under subsidiary rights, the marketing of electronic rights in this era of rapidly expanding capabilities and markets for electronic material can be tricky. Display rights can cover text or images to be used in a CD-ROM or online, or they may cover use of material in formats not even fully developed yet. If a display rights clause is listed in your contract, try to negotiate its elimination. Otherwise, be sure to pin down which electronic rights are being purchased. Demand the clause be restricted to things designed to be read only. By doing this, you maintain your rights to use your work for things such as games and interactive software.

STRICTLY BUSINESS

An essential part of being a freelance writer, illustrator, or photographer is running your freelance business. It's imperative to maintain accurate business records to determine if you're making a profit as a freelancer. Keeping correct, organized records will also make your life easier as you approach tax time.

When setting up your system, begin by keeping a bank account and ledger for your business finances apart from your personal finances. Also, if writing, illustration, or photography is secondary to another freelance career, keep separate business records for each.

You will likely accumulate some business expenses before showing any profit when you start out as a freelancer. To substantiate your income and expenses to the IRS, keep all invoices, cash receipts, sales slips, bank statements, canceled checks, and receipts related to travel expenses and entertaining clients. For entertainment expenditures, record the date, place, and purpose of the business meeting, as well as gas mileage. Keep records for all purchases, big and small. Don't take the small purchases for granted; they can add up to a substantial amount. File all receipts in chronological order. Maintaining a separate file for each month simplifies retrieving records at the end of the year.

Record keeping

When setting up a single-entry bookkeeping system, record income and expenses separately. Use some of the subheads that appear on Schedule C (the form used for recording income from a business) of the 1040 tax form so you can easily transfer information onto the tax form when filing your return. In your ledger include a description of each transaction—the date, source of income (or debts from business purchases), description of what was purchased or sold, the amount of the transaction, and whether payment was by cash, check, or credit card.

Don't wait until January 1 to start keeping records. The moment you first make a business-related purchase or sell an article, book manuscript, illustration, or photo, begin tracking your profits and losses. If you keep records from January 1 to December 31, you're using a calendar-year accounting period. Any other accounting period is called a fiscal year.

There are two types of accounting methods you can choose from—the cash method and the accrual method. The cash method is used more often: You record income when it is received and expenses when they're disbursed.

Using the accrual method, you report income at the time you earn it rather than when it's actually received. Similarly, expenses are recorded at the time they're incurred rather than when you actually pay them. If you choose this method, keep separate records for "accounts receivable" and "accounts payable."

Satisfying the IRS

To successfully—and legally—work as a freelancer, you must know what income you should report and what deductions you can claim. But before you can do that, you must prove to the IRS you're in business to make a profit, that your writing, illustration, or photography is not merely a hobby.

The Tax Reform Act of 1986 says you should show a profit for three years out of a five-year period to attain professional status. The IRS considers these factors as proof of yourprofessionalism:

- accurate financial records
- a business bank account separate from your personal account
- proven time devoted to your profession
- whether it's your main or secondary source of income
- your history of profits and losses
- the amount of training you have invested in your field
- your expertise

If your business is unincorporated, you'll fill out tax information on Schedule C of Form

1040. If you're unsure of what deductions you can take, request the IRS publication containing this information. Under the Tax Reform Act, only 30 percent of business meals, entertainment and related tips, and parking charges are deductible. Other deductible expenses allowed on Schedule C include: car expenses for business-related trips; professional courses and seminars; depreciation of office equipment, such as a computer; dues and publication subscriptions; and miscellaneous expenses, such as postage used for business needs.

If you're working out of a home office, a portion of your mortgage interest (or rent), related utilities, property taxes, repair costs, and depreciation may be deducted as business expenses—under special circumstances. To learn more about the possibility of home office deductions, consult IRS Publication 587, Business Use of Your Home.

The method of paying taxes on income not subject to withholding is called "estimated tax" for individuals. If you expect to owe more than $500 at year's end and if the total amount of income tax that will be withheld during the year will be less than 90 percent of the tax shown on the current year's return, you'll generally make estimated tax payments. Estimated tax payments are made in four equal installments due on April 15, June 15, September 15, and January 15 (assuming you're a calendar-year taxpayer). For more information, request Publication 533, Self-Employment Tax.

The Internal Revenue Service's Web site (www.irs.gov) offers tips and instant access to IRS forms and publications.

For More Info

Social Security tax

Depending on your net income as a freelancer, you may be liable for a Social Security tax. This is a tax designed for those who don't have Social Security withheld from their paychecks. You're liable if your net income is $400 or more per year. Net income is the difference between your income and allowable business deductions. Request Schedule SE, Computation of Social Security Self-Employment Tax, if you qualify.

If completing your income tax return proves to be too complex, consider hiring an accountant (the fee is a deductible business expense) or contact the IRS for assistance. (Look in the White Pages under U.S. Government—Internal Revenue Service or check their Web site, www.irs.gov.) In addition to offering numerous publications to instruct you in various facets of preparing a tax return, the IRS also has walk-in centers in some cities.

Insurance

As a self-employed professional, be aware of what health and business insurance coverage is available to you. Unless you're a Canadian who is covered by national health insurance or a full-time freelancer covered by your spouse's policy, health insurance will no doubt be one of your biggest expenses. Under the terms of a 1985 government act (COBRA), if you leave a job with health benefits, you're entitled to continue that coverage for up to 18 months—you pay 100 percent of the premium and sometimes a small administration fee. Eventually, you must search for your own health plan. You may also choose to purchase disability and life insurance. Disability insurance is offered through many private insurance companies and state governments. This insurance pays a monthly fee that covers living and business expenses during periods of long-term recuperation from a health problem. The amount of money paid is based on the recipient's annual earnings.

Before contacting any insurance representative, talk to other writers, illustrators, or photographers to learn which insurance companies they recommend. If you belong to a writers' or artists' organization, ask the organization if it offers insurance coverage for professionals. (SCBWI has a plan available to members in certain states. Look through the Clubs & Organizationssection for other groups that may offer coverage.) Group coverage may be more affordable and provide more comprehensive coverage than an individual policy.

The Uneasy Marriage of Art & Commerce

by Kathleen Duey

Art vs. Commerce: the wish

A children's writer buys an old brass lamp and tries to rub a little luster back into the dull metal. A genie appears and asks, "To whom am I indebted?" (Genies in children's writers' fantasies are often grammatically correct). The writer, startled, doesn't answer. The genie stretches, looks up at the open sky, then back. "I owe someone one wish. You?"

The writer nods, then begins to ponder. Brilliant writing? Or money? One wish. *One*.

The genie scowls. "So? What's it going to be?"

The writer takes a long breath. A million dollars. No. Two million. Invested wisely, it would provide a great income for life and a big head start for the kids. No money worries, no day job—endless time to work on the YA novels. The writer frowns. But wait. That much money might de-motivate me. I procrastinate writing now. If I could travel, play, watch movies in bed all day, I might. But the day job wears me out and I will never finish a book if I have to keep working the hours I work now.

The writer looks up. "May I have two wishes?"

The genie looks annoyed. "No. Hurry up."

The writer's thoughts reboot. Wishing to be a brilliant writer makes more sense. Or does it? Many wonderfully written books fall out of print after a year of sluggish sales. What if the first two or three tank? How long will everyone put up with the hours of writing, the isolation? How long can I work and write like this? The writer tries frantically to think of a wish that will cover everything. Market prescience? Knowing in advance the picture book market would slump for years while YA took off? Or that a fun, imaginative fantasy epic would hit the cultural sweet-spot, worldwide, in 1996? Then the writer's shoulders drop. Trend-hopping isn't the point. Great writing, true art, that's real success. But if the books don't sell—

"Wish or forfeit!"

The writer looks up. "I just wish I knew what to wish for."

And poof! In that instant, the writer knows. But the genie is gone.

Art and Commerce will never get along, but every successful writer lives with this odd couple. The correct wish? Long life. You are going to need lots of time to figure how to make Art and Commerce work as a team.

KATHLEEN DUEY is happy to report that Art and Commerce remain committed to their relationship and that Art is winning more arguments lately. Their 2007 offspring are *Silence and Lily*, the ninth historical horse novel in her Hoofbeats collection from Dutton/Puffin; *My Animal Family*, a Smartkids Publishing project; and the first title in an edgy YA trilogy, *A Resurrection of Magic: Skin Hunger*, from Atheneum. Visit www.kathleenduey.com.

Art vs. Commerce: the day job derby

Almost every writer struggles to balance Art and Commerce, every single day. We all need food, shelter, and a net-connected computer as well as the time and energy to write. The obvious Art/Commerce solution for your start-up years—or decades, depending on many factors, only a few of which are in your control—is to find your very own writer's dream job.

Here's the basic checklist:

1. Highest possible take-home pay.
2. Lowest possible take-home work, frustration, stress, worry, etc.
3. Health care provided.
4. IRA account provided/matched
5. Work that feeds, or at least doesn't starve, your writing.

The vast majority of writers have day jobs. Over the past year, at conferences and online, I listened to professional writers describe their work/write solutions. In the list above, items one through four were obvious to all. Number five is the slippery one. Different writers have very different requirements.

One technical writer said he jots down plot ideas all day long at his day job, then writes his fiction at night. Another, with similar work, says her novel in progress has stalled; the technical writing dulls her desire to write fiction. Another novelist has several award-winning novels, a growing reputation and is content to write a book every two to three years in exchange for the solid security of her job.

Writers doing ad agency work disagreed on the side effects, too. One reported having "perma-greased creative wheels" for her narrative nonfiction, while another advertiser struggled with "creative depletion." Waitresses, receptionists, doctors, librarians, teachers, real estate agents, a psychologist, three professors, a few attorneys, librarians, a fireman, and an insurance salesperson—all had very personal evaluations of their work's effect on their writing and their larger lives.

Some writers prefer to work for themselves. Entrepreneurs, inventors, house-sitters, dog breeders—the list seems endless. But most self-employed writers use freelance writing to augment their "real" writing income. Traditional publishers sometimes hire writers for li-

A or B?

A Massively Oversimplified (but useful) Quiz

Do you daydream about . . .

A. composing acceptance speeches given to hundreds of dressed-up librarians, booksellers, and other literati. Your reviews praise your vision, your emotional depth, your seamless plots, the grace of your prose—and a few say you might have written a generational classic.

B. having three shelf-feet in B&N of a face-out display of your work, bags of fan mail, monster royalty checks and a movie deal? The reviews you get point out the entertainment value and kid-appeal of the work.

The Massively Oversimplified (but still useful) Results

A. If choice **A** steals your writer's heart, Art should win most of the arguments.
B. If **B** is your idea of success, Commerce should probably lead the way.

brary and classroom friendly nonfiction for beginning readers, educational materials, movie tie-ins, ghostwriting, titles for established series and more. Some published writers critique, edit, and/or teach writing in person and online. Some write résumés, help seniors write memoirs for family keepsake-books, write essays for specialty publishers, Web site text for small businesses. I once condensed legal depositions—a ten to one reduction without losing substantive info or nuance. It improved my fiction. The pay varies and there are no perks. But you chart your own course, arrange your own schedule and can often choose jobs that will enlarge your writing skills.

When you evaluate your day job—whatever form it takes—remember the lessons of Three Mile Island: *Watch your gauges. Believe what they tell you.* Freelancing, if it makes you chronically uneasy and less able to focus, is not for you. A salaried day job that provides money, benefits, and spare time—if it gravely damages your writing—is not your dream job. Keep looking until you find your unique Art/Commerce balance.

> **Commerce:** I'm too tired to write tonight. I did a good day's work. I just want to relax.''
>
> **Art:** ''But Jacob is waiting to hear from his mother in this scene. He doesn't know what's going to happen and . . .''
>
> **Commerce:** ''All right, all right. But only an hour or two. Then we sleep. Can't nod out at work tomorrow.''

Art vs. Commerce: welcome to the book-biz

After your earthly needs are provided and the day job is settled, the Art vs. Commerce tug-of-war continues. Writer-tribe elders tell me that corporate thinking has forever changed publishing—that an idealistic gentleman's endeavor has become a profit-driven machine. Perhaps. But editors and publishers still love all kinds of books—and you still have choices to make. Here is the most fundamental one: what kind of books will you write?

There are two major divergent trajectories in writing for children. There are dozens of sub-categories, but it's like a road system, tree-lined lanes lead to surface streets that connect to the highways inside publishers' offices. Both nonfiction and fiction books are divided into two messy, sometimes overlapping, piles: ''commercial'' and ''literary''.

Literary books are almost always hardcovers—with a paperback edition printed later if sales merit it. They are written for every age group and can be funny, tragic, realistic or fantastic and all hues in between. **Literary nonfiction** tends to have a new take on its subject, or focus on something that has not been much written about. For both literary fiction and nonfiction, excellent writing, depth, and originality are the qualifiers. Literary books are reviewed in children's literature journals and elsewhere. Marketing efforts are usually based on the reviewers' response. Literary books are considered for the many honors and awards bestowed by educators' and literacy organizations each year.

Picture books encompass a world of creative possibilities. Most are released as hardcovers and are reviewed—many are considered literary quality. These can be fact or fiction, silly or serious, wordy or wordless, happy to heartbreaking, and all that lies between. The criteria is excellence and originality for both text and art, and a deft interplay between the written and the visual elements. They are reviewed in educators' journals and elsewhere and considered for awards and other honors.

Softcover originals, both series and single titles, are usually less artful and more commercial. They are sometimes reviewed. A few, thought to have commercial potential, are ''pushed'' by the publisher. They sometimes make state award lists—because children vote to determine the winners.

Mass market properties, movie and TV tie ins, in-house lines, packager' series, etc. are the most commercial of all writing for children. Generally speaking, writers work within specific guidelines using already-developed characters. The books are sometimes packaged with a "value added" gimmick—charm bracelet, a soft-plastic ogre. Some are wonderful. Others gaudy.

The books that make educators and parents cringe are often a child's first real love, and their springboard into lifelong literacy. The books that delight educators and parents don't always attract a large child-audience, at least at first. Sometimes books written to be wildly commercial don't sell. Sometimes literary books have great sales. Go figure.

> **Art:** The YA novel came from my deepest heart.
> **Commerce:** Right. But the dinosaur-dilly-doodles books pay the bills.
> **Both, in unison:** I have to go now—I need to write this afternoon.

Art vs. Commerce: travel & promotion

Once your books, literary or commercial, are published, Art and Commerce will argue about time allotment. A very few lucky (and, usually, very good) writers will be chosen by the publisher's marketing department to be promoted with publicity, ads, signing tours, large giveaways of ARCs (advance readers copies) at library and educators' conferences. Sometimes this catapults sales. Not always. There are many ways to do your own promotion. All of them take time and energy.

School visits, if you enjoy them and speaking doesn't exhaust you, are probably the best grassroots promotion tool available. You will be paid, and hundreds of children and teachers will be introduced to your work. Bookstore signings, especially at stores willing to bring in school students or hold an event that features your book, can help spread the word about your work, too. Speaking at librarians' and teachers' conferences, regional and national, helps introduce your work to the educational community.

Building a Web site where readers can contact you, learn more about your work, and post messages is a wonderful promotional tool. Children love to see pictures of you, your dog,

Articles & Interviews

Art vs. Commerce: The Rematch

I meant to write smart adult and YA fiction with elements of fantasy, SF, magic realism. Long story short, I created and wrote two series of paperback historical novels for third- through seventh-grade readers because I could sell them more easily. Following a trend, I wrote 30 books into those series and many other kid-appeal paperbacks. Every title was well edited, well reviewed (very unusual for series books) and I came to love writing for kids—and every multi-title contract meant the bills would get paid. I write fast. One year, I published 13 books. My books sell well enough, and steadily. It has been 14 years since my last day job.

Four years ago, I wrote an eight-book fantasy saga for early chapterbook readers, based on a recurring grade school dream—one that shaped my life. The work was heartfelt, born of Art more than Commerce—and it woke me up. My first Art-mandated, hardcover novel is scheduled for release June 2007. It is a dark, circular tale, begun 16 years ago, then put aside to make a living. Redefining my competent, kid-popular midlist series writer's career into the career I dreamed about will be an uphill run. I tended short-term Commerce and neglected long-haul Art and I'm not sure I can repair the mistake. I do know it could have been avoided. If I could go back, I would gag Commerce and feed Art more protein.

your yard, the places you have traveled. They love to have a personal connection with the author of books they have enjoyed.

YA writers know the power of a good blog. Their readers are teens, the text-message and MySpace generation—though younger readers love reading blog entries, too. Blogs and Web site message boards are the best and easiest way for writers to converse with their readers.

So. Add it up. Writing an interesting entry in a blog every day or even every week, updating a Web site, answering message board missives, and e-mails from readers, writing speeches, arranging travel, appearing at schools, conferences, book events of all kinds—these all absorb time and energy and conflict with a salaried day job. Are they worth it? Yes, if your books start to pay the daily freight. Many of us carry laptops and try to write a few pages every night on the road, but the distraction and energy-drain of promotion is inarguable. Writers who do nothing to promote—and succeed—are as rare as one legged, chartreuse whooping cranes.

> **Art:** "I need six months of undisturbed writing time. A year would be better."
> **Commerce**: "You won't sell the next book if this one doesn't do well."
> **Art:** "If I don't get time to create, there won't be a next book."
> **Commerce:** "You have an hour before the plane leaves. I see a coffee shop from here. You could finish that scene . . ."

Art & Commerce, sitting in a tree . . .

How can a writer balance all this? To begin the process, you'll need a figurative shotgun— or any other immutable authority symbol. You're a writer: Imagine something meaningful to you. A wooden spoon, a scepter encrusted with elfin gems, I don't care. Just make it an argument-stopper.

The wedding and the interminable counseling sessions that follow it will all take place between your ears. Since you are a writer, important imaginary events in the confines of your own skull should be both frequent and familiar. So, holding your authority object, stand squarely facing the two major elements of your career. "Art, meet Commerce. Commerce, this is Art. Congratulations. You're getting hitched." Raise the scepter/soup ladle/golf club/ copy of *Bird by Bird*/red pencil/whatever and look menacing. This takes grit. "Art, you promise to fly free, high, and fast, even if we are sweating the rent. And Commerce? You can remind Art and me that we have a day job, and that we have to promote the books. But not during work hours. I'll consult with both of you, but I will make all the decisions. Now. Let's get to work."

Making Time for Art

Time/energy management is a pickle. "I need a wife" is a standard quip among married women writers. Managing your family/personal life, writing, and a full time job can be almost impossible. Still, the vast majority of writers who read that last sentence are living it. Art happens when we can somehow steal time from the everyday commerce of life.

Take a week or two and notice where your time goes. Count minutes instead of calories, and see if you can allot more time to write. Make lists, organize/minimize errands, carry a voice activated recorder for idea snippets you can replay to jump-start your writing sessions, take yourself seriously so that others will. Write early; write late. Experiment. Whatever works is fine. Just make sure something does.

Your First Novel

10 (Giant but Essential) Steps to Getting There

by Candie Moonshower

In my debut novel, *The Legend of Zoey*, the character of Grandma Cope tells her granddaughter, "Zoey, it is time for you to face your destiny." By the time I wrote those words, Grandma Cope was talking to me, too. I'd won the SCBWI's Sue Alexander Most Promising New Work Award, based on the first 40 pages of my novel, and editors were calling.

The problem? There were *only* 40 pages of my novel written.

For 25 years, I toyed with writing a novel. I finished many short pieces and even embarked on a freelancing career that I eventually built up to consistent monthly assignments. But my novel writing was going nowhere. Fast. I had a stockpile of excuses, too, about time, kids, family responsibilities, jobs, the muse, money, fear of rejection, fear of success and, oh yes, plain old fear.

(Did I mention fear?)

With editors calling, the rubber had met the road. I realized that I had one chance to take advantage of the golden opportunity I'd been given to leap across the slush pile in a single bound. It was time to finish a novel.

I did finish *Zoey*—in six weeks. And I sold it in short order, too. But I don't recommend what I call the "25-year-overnight-success method." It's too hard on the nerves—and your confidence.

Many people have asked me how I finished, revised and submitted my novel within a three-month period, while working full-time, freelancing, and with a teenager, a kindergartner and a toddler at home. I've often asked myself how I did it!

As it turns out, I was in a decent position to perform such a feat. I'd done a few things right along the way—things that had prepared me for the challenge. I'd studied the craft of writing, and the business of writing, too. Throw in a few positive affirmations, a mantra or two, and some fast-food meals, and you can do it, too.

But how do you start and, especially, how do you make time for the pursuit of writing success?

From my own experience, I've decided that there are five essential steps to pursuing your

CANDIE MOONSHOWER is an Army Brat who grew up in Okinawa and Tennessee. She taught herself to type at age eight, because writers type. She'd seen it on TV, so it had to be true. Her debut novel, *The Legend of Zoey*, won SCBWI's Sue Alexander Most Promising New Work Award. In addition to working on a new novel, she is under contract to write a biography. Visit her online at www.CandieMoonshower.com or http://c-moonshower.livejournal.com.

When Candie Moonshower won the SCBWI's Sue Alexander Most Promising New Work Award based on sample chapters submitted for critique, she had to finish her book in a hurry—just six weeks—while she juggled her freelance writing career and her family life. The mad rush paid off for Moonshower when she got a book contract from Delacorte for her debut novel *The Legend of Zoey*. Her book about modern-girl Zoey's trip to the past "captures the perfect blend of fact and fantasy, past and present, adventure and characterization to make this a compelling first novel," says *School Library Journal*.

craft, and there are five essential steps to approaching the business end of writing. All the steps together will help you find ways to fit writing into your harried life.

CRAFT
#1. Stop writing.

This might sound counter-productive, but it's not! If you haven't read a children's book since you were a child, you're already behind the eight ball. Children change, tastes change, and the market changes, too. What was hot in 1959 or 1984, or even 2001, may not be selling now.

When I decided I wanted to settle down and write a novel for 'tweens or teens, it struck me that the last children's novel I had read was *Heidi*—in 1972! I stopped writing and spent an entire year reading. That year brought me up to date with the last 25 Newbery winners. I discovered the books that had received the Michael L. Printz Awards. I discovered that "malt shop romances" were out, and books about cliques and community pants were in. And some of the books that I had enjoyed as a child were still in print—books by Eleanor Estes and Beverly Cleary.

Take time off from writing and spend it reading:

- What kids are reading—ask librarians what books are always on hold or reserve.
- Recent award winners.
- In the genre you think you might want to write in—you'll know because you'll begin searching out books in a particular genre before too long.

#2. Decide: job or hobby?

Writing for children is hard work. And if you don't seriously pursue publication, it's only a hobby. Writing as a hobby is a wonderful thing, but that kind of attitude is the death knell ringing on a career as a published author. Just as with any career goals you have in mind, failure to plan is planning to fail. Plan your writing time. Plan your future success.

Whether you have a full- or part-time job or work at home, you can help yourself by setting aside time to write—time that is sacred. I get up, shower and dress, and go to my computer every morning just as I previously drove to work every morning. I'm at the desk, and it's time to work.

If writing is going to be your job, then:

- Stop thinking (and reading) about writing and write.
- Act like it's a job—you wouldn't play Spider Solitaire at work all day!
- Take classes and attend workshops.
- Join professional writer's groups and a critique group or two.

I like this attitude! William Faulkner said: "I write only when I'm inspired. Fortunately, I'm inspired at 9 o'clock every morning."

#3. Believe in yourself.

Recently, an old family friend called after he'd seen the publicity in the newspaper about a signing for *The Legend of Zoey* at a local bookstore. "I never knew you wanted to be a writer!" he said.

I've been writing since I was eight years old, but I'm not surprised he didn't know it. I never told anyone that I had serious aspirations to be a writer!

I kept planning to tell people—when I was published.

The moral of the story is that if you don't believe in yourself, no one else will. How to float that balloon? Write, of course (reread the first bullet under #2), but come clean with people, too. This is essential. If you don't treat your writing time with the respect it deserves, neither will your family, your friends or your neighbors.

To earn respect for your writing endeavors, try:

- Acting like a professional—set aside time when everyone understands that you are working. Even the youngest children can be taught to respect your time for 15-minute stretches.
- Cultivating those who will support you.
- Developing your own self-motivational tools.

#4. BIC HOK TAM!

No, don't join a fraternity or sorority! *BIC HOK TAM!* is the motto of a Book-in-a-Week (BIW) challenge group I've belonged to for about ten years. What does it mean? "Butt in the chair, hands on the keyboard, typing away madly!" Or as Jane Yolen said, in her keynote speech at the SCBWI national conference in August of 2006 in Los Angeles, "Write the damn book."

BIW groups, along with the folks over at the National Novel Writing Month Challenge (NaNoWriMo), are wonderful for helping undisciplined writers get over themselves—their search for the muse, their fears and their writers' blocks. That sounds harsh, but (and again with the first bullet under #2) most people spend more time talking about writing—their desire to write, the stories they've thought up, their dreams of future success—than they spend actually writing. The sole purpose of the various BIW groups out there is stacking up pages—quantity over quality is the goal.

When you first begin to write seriously, concentrating on quantity over quality can help you learn to:

- Write a lot of crap, because without mining the rock, you can't find the diamonds. Join some BIW groups, or NaNoWriMo, and train yourself to shut down that infernal internal editor. Check out www.book-in-a-week.com or www.nanowrimo.org.
- Sit on your muse (butt in chair), because if you wait for your muse to come and visit, you'll be worm-dirt before you finish a first draft. The muse is a myth. Pages stacking up beside the computer are a reality.
- Think of writer's block as an urban legend (a rural and suburban one, too). Writer's block is usually fear, resistance or lack of discipline.

> *I've had this quote by novelist Jane Smiley hanging on an index card over my computer for years. It reminds me to forge ahead: "Every first draft is perfect because all the first draft has to do is exist. It's perfect in its existence. The only way it could be imperfect would be not to exist."*

#5. Submit.

After I'd been writing for years, my husband said to me, "Honey, they can't read your mind in New York City." He was tired of looking at my piles of writing—the stacks of work that were hanging around like the in-laws after the holidays.

You've written *The End* on your novel draft. You've revised it. You've had trusted critique group members read it. You've polished it to a high sheen. Now what?

It's time to submit. Yes, it's scary, but it's a necessary part of becoming a published children's writer. If you don't submit, it's only a dream. When you start to send your work out, you're actively pursuing publication.

Because they can't read your mind in New York City, editors will not come a callin' unless they *read* something you've written. If you're not submitting your work, it's a hobby.

Remember, when it comes to submitting:

- Without some "no's," you'll never get a "yes"—and since only one publisher can buy your book, it only takes one yes.
- Rejections aren't personal—these editors aren't rejecting *you*, only your manuscript.
- Rejections won't kill you—and every rejection is one step closer to an acceptance.

BUSINESS

In the first *Rocky* movie, Burgess Meredith's character, the crusty old trainer, Mick, says to Sylvester Stallone's Rocky, "How can you fight the champ when you can't even catch a chicken?"

Of course, writing—and boxing—aren't about catching chickens, but the business of writing is about having the proper mindset to get into the ring with the champ. When you begin to submit your work, you're competing with published authors—the champs. And if you push your work out into the world, unprepared and to the wrong editor or house, it's like sending Tweety Bird into the boxing ring with The Terminator.

Publishing is not a day at the spa designed to help us relax and forget our troubles. *It is a business designed to make money.* After your manuscript leaves your house, it is entering the business world. It's no longer your baby. It's a viable business product.

Don't send your manuscript out to the wrong job interview, dressed in chocolate-stained sweat suit. Familiarize yourself with the business of publishing.

#1. Know the markets.

If you submit a gritty, cutting edge, young adult novel to a house that only publishes sweet board books, you're doing yourself and the rest of us a disservice. Time and again, I've heard editors at conferences say that the number one reason they reject a manuscript isn't that it's badly written—it's that the manuscript isn't right for their list. And the more misdirected manuscripts out there clogging the transoms, the more houses that will close their doors to unagented material.

How do you figure out where to send your manuscripts?

- Know your audience. If you've done your craft homework, you'll know if your book is appropriate for toddlers, young children, 'tweens or teens.
- Submit your work to editors whose houses have published books similar to your manuscript. That doesn't mean that you should sub a wizard story to Scholastic simply because they've published *Harry Potter*, but if your book is a quirky nonfiction book, check out the books put out by a publisher like Darby Creek Publishing.
- Use available resources to find the right houses for your work. Invest in the *Children's Writer's & Illustrator's Market, Writer's Market* and other books that update publishers' wish lists and submission guidelines.

#2. Follow instructions.

Be a maverick with your prose, but not with submission guidelines. When editors post procedural preferences in market listings, it's because they have a good reason for it. Do what the "boss" says!

When researching a publisher, check to see:

- If the house is open to unagented material.
- If the house prefers certain months for submissions.
- If there is a particular editor you can address your sub to (and if there's not, try and find one).
- What they're looking for this season—and what they don't want.
- Exactly what their submission guidelines tell you to send, such as SASEs—and what not to send.

#3. Seize opportunities.

George Steinbrenner, principal owner of the New York Yankees baseball team and known as "The Boss," has been heard to say about the pursuit of success, "The secret is desire. You gotta want to win!" I agree. Writing, like any other activity you want to do well, takes practice, discipline and ongoing effort.

I don't believe in luck. Whenever anyone tells me I'm lucky, I say (with a smile), "Yes, the harder I work, the luckier I get!" Remember: Opportunity can knock all day long, but if you're asleep on the couch, it won't do you much good! If you've worked hard, and circumstances are right, things start to happen.

Make the most of your hard work by:

- Networking through your critique group, online lists, writer's groups and conferences. Children's writers, as a group, are noted for their generosity with information and encouragement of newbies.
- Paying to have your manuscript professionally critiqued at conferences.
- Subbing after conferences. Editors that serve as faculty often allow attendees to submit manuscripts to them, even if their publishing houses are closed to unagented material or not accepting submissions. Don't pass up these chances!
- Sending your manuscript, in a timely fashion, if an editor or an agent requests it during a critique!

#4. Market yourself.

Whether you're a plumber, a financial analyst or a car salesman, you carry cards. If you own a business, you advertise. Writing, like plumbing, is a business. Advertise yourself.

Authors these days know that they are responsible for the bulk of the marketing and promotional activities necessary for selling their books after publication. Post cards, flyers, attendance at book festivals and writer's conferences, school visits and book signings are all integral to creating that sought-after promotional buzz.

But what if you're among the "pre-published"? It is still important to begin the process of advertising yourself.

Get your name in front of people with:

- Business cards—hand them out at writing events. Collect them from other writers.
- Web sites—today's world requires that you have one. Cyber-savvy children surf the Web for information as easily as their grandparents went to the World Book Encyclopedia set.
- A blog, or Web log. Many children's writers (and editors and agents) are blogging these days on MySpace or LiveJournal, connecting with other writers and readers, and sharing information about their books.
- A friendly and genuine schmoozing skill—be that person other writers want to be around. That kind of word-of-mouth is invaluable!

#5 Handle rejection.

Part and parcel of the writing biz are the rejections. You will get them. In fact, you *need* to get them! Because after you've received a few rejections, it dawns on you that rejections aren't personal.

Instead of looking at rejections as overwhelming obstacles, try to view them as part of your development as a professional writer. New writers aren't the only ones who receive rejections. Published authors submit manuscripts that garner rejections, too. If you never submit out of fear of rejection, you'll never allow an editor the opportunity to call you with an offer!

Learn to deal with rejections by:

- Not submitting manuscripts too early. Like fine wine, your manuscript isn't ready until it has been written, rewritten, critiqued, revised and polished. When you send in work that isn't ready for an editorial look-see, you're cheating yourself by knocking that editor off your list of possibilities.
- Replacing worry with work. My mother always says that it's hard to worry when you're scrubbing a floor. I find it hard to worry about rejections when I have another manuscript ready to send out the door.
- Starting on a new project as soon as your manuscript has left the building (again, you're replacing worry with work). Always have a new, exciting project going that will take your mind off your mailbox.
- Never whining, ranting or crying about rejections except to your most trusted writing friends and, perhaps, your spouse. You, especially, never want to complain about rejections to those agents or editors who, potentially, might have one of your manuscripts in their hands someday.

As a signature line in my e-mail program, I have a quote from novelist Rita Mae Brown: "Don't hope more than you're willing to work." I have practiced living in that mindset for years, and I find it keeps me sensible. When you start hoping for something, that's the time to pick up the pace and work harder than ever.

Prepare yourself for a writing career by learning the craft and familiarizing yourself with the publishing business. You will eliminate a number of stumbling blocks that might slow you down later.

Just as you wouldn't want to go under the knife with someone who has never attended medical school, you shouldn't expect to simply write, submit and sell a novel. Talent is good. Talent combined with preparation and knowledge will help you fit writing into your harried life, and build a successful writing career.

Essential Reading on Writing

I always hesitate to suggest "further reading" because I know (from years of experience) how easy it is to get caught up in *reading* about the craft of writing and not *practicing* the craft of writing. I have enough "how-to" books to start a library of my own! The books listed below contain plenty of information, as well as inspirations, however, so I heartily recommend them!

- *On Writing: A Memoir on the Craft*, by Stephen King.
- *Bird by Bird: Some Instructions on Writing and Life*, by Anne Lamott
- *How to Write a Children's Book and Get It Published*, by Barbara Seuling

Writing with Intention

The Heart's Journey

by Justina Chen Headley

I will be brutally honest. I didn't want to write my first novel, *Nothing but the Truth (and a few white lies)*. And to tell you the truth, I didn't particularly want to write my second novel, *Girl Overboard*, either.

Both stories were inspired by experiences that were hard for me to revisit, much less dissect and revise. Which is, after all, what we writers do. For my first novel, it was witnessing some teenagers mock my kids, who are half-Asian and half-white, with *hung-twung-wung* pseudo-Chinese at a children's museum—and being reminded of the time I was spit upon for no other reason than my being Asian. And for my second novel, I truly did not want to relive my feelings of inadequacy during my teenhood.

Wouldn't you know it? After the *hung-twung-wung* incident, the main character for my debut novel introduced herself to me that night: *Hi, I'm Patty Ho. I'm not quite a banana (Asian on the outside, white on the inside) and not quite an egg (a white kid who gets off on all things Asian)*.

Really, who wants to write a book about racism? Not I. But no matter what I did, no matter how much I resisted Patty, she kept yakking to me—in my sleep, when I was supposedly cleansing my mind in yoga, and yes, while I was writing other books.

I'm so glad that Patty compelled me to write her story. Writing what was deeply and personally meaningful to me instead of merely interesting didn't just lead to the auction of my first two novels. Much, much more importantly, it showed me how critical it is to write from my heart instead of to architect a story from my head.

WRITING FROM THE HEART

Whether it's my first rambling discovery draft or my final version, writing for me is about revelations: figuring out who my characters are, what they want, and how they're going to get what they want. Just as importantly, I understand and confront why I feel compelled to tell this story.

Skip this last step—this honest and sometimes painful self-inquiry—and I can write off

JUSTINA CHEN HEADLEY wrote her first novel when she was eight years old. Her debut young adult novel *Nothing But the Truth (and a few white lies)*, was sold at auction, and was named a 2007 IRA Notable Book, New York Public Library Book for the Teen Age and Chicago Public Library Best of the Best. Additionally, it was a Borders' Original Voices nominee, a Book Sense top pick, and received a starred review in *Publishers Weekly*. Her picture book, *The Patch*, was selected as a Notable Social Studies Trade Books for Young People 2007. After graduating from Stanford University with honors, she worked as a marketing executive at Microsoft. She now lives in the Pacific Northwest. Visit her Web site at www.justinachenheadley.com and her online book community at www.readergirlz.com.

another fruitless year. Really. Without thinking deeply about why I'm writing what I write, I might as well consign my work into a desk drawer, forever unfocused, unwanted, and unpublished. I have plenty of unsold manuscripts to prove it, too.

For good reason, I've tacked a quote from Amy Tan's *The Bonesetter's Daughter* in my office and have it scrawled in several of my writing journals: "...when you push an inkstick along an inkstone, you take the first step to cleansing your mind and your heart. You push and you ask yourself, What are my intentions? What is in my heart that matches my mind?"

I never start a writing day, much less a new project, without contemplating this quote and asking myself, Yeah, what are my intentions with this story anyway? What's in my heart that I want to express today?

So let's say I'm beginning a new novel. Or I'm stuck midway through. Or I'm suffering a severe case of self-doubtitis since I've just spent a year researching a story that's going nowhere. I return to these questions and journal until I'm reminded again of why I began in the first place—and why I have to continue:

After an unpleasant incident at the museum, a character introduced herself to Justina Chen Headley: *Hi, I'm Patty Ho. I'm not quite a banana (Asian on the outside, white on the inside) and not quite an egg (a white kid who gets off on all things Asian).* And Patty wouldn't go away, leading Headley through her first novel *Nothing but the Truth (and a few white lies)* which was named a New York Public Library Book for the Teen Age and an IRA Notable Book for 2007.

- What is pulling me to tell this specific story?
- What about the story and/or character touches my heart?
- What happened to me so that I identify with this story/character?
- What about this story am I afraid to write...yet must?
- What am I really trying to say with this story?

I can almost guarantee you, if you take the time to answer these questions, chances are you will finish your story, assuming it's one that you are truly compelled to tell. What happens is this: as tantalizing as it may be to chuck a story and start something new, something easier, something that will tax you less emotionally, you won't. Why? Now, you have a story that you need to get out of your heart. And now you have a story that you must transplant into your reader's.

Maybe your best friend had an eating disorder and as a teen you had no idea how to help her. Or perhaps you were uprooted when you were in first grade and all you wanted was one friend, the person you left behind. Or it could be that your kids were made fun of for no reason other than the way they looked and you remembered your own brother yelling at your parents, "I just wish I were white!"

Something about this character and his heart's journey is calling to you for a reason only you can answer. Chances are it's something deeper than "oh, what a great idea for a story!" So ask yourself this when you feel your writing stamina faltering: how can you shelve this work when you owe it to your character and yourself and your future readers to sit in your chair and type until you reach the last page? How can you stop until you've said what you need to say, and said what only you can say with your unique character in your unique voice with your unique vision?

Creating characters with heart

There are so many manuals about writing that turn writing into manual labor. Honestly! Create elaborate lists of your characters' likes and dislikes. What color looks good on your character? What is his favorite food?

While I think details define characteristics, they don't define character. For me, to create authentic characters—ones that make my readers think, *oh my gosh, I know someone who is just like Patty*, or *I'm Jasmine! How did the author know me?*—the most important things I need to nail are their fears and desires. Their strengths and weaknesses. Everything else—back story, her lucky number, his best subject at school—will reveal themselves to me as I write.

So how do you figure out what's at the heart of your character? The best way I know is (what else?) to write. Here are some prompts that I use in my journal to discover the truth about my character:

- What does your character want most?
- Why doesn't your character have his heart's desire?
- Who and what scares your character? Why?
- What would be the worst thing that could happen to your character?
- What would be your character's moment of purest joy?

Plotting The Heart's Journey

In Christopher Vogler's book, *The Writer's Journey: Mythic Structure for Writers*, he introduced a wonderful way to construct and deconstruct story. He segments story, or the hero's journey, into three parts: the hero's existing world where the story begins; the new world which the hero must successfully navigate; and then the return to the existing world where the hero claims his reward for triumphing on his quest.

Before I write my discovery draft and again before I start the endless rewrite, I take apart my story with my own personal version of Vogler's model, one that I've nicknamed The Heart's Journey. Think of this as just another way to focus story, not on action (what happens to the hero) but on our characters' innermost wants, needs, and fears (why the hero acts the way he does).

We authors talk about knowing the beginning and ending of our stories. Hey, we can set up our stories, no problem. Meet my character, and here's what he wants but can't have. Got it. And the ending? Yay, our character gets what he most wants, or something like it. And if he doesn't, well, there's a darn good reason.

But it's that murky, unwieldy and *long* middle section that stumps us and gives us that blasted disease known as writer's block. It's in this middle section where our writing resolve wilts as we try to answer: so what happens next?

For me, my ideas for this middle section burst free once I know how my character needs to grow. Consider this question: Given my character's most heartfelt desire and deepest fear, what does she need to learn about herself, her family and her world?

See, it all goes back to my character's heart: what she wants but is afraid of receiving. Once I know the "life lessons" my character needs to experience in order to be able to reach for what she wants, I can create plenty of "growth opportunities" for her. (Yes, "growth opportunities" is just the politically correct way to say all the terrible but necessary situations we as writers inflict upon our poor characters.)

Those "life lessons" translate to the many scenes and chapters that move our character's story forward. And I would bet that some of those "life lessons" are the very reasons why you're motivated to tell your story. In my novel, half-and-half Patty Ho needs to learn that she is wholly perfect the way she is—and isn't that what I wanted to assure my kids and my brother? And heck, probably (most likely) my own inner teen?

A case study: *Fat Kid Rules the World*

Let's use one of my favorite young adult novels, K.L. Going's masterful *Fat Kid Rules the World* as another example of The Heart's Journey. Meet my beloved Troy, a grossly obese teen who wants to be loved for himself.

Expressing Your Character's Heart

When I do school visits, one of the top questions from students is about writer's block: how do you avoid it? What do you do when you're stuck in it? What I end up telling the students is that writer's block happens when we as writers lose our way and forget what's at the heart of our story: who is our main character? And what does he want, but is too afraid to reach for?

Before I start to write any new work, I usually spend a week putting together an art project. I think of it as a visual rubric, an easy way to remind me what I'm writing about and why.

So here are a few fun ways to get in touch with your character.

Create a collage board

Take a canvas or piece of cardboard and create a collage with images and words that represent your character. You can find these in ubiquitous catalogs or magazines. Search for quotes that capture your character's mindset. I place my collage board somewhere prominent in my office so that as soon as I sit down to work on my novel, I'm prompted about what truly matters to my character.

Find a mantra

Create a mantra for your character with as few words as possible. Think of this as your before and after slogan. For instance, when I was creating Patty, I thought of her change over the course of the novel as going from the Chinese word of woe "aiyaaa" to her powerful war cry "Hi-YAH!" When I come up with a catch-phrase that encapsulates my character, I'll post it on my computer, the left side for where the character starts, and the right for where she'll end.

Search for a symbol

Novelist Janet Lee Carey always finds an object that symbolizes her character's wish. For her YA fantasy, *Dragon's Keep*, she went beachcombing and found an aged branch that looked like a dragon's claw, a perfect symbol for a princess who was born with a talon instead of a finger on one hand. That branch stayed on Janet's desk until she finished the novel.

Make a playlist

If you love music, be your novel's personal deejay and compile a list of tunes that match your story arc—the struggles and triumphs. Or find songs that remind you of your character. Play the music in the background as you write . . . and again at your book release party.

What does Troy need to learn about himself, his family and his world for him to feel loved and accepted? Well, I'd say that a kid who fits his profile needs to learn that he deserves love and friendship as much as all the super skinny kids he notices, that he's good at something, that he needs to take risks to get what he wants. He has a few lessons to learn about his dysfunctional family: that his dad loves him, and that his seemingly perfect and popular little brother actually does want to have a relationship with him. And finally, I'd say that Fat Kid needs to learn that while the world can be cruel, not everyone judges him because of his weight, and not everybody is staring at him like he's a freak.

Now it's a matter of making sure that the plot (what actually happens in the story) provides Troy with those "growth opportunities" so he learns all of these lessons. Does K.L. Going make Troy endure his worst possible nightmare to test to see if he's learned enough to believe in himself? You bet she does. And does Troy learn enough about who he really is and how his true friends see him and how much his family loves him that by the end of the story he's able to accept himself? What do you think? The answer is: of course! I encourage all writers to study this book to see how K.L. Going accomplishes this so well.

Really, try this exercise on your favorite novel. Distill the main character down to one line: who is he and what he wants. And then brainstorm the lessons you think the character needs to learn in order to gain what he wants: what are the lessons that will change the way he perceives himself and his world? See if the author has provided scenes that give the character those "growth opportunities." And ask yourself whether the character has learned who they really are and where they fit into their world by the final page.

Most important of all, apply The Heart's Journey to your own work. Trust me, this is a great way to see if you've got any holes in your storyline or if you've harped on a lesson that your character has already learned. Once is good, twice is okay, but three or four times and we go from writer to nagging parent. And no reader wants that.

Stories that beat with heart

We may not be Fat Kids or biracial teens or any of the characters we create. But by drawing from the deep well of our own experiences, we can create characters with heart, who feel real to us and real to our readers. How could they not be when they're born from our souls?

So those teen who *hung-twung-wunged* my kids at the children's museum? They found us an hour later to apologize. I thought that was incredibly brave of them and told them so. But I didn't let them off the hook with that nice girl, it's-OK talk. Instead, I told them this: "Now you know. And now you can do better next time."

That's what drove me to write my first novel and my second. This belief that through literature we can all know better. And we can all do better the next time. That's at the heart of my stories. What's at yours?

So go on. Don't just write your heart out. Get your heart down on paper. Let your stories pulse with your raw emotional intensity. Your characters and readers await.

Writing for Boys

*An Editor's Advice on Reaching
These Often Reluctant Readers*

by Krista Marino

As an editor it's frustrating to hear people talk about the need for "boy books." It seems that publishers are always being chided for neglecting this genre, but the fact is that this is simply not true. Every year many books are published for "the boy reader," but that doesn't mean the boy necessarily gets his hands on them to read. It's a well-known fact that teen novels directed at "boys" are a harder sell than teen novels written for girls. I think it's gotten easier to get your boy book published, but it's still hard to get it sold to the public—or have it hit the market and get nearly as much publicity as a girl book can.

The eternal question: *Why is this*? Sadly, the answer to it is easy. Feel free to argue, but the fact of the matter is that teen boys just don't read the same way teen girls do and they certainly aren't reading nearly as much fiction.

WHY WON'T JOHNNY READ?

Studies show that both boys and girls age zero to five are read to the same amount by parents. But by age eight girls already have a higher interest in reading. Of course this difference in behavior has to start somewhere, and I think it's important to understand that there are many acknowledged social and biological and developmental differences between boys and girls. Again—feel free to argue—but these differences seem to me the logical cause for not only *why* boys read differently (specifically *less*) than girls, but *what* they're reading.

Biological differences between the sexes appear in both physical development and emotional development. Then emotional development is further influenced by the different ways the sexes are socialized. Biologically, boys are slower to develop language and fine motor skills than girls and often struggle with reading and writing skills early on. As well, boys are more physically active than girls. And though both sexes are certainly energetic, this physicality boys are prone to is more likely to cause chaos in the classroom for a male student. Boys simply have a harder time sitting down. While girls can sit and concentrate on reading, it's harder for a boy to do this. And the more one is interrupted, the less one can connect to what they're reading.

KRISTA MARINO began her publishing career in San Diego at Harcourt Children's books. After transferring to the New York offices she decided that fiction was her passion and took a position at Random House Children's Books at Delacorte Press, where she is now an Editor. She works on Young Adult and Middle Grade fiction solely and is always looking for new voices, innovative concepts, and great stories for her list. Recent books she has edited include *King Dork*, by Frank Portman; *The Alchemyst: The Secrets of the Immortal Nicholas Flamel*, by Michael Scott; and *Prom Dates from Hell*, by Rosemary Clement-Moore.

THE TRUTH ABOUT FICTION

This is where things get interesting. Despite our differences, many boys *do* grow up to be teenagers that read—just not fiction.

Because of men and women's biological differences and socialization differences, we also have emotional differences. One of the most obvious emotional differences between the sexes is that, because of brain development, it's harder for boys to communicate their feelings at a young age.

Then, as they grow up, as a society, we teach boys to suppress their feelings. Fiction requires an emotional journey that traditionally boys are taught to reject. As a result, instead of reading fiction, boys often gravitate towards publications such as informational texts, magazines, and newspapers. Many boys connect easily with nonfiction about hobbies, sports, and things they might do or be interested in. And what does society basically shove down boys' throats as acceptable reading material? Graphic novels and comic books.

Now, aside from fantasy and science fiction—both traditionally accepted to be "boy-friendly," why *aren't* teenage boys reading fiction? For one, reading is commonly regarded as a passive activity. How many times have you said you are "doing nothing—just reading?" When you have a lot of energy, "nothing" doesn't sound like much fun for a Saturday afternoon. Another reason could go back to the fact that we teach boys to suppress their feelings, they aren't practiced and don't feel comfortable exploring the emotions and feelings found in fiction. But one of the reasons I think boys don't like to read fiction is that they're simply never introduced to books they'd like in school. A reader is born from enjoyment, not from drudgery. High school curriculum is heavily based on fiction and the books teens are being introduced to simply aren't stimulating to teenage boys. As a result, they aren't motivated to want to read and simply become turned-off by the whole activity.

While writing this, I went to my high school's Web site and looked at the current literature curriculum. What I saw was the perfect example of the underwhelming high school reading list. Even scarier is that they are the same books that I read when I went to the high school. And don't get me wrong, classics are important, but a 14-year-old boy cannot be expected to read Daphne du Maurier's *Rebecca* and enjoy it.

WINNING OVER BOY READERS

Lucky for us the books that publishers are fighting to get out there today *are* more boy-friendly. And though our educational system and Western socialization isn't going to change any time soon, you *can* write books that might just turn a teenage boy into a fiction reader.

Relatable main character

When writing for boys it's important that you create a protagonist a boy can identify with. In *The Lord of the Flies*, *A Separate Peace*, and *The Catcher in the Rye*—all popular high school required reading—the characters are all wealthy, Caucasian males who live at boarding schools. How common is this? Be aware that not all readers in 2008 will connect with a story about a rich white boy. Your protagonist could be from a different ethnic and economic background. In *Ball Don't Lie*, by Matt de la Peña, Sticky—the main character—is a boy whose mother was a drug addict and prostitute, then committed suicide. He's now alone—in and out of foster homes. He is gifted on the basketball court, but he has OCD and he's extremely withdrawn.

Simply put, Sticky is not your average kid from the suburbs. But what's average these days?

Relatable challenges

When creating your protagonist think about common adolescent challenges—challenges a teenage boy can identify with. (Being kicked out of boarding school isn't necessarily an issue many kids deal with annually.) In *King Dork*, by Frank Portman, the protagonist is being forced to read *The Catcher in the Rye*—something a lot more kids identify with than boarding school expulsion these days.

Tom Henderson is the main character in this book and, as he says so eloquently (in regard to his high school reading list): "Things were really, really bad in the '60s. You were always getting kicked out of your prep school, or getting into fights at your prep school, or getting marooned on deserted islands on the way to your fancy English boarding school." The bottom line is that most kids want to see glimpses of themselves in the fiction they read.

Unlikely heroes

The third way you can grasp the attention of a boy is to take advantage of the timeless success of the unlikely hero—the underdog or the outsider protagonist. This character many times offers affirmation for the teen reader, who—chances are—feels like he is, himself, an underdog.

Two current books—*I am the Messenger*, by Markus Zuzak, and *Looking for Alaska*, by John Green—are driven by solidly drawn unlikely heroes. In *I Am The Messenger* the protagonist describes himself early on for the reader, then sums it up simply by saying, "Constantly, I'm asking myself, *Well, Ed— what have you really achieved in your nineteen years?* The answer's simple. Jack Shit."

Reprinted with permission of Random House, Inc.

Tom Henderson in *King Dork*, by Frank Portman, goes through an experience that most boys can relate to when he's forced to read *The Catcher in the Rye* for school. Tom verbalizes the feelings many boys have about required reading: "Things were really, really bad in the '60s. You were always getting kicked out of your prep school, or getting into fights at your prep school, or getting marooned on deserted islands on the way to your fancy English boarding school."

Any underdog teen reading this could identify with this protagonists' self-contempt. After all, how many chances are teens given to see what they are capable of? Being unsure of yourself and your power is basically the definition of adolescence, and any reader will see himself in Ed's words.

When a reader can identify with a character/setting/plotline in a narrative it will affirm his own identity. The secret is that this is exactly what every teen is searching for. Ask a teenager what his favorite book is and he will most likely cite one that he really identified with. In the world of YA I think, "That was exactly like my high school!" is the most fantastic compliment a reader can give to an author.

Authentic dialogue

Your next task in writing a book for boys is to create an authentic teen experience. And you may think this one goes without saying, but it's surprising how many adult authors can be out of touch with the teen world. To do this, start by paying special attention to writing believable dialogue. A great exercise I recommend to many writers is to go out to malls or the beach—or anywhere teenagers hang out—and listen to the way kids talk.

An example of this can also be found in *Ball Don't Lie*. It's actually one of the qualities that makes the book feel so real to so many young readers. When he was writing this book, de la Peña would go out to street ball games and listen to the players interact with each other—listen to how they talk. And the result? In the following excerpt it's clear that the author knows his audience: "It's like this, Annie, God puts us here for a reason. We all born with something we could do good, but it's up to us to make sure we use it. That's why I play ball so much. I ain't gonna lie, I think God put me here to play ball."

Convincing characterization

Creating convincing characters, however, goes beyond just knowing how they speak to each other. The next task you must master is to create convincing characterizations and relationships. One of the reasons people connect with *King Dork* is that Frank Portman created a world that feels so real—complete with people and relationships that feel like they truly do exist.

In the book Tom Henderson has an awkward, yet strangely warm relationship with his step-dad. Portman sums up this step-father/step-son relationship easily, but dead on: "Little Big Tom can be annoying, but eventually I got used to him. Amanda, on the other hand, has never accepted his legitimacy. She spent the whole first year of the 'partnership' sobbing."

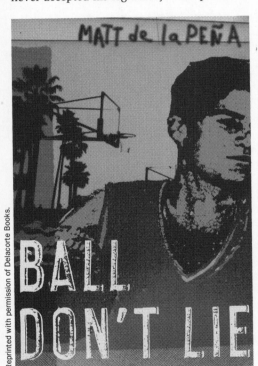

In just three sentences we know how Tom feels and how his sister feels, creating a realistic family life.

Realistic microcosm

Which brings me to the next task—create a realistic high school microcosm. Going back to the "underwhelming" high school reading list; how many teen readers are identifying with the social order of boarding school boys stranded on islands, or getting kicked out of their schools? In all of the contemporary books I've mentioned so far, the author has created concrete social structures.

In *King Dork*, Tom is at the bottom of the social order and is therefore tormented by the "normal people." In *Ball Don't Lie*, Sticky is such an outsider that he only really feels like an equal on the basketball court. In *Looking for Alaska*, the protagonist has a small clique of friends who don't really fit into any other mold—he's an outsider with his own group of fellow outsiders. The truth about being a teenager is that no matter how popular you are, you're never really secure and you never really feel like you can't be dumped from your "group." Capturing this social insecurity is a brilliant way to capture the truth of being a teen.

Reprinted with permission of Delacorte Books.

Ball Don't Lie, by Matt de la Peña, features Sticky, a teen boy with an authentic voice. More like the typical high school boy than the rich boarding school kids in required-reading-list books like *A Separate Peace* or *Lord of the Flies*, readers and critics alike empathize with Sticky and his story. Says *Booklist*, "Teens will be strongly affected by the unforgettable, distinctly male voice; the thrilling, unusually detailed basketball action; and the questions about race, love, self-worth, and what it means to build a life without advantages."

Fast-paced plots

My final piece of advice in writing for boys is to craft your plot with care. It may seem like a no-brainer, but fast paced books will pull the reluctant reader in. From the first line, *Ball Don't Lie* sets the reader up for action, "Dreadlock Man, with his fierce fists and suspect jump shots, sets his stull ($1.45 sandals, key to bike lock, extra T-shirt) on the bleachers and holds his hand out for the ball." There's no fooling around here. We go straight to the game— most-likely exactly what the boy reader has picked up this book for.

It goes without saying that quieter, meditative books are less likely to engage this audience. The more cerebral—or inside the protagonist's head—the quieter the book will feel. This however, is not an absolute. *I Am the Messenger* is a great example of how to get around this. Though a lot of story is the protagonist's inner struggle, he's given actual tasks he must perform throughout the book that take him outside of himself and his own head and force him to interact with others and to actually take action. The reader, in turn, goes on the journey as well.

Writing can't be turned into an equation. There are no guarantees on book sales or good reviews. But it *can* be less of a mystery. All of us were once teenagers. The goal of writing a successful children's book is to go back and capture that voice. In the case of writing fiction for boys, you want to concentrate on that voice and character. Writing books for a boy reader isn't impossible—even if you're a woman. But everyone can use tips. Give the boys what they want—what they identify with—and they will read.

Articles & Interviews

A Guide to Writing Teen Chick Lit

by Farrin Jacobs & Sarah Mlynowski

The Princess Diaries. Gossip Girl. The Sisterhood of the Traveling Pants. If you've followed the world of young adult fiction for the last few years, then you've noticed that some popular teen heroines have dug their Doc Martens/Prada heels into the bestseller lists and aren't stepping off.

If adult chick lit is considered Bridget Jones, then teen chick lit is Bridget Jones' little sister. The types of stories under the teen chick lit umbrella are just as varied as their adult contemporaries, but they're not differentiated in the same way: that is, adult chick lit is often categorized by stage of life (for example, now there's single-girl lit, bride lit, divorce lit, and we'll probably soon be seeing second-marriage lit), whereas teen chick lit is identified more by the characters' lifestyle and relationships. For simplicity's sake, we're going to make vast generalizations and divide teen chick lit into three groups: It Could Be You, the Glamorous Life, and BFF. It Could Be You (ICBY) books focus on a main character, are often in first person, and are about real girls in real situations (think *The Boyfriend List*, and *Angus, Thongs and Full-Frontal Snogging*) or real girls in outlandish situations (think *The Princess Diaries* and *Bras & Broomsticks*). The Glamorous Life books tend to be aspirational stories about multiple characters set in ritzy locations like Beverly Hills or fancy prep schools (*The Au Pairs*, *Gossip Girl*, *The It Girl*), and BFF books often have multiple characters too, but deal with real-life contemporary issues that teen girls face, while focusing on the power of friendship to help them through (*Sisterhood of the Traveling Pants*, *Peaches*, *ttyl*).

No matter which type of teen chick lit novel you're writing, these are some of the things you'll want to consider:

YOUR MAIN CHARACTER(S)

Who your main character is depends on which type of book you're writing. If you're going the ICBY route, then your heroine is the anchor to your book. First, she has to be likeable. If your reader thinks she's too whiny, too bitchy, or too spoiled, she isn't going to care what happens

FARRIN JACOBS, a former chick lit editor and current teen fiction editor, is the co-author of *See Jane Write: A Girl's Guide to Writing Chick Lit.*

SARAH MLYNOWSKI has written three novels for teens (*Bras & Broomsticks, Frogs & French Kisses* and *Spells & Sleeping Bags*), five for adults (*Milkrun, Fishbowl, As Seen on TV, Monkey Business* and *Me Vs. Me*), co-written a guide to writing chick lit (*See Jane Write*), co-edited two bestselling charity collections (*Girls' Night Out* and *Girls' Night In*), and contributed to various anthologies. She is currently writing a new novel called *How to Be Bad* with YA writers Lauren Myracle and E. Lockhart. Originally from Montreal, Sarah now lives in New York City. Visit her online at www.sarahm.com.

to her. She also has to be relatable. This doesn't mean that your character can't experience unusual situations—it just means that your girl has to respond to her circumstances in a way that makes sense to your reader. In Meg Cabot's Princess Diaries series (going strong with the eighth book out this year), down-to-earth Mia finds out in book one that she's actually the Princess of a country called Genovia. But because Mia is such a grounded character (she has boy crushes, an ex-best friend, a best friend and parental trouble just like anyone else) readers can easily see themselves in Mia's royal shoes. Another important element in the ICBY category is that your protagonist has room to grow. These novels are coming of age stories, so the arc of your novel should center around what she learns about herself, and how she changes. Maybe she becomes less self-involved. Maybe she learns the value of true friendship.

If the Glamorous Life is for you, then you probably have more than one heroine. These girls can be a little less likeable, and a little less relatable, but they're always entertaining. Jenny Humphrey, in The It Girl, a series set at a boarding school, might be shallow, maybe hooks up with her roommate's boyfriend, and, OK, is a little image obsessed . . . but people are not reading about her to relate, they're reading to be entertained, to peer into a foreign world. There's often a fish-out-of-water swimming in this rarified world but generally readers want to feel like they have the inside scoop. While character arc is a part of the book, plot and external forces are what drives these characters.

Author Sarah Mlynowski and editor Farrin Jacobs teamed up for *See Jane Write*, an in-depth look at how to write chick lit, with lots of information that carries over into other genres. *School Library Journal* says, "The writing style is quirky and the advice is sound. The main theme is that writing is difficult, but rewarding, and that one can always improve."

In a BFF book, you don't have one main character, you have three or four, and each of them has distinct personal issues/obstacles they have to overcome. They each have a character arc. They each grow in some way. Of course the friendship is probably tested at some point in the novel, but in the end it is usually that friendship that helps them make sense of their world. In Lauren Myracle's TTYL series, Angela, Zoe, and Maddie all deal with their own stuff (a broken heart, an inappropriate teacher relationship, a toxic friendship) but the novel's heart lies in the strength of their relationship with each other.

Watch out for:
A main character that's supposed to be funny and sarcastic, but is kinda just . . . bitchy. Also, a main character that's supposed to be clever and quirky, but is just kinda . . . weird and off-putting.

POINT OF VIEW & STORYTELLING DEVICE
Although it's not a hard and fast rule, usually the ICBY books are written in the first person, while the Glam Life and BFF books are written in the third person. The advantage of first

person is that you feel like you're hearing the character's deepest secrets. Third person, however, allows you to jump back and forth between multiple characters without having to create distinct first-person voices. You should choose the point of view you feel most comfortable writing—and the one that works best for your story.

Storytelling device might also play a role in choosing the point of view, and teen chick lit authors have experimented with many different ones. There's the popular diary format (Megan McCafferty's Sloppy Firsts series, Louise Rennison's Georgia Nicolson series), letter format (all of Jaclyn Moriarty's books) and even instant messages (Lauren Myracle's *ttyl*; *ttfn*; and *L8R, G8R*). Choosing an alternative narrative technique allows you to play with point of view and could add a new twist to a traditional story. (*ttyl* is a BFF story at its heart, but because it's told in IMs it's three alternating first-person voices.)

SECONDARY CHARACTERS

There are certain characters that you're likely to include in your teen chick lit novel. Number one, there are your main character's peers. Whether it's a new friend, or a frienemy, or the popular girl from hell, the girls that she hangs out with/wants to hang out with are probably the most important secondary characters in your book. The key to creating dynamic, believable secondary characters is to not rely on clichés—the mean head cheerleader, the nerdy bookworm. Since these characters have been done again and again, if you want them to leap off the page, then you have to make the mean head cheerleader different from all the mean head cheerleaders that have come before her. Maybe she's a vampire. Maybe the bitchy head cheerleader is a guy. Just because they're secondary doesn't mean they can be two-dimensional. Flesh these characters out. For example, remember that no one is mean just for the sake of being mean. Show the reader what has happened in her life to make her so awful.

Number two, you have the love interest. This can be a crush, a boyfriend, an ex-boyfriend, a best friend, or all of the above. How much you want to develop the relationship depends on how important it is to the crux of your book, but romance will likely be involved in at least a sub plot. What can we say—girls like romance. The key to this relationship is to have the reader fall for the guy at the same time your main character does. If "Robbie" is described as a shallow A-list jerk who trips freshmen as they walk down the hall, your reader is not going to understand why your girl has a thing for him. Make sure you don't make Robbie too good to be true though. A believable character has flaws. Just don't make them deal-breaker flaws. In other words, he can be a Trekkie, but he can't enjoy giving Trekkies wedgies.

Number three is family. Again, making your girl's parents and siblings well-rounded is key. A psycho strict parent is psycho strict for a reason (and might benefit from at least one tender scene). In teen chick lit novels, siblings and parents often serve as foils for the main character. In *Bras & Broomsticks*, for example, not only does main character Rachel *not* have magical powers while her younger sister Miri does—but Miri's calm and introspective nature is juxtaposed against Rachel's hyperactive and outgoing one. Use family members to help the reader better understand what makes your character tick.

SETTING

Yes, most teen chick lit novels are set at school, since that's where teen girls spend five days of the week 10 months of the year, but don't forget about that time off. Many teen chick lit novels take place during the summer, to let their characters roam. Look at the Sisterhood books—the four characters all go their separate ways every summer leading the girls to Greece, to Baja, to art school, to working at Wallmans. Many authors take their girls out of the classroom and into exciting locations by taking advantage of summers off and school vacations and sending them to drama camp (E. Lockhart's *Dramarama*), a bike trip to Ireland (Maryrose Wood's *Why I Let My Hair Grow Out*), or Miami Beach (Aimee Friedman's *South Beach*). If you do decide to set your book at school, don't despair: find interesting and appealing locations in which to set your scenes. Try not to set every scene in the classroom/lunchroom/bedroom. Take your girl to the mall. To her after school job. To the school's roof. Make like *Laguna Beach*, hit the beach, and take advantage of your locale.

Watch out for:

Clichéd settings like the prom. We've all seen the movies. Again. And again. Everything leads up to the prom. Yes, prom is an important rite of passage in an American teen girl's life, but if you're going to write about prom, then you have to write about it in a different way (and make sure it's relevant to your story). Maybe you have a Morp, an anti-prom at your character's house. (Like John Green did in his short story in the anthology *21 Proms*. Couldn't avoid writing about the prom that time!) Maybe your prom is a costume party. Whatever. Just make it your own.

TONE & LANGUAGE

If you think that teen chick lit has to be sweet and fluffy, the equivalent of literary cotton candy, think again. The truth is, your book can be anything from upbeat to dreamy to sarcastic to literary. Jodi Lynn Anderson's *Peaches* has a sweet, nostalgic feel to it, while Melina Marchetta's *Saving Francesca* is more serious (the main character is wrestling with her mother's depression) and *Bad Kitty* by Michele Jaffe is over-the-top hilarious. Keep your tone options open, and go with whatever works with your story. Just make your tone consistent, please.

Reprinted with permission of Delacorte Books.

Spells & Sleeping Bags, by Sarah Mlynowski, is an It Could Be You (ICBY) novel that has a normal girl dealing with some abnormal experiences when main character Rachel, who readers first meet in Mlynowski's *Bras & Broomsticks* and *Frogs & French Kisses*, finally taps into her own magical powers, just in time to go to summer camp.

Watch out for:

1. Trying too hard with the teen speak. Teens are pretty sharp so don't write down to them and don't overuse words such as *totally* and *like*. Yes, teen girls use them, but that doesn't mean anyone wants to see them in print, like, again and again.
2. Not trying hard enough with the teen speak. If your character says "Gosh darn it!" when she stubs her finger, your readers are going to laugh. At you, not with you.
3. Brand names. If it suits your character (say, if it's a Glam Life book), then yes, it makes sense to sprinkle them throughout. But keep in mind that they often come across as a substitute for description, and that they date your book. Fast.

THE END

What makes a good teen chick lit ending? While there aren't too many rules, your grand finale has to fit your story, and should probably be upbeat and hopeful. If your book deals with tough issues, don't feel pressured to solve them outright. Your main character can simply be figuring out how to face them and move forward in her life. She should be growing up. You don't have to fix all her problems, but you also don't want to leave too many loose ends—unless you're planning a series. In that case, cliffhanger-away.

Watch out for:

Hospital corner endings. These are endings where everything is improbably wrapped up *too* quickly, *too* neatly. Yes, you want a tidy, satisfying ending but it should be at least somewhat grounded in reality.

WHAT'S THE NEXT BIG THING?

It's never easy to call trends, and it's always dangerous to write for them at the risk of them being not-trends by the time your book is published, but it helps to stay in the know of what publishers are looking for. Here's what's selling to publishers right now: younger teen chick lit like Leslie Margolis' upcoming *Boys Are Dogs* books and Meg Cabot's next series, which kicks off with *Allie Finkle's Rules for Girls*. Paranormal stories, like *Hex Education*, by Emily Gould and Zareen Jaffery, and Beth Paige's vampire tale, *Jessica's Guide to Dating on the Dark Side* (although if you're writing about vampires, you'd better make sure it's the best vampire book ever because there are a *lot* of them already in the pipeline from many publishers). And of course, a strong, character-driven coming-of-age tale never goes out of style.

Rhyming Right

Crafting Rhyming Stories That Lilt, Dance & March off the Page

by Hope Vestergaard

After attending umpteen local, state, and national children's writers' conferences, I calculate that I have heard the following question at least 72 times: "Why don't children's book editors like rhyming picture books?"

Most editors respond that they don't dislike rhyming texts, just *bad* ones. Sure, there is the occasional curmudgeonly editor who, forced to answer this question for the 423rd time, finally snaps and says, "I hate rhyming books. Don't send me a rhyming picture book, ever." But for the most part, there appears to plenty of room on the shelves for rhyming picture books. New titles are published every season, and classics such as Dr. Seuss have more than withstood the test of time. It's no wonder newbies are confused. If rhyming picture books are being published, why is everyone so discouraging?

Editors are simply responding to what they find in the slush pile. Reading bad verse is excruciating. It's right up there with listening to nails on a chalkboard, fifth grade band recitals, and *American Idol* audition tapes. Bad rhyme, like bad singing, is the opposite of entertainment. In fact, it can turn people *off* to reading. So why on earth do people keep submitting bad rhyme?

The answer is simple: *People keep writing bad rhyme because they don't know what bad rhyme is.* To paraphrase a recent Defense Secretary, "Some folks don't know what they don't know." Is this a hopeless cause? No! Not everyone is an instinctively good poet, but everyone can get better at understanding and, yes, writing poetry.

Great rhyme sounds effortless—it dances off the tongue. This can lead people to believe that it's an easy form to master, but most rhymers I know spend days, weeks, and even months finding the right combination of stresses, sounds, and subjects to make a poem perfect. In the interest of shrinking slush piles and decreasing auditory abominations, I'd like to take a stab at defining bad and good rhyme and give aspiring rhymers specific tips for polishing up their poetry until it gleams.

BEFORE YOU BEGIN

Some story ideas emerge in rhyme. It is always fun to play with sounds and words to see where they'll take you. But whenever you are tempted to write a story in rhyme, think long and hard about whether a rhyming format will enhance or constrict your story. Remember

HOPE VESTERGAARD is the author of many rhyming picture books, most recently, *I Don't Want To Clean My Room: A Mess of Poems About Chores* and *What Do You Do When a Monster Says Boo?*, both published by Dutton. She's a former teacher and curriculum writer. Visit her Web site: www.hopevestergaard.com for more articles on the writing life.

that the rhyme isn't the story, it's a flourish. It's the icing, not the cake. The following subjects are often enhanced by being told in verse:

- **Epic stories** or modern, tongue-in-cheek epics such as Lisa Wheeler's *Seadogs: An Epic Ocean Operetta* (Simon & Schuster)
- **Musical stories:** *Zin! Zin! Zin! A Violin!*, by Lloyd Moss (Simon & Schuster) or my book, *Hillside Lullaby* (Dutton)
- **Movement stories:** *Off We Go!*, by Jane Yolen (Little Brown)
- **Early Readers:** *Sheep in a Jeep*, by Nancy Shaw (Houghton Mifflin)
- **Wordplay books:** *Chicka, Chicka, Boom, Boom*, by Bill Martin, Jr. and John Archambault (Simon & Schuster), or any of John Lithgow's books
- **Interactive stories** that invite readers to chant along: *Louella Mae, She's Run Away*, by Karen Beaumont Alarcon (Henry Holt).

Once a rhyming story you're working on becomes arduous, don't feel you must finish it in rhyme. If you're trying too hard, it's likely to show in strained, forced verse. Reserve the right to change your mind. Once you are confident that your story would be well-served by a rhyming format, you'll need to ensure that your verse is flawless.

THE GOOD
Good meter

You don't need a degree in poetry to recognize good meter. If everyone who reads the verse aloud puts the accents in the same place and can read it without stumbling, a verse is said to "scan." If it takes several tries to read a line correctly, or if it sounds awkward and clunky when read aloud, the meter may have gone awry.

Good meter is not a matter of syllables, but stresses. Paired lines must have stresses in the same place. In addition, the stresses in each word should fall where they do when the word is spoken aloud by an average person. To illustrate this, I use CAPS for stressed syllables and lowercase for unstressed ones. So let's look at a limerick:

> there ONCE was a MAN from PerU
> who DREAMED he was EATing his SHOE
> he aWOKE in the NIGHT
> in a TERRible FRIGHT
> and FOUND it was PERfectly TRUE.

Lines one, two, and five all share the same stresses:

> soft HARD soft soft HARD soft soft HARD

Lines three and four have a different pattern, but they match each other:

> soft soft HARD soft soft HARD

In terms of the natural stresses of individual words that I mentioned above, look at the word *Peru*. It rhymes with *aDIEU* and *PurDUE* and *the FLU* because the end rhymes and the natural stresses match. The word *HAIRdo*, however, has a different natural stress, even though the end syllables sound the same. If you try to pair "hairdo" with Peru in a verse, the reader has to make an adjustment ("PERu") to maintain forward motion as they read aloud. This is not a good thing for your poem.

> *Specific terms are used to describe stressed and unstressed syllables and various metric patterns, but you don't have to know these names to write decent verse.*

To learn more about them, Myra Cohn Livingston's Poem-Making *(HarperCollins) is a useful guide. It's out of print, but is relatively easy to find at libraries or from online used booksellers.*

Good storytelling

No matter how spectacular your verse is, it can't prop up a sagging story. Before you get too involved in fixing your rhyme, you need to ensure that your **story** is solid. Writing a story in rhyme can add extra layers of meaning, but a bunch of rhyming verses don't necessarily make a story. Even wordplay books such as *Jamberry*, by Bruce Degen (Harper) include narrative elements. Many of the bad rhyming stories I read are ones in which the form has dictated the function. The writer chooses words that complete his or her rhymes, rather than choosing the right words to tell the story, and the whole thing runs amok.

A rhyming picture book has to have all the elements of a great prose story. It needs **rich language**: interesting vocabulary, alliteration, metaphors, and onomatopoeia. A story also needs a **compelling plot**. Even slice-of-life stories need clear forward motion and a progression of ideas or feelings or events over the course of the book. All stories for children need to have great **pacing**—perfect page turns and just enough words to tell the story. Kids won't sit still for boring descriptions and flowery prose.

Called "Humorous and amiable" by the *Kirkus Reviews*, *I Don't Want To Clean My Room: A Mess of Poems About Chores*, by Hope Vestergaard, shows how to do rhyming right, combining a compelling storyline with good pacing and meter. See other titles by Vestergaard, like *What Do You Do When a Monster says Boo?* and *Hillside Lullaby* for more examples of well-written rhyme for young readers.

Children's books also need **interesting characters** who are three-dimensional, engaging, and imperfect. For some reason, a rhyming format is often the approach people take when writing preachy and didactic books. If you strip away the rhyme, you don't have a story, just a lecture. And what kid will hang around for that? Last but not least, any story needs to have a **satisfying resolution**. This is often easily overlooked in a rhyming story if you've done all the other things right. If a story doesn't build to something meaningful, kids (and editors!) won't want to read it again. (Speaking of your audience, just as with prose stories, the subject matter and the language you use to tell your story should be developmentally appropriate for the children who will be reading it.)

THE BAD

Now that we've identified essential elements for a good rhyming story, let's get back to the question that inspired this article: what makes bad rhyme bad?

- Unnatural word stresses
- Clunky, meandering meter
- Unimaginative language
- Dull characters and plot

- Stale or overdone subject matter
- Near rhymes

Songwriters can get away with near rhymes because melody and beats often take precedence over the language. Picture book writers can't get away with sloppy rhymes because their audience counts on true rhymes to help them learn to read. Pre-readers love rhyming stories precisely because the rhymes help them predict which word comes next and feel like they are reading. For kids who have just learned to read, rhyming texts make it easier for them to decode words and feel competent. Near rhymes such as *foot/good*, *bird/poured*, and *climb/dine* are confusing.

THE UGLY

I prefer not to pick on bad writing, but in the case of some celebrity projects, I think it's OK to highlight examples of bad rhyme because these are often cases where more strenuous editing could have drastically improved the story. In Katie Couric's *Brand New Kid* (Doubleday), the main character's name is Ellie McSnelly. This isn't a real name and appears to be used for convenience, as do some of the book's forced rhymes: *poodle* and *strudel*, for example. Another no-no is changing the syntax of a sentence to make an end-rhyme work: *"Too different and strange to fit in they all feared."* If it sounds unnatural, it doesn't belong in the story. Even though sub-par books sometimes sneak through the slush pile, if you want to get published, you'll need to do the hard work to get your story right. Don't waste energy looking for an easy out when you have the tools to get the job done yourself.

Quick fixes for rhymes & misdemeanors

My own rhyming manuscripts tend to stumble in predictable ways. The following suggestions will help you polish your own diamonds in the rough.

Near Rhymes:

- A good rhyming dictionary is critical. (Note that some of the entries in rhyming dictionaries include archaic words or regional pronunciations that are too obscure.)
- Avoid online dictionaries. I haven't found one that can match my trusty Merriam-Webster paperback.
- A thesaurus can lead you to words that mean the same thing and are easier to rhyme.
- Try switching word order within a line or moving around lines within a verse, but don't create unnatural syntax. If it sounds stilted or confusing, you haven't solved the problem.

Sing-Song Verse:

- Sometimes meter can be too consistent. Break up the monotony with a chorus, or shift rhythms within a longer piece. Be sure meter shifts are symmetrical: begin and end the story on a similar note, for example.
- It's easy to get stuck on a particular rhythm. Read lots of different authors to get out of the rut. Make sure that every poem in a collection does not have the same meter and structure.
- Some stories are meant to be sung, but remember that not every reader is a singer. Make sure your story works without a melody, too.

Uncooperative Meter:

- If only a few verses in a story are really working, rethink the format. You might write the story in prose with a refrain, as in Lisa Wheeler's *Porcupining* (Little, Brown) or Anita Jeram's *Bunny My Honey* (Candlewick).

- Give the story a rest. It's especially important to get some distance from the manuscript when you are having rhythmic difficulties. Repetitive, physical work such as walking, mowing the lawn, or scrubbing tiles is a good cure for this kind of problem. I set my subconscious brain to the task and it's usually not too long before I have a solution.
- Listen to many other people reading your text aloud.
- If you print the manuscript in the lowercase/UPPERCASE format mentioned above, a quick visual scan will highlight tricky spots.

Cereal fillers

The final step in polishing rhyming text should be checking to make sure that each and every word earns its space on the page. Omit words such as ''very'' and ''so'' and ''just'' and ''really'' that are just holding beats, and replace them with stronger verbs and adjectives. Every single word should be a gem.

SHINING STARS

The best way to learn a new language is to immerse yourself in the sights and sounds of the culture you're studying. The same is true for poetry. Here are some recommendations for a do-it-yourself intensive poetry class. Happy reading!

Poetry collections:

- A.A. Milne's poems: they're full of energy and have interesting metrical jogs and jumps. My favorite: *When We Were Very Young* (Dutton)
- Alice Schertle: Intense language, interesting rhythms, and great personification of characters. Try *How Now, Brown Cow* (Voyager)
- Anything by J. Patrick Lewis, Karla Kuskin, or Douglas Florian.

Narrative picture books:

- *Seven Silly Eaters* (Harcourt) or *A House is a House for Me* (Viking) by MaryAnn Hoberman.
- *Mrs. Biddlebox* or *When Moon Fell Down* by Linda Smith (both published by HarperCollins), two very different kinds of stories told in expert rhyme.
- *Te Amo, Bebe, Little One* by Lisa Wheeler (Little, Brown). Wheeler's always pitch perfect. This is a great example of a simple, elegant story for the youngest readers.
- *What Do You Do When a Monster Says Boo?*, by Hope Vestergaard (Dutton). Pardon me for tooting my own horn, but this participation book works well for its target audience and teaches without preaching.

Interesting rhythms:

- *Grump* by Janet Wong (Margaret McElderry). A tired toddler and his beleaguered mom trudge, tromp and stomp toward a perfect and inevitable conclusion.
- *Hushabye* by John Burningham (Knopf). A quiet and quirky lullaby.
- *The Day the Babies Crawled Away* by Peggy Rathmann (Putnam). Rathmann's best known for her prose but this book is a treat: fun, engaging, and full of delicious turns of phrase.
- *Charlie Parker Played Be Bop* by Chris Raschka (Scholastic) is a great example of lean language that does heavy lifting.

Writing for Beginning Readers

by JoAnn Early Macken

A child who is learning to read faces a challenging task. Beginning readers must be able to identify letters, connect them to sounds, recognize familiar words, learn new words, and understand what they are reading. They need engaging, informative, clearly written books to hold their attention and help them learn.

Both trade and educational publishers publish books for beginning readers, and they publish both fiction and nonfiction. Subjects include biography, science, sports, careers, math, mystery, humor, how-to—almost any topic you would find for older readers.

What makes such books attractive to readers? What makes them easy to read? What does a writer need to know? As an author and former editor of books for beginning readers, I've worked on hundreds of these books. I also recognize the value of research, so I asked eight other authors and editors of books for beginning readers to contribute their thoughts about the process.

WHERE TO BEGIN?

If you're thinking about writing for this age group, start by reading. Look for classics by Dr. Seuss, Arnold Lobel, and Russell Hoban. Study *Nate the Great*, *Mrs. Wishy-Washy*, and *Red-Eyed Tree Frog*. But don't stop there. Explore the abundance of books published by educational publishers. Notice the range of topics and levels of complexity. Seek out award winners such as Dana Meachen Rau's *A Star in My Orange: Looking for Nature's Shapes*. You'll find a wealth of satisfying reading about subjects that appeal to children.

Beginning reader books from trade publishers are typically 32 pages long. Some have 48 or even 60 pages, and some have as few as eight. Many books from educational publishers are 24 pages long. In a typical format, the first three pages include copyright information, a title page, and a Table of Contents. The last three pages contain a glossary, an index, and a list of related books and Web sites.

Of the 24 pages, that leaves 18. In books for the earliest readers, one page of every two-page spread is an illustration. Nine pages remain for text, and each page may include only one or two sentences. A limit of 100 to 200 words is common. Books for slightly more

---

JOANN EARLY MACKEN has written more than eighty books for beginning readers. She is the author of the picture books *Sing-Along Song*; *Waiting Out the Storm*; and *Flip, Float, Fly! Seeds on the Move*, as well as about a dozen biographies, several science books, and a variety of poems. She is a graduate of the M.F.A. in Writing for Children and Young Adults Program at Vermont College. Visit her Web site at www.joannmacken.com.

advanced readers may include both text and illustrations on those 18 pages and a maximum of 500 to 1,000 words.

Although these books appear simple, writing them is not. Lola Schaefer, author of *Loose Tooth*, *Mittens*, and many nonfiction books for beginning readers, says writers may think that writing "one of those simple books for young readers" would be an easy way to break into children's publishing. But they are mistaken.

"The audience, typically children between the ages of four and seven, is intelligent and discerning," Schaefer says. "This readership would immediately spot an insincere attempt to placate them with short, stiff prose or a less than emotional text. I believe that the fewer the words, the more difficult the job. A writer of these texts needs to engage, entertain, and inspire."

Why is it harder to write something shorter? Say you are writing a nonfiction book about wolves for first graders. First, as with any project, you must do your research. The fact that the text is shorter doesn't mean you need to know less about your subject. In fact, you have to find out everything you can about wolves so you can decide which information is most important. Then you must boil it down to its absolute essence and put it in language a first grader can understand—while making it interesting.

SIMPLICITY IS KEY

Sarah Schuette, senior editor at educational publisher Capstone Press, says to keep it simple. "Simple construction, simple word choice, and logical organization are key at this level. Moving the text along from general to specific, making sure it doesn't raise more questions than it answers is important. Repetition of simple phrases and text that builds on that knowledge gives the reader a sense of accomplishment."

"It is also helpful to imagine a child reading aloud when writing for this level," Schuette says. "Simple sentence structure may feel or sound choppy to the writer, but early readers aren't smooth readers. Revisit the Dick and Jane books, they are wonderful examples of books designed to help kids read."

Dori Chaconas, author of the hilarious Cork and Fuzz series and many outstanding picture books, agrees with that priority. "One of the most valuable things I learned about writing beginning readers is to keep a narrow focus on what's happening in the story. In the first version of *Cork and Fuzz*, I had too much going on in the plot. Melanie Cecka [former Viking editor now with Bloomsbury], suggested I focus on only one thing per book, then carry that single thread throughout the story. As these stories are limited to about one thousand words, a narrow focus in the plot left me with time and words to develop the characters more fully."

Lisa Moser, a former teacher and the author of *The Monster in the Backpack* and *Squirrel's World*, says, "It is a great joy to write for children who are learning to read. I have tremendous respect for the work the children must do to decode the words and comprehend a story. As a writer, I want my stories to be fun and entertaining, and most of all, a successful experience."

Moser says simple sentence structure is even more important than controlling the vocabulary. "Write short sentences with distinct nouns and verbs. Avoid compound sentences and sentences with a lot of adjectives or adverbs. Complex sentences make more work for the child who is learning to read. Pave the way for the child. Don't put up obstacles."

"Capturing the beginning reader language can be difficult at first, but the more you work with the genre, the easier it gets," Moser says. "My first suggestion is to read, read, read every beginning reader you can get your hands on. Pretty soon, the language will begin to soak into your writing. Another trick I use is to speak without contractions. Say 'I will' instead of 'I'll.' This technique helps me to quickly find the beginning reader language."

Keep the language spare. Don't slip in a single extra word. Such a brief format has no room for description, background, or dialogue that doesn't move the story forward or provide essential information. Keep sentences short, but do vary the structure so not every sentence follows the same pattern.

Exciting writing

Simple does not mean boring! Joanne Mattern, author of more than 150 books for children, says, "I think the most important thing to keep in mind when writing for beginning readers is not to lose the liveliness of the subject matter. Just because you are using simple words and short sentences doesn't mean that you have to leave out all the details that give the subject depth. You have to not only keep it simple, but keep it fun! I've found the best way to do this is to keep the child in mind as I write and think about what he or she would *really* want to know about the subject."

The language for these readers must be engaging. Use active verbs and specific nouns. Include wordplay if it fits your subject. Alliteration can be appealing, but don't overdo it unless you are aiming for humor. Rhythm and repetition help the early learner. Not all publishers accept rhyme, so be sure to find out before you submit. Even if a publisher prefers to avoid end rhyme, internal rhyme might be acceptable.

Other poetic techniques are also inviting. Use luscious imagery to describe an unfamiliar object. Onomatopoeia adds zip to language. And it's OK to use an occasional unfamiliar term. That's how children learn new words. Just try to define any difficult words, either in the text or in a glossary.

Not all kids this age have a firm grasp of measurements, so use comparisons to give them a clearer picture. Say "as narrow as a pencil" or "the size of a door" to help them understand inches and feet—and include metric equivalents.

Telling the truth

Writers have a responsibility to new readers, who form their first impressions of many subjects when they read. Accuracy is essential. When you must simplify, be careful not to change the meaning or mislead the reader.

Helen Frost is the author of more than 100 nonfiction books for young readers, four novels-in-poems, and *Monarch and Milkweed,* a lyrical nonfiction picture book. She says, "In writing for beginning readers, it can be challenging to speak both truthfully and simply. For example, I don't believe that anyone is 'born a slave.' A baby was born, and then another person made a claim on the child's life and enforced that claim through systematic violence for their own economic gain and power within the larger society. The oversimplification of such hard facts can serve to reinforce inequities that remain today. I don't have an easy answer to the question of how to address this, but I do feel it is important to consider each word we write, and each sentence construction we use, with an awareness of how our language will affect young children as they construct their view of the world."

Ages & reading levels

Beginning reader books are available for a range of ages and reading levels. When you write, be aware of the typical reader's age so you can provide appropriate information and concepts a child that age can understand.

Many different systems measure readability, which does not necessarily correspond to a reader's age or school grade. Vocabulary and sentence structure are important in determining readability. Some formulas, such as the Flesch-Kincaid Grade Level provided by Microsoft® Office Word, measure only these two factors. Other systems also consider typeface, amount of white space per page, repetition, and graphic support from illustrations. An article on the Houghton Mifflin Web site at (www.eduplace.com/state/pdf/author/pikulski.pdf) explains more about reading levels and readability formulas. A chart from Capstone Press at (www.capst onepress.com/aspx/pLeveling.aspx) compares the levels of four systems and provides a brief history of each one. Random House's Step into Reading Web site provides examples of books at five readability levels at www.randomhouse.com/kids/books/step/teachers/index.html.

Children's Writer's Word Book, 2nd edition, by Alijandra Mogilner (Writer's Digest Books) is a valuable reference tool. It lists the grade levels at which many common words are introduced and provides synonyms with their corresponding grade levels.

The role of illustrations

Illustrations in books for beginning readers differ from those in picture books in an important way. In a picture book, illustrations might expand on the text or even show something that isn't mentioned. Illustrations in books for beginning readers must closely match the text to provide clues for the readers. Research shows that children who are learning to read study the pictures to help them understand the text. One study tracked eye movements of young readers. Their eyes continually moved from the words to the illustrations and back again.

What does this mean for writers? Each page needs to be illustratable. Try to provide one concrete picture option on each page. You'll be helping young readers understand what they read.

Following the guidelines

Many educational publishers assign topics to writers rather than accepting submissions as trade publishers do. If you want to write for a particular publisher, find a copy of the company's guidelines. Many are available on the Internet; if not, ask for them. Know the required word count and number of pages for a manuscript at your intended reading level.

Dana Meachen Rau has written almost two hundred books for children, most of them nonfiction for readers in kindergarten through third grade. She explains that with the limited number of words in an easy reader book, every single one must count. "I believe that writing for the youngest readers is probably the most challenging of all the age levels. While I might have grand hopes for any given topic, piles of kid-friendly anecdotes the readers would love, or fabulous metaphors that will help them discover their world, the biggest struggle in writing early readers is the limited nature of the genre. At all turns, I have to take into account their prior knowledge of the topic and vocabulary. In other words, is it worth it to write a kindergarten book on the solar system, when I would have to devote so many precious words to explaining terms such as 'planet,' 'orbit,' and 'rotation,' and therefore have no room left for the fact that Jupiter looks like a big ball of rainbow sherbet? Or if I use a word such as 'crunchy,' am I providing enough clues on the rest of the page so that they can decipher it on their own?"

"I often think of the process as distilling down the information to its most simple level," Rau says. "And while doing that, the challenging part is making sure I am still being completely accurate. I often find I am spending an hour on a seemingly simple issue—Can I say 'bug' when 'insect' is the more correct term? Should I compare lungs to balloons or sponges? So when choosing topics, I try to keep them within a child's realm of experience, or at least connect something new with something they might already know. Stretching a child's world is what books are all about. It is immensely gratifying to take a topic and make it accessible to even the youngest readers—and to find the words for them to discover it on their own."

While it is important to know what a publisher requires, Editor Kristin Daly of HarperCollins warns writers not to get too caught up with format specifications. "The absolutely, positively, most important element in creating a good easy-to-read book is not the ease of vocabulary, nor the simplicity of the sentence structure, nor the length of the lines of text. It is—as with all writing—a good story or plot. Just as in YA, or middle-grade, or picture

Articles & Interviews

books, every author's first concern in writing an easy-to-read book should be to write a good story. While it is good to do your research, and to keep genre guidelines in the back of your mind, in the end, ultimately you have to write a good story. The text can be written in letter-perfect easy-to-read style, but it won't get published if the story itself is not compelling.''

As Lola Schaefer says, "Study the best. Visit a library, bookstore, or school and read at least 10 examples. Read them silently. Read them out loud. Type them in manuscript form and see what they look like on the page. Examine word choice, cadence, and sentence structure. Listen to the pace. Afterward, write and revise and revise until your text rivals those. Then, and only then, send your work to an editor.''

Remember these tips from the experts. Read, read, read. Keep it simple. Make it fun. Tell the truth. Be aware of the guidelines, but don't let them suck the joy out of your work. Beginning readers need engaging, informative, clearly written books. You could be helping them learn.

Getting Your Art Noticed

By the People Who Count

by Laurent Linn

Y ou've heard it said a thousand times, and it's absolutely true: your art must speak for itself. And each illustration has much to say. So . . . why aren't more people listening? No matter what your skills or level of experience, the most daunting challenge for many illustrators isn't an artistic one, but a practical one: How do I get my art noticed?!

As a visual artist interested in illustrating children's books, your *first* job is quite simple: draw! And draw, and draw, and draw. In other words, your main focus should, not surprisingly, be on your art. There are many stellar artists out there creating books and, in order to get published, you must be sure that *your* art is truly outstanding. Yes, there are all sorts of books put out each year that are filled with mediocre illustrations. We always wonder "How did *that* get published when I can draw so much better using only my thumb?" But those books come and go quickly. The ones with staying power—potential classics that become favorites of so many children—are truly beautifully illustrated. The art is unique, deceivingly simple looking, technically masterful, and often offers a brand new use of familiar themes or art techniques.

Once you feel confident with your artistic skills—what's next? Your *second* job as an illustrator is to promote your art. You must think of yourself as a one-person show—creative marketing director, agent, client, and secretary—in the business of selling your art and talents. Even if you have an artist's representative, no one knows your vision and goals better than you.

Think about the big picture

Why do you create art? Why children's books? What are your goals? Your answers are important. As a creative person, you may recoil at the thought of viewing your artistic creations as a business. Indeed, you're not alone—it's hard for most of us to think of our work in commercial terms. But children's books *are* a business. And, while most publishing people respect creative vision, they also must be sure to create books that will sell in an ever more competitive market. But the publishers aren't the only ones in this field . . .

LAURENT LINN, Associate Art Director for Henry Holt Books, began his career as a puppet designer in Jim Henson's Muppet Workshop. With the Muppets for over a decade, he became the Creative Director for *Sesame Street*, winning an Emmy Award. He illustrates; reads over one hundred books a year as a member of the Children's Book Awards Committee at Bank Street College; and collaborates with noted editors, authors, and illustrators on picture books, middle-grade books, and teen novels at Holt.

You are a business!

A business? This may sound strange, especially to those of us who *love* what we do and would do it no matter what. We're not in it for the money. (OK, yes we are—but not *only* for the money). But you must think of yourself in this light in order to best represent your art. And remember, you have an advantage over those who aren't visual people—you can approach your business creatively!

Where to start? First focus on your aim and goals. Who is your audience? What types of books are appropriate to your art style and vision? Who do you want to approach? Who publishes books like what you want to do? Do your homework. Make a plan.

Second, just like any business, create a visual identity for yourself—a brand. Come up with a logo, color palette, and certain fonts to use on all your marketing materials. Having a cohesive look to your art samples, portfolio, Web site, etc. not only shows you are serious and professional, it may help art directors, editors, and designers get to know who you are. However, be sure to keep your logo and overall ''brand'' design simple—you don't want to overpower or distract from your art. For example, type styles should certainly reflect your style, but be clean and not too fussy. If someone can't easily read what you have to say, your effort is wasted.

Now that you've got a visual identity ready, what next?

Getting noticed

There are all sorts of great ways of promoting yourself, including a portfolio and, especially, a Web site. But how will editors and art directors know how to find you? Or that you're even out there? Without a doubt, postcards are the best way to get your art into the publishing world and noticed. They're easy to create, simple to distribute, and fun to design. However, the look and layout is important and should be well thought out.

Select only the best illustrations to showcase and carefully consider which art samples to send out first. As you can imagine, publishers receive hundreds of these each month. A powerful first impression is essential and the competition is formidable, so your postcards need to shine in order to get noticed. Don't be discouraged, though; not everyone sending samples is a great illustrator. Nor has every artist done their homework—many submit art inappropriate for children's books. I can't even count how many postcards I've received showing, for example, a scantily clad woman holding a sword in the air while riding a dragon. Great for adult fantasy book covers, perhaps, but not for kids. No matter what your subject and style just remember: don't be trendy, be yourself.

Postcards as art samples

Think of your postcard as a mini portfolio. When designing *the front*, keep the layout simple. Use your best color piece, making it as large as possible. There are many factors to consider when selecting the illustration. Which is best: an active character portrait or a scene? Will the piece catch someone's attention right away? Does it show your artistic strengths and unique vision? Is it truly your best work? Often we may choose a piece because it has some emotional meaning or the subject is a personal favorite. Don't let your private feelings toward an illustration color your objectivity—put yourself in the place of an editor or art director who doesn't know you at all. Also, keep in mind the subjects most used in children's books and show that you can illustrate those. Children, animals, active scenes, farms and schools, trucks and trains and planes . . . whatever your interests, art showing subjects such as these will be most effective. While static portraits and landscapes may be lovely and fun to draw, they don't make engaging books for children. Books are about *storytelling*.

To keep the focus on the illustration, include only the most important contact information—but do show the basics. When editors and art directors get an art sample they want to share with colleagues, they will often make a color copy of just the front, so including your Web site (or other basic contact information) is essential. In **Examples A & B**, showing two of my own postcards, I use only my logo and Web site address. While the art and placement of the text varies, both cards have a consistent look due to the "branded" elements. Sometimes less really is more, as shown in **Example C** by noted illustrator Sergio Ruzzier. Here he has cleverly taken advantage of the fact that his Web site address consists of his last name, eliminating any need for listing his name and Web site separately.

The back of the postcard is a great place to personalize any information you would like to present. Text-wise, it could simply be your contact details. However, you may also want to briefly bullet point other information, such as if you are published, if your Web site has been updated recently, any book/illustration awards you may have won, professional memberships (like the SCBWI), etc. If you do this, be sure to list only facts that are relevant to illustrating children's books—mentioning unrelated information may sound a bit amateur and color how your art is viewed. Also, don't limit yourself by creating a catch phrase to go with your name like "illustrator" or "creator of art for children." It is unnecessary and can be perceived as cutesy or obvious.

The art you include on *the back* is also important. Often postcards are printed with only black ink on the back—if that's the case, be sure the art you use will look good in grayscale tones. However, whether in color or not, the way you integrate the illustration(s) and the text is another opportunity to show your skills. While the information must be clearly readable and quick to understand, the overall layout can be playful and fun. For example, in **Example D**, Sergio Ruzzier lists his contact information on the back of his postcard in a simple fashion, focusing attention on his humorous drawing. Art and text are nicely integrated in a very straightforward way, with his Web site heating up the skillet.

If you have a unique approach to creating your illustrations, showing some of your process can make your art sample stand out. To develop the characters I used on my postcard **Example A**, I first created clay maquettes of their heads. Doing this sometimes helps me see how to draw faces with unusual features from various angles. So for the back of this postcard, **Example E**, I include photos of the sculptures as well as a rough sketch of a scene involving both characters. I top it off with silhouetted theater curtain art from the same project, hinting at the behind-the-scenes look I'm providing.

Once you have your overall design and look, don't just create one fantastic postcard—create a few. Send out a new art sample about every three months. This will help you get noticed, show the diversity of your talents, and better your chances of becoming recognized over time. It's also an opportunity for you to stretch your skills and create new art. A couple of years ago I decided to create a new promotional illustration every month for a year. Opening up my subject matter to whatever my imagination could conceive of was a great experience. And it gave me a whole new selection of art to choose from—I was able to use the best pieces and send out some great postcards.

Book promotion postcards

Another great way to use postcards is to spread exciting news. And what's more exciting than if you have a new book coming out? These cards can be sent to professional connections you may have, local bookstores and libraries, etc.—anyone that could help your book get noticed. You could even use a postcard like this as an art sample to send to publishers.

To help with the printing costs, often illustrators and authors of a book will team up and make a postcard together. This is what accomplished illustrator Julie Paschkis did for her book *The Talking Vegetables*. She and authors Won-Ldy Paye and Margaret H. Lippert created a single card to promote this picture book, their third collaboration. Seen in **Example F**, the front of the card is quite straightforward—the book cover says it all. A space was left at the

Examples A & B: When creating promotional postcards, use pictures that tell a story, and keep it simple. These two postcards by Laurent Linn feature only an image, his logo and Web site address. The simplicity and similarity give his cards a "branded" look. Reprinted with permission of Laurent Linn.

Example C: When it comes to self promotion, often less is more. Illustrator Sergio Ruzzier allows his last name do double-duty as his Web site address, thereby eliminating extra text and offering a more striking design.

Example D: Incorporating your art into the text of a postcard is a great way to show off your skills. On the back of his postcard illustrator Sergio Ruzzier makes his text part of his illustration, allowing his Web site and e-mail address to add sizzle to the skillet.

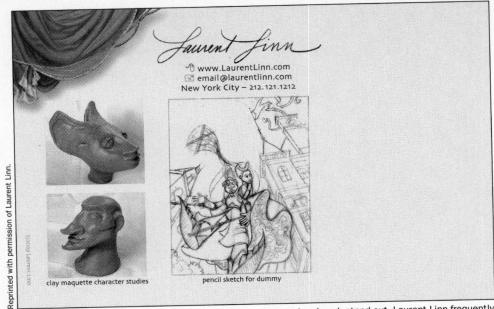

clay maquette character studies   pencil sketch for dummy

Example E: Showing part of your process can help your postcard and work stand out. Laurent Linn frequently creates clay maquettes of the heads of his characters to help him with the drawing process, so in this postcard he includes a "behind the scenes" look at his drawings.

bottom so that Paschkis could customize the cards she personally sends out by adding her Web site address as shown.

The back of this postcard, **Example G**, is also simple. The basic information is all that's needed. By omitting any dated information, such as the book release date, the card can be used again and again. The back is also a good place to show an interior illustration as well as Web site addresses for both the illustrator and the authors. They've even left some room for writing a brief note. The result is a straightforward, quick to read, and professional marketing tool.

Technical tips

You can create effective postcards whether you're computer savvy or not. If you are good at computer design and have access to resources such as a scanner and design software (like Adobe Illustrator® or Adobe Photoshop®), there's no limit to what you can do. If computers are not your forte, however, don't worry—you have many resources available. If you have friends or colleagues who are experienced with computer software, why not ask them to help out? Or you could go the easiest route, which is to have a printer do it all for you. Most postcard printing places (whether found online or in your neighborhood) have all sorts of design options all ready to go—you simply have to supply the text and art. Whether you design them yourself or not, having your postcards professionally printed is probably the best bet to save cost and time. Usually there's a large minimum quantity of cards (250, 500, or 1,000) and, once you've sent one to everyone on your mailing list, you'll probably have many extras. But it sure beats printing them yourself one at a time. And they can become business cards, too.

Size-wise, 4×6 cards are the best. A little larger, like 5×7, is all right too. But no need to spend more for bigger sizes and increased postage—if your card is well designed with your best art, it will stand out at any size. And speaking of postage, the U. S. Postal Service

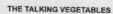

WWW.JULIEPASCHKIS.COM

Example F: Postcards are a great way to promote upcoming titles. Illustrator Julie Paschkis teamed with writers Won-Ldy Paye and Margaret H. Lippert to promote their book, *The Talking Vegetables*, making her marketing efforts more cost-effective.

Articles & Interviews

THE TALKING VEGETABLES
Won-Ldy Paye & Margaret H. Lippert
Illustrated by Julie Paschkis
Henry Holt ~ 2006 ~ ISBN 0-8050-7742-1

Spider wants to pick vegetables from the village farm, even though he didn't help plant them. But the vegetables have their own ideas about this....

Created by the same award-winning team:
HEAD, BODY, LEGS
MRS. CHICKEN AND THE HUNGRY CROCODILE

www.wonldypaye.com • www.storypower.net • www.juliepaschkis.com

Reprinted with permission of Julie Paschkis, Won-Ldy Paye and Margaret H. Lippert.

Example G: The back of a postcard can include a lot of information, but should not include any dated information so the cards don't ''expire.'' A great example is this postcard created by the team of Julie Paschkis, Won-Ldy Paye and Margaret H. Lippert for *The Talking Vegetables*. Simple and clean, all needed information is there and there's still a space for a personalized note.

has strict guidelines as to where printed elements can be placed on the back (address side) of a postcard. Be sure to keep those areas clear or important information may get printed over. For guidelines go to www.usps.com and search for "Physical Standards for Cards"

Enough homework . . . now get going!

Now that you know what to do, go for it. And remember, you may come up with the most fantastic postcard designs, but it won't help you if don't get them printed and mailed! It's a lot of work to get started, but once you get a system going you'll be on a roll. You'll have your promotional side up and running and be able to focus more on your art. And, who knows—one day soon, instead of mailing something to a publisher, a publisher may be mailing something to *you*: a contract!

The Evolution of a Web Site

From Attracting Editors to Hooking Readers

by Jarrett J. Krosoczka

In the late '90s when I was young lad trying to break into the children's publishing market, I used the power of the Internet to my advantage. Back then, using the Internet to promote your illustration work was still looked at as somewhat avant-garde. If you can think way back to 1999, you may remember what it was like to download a single image. From top to bottom, the image would *slowly* appear, line . . . by . . . line. And editors and art directors were just coming around to the idea of looking at illustrator's work online. It was fortuitous timing for me.

I taught myself how to design and launch my own Web site, www.studiojjk.com. I didn't take a single class and learned by trial and error. There were a lot of late nights and the learning curve was steep. However, using a simple click-and-paste program, I was able to send imagery and information over the Web that soon landed me my initial meeting with my publisher and later provided me with a platform to promote my published books. I do regret that I didn't take a class—it would have saved me a lot of time and stress and the early incarnations of my site wouldn't have been plagued by slow load times. I didn't have a clue what DPI meant and didn't even know how to begin to program a loader. What's that you say? You don't know either? You can take a class to learn all that (or at the very least a seminar). But if you would like to learn how my site developed and hear my philosophies on how to effectively promote work via the Internet, please read on.

Inject personality

The Internet is a key tool in promotion for illustrators and writers and a Web site's purpose varies for two distinct groups, the unpublished and the published. Regardless of your standing in the world of ISBNs one thing is universal—your Web site should reflect the personality of your work. Be it with buttons, backgrounds, characters or sounds, one should look at your Web site and instantly think of you. To take it a step further, this design should spill into your printed promotional materials as well. You'll look like a consummate professional when the same font, color scheme, and flavor is found in your business cards, post cards and Web site.

Something else to consider is your domain name (www.whatever.com). The simpler the address is the easier it will be for people to remember it. If you can, try to lock down www.your

JARRETT J. KROSOCZKA is an award-winning author/illustrator with many books to his credit. His work has been short listed by *Newsweek*, *USA Today*, *The Boston Globe* and *New York Times*, among others. His book *Punk Farm*, about a group of raucous farm animals who form an underground rock band, is currently in development as a feature film at DreamWorks Animation. He is a graduate of Rhode Island School of Design and currently lives in Northampton, MA.

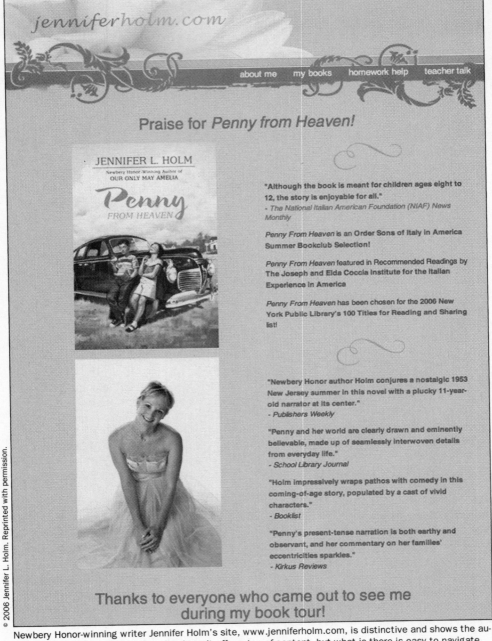

Newbery Honor-winning writer Jennifer Holm's site, www.jenniferholm.com, is distinctive and shows the author's personality and style. The site doesn't offer a ton of content, but what is there is easy to navigate, engaging and visually appealing—a perfect portal for Holm's fans.

name.com. However, if your last name is something impossible to spell like *Krosoczka*, consider creating a site name that can easily be given over the phone or in conversation, as I did will studiojjk.com.

Once my site was up and running, I was able to combine old school tactics and what was then considered to be forward thinking, and run a campaign that led to my first published picture book. My strategy was to create a new illustration every week, design a postcard on my computer, produce 60 postcards at my local copy shop, then mail them off to various publishers. The postcards simply included the illustration with my name, phone number and Web site prominently displayed on the front. It cost me approximately 75 cents to get one image into the hands of an editor or art director, but with my Web site prominently displayed, I had an opportunity to get my entire portfolio in front of the eyes of someone who could make my publishing dreams a reality.

One magical day, I received an e-mail (not a phone call) from an editor at Random House who had seen my postcard, visited my Web site, clicked on my e-mail, and invited me to New York City to show my work and share any potential story ideas. My Web site at the time was nothing fancy—just a Portfolio page, a Bio page, and a Contact page. It was simple and easy to navigate. In short, it was to the point. If you really want to have your online portfolio stand out, don't allow it to get lost in a sea of blogs, non-related art or personal photos.

ERICA WOLF

Illustrator

Portfolio   Books   Other Work

School Visits   About Me   Contact Me

All images on this site are copyrighted, Erica Wolf 2006©

back to start

Illustrator Erica Wolf's Web site, www.ericawolf.com, is clean and simple, just like her illustrative style. With the lack of clutter, it is easy for site visitors to find exactly what they are looking for—particularly Wolf's striking portfolio.

ACTIVITIES
FOR KIDS!

PRESS
MATERIAL!

NEW WORK!

MAILING LIST!

FUN LINKS!

Anna Alter • author and illustrator

Illustrator Anna Alter makes her site interactive by programming the menu icons to change to text as the mouse rolls over an image. The large picture in the middle of www.annaalter.com rotates through various illustrations. These elements add fun without making the site slow to load or confusing.

New audience, new content

Eventually, as my body of work grew and more books were getting published, I realized that my Web site's audience was shifting. My target audience was no longer editors and art directors—it was readers, parents, and librarians. My content *needed* to grow and change. The first new sections I created were a Books section, an Events page and a School Visit page.

The Books section is self-explanatory, a page where readers see and read about all my titles. This section has become more important with time, as new readers come across my newest release and previous books that they may have not been aware of.

On the Events page, readers can obtain up-to-date information on upcoming readings and signings.

The School Visits page offers information on my school visit lectures. School visits (another whole conversation in itself) are an excellent way to promote your work, sell a few books and make some extra money to help you in between advances. This particular section of my Web site has evolved tremendously over time as I've learned what works and what doesn't work during a school visit and I've been able to explain my expectations with schools ahead of my visits. Librarians can obtain information on how to order books for resale and read up on reviews from previous stops. Everything a librarian would need to organize my visit can be found there, even high-resolution pictures of my books and me for their school flyers. And librarians appreciate it! And they are, after all, some of the most powerful people in publishing.

Fancy-schmancy stuff

As time went on, I added more content to my Web site and continued to think outside the box. I added free digital media giveaways, such as IM icons and desktop wallpapers. The most effective content I added was educational material such as childhood drawings and behind-the-scenes stories on how books came into creation. Librarians and teachers *always* love content they can use in their classrooms.

Although I had a working, functional Web site, it still wasn't enough for me. As an emerging author/illustrator—I wanted to stand out; I wanted to raise the bar for myself. My site needed a bit more pep and boisterousness to match the personality of my books, so I taught myself Flash. With Flash I was able to create content that was far more animated than basic HTML or click-and-drag programs could offer. The new features that have garnered the most praise were the faux movie book trailers and video games involving my characters. My goal was to create content that keeps my Web site "sticky" and welcome visitors back again and again.

Keep in mind that including too many bells and whistles on your site will distract visitors and bog down load times. The initial flash version of my site had just those problems. I was too eager to make a sound go "whoosh" or have a button transform into another image just because I could. This led to an aesthetically incoherent Web site that took too long to load. If you leave people waiting, they will generally leave altogether. Another thing that can get under people's skin is too many sounds that get repeated over and over again.

Studio JJK today

With my most recent redesign, my Web site took a step back from its previous incarnation. I simplified the navigation but kept some zaniness to the whole thing. I listened to advice

Author-illustrator Jarrett J. Krosoczka uses Flash animation to keep viewers entertained as they search his site, www.studiojjk.com. This is a far cry from the basic site Krosoczka created in 1999 that started out with not much more than his bio and portfolio. Now visitors can watch previews of the books, get the latest news, free games and more.

that educators and kids had given me and made appropriate changes, adding more educational content and giveaways and speeding up load times. For the first time I cut a section—my portfolio section. At this point in my career, offering a portfolio on my Web site no longer makes sense and isn't necessary. My site has fully evolved from being a vehicle for getting new illustration work to being a promotional tool for my books.

Taking on your own Web design may sound like a lot to learn and a lot of work—and it is. Whenever I finish a redesigning my site, I get the same feeling that I have after meeting a book deadline: I'm relieved and exhausted! Is all this work worth it? I say it is. The beauty of designing your own site is that you can control how and when it gets updated. Hiring someone else to design your site costs money; doing it yourself costs time. But in turn—time is money. If you do choose to hire someone to design your site, make sure it's someone you trust and can be in touch with. And some Web designers can offer you a program through which you can update text-based content, like your book signing schedule, so ask about this option when interviewing potential designers.

In truth, your site doesn't need to be anything too fancy. The point of the Internet in the first place is to transfer information from computer to computer. Your Web site at bare minimum should simply contain information about your work in an organized manner. I started my Web journey using a company called Homestead (www.homestead.com). I signed on with them because their interface was (and still is) easy. They give you a free design program with which you can put together your site and publish it to their server. If you can handle Microsoft Word, you can probably handle Homestead. You can even register your

Good Web Sites to Visit

Check out these great Web sites by authors, illustrators and author/illustrators. Some are simple; some are more complex. Some offer a ton of additional information regarding the creator's books, some are bare bones, but all are exceptional!

- Anna Alter: www.annaalter.com
- Peter Brown: www.somebrownstuff.com
- Tony DiTerlizzi: www.diterlizzi.com
- John Green: www.sparksflyup.com
- Jennifer Holm: www.jenniferholm.com
- David Levithan: www.davidlevithan.com
- Grace Lin: www.gracelin.com
- Kelly Murphy: www.kelmurphy.com
- Robert Sabuda: www.robertsabuda.com
- Nathan Walker: www.nathanwalker.net
- Erica Wolf: www.ericawolf.com
- Jacqueline Woodson: www.jacquelinewoodson.com

domain name with them. I highly recommend them for the novice Web designer. My site is still hosted by Homestead today.

If you're on a Mac, Homestead offers a program called iWeb (www.apple.com/iweb). With the templates offered with iWeb, you are even fewer clicks away from launching your own professional looking site. If you want to go the cheaper route, you could always host your images on Flickr.com or provide info on your books on a site like blogger.com or livejournal.com. There are many free options out there. But like the old saying goes, you often get what you pay for, so choose carefully. And at all costs: avoid ads, especially ads that you don't control!

After designing your site, but before publishing it, ask a friend or family member to open the site, but don't give them any instruction or advice on how to navigate it. If they are getting hung up, you know you have some tweaks and improvements to make. Also ask someone to proofread the text for you. If you have a good relationship with any librarians, get their opinions. Ask other writers or illustrators for input. Just like writing and illustrating, your Web design work will only improve once it has gone through the rigors of critique and revision.

If you're getting a book published, be sure to ask your publisher to print your Web site address on the back flap of your book—don't assume they will do this automatically. And make sure things are spelled correctly!

Even more important than having a Web presence is to work on your writing and illustrations, so don't get too caught up in the dot-com world. A simple site designed with creativity and cleverness will leave the visitor with a far more favorable opinion than any technologically dazzling site ever could.

Articles & Interviews

Market Know-How

Learning Who Is Perfect for Your Book

by Sue Bradford Edwards

Y ou hope Molly Market-right makes it to your critique group meeting tonight. Your latest picture book is ready to submit right down to the cover letter and envelope addressed to Edie Editor. Still, you really want Molly Market-right's OK. Three other people in your group made sales going with her market advice rather than their original plans.

Why can some writers read a manuscript and really and truly *know* who the best editors would be?

START WITH THE BASICS

What do they know that you don't? It might be a little. It might be a lot. Either way, they start out with the same market guides that you do, but that isn't where they stop. Lisa Harkrader most often begins her research with guidebooks, such as *Children's Writer's & Illustrator's Market*. She also checks out *Children's Writer* newsletter for its interview based articles, the SCBWI *Bulletin*, the information found at the Children's Book Council (www.cbc books.org), and the publishers' own Web sites. Susanna Reich makes a point of always reading the *Publishers Weekly Spring and Fall Children's Book Announcements* issues. Sudipta Bardhan-Quallen makes a point of reading the American Library Association's *Booklist* and the *Horn Book* magazine.

They aren't just looking for the basics—who publishes humorous preschool picture books or middle grade nonfiction. If that's all you do before slipping your manuscript into the envelope, you aren't doing nearly enough.

These writers, and those like them, look at these listings with an eye for publishers who are ready to buy. "I look for opportunities—new imprints, new editors, expanding lists, and expanding markets such as graphic novels, teen lit, or fantasy," says Molly Blaisdell.

They look for specific editors who are in the market for talent. "If they have put out a call for submissions, I know that they are acquiring," says Bardhan-Quallen. "I am encouraged to submit to editors who have recently moved to a new publishing house. More often than not, these editors will be looking to build a new list and will be more actively acquiring."

Even with such information in hand, you still need to scour the publisher's catalog. Some

SUE BRADFORD EDWARDS studies the magazine and book markets from her office in St. Louis, Missouri. She writes a variety of nonfiction, specializing in history, archaeology and nature pieces. Her work appears regularly in a variety of testing and educational publications, *Children's Writer* newsletter and the *St. Louis Post-Dispatch*. Visit her Web site at www.SueBradfordEdwards.8m.com.

catalogs are relatively easy to mine for information, especially those of niche publishers who focus on a region or other specific topic.

A major publisher's catalog is much more difficult, but Harkrader has mastered the challenge. "I look for the number of each type of book, picture book, middle-grade novel, YA, fiction, nonfiction, etc., the house publishes, as well as the genres. I read through the catalog copy to get a sense of the tone of each book, even highlighting descriptive words and phrases, such as 'zany adventure,' 'atmospheric tale,' or 'quirky characters.' I match these genres and descriptions against my own manuscript to see if my story would make a good fit."

She also looks at the authors. "Are every one of them well-established, award-winning, best-selling authors? If so, a new writer could have a hard time breaking in," she says. "If I see that the catalog proudly proclaims that they're publishing an author's first novel, I would be encouraged to submit."

Ready to package up your manuscript? Then you're still moving forward too soon. These authors also look at recent acquisitions. "There is a free service called Publishers Lunch which lists some of the new sales," says Bardhan-Quallen. "If you've got a picture book manuscript about a vampire duck, and you read that HarperCollins has recently acquired a picture book about a vampire pig called *Hampire*, by Sudipta Bardhan-Quallen, illustrated by Howard Fine, you probably shouldn't approach Harper since they are unlikely to acquire another vampire animal book. On the other hand, you could be encouraged that animal monsters might be hot right now, and it might be worth approaching other publishers."

Writers who successfully market their work supplement the above through networking. "Whenever possible, I try to meet editors in person. I live in New Jersey, but I've attended conferences in New Hampshire, Virginia, South Carolina, and California, as well as in more local venues like New York and Philadelphia. Each time I had an opportunity to meet editors in some form of in-person way," says Bardhan-Quallen. "This gave me a chance to get to know the editors beyond their formal bios."

Even the smallest piece of information can come in handy. "When networking, I try to learn as much about an editor as I can. For example, knowing that an editor loves basketball or plays the cello might someday come in handy. Write it down," says Reich. "Someday you may write a picture book about basketball or a novel about an cello player, and it might be a perfect fit for that editor."

Supplement your travel budget by networking with other writers either in your area or online. "If you know authors who you trust and who are familiar with your body of work and vice versa, you can share information with each other," says Bardhan-Quallen. "I don't write novels, but I have writing colleagues who do so if I hear of someone in the publishing world looking for novels, I pass that information along. In return, when they hear of a picture book opportunity, they send the word my way."

READ AS A WRITER

You've read market guides, attended a conference where you heard your target editor speak and even chatted up an author who has worked with her. Is it time to send off your manuscript *now*?

No.

Now it is time to read like a *writer*.

First, go for quantity. "Read hundreds of books published in the past five years or so in the same category that you wish to write in. You cannot begin to write until you know the market," says Carol Parenzan Smalley. Writing based on childhood memories of favorite books, won't get you anywhere. "Many of the books you loved as a child would not pass the slush pile today," she says. "They simply do not have the forward movement or action required to capture and hold a child's interest."

There are too many new books each season to know them all, so you'll have to focus. "Follow your passion. If train books aren't your thing, don't read train books," says Blaisdell.

When reading young adult fantasy or humorous picture books, don't let the story suck you in. Read like a writer. "What books draw you in? Why do they do that?" Blaisdell asks. "It's just as important to list books that push you away. Over time you will find that certain houses rise to the top in your opinion." Obviously, these are the houses you should consider.

Are you looking for a manuscript mailer? Sit back down and look at the books again. The books you have focused on might be too like your own. "If the house already has something similar, why would they acquire another manuscript like that?" asks Bardhan-Quallen. "On the other hand, if your manuscript is very different from what already appears on the house's list, would they really be interested in departing from their core program?"

Bardhan-Quallen uses a few simple steps to avoid this situation. "I recommend to people that they think of three or four key words to describe the manuscript they are marketing in particular, and their body of work in general, and then come up with key words to describe the publishing programs of the markets they are considering. For example, my work can generally be summed up by 'humorous,' 'rhyme,' and 'talking animal' so I look for publishers who produce a lot of books like this," she says. "I then remove from my submission list the publishers who have titles that are too similar to my manuscripts."

Blaisdell does something similar. "I search reviews, library databases and publisher catalogues to find similar books. I read these books. I note their publishers and editors. If the book is too similar to my book, I take that house off the list," she says.

From there Blaisdell moves on to find books that are less similar. "Then I look at the competitor's lists and find books that connect with my book. This is a little like that game seven degrees of separation. If my book is nonfiction about elephants, and my target house already has a non-fiction book about circus elephants, but the competitor house has books about protecting endangered animals and hoot owls, I read these books."

Go to Amazon and find the too-similar book. Then scroll to "look for similar items by subject" at the bottom of the page. Select as many search criteria as are applicable and then hit "Find books matching ALL checked subjects." Pick through the results to find less similar titles to read in search of possible publishers. If you like the tone and physical make up of this and other books by this publisher, you still aren't ready to put your manuscript in the mail. You are ready to look for editors.

TRACKING DOWN THOSE EDITORS

Start with the books you enjoyed but are not too-like your own. "Sometimes it is in the book," says Harkrader. If it isn't, the answer is still often easy to find. "Usually a quick Google search will turn up the editor," she says. "Type in the name of the book and the author and the word editor and usually you are there. I might also ask on a board or try SCBWI's 'Edited By.'"

But what if none of this works? "A call to the publishing house or author can reveal this information," says Smalley.

Assemble a list of editors whose work attracts you. If you're lucky, some of these editors will be people you have met. These names should go to the top of your list.

Even a tenuous connection can pay off. "While researching publishers to see where I might sent my manuscript, I recognized a name of an editor as someone I met with when she was at another publisher," says Maryann Cocca-Leffler. "I mailed her a manuscript with a few art samples. I mentioned in my note that I met her many years ago. She rejected my story but liked my art samples enough to offer me a chapter book to illustrate." When the editor encouraged Cocca-Leffler to submit other manuscripts, she did. Her picture books, *Jack's Talent*, will be published in Fall 2007. The connection all of this was built on? Cocca-

Reading Editors Blogs

What do you expect to find on an editor's blog? The top ten things they want to see in a manuscript? What first caught their eye in their most recent acquisition? Why they rejected that near perfect manuscript?

Go in looking for these kinds of specifics, and you'll soon leave disappointed. "I do not write about my work, and very deliberately so," says Sharyn November, Firebird Editorial Director and Puffin and Viking Books senior editor, who maintains a page on her site www.sharyn.org/slush.html specifically for authors.

Although many editors mention their work, that isn't the purpose of the majority of their blogs. "However, writers should also remember that editors aren't necessarily blogging solely for the benefit of writers," says Cheryl Klein, an editor at Arthur Levine books, in an e-mail discussion. "I at least am also blogging for my friends, family, occasional passersby, and own pleasure in writing, so while I sometimes post things writers will find interesting and useful, that isn't the blog's reason for being."

Like everyone else, editors blog for a wide variety of reasons and this variety will vary from one editor to another. "A writer can (I hesitate to say 'should') read an editor's blog as an indication of that editor's tastes, concerns, and personality, and the way that editor thinks and writes," says Klein. "It's useful to see what books the editor loves (because we never shut up about books) and the subjects that come up again and again; the tags on my blog include 'editing,' 'family,' 'poetry,' 'politics,' 'religion,' and 'theatre,' and that's a pretty good list of things I think about a lot and love to think about in the books I work on."

A quick look at other blogs reveals entries on the power writers seek to capture in their work, authors' use of publicists, and "Ugly Betty." So what can you learn from this variety? That like everyone else, editors are motivated by and interested in an incredible range of things. Or as Klein put it, "This may be another useful thing that writers can take from blogs: Editors are human too!"

Just as you wouldn't give Aunt Louise a fly rod for Christmas, you wouldn't send one editor a manuscript that ideally suits another. Find out all you can to achieve a near-perfect fit.

Here is a list of editors' blogs to get you started. Most do not reveal the employer, but with some effort the information can be found online.

- **Aimee Friedman's Amazon Blog:** http://blog.myspace.com/index.cfm?fuseaction=blog.ListAll&friendID=11650519&MyToken=f4eafaeb-187e-4b75-80a8-41469bc88915ML
- **Lisa Graff:** http://lisagraff.blogspot.com
- **Andrew Karre:** http://www.fluxnow.com/index.php
- **Cheryl Klein's Brooklyn Arden:** http//chavelaque.blogspot.com
- **Alvina Ling's Bloomabilities:** http//bloomabilities.blogspot.com
- **Sharon November's sdn's Journal:** http://sdn.livejournal.com
- **Abigail Samoun's Word Pavillion:** http//www.wordpavillion.com/administrator/index.php?option=com_wrapper&Itemid=8
- **Samantha Schutz's I Don't Want to Be Crazy:** http://samanthaschutz.blogspot.com
- **Madeline Smoot's Buried in the Slushpile:** http://cbaybooks.blogspot.com
- **Stacy Whitman's Grimoire:** http://slwhitman.livejournal.com

Leffler met this editor in New York City 18 years earlier. At the time, the editor wanted to buy her manuscript but couldn't get committee approval. "She always remembered my book as 'the one that got away,' " says Cocca-Leffler. "Maintaining connections is important." Even a slight connection is better than none.

Knowing why an editor is at the top of your list comes into play when you prepare your cover or query letter. "When I send a manuscript to an editor, I always state in the cover letter exactly why I chose her, such as 'Since you recently published *I Traveled With Lewis and Clark*, I thought you might be interested in my historical adventure. . . .' or 'At the Kansas SCBWI conference, you expressed interest in quirky animal picture books. . . .,' " says Harkrader. "This tells the editor that you have, in fact, done your research, rather than just opening your Writer's Market at random and pointing to a name." Editors get many manuscripts simply because the author needed to send it to someone. Let the editor know that you have done your research or you have some kind of connection to them.

A slight connection may be better than none, but what if you have *no* connection at all? "Many times I will send something to an editor I do not know. I usually query by email and give a brief bio and my website. I ask them if I may send a manuscript," says Cocca-Leffler who has no agent and does all of her own marketing. "I just made a connection!" In this way she begins building the name recognition and the relationship that helps make sales. Again, tell them why they are your editor of choice and begin building a relationship.

All relationships start somewhere and its up to you to build them with unfamiliar editors. Respond to their encouragement. When does Cocca-Leffler pursue a publisher? "If I received an encouraging 'rejection' letter or a good response to an art sample," she says. "Also when a publisher contacts me for art samples, I would send them manuscripts as well."

If you've gotten a few personal rejections but still aren't sure what your target editor wants. "Ask them!" says Cocca-Leffler. It never hurts to ask an editor what they are looking for or what holes in their list they are trying to fill. This is another way to gain access to more market information and also, through dialogue, to build on a developing relationship with an editor.

The important thing is to be open to the market news that comes your way and to take advantage of it. "I read in the SCBWI newsletter that a certain editor was moving to another publisher and starting her own imprint. It listed that she was looking for 'X, Y & Z.' I happened to have an 'X' dummy that I was shopping around that might fit. I mailed it to her. Unfortunately she rejected it, via email, but encouraged me to send something else. A discussion began as to what exactly she was looking for. Based on our conversation I had a brainstorm, made a dummy and mailed it. She bought it."

The time to submit comes only after you have developed a knowledge of the market, have a relationship or solid groundwork in place to approach an editor, and also have a truly high quality manuscript in hand. "It's really all about the submission, not some mysterious 'need' of an editor," says Blaisdell. "Ask yourself, if this book was on the shelf of Barnes and Noble—as is, no diamonds in the rough, folks—would you buy it? Editors want books that will sell and so do you."

Going beyond a half-page market listing isn't a path to rapid success, but done right, it will work. "I have never seen one dedicated person, who takes time to write a thoughtful book and then truly research the market, fail. The only people who fail are those who do not educate themselves holistically with an eye on craft and marketing," says Blaisdell.

So don't sell yourself short. Learn your market as well as your craft and the effort will pay off as your work makes its way into print.

Roundtable

Top Magazine Editors Discuss
Writing for Their Audience

by I.J. Schecter

While Elmo dolls, electronic gizmos and must-have collectables appear in the market and then vanish faster than you can say "Webkinz," one type of children's entertainment endures the test of time: a good old-fashioned story. Here, editors of three leading kids' magazines discuss the current state of children's publishing, the best part about having a job that involves entertaining kids and why writing for little audiences is harder than most people think.

Daniel Lee started as editor of *Jack and Jill* in November 1994. Previously he'd been a newspaper reporter and had done some outdoor education with kids at a YMCA camp. Lee has a degree is in English and Political Science from Indiana University.

Christine French Clark has been with *Highlights* for 13 years and has served as editor since 2000. For 13 years prior to that, she was with another group of children's magazines. Clark started her career writing and editing preschool curricula. She's worked in children's periodicals her entire career.

Lonnie Plecha became editor of *Cricket* in summer 2006 after five years as editor of *Click* and *Ask*, science and discovery magazines for younger children published by the Cricket Magazine Group. Before that he was a developmental editor of literature and discussion programs for schoolchildren and adults and a college-level philosophy teacher.

When writing for children, what are the most critical things to remember?

Daniel Lee: That their frame of reference is limited. They don't necessarily know, for instance, that the seasons are reversed in the Southern Hemisphere; or that before there were DVDs there were videos, and before videos there were coloring books; or that not everybody celebrates the New Year on January 1. You have to lay the groundwork.

Christine French Clark: The fundamental thing children's writers should remember is that their readers deserve the very best. Children's writers should set the quality bar high and believe that "good enough" is never good enough for children.

Lonnie Plecha: Perhaps the most important thing is not to talk down to them, to respect the validity of their experiences and thoughts about the world.

Christine French Clark: Yes—kids won't tolerate being patronized. I think children do want and need stories and articles that challenge them to think and that leave them somehow changed because of a new insight either into themselves or the world, but this has to happen

I.J. SCHECTER (www.ijschecter) is an award-winning writer, interviewer and essayist. His bestselling collection, *Slices: Observations from the Wrong Side of the Fairway* (John Wiley & Sons), is available in bookstores and online.

Daniel Lee has worked as editor of *Jack and Jill* since 1994. The magazine is geared toward readers ages 7-10.

without heavy moralizing or lecturing, particularly in fiction. The "goodness" in a story has to be organic, not tacked on.

What are the most common flaws you see in manuscripts submitted to your magazine?

Clark: Very often manuscripts are too similar to what we already have in the drawer or to what we've already published. Otherwise, good manuscripts are rejected because they lack that extra spark of creativity, stylish writing or a unique and authentic voice that makes even a familiar theme or subject seem fresh.

Plecha: Often authors, especially new ones, attempt to teach children a lesson through a story. However well-intentioned, children quickly sense the parental voice. A story should be true to the child's experience—young readers will know if it's not, and reject it. By being truthful and genuine, a good story will uplift and inspire.

Lee: We get a surprising number of nostalgia pieces that look back fondly at the joys of childhood. These are fine for adults, but kids don't respond to pieces about the good old days. They're doing all these things for the first time. Also, we've seen enough of the girl-gets-to-play-Little-League story. That battle was fought and won 30 years ago.

Clark: Sometimes a writer's work is rejected because it's clear the writer doesn't understand the magazine. A magazine, by definition, is a package of ideas and biases. We definitely have ours, and every piece we buy has to fit with them and help us further our mission, which is described in every issue of *Highlights*. Writers who fail to study back issues can't begin to know us and will likely waste a lot of time sending material we can't use.

Do you think writing for kids is different today than in the past, or are certain characteristics enduringly important?

Clark: I think the writing has to be tighter and livelier than ever before. Kids have so many distractions pulling them away from reading. But, of course, strong plot, realistic dialogue, compelling characters, humor (when appropriate), themes that are timely and relevant to kids—all of these components of a good story are at least as important as they ever were.

Lee: Since Harry Potter there's been an endless supply of magic, and more and more the books and stories we see push the myth of kids as just shorter, smarter adults. I'd like to see more innocence in kids' stories.

Plecha: I don't think writing literature for children is essentially different today. Society has changed, as have many circumstances of children's lives, but basic themes of childhood—seeking love, justice and friendship, facing adversity with courage, overcoming disappointment, finding a path through the challenges and disorder of everyday life—are perennial.

What makes a great children's story?

Lee: We editors tend to say the usual things: great characters, believable but interesting situations, engaging conflict and sensible resolutions—the same things that make a great adult story, only shorter and faster, like children—and those are all true, but I think kids, unlike grownups, will also focus on one really strong element of a story and fill in the rest with their imaginations. For instance, Beatrix Potter's exquisite art brings her very simple stories to life. Dr. Seuss's wackiness offsets a certain, say, lack of believability in his work. A.A. Milne can get wordy and redundant, but kids love the characters so much they'll follow them through the whole 100-Acre Wood of his prose. The Curious George and Clifford stories are almost vestigial, but what kid can resist a troublesome monkey or a dog big enough to eat parents?

Plecha: For us, it's something that—even if it's humorous—is genuine and true on some profound level, that inspires wonder and leaves the child with a sense that there's something worthwhile in the drama of life and that the world is a fantastic place to explore. A really good story can both challenge and affirm a child's feelings about life; it helps a child grow by giving expression to ideas and feelings that may only have existed on a preconscious level.

Christine French Clark came to *Highlights* with a wealth of editorial experience and has been editor of the magazine, whose motto is "Fun with a Purpose," since 2000.

Clark: The best children's stories are stories that adults like to read, too. I also think the really great children's stories have unforgettable characters—characters readers can relate to, either because they see themselves in the characters or they would like to. At *Highlights*, we also think that the really great children's stories leave a positive impression with readers that remains long after the details of the story are forgotten. Our founders used to call this "moral residue." I often think of it as simply hope. A great children's story leaves readers feeling hopeful.

How long does it take you to know whether a story is a winner—or at least a candidate?

Plecha: The majority of manuscripts are sent to a first reader, who weeds out those that are obviously not right for us, then passes on the rest to me with a brief comment. I read each of these manuscripts carefully. Many I reject immediately after my first reading. They might find a home elsewhere, but they're not for *Cricket*. Others I will re-read and ponder at greater length. I circulate the stories that seem to me wonderful, or that I think could be made wonderful with revision, among several other editors, each of whom comments on the manuscripts, sometimes extensively. If a story seems promising but not yet ready for publication, and if I feel confidence in the author, I will write the author expressing the opinions of the editors and offer to see a revision of the story on spec.

Clark: A winning manuscript often announces itself by the end of the first page, but even if the first page disappoints, I force myself to read on to the second. Sometimes the story actually starts on the second page, and it's great the rest of the way through.

Lee: You can spot a no-go in a sentence or two. A possible in a few paragraphs. A winner by halfway through—sometimes you have to go to the end. It's like panning for gold; the good stuff is what's left after the gravel and mud gets slopped over the side.

Do certain themes come up repeatedly in the submissions you receive? Any you'd like to see less of? More of?

Clark: We sometimes lament the fact that writers tend to send us only what they see we are publishing. While certainly we have an ongoing need for certain kinds of stories and articles, it's also true we are open to seeing something different. We know it frustrates writers when we say, "We can't tell you exactly what we want . . . but we'll know it when we see it," but it's true.

Plecha: We're very interested in seeing more fantasy, science fiction, humor and adventure stories. We would also like a greater number of stories about contemporary children. We receive a great deal of historical fiction, legends and folktales. But while we enjoy, for instance, traditional Chinese legends, we would welcome an insightful story about contemporary China or other cultures.

Clark: Agreed—we could use more articles about contemporary life in cultures around the world. We also seem to have more Halloween stories than we can use, and not enough stories about other holidays.

Is there a general assumption that writing for children is easy? How wrong is that assumption?

Lee: Writing for kids should be easy; the stories are usually short, gratuitous complications should be kept to a minimum and the themes or ideas handled should be relatively accessible. We're not talking Faulkner here, thank goodness. On the other hand, Woodrow Wilson once said, "If I am to speak 10 minutes, I need a week for preparation; if an hour, I am ready now." Cutting and condensing is harder than writing. Writers tend to fall in love with every word they produce, but kids don't have time to read them all.

Plecha: Writing the sorts of stories that are published in our magazine certainly isn't easy. It requires a great deal of effort, dedication, skill, inspiration, research and, especially, empathy for children.

Clark: When I started my career more than 20 years ago, I heard people say this all the time. But the assumption is less common today it seems to me. At any rate, I don't hear it nearly as often from serious new writers. They seem to have gotten the message that becoming a published children's writer requires both skill and talent, a lot of hard work, and perseverance. No doubt, writing for children is hugely challenging. Maybe it looks easy, but I firmly believe it's much harder to write for children than for adults. Children are much less forgiving!

What are the main differences between the way children look at stories and the way adults do?

Plecha: Children are certainly open to being transported to another time and place in a story, to finding heroes to admire and emulate, and reason for hope and optimism even when things don't turn out quite right. They also love a good laugh at life's absurdities. On the other hand, adults are like that, too.

Lee: I think kids probably can manage a willing suspension of disbelief more easily than adults, so you can get right into the meat of a story. The plot devices can be more outlandish, too. Alice went down a rabbit hole, after all, and Toad somehow managed to drive a full-sized automobile in *The Wind in the Willows*. On the other hand, within the frame of reference that they know intimately, the world of childhood, kids are quick to spot faulty or dated details. And details get dated very quickly in their world.

Clark: Writers also need to recognize that a young reader's patience with long narratives and messages is quite limited. New writers of children's magazine stories often struggle with pacing and fitting everything in—a beginning, middle and end, conflict, resolution, character development, and so on. Writing a magazine short story for kids requires a great economy of words, which requires a lot of discipline on the part of the writer.

Editor Lonnie Plecha worked on other Cricket Magazine Group publications before moving to *Cricket* in 2006. The company's flagship magazine was born in 1973.

What are the main difficulties writers of adult fiction usually encounter when they first attempt the transition to kids' stories?

Plecha: I would say not having sufficient respect for the character, intelligence and emotional life of young readers, or perhaps not taking the enterprise of writing for children as seriously as they would writing for adults. And of course, there's the difficulty of writing in a voice that rings true for contemporary children when one isn't a child anymore.

Lee: Writers of adult fiction should also be aware that many kids' magazines have lower pay rates and frequently ask for all rights.

Clark: For many, it's difficult to write from a child's point of view rather than an adult's perspective. They need to ask themselves: "Is the story's problem a child's problem? Is it resolved by the child, or does an adult fix it?" New children's writers must learn how to see their whole story through the eyes of their child protagonist.

What is your favorite aspect of working—indirectly—for children?

Lee: Kids have a natural curiosity that begs for new information and experiences; everything is fresh and new for them. Writing for adults, you have to break through their expectation that everything is just the same old stuff. Also, there's a lot of positive reinforcement; my bulletin board is covered with photos of grinning kids trying the activities and recipes we publish.

Plecha: When I was young I read a great deal, and always found enjoyment in books, so I know how meaningful a great story can be to a child. My favorite aspect of editing *Cricket* is finding a story that I know children will love—one that will linger in their thoughts, as it does in mine.

Clark: I've always loved working with kids, writing and reading—so I feel fortunate to have a career that combines all of these passions. I also remember how books and magazines affected me as a child—very specific things I read that truly helped me figure out who I was and how to make sense of the world. I love that I'm in a position to offer children content that might do the same for them.

Weird Nonfiction

A Great Way to Hook Reluctant Readers

by Kelly Milner Halls

There were other pioneers before her. Dr. Seuss redefined silly. Bruce Coville braved the word "fart." Jon Scieszka warped literary tradition. But when *Grossology* author Sylvia Branzei took her turn at bat in 1995—glossy plastic barf firmly attached to her shocking green, spiral-bound cover—she knocked it out of the park and blew the lid off a largely untapped realm of potential.

Branzei and her gifted illustrator Jack Keely unapologetically opened the door to the wonders of weird through nonfiction. And millions of reluctant readers—and a small group of energized writers—ran joyfully through, right behind them.

What is a reluctant reader? Experts say they are readers slow to develop reading skills and interests, compared to other children their own age. The causes vary from learning disabilities to sheer boredom. But the solution often begins with high interest, non-traditional, nonfiction books.

Do you have what it takes to join the revolution? Can you explore the wonders of weird for kids and still win the support of the grown-ups that love and educate them? As a writer of the weird myself, (*Dinosaur Mummies, Albino Animals, Tales of the Cryptids, Mysteries of the Mummy Kids*), I can say with conviction that, yes you probably can. And seven tips will show you how.

#1: Keep it real.

What made you laugh or gasp or wonder when you were 10? If you analyze your memories, you'll make a life-altering discovery. The sands of time have made you older, but the landmarks of child development remain the same. In other words, what you saw as amazing when you were 10 is probably still newsworthy to your modern counterpart.

For Branzei, authenticity was key to writing *Grossology*. "To get kids interested in science," she said, "I knew I would have to make it fun. And since I find science fun, it was the only way I knew to write it."

I saw my first mummy postcard when I was 10, and I can still see that haunting image in my mind. Is it any wonder I wrote *Mysteries of the Mummy Kids* 40 years later? Maybe not,

KELLY MILNER HALLS is a full-time freelance writer who gets paid for being weird. Her quirky nonfiction has been published in *Highlights for Children, Boy's Life, Teen People, Fox Kids*, and dozens of other publications. Her books include *Dinosaur Mummies, Albino Animals*, and *Mysteries of the Mummy Kids* and others from Darby Creek Publishing. She lives in Spokane, Washington, with two daughters, five cats, three dogs and a five-foot Rock Iguana (caged where her dining room used to be). She lectures regularly at schools and writing conferences, where she confirms she is still weird, and proud of it.

but I see the same astonishment I felt in the eyes of fifth graders at school visits today.

So skip the trendy alternatives. Rely on what you find amazing to keep it real.

#2: Think outside the box.

"I want something just like Harry Potter, only different." Stay in this business long, and you'll hear the underlying theme of that message over and over again. Editors want fresh ideas that sell as well as the old favorites. So get in the habit of thinking outside the box.

When it comes to recommendations, says reluctant reading expert Kathleen Baxter, "The book I most often cite (in presentations all over creation) is *Albino Animals*. The minute I saw that book I grabbed it and sat down and read it. What a great topic! What a superb title! I can hardly imagine a kid who would not want to pick it up and sit down."

Albino Animals is, on the surface, just another animal book. But albinism was a subject not yet described in books for young readers when I saw it published in 2004. It was that unique twist that got the book noticed.

So even an old idea (an animal book) can take on new life (an albino animal book) if you think outside the box.

#3: Do your homework.

It's Disgusting and We Ate It!, by James Solheim, examines quirky food facts from around the world, skillfully enhanced by illustrator Eric Brace's ick-factor drawings.

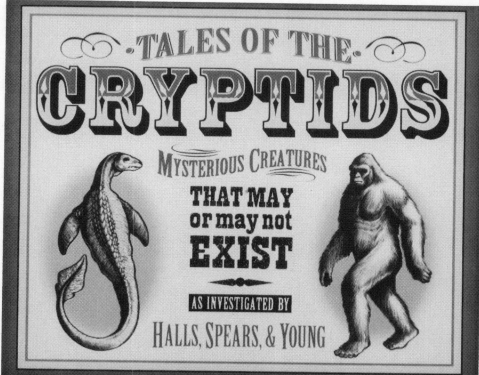

Kelly Milner Halls takes readers through the hall of fame of creatures that may (or may not) exist in *Tales of the Cryptids*. "Readers will scramble to find data on such eerie apparitions as the Chupacabra and the Mongolian Death Worm," says *School Library Journal*. "From old big leaguers like Bigfoot and his kin, and Nessie and her ilk, they pop down to the minors with Mokele-mbembe and Olitu, and on into the bush leagues with the Bunyip and the Caddy."

"In Europe and Asia," Solheim writes, "many kids love to eat fish heads. Americans gulp down tons of live oysters a day. And many Africans know that a properly cooked grasshopper has a delightful crunch." Brace tops the text with an open, metal lunch box, worms, a frog and a grasshopper make their daring escapes.

But how do we know Solheim and Brace can be trusted? Twenty-one items on their "Select Bibliography" offers convincing evidence and emphasizes the point of this tip: Just because you're writing fun nonfiction for young readers doesn't let you off the hook when it comes to careful and thorough research.

#4: Enlist the aid of your allies: kids, teachers and librarians.

You've come up with your weird and wonderful book idea. You've interviewed a dozen experts and read two dozen articles and books. You're writing what you think may be your best work ever. But are you really on track? Don't rely on your own impressions to be certain. Go right to the source.

"When I came up with the concept of *Grossology*," said Branzei, a former teacher and writer, "I passed the idea by my stepchildren, who were 14 and 11 at the time, and by my fourth through sixth grade science enrichment class. For all of my books, I sought input from

Cover design by C. Shane Sykes. © 1999 Planet Dexter. Reprinted with permission.

"The point of this book is that it really sucks. Seriously!" So opens Planet Dexter's ridiculously accurate take on the act of sucking, *This Book Really Sucks!* The book goes on to discuss sucking in all contexts, from a baby sucking his thumb to the earth's gravity sucking us to the ground. Highly irreverent, this book takes a humorous look at the science behind an action kids take for granted.

the young people who were the target audience. I field-tested my experiments as well as my text. The fact that it could be used as a curriculum was not conscious. But once a teacher. . . .''

Before the rough draft of *Tales of the Cryptids* was complete, I carried it with me to 12 different school visits and sought the feedback of over 3,000 teachers, librarians and kids. By the time my editor Tanya Dean got the final text for her brilliant fine tuning, the real critics had already gone over it with a fine-toothed comb. Before I submitted, I knew my readers would like what they saw.

#5: Don't skimp on the visuals.

In the first 21 pages of Steve Parker's *Animal Autopsy* (1997), there are more than 90 full-color illustrations by Rob Shone, not counting the title page, table of contents or introduction. More than 20 full-color photographs dot the first 15 pages of *Albino Animals*.

Why? Because images are crucial in books designed to attract reluctant readers—kids who aren't yet convinced they really love to read. Images help them form pictures in their minds and keep them from getting too frustrated or bored as they navigate the text they're trying to read.

As a writer, you will seldom be asked to provide the artwork. You may be required to assist with all photo research, but it's easier than it sounds. When you interview your topical experts, simply ask them for suggestions on where to get high-quality images. They will very often lead you to your prey.

If your book is fully illustrated, as is *Animal Autopsies*, your publisher will need to select an artist who is fully trained and prepared for the related time commitment—the call to complete the job.

#6: Don't get discouraged.

It's hard to imagine *Grossology* author Sylvia Branzei ever heard a discouraging word, but like most writers, her road hasn't always been smooth. With that wealth of experience behind her, she offers these suggestions to new writers looking for reinforcements, and I quote:

- Some publisher will want to publish your book. Get used to rejection and don't give up.
- Research the publishing houses. It has to be the right fit for your book. In my case, a publishing house that just wanted to be disgusting would have been a terrible fit. My first publisher, Jess Brallier, understood that *Grossology* was an educational book with a quirky edge.
- Stick to your vision. I remember when my publisher, Jess, thought that it might not be a good idea to include the section on farts. We had a long conversation and I explained why we should include the Fart section. I was so passionate in my argument that Jess had to agree.

#7: Wear your inner weirdo with pride.

Once you've married your manuscript to the right publisher and your book is on retail and library shelves, stand tall. You may not always win the top literary awards for children's writers if you take the road less traveled, but you will win the hearts of readers who walk the path with you.

"I have never been presented any 'serious' writing awards," Branzei admits, "but my goal is to get kids excited about learning science. If a child reads my book and says, 'Wow, science is cool. I would like to read more,' I have succeeded because my book is important to my reader and that is what matters."

Author and children's literature professor Teri Lesesne takes that thought a step further. "I am a firm believer in the concept of reading ladders," she says. "You take the kid from where

Guide Your Inner Weirdo. . .

Kathleen Baxter, author of *Gotcha Covered: More Nonfiction Booktalks to Get Kids Excited about Reading* (2005) and *Gotcha for Guys: Nonfiction Books to Get Boys Excited About Reading* (2006) worked in the trenches as a children's services librarian for more than 25 years.

That expertise has helped her become one of the foremost experts in the realm of reluctant readers and nonfiction, and a regular workshop leader for the Bureau of Education and Research. She offers below a look at 15 of her time-tested, favorite nonfiction titles.

- *The American Story: 100 True Tales From American History*, by Jennifer Armstrong, illustrated By Roger Roth (Knopf 2006)
- *Hitler Youth: Growing Up In Hitler's Shadow*, by Susan Campbell Bartoletti (Scholastic 2005)
- *Getting Away With Murder: The True Story of the Emmett Till Case*, by Chris Crowe (Phyllis Fogelman Books 2003)
- *How Bright Is Your Brain? Amazing Games To Play With Your Mindi*, by Michael A. Dispezio, illustrated by Catherine Leary (Sterling 2004)
- *Remember D-Day: The Plan, The Invasion, Survivor Storiesi*, by Ronald. J.Drez (National Geographic 2004)
- *Escape! The Story of the Great Houdini*, by Sid Fleischman (Greenwillow 2006)
- *Bound for the North Star: True Stories of Fugitive Slaves*, by Dennis Brindell Fradin (Clarion 2000)
- *Albino Animals*, by Kelly Milner Halls (Darby Creek 2004)
- *ER Vets: Life in an Animal Emergency Room*, by Donna M. Jackson (Houghton Mifflin 2005)
- *The Wildlife Detectives: How Forensic Scientists Fight Crimes Against Nature*, by Donna M. Jackson, photo by Wendy Shattil & Bob Rozinski (Houghton Mifflin 2000)
- *Harvesting Hope: The Story of Cesar Chavez*, by Kathleen Krull, illustrated by Yuyi Morales (Harcourt 2003)
- *What You Never Knew About Tubs, Toilets, and Showers*, by Patricia Lauber, illustrated by John Manders (Simon & Schuster 2001)
- *George vs. George: The American Revolution as Seen From Both Sides*, by Rosalyn Schanzer (National Geographic 2004)
- *Exploding Ants: Amazing Facts About How Animals Adapt*, by Joanne Settel, Ph.D. (Atheneum 1999)
- *How Dinosaurs Took Flight: The Fossils, The Science, What We Think We Know, and the Mysteries Yet Unsolved*, by Christopher Sloan, foreword by Dr. Xu Xing (National Geographic 2005)

he or she is and move them along slowly. If we ask kids to go from Silverstein to Dickinson, there is a huge gap in between. Too often, they fall into the crevasse, and we lose them.''

Quirky nonfiction books may provide the perfect bridge. ''They can go from reading those wonderful picture books about *Grossology* or snakes,'' where they learn confidence, Lesesne says, ''to essays by Emerson with nary a step lost or wasted along the way.''

Capturing Culture

*Writing the Muslim-American
Experience for Young Readers*

by Asma Mobin-Uddin

As a pediatrician, I have always encouraged new parents in my practice to introduce books to their infants very early in life. When I had my first child, I was excited to do the same. I bought wonderful books for my daughter—fuzzy chicken books, alphabet board books, mommy-loves-you-so-much-she-can't-stand-it books—and together, we shared them all. But there was one type of book I searched and searched for but could not find: books that accurately reflected our cultural and religious experience being a Muslim-American family.

My children and I were all born in and grew up in America as Muslims. We are not alone in combining this national and religious identity. "There are more American Muslims than there are American Episcopalians, Jews, or Presbyterians," Harvard professor Diana Eck notes on the Web site about her book, *A New Religious America*. With America's Muslim population estimated to be about six to eight million people, Islam may very well be the second most common religion in the United States. Yet, in 1999 when I did my initial search, I could not find any picture books about American Muslim children in America's libraries and bookstores.

Many of the books I did find in local libraries about Muslims were stereotypical, and they were often about camels or sultans or something else that is as foreign to the Muslim-American experience as it is to any other American experience. Even when the books were written in a sensitive way, they were almost always set in some far-away location, not in America.

So I had two main reasons for starting to write books for children. I wanted to introduce accurate books about the Muslim-American experience to the general American community, and I wanted to write books that Muslim-American kids would see themselves in.

WHO ARE MUSLIM-AMERICANS?

The stories of America's Muslim families are diverse. They include stories of immigrants who came to America searching for opportunity and believing in the American dream. They include stories of people whose foreparents were brought to this country in chains and who rededicate themselves to a faith of their ancestors, as possibly one quarter of the African slaves brought to America were Muslim. The stories of the American Muslim-American community contain the histories of refugees fleeing wars, violence, and despair, hoping for safety and a new start in their new country. And they include the stories of converts, the sons and daughters of this land who turned to Islam when choosing their spiritual path.

DR. ASMA MOBIN-UDDIN is a pediatrician and author of two children's books on the Muslim-American experience published by Boyds Mills Press. More information about her books can be found on her Web site, www.asmamobinuddin.com.

Coming from these and other diverse backgrounds either recently or in previous generations, these families now face the challenges of forging a common path forward as Americans. Besides sharing a common faith, these families are tied together in the present in America as they all deal with the effects of the horrific events of September 11, 2001. These attacks affected Muslim-Americans the same way they affected other Americans and then some. We face the same emotions and trauma that our fellow Americans have as a result of that horrific day when our country was attacked. But Muslim-Americans also face a double burden as members of our community are often associated with or considered to be part of the same group as the terrorists. Living in post-9/11 America, Muslim-Americans often face regular suspicion and hostility, making many of us feel like strangers in our own land.

But also part of the new reality are the increased opportunities to educate and build bridges of understanding. Many Americans of goodwill have reached out to us in solidarity and support over these difficult years. We have been heartened by the hands extended in warmth and friendship and by the offers of help and support.

My Name Is Bilal

By Asma Mobin-Uddin • *Illustrated by* Barbara Kiwak

Asma Mobin-Uddin is Muslim-American, and she wanted books for her children that reflected her own experiences. When none could be found she decided to write some herself. "The female characters in my books reflect the reality I know," she says. Her first book, *My Name is Bilal*, follows a brother and sister as they try to adjust to being one of the few Muslim families in a new town. Their struggles and success reflect Mobin-Uddin's own experience growing up in a small town, and give a realistic portrait of what it means to be an American Muslim.

Countering prejudices and stereotypes with education and human connections helps to heal some of the divisions we face. Children's books have always been important as ways for kids to learn about others. Books can help children connect with other cultures on a human level, bypassing the walls of mistrust, anger, and ignorance. Educating young children about other cultures lays the groundwork for a lifetime of acceptance, respect, and understanding.

ROOM FOR IMPROVEMENT

Writers and publishers have realized the need for more books about Muslim-American children to bridge the divisions we face, and we are seeing such books reaching the shelves, although they are still few and far between.

Some of these books coming out are good. Others fall short. Can authors from outside the Muslim experience accurately convey the viewpoint of this community? My opinion, as a Muslim-American of Pakistani descent, is that it is very challenging for other authors to be able to be completely authentic, but it is possible. Non-Muslim authors who have succeeded in this area usually have lived in Muslim countries or otherwise experienced first-hand the people and cultures that shaped the stories they later wrote about. In the recent books I've seen, however, there are several areas where I see children's authors from outside the Muslim community not accurately or effectively representing the Muslim experience.

Assimilation or acculturation?

Some authors try too hard to show that Muslim-American children are exactly like their peers or that their goal is to assimilate completely. These books are often about children who come from immigrant families.

While I appreciate the good intentions of the authors, I am uncomfortable with the underlying message of these stories and the way the cultural heritage of the immigrant child is downplayed or even demeaned in some of these books.

As a child of immigrants, I know how much families value the rich and beloved cultural heritage and traditions they bring with them to America. They also celebrate and are grateful for the new traditions they learn and adopt in their new country. The result is a merging of identity and culture into a uniquely American outcome that maintains the flavor of both past and present.

A more authentic representation of the immigrant experience in children's books occurs when cultural distinctions naturally add flavor, identity and realism to the stories. The stories should give voice and authenticity to the experiences of immigrant children by recognizing the influence and value of their backgrounds while also sharing their journey as they adapt to American customs and ways. The goal should not be seen as hurrying up a process of losing one's distinctiveness and merging into a common, homogenous whole.

Stereotypical female characters

The portrayal of female characters is another area of concern in children's books with Muslim characters. Stereotypical girls and women abound, trapped in sensationalized scenarios that perpetuate myths and misunderstanding.

The Muslim women I know, including my mother, community members in America, and my relatives in Pakistan, are educated, confident, independent women who are dedicated to their families and their faith. It is their example I have grown up with and internalized.

The female characters in my books reflect the reality I know. Ayesha, Bilal's older sister in *My Name is Bilal*, is confidant in her approach to the bullies who tease her about her headscarf, and she maintains her sense of humor. Aneesa's grandmother, in my latest book *The Best Eid Ever*, is a wise, loving, independent woman who delights in the special relation ship she shares with her granddaughter. In the same book, the Muslim refugee girls are

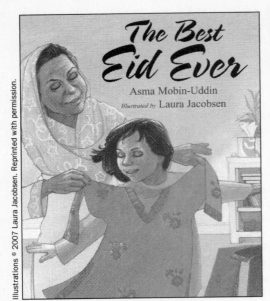

The Best Eid Ever, by Asma Mobin-Uddin, follows Aneesa and her grandmother as they celebrate Eid al-Adha. Aneesa meets some refugee girls at a morning service and decides to help them have a special holiday. The characters in this book were "inspired by my own experiences," says Mobin-Uddin, "these characters help me share with readers a real view into the lives of Muslim girls and women."

not afraid of the resoluteness of their father as they reach out to the warmth and tenderness they know in him. Inspired by my own experiences, these characters help me share with readers a real view into the lives of Muslim girls and women.

Solutions go against Islamic teachings

I've also seen Muslim books for young readers misrepresent Islamic teachings and practices. The Muslims in these books sometimes solve their problems by going against their faith.

These books are obviously written from an outsider's perspective. Many times it just seems as if the author did not know that the actions in question are against the teachings of Islam, because the people in the story appear to be observant Muslims. These mistakes may not be obvious to readers or editors who are unfamiliar with the subject matter, but they are painfully obvious to Muslim readers who immediately appreciate that an observant Muslim would not accept solving the problem in this manner.

In other cases, it seems that instead of being a mistake, the author is purposefully implying that the solution to the problem lies in abandoning the religious observance. In stories like these, the author's critique of the practice and his or her inability to appreciate its value within the other culture is clearly heard between the lines.

To bypass some of the concerns I have mentioned, I believe we need to encourage more Muslim writers to share their stories. Encouraging collaborative efforts between Muslim-Americans and experienced writers outside of the faith might also help meet the need for these books while maintaining authenticity of experience.

Some American Muslim authors have published books through small Muslim presses. These books often have overt religious content and were written to help Muslim families teach their religion to their children. Perhaps some authors who have written for this Islamic religious market can also be tapped to write for a more mainstream American audience.

ACCURATE, AUTHENTIC BOOKS

I've talked about problems in books with Muslim characters. Now I'd like to offer examples of books that succeed. I chose these books because they feel real and authentic, the characters speak to me, and the books are, to the best of my knowledge, accurate representations of their subject matter.

My own book, *My Name is Bilal* is about a Muslim-American boy, Bilal, who is afraid to let his classmates know that he is Muslim. Trying to hide his religious identity, he tells his class that his name is Bill. His sister, who wears the traditional Islamic headscarf, is being harassed, and Bilal is feeling guilty about not standing up for her. As he learns more about his religious heritage and the beloved figure in Islamic history for whom he is named, Bilal

Reading List

Here are some recommended children's books with Islamic themes or Muslim characters broken out by category.

American Muslim experience
- *Ramadan*, by Susan Douglass, illustrated by Jeni Reeves (Carolrhoda 2004).
- *Nadia's Hands*, by Karen English, illustrated by Jonathon Weiner (Boyds Mills Press 1999).
- *Ramadan*, by Suhaib Hamid Ghazi, illustrated by Omar Rayyan (Holiday House 1996).
- *The Color of Home*, by Mary Hoffman, illustrated by Karen Littlewood (Phyllis Fogelman Books 2002).
- *My Muslim Friend: A Young Catholic Learns About Islam*, by Donna Jean Kemmetmueller, illustrated by Laura Jacobsen (Pauline Books and Media 2006).
- *The Stars in My Geddoh's Sky*, by Claire Sidholm Matze, illustrated by Bill Farnsworth (Albert Whitman 1999).
- *My Name is Bilal*, by Asma Mobin-Uddin, illustrated by Barbara Kiwak (Boyds Mills Press 2005).

Muslim children in other countries
- *Snow in Jerusalem*, by Deborah De Casta, illustrated by Cornelius Van Wright and Ying-Hwa Hu (Albert Whitman 2001).
- *Sami and the Time of the Troubles*, by Florence Parry Heide and Judith Heide Gilliland, illustrated by Ted Lewin (Clarion 1992).
- *The Day of Ahmed's Secret*, by Florence Parry Heide and Judith Heide Gilliland, illustrated by Ted Lewin (Lothrop, Lee & Shepard 1990).
- *My Great-Grandmother's Gourd*, by Cristina Kessler, illustrated by Walter Lyon Krudup (Orchard 2000).
- *One Night: A Story from the Desert*, by Cristina Kessler, illustrated by Ian Schoenherr (Philomel 1995).
- *The Roses in My Carpets*, by Rukhsan Kahn, illustrated by Ronald Himler (Holiday House 1998).
- *Sitti's Secrets*, by Naomi Shihab Nye, illustrated by Nancy Carpenter (Simon & Schuster 1994).

History
- *Muhammad*, written and illustrated by Demi (McElderry 2003).
- *A 16th Century Mosque*, by Fiona MacDonald, illustrated by Mark Bergin (Peter Bedrick Books 1994).
- *Traveling Man. The Journey of Ibn Battuta, 1325-1354*, written and illustrated by James Rumsford (Houghton Mifflin 2001).
- *Saladin: Noble Prince of Islam*, by Diane Stanley (HarperCollins 2002).

Holidays
- *Samira's Eid*, by Nasreen Akhtar, illustrated by Enebor Attard (Mantra Publishing, London 1999).
- *The Three Muslim Festivals*, by Aminah Ibrahim Ali, illustrated by Aldin Hadzic (Iqra International Educational Foundation 1998).
- *The Best Eid Ever*, by Asma Mobin-Uddin, illustrated by Laura Jacobson (Boyds Mills Press 2007).

grows more comfortable with his religious identity and finds the courage to be himself.

Part of Bilal's struggles for self-acceptance reflects the struggle for identity that I went through growing up as a Muslim child in a small Ohio town that had few Muslim families.

The specifics of the story in *My Name is Bilal* reflect struggles in the Muslim-American experience. I hope that by encouraging kids and adults to discuss issues relating to religious and ethnic diversity, the book will lead to greater tolerance, understanding, and respect in our communities. However, my overall purpose in writing this book was not limited to raising awareness about this community. I wanted the book to inspire children in general to be true to themselves and to learn to accept and cherish their own identity, instead of being afraid of what others might think about them.

My second book, *The Best Eid Ever* is about a Muslim-American girl on Eid al-Adha, the biggest holiday of the Muslim year. Aneesa's parents are away at the Hajj pilgrimage and her grandmother from Pakistan has come to spend Eid with her. Initially, she misses her parents and feels sad that she has to spend the holiday without them. After meeting a refugee family at the morning prayer service, Aneesa and her grandmother carry out a plan to make sure the family's holiday is special.

More than 70% of the world's refugees are Muslim. *The Color of Home*, by Mary Hoffman (Phyllis Fogelman Books), is an important book that deals with the refugee experience. The book is necessarily intense, as are the experiences children face when fleeing from war. It shares the horror that little Hassan experienced before his family fled from Somalia, but it ends on a hopeful note.

Gratitude to God is an important value in Islam. Cristina Kessler's *One Night: A Story from the Desert* (Philomel), is a coming-of-age story that resonated with me because of the thankfulness with which Muhamad and his family live their lives. They are desert people whose dignity, gratitude, and appreciation for the blessings of their life shine throughout the story.

Donna Jean Kemmetmueller's *My Muslim Friend: A Young Catholic Learns about Islam* (Pauline Books and Media) gives detailed explanations about Catholic and Muslim beliefs and practices as friends Mary and Aisha compare each other's lives. This book contains a wealth of information and is sensitively written.

James Rumsford's *Traveling Man: The Journey of Ibn Battuta, 1325-1354* (Houghton Mifflin) tells the story of Ibn Battuta's travels across the world in the 14th century. His journey through life is beautifully told in words and intricate pictures.

Demi's *Muhammad* (McElderry) is an excellent biography of Islam's Prophet Muhammad for young readers. In keeping with Islamic tradition, the Prophet Muhammad is not depicted in the book.

The books above and in the sidebar are excellent examples of young children's literature with Islamic themes or Muslim characters. More books are needed, especially on the Muslim-American experience. We look to authors with close ties to this community to share with the community at large what it means to be a Muslim-American.

I am pleased to see the inspiring, wonderful books on this topic that are coming out and to be able to share these books with my three children. During my entire childhood growing up in Ohio, I never once read a book that had a Muslim girl in it. For me to see my children's delight in identifying with the characters in these books and recognizing themselves, their traditions, and their heritage in the pages is a beautiful experience, one that all families should have.

Educating the Writer

Learn to Get Your Work into the Classroom

by Sue Bradford Edwards

You enjoy your work but you're not doing it just for fun. You want it to be read and wouldn't turn up your nose at making a living. One of the best ways to increase your readership and your sales is to get your books into the schools.

Although the publisher will list your book in their catalog and it may be reviewed in a journal, you'll stand a better chance of breaking into the schools if you put effort into three areas:

- earning name recognition,
- creating something to make your book work in the classroom,
- and letting reading programs work for you.

Read on to find out how.

WHO ARE YOU?

It's a reality. Schools only have so much money. This limits the number of books they can buy. Want yours to be one of them? Then the buyers have to know who you are because they tend to buy what they are familiar with. You do it when you shop. Teachers and librarians do it when they buy books.

One way to come to the attention of teachers and librarians is to get a starred review. This is great and takes little effort on your part, but it is also something largely out of your control.

Take matters into your own hands and get your name out there.

This doesn't mean crafting a mailing, because the response they draw is often tepid at best. "I've only done a mailing once—to schools in a city where I was picking up an award—and got no response," says author Wendie Old. With hundreds of pieces of paper in circulation, a mailing can easily get lost in the shuffle as a busy teacher or librarian gets ready for their day.

Instead do an excellent signing or school visit and become the talk of the town. It worked when Phyllis and Bradley Harris held the first signing for *My Brother and I* at KD's Books in Lee Summit, Missouri. Cheryl Collier, owner of this independent bookstore, spread the word about their signing and a librarian asked whether they did school visits. This led to an appearance at Young Authors Day where two teachers invited them into the classrooms. Each of

SUE BRADFORD EDWARDS studies the magazine and book markets from her her office in St. Louis, Missouri. She writes a variety of nonfiction, specializing in history, archaeology and nature pieces. Her work appears regularly in a variety of testing and educational publications, *Children's Writer* newsletter and the *St. Louis Post-Dispatch*. Visit her Web site at www.SueBradfordEdwards.8m.com.

these opportunities increased their visibility locally, moving the pair toward becoming a known factor among their local librarians.

To do this in your area, look for stores with scheduled events for educators. ''When I set up signings, I always ask the events coordinator at the bookstore if they have any teacher appreciation events coming up that I can sign at,'' says Cynthia Lord (whose debut book *Rules* has since won a Newbery Honor). In addition to the event in question, your book could get additional face time. ''It's especially nice because my books were often part of the store's teacher display then,'' says Lord. She finds that most books stores host their teacher events during September and October so contact them before this.

But don't limit yourself to bookstore-affiliated events. ''I accept all invitations to come to the state reading association conferences and the state school librarian conferences, even if it's just for a mass author signing and not a speaking gig,'' says Old who has thus earned long term recognition. ''I've discovered that some invitations to speak come several years after the people have seen me at a signing.'' A kind word while signing a book creates memorable face time and name recognition with a teacher or librarian who appreciates the work authors do.

Once you've earned some name recognition at low-pressure events like signings, notch it up by speaking or writing on something related to your book. ''Writing articles for publications that educators read is an effective way to highlight your book, but perhaps more importantly, this offers you an opportunity to speak to any literary topic you may be knowledgable and/or passionate about,'' says author Tanya Stone. ''For example, when *A Bad Boy Can Be Good for a Girl* came out, an article I wrote for *VOYA* followed, called 'Now and Forever: The Power of Sex in Young Adult Literature.' '' Writing on a related topic brings not only another byline but also highlights the effort you put into your work. Effort bespeaks quality.

Louise Jackson works for similar effect when she speaks on topics related to her book. ''I spoke at a Bookfest at Sam Houston State University in Huntsville, Texas in November on the topic 'Eight Great Things to Do with Any Historical Fiction,' '' says Jackson. ''My audience included about 50 elementary librarians and teachers. I sold lots and lots of books, and fully expect to get invitations to speak at some of their schools.'' Why? Because Jackson showed them how versatile, and thus useful, both she and her book can be.

An essential way to increase your name recognition in this day and age is to put up a Web site. Putting up a Web site on your own is an article in and of itself. The why, on the other hand, is much simpler. Unlike human employees and even you yourself, blogs and Web sites work for you round-the-clock. ''The Web site and blog are effective tools because they are always up, and I update them frequently. If someone is looking for me, or wants to learn about a new book of mine, I'm easy to find,'' says Stone.

A teacher or librarian with a catalog or a business card in hand can easily google your name to find out about the book they are thinking about using in the classroom. If you don't have a site, they may very well turn to the work of an author who does have a site and whom they can easily find out more about.

Your site alone isn't enough of a presence on the Web. Get your site and name listed on as many other legitimate sites as you can. ''I belong to groups that have Web sites and get myself listed as a potential speakers,'' says Wendie Old who is listed on the sites of various writers groups. Get your name in as many places as possible and there's a greater chance that you will be the author they find when they need someone.

A final way to gain name recognition online is by joining the same listservs that your audience frequents. ''I did an Internet search and found out that my state (Maine) librarians have a listserv of over 1,000 people, most of whom are public and school librarians,'' says Cynthia Lord. Studying the procedures of the list, Lord found out that anyone could join and that Maine authors were permitted to post concerning their book one time. She knew that a one-time mention would bring her some face time and a small amount of name recognition, but she also realized that the odds of her book being picked up would greatly increase if she offered her audience something more.

GIVE THEM SOMETHING MORE

No matter how you choose to connect with teachers and librarians, you aren't the only writer trying to do so. You are in competition with other writers and illustrators, including big names and local favorites. Once the teachers and librarians have noticed you, how do you get them to pick *your* book? Show them you are serious about what they do. Give them something that will make their jobs as educators easier.

This can mean no more than making sure that the under-financed and often overlooked have basic opportunities. When Lord found the listserv for Maine's librarians, she realized that she had to make her efforts count the one and only time she would be allowed to post about her novel. She contacted her publisher and Scholastic made a set of *Rules* galleys available for

Before You Write

If you really want to get your work into the schools, make certain your idea is a good fit even before you begin to write.

Want to write about the Toltecs? Reconsider your picture book plans. Delaware doesn't cover that topic until sixth grade.

Considering a manuscript on lunar phases? Then a picture book might work better than a middle grade text because many students in Florida learn about this in kindergarten through the second grade.

To find out what grade your topic best fits, review state curriculum guidelines. Check out the state in which you live as well as California (www.cde.ca.gov/be/st/ss/), Texas (www.tea.state.tx.us/curriculum/social/index.html) and New York (www.emsc.nysed.gov/ciai/cores.htm#3ela), which are often referenced because of their large populations. There is some variation from state to state, but also many similarities. For example, magnetism is studied in second grade in Missouri as well as in third grade in both Texas and Tennessee.

Don't shirk studying the guidelines because you plan to submit to a trade publisher versus an educational publisher. Educational sales can still boost your bottom line, and trade authors whose books have strong curriculum ties also do school visits.

Knowing the guidelines can you help prepare a suitable program likely to make you the speaker of choice. "I study the state or district curriculum requirements in writing and social studies and give presentations related to these. Example: In Springfield, a fourth grade benchmark is to write a piece of historical fiction with an identifiable beginning, middle and end. In the fifth grade, they have to write a journal entry with a historical setting. This, of course, involves a first-person situation and asks them to report personal reactions to being an immigrant, etc. I have presentations with handouts the teachers can use and often go year after year," says Louise Jackson. "I also insist that the class has either read my book or had it read to them or I won't come. This ensures at least one book purchased and often more."

The more you know before you craft your manuscript, the better the fit will be.

a give away. "When I blurbed my book, I also included a link to my first chapter and offered those galleys," says Lord. "Many rural school librarians had never received a galley before, and so it was very special to them. They really went to bat for my book." Offering a group of librarians access to something they didn't usually have earned Lord their respect.

You can also do this by developing materials to accompany your book. "I have teacher's guides for most of my books," says Dori Butler, "I had copies of them available at ALA although they're also on my Web site. Everybody's got a book, but I've got a teacher's guide, too." Giving them something ready to use makes teachers' jobs easier and increases the chance that yours will be the book they chose.

Obviously, this works best when they can easily see that it is available. "I made up a teacher's guide that fits neatly in my book, with just the top that says '*Rules* Discussion Guide' sticking out," says Lord, "so it doesn't take up more room on the bookstore shelf." She offers the guide to bookstores when she does a signing. Lord also emphasizes that a guide can be included on your Web site, that of your publisher and sometimes even on sites that feature books and corresponding discussion guides.

Worried that too many authors offer teacher's guides? Go beyond the basics. Lord offers a packet of "behind the scenes" material to any teacher who asks for it. "It includes a timeline of *Rules'* publication, a few pages with my editor's comments on them to show the revision process, my discussion guide, the evolution of my book's cover and design, a story I wrote at the age of six to show how we all start somewhere, etc." It's a lot of work to pull together this much supplemental material but its well worth it. "Teachers love this packet, because they usually don't get to see and show students the process behind a book," Lord says. "It often results in them buying class sets of copies of my book or adding my book to the curriculum." Just as offering something extra sparks interest in overworked editors, it also gets the attention of harried teachers and librarians.

STATE AWARDS

One final way to get your work into the classroom is to get it into reading programs, from state reading lists to Accelerated Reader (AR). Once on these lists, your book will find its way into classroom after classroom.

For many state awards, including the Texas Bluebonnet Award, Florida's Sunshine State Young Readers Award, and the Missouri Building Block award, anyone can nominate a book. Perhaps one of the teachers for whom you've done a drop dead classroom visit will nominate your book, but you can also take matters into your own hands.

Before nominating your own book, study the eligibility requirements. The Texas Bluebonnet Award is for books relevant to grades three to six vs. the Missouri Building Blocks' preschoolers. While those for the Bluebonnet Award may be set anywhere in the world and may have been written by an author living anywhere in the U.S., for the Oklahoma Book Awards the book must have an Oklahoma-based theme or the author or illustrators must live or have lived in Oklahoma. Thus Anna Myer's *Assasin,* is eligible due to her Oklahoma residency although it's about a seamstress who interacted with John Wilkes Booth in Washington, D.C.

Which nominated books are chosen? To help us understand this, Vice Chair Christy Schink shared some insights into the requirements for Missouri Building Block Picture Book Award administered by the Missouri Library Association. "The book must be an appropriate read-aloud for a preschool audience, it must have been published within the past two years, it can't be a holiday book, and either the author or illustrator must live in the U.S.," says Schink. "The main reason that books get knocked off the list early is that they are just too long."

A successful nomination brings increased sales. "These books find their way into libraries across the state after we choose them," says Schink. "They are newer books and so not necessarily already in all the libraries. I know that in my library, I might already have one to four copies of a title. But if it gets chosen as a Building Block nominee, I'll buy nine copies." Given the number of children who vote, such purchases are necessary. In 2005, 8,000 Missouri preschoolers voted to select the winner. That won't translate into 8,000 copies sold, but increased sales even in the hundreds are beneficial to your bottom line.

Exposure in multiple states will obviously bring even more sales and one way to do this is to get your book into the AR program. This program is used to promote reading in schools across the country.

Because Renaissance, the company that produces the AR program, tries to include books in their program that many libraries already have in stock, the criteria they use for choosing which books to add is similar to that used by school libraries. The cover letter for your nomination needs to include information about your book's awards, positive reviews, and whether it is available through major school library suppliers. Another plus is whether or not it has been on any reading lists such as state awards lists. If you have this kind of success behind you, get that package with two copies of your book ready to go!

Gaining face time and name recognition. Showing the teachers your book can work in the classroom. Even getting your book on lists wherever possible. It takes time to do these things. But if you can get your work into the hands of young readers across the country, it is time well spent.

Do Visits for Free

You have no speaking experience and you just can't seem to book a classroom visit. The solution? Chose your venue and volunteer to speak for free. It goes against the common wisdom, but, in the long run, it will pay off.

"I've spoken for free at a few small local book festivals, one of which was sponsored by my state's reading association. I got a nice amount of press in my state's library/educator world as a result of that talk," says Cynthia Lord. This kind of publicity brings with it not only sales but often invitations for more speaking engagements.

"I have found that one free visit generates at least 10 paid visits. It's called 'casting your bread on the waters and being sure it will return to you.' " I have done this as a consultant for years. When a school in Wyoming needed me and couldn't afford much or anything, I would go and, invariably, I was paid back over and over again because they never forgot it and, the minute they got money, they gave me many opportunities. Of course, this assumes that I did a bang-up good job and I always made sure I did," says Louise Jackson. "Good things often take several years to happen. They come one by one and each one seems to generate another. Word of mouth is a useful thing and teachers tend to believe other teachers more than anyone."

Each time you speak, you get your work into the hands of more educators or more young readers. Gain name recognition and see the results.

The Class of 2k7

First-Time Authors Band Together for Book Promotion

by Greg R. Fishbone

I got the call in late 2005. Yes, *that* call, the one that meant a book of mine would finally be published. For years this moment had been the goal of all my writing, revising, and submitting. In my mind, I was in the end zone doing my touchdown dance and everything else would just follow naturally—good reviews, book signings, bestseller status, and publishers stumbling over each other for the opportunity to put additional books of mine into print.

When I'd finished jumping around, shouting for joy, and spiking imaginary footballs, I got a reality check from my publisher. There was no "guaranteed rich and famous" clause in my contract. It would take a lot of work to make my book a success, so my end zone dance had been premature.

Today's authors are expected to shoulder more of the promotional burden than ever. It's not that publishers are looking to shift more work onto us, but there's only so much they can do when thousands of books are published each year and, except for a few select titles each season, marketing budgets are tight. The competition for attention is fierce, and most books don't stand out from the crowd. An author's promotional efforts can mean the difference between success and failure in the marketplace, no matter how well-written or well-reviewed a book is.

For me, it was a major mental shift to go from selling my book to a publisher to selling my book to the world. After a few months of research into the mechanics of book signings, classroom visits, press releases, interviews, online viral marketing, and social networks, I felt like my head was ready to explode. The goal line had moved to a distant horizon, and getting there would require new skills and a large investment of time.

Since there was only one of me, I knew I'd never be able to do all the promotional things I wanted to—but what if there weren't only one of me? One morning, I woke up wondering what might happen if I could gather together a whole group of fellow authors with first books coming out in 2007. Working together, we'd be able to do far more than any one of us could do alone.

A CALL GOES OUT

That morning I registered a domain name (http://classof2k7.com) and put out a call for first-time authors through an SCBWI mailing list, and the Class of 2k7 was born. According to

GREG R. FISHBONE is the author of *The Penguins of Doom* (Blooming Tree Press, Summer 2007), Class President of the Class of 2k7, and ARA/Webmaster of the New England regions of SCBWI. The Class of 2k7 invites you to follow their adventures on their Web site (http://classof2k7.com), forum (http://forum.classof2k7.com), and blog (http://community.livejournal.com/classof2k7).

2k7 Class Historian Alice Bauer, we had seven members and our own Yahoo Group within the first 24 hours.

Early on, we had to decide on a core message for our group. We figured that middle grade and young adult novels were complementary markets for our purposes. We also determined that it would be an absolute requirement for our members to be first-time authors with books coming out in the 2007 calendar year, so that our whole class would be graduating together into the world of professional publishing. Our Class 2k7 "brand" would represent fresh new books from fresh new voices, and our target audience would be booksellers, librarians, and teachers—the BLTs of publishing, as we called them.

Painful as it was, we had to cement our group's identity by turning away authors of non-fiction books, picture books, books that weren't being published in the United States, and books that were not an author's very first published novel. Each time I spoke to any of these authors, I would urge them to start their own marketing group for whatever niche their book

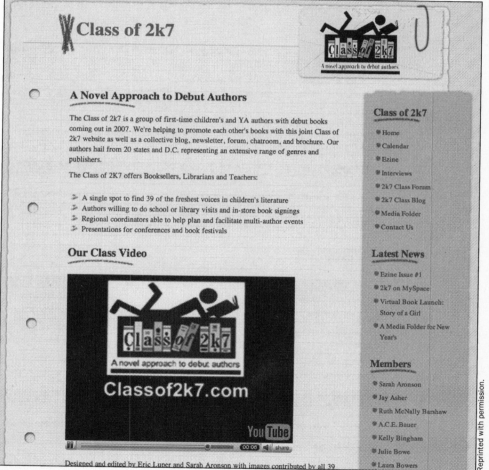

When Greg Fishbone got overwhelmed with the prospect of promoting his first novel, he decided to take a strength-in-numbers approach, and soon the Class of 2k7 was born. Class of 2k7 is a collective of first-time mid-grade and YA authors with books coming out in 2007. One of the first things the group did was create a Web site about their books, http://classof2k7.com, which fuels their effort to market their books to all-important booksellers, librarians and teachers.

fit into. If we could do it, anyone else could do it too, and we all wished them every success.

Also painful was when we met and exceeded our original membership goal and had to turn away some very talented debut authors with amazing-sounding books. Group consensus was that we were in danger of becoming too big and unwieldy.

ONLINE EN MASSE

The Internet is a great and wonderful thing. If you're looking to collaborate with other authors who are located hundreds or thousands of miles away, an e-mail list or forum beats anything you can do with tin cans and a zillion yards of string. And if you're looking to get the word out about your books, a Web site or blog is so much more effective than all that ''shouting from the rooftops'' people used to do back in the olden days. For the Class of 2k7, we used the Internet like it was going out of style—which it probably never will.

We've found that using the Internet as a group offers unique challenges as well as opportunities that are not be available to solo authors. A Web site featuring 38 books will have more information on it than a Web site featuring only one, so a group site might be more interesting and attractive for a book buyer—although it becomes more difficult to make any one book truly stand out.

The Class of 2k7 established a group Web site with the goal of creating a ''one-stop shopping'' destination for BLTs. Each author has a page of biographical and book information, links, cover art, and a headshot, and all pages can be searched by genre, season, publisher or region. As the year has gone on, we've expanded the 2k7 site with an interview archive, e-zine, media folder, and links to our forum and chatroom. No one of us alone could have packed our personal Web sites with so much content!

Our collective blog has an ''Ask a Debut Author'' format that's different from anything else we've seen on the Internet, and plays on our strength of being a diverse group of authors with a wide range of books. Each week we take a question from the audience, discuss it amongst ourselves, and release a collection of answers.

Finally, we've been able to reach out as a group to BLTs on social networking sites like MySpace. What? Didn't you know that there were hundreds of booksellers, librarians, and teachers on MySpace? Like I said, the Internet is a great and wonderful thing.

PLAYING ON STRENGTHS

The members of our Class are all talented authors, but as individuals we also have strengths in many other areas that can help the entire group. Some members are skilled at Web design, some have years of experience drafting press releases, some are especially knowledgeable about school visits, some are great at brainstorming new ideas, and one is a graphic designer who created an amazing logo for us.

Two of our members, Eric Luper (*Big Slick*, Fall 2007) and Sarah Aronson (*Head Case*, Fall 2007), have experience in video production and volunteered to produce a class video. They collected an image from each author that represented the thematic essence of their book, and set the whole thing to music. The result was a movie trailer that the rest of us certainly would never have thought of making on our own. (See it on the Class of 2k7 homepage or search for Class of 2k7 on www.youtube.com.)

ALL ALONE TOGETHER

Because the Class of 2k7 books range from humorous middle grades to edgy YA, including graphic novels and novels in verse, we don't always have readers in common. This was one reason we decided to target BLTs through our group efforts rather than readers. In order to reach our readers, we each still need our own individual Web sites and marketing plans.

All of our group efforts have also been informed by the policies and practices of our

The Class of 2k7 (& Their Books)

Of the 38 authors in the 2k7 collective 13 have written middle grade/tween books and 25 have written YA/Teen titles. Here's a list of the authors, their book titles, and their publishers by season:

Spring 2007 Debuts
- *Ruth McNally Barshaw—*Ellie McDoodle: Have Pen, Will Travel* (Bloomsbury)
- *Kelly Bingham—*Shark Girl* (Candlewick)
- Julie Bowe—*My Last Best Friend* (Harcourt)
- Laura Bowers—*Beauty Shop for Rent* (Harcourt)
- Paula Chase—*So Not The Drama* (Dafina/Kensington)
- Cassandra Clare—*City of Bones* (McElderry Books)
- Rosemary Clement-Moore—*Prom Dates From Hell* (Delacorte)
- Karen Day—*Tall Tales* (Wendy Lamb Books)
- Aimee Ferris—*Girl Overboard* (Penguin)
- Paula Jolin—*In the Name of God* (Roaring Brook)
- *Carrie Jones—*Tips on Having a Gay (ex) Boyfriend* (Flux/Llewellyn)
- *Rose Kent—*Kimchi & Calamari* (HarperCollins)
- Constance Leeds—*The Silver Cup* (Viking)
- Elizabeth Scott—*Bloom* (Simon Pulse)
- Joni Sensel—*Reality Leak* (Henry Holt)
- C.G. Watson—*Quad* (Razorbill)
- Sara Zarr—*Story of a Girl* (Little Brown)

*These authors are all featured in First Books on page 119.

Summer 2007 Debuts
- Sarah Beth Durst—*Into The Wild* (Razorbill)
- Ann Dee Ellis—*This Is What I Did* (Little Brown)
- Greg R. Fishbone—*The Penguins of Doom* (Blooming Tree Press)
- Jeannine Garsee—*Before After and Somebody In Between* (Bloomsbury)
- Judy Gregerson—*Bad Girls Club* (Blooming Tree Press)
- Stephanie Hale—*Revenge of the Homecoming Queen* (Berkley Jam)
- S.A. Harazin—*Blood Brothers* (Delacorte)
- Thatcher Heldring—*Toby Wheeler: Eighth Grade Benchwarmer* (Delacorte)
- Marlane Kennedy—*Me and the Pumpkin Queen* (Greenwillow)
- Melissa Marr—*Wicked Lovely* (HarperCollins)
- G. Neri—*Yummy: The Last Days of a Southside Shorty* (Lee & Low)
- Rebecca Stead—*First Light* (Wendy Lamb Books)

Fall 2007 Debuts
- Sarah Aronson—*Head Case* (Roaring Brook)
- Jay Asher—*Thirteen Reasons Why* (Razorbill)
- A.C.E. Bauer—*No Castles Here* (Random House)
- Autumn Cornwell—*Carpe Diem* (Feiwel)
- Sundee T. Frazier—*Brendan Buckley's Universe & Everything In It* (Delacorte)
- *Jo Knowles—*Lessons from a Dead Girl* (Candlewick)
- Eric Luper—*Big Slick* (Farrar Straus & Giroux)
- Suzanne Selfors—*To Catch a Mermaid* (Little Brown)
- Heather Tomlinson—*The Swan Maiden* (Henry Holt)
- Tiffany Trent—*In the Serpent's Coils* (Mirrorstone)

*This author is featured in an Insider Report on page 352.

Articles & Interviews

publishers. They've been doing this marketing stuff for a lot longer than we have, so it's been important for us to consult and coordinate with them on all of our projects, and to allow members to opt out of any activities that might cause a conflict. Although our members are being published by a wide variety of publishers, from very small to very large, they have all been supportive and excited about what we're doing in our group.

The Class of 2k7 group was meant to supplement the marketing and promotion work that each member has to do, but not to replace it. No matter how effective we have been as a group, each of us has further work to do in promoting or individual books. Still, that part of the business somehow seems less daunting now, and if we get stuck on something we each have 37 online friends who are willing to help us out.

INTO THE FUTURE

When we sent out the first batch of press releases for the Class of 2k7, one of our members received an inquiry assuming that she was a full-time publicist, because a group such as ours apparently could not exist unless it was professionally managed. We all laughed and took it as a sign that our homebrewed Web site and consensus-drafted materials were good enough to fool even a discerning critic. We were like the Folgers crystals of the publishing world!

Then other interviewers assumed that the Class must have been assembled by an industry trade group or as a joint venture of our publishers. One magazine editor even marveled that any authors would want to join because "everyone knows" authors are introverted and ultra-competitive. Someone else remarked that managing a group of authors would be like herding cats.

Luckily, that's not the case. If authors really were the antisocial prima donnas that some people make us out to be, I'd never have been able to find a critique group, participate in online author communities, read helpful author blogs, or join the SCBWI—which is run on the regional level by authors and illustrators volunteering their time and effort. Almost certainly, then, I'd never have been able to finish a book and get it into print.

The reality is that authors not only can work together, but increasingly we must, especially in the areas of marketing and promotion.

The friendships we've formed through participation in this group are perhaps the most important thing we'll take away at the end of the year, and in that way the Class of 2k7 spirit should last deep into our respective publishing careers.

At the time of this writing, a Class of 2k8 is already forming, and several of us 2k7ers have expressed an interest in mentoring them. When available, details will be posted to the Class of 2k7 Web site. With luck, groups such as ours will continue to thrive into the future, and everyone will know how supportive, cooperative, and helpful most authors really are.

School Visits

From Blah to SCBWIdol-Winning

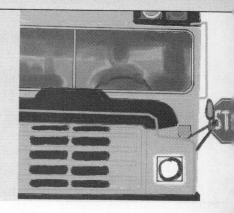

by Claire & Monte Montgomery

Our refrigerator doesn't have any magnets on it. Our carpets are uncluttered by cookie crumbs and action figures. Our white walls are unsmudged by crayons and peanut butter. Our sharp-edged, fragile, midcentury-modern furniture is about as kid-friendly as Laura Wingfield's glass menagerie.

You see, soon after getting married we decided—for various reasons—not to reproduce. Consequently our house, and in many ways our lives, have become virtual monuments to childlessness. So how is it that every week or two we find ourselves up to our necks in a boiling crowd of hyperactive eight- to twelve-year-olds?

Simple: we wrote a children's book.

Hubert Invents the Wheel (Walker/Bloomsbury 2005) began life back in 2002 as a screenplay, which is what we'd been primarily writing up to then. After coming heart-stoppingly close to selling our story about a plucky Bronze Age teenager to not one but *two* movie studios, we decided to retool the tale as a novel and see if we could find a buyer in the publishing world.

Using *Children's Writer's & Illustrator's Market* as our bible, we spent months making the grueling rounds of query letters and manuscript submissions. Sixty-four rejections later (nothing new there, after two decades in the Hollywood trenches), Walker stepped forward with an offer. We whooped with joy, popped a champagne cork, then sailed through the surprisingly pleasant revision process under the guidance of their excellent editors. Eighteen months after the manuscript's acceptance, we held the final product—a real, live book!—in our trembling hands. Nothing to do now but sit back and wait for the royalty checks to come in, right?

Well, not quite. To our astonishment and dismay our *magnum opus*—despite a smattering of uniformly good reviews and Walker's considerable marketing efforts—failed to fly off the shelves! The chains didn't take it. Our Amazon sales rank had as many digits as Bill Gates's salary. All that work, and now this? *Something had to be done!*

We'd been told of a concept called "school visits," which supposedly helped publicize your book, and sometimes even pay a few bucks. We decided to line some up. Lacking children of our own—and hence teachers to bribe or threaten—this turned out to be harder than it sounded. Printing and mailing a few hundred postcards yielded zero results. (We've

CLAIRE & MONTE MONTGOMERY are a wife-and-husband writing team who have seen their work produced on stage, screen and television. Their musical *Flying Colors*, is frequently performed by youth theatre groups around the country. After dark, they can be found playing and singing pop tunes and jazz standards in nightspots throughout Southern California.

Hubert Invents the Wheel got great reviews. The *School Library Journal* praised the writing—"Broad comic scenes are balanced by wordplay and lively dialogue. Juxtapositions between the realities of Hubert's time and today are especially effective"—and the content—"this enjoyable novel demonstrates that ancient history can be surprisingly funny"—but no one seemed to be buying the book. That was when Claire and Monte Montgomery decided to take matters into their own hands—and start doing school visits.

since heard from many successful authors that these cards are a total waste of money.)

At last, after much soul-killing degradation (another experience as familiar to screenwriters as breathing) we booked our first gig, at our tax accountant's kids' school. Our payment? Zero. But we had to start somewhere.

Understand that the last time either of us had set foot in a classroom was under penalty of truancy law. The very smell of chalk dust acted upon us like the sound of sirens upon an escaped convict. Still, we were upbeat. Stage fright wouldn't be a problem—our day job as singers and musicians had erased that impediment years ago—nor, we thought, would lack of content. We worked up a little dog-and-pony show including demonstrations of some wheeled devices, figuring that afterward we'd just open the floor to questions, right?

Again, not quite.

That first visit was a real baptism by fire. To begin with, the class we faced was hardly the gang of naïve, impressionable fifth-graders that we'd expected, eager to sit at our feet and absorb our wisdom like sponges. Far from it. They seemed to know all the answers to our questions and, what was worse, kept asking questions that *we* didn't know the answers to. These baby Einsteins were as sophisticatedly blasé as so many children of law partners and studio heads, which no doubt many were. (Their intellect was atypical, as well: we learned afterward that we'd just addressed a group of highly gifted students who'd been singled out from *other* groups of highly gifted students).

Second, we were cramped. Jammed into one of those classroom/trailers with 30 kids and two teachers, we barely had room to turn around, let alone roam the stage, as our active presentation requires.

Third, we simply hadn't spent enough time rehearsing with our props. At one point we'd planned to demonstrate gyroscopic precession by spinning one of the kids on a lazy Susan. (As a child, Monte had been impressed with this stunt by his physicist father.) But our poor volunteer, a plump, bookish lad, appeared to be nailed to the floor. No amount of effort could coax him into rotation. A quick examination revealed the snag: by sheer bad luck, another of our props—a Frisbee—had gotten stuck in the works, freezing the mechanism! Naturally, we haven't made that mistake again. (Also, we no longer use a volunteer for this—now the petite Claire takes the spin.)

Dripping with flop sweat, we hurtled toward our anticlimactic climax, finished up to meager applause and unenthusiastic thanks, and escaped with our hides, having learned several valuable lessons. (In fact, we've since learned a lot of lessons, some of which appear at the bottom of this article.) We went back to the drawing board.

Our next outing, another freebie, wasn't exactly glitch-free, either. We stumbled a lot, and a grumpy teacher in the next classroom chewed us out for making too much racket. But we were improving.

Each visit went a little better than the last. Neil Simon says that preparing a Broadway show in out-of-town previews is like getting to take the same test over and over until you can't help but ace it. School visits are no different. We cut here, expanded there, took note of when we were going over and when we were bombing.

That said, there was still no predicting how any individual audience would react. The same joke would provoke guffaws one day, crickets the next. The best we could hope for was to improve our odds with constant tinkering. The key was to put in as many appearances as we could possibly schedule, whether paid or free.

After a dozen or so visits we'd established the basis of what has since solidified into a reliably entertaining and educational talk. It's in three sections: "Wheel History," "How We Wrote the Book," and "The Stunts."

In the first part we engage the class by asking them to identify all the wheels in the room, and to guess when and where the wheel was invented. (Typical responses: "1972" and "Indiana.") Next we touch on some aspects of life in 3000 B.C. Mesopotamia including ancient technology, the first cities, and that sixth-grade staple, cuneiform writing.

Part two covers how we came to write the book, drawing obvious parallels with schoolwork. You get an assignment (or give yourself one), then do research, then write, then rewrite, then submit, then get your work back with marks all over it, then rewrite some more.

The third part is about how wheels work, and the "superpowers" they convey, including speed, strength, and "super-silliness." Demonstrations and audience participation really help sell this section: We use yo-yos, juggling rings, and a "Sumerian torture device" that we made out of a broom and some pulleys. Our grand finale is Monte's unicycle ride and inevitable crash, followed by Q&A.

This one-wheeled climax has a bit of history to it. Monte learned to ride a unicycle in his early teens, then lost interest and let his skill atrophy, assuming that—like trigonometry—he'd find no use for it in later life. Thirty years later, while we were working up our act, it occurred to us that a ride on the contraption might provide a satisfying capper to the proceedings. How much trouble could it be to re-learn the skill? It's just like riding a bicycle, right?

In a word, nope. Getting up on one wheel at age 47 turns out to be something else altogether from doing it at 15. There are certain biological differences that we needn't go into here. Plus, one feels like an idiot. Once, while Monte was pedaling up

Photo: Claire and Monte Montgomery.

Monte's unicycle ride—and subsequent crash—is the climax of the Montgomerys' school visits. Monte had ridden the unicycle as a teenager, but he had to relearn the skill for their routine. Many falls and jokes from the neighbors later, Monte's ride became a staple of their program, adding a fun and exciting element that young readers respond to.

our street, a neighborhood wag called out, "Guess that's what happens when you buy a bicycle on the installment plan, huh?" Eight days and many a bloodied shin later he was back in the saddle, and the ride became a permanent part of the show.

But there still remained the challenge of finding venues. We caught a break when recent Newbery winner Susan Patron (*The Higher Power of Lucky*), senior children's librarian of the L.A. system, caught our act in our local branch. She liked what she saw and generously included us in an "author showcase" at LAPL's central library. As a result of that appearance, we booked 17 branch visits all over the city, which to our surprise and delight have been among the most gratifying experiences we've had in connection with this book.

Another high point was the Society of Children's Book Writers and Illustrators' "SCBWI-dol" contest, held at the annual conference in August 2006 at the Century Plaza Hotel in Los Angeles. We'd resolved to enter our presentation this year, despite what was sure to be tough competition. Making things even tougher, Monte had to give the talk himself, because Claire couldn't attend—*and*, do it in three minutes instead of 45!

Here's how hard it is to do the short program instead of the long one: 15 times as hard. After looking at our act from every angle, we opted for cheap theatrics over pedagogy: juggling, riding the "ridiculocipede," and the mono-wheeled ride at the end.

In the finals, Monte was quaking gelatinously in front of 800 people—many of them successful authors and seasoned school visitors themselves—but managed to keep it together for the allotted 180 seconds. The climactic unicycle crash was spectacular, and his howls of pain rang with authenticity, thanks to a broken rib he'd sustained earlier in the week.

Those screams must have done the trick, because our program managed to nose out the other finalists and claim first prize: the new notebook computer on which this article is being written. It just goes to show, you don't need to be a genius to develop an effective book talk;

Photo: Claire and Monte Montgomery.

The Montgomerys' school visit routine has gags and gimmicks, such as juggling and riding the "ridiculoc-ipede," to keep the kids interested, and it has proven effective with adults, too. Monte Montgomery won the "SCBWIdol" contest in 2006 with a short version of their program. Here Claire demonstrates gyroscopic precession with one of the couple's many props.

you just need dedication, a sense of humor, and a willingness to make a complete fool out of yourself.

Now, more than a year after those awkward first steps before the pint-sized brainiacs, we approach each author visit with genuine enthusiasm. It gives us a legitimate excuse to get out of the house and away from working on our next book; the teachers and librarians are great; and the kids are always full of surprises.

Once, after a particularly energetic performance in which we shamelessly pulled out every trick we could think of (including some that were totally unrelated to wheels, let alone our novel), a shy girl raised her hand during the Q&A and asked, "Have you ever made a list of all your talents?" Now, we've written dialogue for Kelly Preston and jokes for Allison Janney, sung for movie stars, governors, and at least one U.S. President, and even performed at the Hollywood Bowl in front of 10,000 people—but in terms of pure satisfaction, nothing has quite equaled that moment.

At the beginning of this piece we said that we didn't have any kids. Now we do—thousands of them. Maybe someday we'll even put a few magnets on the fridge.

SCHOOL VISITS TIPS & TRICKS

Authors making their first school visits will be no doubt face problems totally unlike ours. Every experience is different. Embrace the chaos! It's what keeps things interesting. But here are few pointers that might make them run a bit more smoothly:

Play to your strengths

We aren't particularly good at acting, memorizing, or even reading aloud, so we keep all three to a minimum. We're fairly good at thinking on our feet, however, so we gravitate toward "improvisation within a framework."

If you happen to be a gifted actor, structure your talk to feature your acting. If you can sing, sing. If you can draw, by all means draw. If you're double-jointed, dislocate. The connection between your specialty and the book's subject may be tenuous, but it's far better to force your forte into your presentation than to leave out your strongest suit and give a perfectly integrated, but less entertaining, performance.

Let the kids move

Remember how it felt to be crammed into straight-backed chair for hours a day when you were dying to be racing around a playground or ball field? Invent a reason for everybody to stand, stretch, or jump up and down during your talk—even if it's only once or twice. Of course, too much of this can become counterproductive—if they get *too* wound up, you'll never get them back in their seats. Besides, they'll forget all about the book, which doesn't exactly help sales.

Don't use notes

Try to get "off book," as they say in the theatre world, ASAP. Reading from a sheet breaks eye contact and saps energy; it's better to risk losing your place than losing your audience.

Solicit volunteers

Even among the most reticent classes, we've never had trouble finding a few students willing to participate. If your talk doesn't present opportunities for this, manufacture something. The kids love it.

Microphones

If there's *any* way to avoid one, do so. Most P.A. systems sound lousy, and even the best can't help but distance you from your audience. But if there are more than a hundred kids or if you must be heard over deafening air-conditioning, you're stuck. If so, arrive early and give the mike a dry run. Does it feed back? Ask someone to turn it down a little, or find the volume knob and do it yourself. Does it distort? You're probably too close. Back up and talk louder.

Unruly kids
If some miniature Don Rickles keeps talking or giggling, don't interrupt your presentation. Just keep up your monologue and walk right over to him. Get right in his face, if necessary. He'll clam up.

Label your stuff
In the heat of the moment—especially if you're signing afterward—props and other materials can get left behind. We printed tiny labels including our name, address, phone number and Web site and taped them to everything with the stickiest tape we could find.

Referrals
If your talk has gone over well (or even if you feel that it hasn't), encourage the teacher or librarian to spread the word among his or her fellow wizards. *Nothing* is more effective in lining up future work than word of mouth.

Use a prop box
When you think about it, author visits are nothing but show-and-tell presented by adults. If you have props, drawings, false teeth, whatever, bring them along, but *keep them in a box* until the appropriate time. Even if your stuff isn't all that fascinating, the anticipation of it drives kids nuts.

SPECIAL CONSIDERATIONS FOR STORES & LIBRARIES
Be flexible. In this uncontrolled environment, you may find yourself facing kids outside of your book's intended age group. For the younger set, be prepared to get sillier—if necessary, to the point of "see the shiny, shiny keys." Conversely, if you're trying to hold a jaded 14-year-old's interest with your picture book about floppy bunnies, focus instead on the process of writing or illustrating or submitting the manuscript. (Illustrators obviously have a big advantage here.)

Stores
Bringing the youngsters in is likely to be your biggest challenge. If possible, arrange to take over somebody else's scheduled "storytime"—you'll have a built-in audience. We always do a pared-down version of our talk (20 minutes maximum, instead of 45) because customers, unlike students, have the right to wander off if they're bored. Don't panic if you find yourself addressing laughably small groups. We once did our entire spiel, from soup to nuts, for *one kid*. It was a little weird, but boy, did she feel special. (*And*, she bought a book!)

Libraries
These are wonderful. Although there's generally little or no sales potential, you get to polish your act, you're doing something nice for the community and for literacy in general, and you might even get paid! The librarians we've worked with have invariably been wonderful at organizing and publicizing our visits, and are often willing to play the bad-cop role when crowd-shooshing is required.

(One last hint for both stores and libraries: after your program has been announced, but just before you start, make a quick circuit of the shelves in search of potential audience. We almost always manage to rope in a few last-minute strays. Just be sure to check with mommy or daddy first, or you may end up getting slapped with a restraining order.)

A First-Time Author's Brush with Fame

by Catherine Stier

We all envision what will happen after the publication of our first book—the thrill of paging through our bound work for the first time, the book signings and royalty checks that are sure to follow, and the chance to casually let it slip at dinner parties: "Why yes, darling, I *am* an author."

Yet I never guessed at all the amazing and unexpected experiences—truly cool things—that would occur in the life of ordinary me once my book was published.

My first book, *If I Were President* (Albert Whitman) is still selling steadily nearly a decade after its publication. That's no small feat for this competitive business, I've learned. The book presents a multi-cultural group of children imagining themselves as President of the United States. While playing up the kid-appealing, fun stuff—how the president's house has its own bowling alley and movie theater—it slips in important facts, too, about the State of the Union address and the president's responsibility in approving or vetoing bills. And it hints to the child that perhaps he or she could someday be president.

With its publication came surprises and big changes for me. But first, let me share a bit about how the book came to be.

The story behind the story

For several years, I worked with my local YMCA's preschool program. As Presidents' Day approached one year, I searched the library for a president-themed book suitable for lively four-year-olds. Most picture books I found featured rather long accounts of the lives of individual presidents. But in speaking with the students during a circle time, I soon learned that they first needed some truly basic information. These tots didn't know what a president was or did, or that the president lived in the White House. A quick, fact-packed and light-hearted overview, it seemed to me, would best serve this age group.

Writing the piece, however, proved most challenging. I strived for a balance between fun and informative, humorous while still remaining respectful to the office. I also searched for things about the president to which very young children could relate. Because preschoolers memorize their addresses, I wrote that after becoming president ". . . I'd have to remember my new address: 1600 Pennsylvania Avenue, Washington, D.C."

CATHERINE STIER is an author, a magazine writer, and a columnist and feature writer for her hometown newspaper. She has had more than 250 articles, stories, features and craft projects published in newspapers and magazines including *Highlights for Children*, *Child Life* and *Children's Playmate*. She hopes her second book, *If I Ran for President*—and all the books that may follow—will lead her on more wondrous and astounding adventures.

Illustrations © 1999 DyAnne DiSalvo-Ryan. Reprinted with permission.

Catherine Stier's book shows children what the president does, beginning with "If I were president, I'd promise to 'preserve, protect, and defend the Constitution of the United States,' because that would be my job." Found at many national historic sites, *If I Were President* was an IRA Los Angeles' 100 Best Books and an Honor Book by the Society of School Librarians International, and has taken the author on an unexpected journey.

Around this time, the Society of Children's Book Writers and Illustrators Illinois chapter hosted an event lead by an editor from Albert Whitman & Company. At the program, I asked the editor if her company had any particular subject needs. "Holiday books," came the reply. "Perhaps the lesser covered holidays."

Ahh . . . Presidents' Day! I thought.

And so I polished my manuscript and sent it with a cover letter mentioning their stated interest in holiday books and my experiences with the preschool set. It was accepted. That's when my adventure began.

On my way . . .

I always understood that the publication of a book would transform me from a writer to an author. Yet I was surprised and delighted to learn that I could also claim the title "honor-winning author" when the book was named an IRA Los Angeles' 100 Best Books and an Honor Book by the Society of School Librarians International.

Hometown hoopla

After the book's publication, I made my first tentative steps toward getting the word out. I sent a letter to my town's weekly newspaper. Might they be interested in this bit of local news? Yes, came the response. And they planned to send a photographer to the YMCA during my class time. Yet what hit the paper was no small community item. The paper featured a full-page article with pictures, and plastered a huge, color photo of me on the front page. All over town, my neighbors and friends were pulling pictures of my mug out of their mailboxes. Heady stuff!

Later, I would be asked to appear at a local department store, a school career day and at a brownie meeting where each girl had purchased a hardcover copy of my book.

Emboldened by my success, I tried other things. I contacted a national woman's magazine that had published my freelance work and a major daily newspaper from my childhood hometown in Michigan. Both featured the book, showcasing it as a great read for kids as the upcoming elections approached.

On to the White House . . . sort of

I also ruminated about who might be interested in offering the book for sale. It was available in bookstores and online, of course, but . . . and then I had it! I called the White House Historical Association, which runs a gift shop near the White House, and asked if they might consider stocking the book among their other presidential-themed children's selections. It would have to undergo a review process, I was told, but I was invited to send a copy.

Later I learned from my publisher that the White House Historical Association had ordered 200 copies to stock their shelves. They subsequently ordered more, presumably once those had run out. Children from all over the country, I knew, would be bringing my book home as a souvenir of their trip to our nation's capital.

You're an Author! Now What?

Share your success story. Getting a book published *is* a big deal. Consider which organizations or businesses would be thrilled to be associated with or informed of your accomplishment. Contact your college alumni newsletter, your local newspaper and the newspaper of your childhood hometown. Inform local parenting publications about the author in their area. If you've published articles or stories in magazines, let them know about your book. They may wish to include a success story about one of their contributors, and it certainly builds your reputation as a writer. Call or write your local school district, especially if family members attend or you have ever belonged to the PTA. When appropriate, let your employer know. Because I worked at the YMCA, I phoned the editorial office of their national news magazine, and got coverage with a photo and the headline "Teaching kids by the book."

Brainstorm for new markets. Think about what establishments, besides bookstores and online booksellers, might be interested in carrying your book. Does your book feature ships, pirates, whales, the sea? How about the gift shops of maritime museums? Do you explore, through fiction or nonfiction, the natural world, or feature trees or flowers in your book? Consider contacting nature centers or botanical gardens. Politely request to speak with the person who chooses books for the gift shop, and offer to send your book for review. Your publisher will likely be glad to send a gratis copy to any establishment considering carrying your book among its merchandise.

Polish up a presentation. As soon as you learn your book will be published, start planning a school presentation. For many authors, the presentations, classes and workshops they lead make up a significant portion of their writing income. Jot down ideas about props, interactive segments and other ways to engage kids. Also consider how your book might tie into subjects kids study in class—a great selling point with schools. I was lucky. Exploring the American presidency fits well with an elementary curriculum. For the presentation, I began by writing a script. Then I went to a sign maker, and had faux campaign signs fashioned so I could bring students on stage for a mock presidential campaign—complete with chanting and cheering. I also had a dollar bill sign made with a cut-out in the center so kids, like many presidents, could have their faces "appear" on the country's money. Note, however, that many school administrators also want authors to talk about the writing and publishing process. Therefore, I include a segment about my writing life, followed by an invitation for questions from the kids.

Search the web. What's the best way get a peek at what your book is doing out in the world? Go surfing! By conducting an Internet search on my book's title, I discovered that *If I Were President* was the basis for a home schooling social studies program, appeared on a recommended reading list at a Michigan elementary school, and was shared aloud by a businessman serving as a guest reader in a fifth grade classroom in Maine—to name just a few listings that have popped up over the years.

I repeated the process with the Mount Rushmore gift shop with similar success. And some sites, such as the Smithsonian National Museum of American History shop, picked up the book all on their own.

These days it is not unusual for me to receive excited calls from vacationing friends or relatives who tell me: *I'm standing in the Mount Rushmore gift shop (or wherever) and you won't believe it—I'm holding a copy of your book!*

Friends have shared other good news, too. There was the time my husband received an e-mail from an old school buddy who told him he and his daughters saw *If I Were President* on television on WGN-TV's *Bozo Show*. I called the studio and they confirmed that the Chicago Public Library had recommended the book for a Presidents' Day episode. (I later caught the show, and now treasure a tape of big-haired Bozo sharing my book with his young audience).

But perhaps the biggest thrill came when I received a call *not* from a friend, but from the Literary Office of the Chicago Public School Systems. I was informed that *If I Were President* had been chosen as the premier book to kick off the Chicago Public School's 2005 literacy program. They would purchase 3,500 books to distribute to 127 schools. The idea that my book would be used as a tool to excite children about reading certainly warmed my heart!

Never the same

A successful author once told me a book takes on a life of its own, and it certainly did. But my first published book also led to such big changes for me, that my life has never been the same.

A few months after appearing on the front page of my local paper, I learned that the same newspaper sought a town columnist. I applied, listing my publication credits along with my stint as their "cover girl" and got the job! Now eight years later, strangers who recognize me from the photo that runs alongside my column stop me to comment on my articles—favorably, so far! Pleased with my work, the editor has assigned major feature articles as well.

I also contacted our local college to share my news and thank them for their part in my achievement. I had polished my original manuscript while enrolled in their writing for chil-

Articles & Interviews

Reprinted with permission.

First-time author Catherine Stier was thrilled and amazed with the reception she got for her first book *If I Were President*. Here she poses with the articles, awards and accolades she acquired. Stier's second book, *If I Ran for President*, is a fall 2007 release from Albert Whitman.

dren course. The college representatives were excited and scheduled a professional photo shoot, bringing in a half dozen adorable, wiggly preschoolers to pose with me. Again, I was a cover girl—this time as a success story on the college's course catalog under the heading "Follow Your Dream." They also featured me in ads in the Chicago Tribune and other papers. The same college hired me to instruct adult writing classes and summer picture book classes for children, and paid me an honorarium to appear on a panel with other authors discussing the topic "Publishing Your First Book." I have been invited as a guest author to the Art Institute of Chicago's Festival of Children's Books, the Illinois Authors Literary Weekend in Springfield and the Statewide Young Authors' Event at Illinois State University.

Our town's library hired me to lead a teen writing club and teen writing workshops, and a multi-library organization offered an honorarium for a workshop on "Writing for Kids 101." And after putting together a lively presentation with colorful props, I have been invited (and paid) to appear at school assemblies. Sometimes the media shows up and the next day I'll appear in a newspaper photo, all decked out in my red white and blue outfit.

The journey continues . . .

I am happy to report the adventure has not yet ended. Following the success of *If I Were President*, I have worked with my publisher on a pre-quel to the book, which describes the presidential electoral process in a light-hearted yet informative way for young readers. *If I Ran for President* was recently released, just in time for the 2008 presidential election excitement.

In this new book, I strived to include all the bits of the electoral and campaigning process that would capture a child's imagination such as those big, confetti-flying conventions, and the fun of having one's name appear on buttons and bumper stickers. While I loved the challenge of working on this book, I am both excited and curious about where it may lead me.

Your journey

I urge all writers to keep typing or scribbling away because you love the process. Keep writing because you have something to offer and because no one can express your story, your idea, the way you can. But I also advise you to be prepared—for something you have created can change your life in unexpected ways. After all, I never imagined I'd be a featured writer in the *Children's Writer's & Illustrator's Market*, the guide I have used constantly throughout my writing journey.

So go and create. Send out your best works to share with the world. Just be ready for the ride of your life.

Articles & Interviews

Jack Prelutsky

America's First Children's Poet
Laureate on Waxing Poetic

by Kelly Milner Halls

When Sir James Barrie wrote his timeless classic *Peter Pan*, he gave his character Tinkerbell fairy dust to help well-grounded people learn to fly. When the Poetry Foundation in Chicago, Illinois named Jack Prelutsky their first Children's Poet Laureate in September of 2006, they may have seen that same kind of stardust in his eyes.

For more than 40 years, the Bronx-raised, Seattle-based author has written better than 35 volumes of poetry—not for lofty adults in smoky coffee houses, but almost exclusively for kids. That's not to say his body of work isn't appealing to grown-ups. Thousands of adults buy his books for their own libraries every year. But neither parent, nor librarian, nor book reviewer drives this literary legend. Respect for child-like wonder is what fuels Prelutsky's creative fire.

Discovered by legendary HarperCollins/Greenwillow editor Susan Hirschman in his twenties, Prelutsky didn't learn poetry through study or imitation. He wrote—then and now—courtesy of a magic all his own. Like those dusted by Tink, something indefinable has helped Jack Prelutsky soar. But he's taken thousands of lucky readers along for the ride.

You've often said you weren't a poetry fan as a kid. Why? What was it about your early exposure to poetry that left you feeling disconnected?

At first, I liked poetry the way most kids do. Neither of my parents were avid readers. My father read a book once in a while. My mother read Agatha Christie. It was an average, working class family. But my mother read me *Mother Goose*, and she used to shop at the A&P and buy *Woman's Day* magazine. Every issue featured a poem from *A Child's Garden of Verses*, by Robert Louis Stevenson, and I'd clip them out and save them.

Then in school, in third or fourth grade, I had a teacher who was probably taught that as a matter of curriculum she had to read a poem to her captives once a week—and she did. Badly. She would pick a boring poem from a boring book and recite it in a boring way. She would even look bored, as she would read it. But I was growing up in the Bronx. I wanted to hear poems about myself—about outer space and sports and music, about the kind of kid I was. So I started to think of poetry as punishment. They said it was good for me, but I didn't really believe it.

KELLY MILNER HALLS is a full-time freelance writer. Her nonfiction articles have been published in *U.S. Kids*, the *Chicago Tribune*, the *Atlanta Journal Constitution*, the *Washington Post*, the *Denver Post* and dozens of other publications. Her books include *Wild Dogs* and *Tales of the Cryptids*, both from Darby Creek Publishing. Her 2008 releases include *Dinosaur Parade*, for very young readers (Lark Books), and *Wild Horses* (Darby Creek). She lectures regularly at schools and writing conferences.

It was like eating liver. (I was five or six years old when I came down to supper to this *thing* on my plate. My mother lied to me. She said it was steak, but I knew it wasn't. After one taste, I hid the rest in my pockets. Then I went outside and invented the liver Frisbee.)

Later, in junior high I had an English teacher who would make us do to a poem what my biology teacher would make us do to a frog. We used all the "P" items—pokers, pinchers, pins—to disable the poor frog just so we could determine what once made it hop. It's the same thing with dissecting a poem. If you wring every last drop of life out of a poem, it's never going to hop for you again, either.

I think of that teacher as a dissectionist. Her approach wasn't too exciting, but poetry can be. It comes from human beings—from the human experience and imagination. The poet puts a lot of effort into his or her work, and we should honor that. A word is dead before its said, and that's it. Poetry, my poetry, is made to be read, not dissected.

Jack Prelutsky proves poetry can be fun in *What a Day It Was at School!*, a book of poems that takes children through the realms of pure fantasy with a science project gone awry, and peeks into everyday life with poems about the mundane world of homework, heavy backpacks, and farting in class.

What did writers do wrong in the past that you've helped to correct with your body of work? What old pitfalls should contemporary writers guard against?

For years, I have collected children's poetry books. Not when I first started. Susan advised me against even looking at other poets when I started, because she sensed I might have a unique voice, and she didn't want that influenced. But now I have a lot of books, and I find most of the poetry of my childhood came from the school of thought that said children should be seen and not heard. There were exceptions, of course, like Robert Louis Stevenson and Lewis Carroll. But a lot of the material seemed to fall into two categories—didactic, moralistic and preachy; or syrupy and condescending—as if children didn't have brains. That's the pitfall to avoid. Children are not stupid. They're just short.

Susan Hirschman discovered you and has often said you never write down to young readers. Is there a secret to maintaining that stance, as an adult writer of children's literature, even as the age gap grows wider?

Yes, well, actually, it's like Bob Dylan said. I'm younger than that now. The more I write, the more I get in touch with my own childhood, the more things I remember. So just treat children like people. It's only the subject matter that's different. I'm not writing about Oprah Winfrey or drive-by shootings, but the words are still the same. And I love words. I've always loved words. I wasn't always a writer, but I was a word game player—you know, like how many words can you make from the letters in another word. And I learned the sounds of different words read aloud were just as important as the meanings—words like gelatinous. I include them, because kids who hear them will want to learn more about them. Beyond that, I'd say be yourself—I write for myself—spend time in schools, keep in touch.

You are also known for making innovations—taking risks—when it comes to the subject matter of your works. Did any of your books ever give you pause as you considered its creation? In other words, did you ever think, "This might be pushing it?"

I don't think I've really pushed the envelope. I think the idea that I did may have started when I wrote my book *Nightmares: Poems to Trouble Your Sleep* about 30 years ago (1976). All the books I had done until then were silly or funny—animals, circus stories, fables, maybe a terrible tiger at worst. But I'd reached a point where I didn't want to write the same thing over and over again.

I was doing a summer workshop at a library in Cambridge, Massachusetts for working class kids involved in writing. I'd been there before and I was friends with the librarian, so I asked her, thinking who would know better about what kids want than a librarian. And she said to write about monsters and dinosaurs.

I knew she was right, and I picked monsters first because I remembered when I was a kid and my mom used to threaten me with the boogeyman. So the first poem I wrote for that book was about the boogeyman. I decided to make him a little more remote. You were OK as long as you stayed away from his domain.

Just as the book was published, I moved from Massachusetts to Kirkland, Washington. Lake Washington School District was the first school district in America to ban one of my books, and it was where I was living. An older child had given it to younger kid, which is the parent's responsibility, not mine. But that parent was a friend of the school board. And as soon as they found out I was living there, it made the front page of the paper, and it made me look demonic.

So I called Susan and said, "Now that I have a book that's banned, let's do a sequel," and she said sure.

Basically, I stay away from adult material. I may write about monsters and trolls, but I didn't create those things. I just write what I think I would like to have heard when I was a kid. I don't think that I'm telling kids to be bad. I think I'm writing about what they're already doing, anyhow.

You were selected as the Poetry Foundation's first Children's Poet Laureate in September of 2006. What doors will this endowment open for Jack Prelutsky and for children's poetry as an under-appreciated art form?

I guess it's given me extra cache. All these things have happened, tons of interviews—major news shows, NPR, Voice of America, *USA Today*, *Parade Magazine*. So it's given me a bit more of a voice.

Do you agree that children's poetry is under-appreciated as the Foundation suggests?

I don't know. I think children's poetry is more accessible than adult poetry. I met three-time United States Poet Laureate Robert Pinsky years ago and he knew who I was. He said, "You're that really good selling poet." So I'm not sure it's under-appreciated. I think it's being taught much better in school and some of the best children's poets that ever wrote are being taught today.

Why do you think the selection committee picked you over other stellar children's poets in the industry today?

You know, I've outgrown that, the enthusiasm for competition. I like to think it's because I'm good, but I'm not the only one. There are a couple around who have been at it longer than me, so part of it is luck. If someone else was on the committee, someone else might have been chosen.

I was reading some blogs the Foundation's publicist sent me that mentioned me and the award. Some thought I was the best choice. Some thought I was a good choice. Some thought I was an adequate choice. Some thought the choice was poor. But my favorite was the one that said, "Why do we need this?" There is a whole universe out there. I don't know the process and I don't want to know. Sometimes things just happen.

If you were on the selection committee, who might you submit for consideration?

I would consider Karla Kuskins, Nikki Grimes, J. Patrick Lewis and a number of others. There is some wonderful stuff out there.

You still give presentations to schools and conference audiences regularly. What do you draw from those interactions?

It wears on me a little now, so I can't do as much. But I always get ideas from kids. And just seeing them, listening to them reminds me of why I do it, of who my audience is. When I present to adults at conferences, most of what I get is applause. I do a good presentation, and they enjoy it. But kids really get the most out of the experience. In fact, I can tell you a few little stories.

Behold the Bold Umbrellaphant features animals with a unique twist, for "the Alarmadillos have alarm clocks for bodies, and the Ballpoint Penguins can write with their beaks." Jack Prelutsky is regarded as "one of the best word crafters in the business," says *School Library Journal*, "and this collection does not disappoint."

One little girl, years ago, put her arms around me and said, "I wish you were my father." There is probably a dark side to that, but it was a tender moment.

Then there was the kid who wanted to meet me in a rural town in Pennsylvania. He was about a fourth-grader; I had talked to the whole school. Then he came over to say hello. I said, "Hi, how are you?" and he said, "Good." I said, "Well, you look good," to which he replied, "I'll bet when you were my age, you looked good too."

I was at a school in Honolulu and had laryngitis. I was almost in tears because I didn't want to disappoint, but I couldn't make a sound. I just couldn't do it. A little girl came up to me and said, "Don't worry Mr. Prelutsky. It's not important what you say. It's just important that you are here."

One more. In Portland, Oregon, I was between presentations, making some notes in a notebook, when these two little shy girls came into the library, very politely. One said, "Is that the man who writes the poems?" And the other one said, "Yes, but sh-h-h-h. He's writing one now."

When I do school visits, the kids realize writers aren't just boring dead guys. They're people, just like them.

Do you have any regrets, as a writer?

I wish I wasn't so lazy. I should have about three times as many book out as I have. And I regret that I've only written poetry. I want to write short stories, maybe a novel. I still have goals. But I don't really regret much. I've had a good life.

What advice do you have for writers hoping to follow in your footsteps?

I don't know that anyone is following in my footsteps, and I don't know that they should. I wasn't following anyone. But sure, I'd say carry a notebook, write what you know, write every day, and don't be afraid. Oh, and never pass up the opportunity to go to the bathroom.

Also, listen to kids—listen to what they have to say. And above all, keep your day job. The odds are against you. Then again, I could be polishing chrome at the car wash. I guess you never know.

First Books

Five First-Timers Share Their Stories

by Alice Pope

Putting together this piece, I thought a lot about juggling. Of course I don't mean juggling balls or knives or things that are on fire (although all of those would be pretty cool). I'm talking about juggling the things in your life that are important to you (writing), are necessary evils (um, laundry) or just gotta get taken care of on a regular basis (buying food). Or juggling the parts of your job that are important to you (writing and editing), necessary evils (um, meetings) or just gotta get taken care of on a regular basis (updating the database).

It's natural to want to put the important-to-you things first and put off the other stuff. (Hmmm, blog or do laundry . . . how does one choose?) But it also can be very difficult. (Kids want dinner, attention, and clean socks.) The five women I talked to for this piece do their share of juggling, and managed to put writing and illustrating high up on their priority lists, creating a workable balance between their family lives and their writing lives. They scheduled creative time when they could. They formed writers groups. A couple of them attended an MFA program. And they made things happen. They made *books* happen.

First-time author and mother of five Kelly Bingham, who discusses her experience with debut book *Shark Girl* below, understands "that there is a time for everything." She advises others pursuing publication to "be realistic about what you can accomplish and set a goal. If it's two hours on Tuesdays, and only Tuesdays, then so be it. Just take what you can, and don't fret about what you can't.

"Once you set a goal, even if it's one hour a week, then make it a priority. When your writing time rolls around, don't cave in and take a nap instead. Do it. If it's something you really want to do, then you have to drive yourself a bit. There will always, always be a pull of some kind or another . . . an errand to run, a Boy Scout meeting you didn't want to miss, your child is not feeling well and wants mommy instead of daddy . . . or you simply feel guilty," says Bingham. "Don't make excuses—go write if this is your appointed time. The only way you're going to make your dream come true is to take it seriously, and to show your family that it's important to you."

Read on to learn how these authors (and one author/illustrator) took their writing seriously, found their own ways to make things work, followed their own paths, and, ultimately, made their dreams come true. And when you're finished, check out their books and visit their Web sites to learn more.

Carrie Jones
Tips on Having a Gay (ex) Boyfriend
(Flux)
www.carriejones.com

When author Carrie Jones approached the publisher who later offered her a book contract, "I did everything wrong," she says. "I heard about Flux, and sent in a brand new manuscript on a whim. I changed the name of the book at the last minute, and forgot to change it in the query, which is horrifyingly unprofessional. To make it all worse, I misspelled my own last name in my e-mail address. Instead of cjones I wrote cjonese. So, Andrew Karre, the acquiring editor, kept trying to e-mail me and the e-mail kept bouncing back. Finally, he gave up and called. We quickly learned that I can't spell my own last name. And I quickly learned that I adore Andrew."

Karre (who Jones often refers to as "Sweet Editor Guy") snapped up Jones' book *Tips on Having a Gay (ex) Boyfriend* right away. "We started revisions right away. Everything was right away," says Jones. "It was amazing. Andrew has always made me feel like my opinion mattered, like my book mattered, that he really wanted this book to be the best."

Jones got the idea for *Tips* during her third semester at Vermont College's MFA Program in writing for Young Adults. "There was an incident in a local school (I'm in Maine) where there was a hate crime against a girl because her ex boyfriend was gay," Jones explains. "Unlike in my book, the incident wasn't reported to the police or to the school administration. It made me think about how small-minded people can be. It made me think how ridiculous that girls/women/ladies always get the rap for everything, even their friend's sexuality." And Jones happens to have a gay ex boyfriend herself.

Working on *Tips* as an MFA student was just the tip of the iceberg for Jones. "While in the Vermont College program I read over 700 books and wrote over 3,000 pages (not counting revised pages) in two years. Not all those pages were good, obviously. But some of them are OK," she says. "The tremendously talented mentors at Vermont College are the reason that any of those pages are decent. When there, you learn so much, so fast, and in an intensely supportive community, it's just an incredible experience. I mean, imagine spending five months with Tim Wynne-Jones or Rita Williams Garcia or Sharon Darrow or Kathi Appelt as your personal advisor. It is the best thing in the world. They are all so brilliant and shiny, that as a student, you just want to reach up and touch that shininess, let some of it rub off, even the tiniest bit."

Jones joined the Vermont program after developing an interest in expanding her writing repertoire. "I'd been a newspaper reporter/editor and I was getting really, really tired going to Bar Harbor Planning Board meetings about setback requirements that would last until 2 a.m. Yes. 2 a.m. I swear. It was Bar Harbor, Maine. People like to argue about land use ordinances in Bar Harbor, Maine. It's also hard to jazz that sort of article up with something interesting. You rarely have town planners composing ballads of their undying affection to their Viagra coffee mugs at these things. I was getting really, really bored," she says.

"At the same time, my daughter, Em, wanted me to tell her a story on long car rides to different Maine places. Where we live, almost everything is a long car ride. So, I started making up a story. Every car ride I'd add a little more, and eventually, I thought, 'This would be easier if I wrote it down.' Then I realized I liked writing it down. And I would like it if it became a good story," she says. "So, on a whim, I applied to Vermont. They somehow let me in."

Her experience there, she says, "has everything to do with me landing a contract with Flux. It looks good on a query letter. It makes you look serious about writing, even if you're a total goof about life. It made me a better writer. I should revise that sentence. It made me a *much* better writer and reviser."

According to the Flux staff, Jones' strength as a writer lies in her ability to approach "universal emotions from surprising angles," evident in her handling of *Tips* main character Belle and her reaction to her boyfriend coming out to her. "When I was at Bates College, I was a political science major, but I took some classes with the poet Robert Farnsworth," Jones says. "He always talked about striving for the universal while detailing the every day. I think that must have affected me somehow.

"In the every day there are so many amazing surprises, so many ways to look at things. I love that. There's always a temptation to write in broad strokes, hoping to define something universal, but the beauty in life, I think, comes from individual reactions and values and what they tell us about character, and what they tell us about ourselves. Sometimes those come from surprising angles. For example, my Grammy Barnard would cry over the beauty and miracle of a ripe, good-looking tomato. That says a lot about her. Our reactions to her tears tell us a lot about ourselves. That's something really specific, but it creates much broader strokes about values and the human condition. I think that as writers we have a responsibility to examine the specifics and the surprises as a way to touch the universal."

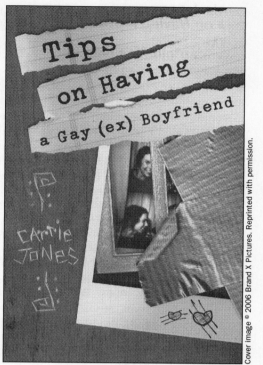

Tips on Having a Gay (ex) Boyfriend was inspired by a hate crime incident in Maine (and by the fact that author Carrie Jones has at least one gay ex boyfriend). As the book opens, main character Belle's boyfriend tells her he's gay. Belle digests the news and soon finds her world turned upside down. "This beautifully-written debut explores what happens when you are suddenly forced to see someone in a different light, and what that can teach you about yourself," says *School Library Journal*.

Cover image © 2006 Brand X Pictures. Reprinted with permission.

As perceptive and confident as Jones' may seem when discussing writing, if you read her livejournal blog (www.carriejones.livejournal.com) or the About the Author in her book, you'll notice unmistakable notes of self-deprecation. "It's like I'm afraid that I'm that girl who keeps entering talent shows and singing those super high songs from *Phantom of the Opera*, even though she's tune deaf, a contra-alto, can't remember the words and has no beat. And every time, people boo her or she doesn't win, or worse, people make fun of her and her arrogance when they are riding home in their cars. I don't want to be that girl.

"And the real truth," says Jones, "is that all writers, especially me, have so much room to grow, to explore, to develop the craft, to become better writers. I really want to become a better writer, and part of that is being able to see where there are flaws in my work, my process, and seeing where there is still room to grow. Sometimes, that journey just takes me back to my first and last sentences, my first and last poems."

Jones is not alone on her journey as an author. In addition to her editor Karre and her agent Edward Necarsulmer IV, at McIntosh and Otis ("Super Agent Guy"), she has amassed a writing community as a member of the Class of 2k7 (http://classof2k7.com) and through livejournal. "I started livejournal because some of my friends from Vermont College were graduating and they had blogs, and I really wanted to stay in touch with them. My publisher pretty much ordered me to have a Web site. MySpace followed, as did 2k7, as ways of being a part of a community. I live way up the coast of Maine in a town of 6,000 people and it's really lonely sometimes, hard to be part of a community of children's authors because we are so scattered," she says. "That's why I've developed a Web presence, not so much to gain readers, although that would be fantastic! It's more to make me feel as if I'm part of a bigger writing community. Community is so important."

Up next for Jones is the tentatively titled *True Grit*, a contemporary novel about a girl who writes letters to John Wayne while dealing with her transition into high school, her own father's gender issues, and the death of her stepfather. Readers will also have the opportunity to revisit Belle and her friends in *Love (And Other Uses for Duct Tape)*, the sequel to the *Tips on Having a Gay (ex) Boyfriend*. "*Love (And Other Uses for Duct Tape)* is about how Belle deals with a lot of identity issue as senior year starts to end. Her mom has a new boyfriend. Her boyfriend and her best friend are acting bizarre," says Jones. "It's a tough time for her. I feel so badly for her."

Perhaps Jones empathizes with Belle so much because they share some qualities. Both Jones and her character have epilepsy—although epilepsy is not a part of the plot of the character's development, just a fact of life for Belle. "I think we are both a little goofy. I think we both struggle to figure out who people are, and how our perceptions of people and ourselves can be wrong, and whether or not that even matters." And, adds Jones, "We both like blue guitars."

Tina Ferraro
Top Ten Uses for an Unworn Prom Dress
(Delacorte Press)
www.tinaferraro.com

"When I decided to get serious about writing," says Tina Ferraro, "I turned to the romance magazines my grandmother used to pass along to me. I went on to sell about 75 stories to them—especially teen stories—and to this day I occasionally submit."

With her success selling to romance mags, Ferraro set her sites on becoming a romance novelist, but with no luck. "I spent many years trying to make my voice and style fit the genre," she says. "Following a particularly disappointing rejection, my critique partners urged me to concentrate on the young adult market, and, buoyed by a life experience and an idea I simply had to write, I decided to do just that."

The idea that compelled Ferraro to write YA evolved into a novel manuscript called *Tour of My Not-So-Normal Life*, which she describes as "a somewhat humorous novel about a 'teen angel' who returns to help her twin sister." When she completed the manuscript, says Ferraro, "I knew, without a doubt, it was the best thing I'd ever written."

Meanwhile, she signed with agent Nadia Cornier after seeing an announcement on a YA loop that Cornier was taking queries. "Soon I told her a title idea that had been floating in my head, *Top Ten Uses for an Unworn Prom Dress*, and I'll never forget what she said: 'I could sell that on the title alone. Start writing now.'"

Ferraro worked on *Prom Dress* for several months while her first novel manuscript made the rounds, and got some interest from editors, but no offers. "Meanwhile *Prom Dress* got requests for exclusives before it was even done," Ferraro says. "But nothing is ever cut-and-dried (at least not for me), so it wasn't until Krista Marino at Delacorte Press requested the book that the real magic happened. Within five days she made an offer, and made me the happiest writer in the world."

Once she got into the publication process, Ferraro was surprised at how long it took from contract to book release—20 months for her—and by the number of steps and people involved in the whole process. "But because of the time element," she says, "nothing was ever rush-rush crazy/scary. I was able to think everything through and make further revisions when necessary. And to enjoy the ride."

The idea for *Top Ten Uses for an Unworn Prom Dress* came to Ferraro after she spotted a book along the lines of *101 Things to Do with a Bridesmaid's Dress*. "I wondered, 'Are there as many things to do with a prom dress? And what if it's an unworn prom dress. Because what if your date dumped you . . .?' And I was off and running."

Ferraro's without-a-prom-date main character Nicolette, the author admits, "entered the first scene bearing a lot of my own traits. She was outgoing, a busy thinker, and could be funny now and them. But early on I sensed a spunk in her that I don't have," says Ferraro. "There was a particular moment near the end of the first chapter where Rascal (the guy who dumps her before the prom) challenges her. Tina at 17 would have backed down and played with my hair or something. But Nic looked him in the eye and gave it back—hard. I remember my heartbeats speeding up, knowing at that moment that she had broken off from me . . . that she had taken on a life of her own, that I really liked the combination of her vulnerability, insecurity—and nerve."

Cover image © 2007 YUKO/www.artscounselinc.com. Reprinted with permission.

What do you do with a prom dress that you never got to wear? That's the question Nicolette explores in *Top Ten Uses for an Unworn Prom Dress*, by Tina Ferraro. "Nicolette is a likable, down-to-earth protagonist who is grappling with a lot of issues, and readers will quickly identify with and understand her," says *School Library Journal*. "Ferraro does a fine job of setting up an interesting plot, funny dialogue and situations, and an engaging lead character."

With a main character like Nic, is *Prom Dress* a teen romance or teen chick lit? Ferraro acknowledges that there's difference between the two, but she isn't sure which category to choose for her debut novel. "To my way of thinking, teen chick-lit refers to a funny, offbeat, quirky teen voice. Teen romance generally means a teen heroine and a potential hero, a conflict keeping them apart, and a satisfying ending which resolves both the plot and the romance," she explains. "I didn't set out to write *Prom Dress* to neatly fit into either category, but I have a tendency to come out with some snarky one-liners, and the only way I could conclude *Prom Dress* was to help Nicolette find what she needed and some joy in the process. And to my way of thinking, a hot guy brings joy."

Guy characters (especially hot ones) are generally an essential element to teen romance and chick-lit alike, and Ferraro writes hers well. Jared, Nic's love interest, is dreamy but still complicated and believable. Rascal, Nic's former prom date, is just a little icky, but not one-dimensional. "I'm a shameless people watcher, and have been studying male behavior for as long as I can remember. Plus I live with my husband and our two teenage sons, and believe me, I use them as sounding boards," she says.

"The single most important thing I can say about writing about males—of any age—is to remember that they generally speak considerable fewer words than females. I always edit my male dialogue for brevity, and then try to fill in the blanks with a look, a shrug, or a well-meaning touch. I also remember that boys go through the same kinds of emotions as girls, but are often either reticent to talk about their feelings, or don't really understand them. Which tends to come out as forced humor or bursts of anger.''

At interview time, *Top Ten Uses for an Unworn Prom Dress* had not yet hit stores, but Ferraro had a number of promotional plans in place, including participating in a blogsite (www.booksboysbuzz.com) with six other authors, starting a "Take Ten with Tina and Kelly" column with her critique partner, YA author Kelly Parra (found at www.tinaferraro.com and www.kellyparra.com), working on a MySpace page where she'll invite readers to post pictures of their prom dresses, and planning her launch party at a local bookstore, where the first 10 people to show up in prom dresses get a free copy of her book.

She's also anticipating the publication of her second book with Delacorte, *How to Hook a Hottie* (spring 2008). "Just like I made a big leap from my 'teen angel' heroine to Nicolette, I took another giant step when I created *How to Hook a Hottie*'s Kate DelVecchio," Ferraro says. "Kate is 17, a serious and driven girl who is determined to be a self-made millionaire before she is 20. When her lab partner—a baseball star—asks her to a sports banquet, people at school take their first real notice of Kate. Suddenly, others are approaching her for her 'secrets' to landing their crushes. And they are willing to pay. Kate is more than happy to take their money, but first she'd better learn a thing or two about hooking hotties.''

Ferraro has learned a thing or two about hooking editors—and readers. (See experts of her books on her Web site for proof.) And she's content and happy writing books for a YA audience even though that's not the original path she chose as a novelist. "I had been writing YA stories for most of my adult life," she says. "I reassessed my writing and realized it was time to put my energy into the YA market. That doesn't mean I'll never write for adults again, but as of now, it's not something I'm considering.''

Ruth McNally Barshaw
Ellie McDoodle: Have Pen, Will Travel
(Bloomsbury)
www.ruthexpress.com

Ruth McNally Barshaw can't seem to stop drawing. "I carry a sketchbook everywhere, never a camera," she says. "I've carried one most of the time since I was 15 years old; there are probably a hundred in the hallway bookcase. If I don't have one on hand and need one, I make one.''

It was one of her sketchbooks that led Barshaw to her first book contract for *Ellie McDoodle: Have Pen, Will Travel*. "I went to the SCBWI national conference in NYC in February, 2005, even though it was nearly impossible to scrape up the money and courage to go," says Barshaw. "While there, I kept a sketch journal of my adventures. I came home discouraged about how soon I might sell a book, and resolved to try even harder to learn all I could about the industry. Meanwhile, I put my sketchbook online, all 150 pages of it, and directed many writer friends to it. They urged me to write a kids' book in that style. I resisted at first, thinking it would never sell. They insisted, so I started one, and within a few days a well-respected agent e-mailed me offering to look at the book when it was ready. I'm told this never happens. She pitched it to Bloomsbury.''

Barshaw says she was surprised by the attention her online sketchbook received. "I was overwhelmed by the response, many hundreds of e-mails. I saved them all and formed some very dear friendships through them. Subsequent sketchbooks have gotten even more buzz. It's all a bit amazing.''

The basis for *Ellie McDoodle*, says Barshaw, was a partial personal essay she'd written about camping as a kid with her family in Northern Michigan. ''I'd been concentrating on picture books and the essay didn't fit that format so I shelved it,'' she says. ''I brought it to my first SCBWI conference in 2003, for the peer group critiques, and other members laughed when I read it, calling it a solid start for a humorous middle-grade novel. This surprised me; I didn't realize I could write funny things. Eighteen months later when I decided to try a sketchbook novel, it was that story that I dug into. My agent and editor have both declared that I am Ellie, but there's a lot of me in all of the characters, particularly the nasty bits.''

What resulted was certainly not a traditional mid-grade novel, not quite a graphic novel, but what her editor calls a ''highly illustrated middle grade novel.'' ''My agent says the publisher had a challenge pricing it out because they'd never bought anything like it before,'' says Barshaw. ''On the back of the book the editor calls it 'part graphic novel, part confessional journal, part wilderness survival guide.' All I know is, it's what I've been doing since I was 15, and I'm delighted anyone has a use for it.''

Ellie McDoodle: Have Pen, Will Travel evolved after writer/illustrator Ruth McNally Barshaw posted her sketchbook of an SCBWI conference online. Before long she had created a story about young Ellie's (mis) adventures on a family camping trip aimed at mid-grade readers. ''On the back of the book the editor calls it 'part graphic novel, part confessional journal, part wilderness survival guide.' All I know is, it's what I've been doing since I was 15, and I'm delighted anyone has a use for it,'' says Barshaw.

While it may sound like Barshaw had an easy time of it—after all, how often do aspiring author/illustrators have agents approach *them*—it was really a long road for her when it came to reaching her goal of being published. ''I quit my job when baby number three was 4 years old, in 1993. It was the right thing to do at the time. I had enough freelance clients to keep busy and wanted to work out of my home,'' Barshaw explains. ''Unfortunately those clients dwindled off into nothing, because I was doing work I didn't enjoy (graphic design, silkscreen t-shirt art, logos) and I didn't *want* to win new clients.

''In 2002, chatting in online writer and illustrator groups, I remembered I'd always wanted to do kids' books. That's when I began to work three years, full time, mostly without a paycheck, learning the children's book industry. I entered a picture book contest and didn't win, but I was hooked,'' she says. ''My family thought I was crazy. I don't recommend that path to anyone.''

Part of Barshaw's children's book research involved closely studying and analyzing 53 picture books. ''I learned where the climax usually falls (page 28), how the text and art work together to become more than the sum of their parts, and how repetition often features in picture books.'' she says. ''I learned layout devices, text treatments, and storyboarding.''

Something else she learned—and preaches on her Web site—is the importance of getting yourself and your work in front of others in the industry, attending conferences and events as often as your time and finances will allow. And she's learned how to make the most of those networking opportunities. "Don't expect one-on-one time with editors, agents and art directors," she advises. "Sometimes your biggest boost in publishing will come from your peers. Push yourself to be friendly and meet new people. Pretend you're an extrovert. Get your work out there, in First Pages, manuscript and portfolio reviews, and critique sessions. If it isn't seen, you won't get valuable feedback from smart people. And that feedback is what makes you grow as a writer and illustrator."

One way Barshaw networks is as a member of the 2k7 collective. She got involved after fellow first-time author Greg Fishbone featured her sketchbook on his blog. (She had drawn him in it). "We e-mailed back and forth, and both had the same idea at the same time: New authors should join together to share marketing resources. I formed a group with Janee Trasler and about 10 other authors and illustrators; it's small and intimate and we share ideas and help each other brainstorm. Greg's group became the Class of 2k7, a more visible group of debut novelists with the specific purpose of reaching librarians, teachers and book-sellers," she says. "I've learned a lot about book marketing from the smart people in 2k7. And I've met some smart librarians directly through 2k7. I have also learned how my pub-lisher measures up to others. It's made me very grateful for Bloomsbury, where I don't have to do every bit of marketing by myself."

In fact Barshaw had a positive experience with Bloomsbury throughout the publishing process for *Ellie McDoodle*. "My publisher's staff is so kind, smart, resourceful and support-ive. I had previously thought authors were thrown out there to sink or swim in the giant pool of publishing, but my editor's a lifesaver. I adore her. She's brilliant," she says. "I was surprised at how intense the revisions process became. I lost two of my closest friends during that short time, both unexpectedly. It was excruciating. I learned I can probably survive anything. Both friends are represented in the book, my tribute to their love."

Barshaw has a second book about Ellie in the works with Bloomsbury. "I am very excited about it," she says. "We'll see Ellie having comical trouble in her new school and with her family at home. Beyond that, I have a million ideas. But Ellie keeps me very busy at the moment."

She's also busy with events to support her book, including a number of school visits. "My presentations include on-the-spot illustration. That's always a crowd-pleaser. I show some of the behind-the-scenes work in developing the Ellie book, characters and theme.

"Teachers love that I talk about revisions. And I show how useful and interesting it can be to keep a journal," she say. "For young audiences, as for older audiences, I think it's important to consider what's in it for them. Why should they listen to the author? I don't talk down to them, and I don't try to be hip. I just try to show them that their unique way of looking at the world can be a very important asset in whatever they do."

This sentiment is echoed in Barshaw's advice to aspiring authors and illustrators: "Trust your instincts. Don't try to do what you think the industry wants; do what you love," she says.

Barshaw also thinks it's important to "find a fabulous critique group. Keep trying until you find the right mix of people who can help you and who you can help in return. You don't want to be the smartest person in your critique group. I joined mine nine months ago and it's the best anywhere."

Finally, she offers, "Only go into this business if you absolutely love it. The revisions process can be very demanding and grueling. It's not worth striving for an excellent product if you don't love the process. And child and teen readers deserve excellence."

Rose Kent
Kimchi & Calamari
(HarperCollins)
www.rosekent.com

A couple days before St. Patrick's Day, Rose Kent, who is "both Irish and a serious foodie," was online looking for a recipe for Irish soda bread, when she read an e-mail containing what she says were some of the most joyful words she ever saw on her computer screen: *Rose, I've been meaning to tell you. I love* Kimchi & Calamari. *Let's talk about it.*

"I had sent *Kimchi & Calamari* to Rachel Orr at HarperCollins about five months prior, after we met at the Rutgers conference (which I highly recommend to beginning writers)," says Kent. "But I hadn't yet heard from Rachel, and true to the writer's neurotic soul, I'd concluded that she hated my story so deeply she couldn't even utter the title. So when I saw the e-mail, I was utterly overjoyed."

When she read Orr's e-mail, Kent says, "I wish I could say that I ran around my house doing a touchdown dance, but I didn't. Tears poured down my cheeks—joyful ones, for the moment that finally arrived, and thankful ones, for all the people in my life who'd helped me get here. And on Saint Patrick's Day I never did get around to baking homemade Irish soda bread, but no one minded. I had a good excuse."

Kent says her path to publication was more like a long and winding road. "I've heard writers joke that they could wallpaper their kitchens with all their rejection letters, and I, too, have had my share," she says. "But my writing improved because of this. I'm referring to rejection that gave constructive feedback (i.e. 'your supporting character feels one-dimensional,' or 'plot needs more twists and turns,' etc.). This gave me something to consider when I delved back into my story. I actually have a special fondness for an editor who passed on *Kimchi & Calamari* in the final review. Her letter offered an insightful critique—even if it broke my heart at the time—and resulted in revisions that ultimately led to publication."

Kimchi & Calamari tells the story of Joseph Calderaro, a 14-year-old of Korean descent who was adopted by an Italian American family, who has just gotten a school assignment titled *Tracing Your Past: A Heritage Essay.* Problem is, Joseph knows nothing of his Korean birth family short of the town in which he was born.

Just as Joseph struggles with his own identity, Kent admits she, too, has struggled when it came to finding her identity as a writer. "I always knew what I wanted to say, but how to say it? Sometimes I felt like an unworthy orchestra conductor. So many parts of a novel need to come together to make pretty music, but could I pull it off? There is no 1-2-3 solution to this dilemma, it's just about putting in the writing time, getting feedback, and prodding on," she says.

"Plus a gremlin inside my head tried to wreak havoc with my confidence, suggesting that my writing was worthless. I've heard this gremlin shows up in other writers' heads as well. Unfortunately there is no magic bullet that can take out this gremlin, but I did choose to ignore him. And in some ways I'm even thankful for that troublemaker because the nervous jitters he provoked turned into adrenaline once I got writing."

Kent was helped through the ups, downs and gremlins of the writing process by her weekly critique group called Writers on Wednesday, which has been meeting for seven years. "WOW, as we call it, has certainly played a vital role in my publishing. Writing is both a solitary and collaborative act, and WOW is one regular way I collaborate," Kent says. "While *Kimchi & Calamari* was already in progress when WOW began, the group provided valuable input during my revisions. I think the secret to a critique group is finding other writers who approach their craft with a similar mindset. In WOW, we all root for each other and we enjoy

Articles & Interviews

In Rose Kent's debut *Kimchi & Calamari*, Joseph Calderaro is given a school assignment to write an essay about his heritage, a difficult task for the Korean adoptee who only knows the Italian family who adopted him. *Kimchi & Calamari* follows Joseph's humorous journey as he figures out where he comes from and who he is. "This will have special appeal for adoptees," says *Booklist*, "but the questions about family roots that Kent raises are universal."

each other's company, but this isn't a social gathering. We show up to work and to help pull the best writing out of each other."

Kent also found a mentor in beloved author Patricia Rielly Giff. "I met Pat when I first started writing for children, and she felt like an angel who'd flown into my life, on the written page and off. Pat became my mentor when I took a children's writing course at her son Jim's bookstore (*The Dinosaur's Paw*—a fabulous children's bookstore in Fairfield, Connecticut). Pat has a gentle yet affirming way of sharing her wisdom, and to this day I often hear her soft voice reminding me that the main purpose of story is to entertain, or that a character must solve her own problem. I'll always be grateful for what she taught me and for believing in me when I wasn't a full believer in my own work."

Her family also played a role as Kent worked through her manuscript for *Kimchi & Calimari*. Kent has two biological teenagers who are part Korean and two younger children who were adopted from Korea, and her kids offered valuable input as she told Joseph's story. "My kids would be first to tell you they deserve mucho credit for Joseph's voice, and they are right," she says. "They forced me to keep it real. I often read sections of *Kimchi & Calamari* to them, and they'd give me feedback on not only the plot, but also if the voice worked. And you know how kids are; they don't mince words. If Joseph didn't sound 14 and boyish, they'd shout out, 'Uggh!' or 'That's goofy, Mom!'

"Creating authentic characters," says Kent, "is about becoming a sponge. Allowing yourself to soak up as much as humanly possible on a topic or a setting. You do this not to be an expert, but to understand. I try to listen and use all my senses, and I ask all sorts of questions."

One sense that Kent relies one as she writes is her sense of taste—food is a powerful tool in her repertoire as a storyteller. "A character's problems, history, family and ethnicity are often revealed in (or over the course of) a meal. In the course of writing *Kimchi & Calamari*, I learned something from food too: that Italian and Korean cultures are, in fact, quite similar. Koreans and Italians both nurture their families with tasty meals that are often labors of love. And they both value the rituals surrounding these foods."

To offer authentic portrayals of Italian and Korean cultures in *Kimchi & Calamari*, Kent relied on both personal experience and research. "I grew up on Long Island, with many close-knit Italian families," she says, "so I had some knowledge of (and tremendous respect for) Italian culture. And of course having adopted Korean children motivated me to learn about their culture. I read whatever I could get my hands on pertaining to Italian and Korean culture, and I attended lectures. I especially enjoyed a presentation given by Sal Primeggia, a sociology professor at Adelphi University, who shared fascinating details about the origins of Italian superstitions. That's where I learned about the curse of the malocchio, or the Italian evil eye, which I have some fun with in *Kimchi & Calamari.*"

She also did a lot of listening, she says. "A dear friend, Sandy Dagliolo, grew up in a small town outside of Venice, Italy. Her recollections helped me appreciate Italian customs and family traditions. And I connected with Jae Kim, a bright young Korean lady who was a student at Yale University at the time. Jae broadened my horizon by sharing her family's story and helping me understand Korea's history, especially during the Japanese occupation."

To promote her debut, Kent has a number of things in the works. She's a member of the Class of 2k7, and, she says, "I'm going to make a lot of noise! I'll be doing interviews and book signings in several states including New York, where I live, and I'll be visiting as many bookstores, schools and libraries as I can. I'll be speaking to teachers and librarians at education conferences. And I'll participate at adoption-related events and outings, including cultural summer camps like the one my children attend in Albany, NY (Go Camp MuJiGae!) And I'm working closely with publicist Melissa Dittmar at HarperCollins on other special promotional events that sound both fun and worthwhile.

"So yes, I'll be doing large group appearances, but you know what I'm *really* excited about? The one-on-one encounters with readers who just love to yack about books. I can't wait for that."

To aspiring, writers, however, Kent says that yacking is simply not enough. "Don't just talk about writing. Don't plan to write or wish you could write if you had more time and talent—just do it. Writing comes from this deep well of pain and joy that all humans experience, and you have a story to tell. Jump in and tell it. Maybe you are afraid. Maybe you have a pesky gremlin bothering you and suggesting your story isn't worth telling. Well tune him out, put your butt in the chair, and write anyway. Just do it."

Kelly Bingham
Shark Girl
(Candlewick Press)
www.kellybingham.net

After two years of work, Kelly Bingham had just finished the first draft of her poetry novel *Shark Girl* when a case of art imitating life imitating art stopped her in her tracks.

Bingham got the idea for *Shark Girl* in the summer of 2001. "At the time, the biggest story in the news was a rash of shark attacks happening around the country. There was one particular story about a young boy who had his arm bitten off and reattached," she says.

"I started thinking, what a terrible tragedy to go through, and worse—to have it so widely publicized. It would follow you around the rest of your life, adding an entire invasive dimension to an already shattering event. You'd forever after be known only for that one moment in your life, not the entire person that you were. And I wondered what that would feel like, trying to put your life back together while under the microscope. So I started writing."

Bingham struggled with her book for about eight months, she says. "I wrote chapter after chapter, but didn't get anywhere . . . I couldn't get a toehold on my story. I felt as though I was holding a locked box, and could not find the key."

The box was sprung one weekend during the Vermont MFA program in which Bingham and her fellow students took a close look at novels in verse. "My friend and author Andrew Auseon said, 'Why don't you try writing your book as a poetry novel?' And instantly, I knew he had found the key," says Bingham. "I went back to my computer and began writing in verse, and the story just poured forth. Writing in verse freed me somehow; it unlocked that box. And once I started, I couldn't imagine writing the story in any other form."

Reprinted with permission.

Written in verse, *Shark Girl* follows 15-year-old Jane Arrowood as she deals with losing a limb in a shark attack, adjusting to a prosthetic arm, and being known for what happened to her instead of who she is. Author Kelly Bingham looked for ways to put Jane in situations that would "require her to face her fears, or face her handicap, and find a way around or through it—challenges such as mowing the lawn, folding laundry, fixing her hair in the mornings, or going out shopping with her best friend." *Shark Girl* has been nominated by the ALA for a Quick Pick for Reluctant Readers for 2008 and received a starred review in *Publishers Weekly*.

Then came the life-imitating-art moment, when 13-year-old surfer Bethany Hamilton had her arm severed in a shark attack. When Bingham heard the news, she felt horrible. "My heart stopped, realizing this had actually happened to someone," she says. "All I could think about was what that poor girl had gone through, and what a horrific experience it must have been, and how terrible a loss she had suffered. It didn't take long to realize that like it or not, this effected my story. This terrible thing had happened, and no matter what the truth, I knew that showing my story to anyone at that point would look as though I was capitalizing on this girl's real life loss. I put the book away in a drawer and let it sit there for a year before I even looked at it again. It seemed like the only thing I could do in the circumstances."

All told, it took four years from the time Bingham began writing *Shark Girl* until the day she got a note from Candlewick editor Liz Bicknell offering a contract. "During that time, I received so much support from my mentors at Vermont, but also steady admonitions that poetry novels really weren't selling well—and I'd have a very hard time finding a home for my story," says Bingham. "I kept writing anyway, because I needed to and wanted to. I wasn't willing to put that story away until I knew it had been told, and my friends, family, and teachers supported me on that. So I wrote with the dim hope of publishing, but not a big hope, and definitely no concrete plan on where to submit.

"When I had nearly finished *Shark Girl*, and began to realize that I had something worth sharing, I thought . . . now what? Where do I send it? I only knew one editor, and I was pretty sure it wasn't the right kind of book for that particular editor's house. But what else to do? I sent it along anyway. And, it was rejected," she says.

Bingham finally submitted to Candlewick at the urging of a writer friend in the Vermont program "who had heard me read from the manuscript several times and said, 'You know, you should send that to my editor, Liz Bicknell—I think she'd really like it.' " So I sent it on to Liz at Candlewick, filled with hope. Candlewick was a dream publisher for me. I love the books they publish, their commitment to excellence, and I was currently reading the Winnie Plays Ball series to my kids! When Candlewick took on *Shark Girl*, I felt so fortunate, I can't even tell you. I would not have chosen anyone else for this book; they are the perfect match."

Once Bingham got into the editorial process for *Shark Girl* she found it quick and painless. "My author friends assure me that it won't happen again; that editing your book is a long, drawn-out and painful process that will drive me insane next time. If that's the case, I'm relieved that the process went so well. Liz and I really saw eye to eye on the manuscript, and the changes we made were minor.''

There are some special considerations when it comes to novels in verse, however, that Bingham hadn't thought about going in. ''One thing I learned is that in a poetry novel, you are somewhat restricted by the number of lines that can fit vertically on one page. You have to look where your breaks fall—does your poem require a page turn right at the last line? If so, it's better in most cases to remove a line or two, so the entire poem can fit on one page. You look at where the breaks fall and what impact they make, and edit accordingly so that the pace and emotion of the moment are not broken up.''

Writing poetry novels is indeed a special skill, drawing characters and all their emotions within a spare text. Bingham advises writers working in this genre to listen to their characters. ''Write down whatever they tell you, what they are seeing, doing, feeling, no matter how small. Don't worry about getting it right on the first draft; ignore trying to make it tight or short or poetic or anything else. Collect these snippets; gather scenes that you imagine, even if they don't make sense quite yet, and even if you don't know where they fit in the book. If your secondary characters are telling or showing you things, write them down as well. It will help you flesh everyone out.

''Once you have a collection of dialogues from your character, sit and look at them. What does she like? What's her slant on life? Where is she coming from, and where does she want to go from there? Where is she on her emotional journey? What's left to discover? For *Shark Girl*, one thing I looked at was the five stages of grief. Then I looked at my poems. Did I shortchange any of the stages? Did they all apply to her particular character, or would she skip through some of them fairly quickly? How would she express herself during each stage?''

Bingham also imagined situations to put her main character Jane into that would require her to face her fears, or face her handicap, and find a way around or through it—challenges such as mowing the lawn, folding laundry, fixing her hair in the mornings, or going out shopping with her best friend. ''I would then explore these situations by writing various poems about the event, each one slightly different, each one with a different emotional outcome. I made myself write out scenarios even if I felt I wasn't going to go that particular way. The more you write, with the eye to just discover your story as you go (and without worrying if you are 'wasting time') the better off you will be in finding your characters, their voices, their feelings, and ultimately, in finding your story.''

Bingham was successful in finding her story and finding her publisher. A member of the Class of 2k7, she does not have an agent and isn't planning on pursuing one. (''I have nothing against agents,'' she says. ''I just don't want one at this time.'') She relocated from California ''for the peace, pollen, and packs of roaming wild dog in the North Georgia mountains,'' and juggles her writing life with a family life including a husband and five kids.

Bingham advises, ''Focus on your work, not on getting published. Take your time writing your story, and be true to yourself when you write. Dig deep. Don't be afraid to 'go there,' if you know what I mean. Put your heart into it. Don't worry about whether or not someone will buy it, the fact that a book exactly like your own has just been released, or what your grandmother would say if she knew you're using a curse word in your story. Write the story you have to tell, worry about the publishing part later. You have to write for the right reasons, and only you will know what those reasons are. But writing strictly because you want to be published is a bad idea. Writing has to be its own reward.''

Book Publishers

There's no magic formula for getting published. It's a matter of getting the right manuscript on the right editor's desk at the right time. Before you submit it's important to learn publishers' needs, see what kind of books they're producing and decide which publishers your work is best suited for. *Children's Writer's & Illustrator's Market* is but one tool in this process. (Those just starting out, turn to Quick Tips for Writers & Illustrators on page 5.)

To help you narrow down the list of possible publishers for your work, we've included several indexes at the back of this book. The **Subject Index** lists book and magazine publishers according to their fiction and nonfiction needs or interests. The **Age-Level Index** indicates which age groups publishers cater to. The **Photography Index** indicates which markets buy photography for children's publications. The **Poetry Index** lists publishers accepting poetry.

If you write contemporary fiction for young adults, for example, and you're trying to place a book manuscript, go first to the Subject Index. Locate the fiction categories under Book Publishers and copy the list under Contemporary. Then go to the Age-Level Index and highlight the publishers on the Contemporary list that are included under the Young Adults heading. Read the listings for the highlighted publishers to see if your work matches their needs.

Remember, *Children's Writer's & Illustrator's Market* should not be your only source for researching publishers. Here are a few other sources of information:

- The Society of Children's Book Writers and Illustrators (SCBWI) offers members an annual market survey of children's book publishers for the cost of postage or free online at www.scbwi.org. (SCBWI membership information can also be found at www.scbwi.org.)
- The Children's Book Council Web site (www.cbcbooks.org) gives information on member publishers.
- If a publisher interests you, send a SASE for submission guidelines or check publishers' Web sites for guidelines *before* submitting. To quickly find guidelines online, visit The Colossal Directory of Children's Publishers at www.signaleader.com.
- Check publishers' Web sites. Many include their complete catalogs that you can browse. Web addresses are included in many publishers' listings.
- Spend time at your local bookstore to see who's publishing what. While you're there, browse through *Publishers Weekly* and *The Horn Book*.

SUBSIDY & SELF-PUBLISHING

Some determined writers who receive rejections from royalty publishers may look to subsidy and co-op publishers as an option for getting their work into print. These publishers ask writers to pay all or part of the costs of producing a book. We strongly advise writers and illustrators to work only with publishers who pay them. For this reason, we've adopted a policy not to include any subsidy or co-op publishers in *Children's Writer's & Illustrator's Market* (or any other Writer's Digest Books market books).

If you're interested in publishing your book just to share it with friends and relatives, self-publishing is a viable option, but it involves time, energy, and money. You oversee all book production details. Check with a local printer for advice and information on cost or check online for print-on-demand publishing options (which are often more affordable).

Whatever path you choose, keep in mind that the market is flooded with submissions, so it's important for you to hone your craft and submit the best work possible. Competition from thousands of other writers and illustrators makes it more important than ever to research publishers before submitting—read their guidelines, look at their catalogs, check out a few of their titles and visit their Web sites.

ADVICE FROM INSIDERS

For insight and advice on getting published from a variety of perspectives, be sure to read the Insider Reports in this section. Subjects include authors and illustrators **Matt Plelan** (page 150), **K.L. Going** (page 174), and **Mo Willems** (page 200).

Information on book publishers listed in the previous edition but not included in this edition of *Children's Writer's & Illustrator's Market* may be found in the General Index.

A/V CONCEPTS CORP.

30 Montauk Blvd., Oakdale NY 11769. (631)567-7227. Fax: (631)567-8745. E-mail: info@edcompublishing.com. Specializes in nonfiction, fiction, educational material. **Writers contact:** Janice Cobas, editorial director. **Illustrators contact:** Janice Cobas, president. Produces 6 young readers/year; 6 middle readers/year; 6 young adult books/year. 20% of books by first-time authors. "Primary theme of books and multimedia is classic literature, math, science, language arts, self-esteem. We also hire writers to adapt classic literature."

Fiction Middle readers: hi-lo. Young adults/teens: hi-lo, multicultural, special needs. Recently published *The Taming of the Shrew*, adaptation by Lewann Sotnak, illustrated by Don Lannon and Ken Landgraf; *The Twelfth Night*, adaptation by Julianne Davidow; *The Merchant of Venice*, adaptation by Rachel Armington; *The Pioneers*, adaptation by Annie Laura Smith, illustrated by Matthew Archambault and Ken Landgraf.

Nonfiction Picture books, young readers, middle readers: activity books. Young adults/teens: activity books, hi-lo, multicultural, science, self help, textbooks. Average word length: middle readers—300-400; young adult books—500-950.

How to Contact/Writers Nonfiction: Submit outline/synopsis and 1 sample chapter. Responds to queries in 1 month.

Illustration Works with 4-6 illustrators/year. Reviews ms/illustration packages from artists. Submit manuscript with 3-4 pieces of final art. Illustrations only: Query with samples. Responds in 1 month. Samples returned with SASE. Samples filed.

Photography Submit samples.

Terms Work purchased outright for $50-1,000. Illustrators paid by the project $50-1,000. Photographers paid per photo $25-250.

ABINGDON PRESS

The United Methodist Publishing House, 201 Eighth Ave. S., Nashville TN 37203. (615)749-6384. Fax: (615)749-6512. E-mail: jstjohn@umpublishing.org. Web site: www.abingdonpress.com. Estab. 1789. **Acquisitions:** Judy Newman-St. John, children's book editor. "Abingdon Press, America's oldest theological publisher, provides an ecumenical publishing program dedicated to serving the Christian community."

Nonfiction All levels: religion.

How to Contact/Writers Query or submit outline/synopsis and 1 sample chapter. Prefers submissions by e-mail. Responds to queries in 3 months; mss in 6 months.

Illustration Uses color artwork only. Reviews ms/illustration packages from artists. Query with photocopies only. Samples returned with SASE; samples not filed.

Photography Buys stock images. Wants scenic, landscape, still life and multiracial photos. Model/property release required. Uses color prints. Submit stock photo list.

Terms Pays authors royalty of 5-10% based on retail price. Work purchased outright from authors ($100-1,000).

HARRY N. ABRAMS BOOKS FOR YOUNG READERS

115 W. 18th St., New York NY 10011. (212)519-1200. Web site: www.abramsbooks.com. **Publisher, Children's Books:** Howard W. Reeves.

Fiction/Nonfiction Picture books, young readers, middle readers, young adult.

How to Contact/Writers Submit complete ms for picture book; for longer works, submit a query with SASE. Responds in 6 months only with SASE. Mail only; no email. Will consider multiple submissions.

Illustration Illustrations only: Do not submit original material; copies only. Contact: Tad Beckerman.

⬚ ABSEY & CO.

23011 Northcrest Dr., Spring TX 77389. (281)257-2340. Fax: (281)251-4676. E-mail: abseyandco@aol.com. Web site: www.absey.com. New York address: 45 W. 21st Street, Suite 5, New York NY 10010. (212)277-8028. (Send mss to Spring TX address only.) **Publisher:** Edward Wilson. "We are looking for education books, especially those with teaching strategies based upon research, for children's picture books and Young Adult fiction. We haven't done much with nonfiction." Publishes hardcover, trade paperback and mass market paperback originals. Publishes 5-10 titles/year. 50% of books from first-time authors; 50% from unagented writers.

Fiction "Since we are a small, new press, we are looking for good manuscripts with a firm intended audience." Recently published *Stealing a Million Kisses* (board book); *Adrift* (YA fiction).

How to Contact/Writers Fiction: Query with SASE. Does not consider simultaneous submissions. Responds to queries in 3 months. No e-mail submissions. "We do not download from unknown sources."

Illustration Reviews ms/illustration packages. Send photocopies, transparencies, etc.

Photography Reviews ms/photo packages. Send photocopies, transparencies, etc.

Terms Pays 8-15% royalty on wholesale price. Publishes book 1 year after acceptance of ms. Manuscript guidelines for #10 SASE.

Tips "Absey publishes a few titles every year. We like the author and the illustrator working together to create something magical. Authors and illustrators have input into every phase of production."

ALADDIN PAPERBACKS/SIMON PULSE PAPERBACK BOOKS

1230 Avenue of the Americas, 4th Floor, New York NY 10020. (212)698-2707. Fax: (212)698-7337. Web site: www.simonsays.com. **Vice President/Associate Publisher, Aladdin:** Ellen Krieger; **Vice President/Editorial Director, Simon Pulse**: Bethany Buck; Mark McVeigh, Editorial Director (Aladdin); Liesa Abrams, senior editor (Aladdin); Jennifer Klonsky, executive editor (Pulse); Michelle Nagler, Senior Editor (Pulse). **Manuscript Acquisitions:** Attn: Submissions Editor. **Art Acquisitions:** Karin Paprocki, Aladdin; Russell Gordon, Simon Pulse. Paperback imprints of Simon & Schuster Children's Publishing Children's Division. Publishes 250 titles/year.

- Aladdin publishes reprints of successful hardcovers from other Simon & Schuster imprints as well as original beginning readers, chapter books, and middle grade single title and series fiction and is looking for graphic fiction and nonfiction. They accept query letters with proposals for originals. Simon Pulse publishes original teen series and single title fiction, as well as reprints of successful hardcovers from other Simon & Schuster imprints. They accept query letters for originals.

Fiction Recently published Robin Hill School beginning reader series (Julia Richardson, editor); Nancy Drew and the Clue Crew chapter book series (Molly McGuire, editor); Pendragon middle grade series (Julia Richardson, editor); Edgar & Ellen middle grade series (Ellen Krieger, editor).

ALASKA NORTHWEST BOOKS

Imprint of Graphic Arts Center Publishing Co., P.O. Box 10306, Portland OR 97296-0306. (503)226-2402. Fax: (503)223-1410. E-mail: editorial@gacpc.com. Web site: www.gacpc.com. **Executive Editor:** Tim Frew. Imprints: Alaska Northwest Books. Publishes 3 picture books/year; 1 young reader/year. 20% of books by first-time authors. "We publish books that teach and entertain as well as inform the reader about Alaska or the western U.S. We're interested in wildlife, adventure, unusual sports, inspirational nature stories, traditions, but we also like plain old silly stories that make kids giggle. We are particular about protecting Native American story-telling traditions, and ask that writers ensure that it's clear whether they are writing from within the culture or about the culture. We encourage Native American writers to share their stories."

Fiction Picture books, young readers: adventure, animal, contemporary, fantasy, history, humor, multicultural, nature/environment, poetry. Middle readers, young adult/teens: adventure, animal, anthology, contemporary, history, humor, multicultural, nature/environment, suspense/mystery. Average word length: picture books—500-1,000; young readers—500-1,500; middle readers—1,500-2,000; young adults—35,000. Recently published *Seldovia Sam and the Wildfire Rescue*, by Susan Woodward Springer, illustrated by Amy Meissner (ages 6-10, early chapter book); *Ten Rowdy Ravens*, by Susan Ewing, illustrated by Evon Zerbetz (age 5 and up, humor); *Berry Magic*, by Teri Sloat and Betty Huffmon, illustrated by Teri Sloat (age 6 and up, legend).

Nonfiction Picture books: animal. Young readers: animal, multicultural, sports. Middle readers, young adults/teens: animal, history, multicultural, nature/environment, sports, Alaska- or Western-themed adventure. Average word length: picture books—500-1,000; young readers—500-1,500; middle readers—1,500-2,000; young adults—35,000. Recently published *Big-Enough Anna: The Little Sled Dog Who Braved the Arctic*, by Pam Flowers and Ann Dixon, illustrated by Bill Farnsworth (5 and up); *Recess at 20 Below*, by Cindy Lou Aillaud (ages 6-10).

How to Contact/Writers Fiction: Submit complete ms for picture books or submit outline/synopsis and 2 sample chapters for YA novels. Nonfiction: Submit complete ms for picture books or submit 2 sample chapters for YA nonfiction chapter books. Responds to queries/mss in 3-5 months. Publishes book 2 years after acceptance. Will consider simultaneous submissions.

Illustration Works with 4-5 illustrators/year. Uses color artwork only. Reviews ms/illustration packages from artists. Submit ms with dummy or scans of final art on CD. Contact: Tricia Brown. Illustrations only: Query with résumé, scans on CD. Responds only if interested. Samples not returned; samples filed.

Photography Buys stock and assigns work. "We rarely illustrate with photos—only if the book is more educational in content." Photo captions required. Uses color and 35mm or 4×5 transparencies. Submit cover letter, résumé, slides, portfolio on CD, color promo piece.

Terms Pays authors royalty of 5-7% based on net revenues. Offers advances (average amount: $2,000). Pays illustrators royalty of 5-7% based on net revenues. Pays photographers royalty of 5-7% based on net revenues. Sends galleys to authors; dummies to illustrators. Originals returned to artist at job's completion. Book catalog available for 9×12 SASE and $3.85 postage; ms, art, and photo guidelines available for SASE. All imprints included in a single catalog. Catalog available on Web site.

Tips "As a regional publisher, we seek books about Alaska and the West. We rarely publish YA novels, but are more interested in the pre-school to early reader segment. A proposal that shows that the author has researched the market, in addition to submitting a unique story, will get our attention."

ALL ABOUT KIDS PUBLISHING √
9333 Benbow Drive, Gilroy CA 95020. (408)846-1833. Fax: (408)846-1835. E-mail: lguevara@aakp.com. Web site: www.aakp.com. **Acquisitions:** Linda Guevara. Publishes 5-10 picture books/year; 3-4 chapter books/year. 80% of books by first-time authors.

Fiction Picture books, young readers: adventure, animal, concept, fantasy, folktales, history, humor, nature, poetry, suspense/mystery. Average word length: picture books—450 words. Recently published *A, My Name is Andrew*, by Mary McManus-Burke (picture book).

Nonfiction Picture books, young readers: activity books, animal, biography, concept, history, nature. Average word length: picture books—450 words. Recently published *Shadowbox Hunt: A Search & Find Odyssey*, by Laura L. Seeley (picture book).

How to Contact/Writers Fiction: Submit complete ms. Nonfiction: Submit complete ms for picture books; outline synopsis and complete ms for young readers. Responds to mss in 3 months. Publishes a book 2-3 years after acceptance. Manuscript returned with SASE only.

Illustration Works with 5-10 illustrators/year. Reviews ms/illustration packages from artists. Submit ms with dummy or ms with 2-3 pieces of final art. Contact: Linda Guevara, editor. Illustrations only: Arrange personal portfolio review or send résumé, portfolio and client list. Responds in 3 months. Samples returned with SASE; samples filed.

Photography Works on assignment only. Contact: Linda Guevara, editor. Model/property releases required. Uses 35mm transparencies. Submit portfolio, résumé, client list.

Terms Pays author royalty. Offers advances (average amount: $1,000). Pays illustrators by the project (range: $3,000 minimum) or royalty of 3-5% based on retail price. Pays photographers by the project (range: $500 minimum) or royalty of 5% based on wholesale price. Sends galleys to authors; dummies to illustrators. All imprints included in a single catalog. Writer's, artist's and photographer's guidelines available for SASE and on Web site.

Tips "Write from the heart and for the love of children. Submit only one manuscript at a time. Not accepting submissions until February 2008. Please check our Web stie for guidelines before submitting."

AMIRAH PUBLISHING
P.O. Box 541146, Flushing NY 11354. E-mail: amirahpbco@aol.com. Web site: www.ifna.net. **Acquisitions:** Yahiya Emerick, president. Publishes 2 young readers/year; 5 middle readers/year; 3 young adult titles/year.

25% of books by first-time authors. "Our goal is to produce quality books for children and young adults with a spiritually uplifting application."

    ● Amirah accepts submissions only through e-mail.

Fiction Picture books, young readers, middle readers, young adults: adventure, animal, history, multicultural, religion, Islamic. Average word length: picture books—200; young readers—1,000; middle readers—5,000; young adults—5,000. Recently published *Ahmad Deen and the Curse of the Aztec Warrior*, by Yahiya Emerick (ages 8-11); *Burhaan Khan*, by Qasim Najar (ages 6-8); *The Memory of Hands*, by Reshma Baig (ages 15 to adult).

Nonfiction Picture books, young readers, middle readers, young adults: history, religion, Islamic. Average word length: picture books—200; young readers—1,000; middle readers—5,000; young adults—5,000. Recently published *Color and Learn Salah*, by Yahiya Emerick (ages 5-7, religious); *Learning About Islam*, by Yahiya Emerick (ages 9-11, religious); *What Islam Is All About*, by Yahiya Emerick (ages 14 and up, religious).

How to Contact/Writers Fiction/nonfiction: Query via e-mail only. Responds to queries in 2 weeks; mss in 3 months. Publishes a book 6-12 months after acceptance. Will consider electronic submissions via disk or modem.

Illustration Works with 2-4 illustrators/year. Reviews ms/illustration packages from artists. Query. Contact: Qasim Najar, vice president. Illustrations only: Query with samples. Contact: Yahiya Emerick, president. Responds in 1 month. Samples returned with SASE.

Photography Works on assignment only. Contact: Yahiya Emerick, president. Uses images of the Middle East, children, nature. Model/property releases required. Uses 4×6, matte, color prints. Submit cover letter.

Terms Work purchased outright from authors for $1,000-3,000. Pays illustrators by the project (range: $20-40). Pays photographers by the project (range: $20-40). Sends galleys to authors; dummies to illustrators. Originals returned to artist at job's completion. Book catalog available for SASE and 2 first-class stamps. All imprints included in a single catalog. Catalog available on Web site.

Tips "We specialize in materials relating to the Middle East and Muslim-oriented culture such as stories, learning materials and such. These are the only types of items we currently are publishing."

AMULET BOOKS

Abrams Books for Young Readers, 115 W. 18th St., New York NY 10001. (212)229-8000. Web site: www.hnabooks.com. Estab. 2004. Specializes in trade books, fiction. **Manuscript Acquisitions:** Susan Van Metre, executive editor. **Art Acquisitions:** Chad Beckerman, art director. Produces 6 middle readers/year, 6 young adult titles/year. 10% of books by first-time authors.

Fiction Middle readers: adventure, contemporary, fantasy, history, science fiction, sports. Young adults/teens: adventure, contemporary, fantasy, history, science fiction, sports, suspense. Recently published *The Sisters Grimm: The Fairy-Tale Detectives*, by Michael Buckley (mid-grade series); *ttyl*, by Lauren Miracle (YA novel); *The Hour of the Cobra*, by Maiya Williams (middle grade novel).

How to Contact/Writers Fiction: Query. Responds to queries in 2-3 months. Publishes book 18-24 months after acceptance. Considers simultaneous submissions.

Illustration Works with 10-12 illustrators/year. Uses both color and b&w. Query with samples. Contact: Chad Beckerman, art director. Samples filed.

Photography Buys stock images and assigns work.

Terms Offers advance against royalties. Illustrators paid by the project . Author sees galleys for review. Illustrators see dummies for review. Originals returned to artist at job's completion. Catalog available for 9×12 SASE and 4 first-class stamps.

ⓦ ATHENEUM BOOKS FOR YOUNG READERS

Imprint of Simon & Schuster Children's Publishing Division, 1230 Avenue of the Americas, New York NY 10020. (212)698-2715. Web site: www.simonsayskids.com. Estab. 1960. **Publisher:** Vice President, Associate Publisher Emma D. Dryden. **Acquisitions:** Ginee Seo, vice president, editorial director; Caitlyn Dloughy, executive editor; Justin Chanda, executive editor; Susan Burke, associate editor; Carol Chou, editorial assistant. **Art Acquisitions:** Ann Bobco, executive art director. Publishes 20-30 picture books/year; 20-25 middle readers/year; 15-25 young adult titles/year. 10% of books by first-time authors; 60% from agented writers. "Atheneum publishes original hardcover trade books for children from pre-school age through young adult. Our list includes picture books, chapter books, mysteries, biography, science fiction, fantasy, graphic novels, middle grade and young adult fiction and nonfiction. The style and subject matter of the books we publish is almost unlimited. We do not, however, publish textbooks, coloring or activity books, greeting cards, magazines or pamphlets or religious publications. The lists of Charles Scribner's Sons Books for Young Readers have been folded into the Atheneum program."

    ● Atheneum title *Copper Sun*, by Sharon Draper, won the Coretta Scott King Author Award in 2007.

Fiction Recently published *Sleepy Boy*, by Polly Kanevsky, illustrated by Stephanie Anderson (picture book);

Olivia Forms a Band, by Ian Falconer (picture book); *Tiger of the Snows*, by Bob Burleigh, illustrated by Ed Young (picture book); *Dooby Dooby Moo*, by Doreen Cronin, illustrated by Betsy Lewin (picture book); *Weedflower*, by Cynthia Kadohata (middle grade); *Alphabet of Dreams*, by Susan Flethcer (middle grade); *The Dragon of Never-Was*, by Ann Downer (middle grade); *The Shadow Thieves*, by Anne Ursa (middle grade); *Copper Son*, by Sharon Draper (teen); *Alice in the Know*, by Phyllis Reynolds Naylor (teen); *Leonardo's Shadow*, by Christopher Grey (teen).

Nonfiction Recently published *Into the West*, by James McPherson.

How to Contact/Writers Send query letters with SASE for picture books; send synopsis and first 3 chapters or first 30 pages with SASE for novels. Responds to queries in 1-2 months; requested mss in 3-4 months. Publishes a book 24-36 months after acceptance. Will consider simultaneous queries from previously unpublished authors and those submitted to other publishers, "though we request that the author let us know it is a simultaneous query." Please do not call to query or follow up.

Illustration Works with 40-50 illustrators/year. Send art samples résumé, tearsheets to Ann Bobco, Design Dept. 4th Floor, 1230 Avenue of the Americas, New York NY 10020. Samples filed. Responds to art samples only if interested.

Terms Pays authors in royalties of based on retail price. Pays illustrators royalty or by the project. Pays photographers by the project. Original artwork returned at job's completion. Manuscript guidelines for #10 SAE and 1 first-class stamp.

Tips "Atheneum has a 40+ year tradition of publishing distinguished books for children. Study our titles."

AVISSON PRESS, INC.

3007 Taliaferro Rd., Greensboro NC 27408. (336)288-6989. Fax: (336)288-6989. **Manuscript Acquisitions:** Martin Hester, publisher. Publishes 5-7 young adult titles/year. 70% of books by first-time authors.

Nonfiction Young adults: biography. Average word length: young adults—25,000. Recently published *I Can Do Anything: The Sammy Davis, Jr. Story*, by William Schoell (ages 12-18, young adult biography); *The Girl He Left Behind: The Life and Times of Libbie Custer*, by Suzanne Middendorf Arruda (ages 12-18, young adult biography); *Randolph Caldecott: An Illustrated Life*, by Claudette Hagel.

How to Contact/Writers Accepts material from residents of U.S. only. Nonfiction: Submit outline/synopsis and 2 sample chapters. Responds to queries/mss in 3 weeks. Publishes a book 9-12 months after acceptance. Will consider simultaneous submissions.

Terms Pays author royalty of 8-10% based on wholesale price. Offers advances (average amount: $400). Sends galleys to authors. Book catalog available for #10 SAE and 1 first-class stamp; ms guidelines available for SASE.

Tips "We publish *only* YA biographies. All artwork is done in-house. We need a few experienced writers for house-generated titles."

Ⓐ AVON BOOKS/BOOKS FOR YOUNG READERS

1350 Avenue of the Americas, New York NY 10019. (212)261-6500. Fax: (212)261-6668. Web site: www.harperc hildrens.com.

• Avon is not accepting unagented submissions. See listing for HarperCollins Children's Books.

Ⓝ AZRO PRESS

PMB 342, 1704 Llano St. B, Santa Fe NM 87505. (505)989-3272. Fax: (505)989-3832. E-mail: books@azropress.c om. Web site: www.azropress.com. Estab. 1997. Specializes in trade books, fiction. **Writers contact:** Gae Eisenhardt. Produces 3-4 picture books/year; 1 young reader/year. 75% of books by first-time authors. "We like to publish illustrated children's books by Southwestern authors and illustrators. We are always looking for books with a Southwestern look or theme."

Fiction Picture books: animal, history, humor, nature/environment. Young readers: adventure, animal, hi-lo, history, humor. Average word length: picture books—1,200; young readers—2,000-2,500. Recently published *Tis for Tortilla*, by Jody Alpers, illustrated by Celeste Johnson; *Cactus Critter Bash*, by Sid Hausman; *Cute As A Button*, by Jeff della Penna, illustrated by Nicole Blau.

Nonfiction Picture books: animal, geography, history. Young readers: geography, history.

How to Contact/Writers Accepts international submissions. Fiction/nonfiction: Query or submit complete ms. Responds to queries/mss in 3-4 months. Publishes book 1½-2 years after acceptance. Considers simultaneous submissions.

Illustration Accepts material from international illustrators. Works with 3 illustrators/year. Uses color artwork only. Reviews ms/illustration packages. Reviews work for future assignments. Query with samples. Submit samples to illustrations editor. Responds in 3-4 months. Samples not returned. Samples not filed.

Terms Pays authors royalty of 10% based on wholesale price. Pays illustrators by the project ($2,000) or royalty of 5%. Author sees galleys for review. Illustrators see dummies for review. Originals returned to artist at job's completion. Catalog available for #10 SASE and 3 first-class stamps. Offers writer's guidelines for SASE. See Web site for artist's, photographer's guidelines.

Tips "We are not currently accepting new manuscripts. Please see our Web site for acceptance date."

☐ BALLYHOO BOOKWORKS INC.

P.O. Box 534, Shoreham NY 11792. E-mail: ballyhoo@optonline.net. **Acquisitions:** Liam Gerrity, editorial director. Publishes 2 picture books/year; 1 young reader/year. 30% of books by first-time authors. "We are a small press, but highly selective and want texts that flow from the tongue with clarity and are infused with the author's passion for the piece."

● Ballyhoo is not accepting new manuscripts until Fall 2007 due to a full schedule and an overwhelming increase in unsolicited submissions. Submissions will be returned unread until that time.

Fiction Young readers: animal, nature/environment. Average word length: picture books—up to 500; young readers—up to 1,000. Recently published *The Alley Cat* and *The Barnyard Cat*, by Brian J. Heinz, illustrated by June H. Blair (ages 5-9, picture books).

Nonfiction Picture books: arts/crafts, how-to. Young readers, middle readers: activity books, arts/crafts, hobbies, how-to. Average word length: picture books—up to 500; young readers—up to 1,000; middle readers—up to 10,000. Recently published *Metal Detecting for Treasure*, by Dorothy B. Francis (ages 10 and up, how-to).

How to Contact/Writers Accepts material from residents of U.S. only. Fiction/nonfiction: Query or submit outline/synopsis or outline/synopsis and 2 sample chapters. Responds to queries in 1 month; mss in 2 months. Publishes book 12-18 months after acceptance. Will consider simultaneous submissions.

Illustration Accepts material from residents of U.S. only. Works with 2-3 illustrators/year. Reviews ms/illustration packages from artists. Query or send ms with dummy. Contact: Editorial Director. Illustrations only: Send résumé, promo sheet and tearsheets. "We file all samples for future reference."

Terms Pays authors royalty of 5% based on retail price. Offers advances (average amount: $1,000-2,500). Pays illustrators 5% based on retail price. Sends galleys to authors. Originals returned to artist at job's completion. Manuscript guidelines available for SASE.

Tips "We don't see any value in trends, only in good writing."

☐ BANCROFT PRESS

P.O. Box 65360, Baltimore MD 21209. (410)358-0658. Fax: (410)637-7377. E-mail: bruceb@bancroftpress.com. Web site: www.bancroftpress.com. **Manuscript Acquisitions:** Bruce Bortz, publisher. **Art Acquisitions:** Bruce Bortz, publisher. Publishes 1 middle reader/year; 2-4 young adult titles/year.

Fiction Middle readers, young adults: adventure, animal, contemporary, fantasy, humor, multicultural, problem novels, religion, science fiction, special needs, sports, suspense/mystery. Average word length: middle readers—40,000; young adults—50,000. Recently published *Finding the Forger: A Bianca Balducci Mystery*, by Libby Sternberg (ages 10 and up); *The Reappearance of Sam Webber*, by Jonathon Scott Fuqua (ages 10 and up); *Jake: The Second Novel in the Gunpowder Trilogy*, by Arch Montgomery (ages 13 and up); *Like We Care*, by Tom Matthews (ages 15 and up).

Nonfiction Middle readers, young adults: animal, biography, concept, health, history, multicultural, music/dance, nature/environment, reference, religion, science, self help, social issues, special needs, sports, textbooks.

How to Contact/Writers Fiction/nonfiction: Submit complete ms or submit outline/synopsis and 3 sample chapters. Responds to queries/mss in at least 6 months. Publishes book 18 months after acceptance. Will consider e-mail submissions, simultaneous submissions or previously published work.

Terms Pays authors royalty of 8% based on retail price. Offers advances (average amount: $1,000-3,000). Sends galleys to authors. Catalog and ms guidelines available on Web site.

Tips "We advise writers to visit our Web site and to be familiar with our previous work. Patience is the number one attribute contributors must have. It takes us a very long time to get through submitted material, because we are such a small company. Also, we only publish 4-6 books per year, so it may take a long time for your optioned book to be published. We like to be able to market our books to be used in schools and in libraries. We prefer fiction that bucks trends and moves in a new direction. We are especially interested in mysteries and humor (especially humorous mysteries)."

☐ BANTAM BOOKS FOR YOUNG READERS

Imprint of Random House Children's Book, Division of Random House, Inc., 1745 Broadway, New York NY 10019. (212)782-9000. Web site: www.randomhouse.com/kids. Book publisher.

● See listings for Random House/Golden Books for Young Readers Group, Delacorte and Doubleday Books for Young Readers, Alfred A. Knopf and Crown Books for Young Readers, and Wendy Lamb Books.

How to Contact/Writers Not seeking manuscripts at this time.

Illustration Contact: Isabel Warren-Lynch, executive director, art & design. Responds only if interested. Samples returned with SASE; samples filed.

Terms Pays illustrators and photographers by the project or royalties. Original artwork returned at job's completion.

BAREFOOT BOOKS

2067 Massachusetts Ave., 5th Floor, Cambridge MA 02140. Web site: www.barefootbooks.com. **Manuscript/ Art Acquisitions:** U.S. editor. Publishes 35 picture books/year; 10 anthologies/year. 35% of books by first-time authors. "At Barefoot Books, we celebrate art and story that opens the hearts and minds of children from all walks of life, inspiring them to read deeper, search further, and explore their own creative gifts. Taking our inspiration from many different cultures, we focus on themes that encourage independence of spirit, enthusiasm for learning, and sharing of the world's diversity. Interactive, playful and beautiful, our products combine the best of the present with the best of the past to educate our children as the caretakers of tomorrow."

Fiction Picture books, young readers: animal, anthology, concept, folktales, multicultural, nature/environment, poetry, spirituality. Middle readers, young adults: anthology, folktales. Average word length: picture books—500-1,000; young readers—2,000-3,000; anthologies—10,000-20,000. Recently published *The Prince's Bedtime*, by Joanne Oppenheim; *The Hare and the Tortoise*, by Ranjit Bolt; *Elusive Moose*, by Clare Beaton.

How to Contact/Writers Fiction: Submit complete ms for picture books; outline/synopsis and 1 sample story for collections. Responds in 4 months if SASE is included. Will consider simultaneous submissions and previously published work.

Illustration Works with 20 illustrators/year. Uses color artwork only. Reviews ms/illustration packages from artists. Send query and art samples or dummy for picture books. Illustrations only: Query with samples or send promo sheet and tearsheets. Responds only if interested. Samples returned with SASE.

Terms Pays authors royalty of 5% based on retail price. Offers advances. Sends galleys to authors. Originals returned to artist at job's completion. Book catalog available for SAE and 5 first-class stamps; ms guidelines available for SASE.

Tips "We are looking for books that inspire and are filled with a sense of magic and wonder. We also look for strong stories from all different cultures, reflecting the ways of the individual culture while also touching deeper human truths that suggest we are all one. We welcome playful submissions for the very youngest children and also anthologies of stories for older readers, all focused around a universal theme. We encourage writers and artists to visit our Web site and read some of our books to get a sense of our editorial philosophy and what we publish before they submit to us. Always, we encourage them to stay true to their inner voice and artistic vision that reaches out for timeless stories, beyond the momentary trends that may exist in the market today."

☐ BARRONS EDUCATIONAL SERIES ✓

250 Wireless Blvd., Hauppauge NY 11788. Fax: (631)434-3723. E-mail: waynebarr@barronseduc.com. Web site: www.barronseduc.com. **Manuscript Acquisitions:** Wayne R. Barr, acquisitions manager. **Art Acquisitions:** Bill Kuchler. Publishes 20 picture books/year; 20 young readers/year; 20 middle readers/year; 10 young adult titles/year. 25% of books by first-time authors; 25% of books from agented writers.

Fiction Picture books: animal, concept, multicultural, nature/environment. Young readers: adventure, multicultural, nature/environment, fantasy, suspense/mystery. Middle readers: adventure, fantasy, multicultural, nature/environment, problem novels, suspense/mystery. Young adults: problem novels. Recently published *Night at the Museum*, by Leslie Goldman; *The Witches of Widdershins Academy*, by Margaret and William Kenda.

Nonfiction Picture books: concept, reference. Young readers: biography, how-to, reference, self help, social issues. Middle readers: hi-lo, how-to, reference, self help, social issues. Young adults: reference, self help, social issues, sports.

How to Contact/Writers Fiction: Query via e-mail. Nonfiction: Submit outline/synopsis and sample chapters. "Submissions must be accompanied by SASE for response." Responds to queries in 2 months; mss in 4 months. Publishes a book 1 year after acceptance. Will consider simultaneous submissions.

Illustration Works with 20 illustrators/year. Reviews ms/illustration packages from artists. Query first; 3 chapters of ms with 1 piece of final art, remainder roughs. Illustrations only: Submit tearsheets or slides plus résumé. Responds in 2 months.

Terms Pays authors royalty of 10-14% based on net price or buys ms outright for $2,000 minimum. Pays illustrators by the project based on retail price. Sends galleys to authors; dummies to illustrators. Book catalog, ms/artist's guidelines for 9×12 SAE.

Tips Writers: "We publish preschool storybooks, concept books and middle grade and YA chapter books. No romance novels." Illustrators: "We are happy to receive a sample illustration to keep on file for future consideration. Periodic notes reminding us of your work are acceptable." Children's book themes "are becoming much more contemporary and relevant to a child's day-to-day activities, fewer talking animals. We have a great interest in children's fiction (ages 7-11 and ages 12-16) with New Age topics."

▢ BEBOP BOOKS

Imprint of Lee & Low Books Inc., 95 Madison Ave., New York NY 10016-7801. (212)779-4400. Web site: www.bebopbooks.com. **Acquisitions:** Jennifer Fox. **Editor-in-Chief:** Louise May. Publishes 10-15 educational market picture books/year. Many books by first-time authors. "Our goal is to publish child-centered stories that support literacy learning and provide multicultural content for children just beginning to learn to read. We make a special effort to work with writers and illustrators of diverse backgrounds. Current needs are posted on Web site."

- Bebop Books acquires manuscripts between August and October only. See Web site for details.

Fiction Picture books: adventure, concept, contemporary, multicultural, nature/environment, sports, culturally specific topics for young children.

Nonfiction Picture books: arts/crafts, careers, concept, cooking, hobbies, how-to, multicultural, music/dance, nature/environment, social issues, sports.

How to Contact/Writers Fiction/nonfiction: Submit complete ms. Responds to mss in up to 4 months . See Web site for specific guidelines; submit between August and October only. We will not respond to manuscripts received when our call for manuscripts is not open."

Illustration Works with 5-10 illustrators/year. Uses color artwork only. Illustrations and photographs: Query with color samples and send client list or cover letter. Responds only if interested. Samples returned with SASE; samples filed. "We are especially interested in submissions from artists of color, and we encourage artists new to the field of children's books to send us samples of their work."

Terms Pays authors royalty. Offers advances. Pays illustrators and photographers royalty and advance. Book catalog available for 9×12 SAE and 89¢ postage, attn: Catalog Request. Catalog available on Web site.

Tips "Bebop Books is currently specializing in beginning readers with multicultural themes. Often called 'little books,' they are used to help young children develop early reading skills and strategies. Each book is a small paperback, with full color illustrations and a story specifically written and illustrated to support beginning readers."

▢ BENCHMARK BOOKS

Imprint of Marshall Cavendish, 99 White Plains Rd., Tarrytown NY 10591. (914)332-8888. Fax: (914)332-1888. E-mail: mbisson@marshallcavendish.com. Web site: www.marshallcavendish.com. **Manuscript Acquisitions:** Michelle Bisson. Publishes about 100 young reader, middle reader and young adult books/year. "We look for interesting treatments of only nonfiction subjects related to elementary, middle school and high school curriculum."

Nonfiction Most nonfiction topics should be curriculum related. Average word length: 4,000-20,000. All books published as part of a series. Recently published First Americans (series), Family Trees (series), Bookworms (series).

How to Contact/Writers Nonfiction: "Please read our catalog or view our Web site before submitting proposals. We only publish series. We do not publish individual titles." Submit outline/synopsis and 1 or more sample chapters. Responds to queries/mss in 3 months. Publishes a book 2 years after acceptance. Will consider simultaneous submissions.

Photography Buys stock and assigns work.

Terms Buys work outright. Sends galleys to authors. Book catalog available online. All imprints included in a single catalog.

THE BENEFACTORY *22. check website*

24 Pine Circle, Pembroke MA 02359. (781)294-4717. Web site: www.thebenefactory.com. **Manuscript/Art Acquisitions:** Cindy Germain, director, creative services. Publishes 6-12 picture books/year with Humane Society and other nonprofits; 6-12 picture books/year. 50% of books by first-time authors. The Benefactory publishes "classic" true stories about real animals, through licenses with many nonprofits. Each title is accompanied by a read-along audiocassette and a plush animal. A percentage of revenues benefits the licensor. Target ages: 4-10.

Nonfiction Picture books: nature/environment; young readers: animal, nature/environment. Average word length: 700-1,500. Recently published *Chessie, the Travelin' Man*, written by Randy Houk, illustrated by Paula Bartlett (ages 5-10, picture book); *Condor Magic*, written by Lyn Littlefield Hoopes, illustrated by Peter C. Stone (ages 5-10, picture book); *Caesar: On Deaf Ears*, written by Loren Spiotta-DiMare, illustrated by Kara Lee (ages 5-10, picture book).

How to Contact/Writers Query only—does not accept unsolicited mss. Responds to queries in 6 weeks. Publishes a book 1 year after acceptance. Will consider simultaneous submissions. Send SASE for writer's guidelines.

Illustration Works with 6-8 illustrators/year. Uses color artwork only. Reviews ms/illustration packages from artists. Query or send ms with dummy. Illustrations only: Send résumé, promo sheet and tearsheets to be kept

on file. Responds in 6 months. Samples returned with SASE; samples filed. Send SASE for artist guidelines.
Terms Pays authors royalty of 3-5% based on wholesale price. Offers advances (average amount: $5,000). Pays illustrators royalty of 3-5% based on wholesale price. Sends galleys to authors; dummies to illustrators. Originals returned to artist at job's completion. Book catalog available for 8½×11 SASE; ms and art guidelines available for SASE.

BESS PRESS

3565 Harding Ave., Honolulu HI 96816. (808)734-7159. Fax: (808)732-3627. E-mail: editor@besspress.com. Web site: www.besspress.com. **Publisher:** Benjamin Bess. **Art Director:** Carol Colbath. Publishes 2 picture books/year; 2 young readers/year. 25% of books by first-time authors. Publishes trade and educational books about Hawaii and Micronesia only. "The perspective should be that of a resident, not a visitor."
Fiction Picture books: Hawaii. Average word length: picture books—600. Recently published *There's a Monster in My Opu*, by Karyn Hopper (ages 3-8, picture books); *The Story of Surfin*, by Carla Golembe (ages 5-10, picture book with CD); *Waltah Melon: Local Kine Hero*, by Carmen Geshell and Jeff Pagat (ages 5-8, picture book).
Nonfiction Picture books, young readers: Hawaii. Recently published *Girls' Day/Boys' Day*, by Minako Ishii (ages 6-10, coloring book).
How to Contact/Writers Fiction/nonfiction: Submit complete ms. Responds to queries in 2-3 weeks; mss in 4-6 weeks. Publishes book 1 year after acceptance. Will consider e-mail submissions, simultaneous submissions, and previously published work.
Illustration Works with 2-3 illustrators/year. Reviews ms/illustration packages from artists. "We prefer to use illustrators and photographers living in the region. We do not encourage samples from freelancers outside the region." Query. Contact: Carol Colbath, art director. Illustrations only: Query. Responds only if interested. Samples returned with SASE; samples filed.
Photography Works on assignment only. Uses Hawaii-Pacific photos only. Model/property releases required. Uses color and various size prints, digital files and transparencies. Submit cover letter.
Terms Pays authors royalty of 4-10% based on wholesale price or work purchased outright from authors. Pays illustrators by the project or royalty of 4-6% based on wholesale price. Pays photographers by the project. Sends galleys to authors; dummies to illustrators. Originals returned to artist at job's completion. Book catalog available for SASE; ms guidelines available for SAE. All imprints included in a single catalog. Catalog available on Web site.
Tips "As a regional publisher, we are looking for material specific to the region (Hawaii and Micronesia), preferably from writers and illustrators living within (or very familiar with) the region."

BICK PUBLISHING HOUSE

307 Neck Rd., Madison CT 06443. (203)245-0073. Fax: (203)245-5990. E-mail: bickpubhse@aol.com. Web site: www.bickpubhouse.com. **Aquisitions Editor:** Dale Carlson. "We publish psychological, philosophical, scientific information on health and recovery, wildlife rehabilitation, living with disabilities, teen psychology and science for adults and young adults."
Nonfiction Young adults: nature/environment, religion, science, self help, social issues, special needs. Average word length: young adults—60,000. Recently published *In and Out of Your Mind* (teen science); *Who Said What?* (philosophy quotes for teens), *What are You Doing with Your Life?*, by J. Krishnamurti (philosophy for teens), *The Teen Brain Book*, by Dale Carlson.
How to Contact/Writers Fiction: Submit outline/synopsis and 3 sample chapters. Nonfiction: Submit outline/synopsis or outline/synopsis and 3 sample chapters. Responds to queries/mss in 2 weeks. Publishes book 1 year after acceptance. Will consider simultaneous submissions and previously published work.
Illustration Works with 1 illustrator/year. Uses b&w artwork only. Reviews ms/illustration packages from artists. Submit sketches of teens or science drawings. Contact: Dale Carlson, president. Illustrations only: Query with photocopies, résumé, SASE. Responds in 2 weeks. Samples returned with SASE.
Terms Pays authors royalty of 5-10%. Pays illustrators by the project (range: up to $1,000). Sends galleys to authors; dummies to illustrators. Book catalog available for SASE with 1 first-class stamp; writer's guidelines available for SAE. Catalog available on Web site.
Tips "Read our books!"

BIRDSONG BOOKS

1322 Bayview Rd., Middletown DE 19709. (302)378-7274. E-mail: Birdsong@BirdsongBooks.com. Web site: www.BirdsongBooks.com. **Manuscript & Art Acquisitions:** Nancy Carol Willis, president. Publishes 1 picture book/year. "Birdsong Books seeks to spark the delight of discovering our wild neighbors and natural habitats. We believe knowledge and understanding of nature fosters caring and a desire to protect the Earth and all living things. Our emphasis is on North American animals and habitats, rather than people."
Nonfiction Picture books, young readers: activity books, animal, nature/environment. Average word length:

picture books—800-1,000. Recently published *Red Knot: A Shorebird's Incredible Journey*, by Nancy Carol Willis (age 6-9, nonfiction picture book); *Raccoon Moon*, by Nancy Carol Willis (ages 5-8, natural science picture book); *The Robins In Your Backyard*, by Nancy Carol Willis (ages 4-7, nonfiction picture book).

How to Contact/Writers Nonfiction: Submit complete manuscript package with SASE. Responds to mss in 3 months. Publishes book 2-3 years after acceptance. Will consider simultaneous submissions (if stated).

Illustration Accepts material from residents of U.S. Works with 1 illustrator/year. Reviews ms/illustration packages from artists. Send ms with dummy (plus samples/tearsheets for style). Illustrations only: Query with brochure, résumé, samples, SASE, or tearsheets. Responds only if interested. Samples returned with SASE.

Photography Uses North American animals and habitats (currently North American animals in winter dens). Submit cover letter, résumé, promo piece, stock photo list.

Tips "We are a small independent press actively seeking manuscripts that fit our narrowly defined niche. We are only interested in nonfiction, natural science picture books or educational activity books about North American animals and habitats. Our books include several pages of back matter suitable for early elementary classrooms. Mailed submissions with SASE only. No e-mail submissions or phone calls, please. Cover letters should sell author/illustrator and book idea."

BLOOMING TREE PRESS ✓

P.O. Box 140934, Austin TX 78714. (512)921-8846. Fax: (512)873-7710. E-mail: email@bloomingtreepress.com. Web site: www.bloomingtreepress.com. Estab. 2000. **Publisher:** Miriam Hees; Madeline Smoot, senior editor, children's division; Judy Gregerson, editor, children's division, Meghan Dietsche, associate editor, children's division; Kay Pluta, accociate edtior, children's division; Bradford Hees, senior editor, graphic novels/comics. **Art Acquisitions:** Regan Johnson. "Blooming Tree Press is dedicated to producing high quality books for the young and the young at heart. It is our hope that you will find your dreams between that pages of our books."

Fiction Picture books: adventure, animal, contemporary, fantasy, folktales, history, humor, multicultural, religion, science fiction, special needs, sports. Young readers: adventure, animal, contemporary, fantasy, folktales, history, humor, multicultural, religion, science fiction, special needs, sports, suspense. Middle readers: adventure, animal, anthology, contemporary, fantasy, folktales, history, humor, multicultural, poetry, religion, science fiction, suspense. Young adults/teens: adventure, animal, anthology, contemporary, fantasy, folktales, history, humor, religion, science fiction, suspense. Average word length: picture books—500-1,000; young readers—800-9,000; middle readers—25,000-40,000; young adult/teens: 40,000-70,000. Recently published *Jessica McBean, Tap Dance Queen*, by Carole Gerger, illustrated by Patrice Barton (chapter book about teasing); *One-Eyed Jack*, by Paula Miller, illustrated by Chris Forrest (mid-grade about a boy and his dog in 1880s Montana); *Summer Shorts*, by multiple authors and illustrators (mid-grade stories about summer); *Kichi in Jungle Jeopardy*, by Lila Guzman, illustrations by Regan Johnson (middle grade about a talking dog in the Mayan temples).

Nonfiction Picture Books: biography, cooking, geography, history, self help, social issues, special needs, sports. Young Readers: animal, biography, careers, cooking, geography, history, music/dance, religion, science, self help, social issues, special needs, sports. Middle Readers: biography, cooking, geography, history, how-to, music/dance, religion, science, self help, social issues, sports. Young Adults/Teens: biography, careers, cooking, geography, history, hobbies, music/dance, religion, science, self help, social issues, sports.

How to Contact/Writers Fiction: Query. Nonfiction: submit outline/synopsis and 3 sample chapters. Responds to queries in 1-3 months; mss in 3-4 months. Publishes ms 18-36 months after acceptance. Will consider simultaneous submissions.

Illustration Works with 6-20 illustrators/year. Reviews ms/illustration packages. Send manuscript with dummy and sample art. Contact: Regan Johnson, publisher. Illustration only: Query with samples to Regan Johnson, publisher. Samples not returned; sample filed.

Terms Pays authors royalty of 10% depending on the project. Pays illustrators by the project. Authors see galleys for review; illustrators see dummies. Send e-mail with mailing address for catalog. Writer's guidelines on Web site.

Tips "Send a crisp and clean one-page query letter stating your project, why it is right for the market, and a little about yourself. Write what you know, not what's 'in.' Remember, every great writer/illustrator started somewhere. Keep submitting . . don't ever give up."

BLOOMSBURY CHILDREN'S BOOKS

Imprint of Bloomsbury PLC, 175 Fifth Avenue, Suite 315, New York NY 10010. (646)307-5858. Fax: (212)982-2837. E-mail: bloomsburykids@bloomsburyusa.co. Web site: www.bloomsbury.com/usa. Specializes in fiction, picture books. Publishes 20 picture books/year; 5 young readers/year; 10 middle readers/year; 15 young adult titles/year. 25% of books by first-time authors.

● See First Books on page 119 for an interview with Ruth McNally Barshaw, author-illustrator of Bloomsbury title *Ellie McDoodle: Have Pen, Will Travel*.

Fiction Picture books: adventure, animal, contemporary, fantasy, folktales, history, humor, multicultural, poetry, suspense/mystery. Young readers: adventure, animal, anthology, concept, contemporary, fantasy, folktales, history, humor, multicultural, suspense/mystery. Middle readers: adventure, animal, contemporary, fantasy, folktales, history, humor, multicultural, poetry, problem novels. Young adults: adventure, animal, anthology, contemporary, fantasy, folktales, history, humor, multicultural, problem novels, science fiction, sports, suspense/mystery. Recently published *Where is Coco Going?*, by Sloone Tanen (picture books); *Once Upon a Curse*, by E.D. Baker (middle reader); *Enna Burning*, by Shannon Hale (young adult fantasy).

How to Contact/Writers Submit synopsis and first 3 chapters with SASE. Responds to queries/mss in 6 months.

Illustration Works with 15 illustrators/year. Reviews ms/illustration packages from artists. Query or submit ms with dummy. Illustrations only: Query with samples. Responds only if interested. Samples returned with SASE; samples filed.

Photography Buys stock and assigns work. Uses color or b&w prints. Submit SASE.

Terms Pays authors royalty or work purchased outright for jackets. Offers advances. Pays illustrators by the project or royalty. Pays photographers by the project or per photo. Sends galleys to authors; dummies to illustrators. Originals returned to artist at job's completion. Writer's and art guidelines available for SASE. Catalog available on Web site.

Tips "Spend a lot of time in the bookstore and library to keep up on trends in market. Always send appropriate SASE to ensure response. Never send originals."

BLUE SKY PRESS

557 Broadway, New York NY 10012-3999. (212)343-6100. Fax: (212)343-4713. Web site: www.scholastic.com. **Acquisitions:** Bonnie Verburg. Publishes 15-20 titles/year. 1% of books by first-time authors. Publishes hardcover children's fiction and nonfiction including high-quality novels and picture books by new and established authors.

- Blue Sky is currently not accepting unsolicited submissions due to a large backlog of books.

Fiction Picture books: adventure, animal, concept, contemporary, fantasy, folktales, history, humor, multicultural, nature/environment, poetry. Young readers: adventure, contemporary, fantasy, folktales, history, humor, multicultural, nature/environment, poetry. Young adults: adventure, anthology, contemporary, fantasy, history, humor, multicultural, poetry. Multicultural needs include "strong fictional or themes featuring non-white characters and cultures." Does not want to see mainstream religious, bibliotherapeutic, adult. Average length: picture books—varies; young adults—150 pages. Recently published *To Every Thing There Is a Season*, illustrated by Leo and Diane Dillon (all ages, picture book); *Bluish*, by Virginia Hamilton; *No, David!*, by David Shannon; *The Adventures of Captain Underpants*, by Dav Pilkey; *How Do Dinosaurs Say Good Night?*, by Jane Yolen, illustrated by Mark Teague.

How to Contact/Writers "Due to large numbers of submissions, we are discouraging unsolicited submissions—send query with SASE only if you feel certain we publish the type of book you have written." Fiction: Query (novels, picture books). Responds to queries in 6 months. Publishes a book 1-3 years after acceptance; depending on chosen illustrator's schedule. Will not consider simultaneous submissions. No electronic submissions or faxes.

Illustration Works with 10 illustrators/year. Reviews illustration packages "only if illustrator is the author." Submit ms with dummy. Illustrations only: Query with samples, tearsheets. Responds only if interested. Samples only returned with SASE. Original artwork returned at job's completion.

Terms Pays 10% royalty based on wholesale price split between author and illustrators. Advance varies.

Tips "Read currently published children's books. Revise—never send a first draft. Find your own voice, style, and subject. With material from new people we look for a theme or style strong enough to overcome the fact that the author/illustrator is unknown in the market."

BOYDS MILLS PRESS ✓✓

815 Church St., Honesdale PA 18431. Web site: www.boydsmillspress.com. Estab. 1990. Imprints: Calkins Creek Books, Front Street, Wordsong. 5% of books from agented writers. "We publish a wide range of quality children's books of literary merit, from preschool to young adult."

Fiction Ages 0-11: adventure, contemporary, humor, multicultural, rhyming. Picture books: all kinds. Multicultural themes include any story showing a child as an integral part of a culture and which provides children with insight into a culture they otherwise might be unfamiliar with.

Nonfiction All levels: nature/environment, history, science. Picture books, young readers, middle readers: animal, multicultural. Does not want to see reference/curricular text.

How to Contact/Writers Fiction/nonfiction: Submit complete ms or submit through agent. Label package "Manucript Submission" and include SASE. Responds to in 3 months.

Illustration Works with 25 illustrators/year. Reviews ms/illustration packages from artists. Submit complete ms with 1 or 2 pieces of art. Illustrations only: Query with samples best suited to the art (postcard, $8^1/_2 \times 11$, etc.). Label package "Art Sample Submission." Responds only if interested. Samples returned with SASE. Samples filed. Originals returned at job's completion.

Photography Assigns work.

Terms Authors paid royalty or work purchased outright. Offers advances. Illustrators paid by the project or royalties; varies. Photographers paid by the project, per photo, or royalties; varies. Manuscripts/artist's guidelines available on Web site.

Tips "Picture books with fresh approaches, not worn themes, are our strongest need at this time. Check to see what's already on the market and on our Web site before submitting your story. Prose fiction for middle-grade through young adult should be submitted to Boyds Mills imprint Front Street—see Front Street listing for submission information. Poetry for all ages should be submitted to Boyds Mills Wordsong imprint—see Wordsong listing for submission information. Historical fiction and nonfiction about the United States for all ages should be submitted to Calkins Creek Books—see Calkins Creek listing for submission information."

☐ BRIGHT RING PUBLISHING, INC.

P.O. Box 31338, Bellingham WA 98228. (360)592-9201. Fax: (360)592-0722. E-mail: maryann@brightring.com. Web site: www.brightring.com. **Editor:** MaryAnn Kohl.

● Bright Ring is no longer accepting manuscript submissions.

CALKINS CREEK BOOKS

Boyds Mills Press, 815 Church St., Honesdale PA 18431. E-mail: Web site: www.calkinscreek.com. Estab. 2004. "We aim to publish books that are a well-written blend of creative writing and extensive research which emphasize important events, people, and places in U.S. history."

Fiction All levels: history. Recently published *Blue*, by Joyce Moyer Hostrtter (ages 10 and up, historical fiction); *Booth's Daughter*, by Raymond Wemmlinger (ages 10 and up, historical fiction).

Nonfiction All levels: history. Recently published *The Printer's Trail*, by Gail Jarrow (ages 10 and up, nonfiction chapter book); *American Slave, American Hero*, by Laurence Pringle (ages 8 and up, nonfiction picture book); *Jeannette Rankin: Political Pioneer*, by Gretchen Woelfle (ages 10 and up, nonfiction biography).

How to Contact/Writers Accepts international submissions. Fiction: Submit outline/synopsis and 3 sample chapters. Nonfiction: Submit outline/synopsis and 3 sample chapters. Considers simultaneous submissions. Responds in 3 months.

Illustration Accepts material from international illustrators. Works with 25 (for all Boyds Mills Press imprints) illustrators/year. Uses both color and b&w. Reviews ms/illustration packages. For ms/illustration packages: Submit ms with 2 pieces of final art. Submit ms/illustration packages to Tim Gillner, art director. Reviews work for future assignments. If interested in illustrating future titles, query with samples. Submit samples to Tim Gillner, art director.

Photography Buys stock images and assigns work. Submit photos to: Tim Gillner, art director. Uses color or b&w 8×10 prints. For first contact, send promo piece (color or b&w).

Terms Authors paid royalty or work purchased outright. Offers advances. Illustrators paid by the project or royalties; varies. Photographers paid by the project, per photo, or royalties; varies. Manuscripts/artist's guidelines available on Web site.

Tips "Read through our recently-published titles and review our catalog. When selecting titles to publish, our emphasis will be on important events, people, and places in U.S. history. Writers are encouraged to submit a detailed bibliography, including secondary and primary sources, and expert reviews with their submissions."

☑ CANDLEWICK PRESS

2067 Massachusetts Ave., Cambridge MA 02140. (617)661-3330. Fax: (617)661-0565. E-mail: bigbear@candlewick.com. Web site: www.candlewick.com. **Manuscript Acquisitions:** Karen Lotz, publisher; Liz Bicknell, editorial director and associate publisher; Joan Powers, editorial director; Mary Lee Donovan, executive editor; Sarah Ketchersid, editor; Deborah Wayshak, senior editor; Andrea Tompa, associate edtior, Kaylan Adair, associate editor; Kate Fletcher, associate editor; Katie Cunningham, associate editor. **Art Acquisitions:** Anne Moore. Publishes 160 picture books/year; 15 middle readers/year; 15 young adult titles/year. 5% of books by first-time authors. "Our books are truly for children, and we strive for the very highest standards in the writing, illustrating, designing and production of all of our books. And we are not averse to risk."

● Candlewick Press is not accepting queries and unsolicited mss at this time. See First Books on page 119 for an interview with Kelly Bingham, author of Candlewick title *Shark Girl*. Candlewick titles *The Astonishing Life of Octavian Nothing, Traitor to the Nation; v. 1: The Pox Party*, by M.T. Anderson and *Surrender*, by Sonya Hartnett, both won Printz Honor Awards in 2007. Their title *The Miraculous Journey of Edward Tulane*, by Kate DiCamillo, illustrated by Bagran Ibatoulline, won the Boston Globe-Horn Book Award for Fiction and Poetry in 2007. Their title *Mercy Watson Goes for a Ride*, by Kate DiCamillo, illustrated by Chris

Van Dusen, won a Geisel Honor Medal in 2007. Their title *Zelda and Ivy: The Runaways*, by Laura McGee Kvasnosky, won the Geisel Medal in 2007.

Fiction Picture books: animal, concept, contemporary, fantasy, history, humor, multicultural, nature/environment, poetry. Middle readers, young adults: contemporary, fantasy, history, humor, multicultural, poetry, science fiction, sports, suspense/mystery. Recently published *The Earth, My Butt, and Other Big Round Things*, by Carolyn Mackler (young adult fiction); *Seeing the Blue Between*, edited by Paul B. Janeczko (young adult poetry collection); *Dragonology*, by Ernest Drake; *Encyclopedia Prehistorica: Dinosaurs*, by Robert Sabuda and Matthew Reinhart.

Nonfiction Picture books: concept, biography, geography, nature/environment. Young readers: biography, geography, nature/environment. Recently published *Top Secret: A Handbook of Codes, Ciphers, and Secret Writing*, by Paul B. Janeczko, illustrated by Jenna LaReau.

Illustration Works with approx. 40 ill ustrators/year. ''We prefer to see a range of styles from artists along with samples showing strong characters (human or animals) in various settings with various emotions.'' Receives unsolicited illustration packages/dummies from artists. Color or b&w copies only, please; no originals. Illustrations only: Submit color samples to Art Resource Coordinator. Samples returned with SASE; samples filed.

Terms Pays authors royalty of 2½-10% based on retail price. Offers advances. Pays illustrators 2½-10% royalty based on retail price. Sends galleys to authors; dummies to illustrators. Pays photographers 2½-10% royalty. Original artwork returned at job's completion.

CAPSTONE PRESS INC.

151 Good Counsel Dr., P.O. Box 669, Mankato MN 55438. Fax: (888)262-0705. Web site: www.capstone-press.com. Book publisher. **Contact:** Kay M. Olson. Imprints: A+ Books, Pebble Books, Edge Books, Blazers books, Snap Books, Capstone High-Interest Books, Fact Finders, First Facts, Pebble Plus, Yellow Umbrella Books. ''Capstone Press books provide new and struggling readers with a strong foundation on which to build reading success. Our nonfiction books are effective tools for reaching readers, with precisely-leveled text tailored to their individual needs.''

• Capstone Press does not accept unsolicited manuscripts.

Nonfiction Publishes only nonfiction books. All elementary levels: animals, arts/crafts, biography, geography, health, history, hobbies, science, and social studies.

How to Contact/Writers Does not accept submissions. Do not send mss. Instead, send query letter, résumé, samples of nonfiction writing to be considered for assignment, and references

Terms Authors paid flat fee. Buys all rights.

Tips ''See Web site prior to sending query letter.''

CAROLRHODA BOOKS, INC.

A division of Lerner Publishing Group, 241 First Ave. N., Minneapolis MN 55401. Web site: www.lernerbooks.com. Contact: Zelda Wagner, submissions editor. Estab. 1969. Publishes hardcover originals. Averages 8-10 picture books each year for ages 3-8, 6 fiction titles for ages 7-18, and 2-3 nonfiction titles for various ages.

• Starting in 2007, Lerner Publishing Group no longer accepts submissions for any of their imprints except Kar-Ben Publishing.

How to Contact/Writers ''We will continue to seek targeted solicitations at specific reading levels and in specific subject areas. The company will list these targeted solicitations on our Web site and in national newsletters, such as the SCBWI Bulletin. Unsoliciteds sent in November 2006 under our previous submissions policy will be read and replied to by November 2007.''

CARTWHEEL BOOKS, for the Very Young

Imprint of Scholastic Inc., 557 Broadway, New York NY 10012. (212)343-4804. Web site: www.scholastic.com. Estab. 1991. Book publisher. Vice President/Editorial Director: Ken Geist. **Manuscript Acquisitions:** Grace Maccarone, executive editor; Cecily Kaiser, executive editor. **Editorial Assistant:** Erika Lo. **Art Acquisitions:** Daniel Martin, executive art director. Publishes 15-20 picture books/year; 20-25 easy readers/year; 40-45 novelty/concept/board books/year.

Fiction Picture books, young readers: humor, seasonal/holiday, family/love. Average word length: picture books—100-500; easy readers—100-500.

Nonfiction Picture books, young readers: seasonal/curricular topics involving animals (polar animals, ocean animals, hibernation), nature (fall leaves, life cycles, weather, solar system), history (first Thanksgiving, MLK Jr., George Washington, Columbus). ''Most of our nonfiction is either written on assignment or is within a series. We do not want to see any arts/crafts or cooking.'' Average word length: picture books—100-1,500; young readers—100-2,000.

How to Contact/Writers Cartwheel Books is no longer accepting unsolicited mss. All unsolicited materials will be returned unread. Fiction/nonfiction: For previously published or agented authors, submit complete ms.

Book Publishers

Responds to mss in 6 months. Publishes a book within 2 years after acceptance. SASE required with all submissions.

Illustration Works with 30 illustrators/year. Reviews ms/illustration packages from artists. Send ms with dummy. Illustrations only: Query with samples; arrange personal portfolio review; send promo sheet, tearsheets to be kept on file. Contact: Executive Art Director. Responds in 6 months. Samples returned with SASE; samples filed. Please do not send original artwork.

Photography Buys stock and assigns work. Uses photos of kids, families, vehicles, toys, animals. Submit published samples, color promo piece.

Terms Pays advance against royalty or flat fee. Sends galley to authors; dummy to illustrators. Originals returned to artist at job's completion.

Tips "With each Cartwheel list, we seek a pleasing balance among board books and novelty books, hardcover picture books and gift books, nonfiction, paperback storybooks and easy readers. Cartwheel seeks to acquire projects that speak to young children and their world: new and exciting novelty formats, fresh seasonal and holiday stories, curriculum/concept-based titles, and books for beginning readers. Our books are inviting and appealing, clearly marketable, and have inherent educational and social value. We strive to provide the earliest readers relevant and exciting books, that will ultimately lead to a lifetime of reading, learning, and wondering. Know what types of books we do. Check out bookstores or catalogs to see where your work would fit best."

CHARLESBRIDGE

85 Main St., Watertown MA 02472. (617)926-0329. Fax: (617)926-5720. E-mail: tradeeditorial@charlesbridge.com. Web site: www.charlesbridge.com. Estab. 1980. Book publisher. **Contact:** Trade Editorial Department. Publishes 60% nonfiction, 40% fiction picture books and early chapter books. Publishes nature, science, multicultural, social studies and fiction picture books.

- Charlesbridge title *A Mother's Journey*, by Sandra Markle, illustrated by Alan Marks, won a Boston Globe-Horn Book Honor Award for Nonfiction in 2007.

Fiction Picture books and chapter books: "Strong, realistic stories with enduring themes." Considers the following categories: adventure, concept, contemporary, health, history, humor, multicultural, nature/environment, special needs, sports, suspense/mystery. Recently published *Vinnie and Abraham*, by Dawn FitzGerald; *Aggie and Ben*, by Lori Ries; *Rickshaw Girl*, by Mitali Perkins.

Nonfiction Picture books: animal, biography, careers, concept, geography, health, history, multicultural, music/dance, nature/environment, religion, science, social issues, special needs, hobbies, sports. Average word length: picture books—1,000. Recently published *Lost Little Bat*, by Sandra Markle; *Super Swimmers*, by Caroline Arnold; *The Bald Eagle's View of American History*, by C.H. Coleman.

How to Contact/Writers Send ms and SASE. Accepts exclusive submissions only. Responds to mss in 3 months. Full mss only; no queries.

Illustration Works with 5-10 illustrators/year. Uses color artwork only. Illustrations only: Query with samples; provide résumé, tearsheets to be kept on file. "Send no original artwork, please." Responds only if interested. Samples returned with SASE; samples filed. Originals returned at job's completion.

Terms Pays authors and illustrators in royalties or work purchased outright. Manuscript/art guidelines available for SASE. Exclusive submissions only.

Tips "We want books that have humor and are factually correct. See our Web site for more tips."

CHELSEA HOUSE PUBLISHERS

Facts on File, 132 West 31st Street, 17th Floor, New York, New York 10001. (800)322-8755. Fax: (917)339-0326. E-mail: authors@chelseahouse.com. Web site: www.chelseahouse.com. Specializes in nonfiction, educational material. **Manuscript Acquisitions:** Laurie Likoff, editor-in-chief. Imprints: Chelsea Clubhouse; Chelsea House. Produces 150 middle readers/year, 150 young adult books/year. 10% of books by first-time authors.

How to contact/Writers "All books are parts of series. Most series topics are developed by in-house editors, but suggestions are welcome. Authors may query with résumé and list of publications."

CHICAGO REVIEW PRESS

814 N. Franklin St., Chicago IL 60610. (312)337-0747. Fax: (312)337-5110. E-mail: frontdesk@chicagoreviewpress.com. Web site: www.chicagoreviewpress.com. **Manuscript Acquisitions:** Cynthia Sherry, associate publisher. **Art Acquisitions:** Gerilee Hundt, art director. Publishes 3-4 middle readers/year; 4 young adult titles/year. 33% of books by first-time authors; 30% of books from agented authors. "Chicago Review Press publishes high-quality, nonfiction, educational activity books that extend the learning process through hands-on projects and accurate and interesting text. We look for activity books that are as much fun as they are constructive and informative."

Nonfiction Young readers, middle readers and young adults: activity books, arts/crafts, multicultural, history, nature/environment, science. "We're interested in hands-on, educational books; anything else probably will be rejected.'' Average length: young readers and young adults—144-160 pages. Recently published *Chicago History for Kids*, by Owen Hurd (ages 9 and up); *Stomp Rockets, Catapults, and Kaleidescopes*, by Curt Gabrielson (ages 9 and up); *Exploring the Solar System*, by Mary Kay Carson (ages 9 and up).

How to Contact/Writers Enclose cover letter and no more than table of contents and 1-2 sample chapters; prefers not to receive e-mail queries. Send for guidelines. Responds to queries/mss in 2 months. Publishes a book 1-2 years after acceptance. Will consider simultaneous submissions and previously published work.

Illustration Works with 6 illustrators/year. Uses primarily b&w artwork. Reviews ms/illustration packages from artists. Submit 1-2 chapters of ms with corresponding pieces of final art. Illustrations only: Query with samples, résumé. Responds only if interested. Samples returned with SASE.

Photography Buys photos from freelancers (''but not often''). Buys stock and assigns work. Wants ''instructive photos. We consult our files when we know what we're looking for on a book-by-book basis.'' Uses b&w prints.

Terms Pays authors royalty of 7½-12½% based on retail price. Offers advances of $3,000-6,000. Pays illustrators by the project (range varies considerably). Pays photographers by the project (range varies considerably). Original artwork ''usually'' returned at job's completion. Book catalog/ms guidelines available for $3.

Tips ''We're looking for original activity books for small children and the adults caring for them—new themes and enticing projects to occupy kids' imaginations and promote their sense of personal creativity. We like activity books that are as much fun as they are constructive. Please write for guidelines so you'll know what we're looking for.''

CHILDREN'S BOOK PRESS

2211 Mission St., San Francisco CA 94110. (415)821-3080. Fax: (415)821-3081. E-mail: submissions@childrensbookpress.org. Web site: www.childrensbookpress.org. **Acquisitions:** Dana Goldberg. ''Children's Book Press is a nonprofit publisher of multicultural and bilingual children's literature. We publish contemporary stories reflecting the traditions and culture of minorities and new immigrants in the United States. Our goal is to help broaden the base of children's literature in this country to include stories from the African-American, Asian-American, Latino/Chicano and Native American communities. Stories should encourage critical thinking about social and/or personal issues. These ideas must be an integral part of the story.''

Fiction Picture books: contemporary, history, multicultural, poetry. Average word length: picture books—750-1,500.

Nonfiction Picture books, young readers: multicultural.

How to Contact/Writers Submit complete ms to Submissions Editor. Responds to mss in roughly 4 months. ''Please do not inquire about your manuscript. We can only return/respond to manuscripts with a SASE.'' Publishes a book 1-2 years after acceptance. Will consider simultaneous submissions.

Illustration Works with 4-5 illustrators/year. Uses color artwork only. Reviews ms/illustration packages from artists. Send ms with 3 or 4 color photocopies. Illustrations only: color copies only, no original artwork. Responds in 8-10 weeks. Samples returned with SASE.

Terms Original artwork returned at job's completion. Book catalog available; ms guidelines available via Web site or with SASE.

Tips ''Vocabulary level should be approximately third grade (eight years old) or below. Keep in mind, however, that many of the young people who read our books may be nine, ten, or eleven years old or older. Their life experiences are often more advanced than their reading level, so try to write a story that will appeal to a fairly wide age range. We are especially interested in humorous stories and original stories about contemporary life from the multicultural communities mentioned above by writers *from* those communities.''

CHRISTIAN ED. PUBLISHERS

P.O. Box 26639, San Diego CA 92196. (858)578-4700. Web site: www.ChristianEdWarehouse.com. Book publisher. **Acquisitions:** Janet Ackelson, assistant editor; Carol Rogers, managing editor; Tim Yen, production coordinator. Publishes 80 Bible curriculum titles/year. ''We publish curriculum for children and youth, including program and student books and take-home papers—all handled by our assigned freelance writers only.''

Fiction Young readers: contemporary. Middle readers: adventure, contemporary, suspense/mystery. ''We publish fiction for Bible club take-home papers. All fiction is on assignment only.''

Nonfiction Publishes Bible curriculum and take-home papers for all ages. Recently published *All-Stars for Jesus*, by Treena Herrington and Letitia Zook, illustrated by Aline Heiser (Bible club curriculum for grades 4-6); *Honeybees Classroom Activity Sheets*, by Janet Miller and Wanda Pelfrey, illustrated by Ron Widman (Bible club curriculum for ages 2-3).

How to Contact/Writers Fiction/nonfiction: Query. Responds to queries in 5 weeks. Publishes a book 1 year after acceptance. Send SASE for guidelines or contact Christian Ed. at cgast@cehouse.com.

Illustration Works with 6-7 illustrators/year. Query by e-mail. Contact: Tim Yen, production coordinator (tyen@cehouse.com). Responds in 1 month. Samples returned with SASE.

Terms Work purchased outright from authors for 3¢/word. Pays illustrators $11-15/page. Book catalog available for 9×12 SAE and 4 first-class stamps; ms and art guidelines available for SASE or via e-mail.

Tips "Read our guidelines carefully before sending us a manuscript or illustrations. All writing and illustrating is done on assignment only and must be age-appropriate (preschool-6th grade)."

CHRONICLE BOOKS ✓✓

680 Second St. San Francisco CA 94107. (415)537-4200. Fax: (415)537-4415. Web site: www.chroniclekids.com. Book publisher. **Acquisitions:** Victoria Rock, associate publisher, children's books. Publishes 50-60 (both fiction and nonfiction) books/year; 5-10% middle readers/year; young adult nonfiction titles/year. 10-25% of books by first-time authors; 20-40% of books from agented writers.

Fiction Picture books, young readers, middle readers: "We are open to a very wide range of topics." Young adults: "We are interested in young adult projects, and do not have specific limitations on subject matter." Recently published *Emily's Balloon*, by Komako Sakai (ages 2-6, picture book); *Ivy and Bean*, by Annie Barrows, illustrated by Sophie Blackall (ages 6-10, chapter book).

Nonfiction Picture books, young readers, middle readers, young adults: "We are open to a very wide range of topics." Recently published *An Egg Is Quiet*, by Dianna Hutts Aston, illustrated by Sylvia Long (ages 4-10, picture book); *Tour America*, by Diane Siebert, illustrated by Stephen Johnson (ages 7-12, picture book).

How to Contact/Writers Fiction/nonfiction: Submit complete ms (picture books); submit outline/synopsis and 3 sample chapters (for older readers). Responds to queries in 1 month; will not respond to submissions unless interested. Publishes a book 1-3 years after acceptance. Will consider simultaneous submissions, as long as they are marked "multiple submissions." Will not consider submissions by fax, e-mail or disk. Do not include SASE; do not send original materials. No submissions will be returned; to confirm receipt, include a SASP.

Illustration Works with 40-50 illustrators/year. Wants "unusual art, graphically strong, something that will stand out on the shelves. Fine art, not mass market." Reviews ms/illustration packages from artists. "Indicate if project *must* be considered jointly, or if editor may consider text and art separately." Illustrations only: Submit samples of artist's work (not necessarily from book, but in the envisioned style). Slides, tearsheets and color photocopies OK. (No original art.) Dummies helpful. Resume helpful. Samples suited to our needs are filed for future reference. Samples not suited to our needs will be recycled. Queries and project proposals responded to in same time frame as author query/proposals."

Photography Purchases photos from freelancers. Works on assignment only.

Terms Generally pays authors in royalties based on retail price, "though we do occasionally work on a flat fee basis." Advance varies. Illustrators paid royalty based on retail price or flat fee. Sends proofs to authors and illustrators. Book catalog for 9×12 SAE and 8 first-class stamps; ms guidelines for #10 SASE.

Tips "Chronicle Books publishes an eclectic mixture of traditional and innovative children's books. We are interested in taking on projects that have a unique bent to them—be it subject matter, writing style, or illustrative technique. As a small list, we are looking for books that will lend us a distinctive flavor. Primarily we are interested in fiction and nonfiction picture books for children ages infant-8 years, and nonfiction books for children ages 8-12 years. We are also interested in developing a middle grade/YA fiction program, and are looking for literary fiction that deals with relevant issues. Our sales reps are witnessing a resistance to alphabet books. And the market has become increasingly competitive. The '80s boom in children's publishing has passed, and the market is demanding high-quality books that work on many different levels."

🔲 CLARION BOOKS ✓

215 Park Ave. S., New York NY 10003. (212)420-5889. Web site: www.clarionbooks.com. **Manuscript Acquisitions:** Dinah Stevenson, publisher; Virginia Buckley, contributing editor; Jennifer Wingertzahn, editor; Marcia Leonard, editor. **Art Acquisitions:** Joann Hill, art director.

- Clarion title *Flotsam*, by David Wiesner, won the Caldecott Medal in 2007.

Fiction Recently published *One Green Apple*, by Eve Bunting (ages 5-8, picture book); *Flotsam*, by David Wiesner (ages 5-8, picture book); *The Loud Silence of Francine Green*, by Karen Cushman (ages 10-14, historical fiction).

Nonfiction Recently published *Jane Addams*, by Judith Bloom Fradin and Dennis Brindell Fradin (ages 10-14, biography).

How to Contact/Writers Fiction and picture books: Send complete mss. Nonfiction: Send query with up to 3 sample chapters. Must include SASE. Will accept simultaneous submissions if informed. "Please no e-mail queires or submissions."

Illustration Send samples (no originals).

Terms Pays illustrators royalty; flat fee for jacket illustration. Pays royalties and advance to writers; both vary. Guidelines available on Web site.

CLEAR LIGHT PUBLISHERS

823 Don Diego, Santa Fe NM 87505. (505)989-9590. Fax: (505)989-9519. Web site: www.clearlightbooks.com. **Acquisitions:** Harmon Houghton, publisher. Publishes 4 middle readers/year; 4 young adult titles/year.

Nonfiction Middle readers and young adults: multicultural, American Indian and Hispanic only.
How to Contact/Writers Fiction/nonfiction: Submit complete ms with SASE. "No e-mail submissions. Authors supply art. Manuscripts not considered without art or artist's renderings." Will consider simultaneous submissions. Responds in 3 months. Only send *copies*.
Illustration Reviews ms/illustration packages from artists. "No originals please." Submit ms with dummy and SASE.
Terms Pays authors royalty of 10% based on wholesale price. Offers advances (average amount: up to 50% of expected net sales within the first year). Sends galleys to authors.
Tips "We're looking for authentic American Indian art and folklore."

CONCORDIA PUBLISHING HOUSE

3558 S. Jefferson Ave., St. Louis MO 63118. (314)268-1187. Fax: (314)268-1329. Web site: www.cph.org. **Contact:** Peggy Kuethe. **Art Director:** Norm Simon. "Concordia Publishing House produces quality resources which communicate and nurture the Christian faith and ministry of people of all ages, lay and professional. These resources include curriculum, worship aids, books, and religious supplies. We publish approximately 30 quality children's books each year. We boldly provide Gospel resources that are Christ-centered, Bible-based and faithful to our Lutheran heritage."
Nonfiction Picture books, young readers, young adults: Bible stories, activity books, arts/crafts, concept, contemporary, religion. "All books must contain explicit Christian content." Recently published *Three Wise Women of Christmas*, by Dandi Daley Mackall (picture book for ages 6-10); *The Town That Forgot About Christmas*, by Susan K. Leigh (ages over 5-9, picture book); *Little Ones Talk With God* (prayer book compilation, aged 5 and up).
How to Contact/Writers Submit complete ms (picture books); submit outline/synopsis and samples for longer mss. May also query. Responds to queries in 1 month; mss in 3 months. Publishes a book 2 years after acceptance. Will consider simultaneous submissions. "Absolutely no phone queries."
Illustration Works with 20 illustrators/year. Illustrations only: Query with samples. Contact: Norm Simon, art director. Responds only if interested. Samples filed.
Terms Pays authors royalties based on retail price or work purchased outright ($750-2,000). Sends galleys to author. Manuscript guidelines for 1 first-class stamp and a #10 envelope. Pays illustrators by the project.
Tips "Do not send finished artwork with the manuscript. If sketches will help in the presentation of the manuscript, they may be sent. If stories are taken from the Bible, they should follow the Biblical account closely. Liberties should not be taken in fantasizing Biblical stories."

Ⓐ JOANNA COTLER BOOKS

HarperCollins Children's Books. 1350 Avenue of the Americas, New York NY 10019. Web site: www.harperchildrens.com. **Senior Vice President and Publisher:** Joanna Cotler. Senior Editor: Karen Nagel. Assistant Editor: Alyson Day. Publishes literary and commercial fiction and nonfiction. Publishes 6 picture books/year; 5 middle readers/year; 2 young adult titles/year. 15% of books by first-time authors.
Fiction Recently published *Psyche in a Dress*, by Francesca Lia Block; *I'm dirty*, by Kate McMullan, illustrated by Jim McMullan; *Grandfather's Dance*, by Patricia MacLachlan.
How to Contact/Writers Only interested in agented material.
Illustration Will review ms/illustration packages. Reviews work of illustrators for possible future assignments. Contact: Alison Day, assistant editor. Sample are not kept on file.
Terms Illustrators see dummies for review. Originals returned to artist at job's completion.

Ⓒ COTTONWOOD PRESS, INC.

109-B Cameron Drive, Fort Collins CO 80525. (907)204-0715. Fax: (907)204-0761. E-mail: cottonwood@cottonwoodpress.com. Web site: www.cottonwoodpress.com. Estab. 1986. Specializes in educational material. **President:** Cheryl Thurston. Cottonwood Press strives "to publish materials that are effective in the classroom and help kids learn without putting them to sleep, specializing in materials for grades 5-12." Publishes 4 middle reader and young adult book/year. 60% of books by first-time authors.
Nonfiction Middle readers: textbooks. Young Adults/Teens: textbooks. Recently published: *Un-Journaling: daily writing exercises that are NOT personal, NOT introspective, NOT boring*; *Singuini: noodling around with silly songs*; *Phunny Stuph: Proofreading exercised with a sense of humor*.
How to Contact/Writers Nonfiction: Submit complete manuscript. Responds to queries in 2 weeks; mss in 2 months. Publishes a book 6 months-1 year after acceptance. Will consider simultaneous submissions if notified.
Terms Pay royalty of 10-15% based on net sales.
Tips "It is essential that writers familiarize themselves with our Web site to see what we do. The most successful of our authors have used our books in the classroom and know how different they are from ordinary textbooks."

Matt Phelan

Create a great portfolio & try everything

Reviewers have described Matt Phelan's illustrations in his debut picture book *The New Girl . . . and Me*, by Jacqui Robbins, as "simple and evocative," and his characters as "masterpieces of button noses, play rumpled grooming, and spot-on body language." His style is soft and loose, spare and warm.

Although *The New Girl* is his first picture book, Phelan has created illustrations for a number of novels including *The Seven Wonders of Sassafras Springs*, by Betty G. Birney, Susan Patron's Newbery winner *The Higher Power of Lucky* (both Atheneum/Richard Jackson), and *Rosa Farm*, by Liz Wu (Knopf), and he's got a number of upcoming books slated for 2007 and 2008 releases including a pair of graphic novels for which he's the writer as well as the illustrator.

Before he pursued illustration as a career, Phelan worked in a bookstore and tried his hand at screenwriting. When that didn't pan out, the then aspiring artist decided to pursue his dream career in children's book illustration and spent several years perfecting his portfolio. After joining the Society of Children's Book Writers and Illustrators (a move he highly recommends), Phelan attended a conference in his hometown of Philadelphia, and dropped the extra dough to have a portfolio review, which he says is "the best 30 bucks I ever spent." His meeting with an Atheneum art director resulted in his first assignments.

Here Phelan talks about his work, his style, and his upcoming projects and offers advice to illustrators looking to get noticed.

Susan Patron described your illustrations in her Newbery-winning book *The Higher Power of Lucky* as having "tender life and immediacy." How would you describe your style? How did you develop your style?

I approach illustrating a character not unlike how an actor approaches playing a role. I try to understand what the character is thinking and feeling at that moment. If I can get that across in the picture, then the other details hopefully will fall into place. Early on, I found that the more I "finish" a picture, the less life it had, so I'm constantly struggling to stay loose enough to retain that spark you get from a quick sketch . . . even if I've drawn the picture 20 times. It's something I'll probably struggle with for the rest of my life.

It's amazing how much expression you can achieve on the faces of your characters using only dots for eyes and a few lines. Did you take an advanced eyebrow-drawing workshop? Or do you teach one?

I spent a good amount of time experimenting with eyes. I lean towards the "less is more" philosophy, so reducing the focal point of a face down to a pair of dots and some eyebrows made sense. It's tricky, though. One millimeter off, and it won't work. I wish there *was* a workshop. In lieu of that, I recommend looking at everything Ernest Shepard and Charles Schulz ever drew.

What did you do as far as training or schooling to prepare for a career as an illustrator?

I haven't really had any formal art school training, but I've drawn and loved illustration since I was kid. The '70s were a great time for classic comic reprints and I devoured many of them, especially Peanuts, Flash Gordon, Prince Valiant, and the Marvel comics of the '60s. Living near the Brandywine River Museum, I also had an early exposure to the work of Howard Pyle and N.C. Wyeth. I've learned a good deal from old art instruction books (from the '50s or earlier, preferably). I like the hardnosed attitude of those books. In college, I studied acting and film, both of which turned out to be very valuable for illustration. Acting for how to approach a character and film for editing/pacing and composition.

The New Girl . . . and Me, by Jacqui Robbins is Matt Phelan's first picture book. *School Library Journal* marvels that "the characters' facial expressions are filled with personality and convey a wide range of emotion," achieved through Phelan's spare illustration style. *The New Girl . . . and Me* chronicles the growing friendship of two young girls as they overcome shyness and bond over a pet iguana name Igabelle.

When you began work on your first picture book, were there any surprises during the production process? How was that experience for you?

Yes, there were a few scary little surprises. Because I used such fine lines and light washes there was some difficulty reproducing the paintings. Luckily, the art director patiently guided me through my many revisions. I learned a great deal from that experience. I'm still learning.

Can you talk a little about the varying challenges in illustrating a picture book versus a novel?

With a picture book, the illustrator has a large role in creating the tone and mood of the reading experience—the world of that book. You are very conscious of the entire book at all times, particularly the pacing and page turns. With novel illustration, you come in now and then to accent something in the prose. I sometimes like to illustrate the moment that occurs after the text, in other words give the reader something to linger over after reading the page, something that will hopefully enhance the story.

You've worked on books with multiple publishers and on different types of projects. Is there much difference from publisher to publisher as far as the process?

The general process is pretty similar as far as sketches, revisions, and final art goes. The difference comes in how the team operates. Sometimes I'm in direct contact with the art director only, sometimes I'm in direct contact with the editor only, other times it's a combination.

How did you land your first book illustration job, *The Seven Wonders of Sassafras Springs* for which you worked in black and white?

Polly Kanevsky, who was then an art director at Atheneum, reviewed my portfolio at a SCBWI Fall Philly regional event and brought my work to the attention of Dick Jackson, who hired me to illustrate *The New Girl . . . and Me*. While I was on the early stages of work on that book, Polly was trying to find an illustrator for *Sassafras*. One day she remembered that my portfolio included some black and white illustrations of kids in the Dust Bowl. She showed them to Caitlyn Dlouhy and Betty Birney (the editor and the author) and I got the job. Since that book had an earlier publication date, I put *The New Girl* on hold and went to work on *Sassafras*.

On your Web site (www.mattphelan.com) you mention that you had a string of jobs that you suppose gave you character. Can you tell me about a few of them? How much more do you like your current job as a full-time illustrator?

I learned something from every job. From being a bookseller, I became convinced that children's books were what I really wanted to do when I grew up. From screenwriting, I learned how to revise and survive rejection. From copywriting, I learned how to work on a tight deadline, multitask, and deal with clients. I'm happy for all of the experience, but being an illustrator is by far the best job I've ever had. Nothing comes close.

What are the best and worst things about being a full-time illustrator?

The best things include getting to do what I love for my living, and working with extraordinary authors, editors, and art directors who all strive to create the very best books we can. Worst things? I miss getting free office supplies . . . and the water cooler. The water cooler was nice.

Matt Phelan illustrated Susan Patron's Newbery winner *The Higher Power of Lucky*, a novel about a young girl trying to cope with her mother's death. Phelan approaches "illustrating a character not unlike how an actor approaches playing a role. I try to understand what the character is thinking and feeling at that moment." Once he captures that feeling, "the other details hopefully will fall into place."

You have a rep to help you market your work. How did that relationship come about? What kind of promotion does your rep handle and what types of self-promotion do you do on your own?

I actually have a literary agent (Rebecca Sherman at Writers House) as opposed to an art rep. She contacted me after seeing a galley of *The New Girl*. I think she was secretly hoping that I'd turn out to be a writer as well as an illustrator, and luckily for both of us, I have. Promotion, other than singing my praises to editors, is mostly up to me. I plan to start visiting schools and libraries soon.

So you haven't yet done any book signings or appearances?

The only signings I've done so far have been at Children's Book World, a great store just outside of Philadelphia. Every year they have a big night where a lot of local writers and illustrators sign and mingle. It's very low pressure being just one of a crowd . . . and when that crowd includes Jerry and Eileen Spinelli, David Wiesner, and Charles Santore, it's easy to fade into the corners if you want. Hopefully, I'll work up the nerve to do my own signings some day.

Do you have any tips for illustrators in regards to creating a good Web site? Putting together an effective portfolio?

Art directors and editors have told me that they like the simplicity of my site. Keep the bells and whistles to a minimum and make it easy to find your pictures. For my portfolio, I tried to create illustrations that—although they weren't—looked like they were from an actual story. If someone asked, ''what book is this from?'' then I knew it was working. It's also good to illustrate a character in three separate situations in order to show that you can consistently draw a character. Also, don't be afraid to draw a few unhappy kids. Most of my books have had characters that rarely smile until the end.

Why did you decide to start your illustration blog, planetham.blogspot.com? Is this a good way for you to accomplish not-quite-daily practice drawing or is it more for feedback or for fun?

All three. At the end of my first year as an illustrator, I realized that I had very little work that wasn't in some way related to the books I had illustrated. So now I try to draw every day, and some of those sketches make it onto the sketch blog. It's important to keep generating your own work. You never know what might be sparked from a sketch. I also love reading comments from people who live all over the world, and then having the opportunity to visit their blogs.

I was excited to hear you've got an upcoming graphic novel, *A Storm in the Barn*, for which you're both the author and the illustrator. Will you be doing more writing in the future? Please tell me about this as well as your other upcoming projects.

I'm currently working on *A Storm in the Barn*, which is a graphic novel set in the Dust Bowl. The story mixes folklore, myth, and the Oz books with the true-life strangeness of Kansas in the dirty '30s. The environment and living conditions of that time were so incredibly bizarre that it's not a far stretch to introduce some supernatural creepiness into the mix. After that, I start work on another graphic novel about three people who took solo journeys around the world at the end of the 19th century. It's based on true stories, but I'll be taking some liberties here and there. Both graphic novels will be published by Candlewick.

Although I'd like to write my own picture books one day, I still love illustrating other people's stories. I've finished three picture books for 2008 releases, including *Big George*, a biography of Washington by Anne Rockwell (Harcourt); *Always*, by Ann Stott (Candlewick); and *Two of a Kind*, the second book by Jacqui Robbins (Atheneum/Richard Jackson).

Have you ever gotten useful career advice? What's your best advice for aspiring illustrators interested in working in children's publishing?

Although I obviously didn't get this advice directly, I've always been inspired by the Goethe quote: ''Whatever you can do or dream you can, begin it. Boldness has genius, power and magic in it.''

As far as advice to aspiring illustrators goes, I really think it comes down to two things. Concentrate on creating the best portfolio you possibly can, then get that portfolio in front of people who can hire you. For the second step, you never know what's going to work, so try everything. I've gotten work as a result of a conference portfolio review, from a slush pile mailing, and from an author seeing my Web site and telling his editor about it. But the most important piece in the puzzle is your portfolio. Fortunately, you have complete control over that.

—Alice Pope

CREATIVE EDUCATION

Imprint of The Creative Company, 123 South Broad St., Mankato MN 56001. (800)445-6209. Fax: (507)388-1364. **Manuscript Acquisitions:** Aaron Frisch. Publishes 5 picture books/year; 20 young readers/year; 30 middle readers/year; 20 young adult titles/year. 5% of books by first-time authors.

Fiction Picture books, young readers, middle readers, young adult/teens: adventure, animal, anthology, contemporary, folktales, history, nature/environment, poetry, sports. Average word length: 1,500. Recently published *The Adventures of Pinocchio*, by Carlo Collodi, illustrated by Roberto Innocanti (ages 10-adult); *A Was an Apple Pie*, illustrated by Etienne Delessert (ages 5-adult); *Galileo's Universe*, by J. Patrick Lewis, illustrated by Tom Curry (ages 12-adult).

Nonfiction Picture books, young readers, middle readers, young adults: animal, arts/crafts, biography, careers, geography, health, history, hobbies, multicultural, music/dance, nature/environment, religion, science, social issues, special needs, sports. Average word length: young readers—500; middle readers—3,000; young adults-6,500. Recently published *My First Look At Science*, by Melissa Gish (age 7, young reader); *The Wild World of Animals*, by Mary Hoff (age 11, middle reader); *Martin Luther King, Jr.*, by Jennifer Fandel (age 14, young adult/teen).

How to Contact/Writers Fiction: Submit complete ms. Nonfiction: Submit outline/synopsis and 2 sample chapters. Responds to queries in 6 weeks; mss in 3 months. Publishes book 2 years after acceptance. Do not accept illustration packages.

Photography Buys stock. Contact: Nicole Becker, photo editor. Model/property releases not required; captions required. Uses b&w prints. Submit cover letter, promo piece. Ms. and photographer guidelines available for SAE.

Tips "We are primarily a nonfiction publisher and are very selective about fiction picture books, publishing five or fewer annually. Nonfiction submissions should be in series (of 4, 6, or 8), rather than single."

CRICKET BOOKS

Carus Publishing Company, 70 East Lake St., Suite 300, Chicago IL 60601. Web site: www.cricketmag.com. **Art Acquisitions:** John Sandford.

 • Cricket books has a moratorium on manuscripts. Queries from agents and authors who have worked with Cricket Books are still welcome. Direct queires to Jenny Gillespie. Watch Web site for updates.

How to Contact Not accepting unsolicited mss. See Web site for details and updates on submissions policy.

Illustration Works with 4 illustrators/year. Use color and b&w. Illustration only: Submit samples, tearsheets. Contact: John Sanford. Responds only if interested. Samples returned with SASE; sample filed.

Tips "You may consider submitting your manuscript to one of our magazines, as we sometimes serialize longer selections and always welcome age-appropriate stories, poems, and nonfiction articles."

CSS PUBLISHING

517 S. Main St., Lima OH 45802-4503. (419)227-1818. Fax: (419)222-4647. E-mail: acquisitions@csspub.com. Web site: www.csspub.com. **Manuscript Acquisitions:** Stan Purdum. Publishes books with religious themes. "We are seeking material for use by clergy, Christian education directors and Sunday school teachers for mainline Protestant churches. Our market is mainline Protestant clergy."

Fiction Young readers, middle readers, young adults: religion, religious poetry and humor. Needs children's sermons (object lesson) for Sunday morning worship services; dramas for Advent, Christmas or Epiphany involving children for church services; activity and craft ideas for Sunday school or mid-week services for children (particularly pre-school and first and second grade). Published *That Seeing, They May Believe*, by Kenneth Mortonson (lessons for adults to present during worship services to pre-schoolers-third graders); *What Shall We Do With This Baby?*, by Jan Spence (Christmas Eve worship service involving youngsters from newborn babies-high school youth); *Miracle in the Bethlehem Inn*, by Mary Lou Warstler (Advent drama involving pre-schoolers-high school youth and adult.)

Nonfiction Young readers, middle readers, young adults: religion. Young adults only: social issues and self help. Needs children's sermons (object lesson) for Sunday morning worship services; dramas for Advent, Christmas or Epiphany involving children for church services; activity and craft ideas for Sunday school or mid-week services for children (particularly pre-school and first and second grade). Published *Mustard Seeds*, by Ellen Humbert (activity bulletins for pre-schoolers-first graders to use during church); *This Is The King*, by Cynthia Cowen.

How to Contact/Writers Responds to queries in 2 weeks; mss in 3 months. Publishes a book 9 months after acceptance. Will consider simultaneous submissions.

Terms Work purchased outright from authors. Manuscript guidelines and book catalog available for SASE and on Web site.

DARBY CREEK PUBLISHING

7858 Industrial Pkwy., Plain City OH 43064. (614)873-7955. Fax: (614)873-7135. E-mail: info@darbycreekpublishing.com. **Manuscript/Art Acquisitions:** Tanya Dean, editorial director. Publishes 10-15 children's books/year.

● Darby Creek does not publish picture books.

Fiction Middle readers, young adult. Recently published *The Warriors*, by Joseph Bruchac (ages 10 and up); *Dog Days*, by David Lubar (ages 10 and up); *Four Things My Geeky-Jock-of-a-Best-Friend Must Do in Europe*, by Jane Harrington.

Nonfiction Middle readers: biography, history, science, sports. Recently published *Albinio Animals*, by Kelly Milner Halls, illustrated by Rick Spears; *Miracle: The True Story of the Wreck of the Sea Venture*, by Gail Karwoski.

How to Contact/Writers Accepts international material only with U.S. postage on SASE for return; no IRCs. Fiction/nonfiction: Submit publishing history and/or résumé and complete ms for short works or outline/synopsis and 2-3 sample chapters for longer works, such as novels. Responds in 6 weeks. Does not consider previously published work.

Illustration Illustrations only: Send photocopies and résumé with publishing history. ''Indicate which samples we may keep on file and include SASE and appropriate packing materials for any samples you wish to have returned.''

Terms Offers advance-against-royalty contracts.

Tips ''We like to see nonfiction with a unique slant that is kid friendly, well researched and endorsed by experts. We're interested in fiction or nonfiction with sports themes for future lists. No series, please. We do not publish picture books of any kind.''

▢ MAY DAVENPORT, PUBLISHERS

26313 Purissima Rd., Los Altos Hills CA 94022-4539. (650)947-1275. Fax: (650)947-1373. E-mail: mdbooks@earthlink.net. Web site: www.maydavenportpublishers.com. **Acquisitions:** May Davenport, editor/publisher. Publishes 1-2 picture books/year; 2-3 young adult titles/year. 99% of books by first-time authors. Seeks books with literary merit. ''We like to think that we are selecting talented writers who have something humorous to write about today's unglued generation in 30,000-50,000 words for teens and young adults in junior/senior high school before they become tomorrow's 'functional illiterates.' We are interested in publishing literature that teachers in middle and high schools can use in their Language Arts, English and Creative Writing courses. There's more to literary fare than the chit-chat Internet dialog and fantasy trips on television with cartoons or humanoids.'' This publisher is overstocked with juvenile books.

Fiction Young readers, young adults: contemporary, humorous fictional literature for use in English courses in junior-senior high schools in U.S. Average word length: 40,000-60,000. Recently published *Charlie and Champ*, by Alysson Wagoner (a fun way to learn phonics coloring book, ages 5-7); *Suriving Sarah, the Sequel: Brown Bug & China Doll*, by Dinah Leigh (novel set in post-WWII Manhattan, ages 15-18);*The Lesson Plan*, by Irvin Gay (about an illiterate black boy who grows up to become a teacher, ages 15-18); *A Life on the Line*, by Michael Horton (about a juvenile delinquent boy who becomes a teacher, ages 15-18); *Making My Escape*, by David Lee Finkle (about a young boy who daydreams movie-making in outer space to escape unhappy family life, ages 12-18); *Matthew Livingston and the Prison of Souls*, by Marco Conelli (about a high-tech solution to a crime, ages 12-18).

Nonfiction Teens: humorous. Recently published *The Runaway Game*, by Kevin Casey (a literary board game of street life in Hollywood, ages 15-18).

How to Contact/Writers Fiction: Query. Responds to queries/mss in 3 weeks. Mss returned with SASE. Publishes a book 6-12 months after acceptance.

Illustration Works with 1-2 illustrators/year. ''Have enough on file for future reference.'' Responds only if interested. Samples returned with SASE; samples filed. Originals returned at job's completion.

Terms Pays authors royalty of 15% based on retail price; negotiable. Pays ''by mutual agreement, no advances.'' Pays illustrators by the project (range: $75-350). Book catalog, ms guidelines free on request with SASE.

Tips ''Write stories with teen narrators and activities that today's teenagers can relate to. Entertain teenagers who don't, can't, won't read printed pages so your book will be useful to teachers in high schools nationwide.''

DAWN PUBLICATIONS

12402 Bitney Springs Rd., Nevada City CA 95959. (530)274-7775. Fax: (530)275-7778. Web site: www.dawnpub.com. Book publisher. Co-Publishers: Muffy Weaver and Glenn J. Hovemann. **Acquisitions:** Glenn J. Hovemann. Publishes works with holistic themes dealing with nature. ''Dawn Publications is dedicated to inspiring in children a deeper appreciation and understanding of nature.''

Fiction Picture books exploring relationships with nature. No fantasy or legend.

Nonfiction Picture books: animal, nature/environment. Prefers ''creative nonfiction.''

How to Contact/Writers Query or submit complete ms. Responds to queries/mss in 3 months maximum. Publishes a book 18 months after acceptance. Will consider simultaneous submissions.

Illustration Works with 5 illustrators/year. Will review ms/illustration packages from artists. Query; send ms with dummy. Illustrations only: Query with samples, résumé.

Terms Pays authors royalty based on net sales. Offers advance. Book catalog and ms guidelines available online.

Tips Looking for "picture books expressing nature awareness with inspirational quality leading to enhanced self-awareness. Usually no animal dialogue."

DELACORTE AND DOUBLEDAY BOOKS FOR YOUNG READERS

Random House Children's Books, 1745 Broadway, Mail Drop 9-2, New York NY 10019. (212)782-9000. Web sites: www.randomhouse.com/kids, www.randomhouse.com/teens. Imprints of Random House Children's Books. 75% of books published through agents.

- Delacorte publishes middle-grade and young adult fiction. See Writing for Boys by Delacorte Editor Krista Marino on page 37. Also see First Books on page 119 for an interview with Tina Ferraro, author of Delacorte title *Top Ten Uses for an Unworn Prom Dress*. Delacorte title *Hattie Big Sky*, by Kirby Larson, won a Newbery Honor Medal in 2007.

How to Contact/Writers Unsolicited mss are only being accepted as submissions to either the Delacorte Dell Yearling Contest for a First Middle-Grade Novel or Delacorte Press Contest for a First Young Adult Novel (contemporary). See Web site for submission guidelines. Query letters for novels are accepted when addresses to a specific editor and must be accompanied by a SASE. No e-mail queires.

DIAL BOOKS FOR YOUNG READERS

Penguin Young Readers Group, 345 Hudson St., New York NY 10014. Web site: www.penguin.com. Vice President and Publisher: Lauri Hornik. **Acquisitions:** Nancy Mercado, senior editor; Liz Waniewski, editor; Alisha Niehaus, editor; Jessica Dandino, assistant editor. **Art Director:** Lily Malcom. Publishes 2 young readers/year; 8 middle readers/year; 12 young adult titles/year.

Fiction Picture books, young readers: adventure, animal, fantasy, folktales, history, humor, multicultural, poetry, sports. Middle readers, young adults: adventure, fantasy, folktales, history, humor, multicultural, poetry, problem novels, science fiction, sports, mystery/adventure. Recently published *Defining Dulcie*, by Paul Acampora (agent 10 and up); *On the Wings of Heroes*, by Richard Peck (ages 10 and up); *The Rules of Survival*, by Nancy Werlin (ages 14 and up); *The Little Red Hen*, by Jerry Pinkney (ages 3-7); *Stick*, by Steve Breen (ages 4-8).

Nonfiction Will consider query letters for submissions of outstanding literary merit. Picture books, young readers, middle readers: biography, history, sports. Young adults: biography, history, sports. Recently published *A Strong Right Arm*, by Michelle Y. Green (ages 10 and up); *We the Kids*, by David Catrow (ages 5 and up).

How to Contact/Writers "Due to the overwhelming number of unsolicited manuscripts we receive, we at Dial Books for Young Readers have had to change our submissions policy: As of August 1, 2005, Dial will no longer respond to your unsolicited submission unless interested in publishing it. Please do not include SASE with your submission. You will not hear from dial regarding the status of your submission unless we are interested, in which case you can expect a reply from us within four months. We accept entire picture book manuscripts and a maximum of 10 pages for longer works (novels, easy-to-reads). When submitting a portion of a longer work, please provide an accompanying cover letter that briefly describes your manuscript's plot, genre (i.e. easy-to-read, middle grade or YA novel), the intended age group, and your publishing credits, if any."

Illustration "Art samples should be sent to attn: Dial Design and will not be returned without SASE. Never send original art. Please do not phone, fax, or email to inquire after your art submission."

Terms Pays authors and illustrators in royalties based on retail price. Average advance payment varies. Catalogue available for 9×12 envelope with four stamps. "This is one way to become informed as to the style, subject matter, and format of our books."

Tips "Because confirmation postcards are easily separated from or hidden within the manuscript, we do not encourage you to include them with your submission. Please send only one manuscript at a time. Never send cassettes, original artwork, marketing plans, or faxes and do not send submissions by e-mail. Please know that we only keep track of requested manuscripts; we cannot track unsolicited submissions due to the volume we receive each day, so kindly refrain from calling, faxing or e-mailing to inquire after the status of an unsolicited submission as we will be unable to assist you. If you have not received a reply from us after four months, you can safely assume that we are not presently interested in publishing your work."

DK PUBLISHING, INC.

375 Hudson St., New York NY 10014. Web site: www.dk.com. **Acquisitions:** submissions editor. "DK publishes photographically illustrated nonfiction for children ages 4 and up."

- DK Publishing does not accept unagented manuscripts or proposals.

☐ DNA PRESS, LLC

P.O. Box 572, Eagleville PA 19408. Fax: (501)694-5495. E-mail: editors@dnapress.com. Web site: www.dnapress.com. **Acquisitions:** Xela Schenk. Publishes 1 picture book/year; 2 middle readers/year; 4 young adult titles/year. 75% of books by first-time authors.

Fiction Picture books: health. Young adults: adventure, contemporary, fantasy.

Nonfiction All levels: science, investing for children, business for children.

How to Contact/Writers Fiction/nonfiction: Submit complete, disposable ms and SASE. Responds to queries in 1 month; mss in 6 weeks. Publishes book 9-12 months after acceptance.

Illustration Works with 1 illustrator/year. Uses b&w artwork only. Reviews ms/illustration packages from artists. Send ms with dummy. Illustrations only: Send Web page. Responds in 1 month. Samples not returned.

Terms Pays authors royalty of 8-15% based on net sales. Pays illustrators and photographers by the project. Sends galleys to authors; dummies to illustrators.

Tips Children's writers and illustrators should pay attention to "how-to books and books in which science knowledge is communicated to the reader. We focus on bringing science to the young reader in various forms of fiction and nonfiction books. For updates, see our Web site or the Web site of our distributor, IPG Book (www.ipgbook.com)."

☐ DOG-EARED PUBLICATIONS

P.O. Box 620863, Middletown WI 53562-0863. (608)831-1410 or (608)831-1410. Fax: (608)831-1410. E-mail: field@dog-eared.com. Web site: www.dog-eared.com. **Art Acquisitions:** Nancy Field, publisher. Publishes 2-3 middle readers/year. 1% of books by first-time authors. "Dog-Eared Publications creates action-packed nature books for children. We aim to turn young readers into environmentally aware citizens and to foster a love for science and nature in the new generation.

Nonfiction Middle readers: activity books, animal, nature/environment, science. Average word length: varies. Recently published *Discovering Sharks and Rays*, by Nancy Field, illustrated by Michael Maydak (middle readers, activity book); *Leapfrogging Through Wetlands*, by Margaret Anderson, Nancy Field and Karen Stephenson, illustrated by Michael Maydak (middle readers, activity book); *Ancient Forests*, by Margaret Anderson, Nancy Field and Karen Stephenson, illustrated by Sharon Torvik (middle readers, activity book).

How to Contact/Writers Nonfiction: **Currently not accepting unsolicited mss**.

Illustration Works with 2-3 illustrators/year. Reviews ms/illustration packages from artists. Submit query and a few art samples. Illustrations only: Query with samples. Responds only if interested. Samples not returned; samples filed. "Interested in realistic, nature art!"

Terms Pays authors royalty based on wholesale price. Offers advances (amount varies). Pays illustrators royalty based on wholesale price. Sends galleys to authors. Originals returned to artist at job's completion. Brochure available for SASE and 1 first-class stamp or on Web site.

☑ DUTTON CHILDREN'S BOOKS

Penguin Group (USA), 345 Hudson St., New York NY 10014-4502. (212)414-3700. Web site: www.penguin.com/youngreaders. **Acquisitions:** Stephanie Owens Lurie (picture books, middle-grade fiction); Lucia Monfried (easy-to-read, middle-grade fiction); Maureen Sullivan (middle-grade fiction, picture books); Julie Strauss-Gabel (picture books, middle-grade fiction, young adult). **Art Acquisitions:** Sara Reynolds, art director. Publishes approximately 50% fiction—fewer picture books, mostly YA and mid-grade novels. 10% of books by first-time authors.

- Dutton is open to query letters only. Dutton title *An Abundance of Katherines*, by John Green, won a Printz Honor Medal in 2007.

Fiction Picture books: adventure, animal, history, humor, multicultural, nature/environment, poetry, contemporary. Young readers: adventure, animal, contemporary, fantasy. Middle readers: adventure, animal, contemporary, fantasy, history, multicultural, nature/environment. Young adults: adventure, animal, contemporary, fantasy, history, multicultural, nature/environment, poetry. Recently published *The Schwa Was Here*, by Neal Shusterman (middle grade); *Skippyjon Jones*, by Juday Schachner (picture book); *Looking for Alaska*, by John Green (young adult).

Nonfiction Picture books. Recently published *With a Little Bit of Luck*, by Dennis Fradin.

How to Contact/Writers Query only. Does not accept unsolicited mss. Responds to queries in 3 months. Publishes a book 12-18 months after acceptance. Will consider simultaneous submissions.

Illustration Works with 40-60 illustrators/year. Reviews ms/illustration packages from artists. Query first. Illustrations only: Query with samples; send résumé, portfolio, slides—no original art please. Responds to art samples only if interested. Samples returned with SASE; samples filed. Original artwork returned at job's completion.

Terms Pays authors royalty of 4-10% based on retail price or outright purchase. Book catalog, ms guidelines for SAE with 8 first-class stamps. Pays illustrators royalty of 2-5% based on retail price unless jacket illustration—then pays by flat fee. Pays photographers by the project or royalty based on retail price.

Tips "Avoid topics that appear frequently. Illustrators: "We would like to see samples and portfolios from potential illustrators of picture books (full color), young novels (b&w) and jacket artists (full color)." Dutton is actively building its fiction lists, particularly upper YA titles. Humor welcome across all genres.

EDCON PUBLISHING

30 Montauk Blvd., Oakdale NY 11769. (631)567-7227. Fax: (631)567-8745. Web site: www.edconpublishing.com. **Manuscript Acquisitions:** Janic Cobes. Publishes 12 young readers/year, 12 middle readers/year, 12 young adult titles/year. 30% of books by first-time authors. Looking for workbooks in the areas of math, science, reading and history that include student activities. All classic adaptations are assigned.

Fiction Young readers, middle readers, young adult/teens: hi-lo. Average word length: young readers—4,000; middle readers—6,000; young adults—8,000. Recently published *A Midsummer Night's Dream*, adaptation by Laura Algieri; *Twelfth Night*, adaptation by Julianne Davidow; *The Merchant of Venice*, adaptation by Rachel Armington.

How to Contact/Writers Fiction and workbooks: Submit outline/synopsis and 1 sample chapter. Responds to queries/mss in 1 month. Publishes book 6 months after acceptance. Will consider simultaneous submissions.

Illustration Works with 6 illustrators/year. Reviews ms/illustration packages from artists. Query. Illustrations only: Send postcard samples, SASE. Responds in 2 weeks. Samples returned with SASE; samples filed.

Terms Work purchased outright from authors for up to $1,000. Pays illustrators by the project (range: $250-$750). Book catalog available for $8^1/_2 \times 11$ SASE and $1.35 postage; ms and art guidelines available for SAE. Catalog available on Web site.

EDUCATORS PUBLISHING SERVICE

Division of School Specialty Publishing, P.O. Box 9031, Cambridge MA 02139-9031. (617)547-6706. Fax: (617)547-3805. E-mail: epsbooks@epsbooks.com. Web site: www.epsbooks.com. **Manuscript Acquisitions:** Charlie Heinle. **Art Acquisitions:** Julie Webster, managing editor. Publishes 30-40 educational books/year. 50% of books by first-time authors.

How to Contact/Writers Responds to only if interested. Publishes book 6-12 months after acceptance. Will consider e-mail submissions, simultaneous submissions, previously published work. See Web site for submission guidelines.

Illustration Works with 12-18 illustrators/year. Reviews ms/illustration packages from artists. Query. Illustrations only: Query with samples; send promo sheet. Responds only if interested. Samples not returned; samples filed.

Photography Buys stock and assigns work. Submit cover letter, samples.

Terms Pays authors royalty of 5-12% based on retail price or work purchased outright from authors. Offers advances. Pays illustrators and photographers by the project. Sends galleys to authors. Book catalog free. All imprints included in a single catalog. Catalog available on Web site.

Tips "We accept queries from educators writing for the school market, primarily in the reading and language arts areas, grades K-8, with a focus on struggling readers. We are interested in materials that follow certain pedagogical constraints (such as decodable texts and leveled readers) and we would consider queries and samples from authors who might be interested in working with us on ongoing or future projects."

EDUPRESS, INC.

W5527 State Road 106, Ft. Atkinson WI 53538. (920)563-9571. Fax: (920)563-7395. E-mail: edupress@highsmith.com. Web site: www.edupressinc.com. **Manuscript Acquisitions:** Sandra Harris, product development manager. "Our mission is to create products that make kids want to go to school!"

How to Contact/Writers Nonfiction: Submit complete ms. Responds to queries/mss in 3 months. Publishes book 1-2 years after acceptance.

Illustration Query with samples. Contact. Contact: Sandra Harris, product development manager. Responds only if interested. Samples returned with SASE.

Photography Buys stock.

Terms Work purchased outright from authors. Pays illustrators by the project. Book catalog available at no cost. Catalog available on Web site.

Tips "We are looking for unique, quality supplemental materials for Pre-K through eighth grade. We publish all subject aread in many different formats, including games. Our materials are intended for classroom and home schooling use."

EERDMAN'S BOOKS FOR YOUNG READERS

An imprint of Wm. B. Eerdmans Publishing Co., 2140 Oak Industrial Dr. NE, Grand Rapids , MI 49505 (616) 459-4591. Fax: (616) 776-7683. E-mail: youngreaders@eerdmans.com. Web site: www.eerdmans.com/youngre

aders. We are an independent book packager/producer. **Writers contact:** Acquisitions Editor. **Illustrators contact:** Gayle Brown, Art director. Produces 16 picture books/year; 3 middle readers/year; 3 young adult books/year. 10% of books by first-time authors. ''We seek to engage young minds with words and pictures that inform and delight, inspire and entertain. From board books for babies to picture books, nonfiction, and novels for children and young adults, our goal is to produce quality literature for a new generation of readers. We believe in books!''

Fiction: Picture books: animal, concept, contemporary, folktales, history, humor, multicultural, nature/environment, poetry, religion, special needs, social issues, sports, suspense. Young readers: animal, concept, contemporary, folktales, history, humor, multicultural, poetry, religion, special needs, social issues, sports, suspense. Middle readers: adventure, contemporary, history, humor, multicultural, nature/environment, problem novels, religion, social issues, sports, suspense. Young adults/teens: adventure, contemporary, folktales, history, humor, multicultural, nature/environment, problem novels, religion, sports, suspense. Average word length: picture books-1,000; middle readers-15,000; young adult-45,000. Recently published *Mr. Ferlinghetti's Poem*, illustrated by David Frampton (picture book, ages 5 and up); *A World of Prayers*, by Jeremy Brooks, illustrated by Elena Gomez (picture book, all ages) *Dancing with Elvis*, by Lynda Stephenson (novel, ages 12 and up); *The Cricket Winter*, by Felice Holman (middle reader fiction, ages 8 and up).

Nonfiction Middle readers: biography, history, multicultural, nature/environment, religion, social issues. Young adults/teens: biography, history, multicultural, nature/environment, religion, social issues. Average word length: middle readers-35,000; young adult books-35,000. Recently published *C.S. Lewis: The Man Behind Narnia* by Beatrice Gormley.

How to Contact/Writers: We only consider submissions send EXCLUSIVELY to Eerdmans. YA and Middle Reader fiction: Please send query, synopsis, and 3 sample chapters. Responds to exclusive queries/mss in 3-5 months. ''We no longer acknowledge or respond to unsolicited manuscripts. Exceptions will be made only for exclusive submissions marked as such on outside envelope.''

Illustration Accepts material from international illustrators. Works with 10-12 illustrators/year. Uses color artwork primarily. Reviews work for future assignments. If interested in illustrating future titles, send promo sheet. Submit samples to Gayle Brown, art director. Samples not returned. Samples filed.

Terms Offers advance against royalties. Author sees galleys for review. Illustrators see proofs for review. Originals returned to artist at job's completion. Catalog available for 8×10 SASE and 4 first-class stamps. Offers writer's guidelines for SASE. See Web site for writer's guidelines. (www.eerdmans.com/youngreaders/submit.htm)

Tips ''Find out who Eerdmans is before submitting a manuscript. Look at our Web site, request a catalog, and check out our books.''

ENSLOW PUBLISHERS INC.

Box 398, 40 Industrial Rd., Berkeley Heights NJ 07922-0398. Fax: (908)771-0925. E-mail: info@enslow.com. Web site: www.enslow.com orwww.myreportlinks.com. **Acquisitions:** Brian D. Enslow, vice president. Imprint: MyReportLinks.com Books. Publishes 30 young readers/year; 70 middle readers/year; 100 young adult titles/year. 30% of books by first-time authors.

● Enslow Imprint MyReportLinks.com Books produces books on animals, states, presidents, continents, countries, and a variety of other topics for middle readers and young adults, and offers links to online sources of information on topics covered in books.

Nonfiction Young readers, middle readers, young adults: animal, arts/crafts, biography, careers, geography, health, history, multicultural, nature/environment, science, social issues, sports. Middle readers, young adults: hi-lo. ''Enslow is moving into the elementary (grades 3-4) level and is looking for authors who can write biography and suggest other nonfiction themes at this level.'' Average word length: young readers—2,000; middle readers—5,000; young adult—18,000. Published *It's About Time! Science Projects*, by Robert Gardner (grades 3-6, science); *Georgia O'Keeffe: Legendary American Painter*, by Jodie A. Shull (grades 6-12, biography); *California: A MyReportLinks.com Book*, by Jeff Savaga (grades 5-8, social studies/history).

How to Contact/Writers Nonfiction: Send for guidelines. Query. Responds to queries/mss in 2 weeks. Publishes a book 18 months after acceptance. Will not consider simultaneous submissions.

Illustration Submit résumé, business card or tearsheets to be kept on file. Responds only if interested. Samples returned with SASE only.

Terms Pays authors royalties or work purchased outright. Pays illustrators by the project. Pays photographers by the project or per photo. Sends galleys to authors. Book catalog/ms guidelines available for $3, along with an 8½×11 SASE and $2 postage or via Web site.

FACTS ON FILE

132 W. 31st St., New York NY 10001. (212)967-8800. Fax: (212)967-9196. E-mail: editorial@factsonfile.com. Web site: www.factsonfile.com. Estab. 1941. Book publisher. Editorial Director: Laurie Likoff. **Acquisitions:**

Frank Darmstadt, science and technology/nature; Nicole Bowen, American history and women's studies; Jeff Soloway, language and literature; Owen Lancer, world studies; Jim Chambers, arts, health and entertainment. "We produce high-quality reference materials for the school library market and the general nonfiction trade." Publishes 25-30 young adult titles/year. 5% of books by first-time authors; 25% of books from agented writers; additional titles through book packagers, co-publishers and unagented writers.

Nonfiction Middle readers, young adults: animal, biography, careers, geography, health, history, multicultural, nature/environment, reference, religion, science, social issues and sports.

How to Contact/Writers Nonfiction: Submit outline/synopsis and sample chapters. Responds to queries in 10 weeks. Publishes a book 10-12 months after acceptance. Will consider simultaneous submissions. Sends galleys to authors. Book catalog free on request. Send SASE for submission guidelines.

Terms Submission guidelines available via Web site or with SASE.

Tips "Most projects have high reference value and fit into a series format."

FAITH KIDZ

Imprint of Cook Communications Ministries, 4050 Lee Vance View, Colorado Springs CO 80918. (719)536-0100. Fax: (719)536-3243. Web site: www.cookministries.com. **Acquisitions:** Mary McNeil, senior acquisitions editor. Publishes 3-5 picture books/year; 6-8 young readers/year; 6-12 middle readers/year. Less than 5% of books by first-time authors; 15% of books from agented authors. "All books have overt Christian values, but there is no primary theme."

  • Visit Web site to see when *Faith Kidz* is accepting manuscripts.

How to Contact/Writers Only accepts online submissions (www.cookministries.com/proposals).

Illustration Works with 15 illustrators/year. "Send color material I can keep." Query with samples; send résumé, promo sheet, portfolio, tearsheets. Responds in 6 months only if interested. Samples returned with SASE; samples filed. Contact: Art Department.

Terms Pays illustrators by the project, royalty or work purchased outright. Sends dummies to illustrators. Original artwork returned at job's completion.

Tips "We're looking for writers willing to writer for fee rather than royalty to contribute stories fo Bible story books."

⊠ FARRAR, STRAUS & GIROUX INC. √√

19 Union Square W., New York NY 10003. (212)741-6900. Fax: (212)633-2427. Web site: www.fsgkidsbooks.com. Estab. 1946. Book publisher. Imprints: Frances Foster Books, Melanie Kroupa Books. Children's Books Editorial Director: Margaret Ferguson. **Manuscript Acquisitions:** Margaret Ferguson, editorial director; Frances Foster, Frances Foster Books; Melanie Kroupa, Melanie Kroupa Books; Beverly Reingold, executive editor; Wesley Adams, executive editor; Janine O'Malley, editor. **Art Director:** Robbin Gourley, art director, Books for Young Readers. Publishes 40 picture books/year; 30 middle readers/year; 10 young adult titles/year. 5% of books by first-time authors; 20% of books from agented writers.

  • FSG title *Wings*, by William Loizeaux, won the Golden Kite Honor Award for Fiction in 2007.

Fiction All levels: all categories. "Original and well-written material for all ages." Recently published *Harlem Hustle*, by Janet McDonald; *So Sleepy Story*, by Uri Shulevitz.

Nonfiction All levels: all categories. "We publish only literary nonfiction."

How to Contact/Writers Fiction/nonfiction: for novels, query with outline/synopsis and 3 sample chapters; for picture books send complete ms. Do not fax or e-mail submissions or queries. Responds to queries/mss in 3 months. Publishes a book 18 months after acceptance. Will consider simultaneous submissions.

Illustration Works with 30-60 illustrators/year. Reviews ms/illustration packages from artists. Submit ms with 1 example of final art, remainder roughs. Do not send originals. Illustrations only: Query with tearsheets. Responds if interested in 2 months. Samples returned with SASE; samples sometimes filed.

Terms "We offer an advance against royalties for both authors and illustrators." Sends galleys to authors; dummies to illustrators. Original artwork returned at job's completion. Book catalog available for 9×12 SASE with $1.95 postage; ms guidelines for SASE1 first-class stamp, or can be viewed at www.fsgkidsbooks.com.

Tips "Study our catalog before submitting. We will see illustrator's portfolios by appointment. Don't ask for criticism and/or advice—due to the volume of submissions we receive, it's just not possible. Never send originals. Always enclose SASE."

⊠ FIRST SECOND BOOKS

Imprint of Roaring Brook Press, 175 5th Ave., New York NY 10010. (646)307-5095. Fax: (646)307-5285. E-mail: mail@firstsecondbooks.com. Web site: www.firstsecondbooks.com. Estab. 2005. **Editorial Director:** Mark Siegel. Publishes 3 young readers/year; 3 middle readers/year; 6 young abult titles/year. "First Second aims fo high-quality, literate graphic novels for a wide range—from middle grade to young adult to adult readers."

  • First Second title *American Born Chinese*, by Gene Luen Yang, won the Printz Award in 2007. *American*

Born Chinese is the first graphic novel to be recognized by the Michael L. Printz Committee.

Fiction Graphic novels. All books 96+ pages. Recently published *Sardine in Outer Space*, by Joann Sfar and Emmanuel Guibert (graphic novel, age 12 and up); *A.L.I.E.E.E.N.*, by Lewis Trondheim (graphic novel, ages 12 and up); *American Born Chinese*, by Gene Yang (graphic novel, teen).

Nonfiction Graphic novels. Recently published *Journey into Mohawk Country*, by George O'Connor (graphic novel, YA); *Kampung Boy*, by Lat (graphic novel, YA); *Missouri Boy*, by Leland Myrick (graphic novel, YA).

How to Contact/Writers Submit outline/synopsis and 1 samply chapter. Repsonds to queries/mss in 1-3 months. Will consider simultaneous submissions and previously published work.

Illustration Works with 12 illustrators/year. Uses color artwork only. Will review ms/illustration packages from artists. Submit ms with 2-3 pieces of final art. Contact: Mark Siegel, editorial director. Illustrations only: Query with samples. Contact: Mark Siegel, editorial director. Responds in 1-3 months. Samples not returned.

Terms Authors see galleys for review. Illustrators see dummies for review. Original artwork returned at job's completion. Book catalog available on Web site. Writer's and artist's guidelines available with SASE and on Web site.

☐ ☐ FIVE STAR PUBLICATIONS, INC.

P.O. Box 6698, Chandler AZ 85246-6698. (480)940-8182. Fax: (480)940-8787. E-mail: art@fivestarpublications.com. Web sites: www.FiveStarPublications.com,www.LittleFivestar.com,www.FiveStarLegends,com,www.FiveStarSleuths.com,www.SixPointsPress.com. **Art Acquisitions:** Sue DeFabis. Publishes 7 middle readers/year.

Nonfiction Recently published *Tic Talk Book: Living with Torette Syndrome*, by Dylan Peters, illustrated by Zachary Wendland (www.TicTalkBook.com); Cooking with Max: 45 Fun and Kind of Messy Recipes Kids Can Make, by Max Nania (www.CookingWithMax.com); Alfie's Bark Mitzvah, by Shari Cohen, songs by Cantor Marcello Gindlin, illustrated by Nadia Komorova (www.AlfiesBarkMitvah.com).

How to Contact/Writers Nonfiction: Query.

Illustration Works with 3 illustrators/year. Reviews ms/illustration packages from artists. Query. Illustrations only: Query with samples. Responds only if interested. Samples filed.

Photography Buys stock and assigns work. Works on assignment only. Submit letter.

Terms Pays illustrators by the project. Pays photographers by the project. Sends galleys to authors; dummies to illustrators.

☒ FLASHLIGHT PRESS ✓

3709 13th Ave., Brooklyn NY 11218. (718)288-8300. Fax: (718)972-6307. E-mail: editor@flashlightpress.com. Web site: www.flashlightpress.com. Estab. 2004. **Editor:** Shari Dash Greenspan. Publishes 2-3 picture books/year. 25% of books by first-time authors.

Fiction Picture books: contemporary, humor, multicultural. Average word length: 1,000. Recently published: *Grandpa for Sale*, by Dotti Enderle and Vicki Sansum, illustrated by T. Kyle Gentry (ages 4-8, picture book); *Getting to Know Ruben Plotnick*, by Roz Rosenbluth, illustrated by Maurie J. Manning (ages 5-9, picture book); *Alley Oops*, by Janice Levy, illustrated by Cynthia B. Decker (ages 5-9, picture book); *Carla's Sandwich*, by Debbie Herman, illustrated by Sheila Bailey (ages 4-8, picture book).

How to Contact/Writers Query by e-mail only. "Do not send queries or manuscripts by mail." Responds to queries in 1 week; mss in 1 month. Publishes a book 2 years after acceptance.

Illustration Works with 2-3 illustrators/year. Uses color artwork only. Query by e-mail with link to online portfolio. Contact: Shari Dash Greenspan, editor.

Terms Pays authors and illustrators royalty of 10% based on wholesale price. Offers advance of $500-1,000. Catalog available through IPG (Independent Publishers Group). E-mail to request catalog or view on Web site.

FLUX

Llewellyn Worldwide, Ltd., 2143 Wooddale Drive, Woodbury MN 55125. (651)312-8613. Fax: (651)291-1908. E-mail: submissions@fluxnow.com. Web site: www.fluxnow.com. **Acquisitions Editor:** Andrew Karre. Imprint estab. 2005; Lllewellyn estab. 1901. Publishes 21 young abult titles/year. 50% of books by first-time authors. "Flux seeks to publish authors who see YA as a point of view, not a reading level. We look for books that try to capture a slice of teenage experience. We are particularly interested in books that tell the stories of young adults in unexpected or surprising situations around the globe."

● See First Books on page 119 for an interview with Carrie Jones, author of Flux title *Tips on Having a Gay (ex) Boyfriend*.

Fiction Young Adults: adventure, contemporary, fantasy, history, humor, problem novels, religion, science fiction, sports, suspense. Average word length: 50,000. Recently published *Blue Is for Nightmares*, by Laurie Faria Stolarz; *Dream Spinner*, by Bonnie Dobkin; *How It's Done*, by Christine Kole MacLean.

How to Contact/Writers Query. Responds to queries in 1-2 weeks; mss in 1-3 months. Will consider simultaneous submissions and previously published work.

Terms Pays royalties of 10-15% based on wholesale price. Offers advance. Authors see galleys for review. Book catalog available on Web site. Writer's guidelines available for SASE or in Web site.

Tips ''Read contemporary teen books. Be aware of what else is out there. If you don't read teen books, you probably shouldn't write them. Know your audience. Write incredibly well. Do not condescend.''

FREE SPIRIT PUBLISHING

217 Fifth Ave. N., Suite 200, Minneapolis MN 55401-1299. (612)338-2068. Fax: (612)337-5050. E-mail: acquisitions@freespirit.com. Web site: www.freespirit.com. **Acquisitions:**Carla Valadez. Publishes 25-30 titles/year for pre-k-12, educators and parents. ''Free Spirit is the leading publisher of learning tools that support young people's social and emotional health. We help children and teens to think for themselves, succeed in life, and make a difference in the world.''

• Free Spirit does not accept fiction, poetry or storybook submissions.

How to Contact/Writers Accepts nonfiction submissions from prospective authors or through agents. ''Please review catalog and authors guidelines (both available online) before submitting proposal. Reponds to queries in 4-6 months. ''If you'd like material returned, enclose an SASE with sufficient postage. Write or e-mail for catalog and submission guidelines before sending submission. Accepts queries only—not submissions—by e-mail.

Illustration Works with 5 illustrators/year. Submit samples to creative director for consideration. If appropriate, samples will be kept on file and artist will be contacted if a suitable project comes up. Enclose SASE if you'd like materials returned.

Photography Submit samples to creative director for consideration. If appropriate, samples will be kept on file and photographer will be contacted if a suitable project comes up. Enclose SASE if you'd like materials returned.

Terms Pays authors royalty based on net receipts. Offers advance. Pays illustrators by the project. Pays photographers by the project or per photo.

Tips ''We do not publish fiction, poetry or picture storybooks, books with animals or mythical characters, books with religious content, or single biographies, autobiographies or memiors. We prefer books written in a practical, pshycologically sound, and positive style.''

FREESTONE/PEACHTREE, JR.

Peachtree Publishers, 1700 Chattahoochee Ave., Atlanta GA 30318-2112. (404)876-8761. Fax: (404)875-2578. E-mail: hello@peachtree-online.com. Web site: www.peachtree-online.com. **Acquisitions:** Helen Harriss. Publishes 4-8 young adult titles/year.

• Freestone and Peachtree, Jr. are imprints of Peachtree Publishers. See the listing for Peachtree for submission information. No e-mail or fax queries or submissions, please.

Fiction Picture books, young readers, middle readers, young adults: history, humor, multicultural, sports. Picture books: animal, folktales, nature/environment, special needs. Picture books, young readers: health. Middle readers, young adults/teens: adventure, contemporary, problem novels, suspense/mystery. Recently published *Dad, Jackie and Me*, by Myron Uhlberg, illustrated by Colin Bootman (ages 4-8, picture book); *Anna's Blizzard*, by Alison Hart, illustrated by Paul Bachem (ages 7-10; early reader); *Dog Sense*, by Sneed Collard (ages 8-12, middle reader).

Nonfiction Picture books, young readers, middle readers, young adults: history, sports. Picture books: animal, health, multicultural, nature/environment, science, social issues, special needs.

How to Contact Responds to queries/mss in 6 months.

Illustration Works with 10-20 illustrators/year. Responds only if interested. Samples not returned; samples filed. Originals returned at job's completion.

Terms Pays authors royalty. Pays illustrators by the project or royalty. Pays photographers by the project or per photo.

FRONT STREET BOOKS

Imprint of Boyds Mills Press, 862 Haywood Rd., Asheville NC 28806. (828)236-5940. Fax: (828)236-5935. E-mail: contactus@frontstreetbooks.com. Web site: www.frontstreetbooks.com. **Acquistions:** Joy Neaves, editor. Publishes 10-15 titles/year. ''We are a publisher of books for children and young adults. We do not publish pablum: we try to publish books that will attract, if not addict, children to literature, and books that are a pleasure to look at and a pleasure to hold, books that will be revelations to young minds.''

• Front Street has merged with and is now an imprint of Boyds Mills Press. See Front Street's Web site for submission guidelines and complete catalog. Front Street focuses on fiction, but will publish poetry, anthologies, nonfiction and high-end picture books.

Fiction Recently published *Keturah and Lord Death*, by Martiine Leavitt; *By the River*, by Steven Herrick; *The Letter Home*, by Timothy Decker.

How to Contact/Writers Fiction: Submit cover letter and complete ms if under 30 pages; submit cover letter, 1 or 2 sample chapters and plot summary if over 30 pages. Nonfiction: Submit detailed proposal and sample

chapters. Poetry: Submit no more than 25 poems. Include SASE with submissions if you want them returned. "Please allow four months for a response. If no response in four months, send a status query by mail."
Illustration "Send sample illustrations."
Terms Pays royalties.

⬚ FULCRUM PUBLISHING

4690 Table Mountain Drive, Suite 100 Golden CO 80403. (303)277-1623. Fax: (303)279-7111. Web site: www.fulcrum-books.com. **Manuscript Acquisitions:** T. Baker, acquisitions editor.
Nonfiction Middle and early readers: activity books, multicultural, nature/environment.
How to Contact/Writers Submit complete ms or submit outline/synopsis and 2 sample chapters. Responds to queries in 3 weeks; mss in 3 months.
Illustration Works with 2 illustrators/year. Reviews ms/illustration packages from artists. Send ms with dummy or submit ms with 3 pieces of final art. Send résumé, promotional literature and tearsheets. Contact: Ann Douden. Responds only if interested. Samples not returned; samples filed.
Photography Works on assignment only.
Terms Pays authors royalty based on wholesale price. Offers advances. Pays illustrators by the project or royalty based on wholesale price. Originals returned to artist at job's completion. Book catalog available for 9×12 SAE and 77¢ postage; ms guidelines available for SASE. Catalog available on Web site.
Tips "Research our line first. We are emphasizing science and nature nonfiction. We look for books that appeal to the school market and trade. Be sure to include SASE."

Ⓐ LAURA GERINGER BOOKS

Imprint of HarperCollins Publishers, 1350 Avenue of the Americas, New York NY 10019. Web site: www.haperchildrens.com. **Manuscript and Art Acquisitions:** Laura Geringer. Publishes 6 picture books/year; 2 young readers/year; 4 middle readers/year; 3 young adult titles/year. 15% of books by first-time authors.
Fiction Picture books, young readers: adventure, folktales, humor, multicultural, poetry. Middle readers: literary, adventure, fantasy, history, humor, poetry, suspense/mystery. Young adults/teens: literary, adventure, fantasy, history, humor, suspense/mystery. Average word length: picture books—500; young readers—1,000; middle readers—25,000; young adults—40,000. Recently published *If You Give a Pig a Party*, by Laura Numeroff, illustrated by Felicia Bond (ages 3-7); *So B.It*, by Sarah Weeks, (ages 10 and up); *Down the Rabbit Hole*, by Peter Abrahams (ages 10 and up).
How to Contact/Writers Only interested in agented material.
Illustration Works with 8 illustrators/year. Reviews ms/illustration packages from artists. Send ms with dummy and 3 pieces of final art. Illustrations only: Query with color photocopies. Contact: Laura Geringer, publisher. Responds only if interested. Samples returned with SASE.
Terms Book catalog available for 11×9 SASE and $2 postage; all imprints included in a single catalog.

GIBBS SMITH, PUBLISHER

P.O. Box 667, Layton UT 84041. (801)544-9800. Fax: (801)544-5582. E-mail: duribe@gibbs-smith.com. Web site: www.gibbs-smith.com. **Manuscript Acquisitions:** Jennifer Grillone, editor; Suzanne Taylor, vice president and editorial director (children's activity books). **Art Acquisitions:** Jennifer Grillone. Book publisher; co-publisher of Sierra Club Books for Children. Imprint: Gibbs Smith. Publishes 2-3 books/year. 50% of books by first-time authors. 50% of books from agented authors. "We accept submissions for picture books with particular interest in those with a Western (cowboy or ranch life style) theme or backdrop."
 ● Gibbs Smith is not accepting fiction at this time.
Nonfiction Middle readers: activity, arts/crafts, cooking, how-to, nature/environment, science. Average word length: picture books—under 1,000 words; activity books—under 15,000 words. Recently published *Hiding in a Fort*, by G. Lawson Drinkard, illustrated by Fran Lee (ages 7-12); *Sleeping in a Sack: Camping Activities for Kids*, by Linda White, illustrated by Fran Lee (ages 7-12).
How to Contact/Writers Nonfiction: Submit an outline and writing samples for activity books; query for other types of books. Responds to queries/mss in 2 months. Publishes a book 1-2 years after acceptance. Will consider simultaneous submissions. Manuscript returned with SASE.
Illustration Works with 2 illustrators/year. Reviews ms/illustration packages from artists. Query. Submit ms with 3-5 pieces of final art. Illustrations only: Query with samples; provide résumé, promo sheet, slides (duplicate slides, not originals). Responds only if interested. Samples returned with SASE; samples filed.
Terms Pays authors royalty of 2% based on retail price or work purchased outright ($500 minimum). Offers advances (average amount: $2,000). Pays illustrators by the project or royalty of 2% based on retail price. Sends galleys to authors; color proofs to illustrators. Original artwork returned at job's completion. Book catalog available for 9×12 SAE and $2.30 postage. Manuscript guidelines available—e-mail duribe@gibbs-smith.com.
Tips "We target ages 5-11. We do not publish young adult novels or chapter books."

Ⓐ DAVID R. GODINE, PUBLISHER

9 Hamilton Place, Boston MA 02108. (617)451-9600. Fax: (617)350-0250. Web site: www.godine.com. Estab. 1970. Book publisher. Publishes 1 picture book/year; 1 young reader/year; 1 middle reader/year. 10% of books by first-time authors; 90% of books from agented writers. "We publish books that matter for people who care."

● This publisher is no longer considering unsolicited manuscripts of any type.

Fiction Picture books: adventure, animal, contemporary, folktales, nature/environment. Young readers: adventure, animal, contemporary, folk or fairy tales, history, nature/environment, poetry. Middle readers: adventure, animal, contemporary, folk or fairy tales, history, mystery, nature/environment, poetry. Young adults/teens: adventure, animal, contemporary, history, mystery, nature/environment, poetry. Recently published *A Cottage Garden Alphabet*, by Andrea Wisnewski (picture book); *Henrietta and the Golden Eggs*, by Hanna Johansen, illustrated by Kathi Bhend.

Nonfiction Picture books: alphabet, animal, nature/environment. Young readers: activity books, animal, history, music/dance, nature/environment. Middle readers: activity books, animal, biography, history, music/dance, nature/environment. Young adults: biography, history, music/dance, nature/environment.

How to Contact/Writers Query. Publishes a book 3 years after acceptance. Include SASE for return of material.
Illustration Only interested in agented material. Works with 4-6 illustrators/year. Reviews ms/illustration packages from artists. "Submit roughs and one piece of finished art plus either sample chapters for very long works or whole ms for short works." Illustrations only: "After query, submit slides, with one full-size blow-up of art." Please do not send original artwork unless solicited. "Almost all of the children's books we accept for publication come to us with the author and illustrator already paired up. Therefore, we rarely use freelance illustrators." Samples returned with SASE; samples filed (if interested).
Tips "Always enclose a SASE. Keep in mind that we do not accept unsolicited manuscripts and that we rarely use freelance illustrators."

Ⓐ GOLDEN BOOKS

1745 Broadway, New York NY 10019. (212)782-9000. **Editorial Directors:** Courtney Silk, color and activity; Chris Angelilli, storybooks; Dennis Shealy, novelty. **Art Acquisitions:** Tracey Tyler, executive art director.

● See listing for Random House-Golden Books for Young Readers Group.

How to Contact/Writers Does not accept unsolicited submissions.
Fiction Publishes board books, novelty books, picture books, workbooks, series (mass market and trade).

GRAPHIA

Houghton Mifflin Company, 222 Berkeley St., Boston MA 02116. (617)351-5000. Web site: www.graphiabooks.com. **Manuscript Acquisitions:** Julia Richardson. "Graphia publishes quality paperbacks for today's teen readers, ages 14 and up. From fiction to nonfiction, poetry to graphic novels, Graphia runs the gamut, all unified by the quality writing that is the hallmark of this imprint."

Fiction Young adults: adventure, contemporary, fantasy, history, humor, multicultural, poetry. Recently published: *A Certain Slant of Light*, by Laura Whitcomb; *Watcha Mean, What's A Zine?*, by Mark Todd and Esther Watson; *Foreign Exposure: The Social Climber Abroad*, by Lauren Mechling and Laura Moser; *The Candy Darlings*, by Christine Walde: *Kid B*, by Linden Dalecki.

Nonfiction Young adults: biography, history, multicultural, nature/environment, science, social issues.

How to Contact/Writers Query. Responds to queries/mss in 3 months. Will consider simultaneous submissions and previously published work.
Illustration Do not send original artwork or slides. Send color photocopies, tearsheets or photos to Art Dept. Include SASE if you would like your samples mailed back to you.
Terms Pays author royalties. Offers advances. Sends galleys to authors. Catalog available on Web site (www.houghtonmifflin.com).

GREENE BARK PRESS

P.O. Box 1108, Bridgeport CT 06601-1108. (203)372-4861. Fax: (203)371-5856. E-mail: greenebark@aol.com. Web site: www.greenebarkpress.com. **Acquisitions:** Thomas J. Greene, publisher. Publishes 1-6 picture books/year; majority of books by first-time or repeat authors. "We publish only quality fictional hardcover picture books for children. Our stories are selected for originality, imagery and color. Our intention is to fire-up a child's imagination, encourage a desire to read in order to explore the world through books."

Fiction Picture books, young readers: adventure, fantasy, humor. Average word length: picture books—650; young readers—1,400. Recently published *Edith Ellen Eddy*, by Julee Ann Granger; *Hey, There's a Gobblin Under My Throne*, by Rhett Ranson Pennell.

How to Contact/Writers Responds to queries in 3 months; mss in 6 months; must include SASE. No response without SASE. Publishes a book 18 months after acceptance. Will consider simultaneous submissions. Prefer to review complete mss with illustrations.

Illustration Works with 1-2 illustrators/year. Uses color artwork only. Reviews ms/illustration packages from artists. Submit ms with 3 pieces of final art (copies only). Illustrations only: Query with samples. Responds in 2 months only if interested. Samples returned with SASE; samples filed. Originals returned at job's completion.
Terms Pays authors royalty of 10-12% based on wholesale price. Pays illustrators by the project (range: $1,500-3,000) or 5-7% royalty based on wholesale price. No advances. Sends galleys to authors; dummies to illustrators. Manuscript guidelines available for SASE or per e-mail request.
Tips "As a guide for future publications look to our latest publications, do not look to our older backlist. Please, no telephone, e-mail or fax queries."

Ⓐ GREENWILLOW BOOKS

1350 Avenue of the Americas, New York NY 10019. (212)261-6500. Web site: www.harperchildrens.com. Book publisher. Imprint of HarperCollins. Vice President/Publisher: Virginia Duncan. **Art Acquisitions:** Paul Zakris, art director. Publishes 40 picture books/year; 5 middle readers/year; 5 young adult books/year. "Greenwillow Books publishes picture books, fiction for young readers of all ages, and nonfiction primarily for children under seven years of age."
- Greenwillow Books is currently accepting neither unsolicited manuscripts nor queries. Unsolicited mail will not be opened and will not be returned. Call (212)261-6627 for an update.
Illustration Art samples (postcards only) should be sent in duplicate to Paul Zakris and Virginia Duncan.
Terms Pays authors royalty. Offers advances. Pays illustrators royalty or by the project. Sends galleys to authors.

GROSSET & DUNLAP PUBLISHERS

Penguin Group (USA), 345 Hudson St., New York NY 10014. Web site: http://us.penguingroup.com/youngreaders. Estab. 1898. **Acquisitions:** Debra Dorfman, president/publisher. Publishes 175 titles/year. "Grosset & Dunlap publishes children's books that show children reading is fun with books that speak to their interests and are affordable so children can build a home library of their own. Focus on licensed properties, series, readers and novelty books."
Fiction Recently published series: Camp Confidential; Hank Zipper; Katie Kazoo; Dish; Dragon Slayers' Academy; Nancy Drew. Upcoming series: Pirate School; The Misadventure of Benjamin Bartholomew Piff. Licensed series: Angelina Ballerina; Strawberry Shortcake; Charlie & Lola; Dick & Jane (brand). Also published the Clear & Simple Workbook series.
Nonfiction Young readers: nature/environment, science. Recently published series: All Aboard Reading sereis; Who Was..? series.
How to Contact/Writers "We do not accept e-mail submissions. Unsolicited manuscripts witll receive a response in 6-8 weeks."

Ⓒ GRYPHON HOUSE

P.O. Box 207, Beltsville MD 20704-0207. (301)595-9500. Fax: (301)595-0051. E-mail: kathyc@ghbooks.com. Web site: www.gryphonhouse.com. **Acquisitions:** Kathy Charner, editor-in-chief.
Nonfiction Parent and teacher resource books—activity books, textbooks. Recently published *Reading Games*, by Jackie Silberg; *Primary Art*, by MaryAnn F. Kohl; *Teaching Young Children's with Autism Spectrum Disorder*, by Clarissa Willis; *The Complete Resource Book for Infants*, by Pam Schiller. "At Gryphon House, our goal is to publish books that help teachers and parents enrich the lives of children from birth through age eight. We strive to make our books useful for teachers at all levels of experience, as well as for parents, caregivers, and anyone interested in working with children."
How to Contact/Writers Query. Submit outline/synopsis and 2 sample chapters. Responds to queries/mss in 6 months. Publishes a book 18 months after acceptance. Will consider simultaneous submissions, e-mail submissions.
Illustration Works with 4-5 illustrators/year. Uses b&w realistic artwork only. Illustrations only: Query with samples, promo sheet. Responds in 2 months. Samples returned with SASE; samples filed.
Photography Buys photos from freelancers. Buys stock and assigns work. Submit cover letter, published samples, stock photo list.
Terms Pays authors royalty based on wholesale price. Offers advances. Pays illustrators by the project. Pays photographers by the project or per photo. Sends edited ms copy to authors. Original artwork returned at job's completion. Book catalog and ms guidelines available via Web site or with SASE.
Tips "Send a SASE for our catalog and manuscript guidelines. Look at our books, then submit proposals that complement the books we already publish or supplement our existing books. We are looking for books of creative, participatory learning experiences that have a common conceptual theme to tie them together. The books should be on subjects that parents or teachers want to do on a daily basis."

HACHAI PUBLISHING

762 Park Place, Brooklyn NY 11216. (718)633-0100. Fax: (718)633-0103. E-mail: info@hachai.com. Web site: www.hachai.com. **Manuscript Acquisitions:** Devorah Leah Rosenfeld, submissions editor. Publishes 4 picture books/year; 1 young reader/year; 1 middle reader/year. 75% of books published by first-time authors. "All books have spiritual/religious themes, specifically traditional Jewish content. We're seeking books about morals and values; the Jewish experience in current and Biblical times; and Jewish observance, Sabbath and holidays."

Fiction Picture books and young readers: contemporary, historical fiction, religion. Middle readers: adventure, contemporary, problem novels, religion. Does not want to see fantasy, animal stories, romance, problem novels depicting drug use or violence. Recently published *Let's Go Visiting*, written and illustrated by Rikki Benenfeld (ages 2-5, picture book); *What Else Do I Say*, by Malky Goldberg, illustrated by Patti Argoff (ages 1-2, lift-the-flap book); *Way Too Much Challah Dough*, by Goldie Shulman, illustrated by Vitaliy Romanenko (ages 3-6, picture book); *Faigy Finds the Way*, by Batsheva Brandeis (ages 7-10, short chapter book).

Nonfiction Recently published *My Jewish ABC's*, by Draizy Zelcer, illustrated by Patti Nemeroff (ages 3-6, picture book); *Shadow Play*, by Leah Pearl Shollar, illustrated by Pesach Gerber (ages 3-6, picture book); *Much Much Better*, by Chaim Kosofsky, illustrated by Jessica Schiffman (ages 5-8).

How to Contact/Wrtiers Fiction/nonfiction: Submit complete ms. Responds to queries/mss in 6 weeks.

Illustration Works with 4 illustrators/year. Uses primary color artwork, some b&w illustration. Reviews ms/illustration packages from authors. Submit ms with 1 piece of final art. Illustrations only: Query with samples; arrange personal portfolio review. Responds in 6 weeks. Samples returned with SASE; samples filed.

Terms Work purchased outright from authors for $800-1,000. Pays illustrators by the project (range: $2,000-3,500). Book catalog, ms/artist's guidelines available for SASE.

Tips "Write a story that incorporates a moral, not a preachy morality tale. Originality is the key. We feel Hachai publications will appeal to a wider readership as parents become more interested in positive values for their children."

HARCOURT, INC.

15 East 26th Street, New York NY 10010. (212)592-1034. Fax: (212)592-1030. Web site: www.harcourtbooks.com. Children's Books Division includes: Harcourt Children's Books—**Editor-in-Chief:** Ms. Allyn Johnston, **Editorial Director:** Liz Van Doren; Voyager Paperbacks, Odyssey Paperbacks, Red Wagon Books. **Children's Book Publisher:** Lori Benton. **Art Director:** Michelle Wetherbee. Publishes 50-75 picture books/year; 10-20 middle readers/year; 25-50 young adult titles/year. 20% of books by first-time authors; 50% of books from agented writers. "Harcourt, Inc. owns some of the world's most prestigious publishing imprints—which distinguish quality products for children's educational and trade markets worldwide."

● Harcourt Children's Books no longer accepts unsolicited manuscripts, queries or illustrations. Recent Harcourt titles *Tails*, by Matthew Van Fleet; *The Leaf Man*, by Lois Ehlert; *The Great Fuzz Frenzy*, by Janet Stevens and Susan Steven Crummel; *How I Became a Pirate*, by Melinda Long illustrated by David Shannon; and *Frankenstein Makes a Sandwich*, by Adam Rex, are all New York Times bestsellers. Their title *Move Over, Rover!*, by Karen Beaumont, illustrated by Jane Dyer, won a Geisel Honor Medal in 2007. Their title *Leaf Man*, by Lois Ehlert, won the Boston Globe-Horn Book Award for Picture Books in 2007. Their title *Yellow Elephant: A Bright Bestiary*, by Julie Larious, illustrated by Julie Paschkis, won the Boston Globe-Horn Book Honor Award for Fiction and Poetry in 2007. Their title *Mama: A True Story in Which a Baby Hippo Loses His Mama During a Tsunami but Finds a New Home and a New Mama*, by Jeanette Winter, won a Boston Globe-Horn Book Honor Award for Picture Books in 2007.

Fiction All levels: Considers all categories. Average word length: picture books—"varies greatly"; middle readers—20,000-50,000; young adults—35,000-65,000. See catalog or visit Web site (www.harcourtbooks.com) for recently published titles.

Nonfiction All levels: animal, biography, concept, history, multicultural, music/dance, nature/environment, science, sports. Average word length: picture books—"varies greatly"; middle readers—20,000-50,000; young adults—35,000-65,000.

How to Contact/Writers Only interested in agented material.

Illustration Only interested in agented material.

Photography Works on assignment only.

Terms Pays authors and illustrators royalty based on retail price. Pays photographers by the project. Sends galleys to authors; dummies to illustrators. Original artwork returned at job's completion. Book catalog available for 8½×11 SAE and 4 first-class stamps; ms/artist's guidelines available for business-size SASE. All imprints included in a single catalog.

HARPERCOLLINS CHILDREN'S BOOKS

1350 Avenue of the Americas, New York NY 10019. (212)261-6500. Web site: www.harperchildrens.com. Book publisher. President and Publisher: Susan Katz. Associate Publisher/Editor-in-Chief: Kate Morgan Jackson.

Associate Publisher, Fiction: Elise Howard. Editorial Directors: Margaret Anastas, Barbara Lalicki, Maria Modugno, Michael Stearns, Phoebe Yeh. **Art Acquisitions:** Martha Rago or Barbara Fitzsimmons, director. Imprints: HarperTrophy, HarperTeen, EOS, HarperFestival, Greenwillow Books, Joanna Cotler Books, Laura Geringer Books, Katherine Tegen Books.

- HarperCollins Children's Books is not accepting unsolicited and/or unagented manuscripts or queries. ''Unfortunately, the volume of these submissions is so large that we cannot give them the attention they deserve. Such submissions will not be reviewed or returned.'' See A Guide to Writing Chick Lit for Teens by HarperCollins Editor Farrin Jacobs and author Sarah Mlynowski on page 42. Also see First Books on page 119 for an interview with Rose Kent, author of HarperCollins title *Kimchi & Calamari.* HarperCollins title *Not a Box,* by Antoinette Portis, won a Geisel Honor Medal in 2007.

Fiction Publishes picture, chapter, novelty, board and TV/movie books.

How to Contact/Writers Only interested in agented material.

Illustration Art samples may be sent to Martha Rago or Stephanie Bart-Horvath. *Please do not send original art.* Works with over 100 illustrators/year. Responds only if interested. Samples returned with SASE; samples filed only if interested.

Terms Art guidelines available for SASE.

☐ HAYES SCHOOL PUBLISHING CO. INC.

321 Pennwood Ave., Wilkinsburg PA 15221-3398. (412)371-2373. Fax: (800)543-8771. E-mail: chayes@hayespub.com. Web site: www.hayespub.com. Estab. 1940. **Acquisitions:** Mr. Clair N. Hayes. Produces folders, workbooks, stickers, certificates. Wants to see supplementary teaching aids for grades K-12. Interested in all subject areas. Will consider simultaneous and electronic submissions.

How to Contact/Writers Query with description or complete ms. Responds in 6 weeks. SASE for return of submissions.

Illustration Works with 3-4 illustrators/year. Responds in 6 weeks. Samples returned with SASE; samples filed. Originals not returned at job's completion.

Terms Work purchased outright. Purchases all rights.

HEALTH PRESS NA INC.

P.O. Box 37470, Albuquerque NM 87176-7479. (505)888-1394 or (877)411-0707. Fax: (505)888-1521. E-mail: goodbooks@healthpress.com. Web site: www.healthpress.com. **Acquisitions:** Editor. Publishes 4 young readers/year. 100% of books by first-time authors.

Fiction Picture books, young readers: health, special needs. Average word length: young readers—1,000-1,500; middle readers—1,000-1,500. Recently published *The Girl With No Hair,* by Elizabeth Murphy-Melas, illustrated by Alex Hernandez (ages 8-12, picture book); *The Peanut Butter Jam,* by Elizabeth Sussman-Nassau, illustrated by Margot Ott (ages 6-12, picture book).

Nonfiction Picture books, young readers: health, special needs, social issues, self help.

How to Contact/Writers Submit complete ms. Responds in 3 month. Publishes a book 9 months after acceptance. Will consider simultaneous submissions.

Terms Pays authors royalty. Sends galleys to authors. Book catalog available.

HENDRICK-LONG PUBLISHING COMPANY

10635 Tower Oaks, Suite D, Houston TX 77070. (832)912-READ. Fax: (832)912-7353. E-mail: hendrick-long@worldnet.att.net. **Acquisitions:** Vilma Long, vice president. Publishes 4 young readers/year; 4 middle readers/year. 20% of books by first-time authors. Publishes fiction/nonfiction about Texas of interest to young readers through young adults/teens.

Fiction Young readers, middle readers: history books on Texas and the Southwest. No fantasy or poetry.

Nonfiction Young readers, middle readers: history books on Texas and the Southwest, biography, multicultural.

How to Contact/Writers Fiction/nonfiction: Query with outline/synopsis and sample chapter. Responds to queries in 5 months. Publishes a book 18 months after acceptance. No simultaneous submissions. Include SASE.

Tips ''Would like to see more workbook-type manuscripts.''

▨ HOLIDAY HOUSE INC.

425 Madison Ave., New York NY 10017. (212)688-0085. Fax: (212)421-6134. Web site: www.holidayhouse.com. Estab. 1935. Book publisher. Vice President/Editor-in-Chief: Regina Griffin. **Acquisitions:** Acquisitions Editor. **Art Director:** Claire Counihan. Publishes 35 picture books/year; 3 young readers/year; 15 middle readers/year; 8 young adult titles/year. 20% of books by first-time authors; 10% from agented writers. Mission Statement: ''To publish high-quality books for children.''

- Holiday House title *Jazz,* by Walter Dean Myers, illustrated by Christopher Myers, won the Golden Kite

Award for Picture Book Illustration in 2007. Christopher Myers also won a Coretta Scott King Illustrator Honor Award for *Jazz*.

Fiction All levels: adventure, contemporary, fantasy, folktales, ghost, historical, humor, literary, multicultural, school, suspense/mystery, sports. Recently published *Jazz*, by Walter Dean Myers, illustrated by Christopher Myers; *Keeper of Soles*, by Teresa Bateman, illustrated by Yayo; *Freedom Walkers*, by Russell Freedman.

Nonfiction All levels, but more picture books and fewer middle-grade nonfiction titles: animal, biography, concept, contemporary, geography, historical, math, multicultural, music/dance, nature/environment, religion, science, social issues.

How to Contact/Writers Send queries only to editor. Responds to queries in 3 months; mss in 4 months. "If we find your book idea suits our present needs, we will notify you by mail." Once a ms has been requested, the writers should send in the exclusive submission, with a SASE, otherwise the ms will not be returned.

Illustration Works with 35 illustrators/year. Reviews ms illustration packages from artists. Send ms with dummy. Do not submit original artwork or slides. Color photocopies or printed samples are preferred. Responds only if interested. Samples filed.

Terms Pays authors and illustrators an advance against royalties. Originals returned at job's completion. Book catalog, ms/artist's guidelines available for a SASE.

Tips "We need books with strong stories, writing and art. We do not publish board books or novelties. No easy readers."

HENRY HOLT & COMPANY

175 Fifth Ave, New York NY 10010. Unsolicited Manuscript Hotline: (646)307-5087. Web site: www.henryholtch ildrensbooks.com. Submissions Web site: www.henryholtchildrensbooks.com/submissions.htm. **Manuscript Acquisitions:** Laura Godwin, vice president and publisher of Books for Young Readers; Christy Ottaviano, executive editor; Reka Simonsen, senior editor; Kate Farrell, editor; Nina Ignatowicz, editor at large. **Art Acquisitions:** Patrick Collins, art director. Publishes 30-35 picture books/year; 6-8 chapter books/year; 10-15 middle readers/year; 8-10 young adult titles/year. 15% of books by first-time authors; 40% of books from agented writers. "Henry Holt and Company Books for Young Readers is known for publishing quality books that feature imaginative authors and illustrators. We tend to publish many new authors and illustrators each year in our effort to develop and foster new talent."

- See Getting Your Art Noticed by the People Who Count, by Henry Holt Associate Art Director Laurent Linn, on page 57.

Fiction Picture books: animal, anthology, concept, folktales, history, humor, multicultural, nature/environment, poetry, special needs, sports. Middle readers: adventure, contemporary, history, humor, multicultural, special needs, sports, suspense/mystery. Young adults: contemporary, humor, multicultural, mystery, historical.

Nonfiction Picture books: animal, arts/crafts, biography, concept, geography, history, hobbies, multicultural, the arts, nature/environment, sports. Middle readers, young readers, young adult: biography, history, multicultural, sports.

How to Contact/Writers Fiction/nonfiction: Submit complete ms, Attn: Submissions; "no SASE please." Responds in 4-6 months only if interested, otherwise mss are not returned or responded to. Will not consider simultaneous or multiple submissions.

Illustration Works with 50-60 illustrators/year. Reviews ms/illustration packages from artists. Random samples OK. Illustrations only: Submit tearsheets, slides. Do *not* send originals. Responds to art samples only if interested. Samples filed but not returned. If accepted, original artwork returned at job's completion. Portfolios are reviewed every Monday.

Terms Pays authors/illustrators royalty based on retail price. Sends galleys to authors; proofs to illustrators.

HOUGHTON MIFFLIN CO.

Children's Trade Books, 222 Berkeley St., Boston MA 02116-3764. (617)351-5000. Fax: (617)351-1111. E-mail: childrens_books@hmco.com. Web site: www.houghtonmifflinbooks.com. **Manuscript Aquisitions:** Submissions Coordinator; Betsy Groban, publisher; Margaret Raymo, editorial director; Ann Rider, senior editor; Mary Wilcox, franchise director, Graphia senior editor; Walter Lorraine, books editor; Kate O'Sullivan, Monica Perez, editors; Erica Zappy, associate editor. **Art Acquisitions:** Sheila Smallwood, creative director. Imprints include Walter Lorraine Books, Clarion Books, and Graphia. Averages 60 titles/year. Publishes hardcover originals and trade paperback reprints and originals. "Houghton Mifflin gives shape to ideas that educate, inform, and above all, delight ."

- Houghton Mifflin title *Team Moon: How 400,000 People Landed Apollo 11 on the Moon*, by Catherine Thimmesh, won the Golden Kite Honor Award for Nonfiction and the Sibert Medal in 2007. Their title *Quest for the Tree Kangaroo: An Expedition to the Cloud Forest of New Guinea*, by Sy Montgomery, photos by Nic

Bishop, won a Sibert Honor Medal in 2007. Their title *Wildfire*, by Taylor Morrison, won a Boston Globe-Horn Honor Award for Nonfiction in 2007.

Fiction All levels: all categories except religion. "We do not rule out any theme, though we do not publish specifically religious material." Recently published *Dairy Queen*, by Catherine Gilbert Murdock (ages 12 and up, YA novel); *Love That Baby*, by Susan Milford (ages 0-3, picture book); *Lights Out*, by Arthur Geisert (ages 4-8, picture book).

Nonfiction All levels: all categories except religion. Recently published *The Forbidden Schoolhouse: The True and Dramatic Story of Prudence Crandall and Her Students*, by Suzanne Jurmain (ages 10 and up); *Prehistoric Actual Size*, by Steve Jenkins (picture book, all ages); *Gorilla Doctors*, by Pamela S. Turner (ages 7-12).

How to Contact/Writers Fiction: Submit complete ms on unfolded white paper. Nonfiction: Submit outline/synopsis and sample chapters. Responds within 4 months *only* if interested—*do not send self-addressed stamped envelope.*

Illustration Works with 60 illustrators/year. Reviews ms/illustration packages from artists. Manuscript/illustration packages or illustrations only: Query with samples (colored photocopies are fine); provide tearsheets. Responds in 4 months. Samples returned with SASE; samples filed if interested.

Terms Pays standard royalty based on retail price; offers advance. Illustrators paid by the project and royalty. Manuscript and artist's guidelines available with SASE.

HUNTER HOUSE PUBLISHERS

P.O. Box 2914, Alameda CA 94501-0914. (510)865-5282. Fax: (510)865-4295. E-mail: acquisitions@hunterhouse .com. Web site: www.hunterhouse.com. **Manuscript Acquisitions:** Jeanne Brondino. Publishes 0-1 nonfiction titles for teenage women/year. 50% of books by first-time authors; 5% of books from agented writers.

Nonfiction Young adults: self help, health, multicultural, violence prevention. "We emphasize that all our books try to take multicultural experiences and concerns into account. We would be interested in a self-help book on multicultural issues." Books are therapy/personal growth-oriented. Does *not* want to see books for young children, fiction, illustrated picture books, autobiography. Published *Turning Yourself Around: Self-Help Strategies for Troubled Teens*, by Kendall Johnson, Ph.D.; *Safe Dieting for Teens*, by Linda Ojeda, Ph.D.

How to Contact/Writers Query; submit overview and chapter-by-chapter synopsis, sample chapters and statistics on your subject area, support organizations or networks and marketing ideas. "Testimonials from professionals or well-known authors are crucial." Responds to queries in 3 months; mss in 6 months. Publishes a book 18 months after acceptance. Will consider simultaneous submissions.

Terms Payment varies. Sends galleys to authors. Book catalog available for 9×12 SAE and $1.25 postage; ms guidelines for standard SAE and 1 first-class stamp.

Tips Wants teen books with solid, informative material. "We do few children's books. The ones we do are for a select, therapeutic audience. No fiction! Please, no fiction."

Ⓐ Ⓥ HYPERION BOOKS FOR CHILDREN

114 Fifth Ave., New York NY 10011-5690. (212)633-4400. Fax: (212)633-4833. Web site: www.hyperionbooksfo rchildren.com. **Manuscript Acquisitions:** Editorial Director. **Art Director:** Anne Diebel. 10% of books by first-time authors.

● Hyperion title *Moses: When Harriet Tubman Led Her People to Freedom*, illustrated by Kadir Nelson, written by Carole Boston Weatherford, won a Caldecott Honor Medal and the Coretta Scott King Illustrator Award in 2007.

Fiction Picture books, young readers, middle readers, young adults: adventure, animal, anthology (short stories), contemporary, fantasy, folktales, history, humor, multicultural, poetry, science fiction, sports, suspense/mystery. Middle readers, young adults: commercial fiction. Recently published *Emily's First 100 Days of School*, by Rosemary Wells (ages 3-6, *New York Times* bestseller); *Artemis Fowl*, by Eoin Colfer (YA novel, *New York Times* bestseller); *Dumpy The Dump Truck*, series by Julie Andrews Edwards and Emma Walton Hamilton (ages 3-7).

Nonfiction All trade subjects for all levels.

How to Contact/Writers Only interested in agented material.

Illustration Works with 100 illustrators/year. "Picture books are fully illustrated throughout. All others depend on individual project." Reviews ms/illustration packages from artists. Submit complete package. Illustrations only: Submit résumé, business card, promotional literature or tearsheets to be kept on file. Responds only if interested. Original artwork returned at job's completion.

Photography Works on assignment only. Publishes photo essays and photo concept books. Provide résumé, business card, promotional literature or tearsheets to be kept on file.

Terms Pays authors royalty based on retail price. Offers advances. Pays illustrators and photographers royalty based on retail price or a flat fee. Sends galleys to authors; dummies to illustrators. Book catalog available for 9×12 SAE and 3 first-class stamps.

▒ IDEALS CHILDREN'S BOOKS AND CANDYCANE PRESS ✓

Imprint of Ideals Publications, 535 Metroplex Dr., Suite 250, Nashville TN 37211. Web site: www.idealsbooks.com. **Manuscript Acquisitions:** Children's Editor. **Art Acquisitions:** Art Director. Publishes 10 picture books/year; 40 board books/year. 50% of books by first-time authors.

Fiction Picture books: animal, concept, history, religion. Board books: animal, history, nature/environment, religion. Average word length: picture books—1,500; board books—200.

ILLUMINATION ARTS

P.O. Box 1865, Bellevue WA 98009. (425)644-7185. Fax: (425)644-9274. E-mail: liteinfo@illumin.com. Web site: www.illumin.com. **Acquisitions:** Ruth Thompson, editorial director.

Fiction Word length: Prefers under 1,000, but will consider up to 1,500 words. Recently published *Just Imagine*, by John M. Thompson and George M. Schultz, illustrated by Wodin; *Mrs. Murphy's Marvelous Mansion*, by Emma Perry Roberts, illustrated by Robert Rogalski.

How to Contact/Writers Fiction: Submit complete ms. Responds to queries in 3 months with SASE only. No electronic or CD submissions for text or art. Publishes a book 1-2 years after acceptance. Will consider simultaneous submissions.

Illustration Works with 3-5 illustrators/year. Uses color artwork only. Reviews ms/illustration packages from artists. Query or send ms with dummy. Illustrations only: Query with color samples, résumé and promotional material to be kept on file or returned with SASE only. Responds in 3 months with SASE only. Samples returned with SASE or filed.

Terms Pays authors and illustrators royalty based on wholesale price. Book fliers available for SASE.

Tips "Read our books and follow our guidelines. Be patient. The market is competitive. We receive 2,000 submissions annually and publish 2-3 books a year. Sorry, we are unable to track unsolicited submissions."

IMPACT PUBLISHERS, INC.

P.O. Box 6016, Atascadero CA 93423-6016. (805)466-5917. Fax: (805)466-5919. E-mail: info@impactpublishers.com. Web site: www.impactpublishers.com. **Manuscript Acquisitions:** Melissa Froehner, children's editor. **Art Acquisitions:** Sharon Skinner, art director. Imprints: Little Imp Books, Rebuilding Books, The Practical Therapist Series. Publishes 1 young reader/year; 1 middle reader/year; 1 young adult title/year. 20% of books by first-time authors. "Our purpose is to make the best human services expertise available to the widest possible audience. We publish only popular psychology and self-help materials written in everyday language by professionals with advanced degrees and significant experience in the human services."

Nonfiction Young readers, middle readers, young adults: self-help. Recently published *Jigsaw Puzzle Family: The Stepkids' Guide to Fitting It Together*, by Cynthia MacGregor (ages 8-12, children's/divorce/emotions).

How to Contact/Writers Nonfiction: Query or submit complete ms, cover letter, résumé. Responds to queries in 12 weeks; mss in 3 months. Will consider simultaneous submissions or previously published work.

Illustration Works with 1 illustrator/year. Uses b&w artwork only. Reviews ms/illustration packages from artists. Query. Contact: Children's Editor. Illustrations only: Query with samples. Contact: Sharon Skinner, production manager. Responds only if interested. Samples returned with SASE; samples filed. Originals returned to artist at job's completion.

Terms Pays authors royalty of 10-12%. Offers advances. Pays illustrators by the project. Book catalog available for #10 SAE with 2 first-class stamps; ms guidelines available for SASE. All imprints included in a single catalog.

Tips "Please do not submit fiction, poetry or narratives."

▒ ▢ INNOVATIVE KIDS

18 Ann St., Norwalk CT 06854. (203)838-6400. Fax: (203)855-5582. E-mail: info@innovativekids.com. Web site: www.innovativekids.com. **Manuscript Acquisitions:** Submissions Editor. **Art Acquisitions:** Art Director. Publishes 30 activity books/year; 20 young readers/year. 5% of books by first-time authors. "IKIDS makes learning fun with Hands-On, Minds-On books, games, and activities!"

Nonfiction/Fiction Beginning readers, activity books, infant/toddler books and games, and science learning tools in a wide range of themes and subjects. Recently published *A Kid's Guide to Giving*, *Phonics Comics* series, *Croovey Tubes* series, and *iBaby* series.

How to Contact innovativeKids works with 30-50 authors and illustrators per year.

Writers Nonfiction/fiction: Submit manuscript or prototype. Contact: Submissions editor. Don't send your only copy. No SASE necessary. iKids responds only if interested.

Illustration Black and white as well as color artwork. Query with brochure, samples, photocopies, résumé or tearsheets. Submit artwork with dummy if appropriate. Contact: Art Director. Don't send your only copy. No SASE necessary. Responds only if interested.

Photography Buys stock and assigns work. Contact: Art Director. Submit résumé, published samples, color promo pieces.

Terms Work purchased outright; payment varies.

Tips "Make sure your project is appropriate to IK prior to sending it. All IK titles are interactive and educational but above all else fun!" Book catalog available with 9×12 SASE with $1.83 postage. Catalog also available on Web site.

JOURNEY STONE CREATIONS ✓

3533 Danbury Rd., Fairfield OH 45014. (513)860-5616. Fax: (513)860-0176. E-mail: pat@jscbooks.com(submissi ons). E-mail: danelle@jscbooks.com. (art dept.). Web site: www.jscbooks.com. Estab. 2004. **Editor:** Patricia Stirnkorb. **Creative Director:** Danelle Pickett. Publishes mass market and trade fiction and nonfiction, Christian, educational and multicultural material. Publishes 40 or more titles/year. 90% of books by first-time authors. Strives to "engage children in the love of reading, while entertaining and educating."

Fiction Picture books: adventure, animal, contemporary, history, humor, multicultural, nature/environment, poetry, religion, sports. Early readers: adventure, animal, contemporary, health, history, humor, multicultural, nature/environment, poetry, religion, sports, suspense. "We are not accepting middle readers at this time." Word length: picture books—1,200 or less; early readers—5,000 or less. Recently published *Stranger Danger*, by Patricia Stirnkorb, illustrated by Claudia Wolf (ages 7-12, childhood saftey); *Camp Limestone*, by Paul Kijinski (ages 10-16, middle reader); *Big Yellow School Bus*, by Sandi Eucks (ages 3-6).

How to Contact/Writers Query or submit complete ms if less than 2,000 words. Reports on queires/mss in 4-6 weeks. Publishes a book up to 2 years after acceptance. Accepts simultaneous and electrionic submissions. "At this time we are only accepting picture books and early reader books with less than 5,000 words. We are reviewing books for publication 12-18 months away."

Illustration Works with 25 illustrators/year. Uses color artwork only. Will review ms/illustrations packages from illustrators. Query; submit ms with 2-3 pieces of final art. Contact: Danelle Pickett, creative director. Illustrations only: Query with samples. Send tearsheets or link to online portfolio. Contact: Danelle Pickett, creative director. Samples not returned, samples filed.

Terms Pays authors negotiable royalty based on wholesale price or work purchased outright. Pay illustrators by the project or negotiable royalty. Book catalog available on Web site. Writer's/artist's guidelines available on Web site.

Tips "Make sure you submit only your best work. For writers, if it is not letter perfect, we don't want to see it. Review our guidelines."

JOURNEYFORTH BOB JONES UNIVERSITY PRESS

Imprint of Bob Jones University Press, 1700 Wade Hampton Blvd., Greenville SC 29614. (864)242-5100, ext. 4350. Fax: (864)298-0268. E-mail: jb@bjup.com. Web site: www.bjup.com. Estab. 1974. Specializes in trade books, Christian material, educational material. **Acquisitions Editor:** Nancy Lohr. Publishes 1 picture book/ year; 2 young readers/year; 4 middle readers/year; 3 young adult titles/year. 10% of books by first-time authors. "We aim to produce well-written books for readers of varying abilities and interests—books excellent in every facet of their presentation and fully consistent with biblical truth."

Fiction Young readers, middle readers, young adults: adventure, animal, contemporary, fantasy, folktales, history, humor, multicultural, nature/environment, problem novels, suspense/mystery. Average word length: young readers—10,000-12,000; middle readers—10,000-40,000; young adult/teens—40,000-60,000. Recently published *Tommy's Race*, by Sharon Hambrick, illustrated by Maurie Manning (ages 6-7, contemporary fiction); *Regina Silsby's Secret War*, by Thomas J. Brodeur (young adult historical ficiton); *Two Sides to Everything*, by Deb Brammer (ages 9-12, contemporary fiction).

Nonfiction Young readers, middle readers, young adult: biography. Average word length: young readers— 10,000-12,000; middle readers—10,000-40,000; young adult/teens—40,000-60,000. Recently published *George Mueller*, by Rebecca Davis (ages 7-9, Christian biography); *Children of the Storm*, by Natasha Vius (young adult autobiography); *Fanny Crosby*, by Rebecca Davis (Christian biography).

How to Contact/Writers Fiction: Query. "Do not send stories with magical elements. We are not currently accepting picture books. We do not publish these genres: romance, science fiction, poetry and drama." Nonfic-tion: Query or submit outline/synopsis and 5 sample chapters. Responds to queries in 4 weeks; mss in 3 months. Publishes book 12-15 months after acceptance. Will consider previously published work.

Illustration Works with 4-6 illustrators/year. Query with samples. Send promo sheet; will review Web site portfolio if applicable. Responds only if interested. Samples returned with SASE; samples filed.

Terms Pays authors royalty based on wholesale price or work purchased outright. Pays illustrators by the project. Originals returned to artist at job's completion. Book catalog and ms guidelines free on request. Send 9×12 SASE with 2 first-class stamps for book catalog and mss guidelines. Writer's guidelines available on Web site.

Tips "Review our backlist and be sure your work is a good fit. Polish your manuscript; only the best writing is going to get our attention. If it reads like a rough draft, we will not be inclined to give it serious consideration."

KAEDEN BOOKS

P.O. Box 16190, Rocky River OH 44116-6190. (440)617-1400. Fax: (440)617-1403. E-mail: lstenger@kaeden.com or curnston@kaeden.com. Web site: www.kaeden.com. **Contact:** Craig Urmston, President or Lisa Stenger, Editor. "Kaeden Books produces high quality, emergent, early, and transitional books for reading teachers, special education teachers, and classroom teachers."

Fiction Young readers: adventure, animal, family, historical, humor, multicultural, sports, suspense/mystery. Average word length: picture books—20-150 words; young readers—20-300 words. Recently published *The Balloon Ride*, by Mary Pearson; *Just One More Mom*, by Kit S. Grady; *Paula's Pickle Picnic*, by Barbara J. Underwood; *Where Is Matt's Cap*, by Beverly Plass.

Nonfiction Young readers: animal, biography, careers, geography, health, history, hobbies, multicultural, music/dance, nature/environment, science, mathematical stories. Multicultural needs include group and character diversity in stories and settings. Average word length: picture books—20-150 words; young readers—20-150 words.

How to Contact/Writers Fiction/nonfiction: Submit complete ms. Do not send original transcripts. Responds to mss in 1 year. Will consider simultaneous submissions.

Illustration Works with 8-10 illustrators/year. Reviews ms/illustration packages from artists. Submit art samples in color. Can be photocopies or tearsheets. Illustrations only: Query with samples. Send résumé, promo sheet, tearsheets, photocopies of work, preferably in color. Responds only if interested. Samples are filed.

Terms Work purchased outright from authors. "Royalties to our previous authors." Pays illustrators by the project (range: $50-150/page). Book catalog available for 8½×11 SAE and 3 first-class stamps.

Tips "We are particularly interested in nonfiction social studies for grades 1 and 2 and mathematical stories for grades 1-3."

KAR-BEN PUBLISHING, INC.

A division of Lerner Publishing Group, 241 First Ave. No., Minneapolis, MN 55401. (612)332-3344. Fax: (612)-332-7615. E-mail: editorial@karben.com. Web site: www.karben.com. **Manuscript Acquisitions:** Joni Sussman, director. Publishes 10-15 books/year (mostly picture books); 20% of books by first-time authors. All of Kar-Ben's books are on Jewish themes for young children and families.

Fiction Picture books: adventure, concept, folktales, history, humor, multicultural, religion, special needs; must be on a Jewish theme. Average word length: picture books—1,000. Recently published *A Grandma Like Yours / A Grandpa Like Yours*, by Andrea Warmflash Rosenbaum, illustrated by Barb Bjornson; *It's Tu B'Shevat*, by Edie Stoltz Zolkower, illustrated by Richard Johnson.

Nonfiction Picture books, young readers: activity books, arts/crafts, biography, careers, concept, cooking, history, how-to, multicultural, religion, social issues, special needs; must be of Jewish interest. Recently published *Paper Clips—The Making of a Children's Holocaust Memorial*, by Peter and Dagmar Schroeder (ages 8-12); *It's Purim Time*, by Latifa Berry Kropf, photos by Tod Cohen (ages 1-4); *Where Do People Go When They Die?*, by Mindy Avra Portnoy, illustrated by Shelly O. Haas (ages 5-10).

How to Contact/Writers Submit complete ms. Responds to queries/mss in 6 weeks. Publishes a book 24-36 months after acceptance. Will consider simultaneous submissions.

Illustration Works with 6-8 illustrators/year. Prefers "four-color art in any medium that is scannable." Reviews illustration packages from artists. Submit sample of art or online portfolio (no originals).

Terms Pays authors royalties of 3-5% of net against advance of $500-1,000; or purchased outright. Original artwork returned at job's completion. Book catalog free on request. Manuscript guidelines on Web site.

Tips Looks for "books for young children with Jewish interest and content, modern, nonsexist, not didactic. Fiction or nonfiction with a Jewish theme can be serious or humorous, life cycle, Bible story, or holiday-related. In particular, we are looking for stories that reflect the ethnic and cultural diversity of today's Jewish family."

KINGFISHER

Imprint of Houghton Mifflin Company, 215 Park Ave. South, New York NY 10003. (212)420-5800. Fax: (212)420-5899. Web site: www.houghtonmifflinbooks.com/kingfisher. **Contact:** Marit Vagstad. Kingfisher is an award-winning publisher of nonfiction and fiction for children of all ages. They publish high-quality books with strong editorial content and world class illustrations at a competitive price, offering value to parents and educators.

- Kingfisher is not currently accepting unsolicited manuscripts. All solicitations must be made by a recognized literary agent.

Fiction Recently published *Flight of the Fire Thief*, by Terry Deary; *Traces: Final Lap*, by Malcolm Rose.

Nonfiction Recently published *New York Times—Deadly Invaders: Virus Outbreaks Around the World, from Marburn Fever to Avian Flu*, by Denise Grady; *Unexplained: An Encyclopedia of Curious Phenomena, Strange Superstitions, and Ancient Mysteries*, by Judy Allen.

K.L. Going

*Crafting compelling characters
for a YA audience*

K L. Going emerged as a strong voice in the world of young adult literature with her 2003 Printz Honor Award-winning novel *Fat Kid Rules the World*, the story of Troy, a pushing-300-pound-17-year-old, and his unlikely friend Curt, a emaciated, semi-homeless, high school dropout guitar genius who saves Troy's life, then goads him into playing the drums in their own punk duo. Going's debut resonated with readers and critics alike. Her follow-up, the middle-grade novel *The Liberation of Gabriel King*, received starred reviews in both *Publishers Weekly* and *Kirkus*.

A *Publishers Weekly* reviewer called Going's latest YA novel *Saint Iggy* "her most impressive achievement yet." *Saint Iggy* invites us into the world of not-so-reliable narrator Iggy Corso—a world of drug-addicted parents, absent mothers, dilapidated housing, and dangerous dealers. When he gets kicked out of school, the only one Iggy can turn to as he works on a plan to make something of himself, is his friend Mo, a law-school dropout rife with his own issues, who fled the upscale side of the tracks for Iggy's.

Before working as a full-time writer, Going worked as an agents' assistant at Curtis Brown and managed an independent bookstore. Here she talks about her work, developing characters, mistakes new authors make, and offers insights from her unique perspective. To learn more about Going, visit www.klgoing.com, http://klgoing.wordpress.com, and www.myspace.com/klgoing.

The world of YA publishing seems to have gotten fairly muddy in recent years. Does YA as a genre defy definition? What draws you to write for this audience?

Yes, I think YA does defy definition. Although teen novels are written for a specific audience, the books that fall into this category are so varied, encompassing every genre from mysteries to literary fiction. That's something I love about writing YA—the openness to ideas and styles.

As for how I got drawn into writing for young adults in the first place, my journey began as a response to an article I read in *Newsweek*. They ran a story about teens in a small town who formed a gay/straight student alliance group. It was the teens featured in the story who propelled me to write my first YA novel. I found them strong, idealistic, and complex, and I thought about them long after I'd put down the magazine. I kept trying to imagine their lives and remember what it felt like to be on the brink between childhood and adulthood—to know your own mind, yet not have many of the freedoms adults take for granted. This period of time is so fleeting, and it captures my imagination in a way that the solid grounding of adulthood does not.

Where did Iggy (and his unique voice) come from? What sparked your idea for _Saint Iggy_?

Saint Iggy, like _Fat Kid Rules the World_, was sparked by a single sentence—in both cases, the first sentence of the book. I often "hear" a character talking in my mind and if their voice is unique enough, it will make me stop and listen. With Iggy and Troy, I found their voices to be very compelling and the single sentences that begin both books held tremendous story potential, leaving me with lots of questions I wanted to answer. In Iggy's case, I also loved the lying-yet-not-lying quality of his voice, as well as the mix of hope and dark reality. These qualities propelled the story forward.

I find the contrast in your characters so interesting—the alternate perspective of Mo, for example, seems to further illuminate Iggy's "Iggy-ness." Is such a foil needed when a writer chooses first-person narration?

This is an interesting question. I wouldn't say that a foil is _needed_ in order to make a unique character work, but it does feel natural since part of establishing someone as unique is showing them interacting with the world around them and contrasting the way they react with the way someone else reacts.

With _Saint Iggy_, I was playing with contrasts throughout the novel, always juxtaposing black and white to illuminate the shades of gray. It's hard to contrast a human being though because we're never just one thing—we're always complex mixtures of goodness and selfishness. So while Mo is to some extent an inversion of Iggy, he's also his own unique person, which is why I think he ultimately works as a character. He may function as a foil, but I didn't use him as a tool. I wrote him as a person—one that I allowed to break my heart in wholly new ways.

Your books have gotten starred reviews and have been included on top-100-books-of-the-year lists and must-read lists. I even saw a K.L. Going title on a list of books someone would take along if stranded on an island. Plus your debut _Fat Kid Rules the World_ won a Printz Honor. What's it like to be so celebrated? Does this ever surprise you?

It surprises me all the time! Mostly because I don't believe things are real until long after they've happened. There's always a lag time between when something good happens to me and when I allow myself to feel excited about it. When I got my first book contract I put every penny of my advance in the bank and didn't touch a cent until the book was in stores because it felt entirely plausible that someone would change their mind about publishing it. I suppose I'm a lot like my first narrator, Troy Billings, because of this way of thinking. When _Fat Kid_ was published I figured everyone would recognize me as the narrator immediately—it was _so_ obvious—but people rarely do. Still, I tend to operate on this level. Usually, by the time one book might be receiving accolades I'm in the thick of agonizing over the next one and I always think everyone will hate the next book. I know, I know . . . I can't help it!

On your blog you've talked about your maternal feelings toward Iggy and having unconditional love for your characters. At what point does a character take on a life of his own? Can you tell me a little about how you tackle character development?

For me, a character takes on a life of his own very early in the process. Often times, I feel that character is alive and "real" long before I write a word. In fact, this is part of how I determine if a given idea ought to be a book. Many writers use note cards to jot down story ideas, but I have always depended on my subconscious to weed out the ideas that aren't meant to stick. I don't take notes but I do turn ideas over in my mind again and again, seeing which ones wait around for months (or in some cases, years). The characters who won't go away, whether written or not, are real to me and they already have a personality. Character development then, is the task of unearthing this personality and revealing it on the page to those who don't live inside my head.

Why have you so often chosen to write male characters?

Honestly, I have no idea. People often ask this question and I wish I had a fabulous intellectual answer, but I don't. I can't figure it out either! My best guess is that I write what I am intrigued by and I find males to be very intriguing. I like the way they reveal a lot without revealing anything.

You have a good Web presence including a Web site, blog and MySpace page. Can a career author get by without the Internet?

I *do* think it's possible to get by without the Internet. I know several authors who don't maintain Web sites or do much online, but generally they are authors who have already made it big and thus can choose to have a Web presence or not and that decision can be independent from the success of their books.

My question is why *wouldn't* you want to have a Web presence? I find it to be a wonderful path to meeting readers. It's another way in which I can be creative and connect to the world around me. On my Web site, I can expand the world of my books by offering deleted scenes, teacher's guides, soundtracks . . . My blog allows me to open a window into my writing process, and the forum is a really fun way to interact with fans. The Web is a fabulous tool, so why not use it?

Is it important for you to get feedback from your audience? Does it effect your writing at all?

Yes, it's important to me to get feedback from my audience, but I try not to let that feedback effect my writing. Maybe that seems contradictory, but I don't think it is. The decision to be published means you want to connect to others and share your work. Without hearing from my audience, that connection is incomplete. Yet at the same time, a book has to be created from someplace deep within you, and sometimes this process can get interrupted if the author's mind is distracted by thoughts of what a book "should" or "should not" be. For example, if I recall a specific piece of criticism from a previous book, I might try to eliminate that element from my next book, but maybe that element would work perfectly in another setting.

It's difficult to do, but I try to keep the voices in my head to a minimum. Sometimes I wonder if that's why so many first books are so powerful. At that point there really are just two voices—yours and your narrator's. After that, the writing process will never again be as pure.

As a full-time writer, do you have a routine? Can you offer advice on juggling projects, events, deadlines, etc.? What keeps you motivated?

I only started writing full-time this past year, so I feel like I'm still in the process of figuring out what works and what doesn't. I don't have a set routine right now, but I generally aim to work from 8 to 5. However, I work many more hours when the ideas are flowing, sometimes writing until I can't stare at the computer screen another second. The biggest thing I've learned so far is to allow myself to work on other projects when one project gets stuck. For a long time I would stare at the pages, trying to force creativity, but finally I admitted this wasn't working. Now, I allow myself to tackle something else if necessary—including reading good books. Many times, taking a break to read a great novel will give me inspiration and improve my mood enough to allow me to write again. That's really what keeps me motivated.

You critique novel manuscripts for aspiring writers when your own writing schedule permits. What are the most common problems with the manuscripts you see?

There are several problems I often see that all fall into one category: trying to do too much. Now, of course writing a book takes tremendous stamina so I'm not referring to the amount of effort a writer puts into their work. I'm a huge advocate for editing again and again and again. What I'm referring to is the tendency new writers have to want to write the next New York Times Best Seller. They often try to combine elements of every popular book on the market, all while writing in a literary fiction style. In the query letter this is revealed in a sentence that usually begins: "My book is _____ meets _____ meets _____." When you read these novels you feel as if the story doesn't know what it wants to be and they are generally crowded with unnecessary adjectives. The irony is that it's the personal, heartfelt stories told in a direct way that often grab us the most.

You've got a rather unique perspective on the publishing world having worked as an agents' assistant, a bookstore manager, and a full-time writer. What's your best advice to writers looking to break in?

My best advice is to persevere and try not to take rejection too personally when it happens. When I worked at Curtis Brown, Ltd. part of my job was reading the slush pile and I was

"So I got kicked out of school today, which is not so great but not entirely unexpected . . ." begins *Saint Iggy*, by Prinz Honor winner K.L. Going. With a drunken father and a mother who is often missing, Iggy enlists the aid of his law-school dropout friend Mo and enacts a plan to change the way people perceive him and keep himself from getting kicked out of school permanently. *Publishers Weekly* calls *Saint Iggy* Going's "most impressive achievement yet."

blown away by how much competition is out there for every single slot on a publisher's list. We turned down many books simply because they didn't match the agent's tastes, and there were definitely times when a book lingered on the "Maybe" pile for a long time before being sent back with a sigh. Those decisions are routine for agents and editors. They have to be made all the time and don't necessarily reflect on your future as a writer.

As a bookstore manager and full-time writer I've seen the same thing operate on a different level with published books. So often great books find their own quiet audiences rather than becoming huge commercial hits and it's not a reflection of the quality of the book. The marketplace is ever changing and unpredictable, so be true to yourself. Write what you love and not what you think will sell.

Do you have any favorite authors to recommend? Or who/what should every aspiring YA writer be reading?

I have many favorite authors including M.T. Anderson, Nancy Werlin, Virginia Euwer Wolf, Susan Cooper, Linda Sue Park, Angela Johnson, Jack Kerouac, J.D. Salinger, David James Duncan, John Irving . . . the list could go on and on. Although many of my favorites are YA authors, I would recommend that writers (aspiring or otherwise) read broadly. You never know what will inspire you or what you can learn from.

Please tell me about your upcoming projects.

I have a new middle grade novel called *The Garden of Eve* coming out this fall. It's the story of a young girl who moves with her father to a town in upstate New York where he's bought an apple orchard that's rumored to be cursed. Since her mom died, Evie hasn't believed in curses or fairy tales, but then she receives a mysterious seed as an eleventh birthday gift and meets a boy who claims to be dead, and she's forced to reevaluate what's real and what's not.

I'm also hard at work on my next novel for teens, which should come out in the fall of 2008. I have a picture book under contract, which I'm excited about, as well as a non-fiction book that I'm working on. It's been a lot of fun to have such varied projects!

—*Alice Pope*

Book Publishers

◪ ALFRED A. KNOPF AND CROWN BOOKS FOR YOUNG READERS

Imprint of Random House Children's Books, 1745 Broadway, New York NY 10019. (212)782-9000. Web site: www.randomhouse.com/kids. See Random House and Delacorte and Doubleday Books for Young Readers listings. Book publisher. "We publish distinguished juvenile fiction and nonfiction for ages 0-18."

• Knopf title *The Book Thief*, by Markus Zusak, won a Printz Honor Medal in 2007.

How to Contact/Writers No query letters, accompanying SASE or reply postcard. Send full picture book mss up to 25 pages plus a 1-page synopsis for longer works. "Please let us know if it is a multiple submission. If we are interested, we will reply withing 6 months of receipt of the manuscript." Address envelope to: Acquisitions Editor, Knopf & Crown/Books for Young Readers, Random House, 1745 Broadway, 9-3, New York, NY 10019.

Illustration Contact: Isabel Warren-Lynch, executive director, art & design. Responds only if interested. Samples returned with SASE; samples filed.

Terms Pays illustrators and photographers by the project or royalties. Original artwork returned at job's completion.

KRBY CREATIONS, LLC

P.O. Box 327, Bay Head NJ 08742. Fax: (815)846-0636. E-mail: info@KRBYCreations.com. Web site: www.KRBYCreations.com. Estab. 2003. Specializes in children's picture books for the trade, library, specialty retail, and educational markets. **Writers contact:** Kevin Burton. 40% of books by first-time authors.

Fiction Recently published *The Snowman in the Moon*, by Stephen Heigh (picture book); *Mulch the Lawnmower*, by Scott Nelson (picture book); *My Imagination*, by Katrina Estes-Hill (picture book).

How to Contact/Writers Fiction/nonfiction: Writers *must* request guidelines by e-mail prior to submitting mss. See Web site. Submissions without annotation found in guidelines will not be considered. Responds to e-mail queries in 1 week; mss in 1-3 months. Publishes book 1 year after acceptance. Considers simultaneous submissions.

Illustrators Detailed contact guidelines available on Web site. Illustrator terms negotiable. Pays advance plus royalties for experienced Illustrators. Avoids work-for-hire contracts. 40-60% of illustrators are first-time children's picture book published.

Terms Pays authors royalty of 6-15% based on wholesale price. Catalog on Web site. Offers writer's guidelines by e-mail.

Tips "Submit as professionally as possible; make your vision clear to us about what you are trying to capture. Know your market/audience and identify it in your proposal. Tell us what is new/unique with your idea. All writers submitting must first request guidelines by e-mail."

WENDY LAMB BOOKS

Imprint of Random House, 1745 Broadway, New York NY 10019. Fax: (212)782-8234. Web site: www.randomhouse.com. **Manuscript Acquisitions:** Wendy Lamb. Receives 300-400 submissions/year. Publishes 12-15 novels/year for middle grade and young adult readers. 15% of books by first-time authors and 10% unagented writers. **Fiction** Recently published *Eyes of the Emperor*, by Graham Salisbury; *Brian's Hunt*, by Gary Paulsen; *Bucking the Sarge*, by Christopher Paul Curtis.

How to Contact/Writers Query with SASE for reply or via e-mail. "At the moment we are not publishing picture books. A query letter should briefly describe the book you want to write, the intended age group, and your publishing credits, if any. If you like, you may send no more than 5 pages of the manuscript of shorter works (i.e. picture books) and a maximum of 10 pages for longer works (i.e. novels). *Please do not send more than the specified amount.* Also, do not send cassette tapes, videos, or other materials along with your query or excerpt. Manuscript pages sent will not be returned. Do not send original art."

Illustration Reviews ms/illustration packages from artists. Query with SASE for reply.

Terms Pays illustrators and photographers by project or royalties. Original artwork returned at job's completion.

LARK BOOKS

Sterling Publishing, 67 Broadway, Ashville NC 28801. (828)253-0467. Fax: (828)253-7952. E-mail: joe@larkbooks.com. Web site: www.larkbooks.com. Specializes in nonfiction. **Writers contact:** Rose McLarney, children's books. **Illustrators contact:** Celia Naranjo, creative director. Produces 3-5 picture book/year. 70% of books by first-time authors. "Lark Books' philisophy is to produce high-quality, content-oriented nonfiction title for ages 0-18 with a focus on art, concept, picture books, humor, science, nature, fun and games, crafts, and activities."

Nonfiction All levels: activity books, animal, arts/crafts, cooking, hobbies, how-to, nature/environment, self help. Recently published *The Boo Boo Book*, by Joy Masoff (ages 0-5, board book); *My Very Favorite Art Book: I Love Collage*, by Jennifer Lipsey (ages 5-9, art instruction); *The Don't-Get-Caught Doodle Notebook*, by Susan McBride (ages 10-110, sneaky art instruction); *Pet Science: 50 Purr-Fectly Woof-Worthy Activities for You & Your Pets*, by Veronika Alice Gunter (ages 8-12, science/activity).

How to Contact/Writers Accepts international submissions. Fiction: Submit complete ms; accept only picture books. Nonfiction: Submit outline/synopsis and 1 sample chapter. Responds to queries in 3 weeks; mss in 3 months. Publishes book 1 year after acceptance. Considers simultaneous submissions, electronic submissions, previously published work.

Illustration Accepts material from international illustrators. Works with 7-10 illustrators/year. Reviews ms/illustration packages. For ms/illustration packages: Send manuscript with dummy. Submit ms/illustration packages to Joe Rhatigan, senior editor. If interested in illustrating future titles, query with samples. Submit samples to Rose McLarney, children's books. Samples returned with SASE.

Terms Offers advance against royalties. Author sees galleys for review. Illustrators see dummies for review. Originals returned upon request. Catalog on Web site. See Web site for writer's guidelines.

Tips "Study the market you're writing for. Let me know why you think now is the right time to publish your book idea. I'm always on the lookout for strong writers with an expertise in an area (science, art, etc.), and even through we publish a lot of books that appeal to teachers and parents, these books are for the kids. Our books have a lot of humor in them as well as a lot of things to do and learn."

LEE & LOW BOOKS INC.

95 Madison Ave., New York NY 10016-7801. (212)779-4400. Fax: (212) 683-1894. E-mail: info@leeandlow.com. Web site: www.leeandlow.com. **Acquisitions:** Louise May, editor-in-chief; Jennifer Fox, senior editor. Publishes 12-14 picture books/year. 25% of books by first-time authors. Lee & Low publishes only books with multicultural themes. "One of our goals is to discover new talent and produce books that reflect the multicultural society in which we live."

● Lee & Low Books is dedicated to publishing culturally authentic literature. The company makes a special effort to work with writers and artists of color and encourages new voices. Also see listings for Bebop Books and New Voices Award.

Fiction Picture books, young readers: anthology, contemporary, history, multicultural, poetry. ''We are not considering folktales or animal stories.'' Picture book, middle reader: contemporary, history, multicultural, nature/environment, poetry, sports. Average word length: picture books—1,000-1,500 words. Recently published *Jazz Baby*, by Carol Boston Weatherford, illustrated by Laura Freeman; *Home at Last*, by Susan Middleton Elya, illustrated by Felipe Davalos.

Nonfiction Picture books: concept. Picture books, middle readers: biography, history, multicultural, science and sports. Average word length: picture books—1,500-3,000. Recently published *George Crum and the Saratoga Chip*, by Gaylia Taylor, illustrated by Frank Morrison by Lynne Barasch; *Rattlesnake Mesa*, by Ednah New Rider Weber, photographed by Richela Renkun.

How to Contact/Writers Fiction/nonfiction: Submit complete ms. No e-mail submissions. Responds in 4 months. Publishes a book 1-2 years after acceptance. Will consider simultaneous submissions. Guidelines on Web site.

Illustration Works with 12-14 illustrators/year. Uses color artwork only. Reviews ms/illustration packages from artists. Contact: Louise May. Illustrations only: Query with samples, résumé, promo sheet and tearsheets. Responds only if interested. Samples returned with SASE; samples filed. Original artwork returned at job's completion.

Photography Buys photos from freelancers. Works on assignment only. Model/property releases required. Submit cover letter, résumé, promo piece and book dummy.

Terms Pays authors advances against royalty. Pays illustrators advance against royalty. Photographers paid advance against royalty. Book catalog available for 9×12 SAE and $1.75 postage; ms and art guidelines available via Web site or with SASE.

Tips ''We strongly urge writers to visit our Web site and familiarize themselves with our list before submitting. Materials will only be returned with SASE.''

LEGACY PRESS

Imprint of Rainbow Publishers, P.O. Box 70130 Richmond VA 23255. (800)638-4428. Web site: www.rainbowpublishers.com. **Manuscript/Art Acquisitions:** Kristen Hughes, editor. Publishes 3 young readers/year; 3 middle readers/year; 3 young adult titles/year. Publishes nonfiction, Bible-teaching books. ''We publish growth and development books for the evangelical Christian from a non-denominational viewpoint that may be marketed primarily through Christian bookstores.''

Nonfiction Young readers, middle readers, young adults: reference, religion. Recently published *Bill the Warthog—Full Metal Trench Coat*, by Dean Anderson, illustrated by Dave Carleson.

How to Contact/Writers Nonfiction: Submit outline/synopsis and 3-5 sample chapters. Responds to queries in 6 weeks; mss in 3 months. Publishes a book 36 months after acceptance. Will consider simultaneous submissions and previously published work.

Illustration Works with 5 illustrators/year. Reviews ms/illustration packages from artists. Submit ms with 5-10 pieces of final art. Illustrations only: Query with samples to be kept on file.

Terms Pays authors royalty or work purchased outright. Offers advances. Pays illustrators per illustration. Sends galley to authors. Book catalog available for business size SASE; ms guidelines for SASE.

Tips ''Get to know the Christian bookstore market. We are looking for innovative ways to teach and encourage children about the Christian life. No picture books please.''

LERNER PUBLISHING GROUP

241 First Ave. N., Minneapolis MN 55401. (612)332-3344. Fax: (612)332-7615. E-mail: info@lernerbooks.com. Web site: www.lernerbooks.com. **Manuscript Acquisitions:** Jennifer Zimian, nonfiction submissions editor; Zelda Wagner, fiction submissions editor. Primarily publishes books for children ages 7-18. List includes titles in geography, natural and physical science, current events, ancient and modern history, high interest, sports, world cultures, and numerous biography series.

● Starting in 2007, Lerner Publishing Group no longer accepts submission for any of their imprints except Kar-Ben Publishing.

How to Contact/Writers ''We will continue to seek targeted solicitations at specific reading levels and in specific subject areas. The company will list these targeted solicitations on our Web site and in national newsletters, such as the SCBWI Bulletin. Unsoliciteds sent in November 2006 under our previous submissions policy will be read and replied to by November 2007.''

◆ ARTHUR A. LEVINE BOOKS

Imprint of Scholastic, Inc., 557 Broadway, New York NY 10012. (212)343-4436. Fax: (212)343-4890. Web site: www.arthuralevinebooks.com. **Acquisitions:** Arthur A. Levine, editorial director. Publishes approximately 8 picture books/year; 8 full-length works for middle grade and young adult readers/year. Approximately 25% of books by first-time authors.

- Arthur A. Levine title *The Adventures of Marco Polo*, by Russell Freedman, won the Golden Kite Award for Nonfiction in 2007.

Fiction Recently published *The End*, by David LaRochelle and Richard Egielski (picture book); *Half the World Away*, by Libby Gleeson and Freya Blackwood (picture book); *Mother Goose's Storytime Nursery Rhymes*, by Axel Scheffler (picture book); *So Totally Emily Ebers*, by Lisa Yee (novel); *The Murder of Bindy Mackenzie*, by Jaclyn Moriarty (novel).

Nonfiction Recently published *A Second is a Hiccup: A Child's Book of Time*, by Hazel Hutchins and Kady MacDonald Denton (picture book), *Dizzy*, by Jonah Winter and Sean Qualls (picture book), and *The Adventures of Marco Polo*, by Russell Freedman and Bagram Ibatoulline (picture book).

How to Contact/Writers Fiction/nonfiction: Accepts queries only. Responds to queries in 1 month; mss in 5 months. Publishes a book 1½ years after acceptance.

Illustration Works with 8 illustrators/year. Will review ms/illustration packages from artists. Query first. Illustrations only: Send postcard sample with tearsheets. Samples not returned.

🅰 🅥 LITTLE, BROWN AND COMPANY BOOKS FOR YOUNG READERS

Hachette Book Group USA, 237 Park Ave, New York NY 10017. (212)364-1100. Fax: (212)364-0925. Web sites:www.lb-kids.com; www.lb-teens.com. **Vice President, Publisher:** Megan Tingley. Editorial Director, Little, Brown Books for Young Readers (core hardcover and paperback list): Andrea Spooner. Editorial Director, Poppy (young women's commercial fiction imprint): Cynthia Eagan; Editorial Director, LB Kids (novelty and licensed books imprint): Liza Baker. Senior Editor: Jennifer Hunt. **Creative Director:** Gail Doobinin. Publishes picture books, board books, chapter books, novelty books, and general nonfiction and novels for middle and young adult readers.

- Little, Brown does not accept unsolicited manuscripts or unagented material. Little, Brown title *Firegirl*, by Tony Abbott, won the Golden Kite Award for Fiction in 2007. Their title *Hippo! No, Rhino!*, illustrated and written by Jeff Newman, won the Golden Kite Honor for Picture Book Illustration in 2007.

Fiction Picture books: humor, adventure, animal, contemporary, history, multicultural, folktales. Young adults: contemporary, humor, multicultural, suspense/mystery, chick lit. Multicultural needs include "any material by, for and about minorities." Average word length: picture books—1,000; young readers—6,000; middle readers—15,000- 50,000; young adults—50,000 and up. Recently published *The Gulps*, by Marc Brown, illustrated by Rosemary Wells; *The Gift of Nothing*, by Patrick McDonnel; *Chowder*, by Peter Brown; *How to Train Your Dragon*, by Cressida Cowell; *Atherton*, by Patrick Carman; *Nothing But the Truth (and a Few White Lies)*, by Justina Chen Headley; *Story of a Girl*, by Sara Zarr.

Nonfiction Middle readers, young adults: arts/crafts, history, multicultural, nature, self help, social issues, sports, science. Average word length: middle readers—15,000-25,000; young adults—20,000-40,000. Recently published *American Dreaming*, by Laban Carrick Hill; *Exploratopia*, by the Exploratorium.

How to Contact/Writers Only interested in solicited agented material. Fiction: Submit complete ms. Nonfiction: Submit cover letter, previous publications, a proposal, outline and 3 sample chapters. Do not send originals. Responds to queries in 2 weeks. Responds to mss in 2 months.

Illustration Works with 40 illustrators/year. Illustrations only: Query art director with b&w and color samples; provide résumé, promo sheet or tearsheets to be kept on file. Does not respond to art samples. Do not send originals; copies only.

Photography Works on assignment only. Model/property releases required; captions required. Publishes photo essays and photo concept books. Uses 35mm transparencies. Photographers should provide résumé, promo sheets or tearsheets to be kept on file.

Terms Pays authors royalties based on retail price. Pays illustrators and photographers by the project or royalty based on retail price. Sends galleys to authors; dummies to illustrators.

Tips "In order to break into the field, authors and illustrators should research their competition and try to come up with something outstandingly different."

🅲 LOLLIPOP POWER BOOKS

Imprint of Carolina Wren Press, 120 Morris Street, Durham NC 27701. (919)560-2738. Fax: (919)560-2759. E-mail: carolinawrenpress@earthlink.net. Web site: www.carolinawrenpress.org. **Manuscript Acquisitions:** Children's Book Editor. **Art Acquisitions**: Art Director. Publishes 1 picture book every two year's. 50% of books by first-time authors. "Carolina Wren Press and Lollipop Power specialize in children's books that counter stereotypes or debunk myths about race, gender, sexual orientation, etc. We are also interested in books that deal with health or mental health issues—our two biggest sellers are *Puzzles* (about a young girl coping with Sickle Cell Disease) and *I like it when you joke with me, I don't like it when you touch me* (about inappropriate touching). Many of our children's titles are bilingual (English/Spanish)."

Fiction Average word length: picture books—500.

How to Contact/Writers Children's lit submissions are read February through June. (Illustrators may send samples any time.) Fiction: Submit outline/synopsis and 3 sample chapters. Responds to queries/mss in 3 months. Publishes book 2 years after acceptance. Will consider simultaneous submissions.

Illustrators We keep a file with artist samples, though we rarely can afford to use illustrators for our books. You are free to send samples to be included in this file. Reviews ms/illustration packages from artists. Submit ms with 5 pieces of final art. Illustrations only: Send photocopies, résumé, samples, SASE. Responds only if interested. Samples not returned; samples filed.

Terms Pays authors royalty of 10% minimum based on retail price or work purchased outright from authors (range: $500-$2,000). Pays illustrators by the project (range: $500-$2,000). Sends galleys to authors; dummies to illustrators. Originals returned to artist at job's completion. Catalog available on Web site.

LUCENT BOOKS

Imprint of Thomson Gale, 27550 Drake Road, Farmington Hills, MI 49331. E-mail: mary.lavey@thomson.com. Web site: www.gale.com/lucent. **Acquisitions:** Mary Lavey. Series publisher of educational nonfiction for junior high school and library markets.

• See also listing for Greenhaven Press.

Nonfiction Young adult and academic reference: current issues, diseases, drugs, biographies, geopolitics, history. Recently launched Library of Black Histiory, Issues That Concern You, and Hot Topics (all series). Recently published *The Ebola Virus*; *Death and Dying*; *Suicide Bombers; Biological Warfare*; *Overweight America*; *History of Latin America*; *and Hilary Swank*.

How to Contact/Writers E-mail query with résumé or list of publications.

Terms Work purchased outright from authors; write-for-hire, flat fee.

Tips No unsolicited manuscripts.

LUNA RISING

Imprint of Rising Moon, P.O. Box 1389, Flagstaff AZ 86002-1389. (928)774-5251. Fax: (928)774-0592. E-mail: editorial@northlandbooks.com. Web site: www.lunarisingbooks.com. Estab. 2004. Published bilingual hardcover and trade paperback originals. **Writers contact:** Theresa Howell. Produces 4-5 picture books/year. 20% of books by first-time authors. "Luna rising publishes high quality original fiction and biographies with Latino themes. Preference is given to Latino writers and illustrators."

Fiction Picture books: multicultural.

Nonfiction Picture books: biography, multicultural. Recently published *My Name is Celia: The Life of Celia Cruz*, by Monica Brown, illustrated by Rafael Lopez; *Playing Loteria*, by Rene Colato Lainez, illustrated by Jill Arena.

How to Contact/Writers Fiction/nonfiction: Submit complete ms. Inculde SASE. "No e-mail submissions please." Responds to queries in 3 months. Publishes book 1-2 years after acceptance. Considers simultaneous submissions.

Terms Authors paid royalty or flat fee. Offers advance against royalties. Offers writer's guidelines for SASE.

Tips "We are looking for original bilingual stories and biographies of Latino role models. Call for book catalog."

MAGINATION PRESS

750 First Street, NE, Washington DC 20002-2984. (202)218-3982. Fax: (202)336-5624. Web site: www.maginationpress.com. **Acquisitions:** Darcie Conner Johnston, managing editor. Publishes 4 picture books/year; 4 young readers/year; 2 middle readers/year; 1 young adult title/year. 75% of books by first-time authors. "We publish books dealing with the psycho/therapeutic resolution of children's problems and psychological issues with a strong self-help component."

• Magination Press is an imprint of the American Psychological Association.

Fiction All levels: psychological and social issues, self-help, health, multicultural, special needs. Picture books, middle readers. Recently published *Mookey the Monkey Gets Over Being Teased*, by Heather Lonczak, illustrated by Marcy Ramsey (ages 4-8); *Ginny Morris and Dad's New Girlfriend*, by Mary Collins Gallagher, illustrated by Whitney Martin (ages 8-12).

Nonfiction All levels: psychological and social issues, special needs, self help. Picture books, young readers, middle readers: activity, workbooks. Recently published *Feeling Better: A Kid's Book About Therapy*, by Rachel Rashkin, illustrated by Bonnie Adamson (ages 8-12); *What to Do When You Worry Too Much: A Kid's Guide to Overcoming Anxiety*, by Dawn Huebner, illustrated by Bonnie Matthews (ages 6-12).

How to Contact/Writers Fiction/nonfiction: Submit complete ms. Responds to queries in 1-2 months; mss in 2-6 months. Will consider simultaneous submissions. Materials returned only with a SASE. Publishes a book 18-24 months after acceptance.

Illustration Works with 10-15 illustrators/year. Reviews ms/illustration packages. Will review artwork for future assignments. Responds only if interested, or immediately if SASE or response card is included. We keep samples on file.

How to Contact/Illustrators Illustrations only: Query with samples; a few samples and Web address are best. Original artwork returned at job's completion.

Photography Buys stock.

Terms Pays authors royalty of 5-15% based on actual revenues (net). Pays illustrators by the project. Book catalog and ms guidelines on request with SASE. Catalog and ms guidelines available on Web site.

☐ MASTER BOOKS

Imprint of New Leaf Press, P.O. Box 726, Green Forest, AR 72638. (870)438-5288. Fax: (870)438-5120. E-mail: nlp@newleafpress.net. Web site: www.masterbooks.net. **Manuscript Acquisitions:** Amanda Price, acquisitions editor. **Art Acquisitions:** Brent Spurlock, art director. Publishes 2 picture books/year; 3 young readers/year; 3 middle readers/year; 2 young adult titles/year. 10% of books by first-time authors.

Nonfiction Picture books: activity books, animal, nature/environment, creation. Young readers, middle readers, young adults: activity books, animal, biography Christian, nature/environment, science, creation. Recently published *Whale of a Story*, by Buddy Davis (middle readers, Bible story); *Dinky Dinosaur*, by Darrell Wiskur (picture book, creation); *For Those Who Dare*, by John Hudson Tiner (young adult, biography).

How to Contact/Writers Nonfiction: Submit outline/synopsis and 3 sample chapters. Responds to queries/mss in 3 months. Publishes book 1 year after acceptance. Will consider simultaneous submissions.

Illustration We are not looking for illustrations.

Terms Pays authors royalty of 3-15% based on wholesale price. Sends galleys to authors. Book catalog available for 9×12 SAE and $1.85 postage; ms guidelines available for SASE. Catalog available on Web site.

Tips "All of our children's books are creation-based, including topics from the Book of Genesis. We look also for homeschool educational material that would be supplementary to a homeschool curriculum."

MARGARET K. MCELDERRY BOOKS

Imprint of Simon & Schuster Children's Publishing Division, 1230 Avenue of the Americas, New York NY 10020. (212)698-7000. Web site: www.simonsayskids.com. **Publisher:** Vice President, Associate Publisher Emma D. Dryden. **Acquisitions:** Karen Wojtyla, executive editor; Sarah Sevier, associate editor; Sarah Payne, editorial assistant. **Art Acquisitions:** Ann Bobco, executive art director. Imprint of Simon & Schuster Children's Publishing Division. Publishes 15 + picture books/year; 8-10 middle readers/year; 8-10 young adult titles/year. 10% of books by first-time authors; 50% of books from agented writers. "Margaret K. McElderry Books publishes original hardcover trade books for children from pre-school age through young adult. This list includes picture books, middle grade and teen fiction, poetry, and fantasy. The style and subject matter of the books we publish is almost unlimited. We do not publish textbooks, coloring and activity books, greeting cards, magazines, pamphlets, or religious publications."

Fiction All levels. "Always interested in publishing humorous picture books, original beginning reader stories, and strong poetry." Average word length: picture books—500; young readers—2,000; middle readers—10,000-20,000; young adults—45,000-50,000. Recently published *Bear's New Friend*, by Karma Wilson, illustrated by Jane Chapman (picture book); *Carrott Soup*, by Jane Chapman (picture book); *Sand Dollar Summer*, by Kimberly Jones (middle-grade); *Victory*, by Susan Cooper (middle grade); *Pirate Curse*, by Kai Meyer (teen); *Burned*, by Ellen Hopkins (teen); *Skin*, by Adrienne Maria Vrettos (teen).

How to Contact/Writers Send query letters with SASE for picture books; send synopsis and first 3 chapters or first 30 pages with SASE for novels. Responds to queries in 1-2 month; mss in 3-4 months. Publishes a book 24-36 months after acceptance. Will consider simultaneous queries from previously unpublished authors and those submitted to other publishers, "though we request that the author let us know it is a simultaneous query." Please do not call to query or follow up.

Illustration Works with 20-30 illustrators/year. Query with samples, resume, tearsheets. Contact: Ann Bobco, executive art director, Design Dept., 4th Floor. Samples filed. Responds only if interested.

Terms Pays authors royalty based on retail price. Pays illustrator royalty of by the project. Pays photographers by the project. Original artwork returned at job's completion. Manuscript guidelines for #10 SASE with one first-class stamp.

Tips "We're looking for strong, original fiction, especially mysteries and middle grade humor. We are always interested in picture books for the youngest age reader. Study our titles."

MEADOWBROOK PRESS

5451 Smetana Dr., Minnetonka MN 55343-9012. (952)930-1100. Fax: (952)930-1940. Web site: www.meadowbrookpress.com. **Manuscript Acquisitions :** Submissions Editor. **Art Acquisitions:** Art Director. 20% of books by first-time authors; 10% of books from agented writers. Publishes children's poetry books, activity books, arts-and-crafts books and how-to books.

• Meadowbrook does not accept unsolicited children's picture books, short stories or novels. They are primarily a nonfiction press. The publisher offers specific guidelines for children's poetry. Be sure to specify the type of project you have in mind when requesting guidelines, or visit their Web site.

Nonfiction Publishes activity books, arts/crafts, how-to, poetry. Average word length: varies. Recently published *Wiggleand Giggle Busy Book*, by Trish Kuffner (activity book); *My Teacher's in Detention*, by Bruce Lansky.

How to Contact/Writers Nonfiction: See guidelines on Web site before submitting. Responds only if interested. Publishes a book 1-2 years after acceptance. Will consider simultaneous submissions.

Illustration Works with 2 illustrators/year. Reviews ms/illustration packages from artists. Submit ms with 2-3 pieces of nonreturnable samples. Responds only if interested. Samples filed.

Photography Buys photos from freelancers. Buys stock. Model/property releases required. Submit cover letter.

Terms Pays authors royalty of 5-7% based on retail price. Offers average advance payment of $2,000-4,000. Pays illustrators per project. Pays photographers by the project. Book catalog available for 5×11 SASE and 2 first-class stamps; ms guidelines and artists guidelines available for SASE.

Tips "Writers should visit our Web site before submitting their work to us. Illustrators should take a look at the books we publish to determine whether their style is consistent with ours. Writers should also note the style and content patterns of our books. No phone calls, please—e-mail us. We work with the printed word and will respond more effectively to your questions if we have something in front of us."

MERIWETHER PUBLISHING LTD.

885 Elkton Dr., Colorado Springs CO 80907-3557. (719)594-9916. Fax: (719)594-9916. E-mail: merpcds@aol.com. Web site: www.meriwetherpublishing.com. **Manuscript Acquisitions:** Ted Zapel, comedy plays and educational drama; Rhonda Wray, religious drama. "We do most of our artwork in-house; we do not publish for the children's elementary market." 75% of books by first-time authors; 5% of books from agented writers. "Our niche is drama. Our books cover a wide variety of theatre subjects from play anthologies to theatrecraft. We publish books of monologs, duologs, short one-act plays, scenes for students, acting textbooks, how-to speech and theatre textbooks, improvisation and theatre games. Our Christian books cover worship on such topics as clown ministry, storytelling, banner-making, drama ministry, children's worship and more. We also publish anthologies of Christian sketches. We do not publish works of fiction or devotionals."

Fiction Middle readers, young adults: anthology, contemporary, humor, religion. "We publish plays, not prose-fiction." Our emphasis is comedy plays instead of educational themes.

Nonfiction Middle readers: activity books, how-to, religion, textbooks. Young adults: activity books, drama/theater arts, how-to church activities, religion. Average length: 250 pages. Recently published *Acting for Life*, by Jack Frakes; *Scenes Keep Happening*, by Mary Krell-Oishi; *Service with a Smile*, by Daniel Wray.

How to Contact/Writers Nonfiction: Query or submit outline/synopsis and sample chapters. Responds to queries in 3 weeks; mss in 2 months or less. Publishes a book 6-12 months after acceptance. Will consider simultaneous submissions.

Illustration Works with 2 illustrators/year. Query first. Query with samples; send résumé, promo sheet or tearsheets. Samples returned with SASE.

Terms Pays authors royalty of 10% based on retail or wholesale price. Book catalog for SAE and $2 postage; ms guidelines for SAE and 1 first-class stamp.

Tips "We are currently interested in finding unique treatments for theater arts subjects: scene books, how-to books, musical comedy scripts, monologs and short comedy plays for teens."

MILET PUBLISHING LTD.

333 N. Michigan Ave., Suite 530, Chicago IL 60601. (312)920-1828. Fax: (312)920-1829. E-mail: info@milet.com. Web site: www.milet.com. Estab. 1995. Specializes in trade books, nonfiction, fiction, multicultural material. **Writers contact:** Editorial Director. **Illustrators contact:** Editorial Director. Produces 30+ picture books, 2 middle readers/year. "Milet publishes a celebrated range of artistic and innovative children's books in English, as well as the leading range of bilingual children's books."

Fiction Picture books: adventure, animal, concept, contemporary, hi-lo, humor, multicultural, poetry. Young readers: adventure, animal, concept, contemporary, fantasy, hi-lo, multicultural, nature/environment, poetry. Middle readers: adventure, animal, contemporary, fantasy, multicultural, nature/environment, poetry, problem novels. Young adults/teens: contemporary, fantasy, multicultural, nature/environment, poetry, problem novels. Recently published *Telling Tales*, by Laura Hambleton & Sedat Turhan (ages 5-7, picture book); *Strawberry Bullfrog*, by Laura Hambleton, Sedat Turhan & Sally Hagin (agest 5-7, picture book); *Monkey Business*, by Laura Hambleton, Sedat Turhan & Herve Tullet; *Bella Balistica and the African Safari*, by Adam Guillain (ages 8-12, novel).

Nonfiction All levels: activity books, animal, arts/crafts, concept, hi-lo, multicultural, nature/environment, social issues. language learning. Recently published *Starting English*, by Tracy Traynor & Anna Wilman (ages 14 and up); *English with Abby and Zak*, by Tracy Traynor & Laura Hambleton (ages 5-7).

How to Contact/Writers Accepts international submissions. Fiction/nonfiction: Submit outline/synopsis and

2-3 sample chapters. Responds to queries in 1 weeks; mss in 1-2 months. Publishes book 12-18 months after acceptance. Considers simultaneous submissions. "Please review the submissions page on our Web site,www.milet.com, for requirements on submitting your work. SASE must be included.

Illustration Accepts material from international illustrators. Works with 4-5 illustrators/year. Uses both color and b&w. Reviews ms/illustration packages. For ms/illustration packages: Submit ms with 2-3 pieces of final art. Reviews work for future assignments. If interested in illustrating future titles, send résumé, promo sheet, client list. Submit samples to Editorial Director. Samples returned with SASE.

Terms Authors paid all terms negotiated depending on type of project. Author sees galleys for review. Illustrators see dummies for review. Catalog on Web site. All imprints included in single catalog. See Web site for writer's, artist's guidelines.

Tips "Please check our list on our Web site to see if your work will be suitable. We are interested only in fresh, imaginative, non-traditional work."

MILKWEED EDITIONS

1011 Washington Ave. S., Suite 300, Minneapolis MN 55415-1246. (612)332-3192. Fax: (612)215-2550. E-mail: editor@milkweed.org. Web site: www.milkweed.org. **Manuscript Acquisitions:** Daniel Slager, editor-in-chief. Publishes 3-4 middle readers/year. 25% of books by first-time authors. "Milkweed Editions publishes with the intention of making a humane impact on society, in the belief that literature is a transformative art uniquely able to convey the essential experiences of the human heart and spirit. To that end, Milkweed Editions publishes distinctive voices of literary merit in handsomely designed, visually dynamic books, exploring the ethical, cultural, and esthetic issues that free societies need continually to address."

Fiction Middle readers: adventure, contemporary, fantasy, multicultural, nature/environment, suspense/mystery. Does not want to see anthologies, folktales, health, hi-lo, picture books, poetry, religion, romance, sports. Average length: middle readers—90-200 pages. Recently published *Perfect,* by Natasha Friend (contemporary); *Trudy,* by Jessica Lee Anderson (contemporary); The Summer of the Pike, by Jutta Richter (contemporary/translation).

How to Contact/Writers Fiction: Submit complete ms. Responds to mss in 6 months. Publishes a book 1 year after acceptance. Will consider simultaneous submissions.

Illustration Works with 2-4 illustrators/year. Reviews ms/illustration packages from artists. Query; submit ms with dummy. Illustrations only: Query with samples; provide résumé, promo sheet, slides, tearsheets and client list. Samples filed or returned with SASE; samples filed. Originals returned at job's completion.

Terms Pays authors royalty of 6% based on retail price. Offers advance against royalties. Illustrators' contracts are decided on an individual basis. Sends galleys to authors. Book catalog available for $1.50 to cover postage; ms guidelines available for SASE or at Web site. Must include SASE with ms submission for its return.

☐ THE MILLBROOK PRESS

A division of Lerner Publishing Group, Inc., 241 First Avenue North Minneapolis, MN 5540. (800)328-4929. Fax: (800)332-1132. Web site: www.lernerbooks.com.

- Starting in 2007, Lerner Publishing Group no longer accepts submission for any of their imprints except Kar-Ben Publishing.

How to Contact/Writers "We will continue to seek targeted solicitations at specific reading levels and in specific subject areas. The company will list these targeted solicitations on our Web site and in national newsletters, such as the SCBWI Bulletin. Unsoliciteds sent in November 2006 under our previous submissions policy will be read and replied to by November 2007."

MIRRORSTONE

Imprint of Wizards of the Coast, P.O. Box 707, Renton WA 98057. (425)254-2287. Web site: www.mirrorstonebooks.com. **Manuscript and Art Acquisitions:** Nina Hess. Publishes 12 middle readers/year; 6 young adult titles/year. 25% of books by first-time authors. "We publish series novels for young readers designed to spur the imagination."

Fiction Young readers, middle readers, young adults: fantasy only. Average word length: middle readers—30,000-40,000; young adults—60,000-75,000. Recently published *A Practical Guide to Dragons*, by Lisa Trumbauer (ages 6 and up); *Time Spies: Secret in the Tower*, by Candice Ransom (ages 6 and up); *Hallomere: In the Serpent's Coils*, by Tiffany Trent (ages 12 and up).

How to Contact/Writers Fiction: Query with samples, writing credits. "No manuscripts, please." Responds to queries in 6-8 weeks. Publishes book 9-24 months after acceptance.

Illustration Works with 4 illustrators/year. Query. Illustrations only: Query with samples, résumé.

Terms Pays authors royalty of 4-6% based on retail price. Offers advances (average amount: $4,000). Pays illustrators by the project. Ms guidelines available on our Web site. All imprints included in a single catalog. Catalog available on Web site.

Tips Editorial staff attended or plans to attend ALA, BEA and IRA conferences.

MITCHELL LANE PUBLISHERS, INC.

P.O. Box 196, Hockessin DE 19707. (302)234-9426. Fax: (302)234-4742. E-mail: mitchelllane@mitchelllane.com. Web site: www.mitchelllane.com. **Acquisitons:** Barbara Mitchell, president. Publishes 80 young adult titles/year. "We publish nonfiction for children and young adults."

Nonfiction Young readers, middle readers, young adults: biography, multicultural. Average word length: 4,000-50,000 words. Recently published *Ashanti, Paris Hilton* (both Blue Banner Biographies); *Jamie Lynn Spears* (A Robbie Reader).

How to Contact/Writers Most assignments are work-for-hire.

Illustration Works with 2-3 illustrators/year. Reviews ms/illustration packages from artists. Query. Illustration only: Query with samples; send résumé, portfolio, slides, tearsheets. Responds only if interested. Samples not returned; samples filed.

Photography Buys stock images. Needs photos of famous and prominent minority figures. Captions required. Uses color prints or digital images. Submit cover letter, résumé, published samples, stock photo list.

Terms Work purchased outright from authors (range: $350-2,000). Pays illustrators by the project (range: $40-400). Sends galleys to authors.

Tips "Most of our assignments are work-for-hire. Submit résumé and samples of work to be considered for future assignments."

MITTEN PRESS ✓

Ann Arbor Media Group, 2500 S. State St., Ann Arbor MI 48104. (734)913-1302. Fax: (734)913-1249. E-mail: ljohnson@mittenpress.com. Web site: www.mittenpress.com. Estab. 2005. **Acquiring Editor:** Lynne Johnson.

Fiction Picture books: adventure, animal, folktales, history, multicultural, nature/environment, sports. Recently published: *The Far-Flung Adventure of Homer the Hummer*, by Cynthia Reynolds & Catherine McClung (ages 6-10, picture book); *The Bird in Santa's Beard*, by Jeffrey Schatzer (ages 3-10, picture book); *Pippa's First Summer*, by Catherine Badgley & Bonnie Miljour.

How to Contact/Writers Submit complete ms.

Illustration Buys 6-8 illustrations/year. Will review mss/illustration packages. Submit manuscript with 3 sample chapters to Lynne Johnson, acquisitions editor. Illustration only: Query with samples. Submit to Lynne Johnson, acquisitions editor. Responds in 12 weeks. Samples not returned; samples filed.

Terms Authors see galley for review; illustrators see dummies. Original artwork returned at job's completion. Book catalog available on Web site. All imprints included in single catalog. Writer's guidelines offered on Web site.

Tips "Think through and provide information on how your book will be marketed."

⬛ MORGAN REYNOLDS PUBLISHING

620 S. Elm St., Suite 223, Greensboro NC 27406. (336)275-1311. Fax: (336)275-1152. E-mail: editorial@morganreynolds.com. Web site: www.morganreynolds.com. **Acquisitions:** Sharon F. Doorasamy, acquisitions editor. Book publisher. Publishes 40 young adult titles/year. 50% of books by first-time authors. Morgan Reynolds publishes nonfiction books for juvenile and young adult readers. "We prefer lively, well-written biographies of interesting figures for our extensive biography series. Subjects may be contemporary or historical. Books for our Great Events series should take an insightful and exciting look at pivotal periods and/or events."

Nonfiction Middle readers, young adults/teens: biography, history. Average word length: 25-35,000. Recently published *No Easy Answers: Bayard Rustin and the Civil Rights Movement*, by Calvin Craig Miller; *Empire in the East: The Story of Genghis Khan*, by Earle Rice, Jr.; *The Mail Must Go Through: The Story of the Pony Express*, by Margaret Rau; *Nikola Tesla and the Taming of Electricity*, by Lisa J. Aldrich.

How to Contact/Writers First-time authors submit entire ms. Query; submit outline/synopsis with at least 2 sample chapters and SASE. Responds to queries in 6 weeks; mss in 2 months. Publishes a book 1-2 years after acceptance. Will consider simultaneous submissions.

Terms Pays authors negotiated price. Sends galleys to authors. Manuscript guidelines available at our Web site or by mail with SASE and 1 first-class stamp. Visit Web site for complete catalog.

Tips Does not respond without SASE. "Familiarize yourself with our titles before sending a query or submission, keeping in mind that we do *not* publish fiction, autobiographies, poetry, memoirs, picture books. We focus on serious-minded, well-crafted, nonfiction books for young adults that will complement school curriculums, namely biographies of significant figures." Editorial staff has attended or plans to attend the following conferences: ALA, TLA, PLA, FAME.

NEW VOICES PUBLISHING

Imprint of KidsTerrain, Inc., P.O. Box 560, Wilmington MA 01887. (978)658-2131. Fax: (978)988-8833. E-mail: rschiano@kidsterrain.com. Web site: www.kidsterrain.com. Estab. 2000. Specializes in fiction. **Manuscript/Art Acquisitions:** Book Editor. Publishes 2 picture books/year. 95% of books by first-time authors.

Fiction Picture books, young readers: multicultural. Average word length: picture books—500; young readers—500-1,200. Recently published *Reaching Home*, by Ron Breazeale.

How to Contact/Writers Fiction: Not accepting unsolicited manuscripts. Publishes book 12-18 months after acceptance. Will consider simultaneous submissions.

Illustration Works with 2 illustrators/year. Uses color artwork only. Reviews ms/illustration packages from artists. No queries accepted until 2008. Responds in 2 weeks. Samples returned with SASE.

Terms Pays authors royalty of 10-15% based on wholesale price. Pays illustrators by the project or royalty. Sends galleys to authors. Offers writer's guidelines for SASE.

NOMAD PRESS

2456 Christain St., White River Junction VT 05001. (802)649-1995. Fax: (802)649-2667. E-mail: lauri@nomadpress.net. Web site: www.nomadpress.net. Estab. 2001. Specializes in nonfiction, educational material. **Contact:** Alex Kahan, publisher. Produces 6-8 young readers/year. 10% of books by first-time authors. "We produce nonfiction children's activity books that bring a particular science or cultural topic into sharp focus."

• Nomad Press does not accept picture books or fiction.

Nonfiction Middle readers: activity books, history, science. Average word length: middle readers—30,000. Recently published *Amazing Leonardo da Vinci Inventions You Can Build Yourself*, by Maxine Anderson (ages 9-12); *Great Colinial America Projects You Can Build Yourself*, by Kris Bordessa (ages 9-12); *Great World War II Projects You Can Build Yourself*, by Sheri Bell-Rehwoldt (ages 9-12); *Tools for Native Americans: A Kid's Guide to the History and Culture of the First Americans*, by Kim Kavin (ages 9-12).

How to Contact/Writers Accepts international submissions. Nonfiction: "Nomad Press does not accept unsolicited manuscripts. If authors are interested in contributing to our children's series, please send a writing resume that includes relevant experience/expertise and publishing credits." Responds to queries in 1-2 months. Publishes book 1 year after acceptance.

Terms Pays authors royalty based on retail price or work purchased outright. Offers advance against royalties. Catalog on Web site. All imprints included in single catalog. See Web site for writer's guidelines.

Tips "We publish a very specific kind of nonfiction children's activity book. Please keep this in mind when querying or submitting."

Ⓐ NORTH-SOUTH BOOKS

350 Seventh Ave., Suite 1400, New York NY 10001. (212)706-4545. Web site: www.northsouth.com. Imprint: Night Sky. U.S. office of Nord-Siid Verlag, Switzerland. Publishes 100 titles/year.

• North-South and its imprints do not accept queries or unsolicited manuscripts.

NORTHWORD BOOKS FOR YOUNG READERS

Imprint of T&N Children's Publishing international, 11571 K-Tel Dr., Minnetonka MN 55343. (982)933-7537. Web site: www.tnkidsbooks.com. Estab. 1984. Specializes in trade books, nonfiction. **Contact:** Submissions Editor. Produces 6-8 picture books/year; 2-4 board books/year; 4-6 young readers/year; 4 middle readers/year. 10-20% of books by first-time authors. NorthWord's mission is publish books for children that encourage a love for the natural world."

Fiction Picture books: animal, concept, history, nature/environment, poetry—all nature-related. Young readers: animal, history, nature/environment, poetry—all nature-related. Average word length: picture books—500-1,000; young readers—1,000-4,000. Recently published *Papa Fish's Lullaby*, by Patricia Hubbell, illustrated by Susan Eaddy (ages 3-5, picture book); *What Does the Wind Say?*, by Wendi Silvano, illustrated by Joan Delehanty (ages 3-5, picture book); *Hungy Beasties*, by Neecy Twinem (ages 0-3, board book).

Nonfiction: activity books, animal, arts/crafts, biography, careers, concept, cooking, geography, history, hobbies, how-to, nature/environment, science, sports. Young readers: activity books, animal, arts/crafts, biography, careers, cooking, geography, history, hobbies, how-to, nature/environment, science, sports. Middle readers: activity books, animal, arts/crafts, biography, careers, cooking, history, hobbies, nature/environment, sports. Average word length picture books—500-1,000; young readers—1,000-4,000. Recently published *What Kinds of Seeds Are These?*, by Heidi Bee Roemer, illustrated by Olena Kassian (ages 5-8, nonfiction picture book); *The Seaside Switch*, by Kathleen V. Kudlinski, illustrated by Lindy Burnett (ages 5-8, nonfiction picture book); *Elephants*, by Jill Anderson (ages 3-6, Wild Ones series); *Rocky Mountains*, by Wayne Lynch (ages 8-11, Our Wild World Ecosystem series).

How to Contact/Writers Accepts international submissions. Submit complete mss for picture books. Nonfiction: Submit outline/synopsis. Responds to queries/mss in 3 months. Publishes book 2 years after acceptance. Considers simultaneous submissions, previously published work.

Illustration Accepts material from international illustrators. Works with 8-10 illustrators/year. Uses color artwork only. For ms/illustration packages: Send ms with dummy. Submit ms/illustration packages to Submission Editor. Reviews work for future assignments. If interested in illustrating future titles, query with samples.

Submit samples to Submissions Editor. Responds in 3 months. Samples returned with SASE. Samples filed.

Photography Buys stock images. Submit photos to Submissions Editor. Looking for animal/nature photography. Model/property releases required. Photo captions required. Uses color prints. Prefers high resolution digital files. For first contact, send cover letter, client list, stock photo list, promo piece (color).

Terms Offers advance against royalties or flat fee. Pays illustrators royalty based on retail price or net receipts. Pays photographers by the project (range: $100). Author sees galleys for review. Illustrators see dummies for review. Originals returned to artist at job's completion. Catalog available for 9x11 SASE and $1.83 postage. Individual catalogs for imprints. Offers writer's, artist's guidelines for SASE; see Web site for guidelines.

Tips "Read our material and mission and what we've recently published."

N ☐ THE OLIVER PRESS, INC.

Charlotte Square, 5707 W. 36th St., Minneapolis MN 55416-2510. (952)926-8981. Fax: (952)926-8965. E-mail: queries@oliverpress.com. Web site: www.oliverpress.com. **Acquisitions:** Denise Sterling, Jenna Anderson, Megan Rocker. Publishes 8 young adult titles/year. 10% of books by first-time authors. "We publish collective biographies of people who made an impact in one area of history, including science, government, archaeology, business and crime.

Nonfiction Middle reader, young adults: biography, history, multicultural, social issues, history of science and technology. "Authors should only suggest ideas that fit into one of our existing series. We would like to add to our Innovators series on the history of technology and our Business Builders series on leaders of industry." Average word length: young adult—20,000 words. Recently published *Business Builders in Toys and Games*, by Nathan Aaseng (ages 10 and up, collective biography); *Women of Adventure*, by Jacqueline McLean (ages 10 and up, collective biography); *Meteorology: Predicting the Weather*, by Susan and Steven Wills (ages 10 and up, collective biography); *Voyageurs, Lumberjacks, and Farmers: Pioneers of the Midwest*, by Kieran Doherty (ages 10 and up, collective biography).

How to Contact/Writers Nonfiction: Query with outline/synopsis via e-mail. Does not accept unsolicited mss. Responds in 6 months. Publishes a book approximately 1 year after acceptance.

Photography Rarely buys photos from freelancers. Please do not send unsolicited materials.

Terms Pays authors flat fee or fee against negotiable royalty. Work purchased outright from authors (fee negotiable). Book catalog and ms guidelines available online or for SASE.

Tips "Authors should read some of the books we have already published before sending an e-mail query to The Oliver Press."

☐ ONSTAGE PUBLISHING

190 Lime Quarry Road, Suite 106J, Madison AL 35601 35758-8962. (256)461-0661. E-mail: onstage123@knology .net. Web site: www.onstagepublishing.com. **Manuscript Acquisitions:** Dianne Hamilton. Publishes 2-4 middle readers/year; 1-2 young adult titles/year. 80% of books by first-time authors.

Fiction Middle readers: adventure, contemporary, fantasy, history, nature/environment, science fiction, suspense/mystery. Young adults: adventure, contemporary, fantasy, history, humor, science fiction, suspense/mystery. Average word length: chapter books—4,000-6,000 words; middle readers—5,000 words and up; young adults—25,00 and up. Recently published *Dorkman*, by Pearch & Story (a boy books for ages 12 and up); *Spies, A Gander's Cove Mystery*, by Mary Ann Taylor (historical fiction for grades 3-5). "We do not produce picture books."

Nonfiction Query first; currently not producing nonfiction.

How to Contact/Writers Fiction: Send complete ms if under 20,000 words, otherwise send synopsis and first 3 chapters. Responds to queries/mss in 6-8 months. Publishes a book 1-2 years after acceptance. Will consider simultaneous submissions.

Illustration Reviews ms/illustration packages from artists. Submit ms with 3 pieces of final art. Contact: Dianne Hamilton, senior editor. Illustrations only: Arrange personal portfolio review. Responds in 6-8 weeks. Samples returned with SASE.

Photography Works on assignment only. Contact: Art Department. Model/property releases required; captions required. Uses color, 5×7, semi gloss prints. Submit cover letter, published samples, stock photo list.

Terms Pays authors/illustrators/photographers advance plus royalties. Sends galleys to authors; dummies to illustrators. Catalog available on Web site.

Tips "Study our titles and get a sense of the kind of books we publish, so that you know whether your project is likely to be right for us."

N OOLIGAN PRESS

P.O. Box 751, Portland OR 97213. (503)725-9410. E-mail: ooliganacquisitions@pdx.edu. Web site: www.ooligan press.pdx.edu. Estab. 2001. **Contact:** Acquisitions Committee. "Ooligan Press is a general trade press at Portland State University. As a teaching press, Ooligan makes as little distinction as possible between the press and the

classroom. Under the direction of professional faculty and staff, the work of the press is done by students enrolled in the Book Publishing graduate program at PSU. We are especially interested in works with social, literary, or educational value. Though we place special value on local authors, we are open to all submissions, including translated works and writings by children and young adults. We do not currently publish picture books, board books, easy readers, or pop-up books.'' 90% of books by first-time authors.
Fiction Middle readers, young adult: open to all categories. Recently published *Ricochet River*, by Robin Cody (YA novel).
Nonfiction Middle reader, young adult: open to all categories.
How to Contact/Writers Query with SASE or submit proposal package including 4 sample chapters, projected page count, intended audience, and marketing ideas. Prefers traditional mail, but will read unattached queries. Do not send proposal package by e-mail. Response to queries in 4-6 weeks. Publishes a book 18 months after acceptance. Will consider simultaneous submissions and previously published work.
Terms Pays negotiable royalty based on retail price. Authors see galleys for review. Book catalog and writer's guidelines available on Web site.

ORCHARD BOOKS
Imprint of Scholastic, Inc., 557 Broadway, New York NY 10012. (212)343-6782. Fax: (212)343-4890. Web site: www.scholastic.com. Book publisher. Editorial Director: Ken Geist. **Manuscript Acquisitions:** Lisa A. Sandell, senior editor. **Art Acquisitions:** David Saylor, creative director. ''We publish approximately 50 books yearly including fiction, poetry, picture books, and young adult novels.'' 10% of books by first-time authors.
• Orchard is not accepting unsolicited manuscripts; query letters only.
Fiction All levels: animal, contemporary, history, humor, multicultural, poetry. Recently published *Children of the Lamp: The Cobra King of Kathmandu*, by P.B. Kerr; *Does My Head Look Big in This?*, by Randa Abdel-Fattah; *Beach*, by Elisha Cooper; *Castle*, by Sabuda & Reinhart's Studio.
Nonfiction ''We publish nonfiction very selectively.''
How to Contact/Writers Query only with SASE. Responds in 3 months.
Illustration Works with 15 illustrators/year. Art director reviews ms/illustration portfolios. Submit ''tearsheets or photocopies or Photostats of the work.'' Responds to art samples in 1 month. Samples returned with SASE. No disks or slides, please.
Terms Most commonly offers an advance against list royalties. Sends galleys to authors; dummies to illustrators. Original artwork returned at job's completion.
Tips ''Read some of our books to determine first whether your manuscript is suited to our list.''

OUR CHILD PRESS ? ✓
P.O. Box 4379, Philadelphia PA 19118. Phone/fax: (610)308-8088. E-mail: ourchildpress@aol.com. Web site: www.ourchildpress.com. **Acquisitions:** Carol Perrott, president. 90% of books by first-time authors.
Fiction/Nonfiction All levels: adoption, multicultural, special needs. Published *Like Me*, written by Dawn Martelli, illustrated by Jennifer Hedy Wharton; *Is That Your Sister?*, by Catherine and Sherry Burin; *Oliver: A Story About Adoption*, by Lois Wichstrom.
How to Contact/Writers Fiction/ nonfiction: Query or submit complete ms. Responds to queries/mss in 6 months. Publishes a book 6-12 months after acceptance.
Illustration Works with 1-5 illustrators/year. Reviews ms/illustration packages from artists. Manuscript/illustration packages and illustration only: Query first. Submit résumé, tearsheets and photocopies. Responds to art samples in 2 months. Samples returned with SASE; samples kept on file.
Terms Pays authors royalty of 5-10% based on wholesale price. Pays illustrators royalty of 5-10% based on wholesale price. Original artwork returned at job's completion. Book catalog for business-size SAE and 67¢ postage.

◻ OUR SUNDAY VISITOR, INC.
200 Noll Plaza, Huntington IN 46750. (260)356-8400. Fax: (260)359-9117. Web site: www.osv.com. For guidelines: booksed@osv.com **Acquisitions:** Jacquelyn Lindsey, Michael Dubruiel, Kelley Renz. **Art Director:** Tyler Ottinger. Publishes primarily religious, educational, parenting, reference and biographies. OSV is dedicated to providing books, periodicals and other products that serve the Catholic Church.
• Our Sunday Visitor, Inc., is publishing only those children's books that tie in to sacramental preparation and Catholic identity. Contact the acquisitions editor for manuscript guidelines.
Nonfiction Picture books, middle readers, young readers, young adults. Recently published *Living the Ten Commandments for Children*, by Rosemarie Gortler and Donna Piscitelli, illustrated by Mimi Sternhagen.
How to Contact/Writers Query, submit complete ms, or submit outline/synopsis and 2-3 sample chapters. Responds to queries/mss in 2 months. Publishes a book 18-24 months after acceptance. Will consider simultaneous submissions, electronic submissions via disk or modem, previously published work.

Illustration Reviews ms/illustration packages from artists. Illustration only: Query with samples. Contact: Acquisitions Editor. Responds only if interested. Samples returned with SASE; samples filed.

Photography Buys photos from freelancers. Contact: Acquisitions Editor.

Terms Pays authors royalty of 10-12% net. Pays illustrators by the project (range: $200-1,500). Sends galleys to authors; dummies to illustrators. Book catalog available for SASE; ms guidelines available for SASE.

Tips "Stay in accordance with our guidelines."

RICHARD C. OWEN PUBLISHERS, INC.

P.O. Box 585, Katonah NY 10536. (800)336-5588. Fax: (914)232-3977. Web site: www.rcowen.com. **Acquisitions:** Janice Boland, children's books editor/art director. 90% of books by first-time authors. We publish "child-focused books, with inherent instructional value, about characters and situations with which five-, six- and seven-year-old children can identify—books that can be read for meaning, entertainment, enjoyment and information. We include multicultural stories that present minorities in a positive and natural way. Our stories show the diversity in America." Is not interested in lesson plans, or books of activities for literature studies or other content areas.

● Due to a high volume of submissions, Richard C. Owen Publishers is currently only accepting nonfiction pieces.

Nonfiction Picture books, young readers: animals, careers, hi-lo, history, how-to, music/dance, geography, multicultural, nature/environment, science, sports. Multicultural needs include: "Good stories respectful of all heritages, races, cultural—African-American, Hispanic, American Indian." Wants lively stories. No "encyclopedic" type of information stories. Average word length: under 500 words. Recently published *The Coral Reef*.

How to Contact/Writers Fiction/nonfiction: Submit complete ms and cover letter. Responds to mss in 1 year. Publishes a book 2-3 years after acceptance. See Web site for guidelines.

Illustration Works with 20 illustrators/year. Uses color artwork only. Illustration only: Send color copies/reproductions or photos of art or provide tearsheets; do not send slides or originals. Include SASE and cover letter. Responds only if interested; samples filed.

Terms Pays authors royalty of 5% based on net price or outright purchase (range: $25-500). Offers no advances. Pays illustrators by the project (range: $100-2,500). Pays photographers by the project (range: $100-2,000) or per photo ($100-150). Original artwork returned 12-18 months after job's completion. Book brochure, ms/artists guidelines available for SASE.

Tips Seeking "authentic nonfiction that has charm, magic, impact and appeal; that children living in today's society will want to read and reread; books with strong storylines, child-appealing characters, events, language, action. Write for the ears and eyes and hearts of your readers—use an economy of words. Visit the children's room at the public library and immerse yourself in the best children's literature."

PACIFIC PRESS

P.O. Box 5353, Nampa ID 83653-5353. (208)465-2500. Fax: (208)465-2531. E-mail: booksubmissions@pacificpress.com. Web site: www.pacificpress.com/writers/books.htm. **Manuscript Acquisitions:** Tim Lale. **Art Acquisitions:** Gerald Monks, creative director. Publishes 1 picture book/year; 2 young readers/year; 2 middle readers/year. 5% of books by first-time authors. Pacific Press brings the Bible and Christian lifestyle to children.

Fiction Picture books, young readers, middle readers, young adults: religious subjects only. No fantasy. Average word length: picture books—100; young readers—1,000; middle readers—15,000; young adults—40,000. Recently published *Plagues in the Palace*, by Bradley Booth; *I Miss Grandpa*, by Karen Holford; *The Secret of Scarlet Cove*, by Charles Mills.

Nonfiction Picture books, young readers, middle readers, young adults: religion. Average word length: picture books—100; young readers—1,000; middle readers—15,000; young adults—40,000. Recently published *Where Did They Come From? Where Did They Go?*, by Elaine Grahan Kennedy; *Beanie: The Horse That Wasn't a Horse*, by Heather Grovet.

How to Contact/Writers Fiction/nonfiction: Query or submit outline/synopsis and 3 sample chapters. Responds to queries in 3 months; mss in 1 year. Publishes a book 6-12 months after acceptance. Will consider e-mail submissions.

Illustration Works with 2-6 illustrators/year. Uses color artwork only. Query. Responds only if interested. Samples returned with SASE.

Photography Buys stock and assigns work. Model/property releases required.

Terms Pays author royalty of 6-15% based on wholesale price. Offers advances (average amount: $1,500). Pays illustrators royalty of 6-15% based on wholesale price. Pays photographers royalty of 6-15% based on wholesale price. Sends galleys to authors. Originals returned to artist at job's completion. Manuscript guidelines for SASE. Catalog available on Web site (www.adventistbookcenter.com).

Tips Pacific Press is owned by the Seventh-day Adventist Church. The Press rejects all material that is not Bible-based.

PACIFIC VIEW PRESS

P.O. Box 2897, Berkeley CA 94702. (510)849-4213. Fax: (510)843-5835. E-mail: pvpress@sprynet.com. Web site: www.pacificviewpress.com. **Acquisitions:** Pam Zumwalt, president. Publishes 1-2 picture books/year. 50% of books by first-time authors. "We publish unique, high-quality introductions to Asian cultures and history for children 8-12, for schools, libraries and families. Our children's books focus on hardcover illustrated nonfiction. We look for titles on aspects of the history and culture of the countries and peoples of the Pacific Rim, especially China, presented in an engaging, informative and respectful manner. We are interested in books that all children will enjoy reading and using, and that parents and teachers will want to buy."

Nonfiction Young readers, middle readers: Asia-related multicultural only. Recently published *Cloud Weavers: Ancient Chinese Legends*, by Rena Krasno and Yeng-Fong Chiang (all ages); *Exploring Chinatown: A Children's Guide to Chinese Culture*, by Carol Stepanchuk (ages 8-12).

How to Contact/Writers Query with outline and sample chapter. Responds in 3 months.

Illustration Works with 2 illustrators/year. Responds only if interested. Samples returned with SASE.

Terms Pays authors royalty of 8-12% based on wholesale price. Pays illustrators by the project (range: $2,000-5,000).

Tips "We welcome proposals from persons with expertise, either academic or personal, in their area of interest. While we do accept proposals from previously unpublished authors, we would expect submitters to have considerable experience presenting their interests to children in classroom or other public settings and to have skill in writing for children."

PARENTING PRESS, INC.

P.O. Box 75267, Seattle WA 98175-0267. (206)364-2900. Fax: (206)364-0702. E-mail: office@parentingpress.com. Web site: www.parentingpress.com. Estab. 1979. Book publisher. Publisher: Carolyn Threadgill. **Acquisitions:** Elizabeth Crary (parenting) and Carolyn Threadgill (children and parenting). Publishes 4-5 books/year for parents or/and children and those who work with them. 40% of books by first-time authors. "Parenting Press publishes educational books for children in story format—no straight fiction. Our company publishes books that help build competence in parents and children. We are known for practical books that teach parents and can be used successfully by parent educators, teachers, and educators who work with parents. We are interested in books that help people feel good about themselves because they gain skills needed in dealing with others. We are particularly interested in material that provides 'options' rather than 'shoulds.'"

• Parenting Press's guidelines are available on their Web site.

Fiction Picture books: concept. Publishes social skills books, problem-solving books, safety books, dealing-with-feelings books that use a "fictional" vehicle for the information. "We rarely publish straight fiction." Recently published *What About Me? 12 Ways to Get Your Parent's Attention (Without Hitting Your Sister)*, by Eileen Kennedy-Moore, illustrated by Mits Katayama (a book offering children options for getting the attention they need in positive ways).

Nonfiction Picture books: health, social skills building. Young readers: health, social skills building books. Middle readers: health, social skills building. No books on "new baby; coping with a new sibling; cookbooks; manners; books about disabilities (which we don't publish at present); animal characters in anything; books that tell children what they should do, instead of giving options." Average word length: picture books—500-800; young readers—1,000-2,000; middle readers—up to 10,000. Published *25 Things to Do When Grandpa Passes Away, Mom and Dad Get Divorced, or the Dog Dies*, by Laurie Kanyer, illustrated by Jenny Williams (ages 2-12).

How to Contact/Writers Query. Responds to queries/mss in 3 months, "after requested." Publishes a book 18 months after acceptance. Will consider simultaneous submissions.

Illustrations Works with 3-5 illustrators/year. Reviews ms/illustration packages from artists. "We do reserve the right to find our own illustrator, however." Query. Illustrations only: Submit "résumé, samples of art/drawings (no original art); photocopies or color photocopies okay." Responds only if interested. Samples returned with SASE; samples filed, if suitable.

Terms Pays authors royalty of 3-12% based on wholesale price. Pays illustrators (for text) by the project; 3-6% royalty based on wholesale price. Pays illustrators 3-6% royalty based on wholesale price, or pays by the project ($250-3,000). Sends galleys to authors; dummies to illustrators.

Tips "Make sure you are familiar with the unique nature of our books. All are aimed at building certain 'people' skills in adults or children. Our publishing for children follows no trend that we find appropriate. Children need nonfiction social skill-building books that help them think through problems and make their own informed decisions. The traditional illustrated story book does not *usually* fit our requirements because it does all the thinking for the child."

PAULINE BOOKS & MEDIA

50 St. Paul's Ave., Jamaica Plain MA 02130-3491. (617)522-8911. E-mail: editorial@paulinemedia.com. Web site: www.pauline.org. **Manuscript Acquisitions:** Sr. Patricia Edward Jablonski, FSP. **Art Acquisitions:** Sr.

Mary Joseph Peterson, FSP, art director. Publishes 2 picture books/year; 5 young readers/year; 3-5 middle readers/year; 1-2 young adult titles/year. 20% of books by first-time authors. "We communicate the Gospel message through our lives and all available forms of media, responding to the needs and hopes of all people in the spirit of St. Paul."

Nonfiction Picture books, young readers, middle readers, young adults: religion. Average word length: picture books—150-500; young readers—8,000-10,000; middle readers—15,000-25,000. Recently published *I Pray the Rosary!*, by Margaret Rose Scarfi (ages 6-9); *Holy Friends: Thirty Saints and Blesseds of the Americas*, by Diane Amadeo (ages 9-12); *Squishy: A Book About My Five Senses*, by Cherie B. Stihler (Ages 4-7).

How to Contact/Writers Nonfiction: Submit query letter with outline/synopsis and 3 sample chapters. Responds to queries in 2 months; mss in 4 months. Publishes book 2-3 years after acceptance. Will consider simultaneous submissions, electronic submissions via disk or modem.

Illustration Works with 20-35 illustrators/year. Uses color artwork only. Illustrations only: Send résumé, promotional literature, client list or tearsheets. Responds only if interested. Samples returned with SASE only or samples filed.

Terms Varies by project. Manuscript and art guidelines available by SASE or on Web site. Catalog available on Web site.

Tips "Please be sure that all material submitted is consonant with Catholic teaching and values. We generally do not accept anthropomorphic stories, fantasy or poetry."

PAULIST PRESS

97 Macarthur Blvd., Mahwah NJ 07430. (201)825-7300. Web site: www.paulistpress.com. Acquisitions: Children's Editor. Publishes 6-8 titles/year. 40% of books by first-time authors. "Our goal is to produce books on Catholic themes."

- Paulist Press does not publish fiction.

Nonfiction "The few books we consider are explicitly Catholic—on Catholic doctrine, biography, prayers, sacraments, or customs—and are meant to be used in a catechetical setting. This means much more than a general reference to 'going to Mass.' " No nonfiction approaches to angels, adoption, grandparents, death, pets, sharing, prejudice, September 11th, etc. No nonfiction books in rhyme. No nonfiction books with animal or angel characters. No retelling of Bible stories. For activity book submissions: Theme-related books are best. Send an outline and a few sample pages. These books are reproducible worksheets and so interiors must be in black and white. Only activity book submissions from writer/illustrators will be considered. Recently published: *Child's Guide to the Seven Sacraments*, by Elizabeth Ficocelli, illustrated by Anne Catharine Blake (picture book; The Catholic Press Association's first-place winner); *My Catholic School Holiday Activity Book*, written and illustrated by Jennifer Galvin (reproducible activity sheets); *The Imitation of Christ for Children*, by Elizabeth Ficocelli (the heart of the Thomas à Kempis classic put in child-friendly terms).

How to Contact/Writers Submit by mail complete mss for short books; query, outline, and sample for longer works. "Please, no e-mail submissions. Please query first on any series or biography because many topics are already in production or under contract." Include SASE with all submissions. Responds in 6 months. "Simultaneous submissions are OK; there's no need to mention it." Publishes a book 2 to 3 years after acceptance.

Terms Usually pays authors royalty of 4 to 8% based on net sales. Average advance payment is $500. Pays illustrators by flat fee or by advance and royalty, depending on the number and type of illustrations.

Tips "This is a niche market and so is very, very difficult to crack. Some of our best writers and illustrators are non-Catholics, but they are willing and able to do the legwork up front to get all the details right. Unfortunately we receive too many inappropriate manuscripts, so please know our books; please know our market. There should be a real reason why you're submitting to a Catholic publisher. Because of our niche market approach, you will be doing yourself a disservice if you submit a general book to us rather than to the religious branch of a children's trade imprint."

PEACHTREE PUBLISHERS, LTD. ✓

1700 Chattahoochee Ave., Atlanta GA 30318-2112. (404)876-8761. Fax: (404)875-2578. E-mail: hello@peachtree-online.com. Web site: www.peachtree-online.com. **Acquisitions:** Helen Harriss. **Art Director:** Loraine Joyner. Production Manager: Melanie McMahon Ives. Publishes 25-30 titles/year.

Fiction Picture books, young readers: adventure, animal, concept, history, nature/environment. Middle readers: adventure, animal, history, nature/environment, sports. Young adults: fiction, mystery, adventure. Does not want to see science fiction, romance.

Nonfiction Picture books: animal, history, nature/environment. Young readers, middle readers, young adults: animal, biography, nature/environment. Does not want to see religion.

How to Contact/Writers Fiction/nonfiction: Submit complete ms (picture books) or 3 sample chapters (chapter books) by postal mail only. Responds to queries/mss in 4-6 months. Publishes a book 1-2 years after acceptance. Will consider simultaneous submissions.

Illustration Works with 8-10 illustrators/year. Illustrations only: Query production manager or art director with samples, résumé, slides, color copies to keep on file. Responds only if interested. Samples returned with SASE; samples filed.

Terms "Manuscript guidelines for SASE, visit Web site or call for a recorded message. No fax or e-mail submittals or queries please."

⬚ PELICAN PUBLISHING CO. INC.

1000 Burmaster St., Gretna LA 70053-2246. (504)368-1175. Web site: www.pelicanpub.com. **Manuscript Acquisitions:** Nina Kooij, editor-in-chief. **Art Acquisitions:** Terry Callaway, production manager. Publishes 19 young readers/year; 6 middle readers/year; 1 young adult title/year. 5% of books from agented writers. "Pelican publishes hardcover and trade paperback originals and reprints. Our children's books (illustrated and otherwise) include history, biography, holiday, and regional. Pelican's mission is "to publish books of quality and permanence that enrich the lives of those who read them."

Fiction Young readers: history, holiday, multicultural and regional. Middle readers: Louisiana history. Multicultural needs include stories about African-Americans, Irish-Americans, Jews, Asian-Americans, and Hispanics. Does not want animal stories, general Christmas stories, "day at school" or "accept yourself" stories. Maximum word length: young readers—1,100; middle readers—40,000. Recently published *The Warlord's Messengers*, by Virginia Walton Pelegard (ages 5-8, fiction).

Nonfiction Young readers: biography, history, holiday, multicultural. Middle readers: Louisiana history, holiday, regional. Recently published *The Buffalo Soldier*, by Sherry Garland; *The Pilgrims' Thanksgiving from A to Z*, by Laura Crawford (ages 5-8, holiday).

How to Contact/Writers Fiction/nonfiction: Query. Responds to queries in 1 month; mss in 3 months. Publishes a book 9-18 months after acceptance.

Illustration Works with 15 illustrators/year. Reviews ms/illustration packages from artists. Query first. Illustrations only: Query with samples (no originals). Responds only if interested. Samples returned with SASE; samples kept on file.

Terms Pays authors in royalties; buys ms outright "rarely." Sends galleys to authors. Illustrators paid by "various arrangements." Book catalog and ms guidelines available on Web site or for SASE.

Tips "No anthropomorphic stories, pet stories (fiction or nonfiction), fantasy, poetry, science fiction or romance. Writers: be as original as possible. Develop characters that lend themselves to series and always be thinking of new and interesting situations for those series. Give your story a strong hook—something that will appeal to a well-defined audience. There is a lot of competition out there for general themes. We look for stories with specific 'hooks' and audiences, and writers who actively promote their work."

PHILOMEL BOOKS √ ?

Penguin Young Readers Group (USA), 345 Hudson St., New York NY 10014. (212)414-3610. Web site: www.penguin.com. **Manuscript Acquisitions:** submissions editor. **Art Acquisitions:** Katrina Damkoehler, design assistant. Publishes 18 picture books/year; 2 middle-grades/year; 2 young readers/year; 4 young adult titles/year. 5% of books by first-time authors; 80% of books from agented writers. "We look for beautifully written, engaging manuscripts for children and young adults."

Fiction All levels: adventure, animal, anthology, contemporary, fantasy, folktales, hi-lo, history, humor, poetry, sports, multicultural. Middle readers, young adults: problem novels, science fiction, suspense/mystery. No concept picture books, mass-market "character" books, or series. Average word length: picture books—1,000; young readers—1,500; middle readers—14,000; young adult—20,000.

Nonfiction Picture books, young readers, middle readers: hi-lo. "Creative nonfiction on any subject." Average word length: picture books—2,000; young readers—3,000; middle readers—10,000.

How to Contact/Writers "As of January 1, 2007, Philomel will no longer respond to your unsolicited submission unless interested in publishing it. Rejected submissions postmarked January 1, 2007, or later will be recycled. Please *do not* include a self-addressed stamped envelope with your submission. You will not hear from Philomel regarding the status of your submission unless we are interested in publishing it, in which case you can expect a reply from us within approximately four months. We regret that we cannot respond personally to each submission, but rest assured that we do make every effort to consider each and every one we receive."

Illustration Works with 20-25 illustrators/year. Reviews ms/illustration packages from artists. Query with art sample first. Illustrations only: Query with samples. Send résumé and tearsheets. Responds to art samples in 1 month. Original artwork returned at job's completion. Samples returned with SASE or kept on file.

Terms Pays authors in royalties. Average advance payment "varies." Illustrators paid by advance and in royalties. Sends galleys to authors; dummies to illustrators. Book catalog, ms guidelines free on request with SASE (9×12 envelope for catalog).

Tips Wants "unique fiction or nonfiction with a strong voice and lasting quality. Discover your own voice and own story and persevere." Looks for "something unusual, original, well-written. Fine art. The genre (fantasy, contemporary, or historical fiction) is not so important as the story itself and the spirited life the story allows its main character. We are also interested in receiving adolescent novels, current, contemporary fiction with voice.''

☐ PIANO PRESS

P.O. Box 85, Del Mar CA 92014-0085. (619)884-1401. Fax: (858)755-1104. E-mail: pianopress@pianopress.com. Web site: www.pianopress.com. **Manuscript Acquisitions:** Elizabeth C. Axford, M.A, editor. ''We publish music-related books, either fiction or nonfiction, coloring books, songbooks and poetry.''

Fiction Picture books, young readers, middle readers, young adults: folktales, multicultural, poetry, music. Average word length: picture books—1,500-2,000. Recently published *Strum a Song of Angels*, by Linda Oatman High and Elizabeth C. Axford; *Music and Me*, by Kimberly White and Elizabeth C. Axford.

Nonfiction Picture books, young readers, middle readers, young adults: multicultural, music/dance. Average word length: picture books—1,500-2,000. Recently published *The Musical ABC*, by Dr. Phyllis J. Perry and Elizabeth C. Axford; *Merry Christmas Happy Hanukkah—A Multilingual Songbook & CD*, by Elizabeth C. Axford.

How to Contact/Writers Fiction/ nonfiction: Query. Responds to queries in 3 months; mss in 6 months. Publishes a book 1 year after acceptance. Will consider simultaneous submissions, electronic submissions via disk or modem.

Illustration Works with 1 or 2 illustrators/year. Reviews ms/illustration packages from artists. Query. Illustrations only: Query with samples. Responds in 3 months. Samples returned with SASE; samples filed.

Photography Buys stock and assigns work. Looking for music-related, multicultural. Model/property releases required. Uses glossy or flat, color or b&w prints. Submit cover letter, résumé, client list, published samples, stock photo list.

Terms Pays authors, illustrators, and photographers royalty of 5-10% based on retail price. Sends galleys to authors; dummies to illustrators. Originals returned to artist at job's completion. Book catalog available for #10 SASE and 2 first-class stamps. All imprints included in a single catalog. Catalog available on Web site.

Tips ''We are looking for music-related material only for any juvenile market. Please do not send nonmusic-related materials. Query first before submitting anything.''

☐ PICTURE ME™ PRESS, LLC

(formerly Playhouse Publishing) 1566 Akron-Peninsula Rd., Akron OH 44313. (330)475-8579. Fax: (330)926-1315. E-mail: webmaster@playhousepublishing.com. Web site: www.playhousepublishing.com. **Acquisitions:** Submissions Editor. Imprints: Picture Me™ Books, Nibble Me™ Books. Publishes 10-15 novelty/board books/year. 25% of books by first-time authors. ''Picture Me™ Press is dedicated to finding imaginative new ways to inspire young minds to read, learn and grow—one book at a time.''

Fiction Picture books: adventure, animal, concept/novelty. Average word length: board books—75. Recently published *Picture Me Dancing*, by Cathy Hapka, illustrated by Monica Pritchard; *Peek-a-Boo, I See You!*, by Merry North, illustrated by Leigh Hughes; *My Halloween*, by Merry North, illustrated by Sara Misconish.

How to Contact/Writers Does not consider unsolicited mss.

Terms Catalog available online.

PIÑATA BOOKS

Imprint of Arte Publico Press, University of Houston, 452 Cullen Performance Hall, Houston TX 77204-2004. (713)743-2843. Fax: (713)743-3080. Web site: www.artepublicopress.com. **Manuscript Acquisitions:** Dr. Nicholas Kanellos; Gabriela Baeza Ventura, executive editor. **Art Acquisitions:** Adelaida Mendoza, production manager. Publishes 6 picture books/year; 2 young readers/year; 5 middle readers/year; 5 young adult titles/year. 80% of books are by first-time authors. ''Arte Publico's mission is the publication, promotion and dissemination of Latino literature for a variety of national and regional audiences, from early childhood to adult, through the complete gamut of delivery systems, including personal performance as well as print and electronic media.''

Fiction Recently published *My Tata's Guitar/La Guitarra De Mi Tata*, by Ethriam Cash Brammer, illustrated by Daniel Lechon (ages 3-7); *Lorenzo's Revolutionary Quest*, by Lila and Rick Guzman (ages 11 and up); *Teen Angel*, by Gloria Velasquez (ages 11 and up).

Nonfiction Recently published *César Chávez: The Struggle for Justice/César Chávez: La Lucha Por La Justicia*, by Richard Griswold del Castillo, illustrated by Anthony Accardo (ages 3-7).

How to Contact/Writers Accepts material from U.S./Hispanic authors only (living abroad OK). Manuscripts, queries, synopses, etc. are accepted in either English or Spanish. Fiction: Submit complete ms. Nonfiction: Query. Responds to queries in 2-4 months; mss in 3-6 months. Publishes a book 2 years after acceptance. Will sometimes consider previously published work.

Illustration Works with 6 illustrators/year. Uses color artwork only. Reviews ms/illustration packages from artists. Query or send portfolio (slides, color copies). Illustrations only: Query with samples or send résumé, promo sheet, portfolio, slides, client list and tearsheets. Responds only if interested. Samples not returned; samples filed.

Terms Pays authors royalty of 10% minimum based on wholesale price. Offers advances (average amount $2,000). Pays illustrators advance and royalties of 10% based on wholesale price. Sends galleys to authors. Catalog available on Web site: ms guidelines available for SASE.

PINEAPPLE PRESS, INC.

P.O. Box 3889, Sarasota FL 34239. (941)739-2219. Fax: (941)739-2296. E-mail: info@pineapplepress.com. Web site: www.pineapplepress.com. **Manuscript Acquisitions:** June Cussen. Publishes 1 picture book/year; 1 young reader/year; 1 middle reader/year; 1 young adult title/year. 50% of books by first-time authors. "Our mission is to publish good books about Florida."

Fiction Picture books, young readers, middle readers, young adults: animal, folktales, history, nature/environment. Recently published *The Old Man and the C*, by Carole Tremblay, illustrated by Angela Donate; *A Land Remembered* (Student Edition), by Patrick Smith, (ages 9 up, Florida historical fiction).

Nonfiction Picture books: animal, history, nature/environmental, science. Young readers, middle readers, young adults: animal, biography, geography, history, nature/environment, science. Recently published *Those Amazing Alligators*, by Steve Weaver (ages 5-9); *The Gopher Tortoise, A Life History*, by Ray and Patricia Ashton (ages 9 up).

How to Contact/Writers Fiction: Query or submit outline/synopsis and 3 sample chapters. Nonfiction: Query or submit outline/synopsis and intro and 3 sample chapters. Responds to queries/samples/mss in 2 months. Will consider simultaneous submissions.

Illustration Works with 2 illustrators/year. Reviews ms/illustration packages from artists. Query with nonreturnable samples. Contact: June Cussen, executive editor. Illustrations only: Query with brochure, nonreturnable samples, photocopies, résumé. Responds only if interested. Samples returned with SASE, but prefers nonreturnable; samples filed.

Terms Pays authors royalty of 10-15%. Pays illustrators royalties. Sends galleys to authors; dummies to illustrators. Originals returned to artist at job's completion. Book catalog available for 9×12 SAE with $1.06 postage; all imprints included in a single catalog. Catalog available on Web site at www.pineapplepress.com.

Tips "Learn about publishing and book marketing in general. Be familiar with the kinds of books published by the publishers to whom you are submitting."

PITSPOPANY PRESS

40 E. 78th St., #16D, New York NY 10021. (212)444-1657. Fax: (866)205-3966. E-mail: pitspop@netvision.net.il. Web site: www.pitspopany.com. Estab. 1992. Specializes in trade books, Judaica, nonfiction, fiction, multicultural material. **Manuscript Acquisitions:** Yaacov Peterseil, publisher. **Art Acquisitions:** Yaacov Peterseil, publisher. Produces 6 picture books/year; 4 young readers/year; 4 middle readers/year; 4 young adult books/year. 10% of books by first-time authors. "Pitspopany Press is dedicated to bringing quality children's books of Jewish interest into the marketplace. Our goal is to create titles that will appeal to the esthetic senses of our readers and, at the same time, offer quality Jewish content to the discerning parent, teacher, and librarian. While the people working for Pitspopany Press embody a wide spectrum of Jewish belief and opinion, we insist that our titles be respectful of the mainstream Jewish viewpoints and beliefs. Most of all, we are committed to creating books that all Jewish children can read, learn from, and enjoy."

Fiction Picture books: animal, anthology, fantasy, folktales, history, humor, multicultural, nature/environment, poetry. Young readers: adventure, animal, anthology, concept, contemporary, fantasy, folktales, health, history, humor, multicultural, nature/environment, poetry, religion, science fiction, special needs, sports, suspense. Middle readers: animal, anthology, fantasy, folktales, health, hi-lo, history, humor, multicultural, nature/environment, poetry, religion, science fiction, special needs, sports, suspense. Young adults/teens: animal, anthology, contemporary, fantasy, folktales, health, hi-lo, history, humor, multicultural, nature/environment, poetry, religion, science fiction, special needs, sports, suspense. Recently published *Hayyim's Ghost*, by Eric Kimmel, illustrated by Ari Binus (ages 6-9); *The Littlest Pair*, by Syliva Rouss, illustrated by Hally Hannan (ages 3-6); *The Converso Legacy*, by Sheldon Gardner (ages 10-14, historial fiction).

Nonfiction All levels: activity books, animal, arts/crafts, biography, careers, concept, cooking, geography, health, history, hobbies, how-to, multicultural, music/dance, nature/environment, reference, religion, science, self help, social issues, special needs, sports.

How to Contact/Writers Accepts international submissions. Fiction/nonfiction: Submit outline/synopsis. Responds to queries/mss in 6 weeks. Publishes book 9 months after acceptance. Considers simultaneous submissions, electronic submissions.

Illustration Accepts material from international illustrators. Works with 6 illustrators/year. Uses color artwork only. Reviews ms/illustration packages. For ms/illustration packages: Submit ms with 4 pieces of final art. Submit ms/illustration packages to Yaacov Peterseil, publisher. Reviews work for future assignments. If interested in illustrating future titles, send promo sheet. Submit samples to Yaacov Peterseil, publisher. Samples returned with SASE. Samples not filed.

Photography Works on assignment only. Submit photos to Yaacov Peterseil, publisher.

Terms Pays authors royalty or work purchased outright. Offers advance against royalties. Author sees galleys for review. Originals returned to artist at job's completion. Catalog on Web site. All imprints included in single catalog. Offers writer's guidelines for SASE.

PLAYERS PRESS, INC.

P.O. Box 1132, Studio City CA 91614-0132. (818)789-4980. **Manuscript Acquisitions:** Robert W. Gordon, vice president/editorial director. **Art Acquisitions:** Attention: Art Director. Publishes 7-25 young readers, dramatic plays and musicals/year; 2-10 middle readers, dramatic plays and musicals/year; 4-20 young adults, dramatic plays and musicals/year. 35% of books by first-time authors; 1% of books from agented writers. Players Press philosophy: "To create is to live life's purpose."

Fiction All levels: plays. Recently published *Play From African Folktales*, by Carol Korty (collection of short plays); *Punch and Judy*, a play by William-Alan Landes; *Silly Soup!*, by Carol Korty (a collection of short plays with music and dance).

Nonfiction Picture books, middle readers, young readers, young adults. "Any children's nonfiction pertaining to the entertainment industry, performing arts and how-to for the theatrical arts only." Needs include activity books related to theatre: arts/crafts, careers, history, how-to, music/dance, reference and textbook. Recently published *Scenery*, by J. Stell (How to Build Stage Scenery); *Monologues for Teens*, by Vernon Howard (ideal for teen performers); *Humorous Monologues*, by Vernon Howard (ideal for young performers); *Actor's Resumes*, by Richard Devin (how to prepare an acting résumé).

How to Contact/Writers Fiction/nonfiction: Submit plays or outline/synopsis and sample chapters of entertainment books. Responds to queries in 2 weeks; mss in 6 months-1 year. Publishes a book 10 months after acceptance. No simultaneous submissions.

Illustration Works with 2-6 new illustrators/year. Use primarily b&w artwork. Illustrations only: Submit résumé, tearsheets. Responds to art samples in 1 week only if interested. Samples returned with SASE; samples filed.

Terms Pays authors royalty based on wholesale price. Pays illustrators by the project (range: $5-1,000). Pays photographers by the project (up to $100); royalty varies. Sends galleys to authors; dummies to illustrators. Book catalog and ms guidelines available for 9×12 SASE.

Tips Looks for "plays/musicals and books pertaining to the performing arts only. Illustrators: send samples that can be kept for our files."

PRICE STERN SLOAN, INC.

Penguin Group (USA), 345 Hudson St., New York NY 10014. (212)414-3590. Fax: (212)414-3396. Web site: http://us.penguingroup.com/youngreaders. Estab. 1963. **Acquisitions:** Debra Dorfman, president/publisher. "Price Stern Sloan publishes quirky mass market novelty series for children's as well as licensed movie tie-in books.

• Price Stern Sloan does not accept e-mail submissions.

Fiction Publishes picture books and novelty/board books including Mad Libs and Movie and Television Tie-ins. "We publish unique novelty formats and fun, colorful paperbacks and activity books. We also publish the Book with Audio Series Wee Sing and Baby Loves Jazz." Recently published: Baby Loves Jazz Board Book With CD Series; New Formats In The Classic Mr. Men/Little Miss Series; Movie/TV tie-in titles Corbin Bleu: To The Limit; Happy Feet; Family Guy Mad Libs; Shrek the Third Mad Libs.

How to Contact/Writers Query. Responds to queries in 6-8 weeks.

Terms Work purchased outright. Offers advance. Book catalog available for 9×12 SASE and 5 first-class stamps; address to Book Catalog. Manuscript guidelines available for SASE; address to Manuscript Guidelines.

Tips "Price Stern Sloan pulbishes unique, fun titles."

N PROMETHEUS BOOKS

59 John Glenn Dr., Amherst NY 14228-2197. (800)421-0351 Fax: (716)564-2711. E-mail: SLMitchell@prometheu sbooks.com. Web site: www.PrometheusBooks.com. **Acquisitions:** Steven L. Mitchell, editor-in-chief. Publishes 1-2 titles/year. 50% of books by first-time authors; 30% of books from agented writers. "We hope more books will be published that focus on real issues children face and real questions they raise. Our primary focus is to publish children's books with alternative viewpoints: humanism, free thought, moral values, critical reasoning, human sexuality, and independent thinking based upon science and reasoning, skepticism toward the paranormal. Our niche is the parent who seeks informative books based on these principles. We are dedicated to offering customers the highest-quality books. We are also committed to the development of new markets both in North America and throughout the world."

Nonfiction All levels: sex education, moral education, critical thinking, nature/environment, science, self help, skepticism, social issues. Average word length: picture books—2,000; young readers—10,000; middle readers—20,000; young adult/teens—60,000. Recently published *A Solstice Tree For Jenny*, by Karen Shrugg (ages 4 and up); *All Families Are Different*, by Sid Gordon (ages 7 and up); *Flat Earth? Round Earth?*, by Theresa Martin (ages 7 and up); *Humanism, What's That?* by Helen Bennett (ages 10 and up); *Dare To Dream* by Sandra McLeod Humphrey (ages 8 and up).

How to Contact/Writers Submit complete ms with sample illustrations (b&w). Responds to queries in 3 weeks; mss in 1-2 months. Publishes a book 12-18 months after acceptance. SASE required for return of ms/proposal.
Illustration Works with 1-2 illustrators/year. "We will keep samples in a freelance file, but freelancers are rarely used." Reviews ms/illustration packages from artists. "Prefer to have full work (ms and illustrations); will consider any proposal." Include résumé, photocopies.
Terms Pays authors royalty of 5-15% based on wholesale price and binding. "Author hires illustrator; we do not contract with illustrators." Pays photographers per photo (range: $50-100). Sends galleys to author. Book catalog is free on request.
Tips "We do not accept projects with anthropomorphic characters. We stress realistic children in realistic situations. "Books should reflect secular humanist values, stressing nonreligious moral education, critical thinking, logic, and skepticism. Authors should examine our book catalog and Web site to learn what sort of manuscripts we're looking for."

PUFFIN BOOKS

Penguin Group (USA), Inc., 345 Hudson St., New York NY 10014-3657. (212)414-3600. Web site: www.penguin.com/youngreaders. **Acquisitions:** Sharyn November, senior editor and editorial director of Firebird. Imprints: Speak, Firebird, Sleuth. Publishes trade paperback originals and reprints. Publishes 175-200 titles/year. Receives 600 queries and mss/year. 1% of books by first-time authors; 5% from unagented writers. "Puffin Books publishes high-end trade paperbacks and paperback originals and reprints for preschool children, beginning and middle readers, and young adults."
Fiction Picture books, young adult novels, middle grade and easy-to-read grades 1-3: fantasy and science fiction, graphic novels, classics. "We publish mostly paperback reprints. We publish some original fiction and nonfiction titles." Recently published *Al Capone Does My Shirts*, by Jennifer Choldenko; *Big Fat Little Lit*, edited by Art Spiegelman and François Mouly; *The Truth About Forever*, by Sarah Dessen.
Nonfiction Biography, illustrated books, young children's concept books (counting, shapes, colors). Subjects include education (for teaching concepts and colors, not academic), women in history. "Women in history books interest us." Publishes Alloy Books series.
Illustration Reviews artwork. Send color copies.
Photography Reviews photos. Send color copies.
How to Contact/Writers Fiction: Submit 3 sample chapters with SASE. Nonfiction: Submit 5 pages of ms with SASE. "It could take up to 5 months to get response." Publishes book 1 year after acceptance. Will consider simultaneous submissions, if so noted. Does not accept unsolicited picture book mss.
Terms Pays royalty. Offers advance (varies). Book catalog for 9 × 12 SASE with 7 first-class stamps; send request to Marketing Department.

Ⓐ PUSH

Scholastic, 557 Broadway, New York NY 10012-3999. Web site: www.thisispush.com. Estab. 2002. Specializes in fiction. Produces 6-9 young adult books/year. 50% of books by first-time authors. PUSH publishes new voices in teen literature.
  • PUSH does not accept unsolicited manuscripts or queries, only agented or referred fiction/memoir.
Fiction Young adults: contemporary, multicultural, poetry. Recently published *Splintering*, by Eireann Corrigan; *Never Mind the Goldbergs*, by Matthue Roth; *Perfect World*, by Brian James.
Nonfiction Young adults: memoir. Recently published *Talking in the Dark*, by Billy Merrell; *You Remind Me of You*, by Eireann Corrigan.
How to Contact/Writers Only interested in agented material. Accepts international submissions. Fiction/nonfiction: Submit complete ms. Responds to queries in 2 months; mss in 4 months. No simultaneous, electronic, or previously published submissions.
Tips "We only publish first-time writers (and then their subsequent books), so authors who have published previously should not consider PUSH. Also, for young writers in grades 7-12, we run the PUSH novel Contest with the Scholastic Art & Writing Awards. Every year it begins in October and ends in March. Rules can be found on our Web site."

Ⓥ G.P. PUTNAM'S SONS ✓

Penguin Putnam Books For Young Readers, 345 Hudson St., New York NY 10014. (212)414-3610. Web site: www.penguinputnam.com. **Manuscript Acquisitions:** Susan Kochan, assistant editorial director; John Rudolph, senior editor; Timothy Travaglini, senior editor. **Art Acquisitions:** Cecilia Yung, art director, Putnam and Philomel. Publishes 25 picture books/year; 15 middle readers/year; 5 young adult titles/year. 5% of books by first-time authors; 50% of books from agented authors.

- G. Putnam's Sons title *The Road to Paris*, by Nikki Grimes, won the Coretta Scott King Author Honor Award in 2007.

Fiction Picture books: animal, concept, contemporary, humor, multicultural. Young readers: adventure, contemporary, history, humor, multicultural, special needs, suspense/mystery. Middle readers: adventure, contemporary, history, humor, fantasy, multicultural, problem novels, special needs, sports, suspense/mystery. Young adults: contemporary, history, fantasy, problem novels, special needs. Does not want to see series. Average word length: picture books—200-1,000; middle readers—10,000-30,000; young adults—40,000-50,000. Recently published *A Place Called Kindergarten*, by Jessica Harper, illustrated by G. Brian Karas (ages 4-8); *Monster Blook Tattoo: Foundline*, by D. M. Cornish (ages 10 and up).

Nonfiction Picture books: animal, biography, concept, history, nature/environment, science. Subject s must have broad appeal but inventive approach. Average word length: picture books—200-1,500. Recently published *The Story of Salt*, by Mark Kurlansky(ages 6 and up, 40 pages).

How to Contact/Writers Accepts unsolicited mss. No SASE required, as will only respond if interested. Picture books: send full mss. Fiction: Query with outline/synopsis and 10 manuscript pages. Nonfiction: Query with outline/synopsis, 10 manuscript pages, and a table of contents. Do not send art unless requested. Responds to mss within 4 months if interested. Will consider simultaneous submissions.

Illustration Write for illustrator guidelines. Works with 40 illustrators/year. Reviews ms/illustration packages from artists. Manuscript/illustration packages and illustration only: Query. Responds only if interested. Samples filed.

Terms Pays authors royalty based on retail price. Pays illustrators by the project or royalty based on retail price. Sends galleys to authors. Original artwork returned at job's completion.

Tips "Study our catalogs and get a sense of the kind of books we publish, so that you know whether your project is likely to be right for us."

RAINBOW PUBLISHERS

P.O. Box 261129, San Diego CA 92196. (858)668-3260. Web site: www.rainbowpublishers.com. **Acquisitions:** Kristen Hughes, editor. Publishes 5 young readers/year; 5 middle readers/year; 5 young adult titles/year. 50% of books by first-time authors. "Our mission is to publish Bible-based, teacher resource materials that contribute to and inspire spiritual growth and development in kids ages 2-12."

Nonfiction Young readers, middle readers, young adult/teens: activity books, arts/crafts, how-to, reference, religion. Does not want to see traditional puzzles. Recently published More Bible Puzzles (series of 4 books for ages 8 and up).

How to Contact/Writers Nonfiction: Submit outline/synopsis and 3-5 sample chapters. Responds to queries in 6 weeks; mss in 3 months. Publishes a book 36 months after acceptance. Will consider simultaneous submissions, submissions via disk and previously published work.

Illustration Works with 2-5 illustrators/year. Reviews ms/illustration packages from artists. Submit ms with 2-5 pieces of final art. Illustrations only: Query with samples. Responds in 6 weeks. Samples returned with SASE; samples filed.

Terms For authors work purchased outright (range: $500 and up). Pays illustrators by the project (range: $300 and up). Sends galleys to authors. Book catalog available for 10×13 SAE and 2 first-class stamps; ms guidelines available for SASE.

Tips "Our Rainbow imprint carries reproducible books for teachers of children in Christian ministries, including crafts, activities, games and puzzles. Our Legacy imprint published titles for children such as devotionals, fiction and Christian living. Please write for guidelines and study the market before submitting material."

RANDOM HOUSE-GOLDEN BOOKS FOR YOUNG READERS GROUP

Random House, Inc., 1745 Broadway, New York NY 10019. (212)782-9000. Estab. 1935. Book publisher. "Random House Books aims to create books that nurture the hearts and minds of children, providing and promoting quality books and a rich variety of media that entertain and educate readers from 6 months to 12 years." Publisher/Vice President: Kate Klimo. VP & Associate Publisher/Art Director: Cathy Goldsmith. **Acquisitions:** Easy-to-Read Books (step-into-reading and picture books), board and novelty books, fiction and nonfiction for young and mid-grade readers: Heidi Kilgras, Editorial Director. Stepping Stones: Jennifer Arena, Executive Editor. Middle grade and youbg adult fiction: Jim Thomas, Editorial Director. Coloring and activity: Courtney Silk, Editorial Director. 100% of books published through agents; 2% of books by first-time authors.

- Random House-Golden Books does not accept unsolicited manuscripts, only agented material. They reserve the right not to return unsolicited material. Random House title *Penny from Heaven*, by Jennifer L. Holm, won a Newbery Honor Medal in 2007. Their title *Sky Boys: How They Built the Empire State Building*, by Deborah Hopkinson, illustrated by James E. Ransome, won a Boston Globe-Horn Book Honor Award for Picture Books in 2007.

How to Contact/Writers Only interested in agented material. Reviews ms/illustration packages from artists through agent only. Does not open or respond to unsolicited submissions.

Terms Pays authors in royalties; sometimes buys mss outright. Sends galleys to authors. Book catalog free on request.

◘ RAVEN TREE PRESS, LLC

P.O. Box 11505, Green Bay WI 54307. (800)909-9901. (920)438-1607. Fax: (800)909-9901. E-mail: raven@ra ventreepress.com. Web site: www.raventreepress.com. Publishes 8-10 picture books/year. 50% of books by first-time authors. "We publish entertaining and educational bilingual materials for families in English and Spanish."

Fiction Picture books: K-3 focus. No word play or rhyme. Work will be translated into Spanish by publisher. Check Web site prior to any submissions for current needs. Average word length: 500.

How to Contact/Writers Check Web site for current needs, submission guidelines and deadlines.

Illustration Check Web site for current needs, submission guidelines and deadlines.

Terms Pays authors and illustrators royalty. Offers advances against royalties. Pays illustrators by the project or royalty. Originals returned to artist at job's completion. Catalog available on Web site.

Tips "Submit only based on guidelines. No e-mail of snail mail queries please. Word count is a definite issue, since we are bilingual." Staff attended or plans to attend the following conferences: BEA, NABE, IRA, ALA and SCBWI.

◘ ▥ RENAISSANCE HOUSE

Imprint of Laredo Publishing, Beverly Hills CA 90210. (800)547-5113. Fax: (310)860-9902. E-mail: laredo@renai ssancehouse.net. Web site: www.renaissancehouse.net. **Manuscript Acquisitions:** Raquel Benatar. **Art Acquisitions:** Sam Laredo. Publishes 5 picture books/year; 10 young readers/year; 10 middle readers/year; 5 young adult titles/year. 10% of books by first-time authors.

Fiction Picture books: animal, folktales, multicultural. Young readers: animal, anthology, folktales, multicultural. Middle readers, young adult/teens: anthology, folktales, multicultural, nature/environment. Recently published *Isabel Allende, Memories for a Story* (English-Spanish, age 9-12, biography); *Stories of the Americas*, a series of legends by several authors (ages 9-12, legend).

How to Contact/Writers Submit outline/synopsis. Responds to queries/mss in 3 weeks. Publishes a book 1 year after acceptance. Will consider simultaneous submissions, e-mail submissions.

Illustration Works with 25 illustrators/year. Uses color artwork only. Reviews ms/illustration packages from artists. Send ms with dummy. Contact: Sam Laredo. Illustrations only: Send tearsheets. Contact: Raquel Benatar. Responds in 3 weeks. Samples not returned; samples filed.

Terms Pays authors royalty of 5-10% based on retail price. Pays illustrators by the project. Sends galleys to authors; dummies to illustrators. Originals returned to artist at job's completion. Book catalog available for 9×12 SASE and $3 postage. All imprints included in a single catalog. Catalog available on Web site.

THE RGU GROUP

560 West Southern Avenue, Tempe AZ 85282. (480)736-9862. Fax: (480)736-9863. E-mail: info@theRGUgroup.c om. Web site: www.theRGUgroup.com. **Manuscript/Art Acquisitions:** Laura Bofinger, Publishing Manager. Publishes 3-4 picture books/year. 30% of books by first-time authors. "The RGU Group publishes entertaining animal-themed children's books with an educational flair, mostly southwestern themes.

Fiction Picture books, board books, young readers: adventure, animal, history, humor, multicultural, nature/ environment. Recently published *Desert Night Shift—A Pack Rat Story*, by Conrad Storad, illustrated by Nathan Jensen (ages 4 and up); *A Wild and Wooly Night*, by Lorraine Lynch Geiger, illustrated by Sharon Vargo. Fiction may include non-fictional elements that complement the southwestern theme. Also will consider bilingual English/Spanish manuscripts.

How to Contact/Writers Fiction/nonfiction: Query or submit complete ms (average 500-1000 words). Responds to queries/mss in 4-5 months. Publishes book 1 year after acceptance. Will consider simultaneous submissions and previously published work.

Illustration Reviews ms/illustration packages from artists. Query or send ms with dummy. Contact: Laura Bofinger, publishing manager. Illustrations only: Query with photocopies, samples, SASE, URL. Responds in 4-5 months. Samples returned with SASE or samples filed.

Terms All contracts negotiated individually.

Tips Looking for fun and dynamic story interaction with well-crafted rising action, climax, and resolution (no flat or abrupt endings). Give the reader a reason to care about the characters. Personify animal characters as much as possible.

Mo Willems

*'Think about your audience,
not for your audience'*

Mo Willems is a bit of a Renaissance man. He creates children's books whose characters resonate with readers and reviewers alike for which he's earned accolades that include Caldecott Honor awards for *Don't Let the Pigeon Drive the Bus!* and *Knuffle Bunny: a cautionary tale* (both Hyperion). His books make frequent appearances on the New York Times Bestseller list. Before delving into children's books, he garnered six Emmy awards for his work as a writer on *Sesame Street. He created the animated series Sheep in the City* for Cartoon Network, and served as head writer for the network's series *Codename: Kid Next Door.* He's a world traveler who chronicled his yearlong voyage in the cartoon journal *You Can Never Find a Rickshaw When It Monsoons.* He's recorded essays for BBC Radio. His work has been shown in galleries, adapted into films and musical theatre productions, and translated into many languages. And he just may have been born in a comedy club while a bunch of clowns were juggling.

Here Willems talks about his work (including the inimitable Pigeon who appears at least once in all of Willem's children's books), offers advice to illustrators, and lets us in on upcoming projects. For more on Willems and his work, visit Mo Willem's Home Studio at www.mowillems.com and his blog, www.mowillemsdoodles.blogspot.com.

The Pigeon seems very demanding—he gets annoyed when you write books that aren't about him. When did you meet said Pigeon? When did he take on a life of his own? Would you say he serves as a muse for you?
I have never been able to control the Pigeon, and doubt that I ever will. He was born fully formed in Oxford, England where I was trying to write the "Great American Picture Book." (I was in Oxford because I hoped it would make me smarter.) None of my projects were any good, so the Pigeon appeared in the margins of the sketches to tell me how bad they were. We've had a distrustful, symbiotic relationship ever since.

I've been enjoying the online Pigeon-drawing instructions. (I appreciate having something new to doodle during meetings.) Why is it important to you that kids can draw your characters?
Hopefully my books will be played, not just read. Being able to make a reasonable drawing of my characters makes it easier for kids to pick up pencil and paper and begin their own adventures. I get a huge kick when kids send me drawings with the Pigeon hanging out with one of their original characters. Too cool.

Did becoming a father affect your career path? How does fatherhood influence your work?

Fatherhood has completely altered my life. To the degree that my career is part of that life, being a dad has changed it, too. I quit television to have more time with my daughter, so in a way she is responsible for my children's book career. While I seek out my daughter's advice, use her stories for my books, and love it when she reads my work, it's important to remember that having a child doesn't make someone a writer for children. I wrote for kids for 15 years before I had my own, and neither Dr. Seuss nor Maurice Sendak have offspring.

When the focus of your career shifted from animation to book publishing, were there any surprises once you got into the process of creating a picture book?

TV is fun, but a grind. TV producers think of writers like safety bars on roller coasters, annoying and pointless. Yet, they demand you knock out story after story after story quickly and consistently. In the book world, authors are treated kindly and given free Coca-colas at meetings. That being said, television is the best place to earn your writing chops.

What's your relationship with your editor like?

My editor and I are on the same team: Team Book. It's not about me, or her. Every conversation, suggestion, critique is focused on how to make a better book. While the relationship is fluid, at its core, my editor finds the problems and I attempt to devise solutions. I cherish working with someone who is both funny and honest.

© 2007 Mo Willems. Reprinted with permission.

Mo Willems' *Today I Will Fly* is "accessible, appealing, and full of authentic emotions about what makes friendships tick," says *Booklist*. One of Mo Willems' Elephant & Piggie Books, the author-illustrator's new series of easy readers, *Today I Will Fly!* centers on the optimistic Piggie, who decides she will take flight—although Elephant is skeptical. With help from a friend Piggie manages to convince Elephant that he wants to fly too.

Don't Let the Pigeon Stay Up Late! is part of the series spawned by Mo Willems' Caldecott Honor winner *Don't Let the Pigeon Drive the Bus!* But Willems' persistent Pigeon somehow manages to find his way into every book by the author-illustrator. Pigeon was born while Willems was working on a project in England. "None of my projects were any good," he says, "so the Pigeon appeared in the margins of the sketches to tell me how bad they were. We've had a distrustful, symbiotic relationship ever since."

How do you get to know your characters as you embark on a new project?

I spend copious time with them, doodling them in all kinds of situations. Once they're done playing in my sketchbooks, I pull them out to do the tough work of putting a story together.

Failure is a recurring theme in your work—tell me about a failure or two of your own.

Oh, I've endured every type of failure, personal, physical, professional . . . While auditioning for *Sesame Street*, I slammed the head writer's head in a door, my cartoon series *Sheep in the Big City* was unceremoniously dumped, as was *The 7th Helper*, a comic book I did for DC Comics a few years back that never saw the light of day. But more importantly, I'm consistently engaging in little failures of miscommunication, temper, and the occasional banging my head against heavy, stationary objects.

Why do you think your books appeal to both young readers and adult readers, to both critics and consumers?

Do they? Cool. Perhaps it's nepotism. Many of my family members are both critics and consumers.

When you traveled abroad for a year, during which time you created the sketchbook diary that became *You Can Never Find a Rickshaw When It Monsoons*, which place that you visited had the biggest impact on you? And why was this book published so long after your travels?

I think I had enough distance from the trip to make the revisiting of it interesting for an audience. Also, a little silver sticker on one of your other books can work wonders when it comes to getting a weird project like this off the ground.

As for impact, the vast scale of the earth and magnitude of divergent cultures on it were shocking. Random moments or events still pop into my head every now and then, producing odd little stories that seem to amuse my family.

What was the most exciting: winning the Caldecott Honor, making the New York Times Bestseller list or being named one of the Hot Men of Children's Literature?

None of the above.

Standing in a library or school and watching 500 kids yell, "NOOOOOOO!!!" at the top of their lungs while giggling incessantly is the coolest accolade I could aspire to. It is a very cool thing.

That is not to underplay the Caldecott Honor, which puts your books on the same shelf as some really excellent, inspiring work. That's cool, too.

(For the record, I have publicly protested my inclusion in the Hot Men of Children's Literature listing, as I am "tepid" on a good day. However, the blogger in question has refused to open categories like "Itchy Men of Children's Literature," "Awkwardly Tall Men of Children's Literature," or "Food Stuck in Their Teeth Men of Children's Literature," so I guess I'm stuck.)

You said; "If I'm funny, everybody should enjoy [my books]. That's my primary goal." Do you think one must be born funny, or is it something a writer/illustrator can learn?

Born funny? Is that like your mother giving birth in a comedy club while a bunch of clowns are juggling?

Any-hoo, most funny people will tell you that humor is learned at the School of Hard Knocks ("Go Knockers!"), but I am of the opinion that a difficult childhood is only helpful, not necessary. What you really need is to be born a comedy club while a bunch of clowns are juggling.

What's harder and why: a book tour or stand up comedy?

Book tours rock! Firstly, the audience wants to be there, and secondly they're so small that they can't throw bottles at you with anywhere near the same velocity that you find in the average comedy club. And, for the record, juice bottles don't bruise as badly as beer bottles.

An Amazon reviewer said: "It would take a human being with the sense of humor of a bowl of moldy tapioca not to find *Edwina: The Dinosaur Who Didn't Know She Was Extinct* one of the funniest picture books of the year." Do you feel there are a lot of moldy tapioca-brained people out there who just don't get you?

If I worried about everyone liking me then I'd have to go back to fifth grade. Please, don't make me go back to fifth grade.

At this point your characters are featured in shows and videos, books, t-shirts and totes, and even mobile phone ring tones. Is Mo Willems becoming a brand or are you on a path to some sort of world domination?

I'm hardly a brand; Charles Schulz's Peanuts was a brand. While he got a kick out of the merch, Schulz believed his job was to focus on the quality of his core work (the daily strip). I agree. No one is going to want a Pigeon doll if the books stink.

As for world domination: with what's going on today, I'd prefer it if the world were run by one of my socks.

You have no siblings and have said you spent a lot of time alone during your formative years. I have a 3-year-old son and don't plan on having any more kids. What advice can you offer my son Murray, only-child-to-only-child?

Never trust anyone over 30 (inches tall).

What's your best advice for illustrators who want to work in children's publishing?

This business requires only two things from its artists: patience and superlative work. I got into books with six Emmy awards, nearly a decade at *Sesame Street*, and two animated television series under my belt, so it merely took me two-and-a-half years to find a publisher for *Don't Let the Pigeon Drive the Bus!* Not that those who rejected me were wrong; my dummy was, well, dumb, and the book was a stretch.

But, I never fretted, as the response to my work was always the same: "It's unusual." I knew it would only take an editor with a bit of vision to change the meaning of unusual from pejorative to positive.

For myself, making books comes down this simple maxim: "Think about your audience, not for your audience."

Please tell me about your upcoming book projects.

I'm quite excited about my slate. Spring 2007 will see the launch of a series of Elephant & Piggie Books, early readers about the mini-adventures of a pessimistic elephant and optimistic pig. In the fall, you'll see the sequel to *Knuffle Bunny: a cautionary tale* entitled *Knuffle Bunny Too: a case of mistaken identity*. The story centers on a pre-school aged Trixie and her bumbling dad. I'm also working on all kinds of new, cool, tip-top secret stuff, so stay tuned!

—*Alice Pope*

RISING MOON

Imprint of Northland Publishing, Inc., P.O. Box 1389, Flagstaff AZ 86002-1389. (928)774-5251. Fax: (928)774-0592. E-mail: editorial@northlandbooks.com. Web site: www.risingmoonbooks.com. Estab. 1988. **Manuscript Acquisitions:** Theresa Howell, kids editor. Publishes hardcover and trade paperback originals. Publishes 8-10 titles/year. Receives 1,000 submissions/year. 20% of books by first-time authors; 20% from unagented writers. "Rising Moon's objective is to provide children with entertaining and spirited picture books with literary integrity and artistic merit."

Fiction Rising Moon is no longer publishing middle-grade children's fiction, only fiction picture books. We are looking for exceptional contemporary fiction with wide appeal to add to our line of Southwest-themed books." Recently published *Do Princesses Wear Hiking Boots?*, by Carmela Lavigna Coyle, illustrated by Mike Gordon.

How to Contact/Writers Accepts simultaneous submissions. Does not accept e-mail submissions. Include SASE. Responds to queries in 3 months. Call for book catalog; ms guidelines online.

Terms Pays authors royalty. Sometimes pays flat fee. Offers advance. Publishes book 1-2 years after acceptance.

Tips "We're always looking for innovative and independently minded stories."

🅰 ROARING BROOK PRESS

143 West St., Suite W, New Milford CT 06776. (860)350-4434. **Manuscript/Art Acquisitions**: Simon Boughton, publisher. Publishes approximately 40 titles/year. 1% of books by first-time authors. This publisher's goal is

''to publish distinctive high-quality children's literature for all ages. To be a great place for authors to be published. To provide personal attention and a focused and thoughtful publishing effort for every book and every author on the list.''

• Roaring Brook Press is an imprint of Holtzbrinck Publishers, a group of companies that includes Henry Holt and Farrar, Straus & Giroux. Roaring Brook is not accepting unsolicited manuscripts.

Fiction Picture books, young readers, middle readers, young adults: adventure, animal, contemporary, fantasy, history, humor, multicultural, nature/environment, poetry, religion, science fiction, sports, suspense/mystery. Recently published *Get Real*, by Betty Hicks.

How to Contact/Writers Primarily interested in agented material. Not accepting unsolicited mss or queries. Will consider simultaneous agented submissions.

Illustration Primarily interested in agented material. Works with 25 illustrators/year. Illustrations only: Query with samples. Do not send original art; copies only through the mail. Samples returned with SASE.

Photography Works on assignment only.

Terms Pays authors royalty based on retail price. Pays illustrators royalty or flat fee depending on project. Sends galleys to authors; dummies to illustrators, if requested.

Tips ''You should find a reputable agent and have him/her submit your work.''

SALINA BOOKSHELF, INC.

1254 W. University Ave., Suite 130, Flagstaff AZ 86001. (928)773-0066. Fax: (928)526-0386. E-mail: sales@salin abookshelf.com. Web site: www.salinabookshelf.com. **Manuscript Acquisitions:** Jessie Ruffenach. **Art Acquisitions:** Art Department. Publishes 10 picture books/year; 4 young readers/year; 1 young adult title/year. 50% of books are by first-time authors.

Fiction Picture books, young readers, middle readers, young adults: adventure, animal, contemporary, folktales, multicultural.

Nonfiction Picture books: multicultural. Young readers, middle readers, young adults: biography, history, multicultural.

How to Contact/Writers Fiction/nonfiction: Query or submit complete ms. Responds to queries in 1 month; mss in 2 months. Publishes a book 1 year after acceptance. Will consider simultaneous submissions and previously published work.

Illustration Works with 8 illustrators/year. Reviews ms/illustration packages from artists. Query. Illustrations only: Query with samples. Responds in 1 month. Samples returned with SASE; samples filed.

Photography Buys stock and assigns work.

Terms Pays authors royalty based on retail price. Offers advances (average amount varies). Pays illustrators and photographers by the project. Originals returned to artist at job's completion. Catalog available for SASE or on Web site; ms guidelines available for SASE.

Tips ''Please note that all our books are Navajo-oriented.''

SASQUATCH BOOKS

119 South Main St., Seattle WA 98104. (800)775-0817. Fax: (206)467-4301. Web site: www.sasquatchbooks.c om. Estab. 1986. Specializes in trade books, nonfiction,children's fiction. **Writers contact:** The Editors. **Illustrators contact:** Lisa-Brire Dahmen, production manager. Produces 5 picture books/year. 20% of books by first-time authors. ''We are seeking quality nonfiction works about the Pacific Northwest and West Coast regions (including Alaska and California). The literature of place includes how-to and where-to as well as history and narrative nonficiton.''

Fiction Young readers: adventure, animal, concept, contemporary, humor, nature/environment. Recently published *Will It Blow?: Become a Volcano Detective at Mount St, Helens*, by Elizabeth Rusch, illustrated by K.E. Lewis (picture book); *Awake to Nap*, written and illustrated by Nikki McClure (board book).

Nonfiction Picture books: activity books, animal, concept, nature/environment. Recently published *Larry Gets Lost in Seattle*, written and illustrated by John Skewes (picture book); *Searching for Sasqatch*, by Nathaniel Lachenmeyer, illustrated by Vicki Bradley (picture book).

How to Contact/Writers Accepts international submissions. Fiction: Query, submit complete ms, or submit outline/synopsis. Nonfiction: Query. Responds to queries in 3 months. Publishes book 6-9 months after acceptance. Considers simultaneous submissions.

Illustration Accepts material from international illustrators. Works with 5 illustrators/year. Uses both color and b&w. Reviews ms/illustration packages. For ms/illustration packages: Query. Submit ms/illustration packages to The Editors. Reviews work for future assignments. If interested in illustrating future titles, query with samples. Samples returned with SASE. Samples filed.

Photography Buys stock images and assigns work. Submit photos to: Lisa-Brire Dahmen, production manager.

Terms Pays authors royalty based on retail price. Offers advance against royalties. Offers a wide range of advances. Author sees galleys for review. Originals not returned. Catalog on Web site. See Web site for writer's guidelines.

SCHOLASTIC INC.

557 Broadway, New York NY 10012. (212)343-6100. Web site: www.scholastic.com. Arthur A. Levine Books, Cartwheel Books®, The Chicken House®, Graphix™, Little Shepherd™, Michael di Capua Books, Orchard Books®, PUSH, Scholastic en español, Scholastic Paperbacks, Scholastic Reference™, and The Blue Sku Press® are imprints of Scholastic Trade Books Division. In addition, Scholastic Trade Books included Klutz®, a highly innovative publisher and creator of "books plus" for childrens.

SCHOLASTIC LIBRARY PUBLISHING

90 Old Sherman Turnpike, Danbury CT 06816. (203)797-3500. Book publisher. Vice President/Publisher: Phil Friedman. **Manuscript Acquisitions:** Kate Nunn, editor-in-chief. **Art Acquisitions:** Marie O'Neil, art director. Imprints: Grolier, Children's Press, Franklin Watts. Publishes more than 400 titles/year. 5% of books by first-time authors; very few titles from agented authors. Publishes informational (nonfiction) for K-12; picture books for young readers, grades 1-3.

Fiction Publishes 1 picture book series, Rookie Readers, for grades 1-2. Does not accept unsolicited mss.

Nonfiction Photo-illustrated books for all levels: animal, arts/crafts, biography, careers, concept, geography, health, history, hobbies, how-to, multicultural, nature/environment, science, social issues, special needs, sports. Average word length: young readers—2,000; middle readers—8,000; young adult—15,000.

How to Contact/Writers Fiction: Does not accept fiction proposals. Nonfiction: Query; submit outline/synopsis, résumé and/or list of publications, and writing sample. SASE required for response. Responds in 3 months. Will consider simultaneous submissions. No phone or e-mail queries; will not respond to phone inquiries about submitted material.

Illustration Works with 15-20 illustrators/year. Uses color artwork and line drawings. Illustrations only: Query with samples or arrange personal portfolio review. Responds only if interested. Samples returned with SASE. Samples filed. Do not send originals. No phone or e-mail inquiries; contact only by mail.

Photography Contact: Caroline Anderson, photo manager. Buys stock and assigns work. Model/property releases and captions required. Uses color and b&w prints; $2\frac{1}{4} \times 2\frac{1}{4}$, 35mm transparencies, images on CD-ROM.

Terms Pays authors royalty based on net or work purchased outright. Pays illustrators at competitive rates. Photographers paid per photo. Sends galleys to authors; dummies to illustrators.

☒ SCHOLASTIC PRESS

557 Broadway, New York NY 10012. (212)343-6100. Web site: www.scholastic.com. **Manuscript Acquisitions:** David Levithan, editorial director; Dianne Hess, executive editor (picture book fiction/nonfiction, 2nd-3rd grade chapter books, some middle grade fantasy that is based on reality); Tracy Mack, executive editor (picture book, middle grade, YA); Kara LaRue, executive editor (picture books, fiction/nonfiction, middle grade); Rachel Griffiths, editor: Jennifer Rees, associate editor (picture book fiction/nonfiction, middle grade, YA). **Art Acquisitions:** Elizabeth Parisi, art director, Scholastic Press; Marijka Kostiw, art director; David Saylor, creative director, all hardcover imprints for Scholastic. Publishes 60 titles/year. 1% of books by first-time authors.

- Scholastic Press title *Rules*, by Cynthia Lord, won a Newbery Honor Medal in 2007. Their title *Dear Mr. Rosenwald*, by Carole Boston Weatherford, illustrated by Gregory Christie, won the Golden Kite Honor for Picture Book Text in 2007. Their title *If You Decide to Go to the Moon*, by Faith McNulty, illustrated by Steven Kellogg, won the Boston Globe-Horn Book Award for Nonfiction in 2007.

Fiction Looking for strong picture books, young chapter books, appealing middle grade novels (ages 8-11) and interesting and well written young adult novels.

Nonfiction Interested in "unusual, interesting, and very appealing approaches to biography, math, history and science."

How to Contact/Writers Fiction/nonfiction: "Send query with 1 sample chapter and synopsis. Don't call! Don't e-mail!" Picture books: submission accepted from agents or previously published authors only.

Illustrations Works with 30 illustrators/year. Uses both b&w and color artwork. Illustrations only: Query with samples; send tearsheets. Responds only if interested. Samples returned with SASE. Original artwork returned at job's completion.

Terms Pays advance against royalty.

Tips "Read *currently* published children's books. Revise, rewrite, rework and find your own voice, style and subject. We are looking for authors with a strong and unique voice who can tell a great story and have the ability to evoke genuine emotion. Children's publishers are becoming more selective, looking for irresistable talent and fairly broad appeal, yet still very willing to take risks, just to keep the game interesting."

SEEDLING PUBLICATIONS

520 E. Bainbridge St., Elizabethtown PA 17022. Web site: www.SeedlingPub.com. **Acquisitions:** Josie Stewart. 20% of books by first-time authors. Publishes books for the beginning reader in English. "Natural language and predictable text are requisite to our publications. Patterned text is acceptable, but must have a unique story

line. Poetry, books in rhyme and full-length picture books are not being accepted at this time. Illustrations are not necessary.''

Fiction Young readers: adventure, animal, folktales, humor, multicultural, nature/environment. Multicultural needs include stories which include children from many cultures and Hispanic-centered storylines. Does not accept texts longer than 16 pages or over 150-200 words or stories in rhyme. Average word length: young readers—100. Recently published *Sherman in the Talent Show*, by Betty Erickson, illustrated by Kristine Dillard; *Moth or Butterfly?*, by Ryan Durney; *The Miller, His Son, and the Donkey*, by Lynn Salem and Josie Stewart (Legends, Fables & Folktales series).

Nonfiction Young readers: animal, arts/crafts, biography, careers, concept, multicultural, nature/environment, science. Does not accept texts longer than 16 pages or over 150-200 words. Average word length: young readers—100.

How to Contact/Writers Fiction/nonfiction: Submit complete ms. Responds in 9 months. Publishes a book 1-2 years after acceptance. Will consider simultaneous submissions. Prefers e-mail submissions from authors or illustrators outside the U.S.

Illustration Works with 8-9 illustrators/year. Uses color artwork only. Reviews ms/illustration packages from artists. Submit ms with dummy. Illustrations only: Send color copies. Responds only if interested. Samples returned with SASE only; samples filed if interested.

Photography Buys photos from freelancers. Works on assignment only. Model/property releases required. Uses color prints and 35mm transparencies. Submit cover letter and color promo piece.

Terms Work purchased outright from authors. Pays illustrators and photographers by the project. Original artwork is not returned at job's completion. Catalog available on Web site.

Tips ''Study our Web site. Follow our guidelines carefully and test your story with children and educators.''

SHEN'S BOOKS

40951 Fremont Blvd., Fremont CA 94538. (510)668-1898. Fax: (510)668-1057. E-mail: info@shens.com. Web site: www.shens.com. Estab. 1986. Specializes in multicultural material. **Acquisitions:** Renee Ting, president. Produces 2 picture books/year. 50% of books by first-time authors.

Fiction Picture books, young readers: folktales, multicultural. Middle readers: multicultural. Recently published *The Wishing Tree*, by Roseanne Thong, illustrated by Connie McLennan (ages 4-8); *The Magical Monkey King*, by Ji-li Jiang (ages 7-10, chapter book); *Many Ideas Open the Way*, by Randy Snook (picture books of proverbs).

Nonfiction Picture books, young readers: multicultural. Recently published *Land of Morning Calm*, by John Stickler, illustrated by Soma Han (ages 7-12, picture book).

How to Contact/Writers Accepts international submissions. Fiction/nonfiction: Submit complete ms. Responds to queries in 1-2 weeks; mss in 6-12 months. Publishes book 1 year after acceptance. Considers simultaneous submissions.

Illustration Accepts material from international illustrators. Works with 2 illustrators/year. Uses color artwork only. Reviews ms/illustration packages. For ms/illustration packages: Send ms with dummy. Submit ms/illustration packages to Renee Ting, president. Reviews work for future assignments. If interested in illustrating future titles, query with samples. Submit samples to Renee Ting, president. Samples not returned. Samples filed.

Photography Works on assignment only. Submit photos to Renee Ting, president.

Terms Authors pay negotiated by the project. Pays illustrators by the project. Pays photographers by the project. Illustrators see dummies for review. Catalog on Web site.

Tips ''Be familiar with our catalog before submitting.''

◻ SILVER MOON PRESS

381 Park Avenue South, Suite 1121,New York NY 10010. (212)802-2890. Fax: (212)802-2893. E-mail: mail@silve rmoonpress.com. Web site: www.silvermoonpress.com. Publisher: David Katz. Managing Editor: Hope Kill-coyne. **Marketing Coordinator:** Karin Lillebo. Book publisher. Publishes 1-2 books for grades 4-6/year. 25% of books by first-time authors; 10% books from agented authors. Publishes mainly American historical fiction and books of educational value. Develops books which fit neatly into curriculum for grades 4-6.'' istory comes alive when children can read about other children who lived when history was being made!''

Fiction Middle readers: historical, multicultural and mystery. Average word length: 14,000. Recently published *Liberty of 23rd Street*, by Jacqueline Glasthal; *A Silent Witness in Harlem*, by Eve Creary; *In the Hands of the Enemy*, by Robert Sheely; *Ambush in the Wilderness*, by Kris Hemphill; *Race to Kitty Hawk*, by Edwina Raffa and Annelle Rigsby; *Brothers of the Falls*, by Joanna Emery.

How to Contact/Writers Fiction: Query. Send synopsis and/or a few chapters, along with a SASE. Responds to queries in 1 month; mss in 2 months. Publishes a book 1-2 years after acceptance. Will consider simultaneous submissions, or previously published work.

Illustration Works with 1-2 illustrators/year. Reviews ms/illustration packages from artists. Query. Illustrations only: Query with samples, résumé, client list. Responds only if interested. Samples returned with SASE; samples filed. Original artwork returned at job's completion.

Photography Buys photos from freelancers. Buys stock and assigns work. Uses archival, historical, sports photos. Captions required. Uses color, b&w prints; 35mm, 2¼×2¼, 4×5, 8×10 transparencies. Submit cover letter, résumé, published samples, client list, promo piece.

Terms Pays authors royalty or work purchased outright. Pays illustrators by the project, no royalty. Pays photographers by the project, per photo, no royalty. Sends galleys to authors; dummies to illustrators. Book catalog available for 8½×11 SAE and $1.11 postage.

Tips "We do not accept biographies, poetry, or romance. We do not accept fantasy, science fiction, or historical fiction with elements of either. Submissions that fit into New York State curriculum topics such as the Revolutionary War, Colonial times, and New York State history in general stand a greater chance of acceptance than those that do not."

SIMON & SCHUSTER BOOKS FOR YOUNG READERS

1230 Avenue of the Americas, New York NY 10020. (212)698-7000. Fax: (212)698-2796. Web site: www.simonsayskids.com. **Manuscript Acquisitions:** Elizabeth Law, vice president and associate publisher; David Gale, vice president, editorial director; Kevin Lewis, executive editor; Paula Wiseman, vice president, editorial director, Paula Wiseman Books. **Art Acquisitions:** Dan Potash, vice president, creative director. Publishes 95 books/year. "We publish high-quality fiction and nonfiction for a variety of age groups and a variety of markets. Above all we strive to publish books that will offer kids a fresh perspective on their world."

- Simon & Schuster Books for Young Readers does not accept unsolicited manuscripts. Queries are accepted via mail. Simon & Schuster title *The Higher Power of Lucky*, by Susan Patron, illustrated by Matt Phelan, won the Newbery Medal in 2007. See page 150 for an Insider Report with Phelan. Their title *To Dance: A Ballerina's Graphic Novel*, by Siena Cherson Siegel, illustrated by Mark Siegel, won a Sibert Honor Medal in 2007.

Fiction Picture books: animal, minimal text/very young readers. Middle readers, young adult: fantasy, adventure, suspense/mystery. All levels: contemporary, history, humor. Recently published *Little Quack's New Friend*, by Lauren Thompson, illustrated by Derek Anderson (picture book, ages 3-7); *Cupcake*, by Rachel Cohn (young adult fiction, ages 13 and up).

Nonfiction Picture books: concept. All levels: narrative, current events, biography, history. "We're looking for picture book or middle grade nonfiction that have a retail potential. No photo essays." Recently published *Our 50 States*, by Lynne Cheney, illustrated by Robin Preiss Glasser (picture book nonfiction, all ages).

How to Contact/Writers Accepting query letters only; please note the appropriate editor. Responds to queries/mss in 3-4 months. Publishes a book 2 years after acceptance. Will not consider simultaneous submissions.

Illustration Works with 70 illustrators/year. Do not submit original artwork. Editorial reviews ms/illustration packages from artists. Submit query letter to Submissions Editor. Illustrations only: Query with samples; samples filed. Provide promo sheet, tearsheets. Responds only if interested.

Terms Pays authors royalty (varies) based on retail price. Pays illustrators or photographers by the project or royalty (varies) based on retail price. Original artwork returned at job's completion. Manuscript/artist's guidelines available via Web site or free on request. Call (212)698-2707.

Tips "We're looking for picture books centered on a strong, fully-developed protagonist who grows or changes during the course of the story; YA novels that are challenging and psychologically complex; also imaginative and humorous middle-grade fiction. And we want nonfiction that is as engaging as fiction. Our imprint's slogan is 'Reading You'll Remember.' We aim to publish books that are fresh, accessible and family-oriented; we want them to have an impact on the reader."

SLEEPING BEAR PRESS

Imprint of Gale Group, 310 N. Main St., Suite 300, Chelsea MI 48118. (734)475-4411. Fax: (734)475-0787. Web site: www.sleepingbearpress.com. **Manuscript Acquisitions:** Heather Hughes. **Art Acquisitions:** Jennifer Bacheller, creative director. Publishes 30 picture books/year. 10% of books by first-time authors.

Fiction Picture books: adventure, animal, concept, folktales, history, multicultural, nature/environment, religion, sports. Young readers: adventure, animal, concept, folktales, history, humor, multicultural, nature/environment, religion, sports. Average word length: picture books—1,800. Recently published *R Is for Rhyme: A Poetry Alphabet*, by Judy Young; *The Last Brother*, by Trinka Hakes; *Grady the Goose*, by Denise Brennan-Nelson.

Nonfiction Average word length: picture books—1,800. Recently published *The Edmund Fitzgerald*; *Mercedes and the Chocolate Pilot*; *P is for Passport*.

How to Contact/Writers Only interested in agented material. Fiction/nonfiction: Submit complete ms. Responds to queries in 1 month; mss in 2 months. Publishes book 2 years after acceptance. Will consider e-mail submissions, simultaneous submissions.

Illustration Only interested in agented material. Works with 30 illustrators/year. Uses color artwork only. Reviews ms/illustration packages from artists. Send ms with dummy. Illustrations only: Send samples, SASE, URL. Responds in 1 month. Samples returned with SASE.

Terms Pays authors royalty. Offers advances. Pays illustrators royalty. Sends galleys to authors. Originals returned to artist at job's completion. Book catalog available. All imprints included in a single catalog. Catalog available on Web site.

Tips ''Please review our book on line before sending material or calling.'' Editorial staff attended or plans to attend the following conferences: BEA, IRA, Regional shows, UMBE, NEBA, AASL, ALA, and numerous local conferences.

SMALLFELLOW PRESS

Imprint of Tallfellow Press, 1180 S. Beverly Dr., Suite 320, Los Angeles CA 90035. E-mail: tallfellow@pacbell.net. Web site: www.smallfellow.com. **Manuscript/Art Acquisitions:** Claudia Sloan.
• Smallfellow no longer accepts manuscript submissions.

🅽 ▢ SOUNDPRINTS/STUDIO MOUSE

Trudy Corporations, 353 Main St., Norwalk CT 06851. (800)228-7839. Fax: (203)864-1776. E-mail: info@soundprints.com. Web site: www.soundprints.com. Estab. 1947. **Manuscript Acquisitions:** Christine Wells, editorial assistant. **Art Aquisitions:** Meredith Campbell Britton, senior designer. 10% of books by first-time authors. Publishes mass market books, educational material, multicultural material.

Fiction Picture books, young readers: adventure, animal, fantasy, history, multicultural, nature/environment, sports. Recently published *Scout Hits the Trail*, by Liam O'Donnell, illustrated by Catherine Huerta (ages preschool-2, paperback available with audio CD and plush toy); *Baby Lamb Finds a Friend*, by Laura Gates Galvin (ages 18 months-3 years, board book available with plush toy); *Captain Jack Sparrow's Secret Journal*, by Jodie Shepherd, designed by Katie Sears (ages 6-10, zippered casebound hardcover with nylon handle, 2 pens, stickers and audio CD).

How to Contact/Writers Query of submit complete manuscript. Responds to queries/mss in 6 months. Publishes a book 1-2 years after acceptance.

Illustration Works with 3-7 illustrators/year. Uses color artwork only. Send tearsheets with contact information, ''especially Web address if applicable.'' Samples not returned; samples filed.

Photography Buys stock and assigns work. Model/property release and captions required. Send color promo sheet.

Terms Original artwork returned at jobs completion. Catalog available on Web site. Offers writer's/artist's/photographer's guidelines with SASE.

STANDARD PUBLISHING

8121 Hamilton Ave., Cincinnati OH 45231. (513)931-4050. Fax: (513)931-0950. Web site: www.standardpub.com. **Editorial Directors:** Matthew Lockhart, director, product development; Ruth Frederick, Children & Youth Ministry Resources. **Creative Services Director:** Julie Diehl. Many projects are written in-house. No young adult novels. 25-40% of books by first-time authors; 10% of books from agented writers. Publishes picture books, board books, nonfiction, devotions and resources for teachers.
• Standard also has a listing in Greeting Card, Puzzles & Games.

Fiction Recently published *Jesus Must Be Really Special*, by Jennie Bishop, illustrated by Amy Wummer.

Nonfiction Recently published *Through the Bible Devotions*, by Mark Littleton.

How to Contact/Writers Responds in 3-6 months.

Illustration Works with 20 new illustrators/year. Illustrations only: Submit cover letter and photocopies. Responds to art samples only if interested. Samples returned with SASE; samples filed.

Terms Pays authors royalty based on net price or work purchased outright (range varies by project). Pays photographers by the photo. Sends galleys to authors on most projects. Book catalog available for $2 and 8½×11 SAE; ms guidelines available on Web site.

Tips ''We look for manuscripts that help draw children into a relationship with Jesus Christ, develop insights about Bible teachings, and make reading fun.''

STARSEED PRESS

Imprint of HJ Kramer in joint venture with New World Library, P.O. Box 1082, Tiburon CA 94920. (415)435-5367. Fax: (415)435-5364. Web site: www.newworldlibrary.com. **Manuscript Acquisitions:** Jan Phillips. **Art Acquisitions:** Linda Kramer, vice president. Publishes 2 picture books/year. 50% of books by first-time authors. ''We publish 4-color, 32-page children's picture books dealing with self-esteem and positive values, with a non-denominational, spiritual emphasis.''

Fiction Picture books: self-esteem, multicultural, nature/environment. Average word length: picture books—

500-1,500. Recently published *Lucky Goose Goes to Texas*, by Holly Bea, illustrated by Joe Boddy (ages 3-10, picture book).

Nonfiction Picture books: multicultural, nature/environment.

How to Contact/Writers Fiction/nonfiction: Submit outline/synopsis. Responds to queries/mss in 10 weeks. Publishes a book 18 months after acceptance. Will consider simultaneous submissions, previously published work.

Illustration Works with 2 illustrators/year. Uses color artwork only. Illustrations only: Query with samples. Responds only if interested. Samples returned with SASE; samples filed.

Terms Negotiates based on publisher's net receipts. Split between author and artist. Originals returned to artist at job's completion. Book catalog available for 9 × 11 SAE with $1.98 postage; ms and art guidelines available for SASE. All imprints included in a single catalog.

STERLING PUBLISHING CO., INC.

387 Park Ave. S., 10th Floor, New York NY 10016-8810. (212)532-7160. Fax: (212)981-0508. E-mail: info@sterlin gweb.com. Web site: www.sterlingpublishing.com. **Manuscript Acquisitions:** Frances Gilbert. **Art Acquisitions:** Karen Nelson, creative director. Publishes 20 picture books/year; 50 young readers/year; 150 middle readers/year; 10 young adult titles/year. 15% of books by first-time authors.

- Sterling title *Poetry for Young People: Langston Hughes*, by Benny Andrews, won a Coretta Scott King Illustrator Honor Award in 2007.

Fiction Picture books.

Nonfiction Young readers: activity books, arts/crafts, cooking, hobbies, how-to, science. Middle readers, young adults: activity books, arts/crafts, hobbies, how-to, science, mazes, optical illusions, games, magic, math, puzzles.

How to Contact/Writers Nonfiction: Submit outline/synopsis and 1 sample chapter. Responds to queries/mss in 6 weeks. Publishes book 1 year after acceptance. Will consider simultaneous submissions, previously published work.

Illustration Works with 50 illustrators/year. Reviews ms/illustration packages from artists. Contact: Frances Gilbert, editorial director. Illustrations only: Send promo sheet. Contact: Karen Nelson, creative director. Responds in 6 weeks. Samples returned with SASE; samples filed.

Photography Buys stock and assigns work. Contact: Karen Nelson.

Terms Pays authors royalty or work purchased outright from authors. Offers advances (average amount: $2,000). Pays illustrators by the project. Pays photographers by the project or per photo. Sends galleys to authors; dummies to illustrators. Originals returned to artist at job's completion. Offers writer's guidelines for SASE. Catalog available on Web site.

Tips "We are primarily a nonfiction activities-based publisher. We have a small picture book list, but we do not publish chapter books or novels. Our list is not trend-driven. We focus on titles that will backlist well."

STONE ARCH BOOKS

7825 Telegraph Rd., Minneapolis MN 55438. (952)224-0514. Fax: (952)933-2410. Web site: www.stonearchbook s.com. **Acquisitions Editor:** Michael Dahl. **Art Director:** Heather Kindseth. Specializes in "high-interest, engaging fiction for struggling and reluctant readers, especially boys."

Fiction Young Readers, middle readers, young adults: adventure, contemporary, fantasy, hi-lo, humor, multicultural, science fiction, sports, suspense. Average word length: young readers—2,000; middle readers—5,000; young adults—7,000-10,000.

How to Contact/Writers Submit outline/synopsis and 3 sample chapters. Responds to mss in 8 weeks. Publishes a book 6-12 months after acceptance. Accepts e-mail submissions and simultaneous submissions.

Illustration Works with 35 illustrators/year. Used both color and b&w. Send manuscript with dummy. Contact: Heather Kindseth, art directorn. Samples not returned; samples filed.

Terms Work purchased outright from authors. Illustrators paid by the project. Book catalog available on Web site.

Tips "A 'high-interest' topic or activity is one that a young person would spend their free time on without adult direction or suggestion."

SYLVAN DELL PUBLISHING

E-mail: donnagerman@sylvandellpublishing.com. Web site: www.sylvandellpublishing.com. Contact: Donna German." Estab. 2004. The books that we publish are usually, but not always, fictional stories that relate to animals, nature, the environment, and science. All books should subtly convey an educational theme through a warm story that is fun to read and that will grab a children's attention. Each book has a 3-5 page "For Creative Minds" section in the back to reinforce the educational component of the book itself. This section will have a craft and/or game as well as "fun facts" to be shared by the parent, teacher, or other adult. Authors do not need to supply this information but may be actively involved in its development if they would like. Please read about our submission guidelines on our Web site.''

● Sylvan Dell only accepts electronic submissions.

Fiction Picture Books: animal, folktales, nature/environment. Word length—picture books: no more than 1500. Spring titles include *In Arctic Waters* by Laura Crawford, illustrated by Ben Hodson; *ABC Safari*, written (first authored book) and illustrated by Karen Lee; *The Rainforest Grew All Around*, written by first-time author Susan K. Mitchell, illustrated by Connie McLennan; *Turtle Summer: A Journal for my Daughter*, written by NY Times bestselling adult novelist Mary Alice Monroe, photographs by Barbara Bergwerf; *Ocean Seasons*, by Ron Hirschi, illustrated by Kirsten Carlson; and *In My Backyard*, by first-time author Valarie Giogas, illustrated by Katherine Zecca.

How to Contact/Writers Submit complete ms. Prefers to work with authors from the US and Canada because of marketing. Responds to mss in 3-4 months. Publishes a book about 2 years after acceptance. Accepts simultaneous submissions. Accepts electronic submissions only.

Illustration Works with 10 illustrators/year. Prefers to work with illustrators from the US and Canada. Uses color artwork only. Reviews ms/illustration packages from illustrators. Submit manuscript with 1-2 pieces of final art. Contact: Donna German. Illustrations only: submit Web link or 2-3 electronic images. Contact: Donna German. ''I generally keep submissions on file until I match the manuscripts to illustration needs.''

Terms Pays authors and illustrators step-up royalty of 7.5% based on wholesale price. Offers $1,000 advance. ''Authors and illustrators see PDFs of book as it goes to the printer. Any concerns or changes are dealt with then. We keep cover art and return all other art to illustrators.'' Catalog available on Web site. Writer's and artist's guidelines available on Web site.

Tips ''Please make sure that you have looked at our Web site to see what we publish and read our complete submission guidelines. Manuscripts must meet all four of our stated criteria. We are currently looking for manuscripts about the Rocky Mt. area (animals, etc.) We look for fairly realistic, bright and colorful art—no cartoons.''

TANGLEWOOD BOOKS

P.O. Box 3009, Terre Haute IN 47803. E-mail: ptierney@tanglewoodbooks.com. Web site: www.tanglewoodbooks.com. Estab. 2003. Specializes in trade books. **Writers contact:** Peggy Tierney, publisher. **Illustrators contact:** Peggy Tierney, publisher. Produces 2-3 picture books/year, 1-2 middle readers/year, 1-2 young adult titles/year. 20% of books by first-time authors. ''Tanglewood Press strives to publishh entertaining, kid-centric books.''

Fiction Picture books: adventure, animal, concept, contemporary, fantasy, humor. Average word length: picture books—800. Recently published *Mystery at Blackbeard's Cove*, by Audrey Penn, illustrated by Josh Miller and Phillip Howard (ages 8-12, adventure); *The Mice of Bistrot des Sept Freres*, written and illustrated by Marie Letourneau; *You Can't Milk a Dancing Cow*, by Tom Dunsmuir, illustrated by Brain Jones (ages 4-8, humorous).

How to Contact/Writers Accepts international submissions. Fiction: Query with 3-5 sample chapters. Responds to mss in 6-9 months. Publishes book 2 years after acceptance. Considers simultaneous submissions.

Illustration Accepts material from international illustrators. Works with 3-4 illustrators/year. Uses both color and b&w. Reviews ms/illustration packages. For ms/illustration packages: Send ms with sample illustrations. Submit ms/illustration packages to Peggy Tierney, publisher. If interested in illustrating future titles, query with samples. Submit samples to Peggy Tierney, publisher. Samples returned with SASE. Samples filed.

Terms Illustrators paid by the project for covers and small illustrations; royalty of 3-5% for picture books. Author sees galleys for review. Illustrators see dummies for review. Originals returned to artist at job's completion.

Tips ''Please see lengthy 'Submissions' page on our Web site.''

TILBURY HOUSE, PUBLISHERS

2 Mechanic St., #3, Gardiner ME 04345. (207)582-1899. Fax: (207)582-8227. E-mail: tilbury@tilburyhouse.com. Web site: www.tilburyhouse.com. **Publisher:** Jennifer Bunting. Children's Book Editor: Audrey Maynard. Publishes 1-3 young readers/year.

Fiction Picture books, young readers, middle readers: multicultural, nature/environment. Special needs include books that teach children about tolerance and honoring diversity. Recently published *Thanks to the Animals*, by Allen Sockabasin; *Playing War*, by Kathy Beckwith; *Say Something*, by Peggy Moss; *The Goat Lady*, by Jane Bregoli.

Nonfiction Picture books, young readers, middle readers: multicultural, nature/environment. Recently published *Life Under Ice*, by Mary Cerullo, with photography by Bill Curtsinger; *Saving Birds*, by Pete Salmansohn and Steve Kress.

How to Contact/Writers Fiction/ nonfiction: Submit outline/synopsis. Responds to queries/mss in 1 month. Publishes a book 1-2 years after acceptance. Will consider simultaneous submissions ''with notification.''

Illustration Works with 2 illustrators/year. Illustrations only: Query with samples. Responds in 1 month. Samples returned with SASE. Original artwork returned at job's completion.

Photography Buys photos from freelancers. Works on assignment only.

Terms Pays authors royalty based on wholesale price. Pays illustrators/photographers by the project; royalty based on wholesale price. Sends galleys to authors. Book catalog available for 6×9 SAE and 57¢ postage.

Tips ''We are primarily interested in children's books that teach children about tolerance in a multicultural society, honor diversity, and make readers curious about the larger world. We are also interested in books that teach children about environmental issues.''

A MEGAN TINGLEY BOOKS

Hachette Book Group USA, 237 Park Ave., New York, NY 10017. (212)364-1100. Fax: (212)364-0925. Web site: www.lb-kids.com,www.lb-teens.com. **Manuscript Acquisitions:** Julie Tony, assistant to the publisher. **Art Acquisitions:** Creative Director. Publishes 10 picture books/year; 1 middle reader/year; 2 young adult titles/year. 2% of books by first-time authors.

- Megan Tingley Books accepts agented material only.

Fiction Average word length: picture books—under 1,000 words. Recently published *You Read to Me, I'll Read to You: Very Short Scary Tales to Read Together*, by Mary Ann Hoberman, illustrated by Michael Emberley (ages 3-6, picture book); *The Peace Book*, by Todd Parr (all ages, picture book); *Between Mom and Jo*, by Julie Anne Peters (ages 12 and up); *New Moon*, by Stephenie Meyer (ages 12 and up).

Nonfiction All levels: animal, biography, history, multicultural, music/dance, nature/environment, science, self help, social issues, special needs. Recently published *My New York* (revised edition), by Kathy Jakobsen; *Harlem Stomp!*, by Laban Carrick Hill (ages 10 and up).

How to Contact/Writers Only interested in agented material. Query. Responds to mss in 2 months. Publishes a book 2 years after acceptance. Will consider simultaneous submissions, previously published work.

Illustration Works with 5 illustrators/year. Reviews ms/illustration packages from artists. Illustrations only: Query with samples. Contact: Assistant to the Publisher. Responds only if interested. Samples not returned; samples kept on file.

Terms Pays illustrators by the project or royalty based on retail price. Sends galleys to authors. Originals returned to artist at job's completion. All imprints included in a single catalog. Responds within 2 months only if interested.

TOKYOPOP INC.

5900 Wilshire Blvd., Los Angeles CA 90036. (323)692-6700. Fax: (323)692-6701. Web site: www.tokyopop.com. Estab. 1996. Specializes in trade books, fiction, multicultural material. **Submissions:** Rob Tokar, editor-in-chief. Produces 75 picture books/year; 6 young readers/year; 6 young adult books/year. 25% of books by first-time authors. ''We are the leading Asian popculture-influenced publisher in the world. Our product lines include manga, cine-manga™, young adult novels, chapter books, and merchandise.''

Fiction Young readers: adventure, contemporary, humor, science fiction, suspense. Middle readers: adventure, contemporary, fantasy, humor, problem novels, science fiction. Young adults/teens: adventure, contemporary, fantasy, humor, problem novels, science fiction, suspense. Average word length: young readers—9,000; middle readers—9,000; young adult—50,000.

Nonfiction Middle readers, young adult/teens: activity books, arts/crafts, hobbies.

How to Contact/Writers Accepts international submissions. Fiction: Submit outline/synopsis and 2 sample chapters. Responds to queries/mss in 6 months. Publishes book 18 months after acceptance.

Illustration Accepts material from international illustrators. Works with 25 illustrators/year. Uses primarily b&w artwork. Reviews ms/illustration packages. Submit ms/illustration packages to Rob Tokar, editor-in-chief. Reviews work for future assignments. If interested in illustrating future titles, query with samples. Submit samples to Rob Tokar, editor-in-chief. Responds in 3 months. Samples not returned.

Terms Pays authors royalty of 8% based on retail price. Pays illustrators by the project (range: $500-5,000). Author sees galleys for review. Illustrators see dummies for review. Originals not returned. Catalog on Web site. See Web site for artist's guidelines.

Tips ''Submit cool, innovative, offbeat, cutting-edge material that captures the essence of teen pop culture.''

N TOR BOOKS

175 Fifth Ave., New York NY 10010-7703. Fax: (212)388-0191. E-mail: Juliet.Pederson@Tor.com. Web site: www.tor.com. **Contact:** Juliet Pederson, assistant to publisher, children's/YA division. Publisher: Kathleen Doherty; Senior Editor: Susan Chang. Imprints: Forge, Orb, Starscape, Tor Teen. Publishes 5-10 middle readers/year; 5-10 young adult titles/year.

- Tor Books is the ''world's largest publisher of science fiction and fantasy, with strong category publishing in historical fiction, mystery, western/Americana, thriller, YA.''

Fiction Middle readers, young adult titles: adventure, animal, anthology, concept, contemporary, fantasy, history, humor, multicultural, nature/environment, problem novel, science fiction, suspense/mystery. Average word length: middle readers—30,000; young adults—60,000-100,000. Published *Hidden Talents, Flip,* by David Lubar (ages 10 and up, fantasy); *Briar Rose,* by Jane Yolen (ages 12 and up).

Nonfiction Middle readers and young adult: geography, history, how-to, multicultural, nature/environment, science, social issues. Does not want to see religion, cooking. Average word length: middle readers—25,000-35,000; young adults—70,000. Published *Strange Unsolved Mysteries,* by Phyllis Rabin Emert; *Stargazer's Guide (to the Galaxy),* by Q.L. Pearce (ages 8-12, guide to constellations, illustrated).

How to Contact/Writers Fiction/nonfiction: Submit outline/synopsis and complete ms. Responds to queries in 1 month; mss in 6 months for unsolicited work; 1 month or less for agented submissions. Note: We do not accept electronic submissions, synopsis or querys of any kind. Do not email your inquiries.

Illustration Query with samples. Contact: Irene Gallo, art director. Responds only if interested. Samples kept on file.

Terms Pays authors royalty. Offers advances. Pays illustrators by the project. Book catalog available for 9×12 SAE and 3 first-class stamps. Submission guidelines available with SASE.

Tips "Know the house you are submitting to, familiarize yourself with the types of books they are publishing. Get an agent. Allow him/her to direct you to publishers who are most appropriate. It saves time and effort."

TRICYCLE PRESS

Imprint of Ten Speed Press, P.O. Box 7123, Berkeley CA 94707. (510)559-1600. Web site: www.tricyclepress.com. **Acquisitions:** Nicole Geiger, publisher. Publishes 12-14 picture books/year; 2-4 middle readers/year; 3 board books/year. 25% of books by first-time authors. "Tricycle Press looks for something outside the mainstream; books that encourage children to look at the world from a different angle. Tricycle Press, like its parent company, Ten Speed Press, is known for its quirky, offbeat books. We publish high-quality trade books."

Fiction Board books, picture books, middle grade: animal, contemporary, fantasy, history, multicultural, nature, poetry, suspense/mystery. Picture books, young readers: concept. Middle readers: literary novels, high-quality fantasy and adventure—no mass market fiction. Average word length: picture books—800-1,000. Recently published *Courage of the Blue Boy,* by Robert Neubecker (ages 3 and up, picture book); *Ceci Ann's Day of Why,* by Christopher Phillips, illustrated by Shino Arihara (ages 4 and up, picture book); *Hugging the Rock,* by Susan Taylor Brown (ages 9-12, novel).

Nonfiction Picture books, middle readers: animal, arts/crafts, biography, careers, concept, cooking, history, how-to, multicultural, music/dance, nature/environment, science. Recently published *Will Fibonacci,* by Joy N. Hulme, illustrated by Carol Schwartz (ages 7 and up, picture book); *Salad People and More Real Recipes: A New Cookbook for Preschoolers and Up,* by Mollie Katzen; *Why Explore?,* by Susan Lendroth, illustrated by Enrique S. Moreiro (agest 6 and up, nonfiction picture book).

How to Contact/Writers Fiction: Submit complete ms for picture books. Submit outline/synopsis and 2-3 sample chapters for chapter book. "No queries!" Nonfiction: Submit complete ms. Responds to mss in 4-6 months. Publishes a book 1-2 years after acceptance. Welcomes simultaneous submissions and previously published work. Do not send original artwork; copies only, please. No electronic or faxed submissions.

Illustration Works with 12 illustrators/year. Uses color and some b&w. Reviews ms/illustration package from artists. Submit ms with dummy and/or 2-3 pieces of final art. Illustrations only: Query with samples, promo sheet, tearsheets. Responds only if interested. Samples returned with SASE; samples filed. Original artwork returned at job's completion unless work for hire.

Photography Works on assignment only. Uses 35mm transparencies or high resolution electronic files. Submit samples.

Terms Pays authors royalty of $7^1/_2$-$8^1/_2$% based on net receipts. Offers advances. Pays illustrators and photographers royalty of $7^1/_2$-$8^1/_2$% based on net receipts. Sends galleys of novels to authors. Book catalog for 9×12 SAE (3 first-class stamps). Manuscript guidelines for SASE (1 first-class stamp). Guidelines available at Web site.

Tips "We are looking for something a bit outside the mainstream and with lasting appeal (no one-shot-wonders)."

▣ TROPHY/HARPER TEEN/EOS PAPERBACKS

1350 Avenue of the Americas, New York NY 10019. (212)261-6500. Fax: (212)261-6668. Web sites:www.harpercollins.com,www.harperteen.com,www.harpertrophy.com. Book publisher. Imprint of HarperCollins Children's Books. Publishes 15-20 chapter books/year, 55-60 middle grade titles/year, 15-20 reprint picture books/year, 60-65 teen titles/year.

- Trophy is a chapter book and middle grade imprint. HarperTeen is a teen imprint. Eos is a fantasy/science fiction imprint. In addition to paperback reprints, Trophy and HarperTeen also publish a number of hardcover and/or paperback originals each year.

How to Contact/Writers Does not accept unsolicited or unagented mss.

TURTLE BOOKS

866 United Nations Plaza, Suite 525, New York NY 10017. (212)644-2020. Web site: www.turtlebooks.com. **Acquisitions:** John Whitman. "Turtle Books publishes only picture books for young readers. Our goal is to publish a small, select list of quality children's books each spring and fall season. As often as possible, we will publish our books in both English and Spanish editions."

• Turtle does a small number of books and may be slow in responding to unsolicited manuscripts.

Fiction Picture books: adventure, animal, concept, contemporary, fantasy, folktales, hi-lo, history, humor, multicultural, nature/environment, religion, sports, suspense/mystery. Recently published *The Legend of Mexicatl*, by Jo Harper, illustrated by Robert Casilla (the story of Mexicatl and the origin of the Mexican people); *Vroom, Chugga, Vroom-Vroom*, by Anne Miranda, illustrated by David Murphy (a number identification book in the form of a race car story); *The Crab Man*, by Patricia VanWest, illustrated by Cedric Lucas (the story of a young Jamaican boy who must make the difficult decision between making an income and the ethical treatment of animals); *Prairie Dog Pioneers*, by Jo and Josephine Harper, illustrated by Craig Spearing (the story of a young girl who doesn't want to move, set in 1870s Texas); *Keeper of the Swamp*, by Ann Garrett, illustrated by Karen Chandler (a dramatic coming-of-age story wherein a boy confronts his fears and learns from his ailing grandfather the secrets of the swamp); *The Lady in the Box*, by Ann McGovern, illustrated by Marni Backer (a modern story about a homeless woman named Dorrie told from the point of view of two children); *Alphabet Fiesta*, by Anne Miranda, illustrated by young school children in Madrid, Spain (an English/Spanish alphabet story).

How to Contact/Writers Send complete ms. "Queries are a waste of time." Response time varies.

Illustrators Works with 6 illustrators/year. Responds to artist's queries/submissions only if interested. Samples returned with SASE only.

Terms Pays royalty. Offers advances.

TWO LIVES PUBLISHING

P.O. Box 736, Ridley Park PA 19078. (609)502-8147. Fax: (610)717-1460. E-mail: bcombs@twolives.com. Web site: www.twolives.com. **Manuscript Acquisitions:** Bobbie Combs. Publishes 1 picture book/year; 1 middle reader/year. 100% of books by first-time authors. "We create books for children whose parents are lesbian, gay, bisexual or transgender."

Fiction Picture books, young readers, middle readers: contemporary.

How to Contact/Writers Fiction: Query. Responds to queries/mss in 3 months. Publishes book 2-3 years after acceptance. Will consider e-mail submissions, simultaneous submissions, previously published work.

Illustration Works with 2 illustrators/year. Uses color artwork only. Query ms/illustration packages. Contact: Bobbie Combs, publisher. Illustrations only: Send postcard sample with brochure, photocopies. Contact: Bobbie Combs, publisher. Responds only if interested. Samples filed.

Terms Pays authors royalty of 5-10% based on retail price. Offers advances (average amount: $250). Pays illustrators royalty of 5-10% based on retail price. Sends galleys to authors. Originals returned to artist at job's completion. Catalog available on Web site.

TWO-CAN PUBLISHING

T & N Children's Publishing, 11571 K-Tel Drive, Minnetonka MN 55343. Web site: www.two-canpublishing.com. Estab. 1990. Specializes in trade books, nonfiction. **Manuscript Acquisitions:** Jill Anderson, editorial director. Produces 10 young readers/year; 5 middle readers/year. 5% of books by first-time authors. "Two-Can's line of nonfiction children's books feature bright, appealing designs, well-researched facts, and fun-to-read texts. Nonfiction does not have to be boring!"

Nonfiction Picture books, young readers, middle readers: animal, geography, health, history, multicultural, nature/environment, reference, science. Average word length: picture books—400-800; young readers—800-3,000; middle readers—2,500-15,000. Recently published *They Ate What?! The Weird History of Food*, by Richard Platt (ages 8-11, history); *Freaky Facts About Mummies*, by Iqbal Hussain (ages 7-10, history); *You Can Write a Story! A Story Writing Recipe for Kids*, by Lisa Bullard (ages 6-9, language arts).

How to Contact/Writers No longer accepting international submissions. Responds to queries/mss in 2 months. Publishes book 1-2 years after acceptance. Considers simultaneous submissions.

Illustration Works with 2 illustrators/year. Uses color artwork only. Reviews ms/illustration packages. For ms/illustration packages: Submit ms/illustration packages to Jill Anderson, editorial director. Reviews work for future assignments. If interested in illustrating future titles, query with samples, photocopies. Submit samples to Art Director. Samples not returned. Samples filed.

Photography Buys stock images. Contact: Jill Anderson, editorial director. Photo needs "depend on project we are working on—nature, culture, how-to—just about anything." Model/property releases required. Photo captions required. Uses high-res scans or color transparencies. For first contact, send cover letter, published samples, stock photo list, promo piece.

Terms Pays authors a royalty based on retail price or work purchased outright. Pays illustrators by the project or royalty. Pays photographers by the project, per photo or royalty. Author sees galleys for review. Illustrators see dummies for review. See Web site for writer's and artist's guidelines.

Ⓐ TYNDALE HOUSE PUBLISHERS, INC.

351 Executive Dr., P.O. Box 80, Wheaton IL 60189. (630)668-8300. Web site: www.tyndale.com. **Manuscript Acquisitions:** Jan Axford. **Art Acquisitions:** Talinda Laubach. Publishes approximately 15 Christian children's titles/year.

- Tyndale House no longer reviews unsolicited manuscripts, only agented material.

Fiction Not acquiring at this time.

Nonfiction Bible, devotionals, Bible storybooks.

Illustration Uses full-color for book covers, b&w or color spot illustrations for some nonfiction. Illustrations only: Query with photocopies (color or b&w) of samples, résumé.

Photography Buys photos from freelancers. Works on assignment only.

Terms Pay rates for authors and illustrators vary.

Tips "All accepted manuscripts will appeal to Evangelical Christian children and parents."

UNITY HOUSE

1901 NW Blue Pkwy., Unity Village MO 64065-0001. (816)524-3550, ext. 3190. (816)251-3552. Web site: www.unityonline.org. Other imprints: Wee Wisdom.

Fiction All levels: religion. Recently published *Henrietta the Homely Duckling*, by Phil Hahn (picture book).

Nonfiction All levels: religion.

How to Contact/Writers Fiction/nonfiction: Submit complete ms. Responds to queries/mss in 6 months. Publishes a book approximately 1 year after acceptance. Will consider simultaneous submissions or previously self-published work. Writer's guidelines upon request.

Illustration Reviews ms/illustration packages from artists. Query.

Terms Pays authors royalty of 10-15% based on net receipts or work purchased outright. Offers advances (average amount: $1,000). Book catalog available.

Tips "Read our Writer's Guidelines and study our catalog before submitting. All of our publications reflect Unity's spiritual teachings, but the presentations and applications of those teachings are wide open."

VIKING CHILDREN'S BOOKS

Penguin Group Inc., 345 Hudson St., New York NY 10014-3657. (212)414-3600. Fax: (212)414-3399. Web site: www.penguin.com. **Acquisitions:** Catherine Frank, senior editor (picture books, middle grade and young adult fiction); Tracy Gates, executive editor (picture books, middle grade, young adult fiction); Joy Peskin, senior editor (picture books, middle grade, young adult fiction); Anne Gunton, editor (picture books, middle grade, young adult); Kendra Levin, assistant editor. **Art Acquisitions:** Denise Cronin, Viking Children's Books. Publishes hardcover originals. Publishes 60 books/year. Receives 7,500 queries/year. 25% of books from first-time authors; 33% from unagented writers. "Viking Children's Books is known for humorous, quirky picture books, in addition to more traditional fiction and publishes the highest quality trade books for children including fiction, nonfiction, and novelty books for pre-schoolers through young adults." Publishes book 1-2 years after acceptance of artwork. Hesitantly accepts simultaneous submissions.

- Viking Children's Books is not accepting unsolicited submissions at this time.

Fiction All levels: adventure, animal, contemporary, fantasy, hi-lo, history, humor, multicultural, nature/environment, poetry, problem novels, religion, romance, science fiction, sports, suspense/mystery. Recently published *Llama Llama Red Pajama*, by Anna Dewdney (ages 2 up, picture book); *Prom*, by Laurie Halse Anderson (ages 12 and up); *Follow the Line*, by Laura Ljungkvist; *Just Listen*, by Sarah Dessen.

Nonfiction Picture books: animal, biography, concept. Young readers, middle readers, young adult: animal, biography, concept, geography, hi-lo, history, multicultural, music/dance, nature/environment, science, sports. Recently published *John Lennon: All I Want Is the Truth*, by Elizabeth Partridge (ages 11 up, nonfiction).

Illustration Works with 30 illustrators/year. Responds to artist's queries/submissions only if interested. Samples returned with SASE only or samples filed. Originals returned at job's completion.

Terms Pays 2-10% royalty on retail price or flat fee. Advance negotiable.

Ⓦ WALKER & COMPANY ✓

Books for Young Readers, 104 Fifth Ave., New York NY 10011. (212)727-8300. Fax: (212)727-0984. Web site: www.walkeryoungreaders.com. **Manuscript Acquisitions:** Emily Easton, publisher; Mary Gruetzke, senior editor. Publishes 20 picture books/year; 5-10 nonfiction books/year; 5-10 middle readers/year; 5-10 young adult titles/year. 5% of books by first-time authors; 65% of books from agented writers.

- Walker title *Gone Wild: An Endangered Animal Alphabet*, by David McLimons, won a Caldecott Honor

Medal in 2007. Their title *Not Afraid of Dogs*, illustrated by Larry Day, written by Susanna Pitzer, won the Golden Kite Award for Picture Book Illustration in 2007.

Fiction Picture books: adventure, history, humor. Middle readers: adventure, contemporary, history, humor, multicultural. Young adults: adventure, contemporary, humor, historical fiction, suspense/mystery. Recently published *Earth Mother*, by Ellen Jackson, illustrated by Leo and Diane Dillon (ages 3-8, picture book); *Once Upon a Cool Motorcycle Dude*, written and illustrated by Kevin O'Malley (ages 6-10, picture book); *Revenge of the Cheerleaders*, by Janette Rallison (12 and up, teen/young adult novel). *Nailed* by Patrice Jones (ages 14 and up).

Nonfiction Picture book, middle readers: biography, history. Recently published *Blood Red Horse*, by K.M. Grant (ages 10-14); *Mutiny on the Bounty*, by Patrick O'Brien (ages 7-12, picture book history); *101 Things to Do Before You're Old and Boring* , by Richard Horne (ages 12 and up). Multicultural needs include ''contemporary, literary fiction and historical fiction written in an authentic voice. Also high interest nonfiction with trade appeal.''

How to Contact/Writers Fiction/nonfiction: Submit outline/synopsis and sample chapters; complete ms for picture books. Responds to queries/mss in 3-4 months. Send SASE for writer's guidelines.

Illustration Works with 20-25 illustrators/year. Editorial department reviews ms/illustration packages from artists. Query or submit ms with 4-8 samples. Illustrations only: Tearsheets. ''Please do not send original artwork.'' Responds to art samples only if interested.

Terms Pays authors royalty of 5-10%; pays illustrators royalty or flat fee. Offers advance payment against royalties. Original artwork returned at job's completion. Sends galleys to authors. Book catalog available for 9×12 SASE; ms guidelines for SASE.

Tips Writers: ''Make sure you study our catalog before submitting. We are a small house with a tightly focused list. Illustrators: Have a well-rounded portfolio with different styles.'' Does not want to see folktales, ABC books, paperback series, genre fiction. ''Walker and Company is committed to introducing talented new authors and illustrators to the children's book field.''

▢ WESTWINDS PRESS/ALASKA NORTHWEST BOOKS

Graphic Arts Center Publishing Company, P.O. Box 10306, Portland OR 97296-0306. (503)226-2402. Fax: (503)223-1410. E-mail: editorial@gacpc.com. Web site: www.gacpc.com. Independent book packager/producer. **Writers contact:** Tim Frew, executive editor. **Illustrators contact:** same. Produces 4 picture books/year, 1-2 young readers/year. 10% of books by first-time authors. ''Graphic Arts Center Publishing Company publishes and distributes regional titles through its three imprints: Graphic Arts Books, Alaska Northwest Books and WestWinds Press. GAB is known for its excellence in publishing high-end photo-essay books. Alaska Northwest, established in 1959, is the premier publisher of nonfiction Alaska books on subjects ranging from cooking, Alaska Native culture, memoir, history, natural history, reference, biography, humor and children's books. WestWinds Press, established in 1999, echoes those themes with content that focuses on the Western States.''

Fiction Picture books: animal, folktales, nature/environment. Young readers: adventure, animal, folktales, nature/environment. Average word length: picture books—1,100; young readers—9,000. Recently published *Kumak's Fish*, by Michael Bania (folktale, ages 6 and up); *Sweet Dreams, Polar Bear*, by Mindy Dwyer (3 and up); *Seldovia Sam and the Sea Otter Rescue*, by Susan Springer, illustrated by Amy Meissner (adventure, beginning chapter book).

Nonfiction Picture books: animal, nature/environment. Young readers: animal, nature/environment. Middle readers: nature/environment. Average word length: picture books—1,100; young readers—9,000. Recently published *Sharkabet*, by Ray Troll (ages 5 and up); *Winter Is*, by Anne Dixon, illustrated by Mindy Dwyer (environment/nature, ages 3-6).

How to Contact/Writers Accepts international submissions. Fiction/nonfiction: Submit complete ms. Responds to queries in 3 months; mss in 6 months. Publishes book 1-2 years after acceptance. Considers simultaneous submissions, electronic submissions, previously published work. ''Please include SASE for response and return of materials.''

Illustration Accepts material from international illustrators. Works with 4 illustrators/year. Uses both color and b&w. Reviews ms/illustration packages. For ms/illustration packages: Send ms with dummy. Submit ms/illustration packages to Tricia Brown, acquisitions editor. Reviews work for future assignments. If interested in illustrating future titles, query with samples. Samples returned with SASE. Samples not filed.

Photography Works on assignment only. Submit photos to Tim Frew, executive editor. Photo captions required. For first contact, send cover letter, portfolio, complete proposal, return postage.

Terms Offers advance against royalties. Originals returned to artist at job's completion. All imprints included in single catalog.

ALBERT WHITMAN & COMPANY

6340 Oakton St, Morton Grove, IL 60053-2723. (847)581-0033. Fax: (847)581-0039. Web site: www.albertwhitman.com. **Manuscript Acquisitions:** Kathleen Tucker, editor-in-chief. Art Acquisitions: Carol Gildar. Publishes 30 books/year. 20% of books by first-time authors; 15% off books from agented authors.

Fiction Picture books, young readers, middle readers: adventure, concept (to help children deal with problems), fantasy, history, humor, multicultural, suspense. Middle readers: problem novels, suspense/mystery. "We are interested in contemporary multicultural stories-stories with holiday themes and exciting distinctive novels. We publish a wide variety of topics and are interested in stories that help children deal with their problems and concerns. Does not want to see, "religion-oriented, ABCs, pop-up, romance, counting." Recently published fiction: *Teeny Weeny Bop*, by Margaret Read MacDonald, illustrated by Diane Greenseid; *My Mom's Having a Baby!*, by Dori Hillestad Butler, illustrated by Carol Thompson; *The Bully-Blockers Club*, by Teresa Bateman, illustrated by Jackie Urbanovic; *Tank Talbot's Guide to Girls*, by Dori Hillestad Butler.

Nonfiction Picture books, young readers, middle readers: animal, arts/crafts, health, history, hobbies, multicultural, music/dance, nature/environment, science, sports, special needs. Does not want to see, "religion, any books that have to be written in, or fictionalized biographies." Recently published *Shelter Dogs*, by Peg Kehret; *An Apple for Harriet Tubman*, by Glennette Tilly Turner; *The Groundhog Day Book of Facts and Fun*, by Wendie Old, illustrated by Paige Billin-Frye.

How to Contact/Writers Fiction/nonfiction: Submit query, outline, and sample chapter. For picture books send entire ms. Include cover letter. Responds to submissions in 4 months. Publishes a book 18 months after acceptance. Will consider simultaneous submissions "if notified."

Illustration "We are not accepting Illustration samples at this time. Submissions will not be returned."

Photography Publishes books illustrated with photos, but not stock photos-desires photos all taken for project. "Our books are for children and cover many topics; photos must be taken to match text. Books often show a child in a particular situation (e.g., kids being home-schooled, a sister whose brother is born prematurely)." Photographers should query with samples; send unsolicited photos by mail.

Terms Pays author's, illustrator's, and photographer's royalties. Book catalog for 8×10 SAE and 3 first-class stamps.

Tips "In both picture books and nonfiction, we are seeking stories showing life in other cultures and the variety of multicultural life in the U.S. We also want fiction and nonfiction about mentally or physically challenged children-some recent topics have been autism, stuttering, and diabetes. Look up some of our books first to be sure your submission is appropriate for Albert Whitman & Co."

JOHN WILEY & SONS, INC.

111 River St., Hoboken NJ 07030. (201)748-6000. Web sites:www.wiley.com,www.josseybass.com. **Senior Editor:** Kate Bradford. Publishes 18 middle readers/year; 2 young adult titles/year. 10% of books by first-time authors. Publishes educational nonfiction: primarily science and math and some history.

Nonfiction Middle readers: activity books, arts/crafts, biography, geography, health, history, hobbies, how-to, nature/environment, reference, science, self help. Young adults: activity books, arts/crafts, health, hobbies, how-to, nature/environment, reference, science, self help. Average word length: middle readers—20,000-40,000. Recently published The Extreme Animal Series: *Animal Planet Extreme Animals*, by Sherry Gerstein; *Animal Planet Extreme Bugs*, by Catherine Nichols; and *Animal Planet Extreme Predators*, by Mary Packard (ages 8-12, science/nature-based on the popular Animal Planet show *The Most Extreme Animals*); *Speed Math for Kids: The Fast, Fun Way to Do Basic Calculations*, by Bill Handley (ages 8-14, math); and *Janice VanCleave's Super Science Challenges: Hands-On Science Inquiry Projects for School, Science Fair, or Just Plain Fun* (ages 8-12, science/activity).

How to Contact/Writers Query. Submit outline/synopsis, 2 sample chapters and an author bio. Responds to queries in 6-8 weeks; mss in 3 months. Publishes a book 1 year after acceptance. Will consider simultaneous and previously published submissions.

Illustration Works with 6 illustrators/year. Uses primarily b&w artwork. Reviews ms/illustration packages from artists. Query. Illustrations only: Query with samples, résumé, client list. Responds only if interested. Samples filed. Original artwork returned at job's completion. No portfolio reviews.

Photography Buys photos from freelancers.

Terms Pays authors royalty of 10-12% based on wholesale price, or by outright purchase. Offers advances. Pays illustrators by the project. Photographers' pay negotiable. Sends galleys to authors. Book catalog available for SASE.

Tips "We're looking for topics and writers that can really engage kids' interest, plus we're always interested in a new twist on time-tested subjects." Nonfiction submissions only; no picture books.

WILLIAMSON PUBLISHING CO.

An imprint of Ideals Publications, 535 Metroplex Drive, Suite 250, Nashville TN 37211. Web site: www.idealspublications.com. **Manuscript and Art Acquisitions:** Williamson Books Submission. Publishes 6-10 titles/year.

50% of books by first-time authors; 10% of books from agented authors. Publishes "very successful nonfiction series (Kids Can!® Series) on subjects such as history, science, arts/crafts, geography, diversity, multiculturalism. Successfully launched *Little Hands*® series for ages 2-6, *Kaleidoscope Kids*® series (age 7 and up) and *Quick Starts for Kids!* ® series (ages 8 and up). "Our goal is to help every child fulfill his/her potential and experience personal growth."

Nonfiction Hands-on active learning books, animals, African-American, arts/crafts, Asian, biography, diversity, careers, geography, health, history, hobbies, how-to, math, multicultural, music/dance, nature/environment, Native American, science, writing and journaling. Does not want to see textbooks, picture books, fiction. "Looking for all things African American, Asian American, Hispanic, Latino, and Native American including crafts and traditions, as well as their history, biographies, and personal retrospectives of growing up in U.S. for grades pre-K-8th. We are looking for books in which learning and doing are inseparable." Recently published *Lighthouses of North America!*, by Lisa Trumbauer, illustrated by Michael Kline (ages 8-14); *Little Hands: Creating Clever Castles and Cars*, by Mari Rutz Mitchell, illustrated by Michael Kline (ages 3 to 8); *Becoming the Best You Can Be!*, by Jill Frankel Hauser, illustrated by Michael Kline (ages 9-14).

How to Contact/Writers Query with annotated TOC/synopsis and 1 sample chapter. Responds to queries/mss in 4 months. Publishes book "about 1 year" after acceptance. Writers may send a SASE for guidelines or e-mail.

Illustration Works with at least 6 illustrators and 6 designers/year. "We're interested in expanding our illustrator and design freelancers." Uses primarily b&w artwork and 2-color and 4-color. Responds only if interested. Samples returned with SASE; samples filed.

Photography Buys photos from freelancers; uses archival art and photos.

Terms Pays authors advance against future royalties based on wholesale price or purchases outright. Pays illustrators by the project. Pays photographers per photo. Sends galleys to authors. Book catalog available for $1 and 6 first-class stamps; ms guidelines available for SASE or download from Web site:www.williamsonbooks.com.

Tips "Please do not send any fiction or picture books of any kind—those should go to Ideals Children's Books. Look at our books to see what we do. We're interested in interactive learning books with a creative approach packed with interesting information, written for young readers ages 3-7 and 8-14. In nonfiction children's publishing, we are looking for authors with a depth of knowledge shared with children through a warm, embracing style. Our publishing philosophy is based on the idea that all children can succeed and have positive learning experiences. Children's lasting learning experiences involve their participation."

WINDWARD PUBLISHING

An imprint of the Finney Company, 8075 215th Street West, Lakeville MN 55044. (952)469-6699. Fax: (952)469-1968. E-mail: feedback@finney-hobar.com. Web site: www.finneyco.com. **Manuscript/Art Acquisitions:** Alan E. Krysan. Publishes 2 picture books/year; 4-6 young readers, middle readers, young adult titles/year. 50% of books by first-time authors.

Fiction Young readers, middle readers, young adults: adventure, animal, nature/environment. Recently published *Nightlight*, by Jeannine Anderson (ages 4-8, picture book); *Daddy Played Music for the Cows*, by Maryann Weidt (ages 4-8, picture book); *Wild Beach*, by Marion Coste (ages 4-8, picture book).

Nonfiction Young readers, middle readers, young adults: activity books, animal, careers, nature/environment, science. Young adults: textbooks. Recently published *My Little Book of Collection*, by Hope Irvin Marston (ages 4-8, introductions to the wonders of nature); *Space Station Science*, by Marianne Dyson (ages 8-13, science).

How to Contact/Writers Fiction: Query. Nonfiction: Submit outline/synopsis and 3 sample chapters. Responds to queries in 1 month; mss in 2 months. Publishes book 6-12 months after acceptance. Will consider simultaneous submissions and previously published work.

Illustration Reviews ms/illustration packages from artists. Send ms with dummy. Query with samples. Responds in 2 months. Samples returned with SASE; samples filed.

Photography Buys stock and assigns work. Photography needs depend on project—mostly ocean and beach subject matter. Uses color, 4×6, glossy prints. Submit cover letter, résumé, stock photo list.

Terms Author's payment negotiable by project. Offers advances (average amount: $500). Illustrators and photographers payment negotiable by project. Sends galleys to authors; dummies to illustrators. Originals returned to artist at job's completion. Book catalog available for 6×9 SAE and 3 first-class stamps; ms guidelines available for SASE. Catalog mostly available on Web site.

PAULA WISEMAN BOOKS

Imprint of Simon & Schuster, 1230 Sixth Ave., New York NY 10020. (212)698-7272. Fax: (212)698-2796. Web site: www.simonsays.com. Publishes 1 picture books/year; 2 middle readers/year; 2 young adult titles/year. 10% of books by first-time authors.

Fiction Considers all categories. Average word length: picture books—500; others standard length. Recently published *Double Pink*, by Kate Feiffer, illustrated by Bruce Ingman.

Nonfiction Picture books: animal, biography, concept, history, nature/environment. Young readers: animal, biography, history, multicultural, nature/environment, sports. Average word length: picture books—500; others standard length.

How to Contact/Writers Submit complete ms.

Illustration Works with 15 illustrators/year. Uses color artwork only. Will review ms/illustration packages from artists. Prefers mail for initial contact. Send manuscript with dummy.

WM KIDS

Imprint of White Mane Publishing Co., Inc., P.O. Box 708, 73 W. Burd St., Shippensburg PA 17257. (717)532-2237. Fax: (717)532-6110. E-mail: marketing@whitemane.com. Web site: www.whitemane.com. **Acquisitions:** Harold Collier, acquisitions editor. Imprints: White Mane Books, Burd Street Press, White Mane Kids, Ragged Edge Press. Publishes 7 middle readers/year. 50% of books are by first-time authors.

Fiction Middle readers, young adults: history (primarily American Civil War). Average word length: middle readers—30,000. Does not publish picture books. Recently published *Lottie's Courage*, by Phyllis Haislip (historical fiction, grades 5 and up); Young Heroes of History series, by Alan Kay (grades 5 and up).

Nonfiction Middle readers, young adults: history. Average word length: middle readers—30,000. Does not publish picture books. Recently published *Slaves Who Dared: The Story of Ten African American Heroes*, by Mary Garrison (young adult).

How to Contact/Writers Fiction: Query. Nonfiction: Submit outline/synopsis and 2-3 sample chapters. Responds to queries in 1 month; mss in 3 months. Publishes a book 12-18 months after acceptance. Will consider simultaneous submissions.

Illustration Works with 3 illustrators/year. Illustrations used for cover art only. Responds only if interested. Samples returned with SASE.

Photography Buys stock and assigns work. Submit cover letter and portfolio.

Terms Pays authors royalty of 7-10%. Pays illustrators and photographers by the project. Sends galleys for review. Originals returned to artist at job's completion. Book catalog and writer's guidelines available for SASE. All imprints included in a single catalog.

Ⓝ WORDSONG

815 Church St., Honesdale PA 18431. Web site: www.wordsongpoetry.com. Estab. 1990. An imprint of Boyds Mills Press, Inc. 5% of books from agented writers. "We publish fresh voices in contemporary poetry."

Fiction/Nonfiction All levels: All types of quality children's poetry.

How to Contact/Writers Fiction/ nonfiction: Submit complete ms or submit through agent. Label package "Manucript Submission" and include SASE. "Please send a book-length collection of your owm poems. Do not sent an initial query." Responds to in 3 months.

Illustration Works with 10 illustrators/year. Reviews ms/illustration packages from artists. Submit complete ms with 1 or 2 pieces of art. Illustrations only: Query with samples best suited to the art (postcard, 8½ × 11, etc.). Label package "Art Sample Submission." Responds only if interested. Samples returned with SASE. Samples filed. Originals returned at job's completion.

Photography Assigns work.

Terms Authors paid royalty or work purchased outright. Offers advances. Illustrators paid by the project or royalties; varies. Photographers paid by the project, per photo, or royalties; varies. Manuscripts/artist's guidelines available on Web site.

Tips "Collections of original poetry, not anthologies, are our biggest need at this time. Keep in mind that the strongest collections demonstrate a facility with multiple poetic forms. Check to see what's already on the market and on our Web site before submitting."

Canadian & International Book Publishers

hile the United States is considered the largest market in children's publishing, the children's publishing world is by no means strictly dominated by the U.S. After all, the most prestigious children's book extravaganza in the world occurs each year in Bologna, Italy, at the Bologna Children's Book Fair and some of the world's most beloved characters were born in the United Kingdom (i.e., Winnie-the-Pooh and Mr. Potter).

In this section you'll find book publishers from English-speaking countries around the world from Canada, Australia, New Zealand and the United Kingdom. The listings in this section look just like the U.S. Book Publishers section; and the publishers listed are dedicated to the same goal—publishing great books for children.

Like always, be sure to study each listing and research each publisher carefully before submitting material. Determine whether a publisher is open to U.S. or international submissions, as many publishers accept submissions only from residents of their own country. Some publishers accept illustration samples from foreign artists, but do not accept manuscripts from foreign writers. Illustrators do have a slight edge in this category as many illustrators generate commissions from all around the globe. Visit publishers' Web sites to be certain they publish the sort of work you do. Visit online bookstores to see if publishers' books are available there. Write or e-mail to request catalogs and submission guidelines.

When mailing requests or submissions out of the United States, remember that U.S. postal stamps are useless on your SASE. Always include International Reply Coupons (IRCs) with your SAE. Each IRC is good for postage for one letter. So if you want the publisher to return your manuscript or send a catalog, be sure to enclose enough IRCs to pay the postage. For more help visit the United State Postal Service Web site at www.usps.com/global. Visit www.timeanddate.com/worldclock and American Computer Resources, Inc.'s International Calling Code Directory at www.the-acr.com/codes/cntrycd.htm before calling or faxing internationally to make sure you're calling at a reasonable time and using the correct numbers.

As in the rest of *Children's Writer's & Illustrator's Market*, the maple leaf 🍁 symbol identifies Canadian markets. Look for International 🌐 symbol throughout *Children's Writer's & Illustrator's Market* as well. Several of the Society of Children's Book Writers and Illustrator's (SCBWI) international conferences are listed in the Conferences & Workshops section along with other events in locations around the globe. Look for more information about SCBWI's international chapters on the organization's Web site, www.scbwi.org. You'll also find international listings in Magazines and Young Writer's & Illustrator's Markets. See Useful Online Resources on page 367 for sites that offer additional international information.

Information on Canadian and international book publishers listed in the previous edition but not included in this edition of *Children's Writer's & Illustrator's Market* may be found in the General Index.

ALLEN & UNWIN

406 Albert St., East Melbourne VIC 3002 Australia. E-mail: frontdesk@allenandunwin.com. Web site: www.allenandunwin.com. **Contact:** Children's Editor.

- Allen & Unwin was voted Publisher of the Year by Australian booksellers in 1992, 1996, 2001, 2002, 2003, 2004 and 2006. They do not accept unsolicited picture book manuscripts.

Fiction Junior novels: For beginner readers ages 5-8, word length: 5,000-10,000; for confident readers ages 7-10, word length: 10,000-20,000. "Looking for fresh original storylines, strong engaging characters, a flair for language and an authentic voice." Inbetween novels: for middle readers ages 11-14, word length: 35,000-55,000. "Looking for great storytelling, popular or literary. Highly entertaining narratives avoiding heavy teenage issues preferred." Young adult novels: for teenage readers ages 13-16, word length: 40,000-60,000; for mature teenagers and older readers, ages 15 + , word length: 40,000-100,000. "Need to be extremely well-written and engrossing. Looking for stories which are groundbreaking, challenging and experimental."

Nonfiction Considers nonfiction for children and teenagers "if it is imaginative, timely and authoritative."

How to Contact/Writers Fiction: Submit complete ms (5,000 words or more) and SASE "of suitable size." Nonfiction: Send proposal, detailed chapter outline and 3 sample chapters. "Receipt of manuscript is acknowledged immediately by card but may take up to three months for a response to you manuscript."

Tips "Do not send e-mail submissions."

ANNICK PRESS LTD.

15 Patricia Ave., Toronto ON M2M 1H9 Canada. (416)221-4802. Fax: (416)221-8400. E-mail: annickpress@annickpress.com. Web site: www.annickpress.com. **Creative Director:** Sheryl Shapiro. Publishes 8 picture books/year; 4 young readers/year; 4 middle readers/year; 9 young adult titles/year. 25% of books by first-time authors. "Annick Press maintains a commitment to high-quality books that entertain and challenge. Our publications share fantasy and stimulate judgment and abilities."

- Annick Press does not accept unsolicited manuscripts.

Fiction No unsolicited mss. Recently published *Torrie & the Firebird*, by K.V. Johanson (ages 9-11); *Strange Times at Western High*, by Emily Pohl-Weary (ages 12 and up); *The Couch Was a Castle*, by Ruth Ohi (picture book).

Nonfiction Recently published *Into the World of the Dead*, by Michael Boughn (ages 9-12); *Flat-Out Rock*, by Mike Tanner (ages 12 and up); *I Did It Because..: How a Poem Happens*, by Loris Lesynski, illustrated by Michaek Martchenko (ages 7 and up).

Illustration Works with 20 illustrators/year. Illustrations only: Query with samples. Contact: Creative Director. Responds in 6 months with SASE. Samples returned with SASE or kept on file.

Terms Pays authors royalty of 5-12% based on retail price. Offers advances (average amount: $3,000). Pays illustrators royalty of 5% minimum. Originals returned to artist at job's completion. Book catalog available on Web site.

BOARDWALK BOOKS

Imprint of The Dundurn Group, 3 Church St., Suite 500, Toronto ON M5E 1M2 Canada. (416)214-5544. Fax: (416)214-5556. E-mail: info@dundurn.com. Web site: www.dundurn.com. **Manuscript Acquisitions:** Barry Jowett. Boardwalk Books is the YA imprint of The Dundurn Group. Publishes 6 young adult titles/year. 25% of books by first-time authors. "We aim to publish sophisticated literary fiction for youths aged 12 to 16."

Fiction Young adults: contemporary, history, suspense/mystery. Average word length: young adults—40,000-45,000. Recently published *Sophie's Rebellion*, by Beverley Boissery (ages 12-16, fiction), *Deconstructing Dylan*, by Lesley Choyce (ages 12-16, fiction), *Viking Terror*, by Tom Henighan (ages 12-16, fiction).

How to Contact/Writers Accepts material from residents of Canada only. Fiction: Submit outline/synopsis and 3 sample chapters (or approximately 50 pages). Responds to queries/mss in 3 months. Publishes book 1 year after acceptance. Will consider simultaneous submissions.

Terms Offers advances. Sends galleys to authors. Book catalog available for 9×12 SAE with sufficient Canadian postage or international coupon. All imprints included in a single catalog. Writer's guidelines available on Web site.

Tips "Be sure your submission suits our list. We do not accept picture books."

N 🌐 BUSTER BOOKS

Imprint of Michael O'Mara Books, 9 Lion Yard, Tremadoc Rd., London SW4 7NQ United Kingdom. (44)(207)772-8643. Fax: (44)(207)819-5934 E-mail: enquiries@mombooks.com. Web site: www.mombooks.com/busterbooks. "We are dedicated to providing irresistible and fun books for children of all ages. We typically publish novelty books, sets of board books for preschoolers, and a variety of nonfiction for children ages 8-12."

Nonfiction Picture books, young readers, middle readers.

How to Contact/Writers Prefers synopsis and sample text over complete mss. Responds to queries/mss in 6 weeks. Will consider e-mail submissions.

Tips "We do not accept fiction submissions. Please do no send original artwork as we cannot guarantee its safety." Visit Web site before submitting.

🌐 CHILD'S PLAY (INTERNATIONAL) LTD.

Child's Play International, Ashworth Rd., Bridgemead, Swindon, Wiltshire SN5 7YD United Kingdom. (44)(179)361-6286. Fax: (44)(179)351-2795. E-mail: office@childs-play.co. Web site: www.childs-play.com. Estab. 1972. Specializes in nonfiction, fiction, educational material, multicultural material. **Manuscript Acquisitions:** Sue Baker, Neil Burden. **Art Acquisitions:** Annie Kubler, art director. Produces 30 picture books/year; 10 young readers/year; 2 middle readers/year. 20% of books by first-time authors. "A child's early years are more important than any other. This is when children learn most about the world around them and the language they need to survive and grow. Child's Play aims to create exactly the right material for this all-important time."

Fiction Picture books: adventure, animal, concept, contemporary, folktales, multicultural, nature/environment. Young readers: adventure, animal, anthology, concept, contemporary, folktales, humor, multicultural, nature/environment, poetry. Average word length: picture books—0-1,500; young readers—2,000. Recently published *The Cockerel, the Mouse and the Little Red Hen*, by Jess Stockham (ages 3-6, fairy tale); *The Bear and Turtle and the Great Lake Race*, by A. Fusek-Peters, illustrated by Alison Edgson (ages 4-8, traditional tale); *Five Little Men in a Flying Saucer*, by Dan Crisp (ages 0-6, novelty board).

Nonfiction Picture books: activity books, animal, concept, multicultural, music/dance, nature/environment, science. Young readers: activity books, animal, concept, multicultural, music/dance, nature/environment, science. Average word length: picture books—2,000; young readers—3,000. Recently published lang2057*Little Drivers*, by Dan Crisp (ages 6 months+, novelty board); *My First Animal Signs*, by A. Kubler (ages 0-3, sign language for hearing babies); *Ocean Deep*, by R. Hatfield (ages 3-8, underwater tunnel book).

How to Contact/Writers Accepts international submissions. Fiction/nonfiction: Query or submit complete ms. Responds to queries in 10 weeks; mss in 15 weeks. Publishes book 2 years after acceptance. Considers simultaneous submissions, electronic submissions.

Illustration Accepts material from international illustrators. Works with 10 illustrators/year. Uses color artwork only. Reviews ms/illustration packages. For ms/illustration packages: Query or submit ms/illustration packages to Sue Baker, editor. Reviews work for future assignments. If interested in illustrating future titles, query with samples, CD, Web site address. Submit samples to Annie Kubler, art director. Responds in 10 weeks. Samples not returned. Samples filed.

Terms Work purchased outright from authors (range: $500-15,000). Pays illustrators by the project (range: $500-15,000). Author sees galleys for review. Originals not returned. Catalog on Web site. Offers writer's, artist's guidelines for SASE.

Tips "Look at our Web site to see the kind of work we do before sending. Do not send cartoons. We do not publish novels. We do publish lots of books with pictures of babies/toddlers."

▣ COTEAU BOOKS LTD.

2517 Victoria Ave., Regina SK S4P 0T2 Canada. (306)777-0170. E-mail: coteau@coteaubooks.com. Web site: www.coteaubooks.com. **Acquisitions:** Barbara Sapergia, children's editor. Publishes 8-10 juvenile and/or young adult books/year; 18-20 books/year; 40% of books by first-time authors. "Coteau Books publishes the finest Canadian fiction, poetry, drama and children's literature, with an emphasis on western writers."

● Coteau Books publishes Canadian writers and illustrators only; mss from the U.S. are returned unopened.

Fiction Young readers, middle readers, young adults: adventure, contemporary, fantasy, history, humor, multicultural, nature/environment, science fiction, suspense/mystery. "No didactic, message pieces, nothing religious, no horror. No picture books. Recently published *New: Terror at Turtle Mountain*, by Penny Draper (ages 9 and up); *The Weathermage: Tales of Three Lands, Book III*, by Linda Smith (ages 10 and up); *Mud Girl*, by by Alison Acheson (ages 13 and up).

Nonfiction Young readers, middle readers, young adult/teen: biography, history, multicultural, nature/environment, social issues.

How to Contact/Writers Fiction: Submit complete ms or sample chapters to acquisitions editor. No e-mail submissions or queries. Include SASE. Responds to queries/mss in 4 months. Publishes a book 1-2 years after acceptance.

Illustration Works with 1-4 illustrators/year. Illustrations only: Submit nonreturnable samples. Responds only if interested. Samples returned with SASE; samples filed.

Photography ''Very occasionally buys photos from freelancers.'' Buys stock and assigns work.

Terms Pays authors royalty based on retail price. Pays illustrators and photographers by the project. Sends galleys to authors; dummies to illustrators. Original artwork returned at job's completion. Book catalog free on request with 9×12 SASE.

Tips ''Truthfully, the work speaks for itself! Be bold. Be creative. Be persistent! There is room, at least in the Canadian market, for quality novels for children, and at Coteau, this is a direction we will continue to take.''

🌐 Ⓐ EMMA TREEHOUSE

Treehouse Children's Books, Little Orchard House, Mill Lane, Beckington, Somerset BA11 6SN United Kingdom. (44)(137)383-1215. Fax: (44)(137)383-1216. E-mail: sales@emmatreehouse.com. Web site: www.emmatreehouse.com. Estab. 1992. Publishes mass market books, trade books. We are an independent book packager/producer. **Manuscript Acquisitions:** David Bailey, director. **Art Acqusitions:** Richard Powell, creative director. Imprints: Treehouse Children's Books. Produces 100 young readers/year.

Fiction Picture books: adventure, animal, concept, folktales, humor.

Nonfiction Picture books: activity books, animal, concept.

How to Contact/Writers Only interested in agented material. Accepts international submissions. Fiction: Submit outline/synopsis. Nonfiction: Submit complete ms. Responds to queries in 3 weeks. No simultaneous, electronic, or previously published submissions.

Illustration Only interested in agented illustration submissions. Accepts material from international illustrators. Works with 10 illustrators/year. Uses color artwork only. Reviews ms/illustration packages. For ms/illustration packages: Send ms with dummy. Submit ms/illustration packages to Richard Powell, creative director. Reviews work for future assignments. If interested in illustrating future titles, arrange personal portfolio review. Submit samples to Richard Powell, creative director. Responds in 3 weeks. Samples returned with SASE. Samples not filed.

Terms Work purchased outright. Pays illustrators by the project. Illustrators see dummies for review. Catalog available for SASE. All imprints included in single catalog.

🌐 FABER AND FABER

3 Queen Square, London WC1N 3AU United Kingdom. Web site: www.faber.co.uk. **Contact:** The Editorial Department.

Fiction Recently published *Heir of Mystery*, by Philip Ardagh (ages 8-11, fiction); *Virtutopia*, by Russell Stannard (ages 12 and up); *Rocket Science*, by Jeanne Willis (ages 8-11).

Nonfiction Recently published *The Spy's Handbook*, by Herbie Brennan; *The Hieroglyph's Handbook*, by Philip Ardagh.

How to Contact/Writers Submit synopsis and 20 pages of sample text with SASE. Responds in 8-10 weeks.

Tips ''Try to discern whether or not your work is suitable for our list by looking on our Web site or in bookshops at the types of books we publish. We do not, for example, publish in fields such as fantasy, science fiction, or photography, all of which we regularly receive.''

🌐 DAVID FICKLING BOOKS

31 Beaumont St., Oxford OX1 2NP United Kingdom. (018)65-339000. Fax: (018)65-339009. E-mail: tburgess@randomhouse.co.uk. Web site: www.davidficklingbooks.co.uk/. Publishes 12 fiction titles/year.

Fiction Considers all categories. Recently published *Lyra's Oxford*, by Phillip Pullman; *The Curious Incident of the Dog in the Night-time*, by Mark Haddon; *The Boy in the Striped Pyjamas*, by John Boyne.

How to Contact/Writers Submit 3 sample chapters. Responds to mss in 2-3 months.

Illustration Reviews ms/illustration packages from artists. Illustrations only: query with samples.

Photography Submit cover letter, résumé, promo pieces.

🔳 FITZHENRY & WHITESIDE LTD.

195 Allstate Pkwy., Markham ON L3R 4T8 Canada. (905)477-9700. Fax: (905)477-9179. E-mail: godwit@fitzhenry.ca. Web site: www.fitzhenry.ca. Book publisher. **President:** Sharon Fitzhenry; Children's Publisher: Gail Winskill; Nonfiction children's editor: Linda Biesenthal. Publishes 10 picture books/year; 5 early readers and early chapter books/year; 6 middle novels/year; 7 young adult titles/year. 10% of books by first-time authors. Publishes fiction and nonfiction—social studies, visual arts, biography, environment. Emphasis on Canadian authors and illustrators, subject or perspective.

How to Contact/Writers Fiction/nonfiction. Publishes a book 12-18 months after acceptance. No longer accepting unsolicited mss.

Illustration Works with 15 illustrators/year. Reviews ms/illustration packages from artists. Submit outline and sample illustration (copy). Illustrations only: Query with samples and promo sheet. Samples not returned unless requested.

Photography Buys photos from freelancers. Buys stock and assigns work. Captions required. Uses b&w 8×10 prints; 35mm and 4×5 transparencies. Submit stock photo list and promo piece.

Terms Pays authors royalty of 10%. Offers "respectable" advances for picture books, 5% to author, 5% to illustrator. Pays illustrators by the project and royalty. Pays photographers per photo. Sends galleys to authors; dummies to illustrators.

Tips "We respond to quality."

GROUNDWOOD BOOKS

110 Spadina., Suite 801, Toronto ON M5V 2K4 Canada. (416)363-4343. Fax: (416)363-1017. Web site: www.grou ndwoodbooks.com. **Manuscript Acquisitions:** Acquisitions Editor. **Art Acquisitions:** Art Director. Publishes 10 picture books/year; 3 young readers/year; 5 middle readers/year; 5 young adult titles/year, approximately 2 nonfiction titles/year. 10% of books by first-time authors.

Fiction Recently published *I am a Taxi*, by Deborah Ellis (ages 10-14); *Skinybones and the Wrinkle Queen*, by Glen Huser (young adult); *Ancient Thunder*, by Leo Yerxa (picture book); Groundwork Guided series: *Being Muslim* by Haroon Siddiqui, *Climate Change* by Skelley Tanaka, *Empire* by James Laxer and *Genocide* by Jane Springer.

How to Contact/Writers Fiction: Submit synopsis and sample chapters. Responds to mss in 6-8 months. Will consider simultaneous submissions.

Illustration Works with 20 illustrators/year. Reviews ms/illustration packages from artists. Illustrations only: Send résumé, promo sheet, slides, color or b&w copies, and tearsheets. Responds only if interested. Samples not returned.

Terms Offers advances. Pays illustrators by the project for cover art; otherwise royalty. Sends galleys to authors; dummies to illustrators. Originals returned to artist at job's completion. Backlist available on Web site.

Tips "Try to familiarize yourself with our list before submitting to judge whether or not your work is appropriate for Groundwood. Visit our Web site for guidelines."

HINKLER BOOKS

17-23 Redwood Dr., Dingley, Victoria Australia 3172. (61)(3)9552-1333. Fax: (61)(3)9552-2588. E-mail: tracey.A hern@hinkler.com.au. Web site: www.hinklerbooks.com. **Acquisitions:** Tracey Ahern, publisher. "Hinkler Books publishes quality books affordable to the average family."

HYPERION PRESS LIMITED

300 Wales Ave., Winnipeg MB R2M 2S9 Canada. (204)256-9204. Fax: (204)255-7845. **Acquisitions:** Dr. M. Tutiah, editor. Publishes authentic-based, retold folktales/legends for ages 4-9. "We are interested in a good story that is well researched and how-to craft material."

Fiction Recently published *Mo & Jo*, by Katherine Ink Setter; *The Little Match Girl*, written and digitally illustrated by Helena Maria Stankiewicz; *Cossack Tales*, illustrated by Stefan Czernecki.

Nonfiction Recently published *Making Drums*, by Dennis Waring.

How to Contact/Writers Fiction/nonfiction: Query. Responds usually within 3 months.

Illustration Reviews ms/illustration packages from artists. Manuscript/illustration packages and illustration only: Query. Samples returned with SASE.

Terms Pays authors royalty. Pays illustrators by the project. Sends galleys to authors; dummies to illustrators. Book catalog available for SAE and $2 postage (Canadian).

KEY PORTER BOOKS

6 Adelaide St. E, Toronto ON M5C 1H6 Canada. (416)862-7777. Fax: (416)862-2304. E-mail: info@keyporter.c om. Web site: www.keyporter.com. Book publisher. Key Porter Books is the largest independent, 100% Canadian-owned trade publisher.

Fiction Picture books, middle readers, young adult: adventure, anthology, sports. Recently published *Past Crimes*, by Carol Matas; *Carew*, by J. C. Mills; *Where Soldiers Lie*, by John Wilson; *Sundancer*, by Shelley Peterson; *Alligator Tales: Alligator Pie, The Dreadful Doings of Jelly Belly, Willoughby Wallaby Woo, Silverly/ Good Night, Good Night*, all by Dennis Lee, illustrated by Nora Hilb (board books).

Nonfiction Picture books: animal, arts/crafts, cooking, geography, nature/environment, reference, science. Middle readers: animal, nature/environment, reference, science. Recently published *Dancing Elephants & Floating Continents*, by John Wilson;, *Being a Girl*, by Kim Cattrall.

How to Contact/Writers Only interested in agented material; *no unsolicited mss*. "Although Key Porter Books does not review unsolicited manuscript submissions, we do try and review queries and proposals." Responds to queries/proposals in 6 months.

Photography Buys photos from freelancers. Buys stock and assigns work. Captions required. Uses 35mm transparencies. Submit cover letter, résumé, duplicate slides, stock photo list.

Tips "Please note that all proposals and accompanying materials will be discarded unless sufficient postage has been provided for their return. Please do not send any original artwork or other irreplaceable materials. We do not accept responsibility for any materials you submit."

KIDS CAN PRESS

29 Birch Ave., Toronto ON M4V 1E2 Canada. (800)265-0884. E-mail: info@kidscan.com. Web site: www.kidscanpress.com. **Manuscript Acquisitions:** Acquisitions Editor. **Art Acquisitions:** Art Director. Publishes 6-10 picture books/year; 10-15 young readers/year; 2-3 middle readers/year; 2-3 young adult titles/year. 10-15% of books by first-time authors.

• Kids Can Press is currently accepting unsolicited manuscripts from Canadian authors only.

Fiction Picture books, young readers: concept. All levels: adventure, animal, contemporary, fantasy, folktales, history, humor, multicultural, nature/environment, poetry, special needs, sports, suspense/mystery. Average word length: picture books—1,000-2,000; young readers—750-1,500; middle readers—10,000-15,000; young adults—over 15,000. Recently published *Suki's Kimono*, by Chieri Ugaki, illustrated by Stephane Jorisch (picture book); *The Mob*, by Clem Martini (novel); *Stanley's Party*, by Linda Bailey, illustrated by Bill Slavin (picture book).

Nonfiction Picture books: activity books, animal, arts/crafts, biography, careers, concept, health, history, hobbies, how-to, multicultural, nature/environment, science, social issues, special needs, sports. Young readers: activity books, animal, arts/crafts, biography, careers, concept, history, hobbies, how-to, multicultural. Middle readers: cooking, music/dance. Average word length: picture books—500-1,250; young readers—750-2,000; middle readers—5,000-15,000. Recently published *The Kids Book of the Night Sky*, by Jane Drake and Ann Love, illustrated by Heather Collins (informational activity); *Animals at Work*, by Etta Kaner, illustrated by Pat Stephens (animal/nature); *Quilting*, by Biz Storms, illustrated by June Bradford (craft book).

How to Contact/Writers Fiction/nonfiction: Submit outline/synopsis and 2-3 sample chapters. For picture books submit complete ms. Responds in 6 months. Publishes a book 18-24 months after acceptance.

Illustration Works with 40 illustrators/year. Reviews ms/illustration packages from artists. Send color copies of illustration portfolio, cover letter outlining other experience. Contact: Art Director. Illustrations only: Send tearsheets, color photocopies. Contact: Art Director, Kids Can Press, 2250 Military Rd., Tonawanda NY 14150. Responds only if interested. Samples returned with SASE; samples filed.

KOALA BOOKS

P.O. Box 626, Mascot NSW 1460 Australia. (61)02 9667-2997. Fax: (61)02 9667-2881. E-mail: admin@koalabooks.com.au. Web site: www.koalabooks.com.au. **Manuscript Acquisitions:** Children's Editor. Art Acquisitions: Children's Designer, deb@koalabooks.com.au. "Koala Books is an independent wholly Australian-owned children's book publishing house. Our strength is providing quality books for children at competitive prices."

How to Contact/Writers Accepts material from residents of Australia only. Hard copy only. Picture books only: Submit complete ms, blurb, synopsis, brief author biography, list of author's published works. Also SASE large enough for ms return. Responds to mss in 3 months.

Illustration Accepts material from residents of Australia only. Illustrations only: Send cover letter, brief bio, list of published works and samples (color photographs or photocopies) in "an A4 folder suitable for filing." Contact: Children's Designer. Responds only if interested. Samples not returned; samples filed.

Terms Pays authors royalty of 10% based on retail price or work purchased outright occasionally (may be split with illustrator).

Tips "Take a look at our Web site to get an idea of the kinds of books we publish. A few hours research in a quality children's bookshop would be helpful when choosing a publisher."

LITTLE TIGER PRESS

Imprint of Magi Publications, 1 The Coda Centre, 189 Munster Rd., London SW6 6AW United Kingdom. (44)20-7385 6333. Fax: (44)20 7385 7333. Web site: www.littletigerpress.com. "Our aim is to create books that our readers will love as much as we do-helping them develop a passion for books that offer laughter, comfort, learning or exhilarating flights of the imagination!"

Fiction Picture books: animal, concept, contemporary, humor. Average word length: picture books-1,000 words or less. Recently published *Cuddly Cuffs*, by Lucy Richards (ages 0-3, cloth, chewable, washable books); *Quiet!*, by Paul Bright and Guy Parker-Rees (ages 3-7, picture book).

Nonfiction Picture books. Average word length: picture books-1,000 words or less.

How to Contact/Writers Fiction/nonfiction: Submit complete ms. Responds to queries/mss in 2 months.

Illustration Illustrations only: Query with samples (include SASE with IRCs). Do not send originals. Color photocopies are best. Responds only if interested. Samples returned with SASE.

Tips "Every reasonable care is taken of the manuscripts and samples we receive, but we cannot accept responsibility for any loss or damage. Try to read or look at as many books a publisher has published before sending in your material."

☐ LOBSTER PRESS

1620 Sherbrooke St. W., Suites C&D, Montreal QC H3H 1C9 Canada. (514)904-1100. Fax: (514)904-1101. E-mail: editorial@lobsterpress.com. Web site: www.lobsterpress.com. **Assistant Editor:** Meghan Nolan. Publishes picture books, young readers and YA fiction and nonfiction. "Driven by a desire to produce quality books that bring families together."

• Lobster Press is currently accepting manuscripts and queries.

Fiction Picture books, young readers, middle readers, young adults: adventure, animal, contemporary, health, history, multicultural, nature/environment, special needs, sports, suspense/mystery, science fiction, historical fiction, teen issues. Average word length: picture books—200-1,000. Average word length: middle, YA readers—40,000-70,000. Recently published *Oliver Has Something to Say!* by Pamela Edwards, illustrated by Louis Pilon (picture book, 3+); *Zibby Payne & The Drama Trauma* by Alison Bell (ages 7+); *Dear Jo: The story of losing Leah. .and searching for hope* by Christina Kilbourne (novel, 10+).

Nonfiction Young readers, middle readers and adults/teens: animal, biography, Canadian history/culture, careers, geography, hobbies, how-to, multicultural, nature/environment, references, science, self-help, social issues, sports, travel. Recently published *Don't Squash That Bug! The Curious Kid's Guide to Insects* by Natalie Rompella (ages 3+); *Island of Hope and Sorrow: The Story of Grosse Ile* by Anne Renaud (ages 8+).

How to Contact/Writers "Please address all submissions to Editorial, Lobster Press and specify the genre of your work on the envelope; e-mailed or faxed submissions will not be considered. No editorial comment will be forthcoming unless Lobster Press feels that a manuscript is publishable."

Illustration Works with 5 illustrators/year. Uses line drawings as well as digital and color artwork. Reviews ms/illustration packages from artists. Query with samples. Illustrations only: query with samples. Samples not returned; samples kept on file.

Terms Pays authors 5-10% royalty based on retail price. Original artwork returned to artist at job's completion. Writer's and artist's guidelines available on Web site.

⊕ MANTRA LINGUA

Global House, 303 Ballards Lane, London N12 8NP United Kingdom. (44)(208)445-5123. Web site: www.mantralingua.com. **Manuscript Acquisitions:** Series Editor. Mantra Lingua "connects and transcends national differences in a way that is respectful and appreciative of local cultures."

• Mantra Lingua publishes books in English and more than 42 languages, including sign language. They are currently seeking fables, contemporary stories and folklore for picture books only.

Fiction Picture books, young readers, middle readers: folktales, multicultural, myths. Average word length: picture books—1,000-1,500; young readers—1,000-1,500. Recently published *Little Red Hen and the Grains of Wheat*, retold by Henriette Berkow, illustrated by Jago (ages 3-7); *Ali Baba and the Forty Thieves*, by Enebor Attard, illustrated by Richard Holland (ages 6-10).

How to Contact/Writers Accepts material from residents of United Kingdom only. Fiction: Myths only. Submit outline/synopsis (250 words, describe myth, "where it is from, whether it's famous or unknown, and why it would make a great picture book." Will consider e-mail and mail submissions. Include SASE if you'd like ms returned.

Illustration Uses 2D animations for CD-ROMs. Query with samples. Responds only if interested. Samples not returned; samples filed.

☒ ⊕ ☐ MILES KELLY PUBLISHING

The Bardfield Centre, Great Bardfield, Essex CM7 4SL United Kingdom. (44)(137)181-1309. Fax: (44)(173)181-1393. E-mail: info@mileskelly.net. Web site: www.mileskelly.net. **Art Acquisitions:** Jim Miles, director. Publishes 6 picture books/year; 30-40 young readers/year; 40-50 middle readers/year; 3-6 young adult titles/year. Produces "top-quality illustration and design complementing sound and well-written information."

How to Contact/Writers Responds to queries in 2 weeks.

Illustration Works with 100 illustrators/year. Illustrations only. Contact: Jim Miles, director. Responds in 3 weeks only if interested.

Terms Pays authors by the word only. Pays Illustrators 30 minimum. Catalog available online.

Tips "Check our Web site first. Be aware that most UK publishers need international sales to make books viable—so appeal to international tastes."

☐ MOOSE ENTERPRISE BOOK & THEATRE PLAY PUBLISHING

Imprint of Moose Hide Books, 684 Walls Rd., Sault Ste. Marie ON P6A 5K6 Canada. E-mail: mooseenterprises@on.aibn.com. Web site: www.moosehidebooks.com. **Manuscript Acquisitions:** Edmond Alcid. Publishes 2 middle readers/year; 2 young adult titles/year. 75% of books by first-time authors. Editorial philosophy: "To assist the new writers of moral standards."

- This publisher does not offer payment for stories published in its anthologies and/or book collections. Be sure to send a SASE for guidelines.

Fiction Middle readers, young adults: adventure, fantasy, humor, suspense/mystery, story poetry. Recently published *Realm of the Golden Feather*, by C.R. Ginter (ages 12 and up, fantasy); *Tell Me a Story*, short story collection by various authors (ages 9-11, humor/adventure); *Spirits of Lost Lake*, by James Walters (ages 12 and up, adventure); *Rusty Butt—Treasure of the Ocean Mist*, by R.E. Forester.

Nonfiction Middle readers, young adults: biography, history, multicultural.

How to Contact/Writers Fiction/nonfiction: Query. Responds to queries in 1 month; mss in 3 months. Publishes book 1 year after acceptance. Will consider simultaneous submissions.

Illustration Uses primarily b&w artwork for interiors, cover artwork in color. Illustrations only: Query with samples. Responds in 1 month, if interested. Samples returned with SASE; samples filed.

Terms Originals returned to artist at job's completion. Manuscript and art guidelines available for SASE.

Tips "Do not copy trends, be yourself, give me something new, something different."

🌐 🖪 🕮 NEATE PUBLISHING LTD.

33 Downside Rd., Winchester SO22 5LT United Kingdom. (44)(196)284-1479. Fax: (44)(196)284-1743. E-mail: sales@neatepublising.co.uk. Web site: www.neatepublishing.co.uk. **Art Acquisitions:** Bobbie Neate. Publishes 5 young readers/year; 5 middle readers/year; 5 young adult titles/year. 50% of books by first-time authors. "Quality nonfiction and exciting educational materials always wanted."

Nonfiction Recently published Role Play Packs—Pet Shop and Café; *Colours Around Us*, by Carole Roberts and Ann Langran (ages 4-7, nonfiction); *Learning How to Learn*, by Bobby Neate (ages 6-16, skill sheets); *Letters, Words and Fun*, by Tracy Spice (ages 3-6, dictionary).

How to Contact/Writers Sumbit material through postal mail, no e-mail sumbissions. Responds to queries in 1 week; mss in 1 month. Publishes book 6 months after acceptance. Will only consider e-mail submissions after initial discussion; previously published work OK.

Terms Sends galleys to authors. Catalog available on Web site.

Tips "We want adventurous and original ideas. Make sure your write for the age groups intended."

🖪 ORCA BOOK PUBLISHERS

1016 Balmoral St., Victoria BC V8T 1A8 Canada. (250)380-1229. Fax: (250)380-1892. Web site: www.orcabook.com. **Acquisitions:** Maggie deVries, children's book editor (young readers); Andrew Woolridge, editor (Orca Soundings); Bob Tyrrell, editor (teen fiction); Sarah Harvey, editor (juvenile fiction); Melanie Jeffs, editor (Orca Currents). Publishes 7 picture books/year; 16 middle readers/year; 10 young adult titles/year. 25% of books by first-time authors.

- Orca only considers authors who are Canadian or who live in Canada.

Fiction Picture books: animals, contemporary, history, nature/environment. Middle readers: contemporary, history, fantasy, nature/environment, problem novels, graphic novels. Young adults: adventure, contemporary, hi-lo (Orca Soundings), history, multicultural, nature/environment, problem novels, suspense/mystery, graphic novels. Average word length: picture books—500-1,500; middle readers—20,000-35,000; young adult—25,000-45,000; Orca Soundings—13,000-15,000; Orca Currents—13,000-15,000. Published *Tall in the Saddle*, by Anne Carter, illustrated by David McPhail (ages 4-8, picture book); *Me and Mr. Mah*, by Andrea Spalding, illustrated by Janet Wilson (ages 5 and up, picture book); *Alone at Ninety Foot*, by Katherine Holubitsky (young adult).

How to Contact/Writers Fiction: Submit complete ms if picture book; submit outline/synopsis and 3 sample chapters. "All queries or unsolicited submissions should be accompanied by a SASE." Responds to queries in 2 months; mss in 3 months. Publishes a book 18-36 months after acceptance. Submission guidelines available online.

Illustration Works with 8-10 illustrators/year. Reviews ms/illustration packages from artists. Submit ms with 3-4 pieces of final art. "Reproductions only, no original art please." Illustrations only: Query with samples; provide résumé, slides. Responds in 2 months. Samples returned with SASE; samples filed.

Terms Pays authors royalty of 5% for picture books, 10% for novels, based on retail price. Offers advances (average amount: $2,000). Pays illustrators royalty of 5% minimum based on retail price and advance on royalty. Sends galleys to authors. Original artwork returned at job's completion if picture books. Book catalog available for SASE with $2 first-class postage. Manuscript guidelines available for SASE. Art guidelines not available.

Tips "We are not seeking seasonal stories, board books, or 'I Can Read' Books. Orca Sounding/Currents lines offer high interest teen novels aimed at reluctant readers. The story should reflect the universal struggles young people face, but need not be limited to 'gritty' urban tales. Can include adventure, mystery/suspense, fantasy, etc. There's a definite need for humorous stories that appeal to boys and girls. Protagonists are between 14 and 17 years old."

🌐 PICCADILLY PRESS

5 Castle Rd., London NW1 8PR United Kingdom. (44)(207)267-4492. Fax: (44)(207)267-4493. E-mail: books@piccadillypress.co.uk Web site: www.piccadillypress.co.uk.

Fiction Picture books: animal, contemporary, fantasy, nature/environment. Young adults: contemporary, humor, problem novels. Average word length: picture books-500-1,000; young adults-25,000-35,000. Recently published *Style Sisters*, by Liz Elwes (young adult); *Cinnamon Girl*, by Cathy Hopkins (young adult); *Hurray Up, Birthday*, by Paeony Lewis and Sarah Gill (picture book).

Nonfiction Young adults: self help (humorous). Average word length: young adults-25,000-35,000. Recently published *Body Blips, Wobbly Bits and Great Big Zits*, by Anita Naik; *Do the Right Thing*, by Jane Goldman.

How to Contact/Writers Fiction: Submit complete ms for picture books or submit outline/synopsis and 2 sample chapters for YA. Enclose a brief cover letter and SASE for reply. Nonfiction: Submit outline/synopsis and 2 sample chapters. Responds to mss in approximately 6 weeks.

Illustration Illustrations only: Query with samples (do not send originals).

Tips ''Keep a copy of your manuscript on file.''

🌐 PIPERS' ASH LTD.

Church Rd., Christian Malford, Chippenham Wiltshire SN15 4BW United Kingdom. (44) (124)972 -0563. Fax: (44) (870)056 -8916. E-mail: pipersash@supamasu.com. Web site: www.supamasu.com. **Manuscript Acquisitions:** Manuscript Evaluation Desk. Publishes 1 middle reader/year; 2 young adult titles/year. 90% of books by first-time authors. Editorial philosophy is ''to discover new authors with talent and potential.''

Fiction Young readers, middle readers: adventure. Young adults: problem novels. Average word length: young readers—10,000; middle readers—20,000; young adults—30,000. Visit Web site or send for catalog for published titles.

Nonfiction Young readers: history, multicultural, nature/environment. Middle readers: biography, history, multicultural, nature/environment, sports. Young adults: self help, social issues, special needs. Average word length: young readers—10,000; middle readers—20,000; young adults—30,000.

How to Contact/Writers Fiction/nonfiction: Query. Responds to queries in 1 week; mss in 3 months. Publishes book 2 months after acceptance. Will consider e-mail submissions, previously published work.

Terms Pays authors royalty of 10% based on wholesale price. Sends galleys to authors. Book catalog available for A5 SASE. Offers ms guidelines for SASE. ''Include adequate postage for return of manuscript plus publisher's guidelines.''

Tips ''Visit our Web site—note categories open to writers and word link to pages of submission guidelines.''

🌐 📖 PLAYNE BOOKS LIMITED

Park Court Barn, Trefin, Haverfordwest, Pembrokeshire SA62 5AU United Kingdom. (44)(134)883-7073. Fax: (44)(134)883-7063. E-mail: playne.books@virgin.net. Web site: www.playnebooks.com. **Manuscript Acquisitions:** Gill Davies. **Art Acquisitions:** David Playne, design and production. Publishes 2 picture books/year; 4 young readers/year.

Fiction Picture books: fantasy, early learning ''fun encapsulated in a story—and humorous.'' Young readers: early learning ''fun encapsulated in a story—and humorous.'' Recently published *A Bug is Very Little*; *One Happy Hippo*, by Gill Davies (ages 3-5, novelty/educational).

Nonfiction Picture books: activity books. Young readers: activity books, animal, nature/environment. Young adults: animal, history, theatre. Recently published *Create Your Own Stage Make-Up*, by Gill Davies (ages 13 and up, How-to achieve state make-up, step by step).

How to Contact/Writers Fiction/nonfiction: Query or submit outline/synopsis. Responds to queries in 2 weeks. Will consider e-mail submissions, simultaneous submissions.

Illustration Works with 2 illustrators/year. Reviews ms/illustration packages from artists. Query. Contact: Gill Davies, editor. Illustrations only: Query with photocopies. Responds in 2 weeks.

Photography Buys stock and assigns work. Contact: David Playne, art director. Photo captions required. Uses color, 35mm, 60×70 or 4×5 transparencies. Submit cover letter, stock photo list.

Terms Work purchased outright from authors. Pays illustrators and photographers by the project. Sends galleys to authors; dummies to illustrators. Book catalog available. All imprints included in a single catalog. Information available on Web site.

Tips ''Be adaptable, persevere—keep optimistic!''

🌐 MATHEW PRICE LTD.

The Old Glove Factory, Bristol Rd., Sherborne Dorset DT94EP United Kingdom. (44)(193)581-6010. Fax: (44)(193)581-6310. E-mail: mathewp@mathewprice.com. Web site: www.mathewprice.com. **Manuscript Acquisitions:** Mathew Price, chairman. Publishes 2 picture books/year; 2 young readers/year; 3 novelties/year; 1 gift book/year. Looking especially for stories for 2- to 4-year-olds. ''Mathew Price Ltd. works to bring to market talented authors and artists profitably by publishing books for children that lift the hearts of people young and old all over the world.''

Fiction/Nonfiction Will consider any category.

Illustration Accepts material from artists in other countries. Uses color artwork only. Reviews ms/illustration packages from artists. Send ms with dummy or submit ms with 2 pieces of final art. Nothing returned without prepaid envelope. Do not send orginals—please only send PDFs or JPEGs and only by e-mail.

Terms Originals returned to artist at job's completion. Book catalog available. All imprints included in a single catalog. Catalog available on Web site.

Tips ''Study the market, keep a copy of all your work, and include a SAE if you want materials returned.''

QED PUBLISHING

Quarto Publishing plc, 226 City Road, London EC1V 2TT United Kingdom. (44)(207)812-8631. Fax: (44)(207)253-4370. E-mail: zetad@quarto.com. Web site: www.qed-publishing.co.uk. Estab. 2003. Specializes in trade books, educational material, multicultural material. **Manuscripts Acquisitions:** Hannah Ray, senior editor. **Art Acquisitions:** Zeta Davies, creative director. Produces 8 picture books/year; 20 nonfiction readers/year. Strives for ''editorial excellence with ground-breaking design.''

Fiction Average word length: picture books—500; young readers—3,000; middle readers—3,500. Recently published *Said Mouse to Mole*, by Clare Bevan, illustrated by Sanja Rescek (ages 4 and up); *Lenny's Lost Spots*, by Celia Warren, illustrated by Genny Haines (ages 2 and up); *Pet the Cat*, by Wes Magee, illustrated by Pauline Siewert (ages 5 and up, poetry).

Nonfiction Picture books: animal, arts/crafts, biography, geography, reference, science. Young readers: activity books, animal, arts/crafts, biography, geography, reference, science. Middle readers: activity books, animal, arts/crafts, biography, geography, science. Average word length: picture books—500; young readers—3,000; middle readers—3,500. Recently published *You and Your Pet Kitten*, by Jean Coppendale (ages 7 and up, animal); *Travel Through India*, by Elaine Jackson (ages 7 and up, geography); *Cartooning*, by Deri Robins (ages 7 and up, art).

How to Contact/Writers Fiction/nonfiction: Query.

Illustration Accepts material from international illustrators. Works with 25 illustrators/year. For ms/illustration packages: Submit ms with 2 pieces of final art. Submit ms/illustration packages to Zeta Davies, creative director. Reviews work for future assignments. Submit samples to Hannah Ray, senior editor. Responds in 2 weeks. Samples filed.

Photography Buys stock images and assigns work. Submit photos to Zeta Davies, creative director. Uses step-by-step photos. For first contact, send CD of work or online URL.

Tips ''Be persistent.''

RAINCOAST BOOKS

9050 Shaughnessy St., Vancouver BC V6P 6E5 Canada. (604)323-7100. Fax: (604)323-2600. E-mail: info@raincoast.com. Web site: www.raincoast.com. **Manuscript Acquisitions:** Editorial Department. Imprints: Polestar. Publishes 4 picture books/year; 4 young adult titles/year.

• Raincoast Books does not accept unsolicited manuscripts or e-mail queries. They accept material from Canadian residents only.

Fiction Picture books, young readers, young adults: contemporary, history. Recently published *Gretzky's Game*, by Mike Leonetti; *The Freedom of Jenny*, by Julie Burtinshaw; *The Quirky Girls'Guide to Rest Stops and Road Trips*, by Karen Rivers.

Nonfiction Picture books, young readers: science, sports, natural history. Recently published *Wild Science*, by Victoria Miles; *Sensational Scientists*, by Barry Shell.

How to Contact/Writers Fiction/nonfiction: query letter with ''details about the work including word count, subject matter and your publication history for picture books and young readers.'' For young adult fiction submit query letter with list of publication credits plus 1-page outline of the plot. Responds to queries in 9 months is SASE with sufficient Canadian postage is included (universal postal coupons not accepted). Will consider simultaneous submissions (indicate in query letter).

Illustration Illustrations only: Query with samples; ''no more than 10, nonreturnable color photocopies. Do not send original artwork or slides. Submit new samples to us as they become available.'' Contact: Editorial Department. Responds only if interested. Samples not returned.

Terms Book catalog available online.

Tips ''For older (teen readers) we're looking for subject matter that pushes the boundaries a little. For children's illustrative work, we are interested in illustrators who can successfully convey an artistic, painterly, whimsical style. Please refer to our catalogue for examples.''

🌐 RANDOM HOUSE CHILDREN'S BOOKS

61-63 Uxbridge Rd., London W5 5SA England. (44)(208)579-2652. Fax: (44)(208)579-5476. E-mail: enquiries@r andomhouse.co.uk. Web site: www.kidsatrandomhouse.co.uk. Book publisher. **Manuscript Acquisitions:** Philippa Dickinson, managing director. Imprints: Doubleday, Corgi, Johnathan Cape, Hutchinson, Bodley Head, Red Fox, David Fickling Books. Publishes 120 picture books/year; 120 fiction titles/year.

Fiction Picture books: adventure, animal, anthology, contemporary, fantasy, folktales, humor, multicultural, nature/environment, poetry, suspense/mystery. Young readers: adventure, animal, anthology, contemporary, fantasy, folktales, humor, multicultural, nature/environment, poetry, sports, suspense/mystery. Middle readers: adventure, animal, anthology, contemporary, fantasy, folktales, humor, multicultural, nature/environment, problem novels, romance, sports, suspense/mystery. Young adults: adventure, contemporary, fantasy, humor, multicultural, nature/environment, problem novels, romance, science fiction, suspense/mystery. Average word length: picture books—800; young readers—1,500-6,000; middle readers—10,000-15,000; young adults—20,000-45,000.

How to Contact/Writers Only interested in agented material. No unsolicited mss or picture books.

Illustration Works with 50 illustrators/year. Reviews ms/illustration packages from artists. Query with samples. Contact: Margaret Hope. Samples are returned with SASE (IRC).

Photography Buys photos from freelancers. Contact: Alison Gadsby. Photo captions required. Uses color or b&w prints. Submit cover letter, published samples.

Terms Pays authors royalty. Offers advances. Pays illustrators by the project or royalty. Pays photographers by the project or per photo.

Tips "Although Random House is a big publisher, each imprint only publishes a small number of books each year. Our lists for the next few years are already full. Any book we take on from a previously unpublished author has to be truly exceptional. Manuscripts should be sent to us via literary agents."

🍁 RED DEER PRESS

#1512, 1800 4th Street SW, Calgary AB T2S 2S5 Canada. (403)509-0802. Fax: (403)228-6503. E-mail: rdp@redde erpress.com. Web site: www.reddeerpress.com. **Manuscript/Art Acquisitions:** Peter Carver, children's editor. Publishes 3 picture books/year; 4 young adult titles/year. 20% of books by first-time authors. Red Deer Press is known for their "high-quality international children's program that tackles risky and/or serious issues for kids."

• Red Deer only publishes books written and illustrated by Canadians and books that are about or of interest to Canadians.

Fiction Picture books, young readers: adventure, contemporary, fantasy, folktales, history, humor, multicultural, nature/environment, poetry. Middle readers, young adult/teens: adventure, contemporary, fantasy, folktales, hi-lo, history, humor, multicultural, nature/environment, problem novels, suspense/mystery. Recently published *Courage to Fly*, by Troon Harrison, illustrated by Zhong-Yang Huung (ages 4-7, picture book); *Amber Waiting*, by Nan Gregory, illustrated by Macdonald Denton (ages 4-7, picture book); *Tom Finder*, by Martine Leavitt (ages 14 and up).

How to Contact/Writers Fiction/nonfiction: Query or submit outline/synopsis. Responds to queries in 6 months; mss in 8 months. Publishes a book 18 months after acceptance. Will consider simultaneous submissions.

Illustration Works with 4-6 illustrators/year. Illustrations only: Query with samples. Responds only if interested. Samples not returned; samples filed for six months. Canadian illustrators only.

Photography Buys stock and assigns work. Model/property releases required. Submit cover letter, résumé and color promo piece.

Terms Pays authors royalty (negotiated). Occasionally offers advances (negotiated). Pays illustrators and photographers by the project or royalty (depends on the project). Sends galleys to authors. Originals returned to artist at job's completion. Guidelines not available on Web site.

Tips "Writers, illustrators, and photographers should familiarize themselves with Red Deer Press's children's publishing program, including the kinds of books we do and do not publish."

🍁 RONSDALE PRESS

3350 W. 21st Ave., Vancouver BC V6S 1G7 Canada. (604)738-4688. Fax: (604)731-4548. E-mail: ronsdale@shaw .ca. Web site: ronsdalepress.com. Estab. 1988. Book publisher. **Manuscript/Art Acquisitions:** Veronica Hatch, children's editor. Publishes 2 children's books/year. 40% of titles by first-time authors. "Ronsdale Press is a Canadian literary publishing house that publishes 8-10 books each year, two of which are children's titles. Of particular interest are books involving children exploring and discovering new aspects of Canadian history."

Fiction Young adults: Canadian historical novels. Average word length: middle readers and young adults—50,000. Recently published *Red Goodwin*, by John Wilson (ages 10-14); *Shadows of Disaster*, by Cathy Beveridge (ages 10-14); *Dark Times*, edited by Ann Walsh (anthology of short stories, ages 10 and up); *Rosie's Dream Cape*, by Zelsa Freedman (ages 8-14); *Hurricanes over London*, by Charles Reid (ages 10-14).

Nonfiction Middle readers, young adults: animal, biography, history, multicultural, social issues. Average word length: young readers—90; middle readers—90.

How to Contact/Writers Accepts material from residents of Canada only. Fiction/nonfiction: Submit complete ms. Responds to queries in 2 weeks; mss in 2 months. Publishes a book 1 year after acceptance. Will consider simultaneous submissions.

Illustrations Works with 2 illustrators/year. Reviews ms/illustration packages from artists. Requires only cover art. Responds in 2 weeks. Samples returned with SASE. Originals returned to artist at job's completion.

Terms Pays authors royalty of 10% based on retail price. Pays illustrators by the project $800-1,200. Sends galleys to authors. Book catalog available for 8½ × 11 SAE and $1 postage; ms and art guidelines available for SASE.

Tips ''Ronsdale Press publishes well-written books that have a new slant on things and that can take an age-old story and give it a new spin. We are particularly interested in novels for young adults with a historical component that offers new insights into a part of Canada's history. We publish only Canadian authors.''

SCHOLASTIC AUSTRALIA

Scholastic Press and Scholastic Press, P.O. Box 579, Lindfield NSW 2070 Australia. Omnibus Books, 225 Unley Road, Malvern SA 5061 Australia. Web site: www.scholastic.com.au. ''Communicating with children around the world.''

• Scholastic Australia accepts material from residents of Australia only. Visit thier Web site for manuscript guidelines (www.scholastic.com.ay/common/about/manuscript.asp).

Fiction Picture books, young readers. Recently published *After Alice*, by Jane Carroll (ages 8-12, fiction); *Amelia Ellicott's Garden*, by Lilianna Stafford, illustrated by Stephen Michael King (ages 5-7, picture book); *An Ordinary Day*, by Libby Gleeson, illustrated by Armin Greder (ages 5-15, picture book).

Nonfiction Omnibus and Scholastic Press will consider nonfiction. Recently published *Bass and Flinders*, by Cathy Dodson, illustrated by Roland Harvey (ages 9-12, history); *The Cartoon Faces Book*, by Robert Ainsworth (ages 7-14, art & craft); *Excuse Me, Captain Cook, Who Did Discover Australia?*, by Michael Salmon (ages 7-12, history).

How to Contact/Writers Fiction/nonfiction: Submit complete ms. For picture books, submit only ms, no art. Responds to mss in 2 months.

Illustration Illustrations only: Send portfolio. Contact appropriate office for more information on what to include with portfolio.

Tips ''Scholastic Australia publishes books for children under three publishing imprints—Scholastic Press, Omnibus Books and Margaret Hamilton Books. To get a more specific idea of the flavor of each list, you will need to visit your local bookstore. Don't be too surprised or disappointed if your first attempts are not successful. Children's book publishing is a highly competitive field, and writing children's books is not quite as easy as some might imagine. But we are always ready to find the next Harry Potter or Paddington Bear, so if you believe you can write it, we're ready to hear from you.''

SCHOLASTIC CANADA LTD.

604 King St. West, ON M5V 1E1 Canada. (416)915-3500. Fax: (416)849-7912. Web site: www.scholastic.ca; for ms/artist guidelines: www.scholastic.ca/aboutscholastic/manuscripts.htm. **Acquisitions:** Editor, children's books. Publishes hardcover and trade paperback originals. Imprints: Scholastic Canada; North Winds Press; Les Editions Scholastic. Publishes 30 titles/year; imprint publishes 4 titles/year. 3% of books from first-time authors; 50% from unagented writers. Canadian authors, theme or setting required.

• At presstime Scholastic Canada was not accepting unsolicited manuscripts. For up-to-date information on their current submission policy, call their publishing status line at (905)887-7323, ext. 4308 or view their submission guidelines on their Web site.

Fiction Picture books, young readers, young adult. Average word length: picture books—under 1,000; young readers—7,000-10,000; young adult—25,000-40,000.

Nonfiction Animals, biography, history, hobbies, nature, recreation, science, sports. Reviews artwork/photos as part of ms package. Send photocopies.

How to Contact/Writers Query with synopsis, 3 sample chapters and SASE. Nonfiction: Query with outline, 1-2 sample chapters and SASE (IRC or Canadian stamps only). Responds in 3 months. Publishes book 1 year after acceptance.

Illustration Illustrations only: Query with samples; send résumé. Never send originals. Contact: Ms. Yuksel Hassan.

Terms Pays authors royalty of 5-10% based on retail price. Offers advances (range: $1,000-5,000, Canadian). Book catalog for 8½ × 11 SAE with $2.05 postage stamps (IRC or Canadian stamps only).

⊕ SCHOLASTIC CHILDREN'S BOOKS UK

Euston House, 24 Eversholt St., London NW1 1DB United Kingdom. Web site: www.scholastic.co.uk. **Submissions:** The Editorial Department.

• Scholastic UK accepts material from residents of United Kingdom only.

Fiction Recently published *A Darkling Plain*, by Philip Reeve; *Storm Thief*, by Chris Wooding; *Looking for JJ*, by Anne Cassidy; *Captain Underpants*.

Nonfiction Recently published *The Horrible Science of Everything*, by Nick Arnold and Tony de Saulles; *Horrible Histories: Horrible Geography, Foul Football*, and *My Story*, by Terry Deary.

Picture Book and Novelty Recently published *Chuckling Ducklings* and *My Little Star*.

How to Contact/Writers Fiction/nonfiction: Query or submit complete ms and SASE. Responds to queries/ mss in 6 months. Does not accept electronic submissions.

Tip "Do not be depressed if your work is not accepted. Getting work published can be a frustrating process, and it's often best to be prepared for disappointment."

⬛ SECOND STORY PRESS

20 Maud St., Suite 401, Toronto ON M5V 2M5 Canada. (416)537-7850. Fax: (416)537-0588. E-mail: info@second storypress.ca. Web site: www.secondstorypress.ca.

Fiction Considers nonsexist, nonracist, and nonviolent stories, as well as historical fiction, chapter books, picture books. Recently published *Mom and Mum Are Getting Married!*, by Ken Setterington.

Nonfiction Picture books: biography. Recently published *The Underground Reporters: A True Story*, by Kathy Kacer (a new addition to our Holocaust remembrance series for young readers).

How to Contact/Writers Accepts appropriate material from residents of Canada only. Fiction and nonfiction: Submit complete ms or submit outline and sample chapters by postal mail only. No electronic submissions or queries.

⬛ THISTLEDOWN PRESS LTD.

633 Main St., Saskatoon SK S7H 0J8 Canada. (306)244-1722. Fax: (306)244-1762. E-mail: tdpress@thistledown.s k.com. Web site: www.thistledown.com. **Acquisitions:** Allan Forrie, publisher. Publishes numerous middle reader and young adult titles/year. "Thistledown originates books by Canadian authors only, although we have co-published titles by authors outside Canada. We do not publish children's picture books."

• Thistledown publishes books by Canadian authors only.

Fiction Middle readers, young adults: adventure, anthology, contemporary, fantasy, humor, poetry, romance, science fiction, suspense/mystery, short stories. Average word length: young adults—40,000. Recently published *Up All Night*, edited by R.P. MacIntyre (young adult, anthology); *Offside*, by Cathy Beveridge (young adult, novel); *Cheeseburger Subversive*, by Richard Scarsbrook; *The Alchemist's Daughter*, by Eileen Kernaghan.

How to Contact/Writers Submit outline/synopsis and sample chapters. "We do not accept unsolicted full-length manuscripts. These will be returned." Responds to queries in 4 months. Publishes a book about 1 year after acceptance. No simultaneous submissions.

Illustration Prefers agented illustrators but "not mandatory." Works with few illustrators. Illustrations only: Query with samples, promo sheet, slides, tearsheets. Responds only if interested. Samples returned with SASE; samples filed.

Terms Pays authors royalty of 10-12% based on retail price. Pays illustrators and photographers by the project (range: $250-750). Sends galleys to authors. Original artwork returned at job's completion. Book catalog free on request. Manuscript guidelines for #10 envelope and IRC.

Tips "Send cover letter including publishing history and SASE."

ℕ ⬛ TRADEWIND BOOKS

202-1807 Maritime Mews, Vancouver BC V6H 3W7 Canada. (604)662-4405. Fax: (604)730-0454. E-mail: tradewi ndbooks@yahoo.com. Web site: www.tradewindbooks.com. **Manuscript Acquisitions:** Michael Katz, publisher. **Art Acquisitions:** Carol Frank, art director. Senior Editor: R. David Stephens. Publishes 2 picture books; 2 young adult titles/year; 1 book of poetry. 15% of books by first-time authors.

Fiction Picture books: adventure, multicultural, folktales. Average word length: 900 words. Recently published *The Clone Emerald Curse*, by Simon Rose; *Crocodiles Say*, by Robert Heidbreder; *If I had a Million Onions*, by Sheree Fitch.

How to Contact/Writers Picture books: Submit complete ms. YA novels by Canadian authors only. Will consider simultaneous submissions. Do not send query letter. Responds to mss in 6 weeks. Unsolicited submissions accepted only if authors have read a selection of books published by Tradewind Books. Submissions must include a reference to these books.

Illustration Works with 3-4 illustrators/year. Reviews ms/illustration packages from artists. Send ms with dummy. Illustrations only: Query with samples. Responds only if interested. Samples returned with SASE; samples filed.

Terms Royalties negotiable. Offers advances against royalties. Originals returned to artist at job's completion. Catalog available on Web site.

⊕ USBORNE PUBLISHING
83-85 Saffron Hill, London EC1N 8RT United Kingdom. Fax: (44)(20)743-1562. Web site: www.usborne.com. **Manuscript Acquisitions:** Fiction Editorial Director. **Art Acquisitions:** Usborne Art Department. "Usborne Publishing is a multiple-award winning, world-wide children's publishing company specializing in superbly researched and produced information books with a unique appeal to young readers."

Fiction Young readers, middle readers: adventure, contemporary, fantasy, history, humor, multicultural, nature/environment, science fiction, suspense/mystery. Average word length: young readers—3,500-8,000; middle readers—10,000-30,000. Recently publshed Oliver Moon series, by Sue Mongredien (ages 6 and up); Fame School series, by Cindy Jefferies (ages 8 and up).

How to Contact/Writers Refer to guidelines on Web site or request from above address. Fiction: Submit 3 sample chapters and a full synopsis with SASE. Does not accept submissions for nonfiction or picture books. Responds to queries in 1 month; mss in 4 months.

Illustration Works with 100 illustrators per year. Illustrations only: Query with samples. Samples not returned; samples filed.

Photography Contact: Usborne Art Department. Submit samples.

Terms Pays authors royalty.

Tips "Do not send any original work and, sorry, but we cannot guarantee a reply."

Magazines

Children's magazines are a great place for unpublished writers and illustrators to break into the market. Writers, illustrators and photographers alike may find it easier to get book assignments if they have tearsheets from magazines. Having magazine work under your belt shows you're professional and have experience working with editors and art directors and meeting deadlines.

But magazines aren't merely a breaking-in point. Writing, illustration and photo assignments for magazines let you see your work in print quickly, and the magazine market can offer steady work and regular paychecks (a number of them pay on acceptance). Book authors and illustrators may have to wait a year or two before receiving royalties from a project. The magazine market is also a good place to use research material that didn't make it into a book project you're working on. You may even work on a magazine idea that blossoms into a book project.

TARGETING YOUR SUBMISSIONS

It's important to know the topics typically covered by different children's magazines. To help you match your work with the right publications, we've included several indexes in the back of this book. The **Subject Index** lists both book and magazine publishers by the fiction and nonfiction subjects they're seeking.

If you're a writer, use the Subject Index in conjunction with the **Age-Level Index** to narrow your list of markets. Targeting the correct age group with your submission is an important consideration. Many rejection slips are sent because a writer has not targeted a manuscript to the correct age. Few magazines are aimed at children of all ages, so you must be certain your manuscript is written for the audience level of the particular magazine you're submitting to. Magazines for children (just as magazines for adults) may also target a specific gender.

If you're a poet, refer to the **Poetry Index** to find which magazines publish poems.

Each magazine has a different editorial philosophy. Language usage also varies between periodicals, as does the length of feature articles and the use of artwork and photographs. Reading magazines *before* submitting is the best way to determine if your material is appropriate. Also, because magazines targeted to specific age groups have a natural turnover in readership every few years, old topics (with a new slant) can be recycled.

If you're a photographer, the **Photography Index** lists children's magazines that use photos from freelancers. Using it in combination with the subject index can narrow your search. For instance, if you photograph sports, compare the Magazine list in the Photography Index with the list under Sports in the Subject Index. Highlight the markets that appear on both lists, then read those listings to decide which magazines might be best for your work.

Since many kids' magazines sell subscriptions through direct mail or schools, you may not be able to find a particular publication at bookstores or newsstands. Check your local library, or send for copies of the magazines you're interested in. Most magazines in this section have sample copies available and will send them for a SASE or small fee.

Also, many magazines have submission guidelines and theme lists available for a SASE. Check magazines' Web sites, too. Many offer excerpts of articles, submission guidelines, and theme lists and will give you a feel for the editorial focus of the publication.

Watch for the Canadian ✂ and International 🌐 symbols. These publications' needs and requirements may differ from their U.S. counterparts.

For some great advice on children's magazine writing, see the Insider Report with writer and e-zine editor **Jan Fields** on page 254.

Information on magazines listed in the previous edition but not included in this edition of *Children's Writer's & Illustrator's Market* may be found in the General Index.

ADVENTURES
WordAction Publishing Company, 6401 The Paseo, Kansas City MO 64131. (816)333-7000. Fax: (816)333-4439. E-mail: jjsmith@nazarene.org. **Articles Editor:** Julie J. Smith. Weekly magazine. "Adventures is a full-color story paper for first and second graders. It is designed to connect Sunday School learning with the daily living experiences of the early elementary child. The intent of Adventures is to provide a life-related paper that will promote Christian values, encouraging good choices and providing reinforcement for biblical concepts taught in Faith Connections curriculum published by WordAction Publishing." Entire publication aimed at juvenile market.
- Adventures is accepting new submissions.

ADVOCATE, PKA'S PUBLICATION
PKA Publication, 1881 Little Westkill Rd., Prattsville NY 12468. (518)299-3103. **Publisher:** Patricia Keller. Bimonthly tabloid. Estab. 1987. Circ. 12,000. "*Advocate* advocates good writers and quality writings. We publish art, fiction, photos and poetry. *Advocate*'s submitters are talented people of all ages who do not earn their livings as writers. We wish to promote the arts and to give those we publish the opportunity to be published."
- Gaited Horse Association newsletter is included in this publication. Horse-oriented stories, poetry, art and photos are currently needed.

Fiction Middle readers, young adults/teens: adventure, animal, contemporary, fantasy, folktales, health, humorous, nature/environment, problem-solving, romance, science fiction, sports, suspense/mystery. Looks for "well written, entertaining work, whether fiction or nonfiction." Buys approximately 42 mss/year. Prose pieces should not exceed 1,500 words. Byline given. Wants to see more humorous material, nature/environment and romantic comedy.

Nonfiction Middle readers, young adults/teens: animal, arts/crafts, biography, careers, concept, cooking, fashion, games/puzzles, geography, history, hobbies, how-to, humorous, interview/profile, nature/environment, problem-solving, science, social issues, sports, travel. Buys 10 mss/year. Prose pieces should not exceed 1,500 words. Byline given.

Poetry Reviews poetry any length.

How to Contact/Writers Fiction/nonfiction: send complete ms. Responds to queries in 6 weeks; mss in 2 months. Publishes ms 2-18 months after acceptance.

Illustration Uses b&w artwork only. Uses cartoons. Reviews ms/illustration packages from artists. Submit a photo print (b&w or color), an excellent copy of work (no larger than 8×10) or original. Illustrations only: "Send previous unpublished art with SASE, please." Responds in 2 months. Samples returned with SASE; samples not filed. Credit line given.

Photography Buys photos from freelancers. Model/property releases required. Uses color and b&w prints (no slides). Send unsolicited photos by mail with SASE. Responds in 2 months. Wants nature, artistic and humorous photos.

Terms Pays on publication with contributor's copies. Acquires first rights for mss, artwork and photographs. Pays in copies. Sample copies for $4. Writer's/illustrator/photo guidelines with sample copy.

Tips "Please, no simultaneous submissions, work that has appeared on the Internet, po rnography, overt religiosity, anti-environmentalism or gratuitous violence. Artists and photographers should keep in mind that we are a b&w paper. Please do not send postcards. Use envelope with SASE."

AIM MAGAZINE, America's Intercultural Magazine

P.O. Box 390, Milton WA 98354-0390. Web site: www.aimmagazine.org. **Contact:** Ruth Apilado, associate editor. Quarterly magazine. Circ. 8,000. "Readers are high school and college students, teachers, adults interested in helping to purge racism from the human blood stream by the way of the written word—that is our goal!" 15% of material aimed at juvenile audience.

Fiction Young adults/teens: adventure, folktales, humorous, history, multicultural, "stories with social significance." Wants stories that teach children that people are more alike than they are different. Does not want to see religious fiction. Buys 20 mss/year. Average word length: 1,000-4,000. Byline given.

Nonfiction Young adults/teens: biography, interview/profile, multicultural, "stuff with social significance." Does not want to see religious nonfiction. Buys 20 mss/year. Average word length: 500-2,000. Byline given.

How to Contact/Writers Fiction: Send complete ms. Nonfiction: Query with published clips. Responds to queries/mss in 1 month. Will consider simultaneous submissions.

Illustration Buys 6 illustrations/issue. Preferred theme: Overcoming social injustices through nonviolent means. Reviews ms/illustration packages from artists. Query first. Illustrations only: Query with tearsheets. Responds to art samples in 1 month. Samples filed. Original artwork returned at job's completion "if desired." Credit line given.

Photography Wants "photos of activists who are trying to contribute to social improvement."

Terms Pays on acceptance. Buys first North American serial rights. Pays $15-25 for stories/articles. Pays in contributor copies if copies are requested. Pays $25 for b&w cover illustration. Photographers paid by the project. Sample copies for $5.

Tips "Write about what you know."

AMERICAN CAREERS

Career Communications, Inc., 6701 W. 64th St., Overland Park KS 66202. (913)362-7788. Fax: (913)362-4864. Web site: www.carcom.com. **Articles Editor:** Mary Pitchford. **Art Director:** Jerry Kanabel. Published 1 time/year. Estab. 1990. Circ. 400,000. Publishes career and education information for students in grades 8-10.

Nonfiction Buys 10 mss/year. Average word length: 300-800. Byline given.

How to Contact/Writers Nonfiction: Query with résumé and published clips. Acknowledges queries within 30 days. Keeps queries on file up to 2 years. Accepts simultaneous submissions with notification.

Terms Pays on acceptance. Pays writers variable amount.

Tips Send a query in writing with résumé and clips.

AMERICAN CHEERLEADER

Lifestyle Ventures LLC, 250 W. 57th St., Suite 420, New York NY 10107. (212)265-8890. Fax: (212)265-8908. E-mail: editors@americancheerleader.com. Web site: www.americancheerleader.com. **Publisher:** Sheila Noone. **Editor:** Marisa Walker. Bimonthly magazine. Estab. 1995. Circ. 200,000. Special interest teen magazine for kids who cheer.

Nonfiction Young adults: biography, interview/profile (sports personalities), careers, fashion, beauty, health, how-to (cheering techniques, routines, pep songs, etc.), problem-solving, sports, cheerleading specific material. "We're looking for authors who know cheerleading." Buys 20 mss/year. Average word length: 750-2,000. Byline given.

How to Contact/Writers Query with published clips. Responds to queries/mss in 3 months. Publishes ms 3 months after acceptance. Will consider electronic submission via disk or e-mail.

Illustration Buys 2 illustrations/issue; 12-20 illustrations/year. Works on assignment only. Reviews ms/illustration packages from artists. Illustrations only: Query with samples; arrange portfolio review. Responds only if interested. Samples filed. Originals not returned at job's completion. Credit line given.

Photography Buys photos from freelancers. Looking for cheerleading at different sports games, events, etc. Uses 35mm, 2¼×2¼ transparencies and 5×7 prints. Query with samples; provide résumé, business card, tearsheets to be kept on file. "After sending query, we'll set up an interview." Responds only if interested.

Terms Pays on publication. Buys all rights for mss, artwork and photographs. Pays $100-500 for stories. Pays illustrators $50-200 for b&w inside, $100-300 for color inside. Pays photographers by the project $300-750; per photo (range: $25-100). Sample copies for $4.

Tips "Authors: We invite proposals from freelance writers who are involved in or have been involved in cheerleading—i.e. coaches, sponsors or cheerleaders. Our writing style is upbeat, and 'sporty' to catch and hold the attention of our teen readers. Articles should be broken down into lots of sidebars, bulleted lists, etc. Photographers and illustrators must have teen magazine experience or high profile experience."

AMERICAN GIRL

8400 Fairway Place, Middleton WI 53562-0984. (608)836-4848. Web site: www.americangirl.com. **Contact:** Editorial Dept. Assistant. Bimonthly magazine. Estab. 1992. Circ. 750,000. "For girls ages 8-12. We use fiction and nonfiction."

Fiction Middle readers: contemporary, multicultural, suspense/mystery, good fiction about anything. No romance, science fiction or fantasy. No preachy, moralistic tales or stories with animals as protagonists. Only girl characters—no boys. Buys approximately 2 mss/year. Average word length: 2,300. Byline given.

Nonfiction How-to, interview/profile, history. Any articles aimed at girls ages 8-12. Buys 3-10 mss/year. Average word length: 600. Byline sometimes given. No historical profiles about obvious female heroines—Annie Oakley, Amelia Earhart; no romance or dating.

How to Contact/Writers Fiction: Query with published clips. Nonfiction: Query. Responds to queries/mss in 3 months. Will consider simultaneous submissions.

Illustration Works on assignment only.

Terms Pays on acceptance. Buys first North American serial rights. Pays $500 minimum for stories; $300 minimum for articles. Sample copies for $4.50 and 9×12 SAE with $1.98 in postage (send to Magazine Department Assistant). Writer's guidelines free for SASE.

Tips ''Keep (stories and articles) simple but interesting. Kids are discriminating readers, too. They won't read a boring or pretentious story. We're looking for short (maximum 175 words) how-to stories and short profiles of girls for 'Girls Express' section, as well as word games, puzzles and mazes.''

APPLESEEDS, The Magazine for Young Readers

Cobblestone Publishing, A Division of Carus Publishing, 140 E. 83rd St., New York NY 10028. E-mail: (for writers queries): swbuc@aol.com. Web site: www.cobblestonepub.com. **Editor:** Susan Buckley. Magazine published monthly except June, July and August. *AppleSeeds* is a 36-page, multidisciplinary, nonfiction social studies magazine from Cobblestone Publishing for ages 8-10. Published 9 times/year.

• Above address is for *AppleSeeds* editorial submissions only. Cobblestone address is: 30 Grove St., Petersborough NH 03458. Requests for sample issues should be mailed to Cobblestone directly. *AppleSeeds* is aimed toward readers ages 8-10. See Web site for current theme list.

How to Contact/Writers Nonfiction: Query only. Send all queries to Susan Buckley. See Web site for submission guidelines and theme list. E-mail queries are preferred. See Web site for editorial guidelines.

Illustration Contact Ann Dillon. See Web site for illustration guidelines.

Tips ''Submit queries specifically focused on the theme of an upcoming issue. We generally work 6 months ahead on themes. We look for unusual perspectives, original ideas, and excellent scholarship. We accept **no unsolicited manuscripts**. Writers should check our Web site at cobblestonepub.com/pages/writersAPPguides/ html for current guidelines, topics, and query deadlines. We use very little fiction. Illustrators should not submit unsolicited art.''

⊕ AQUILA

New Leaf Publishing, P.O. Box 2518, Eastbourne BN22 8AP United Kingdom. (44)(132)343-1313. Fax: (44)(132)373-1136. E-mail: info@aquila.co.uk. Web site: www.aquila.co.uk. **Submissions Editor:** Jackie Berry and Karen Lutener. Monthly magazine. Estab. 1993. ''Aquila is an educational magazine for readers ages 8-13 including factual articles (no pop/celebrity material), arts/crafts and puzzles.'' Entire publication aimed at juvenile market.

Fiction Young Readers: animal, contemporary, fantasy, folktales, health, history, humorous, multicultural, nature/environment, problem solving, religious, science fiction, sports, suspense/mystery. Middle Readers: animal, contemporary, fantasy, folktales, health, history, humorous, multicultural, nature/environment, problem solving, religious, romance, science fiction, sports, suspense/mystery. Buys 6-8 mss/year. Byline given.

Nonfiction Considers Young Readers: animal, arts/crafts, concept, cooking, games/puzzles, health, history, how-to, interview/profile, math, nature/environment, science, sports. Middle Readers: animal, arts/crafts, concept, cooking, games/puzzles, health, history, interview/profile, math, nature/environment, science, sports. Buys 48 mss/year. Average word length: 350-750.

How To Contact/Writers Fiction: Query with published clips. Nonfiction: Query with published clips. Responds to queries in 6-8 weeks.Publishes ms 1 year after acceptance. Considers electronic submissions via disk or e-mail, previously published work.

Illustration Color artwork only.Works on assignment only. For first contact, query with samples. Submit samples to Jackie Berry, Editor. Responds only if interested. Samples not returned. Samples filed.

Terms Buys exclusive magazine rights. Buys exclusive magazine rights rights for artwork. Pays 150-200 for stories; 50-100 for articles. Additional payment for ms/illustration packages. Additional payment for ms/photo packages. Pays illustrators $130-150 for color cover. Sample copies free for SASE. Writer's guidelines free for SASE. Publishes work by children.

Tips ''We only accept a high level of educational material for children ages 8-13 with a good standard of literacy and ability.''

ASK, Arts and Sciences for Kids

Carus Publishing, 70 E. Lake Sreet, Suite 300, Chicago IL 60601. (312)701-1720. E-mail: ask@caruspub.com. Web site: www.cricketmag.com. **Editor:** Lonnie Plecha. **Art Director:** Karen Kohn. Magazine published 9 times/year. Estab. 2002. "ASK encourages children between the ages of 7 and 10 to inquire about the world around them."

Nonfiction Young readers, middle readers: animal, history, nature/environment, science. Average word length: 150-1,500. Byline given.

How to Contact/Writers *Ask* does not accept unsolicited mss or queries. All articles are commissioned. To be considered for assignments, experienced science writers may send a résumé and 3 published clips.

Illustration Buys 10 illustrations/issue; 60 illustrations/year. Works on assignment only. Illustrations only: Query with samples.

BABAGANEWZ

Jewish Family & Life, 11141 Georgia Ave. #406, Wheaton MD 20902. (301)962-9636. Fax: (301)962-9635. Web site: www.babaganewz.com. **Articles Editor:** Mark Levine. **Managing Editor:** Aviva Werner. Monthly magazine. Estab. 2001. Circ. 40,000. "*BabagaNewz* helps middle school students explore Jewish values that are at the core of Jewish beliefs and practices."

Fiction Middle readers: religious, Jewish themes. Buys 1 ms/year. Average word length: 1,000-1,500. Byline given.

Nonfiction Middle readers: arts/crafts, concept, games/puzzles, geography, history, humorous, interview/profile, nature/environment, religion, science, social issues. Most articles are written by assignment. Average word length: 350-1,000. Byline given.

How to Contact/Writers Queries only for fiction; queries preferred for nonfiction. No unsolicited manuscripts.

Illustration Uses color artwork only. Works on assignment only. Illustrations only: Send postcard sample with promo sheet, resume, URL. Responds only if interested. Credit line given.

Photography Photos by assignment.

Terms Pays on acceptance. Usually buys all rights for mss. Original artwork returned at job's completion only if requested. Sample copies free for SAE 9×12 and 4 first-class stamps.

Tips "Most work is done on assignment. We are looking for freelance writers with experience writing nonfiction for 9- to 13-year-olds, especially on Jewish-related themes. No unsolicited manuscripts."

BABYBUG

Carus Publishing Company, 70 E. Lake St., Suite 300, Chicago IL 60601. **Editor:** Alice Letvin. **Art Director:** Suzanne Beck. Published 10 times/year (monthly except for combined May/June and July/August issues). Estab. 1994. "A listening and looking magazine for infants and toddlers ages 6 to 24 months, *Babybug* is 6×7, 24 pages long, printed in large type on high-quality cardboard stock with rounded corners and no staples."

Fiction Looking for very simple and concrete stories, 4-6 short sentences maximum.

Nonfiction Must use very basic words and concepts, 10 words maximum.

Poetry Maximum length 8 lines. Looking for rhythmic, rhyming poems.

How to Contact/Writers "Please do not query first." Send complete ms with SASE. "Submissions without SASE will be discarded." Responds in 6 months.

Illustration Uses color artwork only. Works on assignment only. Reviews ms/illustration packages from artists. "The manuscripts will be evaluated for quality of concept and text before the art is considered." Contact: Suzanne Beck. Illustrations only: Send tearsheets or photo prints/photocopies with SASE. "Submissions without SASE will be discarded." Responds in 3 months. Samples filed.

Terms Pays on publication for mss; after delivery of completed assignment for illustrators. Rights purchased vary. Original artwork returned at job's completion. Rates vary ($25 minimum for mss; $250 minimum for art). Sample copy for $5. Guidelines free for SASE or available on Web site, FAQ atwww.cricketmag.com.

Tips "*Babybug* would like to reach as many children's authors and artists as possible for original contributions, but our standards are very high, and we will accept only top-quality material. Before attempting to write for *Babybug*, be sure to familiarize yourself with this age child."

BOYS' LIFE

Boy Scouts of America, 1325 W. Walnut Hill Lane, Irving TX 75015-2079. (972)580-2366. Fax: (972)580-2079. Web site: www.boyslife.org. **Managing Editor:** Michael Goldman. **Senior Writer:** Aaron Derr. **Fiction Editor:** Paula Murphey. **Director of Design:** Scott Feaster. Monthly magazine. Estab. 1911. Circ. 1,300,000. *Boys' Life* is "a 4-color general interest magazine for boys 8 to 18 who are members of the Cub Scouts, Boy Scouts or Venturers."

Fiction Young readers, middle readers, young adults: adventure, animal, contemporary, history, humor, multicultural, nature/environment, problem-solving, sports, science fiction, spy/mystery. Does not want to see "talking animals and adult reminiscence.'' Buys only 12-16 mss/year. Average word length: 1,000-1,500. Byline given.

Nonfiction Young readers, middle readers, young adult: animal, arts/crafts, biography, careers (middle readers and young adults only), cooking, health, history, hobbies, how-to, interview/profile, multicultural, nature/environment, problem-solving, science, sports. ''Subject matter is broad. We cover everything from professional sports to American history to how to pack a canoe. A look at a current list of the BSA's more than 100 merit badge pamphlets gives an idea of the wide range of subjects possible. Even better, look at a year's worth of recent issues. Column subjects are science, nature, earth, health, sports, space and aviation, cars, computers, entertainment, pets, history, music and others.'' Average word length: 500-1,500. Columns 300-750 words. Byline given.

How to Contact/Writers Fiction: Send complete ms with cover letter and SASE to fiction editor. Nonfiction: Major articles query senior editor. Columns query associate editor with SASE for response. Responds to queries/mss in 2 months.

Illustration Buys 10-12 illustrations/issue; 100-125 illustrations/year. Works on assignment only. Reviews ms/illustration packages from artists. ''Query first.'' Illustrations only: Send tearsheets. Responds to art samples only if interested. Samples returned with SASE. Original artwork returned at job's completion. Credit line given.

Terms Pays on acceptance. Buys first rights. Pays $750 and up for fiction; $400-1,500 for major articles; $150-400 for columns; $250-300 for how-to features. Pays illustrators $1,500-3,000 for color cover; $100-1,500 color inside. Pays photographers by the project. Sample copies for $3.60 plus 9×12 SASE. Writer's/illustrator's/photo guidelines available for SASE.

Tips ''We strongly urge you to study at least a year's issues to better understand the type of material published. Articles for *Boys' Life* must interest and entertain boys ages 8 to 18. Write for a boy you know who is 12. Our readers demand crisp, punchy writing in relatively short, straightforward sentences. The editors demand well-reported articles that demonstrate high standards of journalism. We follow *The New York Times* manual of style and usage. All submissions must be accompanied by SASE with adequate postage.''

BOYS' QUEST

P.O. Box 227, Bluffton OH 45817-0227. (419)358-4610. Fax: (419)358-5027. Web site: www.boysquest.com. **Articles Editor:** Marilyn Edwards. Bimonthly magazine. Estab. 1995. ''*Boys' Quest* is a magazine created for boys from 6 to 13 years, with youngsters 8, 9 and 10 the specific target age. Our point of view is that every young boy deserves the right to be a young boy for a number of years before he becomes a young adult. As a result, *Boys' Quest* looks for articles, fiction, nonfiction, and poetry that deal with timeless topics, such as pets, nature, hobbies, science, games, sports, careers, simple cooking, and anything else likely to interest a young boy.''

Fiction Picture-oriented material, young readers, middle readers: adventure, animal, history, humorous, multicultural, nature/environment, problem-solving, sports. Does not want to see violence, teenage themes. Buys 30 mss/year. Average word length: 200-500. Byline given.

Nonfiction Picture-oriented material, young readers, middle readers: animal, arts/crafts, cooking, games/puzzles, history, hobbies, how-to, humorous, math, problem-solving, sports. Prefer photo support with nonfiction. Buys 30 mss/year. Average word length: 200-500. Byline given.

Poetry Reviews poetry. Maximum length: 21 lines. Limit submissions to 6 poems.

How to Contact/Writers All writers should consult the theme list before sending in articles. To receive current theme list, send a SASE. Fiction/Nonfiction: Query or send complete ms (preferred). Send SASE with correct postage. No faxed or e-mailed material. Responds to queries in 2 weeks; mss in 2 weeks (if rejected); 5 weeks (if scheduled). Publishes ms 3 months-3 years after acceptance. Will consider simultaneous submissions and previously published work.

Illustration Buys 10 illustrations/issue; 60-70 illustrations/year. Uses b&w artwork only. Works on assignment only. Reviews ms/illustration packages from artists. Illustrations only: Query with samples, tearsheets. Responds in 1 month only if interested and a SASE. Samples returned with SASE; samples filed. Credit line given.

Photography Photos used for support of nonfiction. ''Excellent photographs included with a nonfiction story is considered very seriously.'' Model/property releases required. Uses b&w, 5×7 or 3×5 prints. Query with samples; send unsolicited photos by mail. Responds in 3 weeks.

Terms Pays on publication. Buys first North American serial rights for mss. Buys first rights for artwork. Pays 5/word for stories and articles. Additional payment for ms/illustration packages and for photos accompanying articles. Pays $150-200 for color cover; $25-35 for b&w inside. Pays photographers per photo (range: $5-10). Originals returned to artist at job's completion. Sample copies for $6 (includes postage); $7.50 outside U.S. Writer's/illustrator's/photographer's guidelines and theme list are free for SASE.

Tips ''First be familiar with our magazines. We are looking for lively writing, most of it from a young boy's point of view—with the boy or boys directly involved in an activity that is both wholesome and unusual. We need nonfiction with photos and fiction stories—around 500 words—puzzles, poems, cooking, carpentry projects, jokes and riddles. Nonfiction pieces that are accompanied by black and white photos are far more likely to be accepted than those that need illustrations. We will entertain simultaneous submissions as long as that fact is noted on the manuscript.''

BREAD FOR GOD'S CHILDREN

Bread Ministries, Inc., P.O. Box 1017, Arcadia FL 34265-1017. (863)494-6214. Fax: (863)993-0154. E-mail: bread@sunline.net. Web site: www.breadministries.org. **Editor:** Judith M. Gibbs. Bimonthly magazine. Estab. 1972. Circ. 10,000 (U.S. and Canada). ''*Bread* is designed as a teaching tool for Christian families.'' 85% of publication aimed at juvenile market.

Fiction Young readers, middle readers, young adult/teen: adventure, religious, problem-solving, sports. Looks for ''teaching stories that portray Christian lifestyles without preaching.'' Buys approximately 20 mss/year. Average word length: 900-1,500 (for teens); 600-900 (for young children). Byline given.

Nonfiction All levels: how-to. ''We do not want anything detrimental to solid family values. Most topics will fit if they are slanted to our basic needs.'' Buys 3-4 mss/year. Average word length: 500-800. Byline given.

Illustration ''The only illustrations we purchase are those occasional good ones accompanying an accepted story.''

How to Contact/Writers Fiction/nonfiction: Send complete ms. Responds to mss in 6 months ''if considered for use.'' Will consider simultaneous submissions and previously published work.

Terms Pays on publication. Pays $30-50 for stories; $30 for articles. Sample copies free for 9×12 SAE and 5 first-class stamps (for 2 copies).

Tips ''We want stories or articles that illustrate overcoming obstacles by faith and living solid, Christian lives. Know our publication and what we have used in the past. Know the readership and publisher's guidelines. Stories should teach the value of morality and honesty without preaching. Edit carefully for content and grammar.''

BRILLIANT STAR

National Spiritual Assembly of the Bahá'ís of the U.S., 1233 Central St., Evanston IL 60201. (847)853-2354. Fax: (847)256-1372. E-mail: brilliantstar@usbnc.org. Web site: www.brilliantstar.org. **Associate Editor:** Susan Engle. **Art Director:** Amethel Parel-Sewell. Publishes 6 issues/year. Estab. 1969. ''Our magazine is designed for children ages 8-12. *Brilliant Star* presents Bahá'í history and principles through fiction, nonfiction, activities, interviews, puzzles, cartoons, games, music, and art. Universal values of good character, such as kindness, courage, creativity, and helpfulness are incorporated into the magazine.

Fiction Middle readers: contemporary, fantasy, folktale, multicultural, nature/environment, problem-solving, religious. Average word length: 700-1,400. Byline given.

Nonfiction Middle readers: arts/crafts, games/puzzles, geography, how-to, humorous, multicultural, nature/environment, religion, social issues. Buys 6 mss/year. Average word length: 300-700. Byline given.

Poetry ''We only publish poetry written by children at the moment.''

How to Contact/Writers Fiction: Send complete ms. Nonfiction: Query. Responds to queries/mss in 6 weeks. Publishes ms 6 months-1 year after acceptance. Will consider e-mail submissions.

Illustration Works on assignment only. Reviews ms/illustration packages from artists. Illustrations only: Query with samples. Contact: Aaron Kreader, graphic designer. Responds only if interested. Samples kept on file. Credit line given.

Photography Buys photos with accompanying ms only. Model/property release required; captions required. Responds only if interested.

Terms Pays 2 copies of issue. Buys first rights and reprint rights for mss. Buys first rights and reprint rights for artwork; first rights and reprint rights for photos. Sample copies for $3. Writer's/illustrator's/photo guidelines for SASE.

Tips ''*Brilliant Star's* content is developed with a focus on children in their 'tween' years, ages 8-12. This is a period of intense emotional, physical, and psychological development. Familiarize yourself with the interests and challenges of children in this age range. Protaganists in our fiction are usually in the upper part of our age-range: 10-12 years old. They solve their problems without adult intervention. We appreciate seeing a sense of humor but not related to bodily functions or put-downs. Keep your language and concepts age-appropriate. Use short words, sentences, and paragraphs. Activities and games may be submitted in rough or final form. Send us a description of your activity along with short, simple instructions. We avoid long, complicated activities that require adult supervision. If you think they will be helpful, please try to provide step-by-step rough sketches of the instructions. You may also submit photographs to illustrate the activity.''

CADET QUEST

Calvinist Cadet Corps, P.O. Box 7259, Grand Rapids MI 49510. (616)241-5616. E-mail: submissions@calvinistcadets.org. Web site: www.calvinistcadets.org. **Editor:** G. Richard Broene. Magazine published 7 times/year. Circ.

9,000. "Our magazine is for members of the Calvinist Cadet Corps—boys aged 9-14. Our purpose is to show how God is at work in their lives and in the world around them. Our magazine offers nonfiction articles and fast-moving fiction—everything to appeal to the interests and concerns of boys and teach Christian values."

Fiction Middle readers, boys/early teens: adventure, humorous, multicultural, problem-solving, religious, sports. Buys 12 mss/year. Average word length: 900-1,500.

Nonfiction Middle readers, boys/early teens: arts/crafts, games/puzzles, hobbies, how-to, humorous, interview/profile, problem-solving, science, sports. Buys 6 mss/year. Average word length: 400-900.

How to Contact/Writers Fiction/nonfiction: Send complete ms by mail with SASE or by e-mail. "Please note: e-mail submissions must have material in the body of the e-mail. Will not open attachments." Responds to mss in 2 months. Will consider simultaneous submissions.

Illustration Buys 2 illustration/issue; buys 12 illustrations/year. Works on assignment only. Reviews ms/illustration packages from artists. Responds in 5 weeks. Samples returned with SASE. Originals returned to artist at job's completion. Credit line given.

Photography Buys photos from freelancers. Wants nature photos and photos of boys.

Terms Pays on acceptance. Buys first North American serial rights; reprint rights. Pays 4-5 ¢/word for stories/articles. Pays illustrators $50-200 for b&w/color cover or b&w/color inside. Sample copy free with 9×12 SAE and 4 first-class stamps.

Tips "Our publication is mostly open to fiction; look for new themes at our Web site. We use mostly fast-moving fiction from a Christian persespective and based on our themes for each issue. Articles on sports, outdoor activities, science, crafts, etc. should emphasize a Christian perspective. Best time to submit material is February-April. Themes available on our Web site February 1."

CALLIOPE, Exploring World History

Cobblestone Publishing Company, 30 Grove St., Peterborough NH 03458. (603)924-7209. Fax: (603)924-7380. Web site: www.cobblestonepub.com. **Editorial Director:** Lou Waryncia. **Co-editors:** Rosalie Baker and Charles Baker. **Art Director:** Ann Dillon. Magazine published 9 times/year. "*Calliope* covers world history (East/West), and lively, original approaches to the subject are the primary concerns of the editors in choosing material."

- *Calliope* themes for 2007-2008 include Greek Olympics, Maps, Mythical Monsters, Genghis Khan and Joan of Arc. For additional themes and time frames, visit their Web site.

Fiction Middle readers and young adults: adventure, folktales, plays, history, biographical fiction. Material must relate to forthcoming themes. Word length: up to 800.

Nonfiction Middle readers and young adults: arts/crafts, biography, cooking, games/puzzles, history. Material must relate to forthcoming themes. Word length: 300-1,000.

How to Contact/Writers "A query must consist of the following to be considered (please use nonerasable paper): a brief cover letter stating subject and word length of the proposed article; a detailed one-page outline explaining the information to be presented in the article; an bibliography of materials the author intends to use in preparing the article; a self-addressed stamped envelope. Writers new to *Calliope* should send a writing sample with query. In all correspondence, please include your complete address as well as a telephone number where you can be reached. A writer may send as many queries for one issue as he or she wishes, but each query must have a separate cover letter, outline and bibliography as well as a SASE. Telephone and e-mail queries are not accepted. Handwritten queries will not be considered. Queries may be submitted at any time, but queries sent well in advance of deadline *may not be answered for several months*. Go-aheads requesting material proposed in queries are usually sent five months prior to publication date. Unused queries will be returned approximately three to four months prior to publication date."

Illustration Illustrations only: Send tearsheets, photocopies. Original work returned upon job's completion (upon written request).

Photography Buys photos from freelancers. Wants photos pertaining to any forthcoming themes. Uses b&w/color prints, 35mm transparencies. Send unsolicited photos by mail (on speculation).

Terms Buys all rights for mss and artwork. Pays 20-25¢/word for stories/articles. Pays on an individual basis for poetry, activities, games/puzzles. "Covers are assigned and paid on an individual basis." Pays photographers per photo ($15-100 for b&w; $25-100 for color). Sample copy for $5.95 and SAE with $2 postage. Writer's/illustrator's/photo guidelines for SASE.

CAMPUS LIFE'S IGNITE YOUR FAITH

Christianity Today, International, 465 Gundersen Dr., Carol Stream IL 60188. (630)260-6200. Fax: (630)260-2004. E-mail: iyf@igniteyourfaith.com. Web site: www.igniteyourfaith.com. **Articles and Fiction Editor:** Chris Lutes. Magazine published 5 times yearly. Estab. 1944. Circ. 100,000. "Our purpose is to creatively engage and empower Christian teens to become fully devoted followers of Jesus Christ."

Fiction Young adults: humorous, problem-solving with a Christian worldview. Buys 1-3 mss/year. Byline given.

Poetry Reviews poetry.

How to Contact/Writers Fiction/nonfiction: Query only.

Terms Pays on acceptance. Writer's guidelines available on Web site.

CAREER WORLD

Weekly Reader Corp., 200 First Stamford Place, P.O. Box 120023, Stamford CT 06912-0023. E-mail: careerworld @weeklyreader.com. **Articles Editor:** Anne Flounders. **Art Director:** Kimberly Shake. Monthly (school year) magazine. Estab. 1972. A guide to careers, for students grades 6-12.

Nonfiction Young adults/teens: education, how-to, interview/profile, career awareness and development. Byline given.

How to Contact/Writers Nonfiction: Query with published clips and résumé. Does not accept unsolicited manuscripts. Responds to queries only if interested.

Illustration Buys 5-10 illustrations/year. Works on assignment only. Reviews ms/illustration packages from artists. Manuscript/illustration packages and illustration only: Query; send promo sheet and tearsheets. Credit line given.

Photography Purchases photos from freelancers.

Terms Pays on publication. Buys all rights for mss. Pays $150 and up for articles. Pays illustrators by the project. Writer's guidelines free, but only on assignment.

CAREERS AND COLLEGES

A division of Alloy Education, an Alloy Media + Marketing Company, 10 Abeel Road, Cranbury NJ 08512. (609) 619-8739. Web site: www.careersandcolleges.com. **SVP/Managing Director:** Jayne Pennington. Editor: Don Rauf. Magazine published 3 times a year (2 issues direct-to-home in July and 1 to 10,000 high schools in December). Circulation: 760,000. Distributed to 760,000 homes of 15- to 17-year-olds and college-bound high school graduates, and 10,000 high schools. *Careers and Colleges* magazine provides juniors and seniors in high school with editorial, tips, trends, and Web sites to assist them in the transition to college, career, young adulthood, and independence.

Nonfiction Young adults/teens: careers, college, health, how-to, humorous, interview/profile, personal development, problem-solving, social issues, sports, travel. Buys 10-20 mss/year. Average word length: 1,000-1,500. Byline given.

How to Contact/Writers Nonfiction: Query. Responds to queries in 6 weeks. Will consider electronic submissions.

Illustration Buys 2 illustrations/issue; buys 8 illustrations/year. Works on assignment only. Reviews samples online. Query first. Credit line given.

Terms Pays on acceptance plus 45 days. Buys all rights. Pays $100-600 for assigned/unsolicited articles. Additional payment for ms/illustration packages "must be negotiated." Pays $300-1,000 for color illustration; $200-700 for b&w/color inside illustration. Pays photographers by the project. Sample copy $5. Contributor' s Guidelines are available electronically.

Tips "Articles with great quotes, good reporting, good writing. Rich with examples and anecdotes. Must tie in with the objective to help teenaged readers plan for their futures. Current trends, policy changes and information regarding college admissions, financial aid, and career opportunities."

CARUS PUBLISHING COMPANY

P.O. Box 300, Peru IL 61354.

● See listings for *Babybug, Cicada, Click, Cricket, Ladybug, Muse, Spider* and *ASK.* Carus Publishing owns Cobblestone Publishing, publisher of *AppleSeeds, Calliope, Cobblestone, Dig, Faces* and *Odyssey.*

CATHOLIC FORESTER

Catholic Order of Foresters, P.O. Box 3012, 355 Shuman Blvd., Naperville IL 60566-7012. (630)983-4900. E-mail: magazine@CatholicForester.com. Web site: www.catholicforester.com. **Articles Editor:** Patricia Baron. **Assistant V.P. Communication:** Mary Ann File. **Art Director:** Keith Halla. Quarterly magazine. Estab. 1883. Circ. 85,000. Targets members of the Catholic Order of Foresters. In addition to the organization's news, it offers general interest pieces on health, finance, family life. Also use inspirational and humorous fiction.

Fiction Buys 6-10 mss/year. Average word length: 500-1,500.

How to Contact/Writers Fiction: Submit complete ms. Responds in 4 months. Will consider previously published work.

Illustration Buys 2-4 illustrations/issue. Uses color artwork only. Works on assignment only.

Photography Buys photos with accompanying ms only.

Terms Pays on acceptance. Buys first North American serial rights, reprint rights, one-time rights. Sample copies for 9×12 SASE with 3 first-class stamps. Writer's guidelines free for SASE.

CELEBRATE

Word Action Publishing Co., Church of the Nazarene, 2923 Troost Ave, Kansas City MO 64109. (816)931-1900, ext. 8228. Fax: (816)412-8306. E-mail: alt@nph.com. Web site: www.wordaction.com. **Editor:** Melissa K. Hammer. **Assistant Editor:** Abagail Takala. Weekly publication. Estab. 2001. Circ. 30,000. ''This weekly take-home paper connects Sunday School learning to life for preschoolers (age 3 and 4), kindergartners (age 5 and 6) and their families.'' 75% of publication aimed at juvenile market; 25% parents.

Nonfiction Picture-oriented material: arts/crafts, cooking, poems, action rhymes, piggyback songs (theme based). 50% of mss nonfiction. Byline given.

Poetry Reviews poetry. Maximum length: 4-8 lines. Unlimited submissions.

How to Contact/Writers Nonfiction: query. Responds to queries in 1 month. Responds to mss in 6 weeks. Publishes ms 1 year after acceptance. Will accept electronic submission via e-mail.

Terms Pays on acceptance. Buys all rights, multi-use rights. Pays $15 for activities, crafts, recipes, songs, rhymes, and poems. Compensation includes 2 contributor copies. Sample copy for SASE.

Tips ''We are accepting submissions at this time.''

☐ CHEMMATTERS

American Chemical Society, 1155 16th Street, NW, Washington DC 20036. (202)872-6164. Fax: (202)833-7732. E-mail: chemmatters@acs.org. Web site: www.chemistry.org/education/chemmatters.html. **Articles Editor:** Carl Heltzel. **Art Director:** Cornithia Harris. Quarterly magazine. Estab. 1983. Circ. 35,000. ''*ChemMatters* is a magazine for connecting high school readers with the fascinating chemistry of their everyday lives.''

• *ChemMatters* only accepts e-mail submissions.

Nonfiction Young adults: biography, health, history, nature/environment, problem-solving, science. Must be related to chemistry. Buys 20 mss/year. Average word length: 1,400-2,100. Byline given.

How to Contact/Writers Nonfiction: Query with published clips. Only e-mail submissions will be considered. Responds to queries/mss in 2 weeks. Publishes ms 6 months after acceptance. Will consider simultaneous submissions, e-mail submissions.

Illustration Buys 3 illustrations/issue; 12 illustrations/year. Uses color artwork only. Works on assignment only. Reviews ms/illustration packages from artists. Query. Contact: Cornithia Harris, art director *ChemMatters*. Illustrations only: Query with promo sheet, résumé. Responds in 2 weeks. Samples returned with SASE; samples not filed. Credit line given.

Photography Looking for photos of high school students engaged in science-related activities. Model/property release required; captions required. Uses color prints, but prefers high-res PDFs. Query with samples. Responds in 2 weeks.

Terms Pays on acceptance. Minimally buys first North American serial rights, but prefers to buy all rights, reprint rights, electronic rights for mss. Buys all rights for artwork; non-exclusive first rights for photos. Pays $500-$1,000 for articles. Additional payment for ms/illustration packages and for photos accompanying articles. Sample copies free for SAE 10×13 and 3 first-class stamps. Writer's guidelines free for SASE (available as e-mail attachment upon request).

Tips ''Be aware of the content covered in a standard high school chemistry textbook. Choose themes and topics that are timely, interesting, fun, mystifying, *and* that relate to the content and concepts of the first-year chemistry course. Articles should describe real people involved with real science. Best articles feature young people making a difference or solving a problem.''

CHILDREN'S BETTER HEALTH INSTITUTE

1100 Waterway Blvd., P.O. Box 567, Indianapolis IN 46206. See listings for *Children's Digest*, *Children's Playmate*, *Humpty Dumpty's Magazine*, *Jack and Jill*, *Turtle* and *U*S* Kids*.

CHILDREN'S DIGEST

Children's Better Health Institute, 1100 Waterway Blvd., P.O. Box 567, Indianapolis IN 46206. (317)634-1100. Fax: (317)684-8094. Web site: www.childrensdigestmag.org. For children ages 10-12.

• See Web site for submission guidelines.

CHILDREN'S PLAYMATE

Children's Better Health Institute, 1100 Waterway Blvd., Box 567, Indianapolis IN 46206. (317)634-1100. Fax: (317)684-8094. Web site: www.childrensplaymatemag.org. **Editor:** Terry Harshman. **Art Director:** Rob Falco. Magazine published 6 times/year. Estab. 1929. Circ. 135,000. For children ages 6-8 years; approximately 50% of content is health-related.

Fiction Average word length: 100-300. Byline given. Sample copies $2.95.

Nonfiction Young readers: easy recipes, games/puzzles, health, medicine, safety, science. Buys 16-20 mss/year. Average word length: 300-500. Byline given.

Poetry Maximum length: 20-25 lines.

How to Contact/Writers Fiction/nonfiction: Send complete ms. Responds to mss in 3 months. Do not send queries.

Illustration Works on assignment only. Reviews ms/illustration packages from artists. Query first.

Terms Pays on publication for illustrators and writers. Buys all rights for mss and artwork. Pays 17¢/word for stories. Pays minimum $25 for poems. Pays $275 for color cover illustration; $90 for b&w inside; $70-155 for color inside. Sample copy $3.95. Writer's/illustrator's guidelines for SASE.

CICADA

Carus Publishing Company, P.O. Box 300, 315 Fifth St., Peru IL 61354. (815)224-5803. Fax: (815)224-6615. Submissions address: 70 East Lake Street, Suite 300, Chicago IL 60601. E-mail: cicada@caruspub.com. Web site: www.cricketmag.com. **Editor-in-Chief:** Marianne Carus. **Executive Editor:** Deborah Vetter. **Editorial Assistant:** Pete Coco. **Art Director:** John Sandford. Bimonthly magazine. Estab. 1998. *Cicada* publishes fiction and poetry with a genuine teen sensibility, aimed at the high school and college-age market. The editors are looking for stories and poems that are thought-provoking but entertaining.

Fiction Young adults: adventure, animal, contemporary, fantasy, history, humorous, multicultural, nature/environment, romance, science fiction, sports, suspense/mystery, stories that will adapt themselves to a sophisticated cartoon, or graphic novel format. Buys up to 60 mss/year. Average word length: about 5,000 words for short stories; up to 15,000 for novellas (one novella per issue).

Nonfiction Young adults: first-person, coming-of-age experiences that are relevant to teens and young adults (example: life in the Peace Corps). Buys 6 mss/year. Average word length: about 5,000 words. Byline given.

Poetry Reviews serious, humorous, free verse, rhyming (if done well) poetry. Maximum length: up to 25 lines. Limit submissions to 5 poems.

How to Contact/Writers Fiction/nonfiction: send complete ms. Responds to mss in 3 months. Publishes ms 1-2 years after acceptance. Will consider simultaneous submissions if author lets us know.

Illustration Buys 20 illustrations/issue; 120 illustrations/year. Uses color artwork for cover; b&w for interior. Works on assignment only. Reviews ms/illustration packages from artists. Send ms with 1-2 sketches and samples of other finished art. Illustrations only: Query with samples. Responds in 6 weeks. Samples returned with SASE; samples filed. Credit line given.

Photography Wants documentary photos (clear shots that illustrate specific artifacts, persons, locations, phenomena, etc., cited in the text) and "art" shots of teens in photo montage/lighting effects etc. Uses b&w 4×5 glossy prints. Submit portfolio for review. Responds in 6 weeks.

Terms Pays on publication. Rights purchased vary. Pays up to 25¢/word for mss; up to $3/line for poetry. Pays illustrators $750 for color cover; $50-150 for b&w inside. Pays photographers per photo (range: $50-150). Sample copies for $8.50. Writer's/illustrator's/photo guidelines for SASE.

Tips "Please don't write for a junior high audience. We're seeing too many young protagonists (ages 14 and under)—would like more stories about older teens. We're looking for complex character development, strong plots, and thought-provoking themes for young people in high school and college. Don't forget humor and romance! We're getting too many cancer-related stories and too much depressing fiction in general. We'd like to publish more nonfiction first-person experiences. Please note that this is a separate category from the shorter, teen-written 'expressions' feature."

THE CLAREMONT REVIEW

4980 Wesley Road, Victoria BC V8Y 1Y9 Canada. (250)685-5221. Fax: (250)658-5387. E-mail: editor@theClaremontReview.ca. Web site: www.theClaremontReview.ca. Magazine 2 times/year. Estab. 1992. Circ. 500. "Publish quality fiction and poetry of emerging writers aged 13 to 19."

Fiction Young adults: multicultural, problem-solving, social issues, relationships. Average word length: 1,500-3,000.

Poetry Maximum length: 60 lines. No limit on submissions.

How to Contact/Writers Fiction: Send complete ms. Responds to queries in 2 weeks; mss in 2 months. Publishes ms 6 months after acceptance.

Illustration Illustrations only: Send postcard sample with samples, SASE. Contact: Janice McCachen, editor. Responds in 2 months. Samples returned with SASE. Credit line given.

Terms Buys first North American rights for mss. Pays contributor's copies when published. Sample copies for $10. Writer's guidelines for SASE.

Tips "Looking for good, concrete narratives with credible dialogue and solid use of original detail. It must be unique, honest and have a glimpse of some truth. Send an error-free final draft with a short covering letter and bio. Read our magazine first to familiarize yourself with what we publish."

CLICK

140 S. Dearborn, Suite 1450, Chicago IL 60603. (312)701-1720. Fax: (312)701-1728. E-mail: click@caruspub.com. Web site: www.cricketmag.com. **Editor:** Lonnie Plecha. **Art Director:** Amy Tao. 9 issues/year. Estab. 1998. "*Click* is a science and exploration magazine for children ages 3 to 7. Designed and written with the idea that it's never too early to encourage a child's natural curiosity about the world, *Click*'s 40 full-color pages are filled with amazing photographs, beautiful illustrations, and stories and articles that are both entertaining and thought-provoking."

Nonfiction Young readers: animals, nature/environment, science. Average word length: 300-1000. Byline given.

How to Contact Writers *Click* does not accept unsolicited manuscripts or queries. All articles are commissioned. To be considered for assignments, experienced science writers may send a résumé and three published clips.

Illustration Buys 10 illustrations/issue; 60 illustrations/year. Works on assignment only. Query with samples. Responds only if interested. Credit line given.

COBBLESTONE: Discover American History

Cobblestone Publishing, 30 Grove St., Suite C, Peterborough NH 03458. (603)924-7209. Fax: (603)924-7380. Web site: www.cobblestonepub.com. **Editor:** Meg Chorlian. **Art Director:** Ann Dillon. **Editorial Director:** Lou Waryncia. Magazine published 9 times/year. Circ. 27,000. "*Cobblestone* is theme-related. Writers should request editorial guidelines which explain procedure and list upcoming themes. Queries must relate to an upcoming theme. It is recommended that writers become familiar with the magazine (sample copies available)."

• *Cobblestone* themes and deadline are available on Web site or with SASE.

Fiction Middle readers, young adults: folktales, history, multicultural.

Nonfiction Middle readers (school ages 9-14): arts/crafts, biography, geography, history (world and American), multicultural, social issues. All articles must relate to the issue's theme. Buys 120 mss/year. Average word length: 600-800. Byline given.

Poetry Up to 100 lines. "Clear, objective imagery. Serious and light verse considered." Pays on an individual basis. Must relate to theme.

How to Contact/Writers Fiction/nonfiction: Query. "A query must consist of all of the following to be considered: a brief cover letter stating the subject and word length of the proposed article, a detailed one-page outline explaining the information to be presented in the article, an extensive bibliography of materials the author intends to use in preparing the article, a SASE. Writers new to *Cobblestone* should send a writing sample with query. If you would like to know if your query has been received, please also include a stamped postcard that requests acknowledgment of receipt. In all correspondence, please include your complete address as well as a telephone number where you can be reached. A writer may send as many queries for one issue as he or she wishes, but each query must have a separate cover letter, outline, bibliography and SASE. Telephone queries are not accepted. Handwritten queries will not be considered. Queries may be submitted at any time, but queries sent well in advance of deadline *may not be answered for several months.* Go-aheads requesting material proposed in queries are usually sent five months prior to publication date. Unused queries will not be returned."

Illustration Buys 5 color illustrations/issue; 45 illustrations/year. Preferred theme or style: Material that is fun, clear and accurate but not too juvenile. Historically accurate sources are a must. Works on assignment only. Reviews ms/illustration packages from artists. Query. Illustrations only: Send photocopies, tearsheets, or other nonreturnable samples. "Illustrators should consult issues of *Cobblestone* to familiarize themselves with our needs." Responds to art samples in 1 month. Samples are not returned; samples filed. Original artwork returned at job's completion (upon written request). Credit line given.

Photography Photos must relate to upcoming themes. Send transparencies and/or color prints. Submit on speculation.

Terms Pays on publication. Buys all rights to articles and artwork. Pays 20-25¢/word for articles/stories. Pays on an individual basis for poetry, activities, games/puzzles. Pays photographers per photo ($50-100 for color). Sample copy $5.95 with 9×12 SAE and 4 first-class stamps; writer's/illustrator's/photo guidelines free with SAE and 1 first-class stamp.

Tips Writers: "Submit detailed queries which show attention to historical accuracy and which offer interesting and entertaining information. Study past issues to know what we look for. All feature articles, recipes, activities, fiction and supplemental nonfiction are freelance contributions." Illustrators: "Submit color samples, not too juvenile. Study past issues to know what we look for. The illustration we use is generally for stories, recipes and activities." (See listings for *AppleSeeds, Calliope, Dig, Faces, Footsteps,* and *Odyssey.*)

CRICKET

Carus Publishing Company, P.O. Box 300, Peru IL 61354. (815)224-5803, ext. 656. Web site: www.cricketmag.com. **Editor-in-Chief:** Marianne Carus. **Executive Editor:** Lonnie Plecha. **Senior Art Director:** Karen Kohn. Monthly magazine. Estab. 1973. Circ. 72,000. Children's literary magazine for ages 9-14.

• See Roundtable on page 77 for an interview with *Cricket* editor Lonnie Plecha.

Fiction Middle readers, young adults/teens: contemporary, fantasy, folk and fairy tales, history, humorous, science fiction, suspense/mystery. Buys 140 mss/year. Maximum word length: 2,000. Byline given.

Nonfiction Middle readers, young adults/teens: adventure, architecture, archaeology, biography, foreign culture, games/puzzles, geography, natural history, science and technology, social science, sports, travel. Multicultural needs include articles on customs and cultures. Requests bibliography with submissions. Buys 40 mss/year. Average word length: 200-1,500. Byline given.

Poetry Reviews poems, 1-page maximum length. Limit submission to 5 poems or less.

How to Contact/Writers Send complete ms. Do not query first. Responds to mss in 4-6 months. Does not like but will consider simultaneous submissions. SASE required for response, IRCs for international submissions.

Illustration Buys 35 illustrations (14 separate commissions)/issue; 425 illustrations/year. Preferred theme for style: "strong realism; strong people, especially kids; good action illustration; no cartoons. All media, but prefer other than pencil." Reviews ms/illustration packages from artists, "but reserves option to re-illustrate." Send complete ms with sample and query. Illustrations only: Provide tearsheets or good quality photocopies to be kept on file. SASE required for response/return of samples. Responds to art samples in 2 months.

Photography Purchases photos with accompanying ms only. Model/property releases required. Uses color transparencies, b&w glossy prints.

Terms Pays on publication. Rights purchased vary. Do not send original artwork. Pays up to 25¢/word for unsolicited articles; up to $3/line for poetry. Pays $750 for color cover; $75-150 for b&w, $150-250 for color inside. Writer's/illustrator's guidelines for SASE. Sample issue for $5, check made out to Cricket Magazine Group.

Tips Writers: "Read copies of back issues and current issues. Adhere to specified word limits. *Please* do not query." Illustrators: "Edit your samples. Send only your best work and be able to reproduce that quality in assignments. Put name and address on *all* samples. Know a publication before you submit is your style appropriate?"

CURRENT SCIENCE

Weekly Reader Corp. E-mail: science@weeklyreader.com. Web site: www.weeklyreader.com. **Managing Editor:** Hugh Westrup. 16 times/year magazine. Estab. 1927. "*Current Science* uses today's new to make science relevant to students in grades 6-10. Each issue covers every area of the science curriculum—life, earth, and physical science, plus health and technology."

● *Current Science* is no longer accepting unsolicited submissions.

DANCE MAGAZINE

333 Seventh Ave., 11th Floor, New York NY 10001. (212)979-4803. Fax: (646)674-0102. Web site: www.dancemagazine.com. **Editor-in-Chief:** Wendy Perron. **Art Director:** Ragnar Johnson. Monthly magazine. Estab. 1927. Circ. 45,000. Covers "all things dance—features, news, reviews, calendar."

How to Contact Query with published clips.

Photography Uses dance photos.

Terms Pays on publication. Buys first rights. Additional payment for ms/illustration packages and for photos accompanying articles. Pays photographers per photo. Byline given. Sample copies for $4.95. (Go to Web site and click on subscription services.)

Tips "Study the magazine for style."

DAVEY AND GOLIATH'S DEVOTIONS

Augsburg Fortress Publishers, P.O. Box 1209, Minneapolis MN 55440-1209. E-mail: cllsub@augsburgfortress.org. Web site: www.augsburgfortress.org. **Editor:** Dawn Rundman. Quarterly magazine. Circ. approximately 40,000. This is a booklet of interactive conversations and activities related to weekly devotional material. Used primarily by Lutheran families with elementary school-aged children." avey and Goliath is a magazine with concrete ideas that families can use to build biblical literacy and share faith and serve others. It includes bible stories, family activities, crafts, games, and a section of puzzles, mazes, and other kid-stuff."

How to Contact/Writers Visit www.augsburgfortress.org/media/company/downloads/FamilyDevotionalSampleBriefing.doc to view sample briefing. Follow instructions in briefing if interested in submitting a sample for the devotional. Published material is 100% assigned.

Terms Pays on acceptance of final ms assignment. Buys all rights. Pays $40/printed page on assignment. Free sample and information for prospective writers. Include 6×9 SAE and postage.

Tips "Pay attention to details in the sample devotional. Follow the process laid out in the information for prospective writers. Ability to interpret Bible texts appropriately for children is required. Content must be doable and fun for families on the go."

DIG

Cobblestone Publishing, 30 Grove St., Suite C, Peterborough NH 03450. (603)924-7209. Fax: (603)924-7380. E-mail: cfbakeriii@meganet.net. Web site: www.digonsite.com. **Editor:** Rosalie Baker. **Editorial Director:** Lou Waryncia. **Art Director:** Ann Dillon. Magazine published 9 times/year. Estab. 1999. Circ. 20,000. An archaeology magazine for kids ages 8-14. Publishes entertaining and educational stories about discoveries, artifacts, archaeologists.

• *Dig* was purchased by Cobblestone Publishing, a division of Carus Publishing.

Nonfiction Middle readers, young adults: biography, games/puzzles, history, science, archaeology. Buys 50 mss/year. Average word length: 400-800. Byline given.

How to Contact/Writers Fiction/nonfiction: Query. "A query must consist of all of the following to be considered: a brief cover letter stating the subject and word length of the proposed article, a detailed one-page outline explaining the information to be presented in the article, a bibliography of materials the author intends to use in preparing the article, and a SASE. Writers new to *Dig* should send a writing sample with query. If you would like to know if a query has been received, include a stamped postcard that requests acknowledgement of receipt." Multiple queries accepted (include separate cover letter, outline, bibliography, SASE) may not be answered for many months. Go-aheads requesting material proposed in queries are usually sent 5 months prior to publication date. Unused queries will be returned approximately 3-4 months prior to publication date.

Illustration Buys 10-15 illustrations/issue; 60-75 illustrations/year. Prefers color artwork. Works on assignment only. Reviews ms/illustration packages from artists. Query. Illustrations only: Query with samples. Arrange portfolio review. Send tearsheets. Responds in 2 months only if interested. Samples not returned; samples filed. Credit line given.

Photography Uses anything related to archaeology, history, artifacts, and current archaeological events that relate to kids. Uses color prints and 35mm transparencies. Provide résumé, promotional literature or tearsheets to be kept on file. Responds only if interested.

Terms Pays on publication. Buys all rights for mss. Buys first North American rights for photos. Original artwork returned at job's completion. Pays 20-25¢/word. Additional payment for ms/illustration packages and for photos accompanying articles. Pays per photo.

Tips "We are looking for writers who can communicate archaeological concepts in a conversational, interesting, informative and *accurate* style for kids. Writers should have some idea where photography can be located to support their articles."

DISCOVERIES

WordAction Publishing Co., 2923 Troost Ave., Kansas City MO 64109. (816)931-1900. Fax: (816)412-8306. E-mail: kdadama@wordaction.com. **Editor:** Virginia L. Folsom. **Senior Editor:** Donna L. Fillmore. **Assistant Editor:** Kimberly Adams. Take-home paper. "*Discoveries* is a leisure-reading piece for third- and fourth-graders. It is published weekly by WordAction Publishing. The major purpose of the magazine is to provide a leisure-reading piece which will build Christian behavior and values and provide reinforcement for Biblical concepts taught in the Sunday School curriculum. The focus of the reinforcement will be life-related, with some historical appreciation. *Discoveries'* target audience is children ages eight to ten in grades three and four. The readability goal is third to fourth grade." Request guidelines and theme list by e-mail or send SASE.

DRAMATICS MAGAZINE

Educational Theatre Association, 2343 Auburn Ave., Cincinnati OH 45219. (513)421-3900. E-mail: dcorathers@edta.org. Web site: www.edta.org. **Articles Editor:** Don Corathers. **Graphic Design:** Kay Walters. Published monthly September-May. Estab. 1929. Circ. 35,000. "Dramatics is for students (mainly high school age) and teachers of theater. Mix includes how-to (tech theater, acting, directing, etc.), informational, interview, photo feature, humorous, profile, technical. We want our student readers to grow as theater artists and become a more discerning and appreciative audience. Material is directed to both theater students and their teachers, with strong student slant."

Fiction Young adults: drama (one-act and full-length plays). Does not want to see plays that show no understanding of the conventions of the theater. No plays for children, no Christmas or didactic "message" plays. "We prefer unpublished scripts that have been produced at least once." Buys 5-9 plays/year. Emerging playwrights have better chances with résumé of credits.

Nonfiction Young adults: arts/crafts, careers, how-to, interview/profile, multicultural (all theater-related). "We try to portray the theater community in all its diversity." Does not want to see academic treatises. Buys 50 mss/year. Average word length: 750-3,000. Byline given.

How to Contact/Writers Send complete ms. Responds in 3 months (longer for plays). Published ms 3 months after acceptance. Will consider simultaneous submissions and previously published work occasionally.

Illustration Buys 0-2 illustrations/year. Works on assignment only. Arrange portfolio review; send résumé, promo sheets and tearsheets. Responds only if interested. Samples returned with SASE; sample not filed. Credit line given.

Photography Buys photos with accompanying ms only. Looking for "good-quality production or candid photography to accompany article. We very occasionally publish photo essays." Model/property release and captions required. Uses 5×7 or 8×10 b&w glossy prints and 35mm transparencies. Also uses high resolution digital files or Zip disk or CD (JPEG or TIFF files). Query with résumé of credits. Responds only if interested.

Terms Pays on acceptance. Buys one-time print and short term Web rights. Buys one-time rights for artwork and photos. Original artwork returned at job's completion. Pays $100-500 for plays; $50-500 for articles; up to $100 for illustrations. Pays photographers by the project or per photo. Sometimes offers additional payment for ms/illustration packages and photos accompanying a ms. Sample copy available for 9×12 SAE with 4 ounces first-class postage. Writer's and photo guidelines available for SASE or via Web site.

Tips "Obtain our writer's guidelines and look at recent back issues. The best way to break in is to know our audience—drama students, teachers and others interested in theater—and write for them. Writers who have some practical experience in theater, especially in technical areas, have an advantage, but we'll work with anybody who has a good idea. Some freelancers have become regular contributors."

FACES, People, Places & Cultures

Cobblestone Publishing Company, 30 Grove St., Peterborough NH 03458. (603)924-7209. Fax: (603)924-7380. E-mail: facesmag@yahoo.com. Web site: www.cobblestonepub.com. **Editor:** Elizabeth Crooker Carpentiere. **Editorial Director:** Lou Warnycia. **Art Director:** Ann Dillon. Magazine published 9 times/year (September-May). Circ. 15,000. *Faces* is a theme-related magazine; writers should send for theme list before submitting ideas/queries. Each month a different world culture is featured through the use of feature articles, activities and photographs and illustrations.

- See Web site for 2007-2008 theme list for *Faces*.

Fiction Middle readers, young adults/teens: adventure, folktales, history, multicultural, plays, religious, travel. Does not want to see material that does not relate to a specific upcoming theme. Buys 9 mss/year. Maximum word length: 800. Byline given.

Nonfiction Middle readers and young adults/teens: animal, anthropology, arts/crafts, biography, cooking, fashion, games/puzzles, geography, history, how-to, humorous, interview/profile, nature/environment, religious, social issues, sports, travel. Does not want to see material not related to a specific upcoming theme. Buys 63 mss/year. Average word length: 300-600. Byline given.

Poetry Clear, objective imagery; up to 100 lines. Must relate to theme.

How to Contact/Writers Fiction/nonfiction: Query with published clips and 2-3 line biographical sketch. "Ideas should be submitted six to nine months prior to the publication date. Responses to ideas are usually sent approximately four months before the publication date." Guidelines on Web site.

Illustration Buys 3 illustrations/issue; buys 27 illustrations/year. Preferred theme or style: Material that is meticulously researched (most articles are written by professional anthropologists); simple, direct style preferred, but not too juvenile. Works on assignment only. Roughs required. Reviews ms/illustration packages from artists. Illustrations only: Send samples of b&w work. "Illustrators should consult issues of *Faces* to familiarize themselves with our needs." Responds to art samples only if interested. Samples returned with SASE. Original artwork returned at job's completion (upon written request). Credit line given.

Photography Wants photos relating to forthcoming themes.

Terms Pays on publication. Buys all rights for mss and artwork. Pays 20-25¢/word for articles/stories. Pays on an individual basis for poetry. Covers are assigned and paid on an individual basis. Pays illustrators $50-300 for color inside. Pays photographers per photo ($25-100 for color). Sample copy $5.95 with $7^1/_2 \times 10^1/_2$ SAE and 5 first-class stamps. Writer's/illustrator's/photo guidelines via Web site or free with SAE and 1 first-class stamp.

Tips "Writers are encouraged to study past issues of the magazine to become familiar with our style and content. Writers with anthropological and/or travel experience are particularly encouraged; *Faces* is about world cultures. All feature articles, recipes and activities are freelance contributions." Illustrators: "Submit b&w samples, not too juvenile. Study past issues to know what we look for. The illustration we use is generally for retold legends, recipes and activities."

THE FRIEND MAGAZINE

The Church of Jesus Christ of Latter-day Saints, 50 E. North Temple, Salt Lake City UT 84150-3226. (801)240-2210. **Editor:** Vivian Paulsen. **Art Director:** Mark Robison. Monthly magazine for 3-11 year olds. Estab. 1971. Circ. 275,000.

Nonfiction Publishes children's/true stories—adventure, ethnic, some historical, humor, mainstream, religious/inspirational, nature. Length: 1,000 words maximum. Also publishes family- and gospel-oriented puzzles, games and cartoons. Simple recipes and handicraft projects welcome.

Poetry Reviews poetry. Maximum length: 20 lines.

How to Contact/Writers Send complete ms. Responds to mss in 2 months.

Illustration Illustrations only: Query with samples; arrange personal interview to show portfolio; provide résumé and tearsheets for files.

Terms Pays on acceptance. Buys all rights for mss. Pays $100-250 (400 words and up) for stories; $30 for poems; $20 minimum for activities and games. Contributors are encouraged to send for sample copy for $1.50, 9×11 envelope and four 37-cent stamps. Free writer's guidelines.

Tips *"The Friend* is published by The Church of Jesus Christ of Latter-day Saints for boys and girls up to eleven years of age. All submissions are carefully read by the *Friend* staff, and those not accepted are returned within two months for SASE. Submit seasonal material at least one year in advance. Query letters and simultaneous submissions are not encouraged. Authors may request rights to have their work reprinted after their manuscript is published."

FUN FOR KIDZ

P.O. Box 227, Bluffton OH 45817-0227. (419)358-4610. Fax: (419)358-5027. Web site: www.funforkidz.com. **Articles Editor:** Marilyn Edwards. Bimonthly magazine. Estab. 2002. *"Fun for Kidz* is a magazine created for boys and girls ages 6-13, with youngsters 8, 9, and 10 the specific target age. The magazine is designed as an activity publication to be enjoyed by both boys and girls on the alternative months of *Hopscotch* and *Boys' Quest* magazines."

• *Fun for Kidz* is theme-oriented. Send SASE for theme list and writer's guidelines.

Fiction Picture-oriented material, young readers, middle readers: adventure, animal, history, humorous, problem-solving, multicultural, nature/environment, sports. Average word length: 300-700.

Nonfiction Picture-oriented material, young readers, middle readers: animal, arts/crafts, cooking, games/puzzles, history, hobbies, how-to, humorous, problem-solving, sports, carpentry projects. Average word length: 300-700. Byline given.

Poetry Reviews poetry.

How to Contact/Writers Fiction/nonfiction: Send complete ms. Responds to queries in 2 weeks; mss in 5 weeks. Will consider simultaneous submissions. "Will not respond to faxed/e-mailed queries, mss, etc."

Illustration Works on assignment mostly. "We are anxious to find artists capable of illustrating stories and features. Our inside art is pen & ink." Query with samples. Samples kept on file.

Photography "We use a number of back & white photos inside the magazine; most support the articles used."

Terms Pays on publication. Buys first American serial rights. Buys first American serial rights and photos for artwork. Pays 5/word; $10/poem or puzzle; $35 for art (full page); $25 for art (partial page). Pays illustrators $5-10 for b&w photos. Sample copies available for $6 (includes postage); $7 outside U.S.

Tips "Our point of view is that every child deserves the right to be a child for a number of years before he or she becomes a young adult. As a result, *Fun for Kidz* looks for activities that deal with timeless topics, such as pets, nature, hobbies, science, games, sports, careers, simple cooking, and anything else likely to interest a child."

GIRLS' LIFE

Monarch, 4529 Harford Rd., Baltimore MD 21214. (410)426-9600. Fax: (410)254-0991. Web site: www.girlslife.com. **Executive Editor:** Kelly White. Bimonthly magazine. Estab. 1994. General interest magazine for girls, ages 10-15.

Fiction Teen and 'tween.

Nonfiction Arts/crafts, fashion, interview/profile, social issues, sports, travel, hobbies, relationships, quizzes, friendship, school. Buys appoximately 25 mss/year. Word length varies. Byline given.

How to Contact/Writers Nonfiction: Query with descriptive story ideas, résumé and published writing samples. Responds in 6 weeks. Publishes ms 3 months after acceptance. Will consider simultaneous submissions. No phone calls. No e-mails.

Illustration Uses color artwork only. Works on assignment only. Reviews ms/illustration packages from artists. Send ms with dummy. Illustration only: Query with samples; send tearsheets. Contact: Chun Kim, creative director. Responds only if interested. Samples returned with SASE; samples filed. Credit line given.

Photography Hires photographers. Send portfolio. Responds only if interested.

Terms Pays on publication. Original artwork returned at job's completion. Pays $500-800 for features; $150-350 for departments. Sample copies available for $5. Writer's guidelines for SASE or via Web site.

Tips "Don't call with queries. Make query short and punchy."

GUIDE MAGAZINE

Review and Herald Publishing Association, 55 W. Oak Ridge Dr., Hagerstown MD 21740. (301)393-4037. Fax: (301)393-4055. E-mail: guide@rhpa.org. Web site: www.guidemagazine.org. **Editor:** Randy Fishell. **Designer:** Brandon Reese. Weekly magazine. Estab. 1953. Circ. 32,000. "Ours is a weekly Christian journal written for middle readers and young teens (ages 10-14), presenting true stories relevant to the needs of today's young person, emphasizing positive aspects of Christian living."

Nonfiction Middle readers, young adults/teens: adventure, animal, character-building, contemporary, games/puzzles, humorous, multicultural, problem-solving, religious. "We need true, or based on true, happenings, not merely true-to-life. Our stories and puzzles must have a spiritual emphasis." No violence. No articles. "We always need humor and adventure stories." Buys 150 mss/year. Average word length: 500-600 minimum, 1,200-1,300 maximum. Byline given.

How to Contact/Writers Nonfiction: Send complete ms. Responds in 6 weeks. Will consider simultaneous submissions. "We can pay half of the regular amount for reprints." Responds to queries/mss in 6 weeks. Credit line given. "We encourage e-mail submissions."

Terms Pays on acceptance. Buys first North American serial rights; first rights; one-time rights; second serial (reprint rights); simultaneous rights. Pays 6-12¢/word for stories and articles. "Writer receives several complimentary copies of issue in which work appears." Sample copy free with 6×9 SAE and 2 first-class stamps. Writer's guidelines for SASE.

Tips "Children's magazines want mystery, action, discovery, suspense and humor—no matter what the topic. For us, truth is stronger than fiction."

GUIDEPOSTS SWEET 16

1050 Broadway, Suite 6, Chesterton IN 46304. (219)929-4429. Fax: (219)926-3839. E-mail: writers@sweet16mag.com. Web site: www.sweet16mag.com. **Editor-in-Chief:** Mary Lou Carney. **Art Director:** Meghan McPhail. **Art Coordinator:** Rose Pomeroy. Bimonthly magazine. Estab. 1998. "*Guideposts Sweet 16* is a general-interest magazine for teenage girls, ages 11-17. We are an inspirational publication that offers true, first-person stories about real teens. Our watchwords are 'wholesome,' 'current,' 'fun,' and 'inspiring.' We also publish shorter pieces on fashion, beauty, celebrity, boys, embarrassing moments, and advice columns."

Nonfiction Young adults: quizzes, DIYs, celebrity interviews, true stories, fashion and beauty. Average word length: 200-1,500. Byline sometimes given.

How to Contact/Writers Nonfiction: Query. Responds to queries/mss in 6 weeks. Will consider simultaneous submissions or electronic submission via e-mail. Send SASE for writer's guidelines or visit Web site.

Illustration Uses color artwork only. Works on assignment only. Reviews ms/illustration packages from artists. Query. Contact: Rose Pomeroy, art coordinator. Illustrations only: Query with samples. Responds only if interested. Samples kept on file. Credit line given.

Photography Buys photos separately. Wants location photography and stock; digital OK. Uses color prints and 35mm, 2¼×2¼, or 8×10 transparencies. Query with samples; provide Web address. Responds only if interested.

Terms Pays on acceptance. Buys all rights for mss. Buys one-time rights for artwork. Original artwork returned at job's completion. Pays $300-500 for true stories; $100-300 for articles. Additional payment for photos accompanying articles. Pays illustrators $125-1,500 for color inside (depends on size). Pays photographers by the project (range: $100-1,000). Sample copies for $4.50 from: Guideposts, 39 Seminary Hill Rd., Carmel NY 10512. Attn: Special Handling.

Tips "Study our magazine! Language and subject matter should be current and teen-friendly. No preaching, please! (Your 'takeaway' should be inherent.) We are most in need of inspirational action/adventure, and relationship stories written in first-person and narrated by teenage girls. We need 'light' stories about finding a date and learning to drive, as well as catch-in-the-throat stories. We also need short (250-word) true stories with a miracle/'aha' ending for our 'Mysterious Moments' department. For illustrators: We get illustrators from two basic sources: submissions by mail and submissions by Internet. We also consult major illustrator reference books. We prefer color illustrations, 'on-the-edge' style. We accept art in almost any digital or reflective format.'"

HIGHLIGHTS FOR CHILDREN

803 Church St., Honesdale PA 18431. (570)253-1080. E-mail: eds@highlights-corp.com. Web site: www.highlights.com. **Contact:** Manuscript Coordinator. **Editor:** Christine French Clark. **Art Director:** Cindy Smith. Monthly magazine. Estab. 1946. Circ. 2.5 million. "Our motto is 'Fun With a Purpose.' We are looking for quality fiction and nonfiction that appeals to children, encourages them to read, and reinforces positive values. All art is done on assignment."

• See Roundtable on page 77 for an interview with *Highlights* editor Christine French Clark.

Fiction Picture-oriented material, young readers, middle readers: adventure, animal, contemporary, fantasy, folktales, history, humorous, multicultural, problem-solving, sports. Multicultural needs include first person accounts of children from other cultures and first-person accounts of children from other countries. Does not want to see war, crime, violence. "We see too many stories with overt morals." Would like to see more contemporary, multicultural and world culture fiction, mystery stories, action/adventure stories, humorous stories, and fiction for younger readers. Buys 150 mss/year. Average word length: 500-800. Byline given.

Nonfiction Picture-oriented material, young readers, middle readers: animal, arts/crafts, biography, careers, games/puzzles, geography, health, history, hobbies, how-to, interview/profile, multicultural, nature/environment, problem-solving, science, sports. Multicultural needs include articles set in a country *about* the people of the country. Does not want to see trendy topics, fads, personalities who would not be good role models for children, guns, war, crime, violence. "We'd like to see more nonfiction for younger readers—maximum of 500 words. We still need older-reader material, too—500-800 words." Buys 200 mss/year. Maximum word length: 800. Byline given.

How to Contact/Writers Send complete ms. Responds to queries in 1 month; mss in 6 weeks.

Illustration Buys 25-30 illustrations/issue. Preferred theme or style: Realistic, some stylization. Works on assignment only. Reviews ms/illustration packages from artists. Illustrations only: photocopies, promo sheet, tearsheets, or slides. Résumé optional. Portfolio only if requested. Contact: Art Director. Responds to art samples in 2 months. Samples returned with SASE; samples filed. Credit line given.

Terms Pays on acceptance. Buys all rights for mss. Pays $50 and up for unsolicited articles. Pays illustrators $1,000 for color cover; $25-200 for b&w inside, $100-500 for color inside. Sample copies $3.95 and 9×11 SASE with 4 first-class stamps. Writer's/illustrator's guidelines free with SASE and on Web site.

Tips "Know the magazine's style before submitting. Send for guidelines and sample issue if necessary." Writers: "At *Highlights* we're paying closer attention to acquiring more nonfiction for young readers than we have in the past. We're also looking for more material for kids ages 2-6." Illustrators: "Fresh, imaginative work encouraged. Flexibility in working relationships a plus. Illustrators presenting their work need not confine themselves to just children's illustrations as long as work can translate to our needs. We also use animal illustrations, real and imaginary. We need crafts, puzzles and any activity that will stimulate children mentally and creatively. We are always looking for imaginative cover subjects. Know our publication's standards and content by reading sample issues, not just the guidelines. Avoid tired themes, or put a fresh twist on an old theme so that its style is fun and lively. We'd like to see stories with subtle messages, but the fun of the story should come first. Write what inspires you, not what you think the market needs."

HOPSCOTCH, The Magazine for Girls

The Bluffton News Publishing and Printing Company, P.O. Box 164, Bluffton OH 45817-0164. (419)358-4610. Fax: (419)358-5027. Web site: hopscotchmagazine.com. **Editor:** Marilyn Edwards. Bimonthly magazine. Estab. 1989. Circ. 14,000. For girls from ages 6-12, featuring traditional subjects—pets, games, hobbies, nature, science, sports, etc.—with an emphasis on articles that show girls actively involved in unusual and/or worthwhile activities."

Fiction Picture-oriented material, young readers, middle readers: adventure, animal, history, humorous, nature/environment, sports, suspense/mystery. Does not want to see stories dealing with dating, sex, fashion, hard rock music. Buys 30 mss/year. Average word length: 300-700. Byline given.

Nonfiction Picture-oriented material, young readers, middle readers: animal, arts/crafts, biography, cooking, games/puzzles, geography, hobbies, how-to, humorous, math, nature/environment, science. Does not want to see pieces dealing with dating, sex, fashion, hard rock music. "Need more nonfiction with quality photos about a *Hopscotch*-age girl involved in a worthwhile activity." Buys 46 mss/year. Average word length: 400-700. Byline given.

Poetry Reviews traditional, wholesome, humorous poems. Maximum word length: 300; maximum line length: 20. Will accept 6 submissions/author.

How to Contact/Writers All writers should consult the theme list before sending in articles. To receive a current theme list, send a SASE. Fiction: Send complete ms. Nonfiction: Query or send complete ms. Responds to queries in 2 weeks; mss in 5 weeks. Will consider simultaneous submissions.

Illustration Buys approximately 10 illustrations/issue; buys 60-70 articles/year. "Generally, the illustrations are assigned after we have purchased a piece (usually fiction). Occasionally, we will use a painting—in any given medium—for the cover, and these are usually seasonal." Uses b&w artwork only for inside; color for cover. Reviews ms/illustration packages from artists. Query first or send complete ms with final art. Illustrations only: Send résumé, portfolio, client list and tearsheets. Responds to art samples only if interested and SASE in 1 month. Samples returned with SASE. Credit line given.

Photography Purchases photos separately (cover only) and with accompanying ms only. Looking for photos to accompany article. Model/property releases required. Uses 5×7, b&w prints; 35mm transparencies. Black & white photos should go with ms. Should show girl or girls ages 6-12.

Terms For mss: pays on publication. For mss, artwork and photos, buys first North American serial rights; second serial (reprint rights). Original artwork returned at job's completion. Pays 5¢/word and $5-10/photo. "We always send a copy of the issue to the writer or illustrator." Text and art are treated separately. Pays $200 maximum for color cover; $25-35 for b&w inside. Sample copy for $6 and 8×12 SASE. Writer's/illustrator's/photo guidelines, theme list free for #10 SASE.

Tips "Remember we publish only six issues a year, which means our editorial needs are extremely limited.

Please look at our guidelines and our magazine . . . and remember, we use far more nonfiction than fiction. Guidelines and current theme list can be downloaded from our Web site. If decent photos accompany the piece, it stands an even better chance of being accepted. We believe it is the responsibility of the contributor to come up with photos. Please remember, our readers are 6-12 years—most are 8-10—and your text should reflect that. Many magazines try to entertain first and educate second. We try to do the reverse. Our magazine is more simplistic, like a book to be read from cover to cover. We are looking for wholesome, non-dated material.''

HORSEPOWER, Magazine for Young Horse Lovers

Horse Publications Group, P.O. Box 670, Aurora ON L4G 4J9 Canada. (800)505-7428. Fax: (905)841-1530. E-mail: info@horse-canada.com. Web site: www.horse-canada.com. **Editor:** Susan Stafford. Bimonthly 16-page magazine, bound into Horse Canada, a bimonthly family horse magazine. Estab. 1988. Circ. 17,000. *"Horsepower* offers how-to articles and stories relating to horse care for kids ages 6-16, with a focus on safety.''

- *Horsepower* no longer accepts fiction.

Nonfiction Middle readers, young adults: arts/crafts, biography, careers, fashion, games/puzzles, health, history, hobbies, how-to, humorous, interview/profile, problem-solving, travel. Buys 6-10 mss/year. Average word length: 500-1,200. Byline given.

How to Contact/Writers Fiction: query. Nonfiction: send complete ms. Responds to queries in 6 months; mss in 3 months. Publishes ms 6 months after acceptance. Will consider simultaneous submissions, electronic submission via disk or e-mail, previously published work.

Illustration Buys 3 illustrations/year. Reviews ms/illustration packages from artists. Contact: Editor. Query with samples. Responds only if interested. Samples returned with SASE; samples kept on file. Credit line given.

Photography Look for photos of kids and horses, instructional/educational, relating to riding or horse care. Uses b&w and color 4×6, 5×7, matte or glossy prints. Query with samples. Responds only if interested. Accepts TIFF or JPEG 300 dpi, disk or e-mail. Children on horseback must be wearing riding helmets or photos cannot be published.

Terms Pays on publication. Buys one-time rights for mss. Original artwork returned at job's completion if SASE provided. Pays $50-75 for stories. Additional payment for ms/illustration packages and for photos accompanying articles. Pays illustrators $25-50 for color inside. Pays photographers per photo (range: $10-15). Sample copies for $4.50. Writer's/illustrator's/photo guidelines for SASE.

Tips ''Articles must be easy to understand, yet detailed and accurate. How-to or other educational features must be written by, or in conjunction with, a riding/teaching professional. Fiction is not encouraged, unless it is outstanding and teaches a moral or practical lesson. Note: preference will be given to Canadian writers and photographers due to Canadian content laws. Non-Canadian contributors accepted on a very limited basis.''

HUMPTY DUMPTY'S MAGAZINE

Children's Better Health Institute, 1100 Waterway Blvd., Indianapolis IN 46206. (317)636-8881. Fax: (317)684-8094. Web site: www.humptydumptymag.org. **Editor/Art Director:** Phyllis Lybarger. Magazine published 6 times/year. *HDM* is edited for children ages 4-6. It includes fiction (easy-to-reads; read alouds; rhyming stories; rebus stories), nonfiction articles (some with photo illustrations), poems, crafts, recipes, and puzzles. Content encourages development of better health habits.

- *Humpty Dumpty's* publishes material promoting health and fitness with emphasis on simple activities, poems and fiction.

Fiction Picture-oriented stories: adventure, animal, contemporary, fantasy, folktales, health, humorous, multicultural, nature/environment, problem-solving, science fiction, sports. Also, talking inanimate objects are very difficult to do well. Beginners (and maybe everyone) should avoid these.'' Buys 8-10 mss/year. Maximum word length: 300. Byline given.

Nonfiction Picture-oriented articles: animal, arts/crafts, concept, games/puzzles, health, how-to, humorous, nature/environment, no-cook recipes, science, social issues, sports. Buys 6-10 mss/year. Prefers very short nonfiction pieces—200 words maximum. Byline given. Send ms with SASE if you want ms returned.

How to Contact/Writers Send complete ms. Nonfiction: Send complete ms with bibliography if applicable. ''No queries, please!'' Responds to mss in 3 months. Send seasonal material at least 8 months in advance.

Illustration Buys 5-8 illustrations/issue; 30-48 illustrations/year. Preferred theme or style: Realistic or cartoon. Works on assignment only. Illustrations only. Query with slides, printed pieces or photocopies. Samples are not returned; samples filed. Responds to art samples only if interested. Credit line given.

Terms Writers: Pays on publication. Artists: Pays within 2 months. Buys all rights. ''One-time book rights may be returned if author can provide name of interested book publisher and tentative date of publication.'' Pays up to 22¢/word for stories/articles; payment varies for poems and activities. 10 complimentary issues are provided to author with check. Pays $275 for color cover illustration; $35-90 per page b&w inside; $70-155 for color inside. Sample copies for $3.95. Writer's/illustrator's guidelines free with SASE.

INSIGHT

Because Life is Full of Decisions, 55 W. Oak Ridge Dr., Hagerstown MD 21740. (301)393-4038. Fax: (301)393-4055. E-mail: insight@rhpa.org. Web site: www.insightmagazine.org. **Contact:** Dwain Nielson Esmond. Weekly magazine. Estab. 1970. Circ. 14,000. "Our readers crave true stories written by teens or written about teens that convey a strong spiritual point or portray a spiritual truth." 100% of publication aimed at teen market.

Nonfiction Young adults: animal, biography, fashion, health, humorous, interview/profile, multicultural, nature/environment, problem-solving, social issues, sports, travel: first-person accounts preferred. Buys 200 mss/year. Average word length: 500-1,500. Byline given.

Poetry Publishes poems written by teens. Maximum length: 250-500 words.

How to Contact/Writers Nonfiction: Send complete ms. Responds to queries in 2 months. Publishes ms 6-12 months after acceptance. Will consider simultaneous submissions, electronic submission via disk or modem, previously published work.

Illustration Works on assignment only. Reviews ms/illustration packages from artists. Query. Illustrations only: Query with samples. Samples kept on file. Credit line given.

Photography Looking for photos that will catch a young person's eye with unique elements such as juxtaposition. Model/property release required; captions not required but helpful. Uses color prints and 35mm, $2\frac{1}{4} \times 2\frac{1}{4}$, 4×5, 8×10 transparencies. Query with samples; provide business card, promotional literature or tearsheets to be kept on file. Responds only if interested.

Terms Pays on publication. Buys first North American serial rights for mss. Buys one-time rights for artwork and photos. Original artwork returned at job's completion. Pays $10-100 for stories/articles. Pays illustrators $100-300 for b&w (cover), color cover, b&w (inside), or color inside. Pays photographers by the project. Sample copies for 9×14 SAE and 4 first-class stamps.

Tips "Do your best to make your work look 'hip,' 'cool,' appealing to young people."

JACK AND JILL

Children's Better Health Institute, 1100 Waterway Blvd., P.O. Box 567, Indianapolis IN 46202. (317)634-1100. Fax: (317)684-8094. Web site: www.cbhi.org/magazines/jackandjill/index.shtml. **Editor:** Daniel Lee. **Art Director:** Jennifer Webber. Magazine for children ages 7-10, published 6 times/year. Estab. 1938. Circ. 360,000. "Write entertaining and imaginative stories *for* kids, not just *about* them. Writers should understand what is funny to kids, what's important to them, what excites them. Don't write from an adult 'kids are so cute' perspective. We're also looking for health and healthful lifestyle stories and articles, but don't be preachy."

● See Roundtable on page 77 for an interview with *Jack and Jill* editor Daniel Lee.

Fiction Young readers and middle readers: adventure, contemporary, folktales, health, history, humorous, nature, sports. Buys 30-35 mss/year. Average word length: 700. Byline given.

Nonfiction Young readers, middle readers: animal, arts/crafts, cooking, games/puzzles, history, hobbies, how-to, humorous, interview/profile, nature, science, sports. Buys 8-10 mss/year. Average word length: 500. Byline given.

Poetry Reviews poetry.

How to Contact/Writers Fiction/nonfiction: Send complete ms. Queries not accepted. Responds to mss in 3 months. Guidelines by request with a #10 SASE.

Illustration Buys 15 illustrations/issue; 90 illustrations/year. Responds only if interested. Samples not returned; samples filed. Credit line given.

Terms Pays on publication; up to 17¢/word. Pays illustrators $275 for color cover; $35-90 for b&w, $70-155 for color inside. Pays photographers negotiated rate. Sample copies $1.25. Buys all rights to mss and one-time rights to photos.

Tips Publishes writing/art/photos by children.

KEYS FOR KIDS

CBH Ministries, Box 1001, Grand Rapids MI 49501-1001. (616)647-4971. Fax: (616)647-4950. E-mail: hazel@cbh ministries.org. Web site: www.cbhministries.org. **Fiction Editor:** Hazel Marett. Bimonthly devotional booklet. Estab. 1982. "This is a devotional booklet for children and is also widely used for family devotions."

Fiction Young readers, middle readers: religious. Buys 60 mss/year. Average word length: 400.

How to Contact/Writers Fiction: Send complete ms. Will consider simultaneous submissions, e-mail submissions, previously published work.

Terms Pays on acceptance. Buys reprint rights or first rights for mss. Pays $25 for stories. Sample copies free for SAE 6×9 and 3 first-class stamps. Writer's guidelines for SASE.

Tips "Be sure to *follow* guidelines after studying sample copy of the publication."

Jan Fields

Advice on children's magazine writing:
'Have fun with it'

Jan Fields loves to write. "For me, writing is much more like trying to control flood waters." Fields took a circuitous approach to children's literature. She started with newspaper writing, then moved on to freelance writing and manuscript editing. Next came being a writing instructor at the local community college. Finally Fields realized what she really loved was writing for and about children. "I am fascinated by the whole beast—the whole world that is children's publishing."

Fields kept herself diversified even after she figured out what she loves to do. A wife and mother, Fields balances many roles. Not only has she written several books and hundreds of articles, she teaches for the Institute of Children's Literature and runs *Kid Magazine Writers*.

Kid Magazine Writers (*KMW*) is an e-zine Fields started several years ago when she realized there was a need for a resource for people who write for children's magazines. "I waited for someone else to discover that and launch a magazine," she says. "I eventually figured out that wasn't happening. So, I started *KMW* because I felt that if I'm going to complain about something, I should be part of fixing it." Fields got her husband to help her with the technical stuff and launched the e-zine into her already busy life.

Working online has been a new experience for Fields. "It's much easier and faster for me to create a Web page than it was (back in the early '80s when I was learning print publication) to lay out a newspaper page. And one person can do a lot more." Yet the digital age has raised some difficulties. "Expectations have risen. People e-mail me and if I don't answer in an hour, they'll e-mail again. Folks just expect a quick answer to anything they need to know." Something that most people don't realize is that "the cost in time is incredible."

The online format gives Fields enough of an advantage over print publications to keep her going. For example, "I can 'scoop' print magazines on market news because I don't have long lead times from printing." But probably the best part of having the magazine online is that it gets to exist at all. Fields didn't have the money to invest in a print publication, but she could afford the time. "*Kid Magazine Writers* couldn't survive as a print publication, but it thrives online."

KMW thrives because it can change constantly. The content and features change monthly, and what gets published is determined by a couple factors. "Partly it's determined by what comes in," Fields explains, "but I also write part of the content for virtually every month and my contribution totally depends upon what high horse I'm up on." There are some things that do stay constant. "Every month I have industry information. Every month I have something on the writing life—either practical or philosophical/inspirational. And every month I have something on technique. I think these are the three sides of a successful

Kid Magazine WRITERS

MARKET GUIDE

Choose a Title Category ▼

ABOUT US   WRITE FOR US   ISSUE 30, FEBRUARY 2007   CONTACT US   PRIVACY POLICY

MARKET INFO

Editor Speak

Special Report

Inside Markets

WORKING DAY

Kids Write

In My Office

In the Beginning

I'm Published

TECHNIQUE

Meter Readers

Storytellers

That's A Fact

ARCHIVES

Editors Speak

Special Report

HOME

Writer's Digest 101 TOP WEB SITES 2006

Sign up to receive update notifications

Email address here

Submit   Reset

IN THIS ISSUE

We're finally having winter here in New England and winter's chill is a great time to write. It's also a great time to explore new magazines. This month we mention several new magazines in Inside Markets, and we really get to know one new market with both a Special Report and an Editors Speak interview. So click on over to get a peek at *Relate* magazine and its delightful editor, Mary Dohack. This is one market you'll be glad to know.

ALSO IN THIS FEBRUARY ISSUE:

Check out Kids Write for an example of one young writer who found out the key to success isn't age specific – it's all in the work and the determination!

Then, click on over to In the Beginning for a great look at writing at home – how does a work at home writer keep life from pushing aside writing?

Never get enough info on tracking submissions? Check out In My Office for a look at manuscript tracking for old-fashioned writers – like me.

And don't miss I'm Published, for an inspiring story of how one writer found publication early and often!

If you read our Technique pieces this month, you may get a flash of déjà vu! They're all from past issues of *Kid Magazine Writers* while we wait from some fresh wisdom from our readers – how do you perfect your technique in fiction, nonfiction, and poetry? We'd love to know.

Kid Magazine Writers is a monthly e-zine for writers of children's literature run by Jan Fields. It features articles on writing techniques, business tips, and advice—both practical and inspirational—on the writer's life. Fields especially loves the "Working Day" area of her site because it has "very cozy, writer-to-writer chatty stuff. The things there help people feel less alone."

writing career. I will always feed those three sides, but the subcategories can vary.''

While some of the specifics in *KMW* may change, some things remain in constant demand. ''We get the most hits to the editor area. Everyone wants to hear from editors. The whole market section is probably the first stop of most of our more successful writers because once you're selling regularly—you're always looking for new markets, better market info, and insider tips.'' Visitors can find tips on how to write better query letters to some new publishing opportunities.

One of Field's favorite sections is the technique area. ''Within whatever your target specialty is—it's so important to always be honing your technique.'' Fields has reason to be proud of this area. ''When I get positive e-mails from editors of magazines, it's nearly always about articles in this area.''

What many new writers really love is the ''Working Day'' area. ''I think that much of the 'Working Day' area is just very cozy, writer-to-writer chatty stuff. The things in there help people feel less alone. We get a lot of e-mail about that section too and how inspirational it is for writers who are struggling with fitting writing and life into a smooth whole.''

One of the difficulties both new and seasoned writers have with the rise of Internet publishing is figuring out which sites and e-zines are reputable. Fields suggests these guidelines:

- How long has it been online? Anything new stands the chance of folding quickly. Also, the quality of submissions grows over time so an older magazine tends to have a better reputation for quality.
- Who is running it? If the site is run by someone with real experience in the business, I'm much more confident about how good the material will be and how good the editing will be.
- Does it pay? That seems snobbish coming from an editor who doesn't pay, but for children's e-magazines, pay is a big part of reputation. Paying writers is a big commitment so magazines that pay are either picky about quality or sadly transient.

Writing for children's magazines is different from writing for adults. Fields maintains that one thing is vital if you want to write for children's magazines: ''Read children's magazines. There is nothing, nothing, *nothing* you can do that is more important in this field. If you're not reading children's magazines, you're likely to get more rejections than acceptances. Reading fuels your creativity in the directions that will work for the magazines. And you'll internalize the unique pacing, plot and scene structure of the short story.''

While reading to see what is there is important, Fields warns writers to be aware of what is *not* there as well. ''I'm sometimes startled by folks who target *Highlights*, for example, by saying they've read the magazine since they were kids—but they're sending a story where a bully smacks a kid around in the school yard. *Highlights* has a very strict 'no violence' policy.'' If you don't want more rejections slips, be aware of each magazine's standards and guidelines.

That advice extends to writing activities for children's magazines. ''You need to be familiar with your target magazine (that's code for *read it*) to send the right activity.'' Along with knowing the magazine, ''lively and fun should be your watch words.'' These watch words apply to nonfiction writing as well, with one twist. ''You have to be tightly focused. Don't write about camels—write about the feral camels of Australia. Drill down to the most fascinating aspect of the subject, the part that captures you, and expand that into your article.''

For Fields, the key to writing for children is to have fun with it. ''If you're reading what's being published and not enjoying it, you're probably not destined to write for children. Find the magazines that still catch your imagination and excite you and learn from them. You're probably the right person to write for them. There is an incredible amount of joy in writing for children and reading is the key to finding it.''

—*Rachel McDonald*

KID ZONE

Scott Publications, LLC, 801 W. Norton Ave., Suite 200, Muskegon, MI 49441. (616)475-0414. Fax: (616)475-0411. E-mail: ahuizenga@scottpublications.com. Web site: www.scottpublications.com. **Articles Editor:** Anne Huizenga. Bi-monthly magazine. Estab. 2000. Circ. 65,000. Kid Zone is a crafts and activities magazine for 4-12 year olds. "We publish projects, trivia, recipes, games, puzzles, and kid-friendly features on a variety of topics."

Nonfiction Picture-oriented material, middle readers: animal, arts/crafts, cooking, how-to, multicultural, nature/environment, science. Buys 20 mss/year. Average word length: 300-700. Byline given.

How to Contact/Writers Nonfiction: Send complete ms. Publishes ms 6-12 months after acceptance. Will consider simultaneous submissions, e-mail submissions.

Illustration Buys 6 illustrations/issue. Uses color artwork only. Works on assignment only. Illustrations only: Send postcard sample. Contact: Anne Huizenga, editor. Responds only if interested. Samples filed. Credit line sometimes given.

Photography Uses photos with accompanying ms only. Model/property release required. Uses color prints or digital images. Responds only if interested.

Terms Pays on publication. Buys world rights for mss. Buys first world rights for artwork. Pays $10-$50 for stories. Sample copies for $4.95 plus SASE. Writer's guidelines for SASE.

Tips "Nonfiction writers who can provide extras to coincide with their submission (photos, games, project ideas, recipes) are more likely to be selected also make sure that you have actually looked at our magazine."

▣ THE KIDS HALL OF FAME NEWS

The Kids Hall of Fame, 3 Ibsen Court, Dix Hills NY 11746. (631)242-9105. Fax: (631)242-8101. E-mail: VictoriaNesnick@TheKidsHallofFame.com. Web site: www.TheKidsHallofFame.com. **Publisher:** Dr. Victoria Nesnick. **Art/Photo Editor:** Amy Gilvary. Online publication. Estab. 1998. "We spotlight and archive extraordinary positive achievements of contemporary and historical kids internationally under age 20. These inspirational stories are intended to provide positive peer role models and empower others to say, 'If that kid can do it, so can I,' or 'I can do better.' Our magazine is the prelude to The Kids Hall of Fame set of books (one volume per age) and museum."

How to Contact/Writers Query with published clips or send complete mss with SASE for response. Go to Web site for sample stories and for The Kids Hall of Fame nomination form.

Tips "Nomination stories must be positive and inspirational, and whenever possible, address the 7 items listed in the 'Your Story and Photo' page of our Web site. Request writers' guidelines and list of suggested nominees. Day and evening telephone queries acceptable."

KIDZ CHAT®

Standard Publishing. Web site: www.standardpub.com. **Editor:** Elaina Meyers. Weekly magazine. Circ. 55,000.
- *Kidz Chat®* has decided to reuse much of the material that was a part of the first publication cycle. They will not be sending out theme lists, sample copies or writers guidelines or accepting any unsolicited material because of this policy.

LADYBUG, The Magazine for Young Children

70 E. Lake St., Suite 300, Chicago IL 60603. (312)701-1720. **Editor:** Alice Letvin. **Art Director:** Suzanne Beck. Monthly magazine. Estab. 1990. Circ. 130,000. Literary magazine for children 2-6, with stories, poems, activities, songs and picture stories.

Fiction Picture-oriented material: adventure, animal, fantasy, folktales, humorous, multicultural, nature/environment, problem-solving, science fiction, sports, suspense/mystery. "Open to any easy fiction stories." Buys 50 mss/year. Story length: limit 800 words. Byline given.

Nonfiction Picture-oriented material: activities, animal, arts/crafts, concept, cooking, humorous, math, nature/environment, problem-solving, science. Buys 35 mss/year. Story length: limit 800 words.

Poetry Reviews poems, 20-line maximum length; limit submissions to 5 poems. Uses lyrical, humorous, simple language , action rhymes.

How to Contact/Writers Fiction/nonfiction: Send complete ms. Queries not accepted. Responds to mss in 6 months. Publishes ms up to 3 years after acceptance. Will consider simultaneous submissions if informed. Submissions without SASE will be discarded.

Illustration Buys 12 illustrations/issue; 145 illustrations/year. Prefers "bright colors; all media, but use watercolor and acrylics most often; same size as magazine is preferred but not required." To be considered for future assignments: Submit promo sheet, slides, tearsheets, color and b&w photocopies. Responds to art samples in 3 months. Submissions without SASE will be discarded.

Terms Pays on publication for mss; after delivery of completed assignment for illustrators. Rights purchased vary. Original artwork returned at job's completion. Pays 25¢/word for prose; $3/line for poetry. Pays $750 for color (cover) illustration, $50-100 for b&w (inside) illustration, $250/page for color (inside). Sample copy for $5. Writer's/illustrator's guidelines free for SASE or available on Web site, FAQ at www.cricketmag.com.

Tips Writers: "Get to know several young children on an individual basis. Respect your audience. We want less cute, condescending or 'preachy-teachy' material. Less gratuitous anthropomorphism. More rich, evocative language, sense of joy or wonder. Keep in mind that people come in all colors, sizes, physical conditions. Be inclusive in creating characters. Set your manuscript aside for at least a month, then reread critically." Illustrators: "Include examples, where possible, of children, animals, and—most important—action and narrative (i.e., several scenes from a story, showing continuity and an ability to maintain interest)." (See listings for *Babybug*, *Cicada*, *Cricket*, *Muse* and *Spider*.)

LIVE WIRE®

Standard Publishing. Web site: www.standardpub.com. **Editor:** Elaina Meyers. Published quarterly in weekly parts. Circ. 40,000.
- *Live Wire*® has decided to reuse much of the material that was a part of the first publication cycle. They will not be sending out theme lists, sample copies, or writers guidelines or accepting any unsolicited material because of this policy.

MUSE

Carus Publishing, 140 S. Dearborn St., Suite 1450, Chicago IL 60603. (312)701-1720. Fax: (312)701-1728. E-mail: muse@caruspub.com. Web site: www.cricketmag.com. **Editor:** Diana Lutz. **Art Director:** Karen Kohn. **Photo Editor:** Carol Parden. Estab. 1996. Circ. 50,000. "The goal of *Muse* is to give as many children as possible access to the most important ideas and concepts underlying the principal areas of human knowledge. Articles should meet the highest possible standards of clarity and transparency aided, wherever possible, by a tone of skepticism, humor, and irreverence."

Nonfiction Middle readers, young adult: animal, arts, history, math, nature/environment, problem-solving, science, social issues.

How to Contact/Writers *Muse* is not accepting unsolicited mss or queries. All articles are commissioned. To be considered for assignments, experienced science writers may send a résumé and 3 published clips.

Illustration Buys 6 illustrations/issue; 40 illustrations/year. Uses color artwork only. Works on assignment only. Responds only if interested. Samples returned with SASE. Credit line given.

Photography Needs vary. Query with samples to photo editor.

NATIONAL GEOGRAPHIC KIDS

National Geographic Society, 1145 17th St. NW, Washington DC 20036-4688. (202)857-7000. Fax: (202)775-6112. Web site: www.nationalgeographic.com/ngkids. **Editor:** Melina Gerosa Bellows. **Art Director:** Jonathan Halling. **Photo Director:** Jay Sumner. Monthly magazine. Estab. 1975. Circ. 1.3 million.

NATURE FRIEND MAGAZINE

4253 Woodcock Lane, Dayton, VA 22821 (540)867-0764. Fax: (540)867-9516. Web site: www.naturefriendmaga zine.com. **Articles Editor:** Kevin Shank. Monthly magazine. Estab. 1983. Circ. 10,000.

Fiction Picture-oriented material, conversational, no talking animal stories.

Nonfiction Picture-oriented material: animal, how-to, nature, photo-essays. No talking animal stories. No evolutionary material. Buys 50 mss/year. Average word length: 500. Byline given.

Photography Submit on CD with a color printout. Photo guidelines free with SASE.

Terms Pays on publication. Buy one-time rights. Pays $75 for front cover photo; $50 for back cover photo, $25 inside photo. Offers sample copy is and writer's/photographer's guidelines for $8.

Tips Needs stories about unique animals or nature phenomena. "Please examine samples and writer's guide before submitting." The best way to learn what we use is to be a subscriber.

NEW MOON: The Magazine for Girls & Their Dreams

New Moon Publishing, Inc., 2 W. First St., #101, Duluth MN 55802. (218)728-5507. Fax: (218)728-0314. E-mail: girl@newmoon.org. Web site: www.newmoon.org. **Executive Editor:** Kate Freeborn. Bimonthly magazine. Estab. 1992. Circ. 30,000. "*New Moon* is for every girl who wants her voice heard and her dreams taken seriously. *New Moon* portrays strong female role models of all ages, backgrounds and cultures now and in the past."

Fiction Middle readers, young adults: adventure, contemporary, fantasy, folktales, history, humorous, multicultural, nature/environment, problem-solving, religious, science fiction, sports, suspense/mystery, travel. Buys 6 mss/year. Average word length: 1,200-1,600. Byline given.

Nonfiction Middle readers, young adults: animal, arts/crafts, biography, careers, cooking, games/puzzles, health, history, hobbies, humorous, interview/profile, math, multicultural, nature/environment, problem-solving, science, social issues, sports, travel, stories about real girls. Does not want to see how-to stories. Wants more stories about real girls doing real things written *by girls*. Buys 6-12 adult-written mss/year; 30 girl-written mss/year. Average word length: 600. Byline given.

How to Contact/Writers Fiction/Nonfiction: Does not return or acknowledge unsolicited mss. Send copies only. Responds only if interested. Will consider simultaneous and e-mail submissions.

Illustration Buys 6-12 illustrations/year from freelancers. *New Moon* seeks 4-color cover illustrations. Reviews ms/illustrations packages from artists. Query. Submit ms with rough sketches. Illustration only: Query; send portfolio and tearsheets. Samples not returned; samples filed. Responds in 6 months only if interested. Credit line given.

Terms Pays on publication. Buys all rights for mss. Buys one-time rights, reprint rights, for artwork. Original artwork returned at job's completion. Pays 6-12¢/word for stories and articles. Pays in contributor's copies. Pays illustrators $400 for color cover; $50-300 for color inside. Sample copies for $7. Writer's/cover art guidelines for SASE or available on Web site.

Tips "Please refer to a copy of *New Moon* to understand the style and philosophy of the magazine. Writers and artists who understand our goals have the best chance of publication. We're looking for stories about real girls, women's careers, and historical profiles. We publish girl's and women's writing only." Publishes writing/art/ photos by girls.

NICK JR. FAMILY MAGAZINE

Nickelodeon Magazine Group, 1515 Broadway, 37th Floor, New York NY 10036. (212)846-4985. Fax: (212)846-1690. Web site: www.nickjr.com/magazine. **Deputy Editor:** Wendy Smolen. **Creative Director:** Don Morris. Published 9 times/year. Estab. 1999. Circ. 1,100,000. A magazine where kids play to learn and parents learn to play. 30% of publication aimed at juvenile market.

Fiction Picture-oriented material: adventure, animal, contemporary, humorous, multicultural, nature/environment, problem-solving, sports. Byline sometimes given.

Nonfiction Picture-oriented material: animal, arts/crafts, concept, cooking, games/puzzles, hobbies, how-to, humorous, math, multicultural, nature/environment, problem-solving, science, social issues, sports. Byline sometimes given.

How to Contact/Writers Fiction/nonfiction: Query or submit complete ms. Responds to queries/mss in 3-12 weeks.

Illustration Only interested in agented material. Works on assignment only. Reviews ms/illustration packages from artists. Query or send ms with dummy. Contact: Don Morris, creative director. Illustrations only: arrange portfolio review; send résumé, promo sheet and portfolio. Responds only if interested. Samples not returned; samples kept on file. Credit line sometimes given.

Tips "Writers should study the magazine before submitting stories. Read-Together Stories must include an interactive element that invited children to participate in telling the story: a repeating line, a fill-in-the-blank rhyme, or rebus pictures."

ODYSSEY, Adventures in Science

Cobblestone Publishing Company, 30 Grove St., Suite C, Peterborough NH 03458. (603)924-7209. Fax: (603)924-7380. E-mail: odyssey@ caruspub.com. Web site: www.odysseymagazine.com. **Editor:** Elizabeth E. Lindstrom. **Executive Director:** Lou Waryncia. **Art Director:** Ann Dillon. Magazine published 9 times/year. Estab. 1979. Circ. 22,000. Magazine covers general science and technology for children ages 10-16. All material must relate to the theme of a specific upcoming issue in order to be considered.

• *Odyssey* themes can be found on Web site: www.odysseymagazine.com.

Fiction Middle readers and young adults/teens: science fiction, science, astronomy. Does not want to see anything not theme-related. Average word length: 900-1,200 words.

Nonfiction Middle readers and young adults/teens: interiors, activities. Don't send anything not theme-related. Average word length: 750-1,200, depending on section article is used in.

How to Contact/Writers Query by mail. "A query must consist of all of the following to be considered (please use nonerasable paper): a brief cover letter stating the subject and word length of the proposed article; a detailed one-page outline explaining the information to be presented in the article; an extensive bibliography of materials/interviews the author intends to use in preparing the article; a SASE. Writers new to *Odyssey* should send a writing sample with query. If you would like to know if your query has been received, please also include a stamped postcard that requests acknowledgment of receipt. In all correspondence, please include your complete address as well as a telephone number and e-mail address where you can be reached. A writer may send as many queries for one issue as he or she wishes, but each query must have a separate cover letter, outline, bibliography, and SASE. Telephone queries are not accepted. Handwritten queries will not be considered. Queries may be submitted at any time ."

Illustration Buys 4 illustrations/issue; 36 illustrations/year. Works on assignment only. Reviews ms/illustration packages from artists. Query. Contact: Beth Lindstrom, editor. Illustration only: Query with samples. Send tearsheets, photocopies. Responds in 2 weeks. Samples returned with SASE; samples not filed. Original artwork returned upon job's completion (upon written request).

Photography Wants photos pertaining to any of our forthcoming themes. Uses color prints; 35mm transparencies, digital images. Photographers should send unsolicited photos by mail on speculation.

Terms Pays on publication. Buys all rights for mss and artwork. Pays 20-25¢/word for stories/articles. Covers are assigned and paid on an individual basis. Pays photographers per photo ($15-100 for b&w; $25-100 for color). Sample copy for $4.95 and SASE with $2 postage. Writer's/illustrator's/photo guidelines for SASE. (See listings for *AppleSeeds, Calliope, Cobblestone, Dig,* and *Faces*.)

ON COURSE, A Magazine for Teens

General Council of the Assemblies of God, 1445 Boonville Ave., Springfield MO 65802-1894. (417)862-2781. Fax: (417)862-1693. E-mail: oncourse@ag.org. Web site: www.oncourse.ag.org. **Editor:** Amber Weigand-Buckley. **Art Director:** Ryan Strong. Quarterly magazine. Estab. 1991. Circ. 160,000. *On Course* is a magazine to empower students to grow in a real-life relationship with Christ.

● *On Course* no longer uses illustrations, only photos.

Fiction Young adults: Christian discipleship, contemporary, humorous, multicultural, problem-solving, sports. Average word length: 800. Byline given.

Nonfiction Young adults: careers, interview/profile, multicultural, religion, social issues, college life, Christian discipleship.

How to Contact/Writers Works on assignment basis only. Resumes and writing samples will be considered for inclusion in Writer's File to receive story assignments.

Photography Buys photos from freelancers. "Teen life, church life, college life; unposed; often used for illustrative purposes." Model/property releases required. Uses color glossy prints and 35mm or $2\frac{1}{4} \times 2\frac{1}{4}$ transparencies. Query with samples; send business card, promotional literature, tearsheets or catalog. Responds only if interested.

Terms Pays on acceptance. Buys first or reprint rights for mss. Buys one-time rights for photographs. Pays 10¢/word for stories/articles. Pays illustrators and photographers "as negotiated." Sample copies free for 9×11 SAE. Writer's guidelines for SASE.

Ⓝ PASSPORT

Sunday School Curriculum, 6401 The Paseo, Kansas City MO 64131-1284. (816)333-7000. Fax: (816)333-4439. E-mail: sweatherwax@nazarene.org. Web site: www.nazarene.org. **Editor:** Ryan R. Pettit. Weekly take-home paper. "*Passport* looks for a casual, witty approach to Christian themes. We want hot topics relevant to preteens."

POCKETS, Devotional Magazine for Children

The Upper Room, 1908 Grand Ave., P.O. Box 340004, Nashville TN 37203-0004. (615)340-7333. Fax: (615)340-7267. E-mail: pockets@upperroom.org. Web site: www.pockets.org. **Articles/Fiction Editor:** Lynn W. Gilliam. **Art Director:** Chris Schechner, 408 Inglewood Dr., Richardson TX 75080. Magazine published 11 times/year. Estab. 1981. Circ. 99,000. "*Pockets* is a Christian devotional magazine for children ages 6-11. Stories should help children experience a Christian lifestyle that is not always a neatly wrapped moral package but is open to the continuing revelation of God's will."

Fiction Picture-oriented, young readers, middle readers: adventure, contemporary, occasional folktales, multicultural, nature/environment, problem-solving, religious. Does not accept violence or talking animal stories. Buys 25-30 mss/year. Average word length: 600-1,400. Byline given. *Pockets* also accepts short-short stories (no more than 600 words) for children 5-7. Buys 11 mss/year.

Nonfiction Picture-oriented, young readers, middle readers: cooking, games/puzzles. "*Pockets* seeks biographical sketches of persons, famous or unknown, whose lives reflect their Christian commitment, written in a way that appeals to children." Does not accept how-to articles. "Nonfiction reads like a story." Multicultural needs include: stories that feature children of various racial/ethnic groups and do so in a way that is true to those depicted. Buys 10 mss/year. Average word length: 400-1,000. Byline given.

How to Contact/Writers Fiction/nonfiction: Send complete ms. "We do not accept queries." Responds to mss in 6 weeks. Will consider simultaneous submissions.

Illustration Buys 25-35 illustrations/issue. Preferred theme or style: varied; both 4-color. Works on assignment only. Illustrations only: Send promo sheet, tearsheets.

POGO STICK

Stone Lightning Press, 1300 Kicker Rd., Tuscaloosa AL 35404. (205)553-2284. E-mail: lillskm@gmail.com. **Articles Editor:** Lillian Kopaska-Merkel. **Art Director:** Lillian Kopaska-Merkel. Quarterly digest-sized with saddle stitching. Estab. 2005. Publishes "fantasy and realistic fiction, poems, short stories, jokes, riddles, and art for and by kids under 17." Entire publication aimed at (and written by) juvenile market.

Fiction Young Readers: adventure, animal, fantasy, humorous, multicultural, nature/environment, problem-solving, suspense/mystery. Middle Readers: adventure, animal, fantasy, humorous, multicultural, nature/environment, suspense/mystery. Young Adults/Teens: adventure, animal, fantasy, humorous, multicultural, nature/environment, suspense/mystery. Average word length: 50-2,000. Byline given.

Nonfiction Young readers, middle readers, young adults/teens: arts/crafts, games/puzzles.

Poetry Seeks fantasy, child-appropriate poetry. Max length: 100 words. Max of 6 poems/submission.

How To Contact/Writers Fiction: Send complete ms. Responds to queries in 2 months. Considers simultaneous submissions.

Illustration Black & white artwork only. For first contact, query with samples. Contact: Rain Kennedy, art director. Responds in 2 months. Samples returned with SASE. Credit line given.

Terms Pays on publication. Buys first North American serial rights.Pays with contributor copies. Sample copies available for $3.50. Writer's guidelines free for SASE. Illustrator's guidelines free for SASE. Publishes work by children.

Tips "Always read guidelines first."

POSITIVE TEENS

Accentuating the Positive in Today's Teens, P.O. Box 301126, Boston MA 02130-0010. (617)522-2961. Fax: (617)522-2961. E-mail: info@positiveteensmag.com. Web site: www.positiveteensmag.com. **Contact:** Susan Manning, publisher/editor-in-chief. Bimonthly magazine. Estab. 1997. Circ. 60,000. "*Positive Teens* magazine uses its pages to accentuate the positive in the talents, lives, skill and voices of the youth of today. *Positive Teens* encourages young adults from 12-21 to take an interest in issues directly or indirectly affecting their schools and community, their future and the world. *Positive Teens* magazine is inclusive of all youth, male and female, of all ethnic, racial and religious groups, of all sexual orientations and all physical abilities."

Fiction Buys 2-5 mss/year. 1,200 words max.

Nonfiction Young adults/teens: biography, careers, games/puzzles, health, history, hobbies, how-to, interview/profile, multicultural, problem-solving, social issues, sports, travel. Buys 3-10 mss/year from freelancers. Average word length/articles: 500-1,200. Byline given.

Poetry No length requirements. Limit submissions to 6-8 poems.

How to Contact/Writers Fiction: query; nonfiction: Send complete mss. Responds to queries/mss in 2-3 months. Publishes ms 1-3 months after acceptance. Will consider simultaneous submission and e-mail submissions.

Illustration Buys 2-4 illustrations/year. Review ms/illustration packages from youth only. Send ms with dummy to Susan Manning, publisher. Responds in 1-2 months only if interested. Samples returned with SASE; samples filed. Credit line given.

Photography Uses photos relating to teen and young adult interests. Model/property release required; captions required. Uses 4×6 and 8¾×11½ prints. Send unsolicited photos by mail. Responds in 1-2 months only if interested.

Terms Pays on publication. Buys reprint rights, exclusive for 18 months. Originals returned at job's completion with SASE. Pays $5-35 for stories/articles. Pays illustrators $5-25 for b&w color/insider. Pays photographers $5-25. Sample $3 for back issues; $4.50 for new issues plus $1.35 postage. Writer's/illustrator's/photographer's guidelines for SASE.

Tips "Adult writers (those over the age of 25) should understand that the audience *Positive Teens* is targeting is teens and young adults, not children. Articles that we receive with a child's theme would never be considered for publication. Also, we prefer nonfiction article from adult writers—interviews, lifestyle, sports, etc. *Positive Teens* magazine featured artwork created by teenagers and young adults, but we would consider illustrations or photographs that would be an accompaniment to a written article."

⃞Ⓝ RAINBOW RUMPUS, The Magazine for Kids with LGBT Parents

P.O. Box 6881, Minneapolis MN 55406. (612)721-6442. Fax: (621)729-1420. E-mail: fictionandpoetry@rainbowrumpus.org. Web site: www.rainbowrumpus.org. **Articles Editor:** Laura Matanah. **Fiction Editor:** Beth Wallace. **Art/photo Acquisitions:** Laura Matanah. Monthly online magazine. Estab. 2005. Circ. 100 visits/day. "*Rainbow Rumpus* is an online children's magazine for 4- to 14-year-old children with lesbian, gay, bisexual or transgender parents. We are looking for children's fiction, nonfiction and poetry. *Rainbow Rumpus* publishes and reviews work that is written from the point of view of children with LGBT parents of who are connected to the LGBT community, celebrates the diversity of LGBT-headed families, and is of high quality." 90% of publication aimed at young readers.

Fiction All levels: adventure, animal, contemporary, fantasy, folktales, history, humorous, multicultural, nature/environment, problem solving, science fiction, sports, suspense/mystery. Buys 12 mss/year. Average word length: 800-5,000. Byline given.

Nonfiction All levels: interview/profile, social issues. Buys 12 mss/year. Average word length: 800-5,000. Byline given.

Poetry Maximum of 5 poems per submission.

How To Contact/Writers Send complete ms. Responds to mss in 6 weeks. Considers electronic submission and previously published work.

Illustration Buys 2 illustrations/issue. Uses both b&w and color artwork. Reviews ms/illustration packages from artists: Query. Illustrations only: query with samples. Contact: Laura Matanah, publisher. Samples not returned; samples filed depending on the level of interest. Credit line given.

Terms Pays on publication. Buys first rights for mss; may request print anthology and audio or recording rights. Buys first rights rights for artwork. Pays $15 or 3¢ a word (whichever is greater) for stories and aritcles. Pays illustrators $100 for b&w; $300 for color. Writer's guidelines available on Web site.

Tips "If you wish to submit nonfiction, please query by e-mail to editor@rainbowrumpus.org."

RANGER RICK

National Wildlife Federation, 11100 Wildlife Center Dr., Reston VA 20190. (703)438-6000. Web site: www.nwf. org/rangerrick. **Editor:** Mary Dalheim. **Design Director:** Donna Miller. Monthly magazine. Circ. 550,000. "Our audience ranges from ages 7 to 12, though we aim the reading level of most material at 9-year-olds or fourth graders."

● Ranger Rick does not accept submissions or queries.

Fiction Middle readers: animal (wildlife), fables, fantasy, humorous, multicultural, plays, science fiction. Average word length: 900. Byline given.

Nonfiction Middle readers: animal (wildlife), conservation, humorous, nature/environment, outdoor adventure, travel. Buys 15-20 mss/year. Average word length: 900. Byline given.

How to Contact/Writers No longer accepting unsolicited queries/mss.

Illustration Buys 5-7 illustrations/issue. Preferred theme: nature, wildlife. Works on assignment only. Illustrations only: Send résumé, tearsheets. Responds to art samples in 2 months.

Terms Pays on acceptance. Buys exclusive first-time worldwide rights and non-exclusive worldwide rights thereafter to reprint, transmit, and distribute the work in any form or medium. Original artwork returned at job's completion. Pays up to $700 for full-length of best quality. For illustrations, buys one-time rights. Pays $150-250 for b&w; $250-1,200 for color (inside, per page) illustration. Sample copies for $2.15 plus a 9×12 SASE.

READ

Weekly Reader Corporation, 200 First Stamford Place, P.O. Box 120023, Stamford CT 06912-0023. Fax: (203)705-1661. Web site: www.weeklyreader.com.

● *READ* no longer accepts unsolicited manuscripts. Those that are sent will not be read, responded to, or returned.

ℕ READ AMERICA, The Place in the Woods

(The Quarterly Newsletter for Reading Coordinators), 3900 Glenwood Ave., Golden Valley MN 55422-5302. (763)374-2120. **Articles Editor:** Roger Hammer. **Fiction Editor:** Susan Brudos. **Art Director:** Alisa Rubino. Quarterly newsletter. Estab. 1979. Circ. 10,000 + . "Two sections: one is news about reading; the other is stories and poetry for children (to read or be read to)." 50% of publication aimed at juvenile market.

Fiction Picture-oriented material, young readers, middle readers, young adults: adventure, animal, fantasy, folktale, history, humorous, multicultural, sports, suspense/mystery, main characters with disabilities who overcome adversity. Average word length: 300-1,500. Byline given.

Nonfiction Picture-oriented material, young readers, middle readers, young adults: animal, biography, humorous, multicultural, sports. Buys 6 mss/year. Average word length: 500-1,500. Byline given.

Poetry "No restrictions other than it needs to communicate with the reader—not be just purging of author's issues." Maximum length: 300-500 words. Limit submissions to 3-6 poems.

How to Contact/Writers Fiction/Nonfiction: Send complete ms. Responds to queries/mss in 6-12 months. Publishes ms 6 months to 1 year after acceptance.

Illustration Buys 100% illustrations/issue; 100% illustrations/year. Reviews ms/illustration packages from artists. Query or a manuscript with dummy. Contact: Roger Hammer, publisher. Illustrations only: Send postcard sample with samples, SASE. Contact: Roger Hammer. Responds only if interested. Samples returned with SASE; samples filed. Credit line given.

Photography Buys photos with accompanying ms only. Model/property release required. Uses b&w prints. Query with samples. Responds only if interested.

Terms Pays on acceptance. Buys all rights for mss. Buys all rights for artwork. Liberal reprint permission. Pays

$50-$250 for stories; $50 for articles. Pays photographers per photo (range: $10 flat). Sample copies for $7.50. Writer's/illustrator's/photo guidelines for SASE.

Tips "No e-mail queries. No multiple submissions. Put enough postage to cover return if you want manuscript back. Indicate when you need a response (return deadline). If you have an illustrator in mind, send examples and contact data. Nonfiction: Indicate your particular qualifications for the subject about which you write."

SCIENCE WEEKLY

P.O. Box 70638, Chevy Chase MD 20813. (301)680-8804. Fax: (301)680-9240. E-mail: scienceweekly@erols.com. Web site: www.scienceweekly.com. **Publisher:** Dr. Claude Mayberry, CAM Publishing Group, Inc. Magazine published 14 times/year. Estab. 1984. Circ. 200,000.

• *Science Weekly* uses freelance writers to develop and write an entire issue on a single science topic. Send résumé only, not submissions. Authors must be within the greater D.C., Virginia, Maryland area. *Science Weekly* works on assignment only.

Nonfiction Young readers, middle readers, (K-6th grade): science/math education, education, problem-solving.

Terms Pays on publication. Prefers people with education, science and children's writing background. *Send resume only.* Samples copies free with SAE and 3 first-class stamps.

N SCIENCE WORLD

Scholastic Inc., 557 Broadway, New York NY 10012-3999. (212)343-6100. Fax: (212)343-6945. E-mail: scienceworld@scholastic.com. **Editor:** Patty Janes. **Art Director:** Brenda Jackson. Magazine published biweekly during the school year. Estab. 1959. Circ. 400,000. Publishes articles in Life Science/Health, Physical Science/Technology, Earth Science/Environment/Astronomy for students in grades 7-10. The goal is to make science relevant for teens.

• *Science World* publishes a separate teacher's edition with lesson plans and skills pages to accompany feature articles.

Nonfiction Young adults/teens: animal, concept, geography, health, nature/environment, science. Multicultural needs include: minority scientists as role models. Does not want to see stories without a clear news hook. Buys 20 mss/year. Average word length: 800-1,000. Byline given. Currently does not accept unsolicited mss.

How to Contact/Writers Nonfiction: Query with published clips and/or brief summaries of article ideas. Responds only if interested. No unsolicited mss.

Illustration Buys 2 illustrations/issue; 28 illustrations/year. Works on assignment only. Illustration only: Query with samples, tearsheets. Responds only if interested. Samples returned with SASE; samples filed "if we use them." Credit line given.

Photography Model/property releases required; captions required including background information. Provide résumé, business card, promotional literature or tearsheets to be kept on file. Responds only if interested.

Terms Pays on acceptance. Buys all rights for mss/artwork. Originals returned to artist at job's completion. For stories/articles, pays $200. Pays photographers per photo.

A SEVENTEEN MAGAZINE

Hearst Magazines, 1440 Broadway, 13th Floor, New York NY 10018. (917)934-6500. Fax: (917)934-6574. Web site: www.seventeen.com. Monthly magazine. Estab. 1944. "We reach 14.5 million girls each month. Over the past five decades, *Seventeen* has helped shape teenage life in America. We represent an important rite of passage, helping to define, socialize and empower young women. We create notions of beauty and style, proclaim what's hot in popular culture and identify social issues."

Nonfiction Young adults: careers, cooking, hobbies, how-to, humorous, interview/profile, multicultural, social issues. Buys 7-12 mss/year. Word length: Varies from 200-2,000 words for articles. Byline sometimes given.

Illustration Only interested in agented material. Buys 10 illustrations/issue; 120 illustrations/year. Works on assignment only. Reviews ms/illustration packages. Illustrations only: Query with samples. Responds only if interested. Samples not returned; samples filed. Credit line given.

Photography Looking for photos to match current stories. Model/property releases required; captions required. Uses color, 8×10 prints; 35mm, $2\frac{1}{4} \times 2\frac{1}{4}$, 4×5 or 8×10 transparencies. Query with samples or résumé of credits, or submit portfolio for review. Responds only if interested.

Terms Pays on publication. Buys first North American serial rights, first rights or all rights for mss. Buys exclusive rights for 3 months; online rights for photos. Original artwork returned at job's completion. Pays $1/word for articles/stories (varies by experience). Additional payment for photos accompanying articles. Pays illustrators/photographers $150-500. Sample copies not available. Writer's guidelines for SASE.

Tips Send for guidelines before submitting.

SHARING THE VICTORY, Fellowship of Christian Athletes

8701 Leeds, Kansas City MO 64129. (816)921-0909. Fax: (816)921-8755. Web site: www.sharingthevictory.com. **Articles/Photo Editor:** Jill Ewert. **Art Director:** Mat Casner. Magazine published 9 times a year. Estab. 1982.

Circ. 80,000. Purpose is to serve as a ministry tool of the Fellowship of Christian Athletes (FCA) by aligning with its mission to present to athletes and coaches and all whom they influence, the challenge and adventure of receiving Jesus Christ as Savior and Lord.

Nonfiction Young adults/teens: religion, sports. Average word length: 700-1,200. Byline given.

How to Contact/Writers Nonfiction: Query with published clips. Publishes ms 3 months after acceptance. Will consider electronic submissions via e-mail.

Photography Purchases photos separately. Looking for photos of sports action. Uses color prints and high resolution electronic files of 300 dpi or higher.

Terms Pays on publication. Buys first rights and second serial (reprint) rights. Pays $150-400 for assigned and unsolicited articles. Photographers paid per photo. Sample copies for 9×12 SASE and $1. Writer's/photo guidelines for SASE.

Tips "All stories must be tied to FCA ministry."

☑ SKIPPING STONES, A Multicultural Children's Magazine

P.O. Box 3939, Eugene OR 97403. (541)342-4956. E-mail: editor@skippingstones.org. Web site: www.skippingst ones.org. **Articles/Photo/Fiction Editor:** Arun N. Toke. Bimonthly magazine. Estab. 1988. Circ. 2,500. "*Skipping Stones* is an award-winning multicultural, nonprofit magazine designed to encourage cooperation, creativity and celebration of cultural and ecological richness. We encourage submissions by children of color, minorities and under-represented populations."

- Send SASE for *Skipping Stones* guidelines and theme list for detailed descriptions of the topics they want. *Skipping Stones*, now in it's 19th year, has won EDPRESS, N.A.M.E. (National Association for Multicultural Education) and Parent's Choice Awards.

Fiction Middle readers, young adult/teens: contemporary, meaningful, humorous. All levels: folktales, multicultural, nature/environment. Multicultural needs include: bilingual or multilingual pieces; use of words from other languages; settings in other countries, cultures or multi-ethnic communities.

Nonfiction All levels: animal, biography, cooking, games/puzzles, history, humorous, interview/profile, multicultural, nature/environment, creative problem-solving, religion and cultural celebrations, sports, travel, social and international awareness. Does not want to see preaching, violence or abusive language; no poems by authors over 18 years old; no suspense or romance stories. Average word length: 500-750. Byline given.

How to Contact/Writers Fiction: Query. Nonfiction: Send complete ms. Responds to queries in 1 month; mss in 4 months. Will consider simultaneous submissions; reviews artwork for future assignments. Please include your name and address on each page.

Illustration Prefers illustrations by teenagers and young adults. Will consider all illustration packages. Manuscript/illustration packages: Query; submit complete ms with final art; submit tearsheets. Responds in 4 months. Credit line given.

Photography Black & white photos preferred, but color photos with good contrast are welcome. Needs: youth 7-17, international, nature, celebration.

Terms Acquires first and reprint rights for mss and photographs. Pays in copies for authors, photographers and illustrators. Sample copies for $5 with SAE and 4 first-class stamps. Writer's/illustrator's guidelines for 4×9 SASE.

Tips "We want material meant for children and young adults/teenagers with multicultural or ecological awareness themes. Think, live and write as if you were a child, 'tween or teen." Wants "material that gives insight to cultural celebrations, lifestyle, custom and tradition, glimpse of daily life in other countries and cultures. Photos, songs, artwork are most welcome if they illustrate/highlight the points. Translations are invited if your submission is in a language other than English. Upcoming themes will include cultural celebrations, living abroad, disability, hospitality customs of various cultures, cross-cultural understanding, African, Asian and Latin American cultures, humor, international, turning points and magical moments in life, caring for the earth, spirituality, and Multicutural Awareness."

SPARKLE

GEMS Girls' Clubs, 1333 Alger SE, P,P. Box 7295, Grand Rapids MI 49510. (616)241-5616. Fax: (616)241-5558. E-mail: senicecenter@gemsgc.org. Web site: www.gemsgc.org. **Articles/Fiction Editor:** Sarah Vanderaa. **Art Director/Photo Editor:** Sara DeRidder. Magazine published 3 times/year. Estab. 2002. Circ. 5,119. "Our mission is to prepare young girls to live out their faith and become world-changers—to help girls make a difference in the world. We look at the application of scripture to everyday life; strive to delight the reader and cause the reader to evalute her own life in lifhg of the truth presented; teach practical life skills.

Fiction Young readers: adventure, animal, contemporary, fantasy, folktale, health, history, humorous, multicultural, music and musicians, nature/environment, problem-solving, religious, recipes, service projects, sports, suspense/mystery, interacting with family and friends. Buys 10 mss/year. Average word length: 100-400. Byline given.

Nonfiction Young readers: animal, arts/crafts, biography, careers, cooking, concept, games/puzzles, geography, health, history, hobbies, how-to, interview/profile, math, multicultural, nature/environment, problem-solving, quizzes, science, social issues, sports, travel, personal experience, inspirational, music/drama/art. Buys 15 mss/year. Average word length: 100-400. Byline given.

Poetry Looks for simple poems about God's creation or free verse haiku, traditional Bible truths. Maximum lenth: 20 words or 5 lines.

How to Contact/Writers Fiction/nonfiction: Send complete ms. Responds to ms in 3 weeks. Publishes ms 6 months after acceptance. Will consider simultaneous submissions, electronic submissions, and previously published work.

Illustration Buys 1-2 illustrations/issue; 8-10 illustrations/year. Uses color artwork only. Works on assignment only. Reviews ms/illustration packages from artists. Send ms with dummy. Contact: Sara DeRidder, graphic and web designer. Illustrations only: send promo sheet. Contact: Sara DeRidder. Responds in 3 weeks only if interested. Samples returned with SASE; samples filed. Credit line given.

Photography Looking for close-up photos of girls, grades 1-3, variety of ethnicities of girls being active, serving, playing. Identity of subjects required. Uses 5×7 clear color glossy prints, GIF/JPEG files on CD. Send unsolicited photos by mail with business card and tearsheets. Responds in 3 weeks only if interested.

Terms Pays on publication. Buys first North American serial rights, second serial (reprint rights) or simultaneous rights for mss, artwork and photos. Pays $20 minimum for stories and articles. Pays illustrators $50 for color cover; $25 for color inside. Pays photographers per photo (range: $25-50). Additional payment for ms/illustration packages and for photos accompanying articles. Original artwork not returned at job's completion. Sample copies for $1. Writer's/illustrator/photo guidelines free for SASE or available on Web site.

Tips "Keep it simple. We are writing to 1st-3rd graders. It must be simple yet interesting. Manuscripts should build girls up in Christian character but not be preachy. They are just learning about God and how He wants them to live. Manuscripts should be delightful as well as educational and inspirational."

SPIDER, The Magazine for Children

Carus Publishing Company, 70 E. Lake St., Suite 300, Chicago IL 60603. (312) 701-1720. Web site: www.cricketmag.com. **Editor-in-Chief:** Alice Letvin. **Editor:** May-May Sugihara. **Art Director:** Sue Beck. Monthly magazine. Estab. 1994. Circ. 70,000. *Spider* publishes high-quality literature for beginning readers, primarily ages 6-9.

Fiction Young readers: adventure, contemporary, fantasy, folktales, humor, science fiction. "Authentic stories from all cultures are welcome. No didactic, religious, or violent stories, or anything that talks down to children." Average word length: 300-1,000. Byline given.

Nonfiction Young readers: animal, arts/crafts, cooking, games/puzzles, geography, history, human interest, math, multicultural, nature/environment, problem-solving, science. "Well-researched articles on topics are welcome. Would like to see more games, puzzles and activities, especially ones adaptable to *Spider*'s takeout pages. No encyclopedic or overtly educational articles." Average word length: 300-800. Byline given.

Poetry Serious, humorous. Maximum length: 20 lines.

How to Contact/Writers Fiction/nonfiction: Send complete ms with SASE. Do not query. Responds to mss in 6 months. Publishes ms 2-3 years after acceptance. Will consider simultaneous submissions and previously published work.

Illustration Buys 20 illustrations/issue; 240 illustrations/year. Uses color artwork only. "We prefer that you work on flexible or strippable stock, no larger than 20×22 (image area 19×21). This will allow us to put the art directly on the drum of our separator's laser scanner. Art on disck CMYK, 300 dpi. We use more realism than cartoon-style art." Works on assignment only. Reviews ms/illustration packages from artists. Illustrations only: Send promo sheet and tearsheets. Responds in 3 months. Samples returned with SASE; samples filed. Credit line given.

Photography Buys photos from freelancers. Buys photos with accompanying ms only. Model/property releases and captions required. Uses 35mm, $2^1/_4 \times 2^1/_4$ transparencies or digital files. Send unsolicited photos by mail; provide résumé and tearsheets. Responds in 3 months.

Terms Pays on publication. Rights purchased vary. Buys first and promotional rights for artwork; one-time rights for photographs. Original artwork returned at job's completion. Pays up to 25¢/word for previously unpublished stories/articles. Authors also receive 6 complimentary copies of the issue in which work appears. Additional payment for ms/illustration packages and for photos accompanying articles. Pays illustrators $750 for color cover; $200-300 for color inside. Pays photographers per photo (range: $25-75). Sample copies for $5. Writer's/illustrator's guidelines online atwww.cricketmag.com or for SASE.

Tips Writers: "Read back issues before submitting." (See listings for *Babybug*, *Cicada*, *Cricket*, *Ladybug*, *Click* and *ASK*.)

[N] [picture] TC MAGAZINE (Teenage Christian)

Institute for Church & Family, 915 E. Market #10750 Searcy, AR. (501)279-4530. E-mail: editor@tcmagazine.org. Web site: www.tcmagazine.org. **Articles Editor:** Laura Kaiser. Quarterly magazine (published March, June, Sept., Dec.). Estab. 1961. Circ. 8,000. "Music. Movies. Style. Sports. Humor. Friends. Art. Faith. All in one."

Fiction "We are not accepting fiction at this time."

Nonfiction Young adults: interview/profile, first person articles, college, style/fashion, humor. We are especially interested in articles written by teenagers. Buys 2-4 mss/year. Average word length: 500-1,000. Byline sometimes given.

Poetry Maximum length: we are not accepting poetry at this time.

How to Contact/Writers Nonfiction: send complete ms. Responds only if interested. Publishes ms 6 mons after acceptance. Will consider simultaneous submissions, e-mail submissions, no previously published work.

Illustration Works on assignment only. Send ms with dummy. Illustrations only: URL. Responds only if interested.

Photography Buys photos separately. Model/property release required. Uses hi-res color digital photos. E-mail or URL. Responds only if interested.

Terms Pays on publication. Buys one-time rights for mss. Buys all rights for artwork; all rights for photos. Payment varies.

TEEN MAGAZINE

Hearst Magazines, 3000 Ocean Park Blvd., Suite 3048, Santa Monica CA 90405. (310)664-2950. Fax: (310)664-2959. Web site: www.teenmag.com. **Contact:** Jane Fort, editor-in-chief (fashion, beauty, TeenPROM); Kelly Bryant, deputy editor (entertainment, movies, TV, music, books, covers, photo editor); Heather Hewitt, managing editor (manufacturing, advertising, new products, what's hot, intern coordinator). Quarterly magazine. Estab. 1957. "We are a pure junior high school female (ages 10-15) audience. *TEEN*'s audience is upbeat and wants to be informed."

Fiction Young adults: romance. Does not want to see "that which does not apply to our market , i.e., science fiction, history, religious, adult-oriented."

Nonfiction Young adults: how-to, arts/crafts, fashion, interview/profile, games/puzzles. Does not want to see adult-oriented, adult point of view.

How to Contact/Writers No unsolicited materials accepted.

Illustration Buys 10 illustrations/issues; 50 illustrations/year. Uses various styles. "Light, upbeat." Illustrations only: "Want to see samples whether it be tearsheets, slides, finished pieces showing the style." Responds only if interested. Credit line given.

Terms Pays on acceptance. Buys all rights. Bylines not guaranteed. Pays $200-800 for fiction; $200-600 for quizzes; $ 500-1,000 for illustrations.

Tips Illustrators: "Present professional finished work. Get familiar with our magazine and send samples that would be compatible with the style of publication." There is a need for artwork with "fiction/specialty articles. Send samples or promotional materials on a regular basis."

TURTLE MAGAZINE, For Preschool Kids

Children's Better Health Institute, 1100 Waterway Blvd., Indianapolis IN 46206-0567. (317)636-8881. Fax: (317)684-8094. Web site: www.turtlemag.org. **Editor:** Terry Harshman. **Art Director:** Bart Rivers. Bimonthly magazine published 6 times/year. Circ. 300,000. *Turtle* uses read-aloud stories, especially suitable for bedtime or naptime reading, for children ages 2-5. Also uses poems, simple science experiments, easy recipes and health-related articles.

Fiction Picture-oriented material: health-related, medical, history, humorous, multicultural, nature/environment, problem-solving, sports, recipes, simple science experiments. Avoid stories in which the characters indulge in unhealthy activities. Buys 20 mss/year. Average word length: 150-300. Byline given. Currently accepting submissions for Rebus stories only.

Nonfiction Picture-oriented material: cooking, health, sports, simple science. "We use very simple experiments illustrating basic science concepts. These should be pretested. We also publish simple, healthful recipes." Buys 24 mss/year. Average word length: 100-300. Byline given.

Poetry "We're especially looking for short poems (4-8 lines) and slightly longer action rhymes to foster creative movement in preschoolers. We also use short verse on our inside front cover and back cover."

How to Contact/Writers Fiction/nonfiction: Send complete mss. Queries are not accepted. Responds to mss in 3 months.

Terms Pays on publication. Buys all rights for mss. Pays up to 22¢/word for stories and articles (depending upon length and quality) and 10 complimentary copies. Pays $25 minimum for poems. Sample copy $ 3.95. Writer's guidelines free with SASE and on Web site.

Tips "Our need for health-related material, especially features that encourage fitness, is ongoing. Health subjects must be age-appropriate. When writing about them, think creatively and lighten up! Always keep in mind that in order for a story or article to educate preschoolers, it first must be entertaining—warm and engaging, exciting, or genuinely funny. Here the trend is toward leaner, lighter writing. There will be a growing need for interactive activities. Writers might want to consider developing an activity to accompany their concise manuscripts." (See listings for *Children's Digest, Children's Playmate, Humpty Dumpty's Magazine, Jack and Jill* and *U*S* Kids*.)

U*S* KIDS
Children's Better Health Institute, 1100 Waterway Blvd., P.O. Box 567, Indianapolis IN 46202. (317)636-8881. Web site: www.uskidsmag.org. **Editor:** Daniel Lee. **Art Director:** Greg Vanzo. Magazine for children ages 6-11, published 6 times a year. Estab. 1987. Circ. 230,000.
Fiction Young readers: adventure, animal, contemporary, health, history, humorous, multicultural, nature/environment, problem-solving, sports, suspense/mystery. Buys limited number of stories/year. Query first. Average word length: 500-800. Byline given.
Nonfiction Young readers: animal, arts/crafts, cooking, games/puzzles, health, history, hobbies, how-to, humorous, interview/profile, multicultural, nature/environment, science, social issues, sports, travel. Wants to see interviews with kids ages 5-10, who have done something unusual or different. Buys 30-40 mss/year. Average word length: 400. Byline given.
Poetry Maximum length: 8-24 lines.
How to Contact/Writers Fiction: Send complete ms. Responds to queries and mss in 3 months.
Illustration Buys 8 illustrations/issue; 70 illustrations/year. Color artwork only. Works on assignment only. Reviews ms/illustration packages from artists. Query. Illustrations only: Send resume and tearsheets. Responds only if interested. Samples returned with SASE; samples kept on file. Does not return originals. Credit line given.
Photography Purchases photography from freelancers. Looking for photos that pertain to children ages 5-10. Model/property release required. Uses color and b&w prints; 35mm, $2\frac{1}{4} \times 2\frac{1}{4}$, 4×5 and 8×10 transparencies. Photographers should provide resume, business card, promotional literature or tearsheets to be kept on file. Responds only if interested.
Terms Pays on publication. Buys all rights for mss. Purchases all rights for artwork. Purchases one-time rights for photographs. Pays 17¢/word minimum. Additional payment for ms/illustration packages. Pays illustrators $155/page for color inside. Photographers paid by the project or per photo (negotiable). Sample copies for $3.95. Writer's/illustrator/photo guidelines for #10 SASE.
Tips "Write clearly and concisely without preaching or being obvious." (See listings for *Child Life, Children's Digest, Children's Playmate, Humpty Dumpty's Magazine, Jack and Jill* and *Turtle Magazine*.)

WHAT IF?, Canada's Fiction Magazine for Teens
What If Publications, 19 Lynwood Place, Guelph ON N1G 2V9 Canada. (519)823-2941. Fax: (519)823-8081. E-mail: editor@whatifmagazine.com. Web site: www.whatifmagazine.com. **Articles/Fiction Editor:** Mike Leslie. **Art Director:** Jean Leslie. Quarterly magazine. Estab. 2003. Circ. 3,000. "The goal of *What If?* is to help young adults get published for the first time in a quality literary setting."
Fiction Young adults: adventure, contemporary, fantasy, folktale, health, humorous, multicultural, nature/environment, problem-solving, science fiction, sports, suspense/mystery. Buys 48 mss/year. Average word length: 500-3,000. Byline given.
Nonfiction Young adults: editorial. "We publish editorial content from young adult writers only—similar to material seen on newspapers op-ed page." Average word length: 500. Byline given.
Poetry Reviews poetry: all styles. Maximum length: 20 lines. Limit submissions to 4 poems.
How to Contact/Writers Fiction/Nonfiction: Send complete ms. Responds to mss in 3 months. Publishes ms 4 months after acceptance. Will consider e-mail submissions, previously published work if the author owns all rights.
Illustration Uses approximately 150 illustrations/year. Reviews ms/illustration packages from young adult artists. Send ms with dummy. Query with samples. Contact: Jean Leslie, production manager. Responds in 2 months. Samples returned with SASE. Credit line given.
Terms Pays on publication. Acquires first rights for mss and artwork. Original artwork returned at job's completion. Pays 3 copies for stories; 1 copy for articles; 3 copies for illustration. Sample copies for $7.50. Writer's/illustrator's guidelines for SASE or available by e-mail.
Tips "Read our magazine. The majority of the material we publish (90%) is by Canadian young adults. Another 10% is staff written. We are currently accepting material from Canadian teens only."

WINNER
The Health Connection, 55 W. Oak Ridge Dr., Hagerstown MD 21740. (301)393-4017. Fax: (301)393- 4055. E-mail: jschleifer@rhpa.org. Web site: www.winnermagazine.org. **Editor:** Jan Schleifer. **Art Director:** Madelyn Gatz. Monthly magazine (September-May). Estab. 1958. Publishes articles that will promote children in grades 4-6 choosing a positive lifestyle and choosing to be drug-free.

Fiction Young readers, middle readers: contemporary, health, nature/environment, problem-solving, anti tobacco, alcohol, and drugs. Byline given.

Nonfiction Young readers, middle readers: positive role model personality features, health. Buys 10-15 mss/year. Average word length: 600-650 (in addition, needs 3 related thought questions and one puzzle/activity). Byline given.

How to Contact/Writers Fiction/nonfiction: Send complete ms; prefers e-mail submissions. Responds in 2 months. Publishes ms 6-12 months after acceptance. Will consider simultaneous.

Illustration Buys up to 3 illustrations/issue; up to 30 illustrations/year. Uses color artwork only. Works on assignment only. Reviews ms/illustration packages from artists ; send ms with dummy. Responds only if interested. Samples returned with SASE.

Terms Pays on acceptance. Buys first rights for mss. Original artwork returned at job's completion. Additional payment for ms/illustration packages. Sometimes additional payment when photos accompany articles. Pays $300 for color inside. Writer's guidelines for SASE. Sample magazine $2; include 9 × 12 envelope with 3 first-class stamps.

☑ YES MAG, Canada's Science Magazine for Kids

Peter Piper Publishing Inc., 3968 Long Gun Place, Victoria BC V8N 3A9 Canada. Fax: (250)477-5390. E-mail: editor@yesmag.ca. Web site: www.yesmag.ca. **Editor:** Shannon Hunt. **Art/Photo Director:** David Garrison. Managing Editor: Jude Isabella. Bimonthly magazine. Estab. 1996. Circ. 22,000. "*YES Mag* is designed to make science accessible, interesting, exciting, and fun. Written for children ages 9 to 14, *YES Mag* covers a range of topics including science and technology news, environmental updates, do-at-home projects and articles about Canadian s cience and scientists."

Nonfiction Middle readers: all the sciences—math, engineering, biology, physics, chemistry, etc. Buys 70 mss/year. Average word length: 250-1,250. Byline given.

How to Contact/Writers Nonfiction: Query with published clips. "We prefer e-mail queries." Responds to queries/mss in 6 weeks. Generally publishes ms 3 months after acceptance.

Illustration Buys 2 illustrations/issue; 10 illustrations/year. Uses color artwork only. Works on assignment only. Reviews ms/illustration packages from artists. Query. Illustration only: Query with samples. Responds in 6 weeks. Samples filed. Credit line given.

Photography "Looking for science, technology, nature/environment photos based on current editorial needs." Photo captions required. Uses color prints. Provide résumé, business card, promotional literature, tearsheets if possible. Will buy if photo is appropriate. Usually uses stock agencies.

Terms Pays on publication. Buys one-time rights for mss. Buys one-time rights for artwork/photos. Original artwork returned at job's completion. Pays $ 70-2 00 for stories and articles. Sample copies for $4 .50. Writer's guidelines available on the Web site under "contact" information.

Tips "Articles relating to the physical sciences and mathematics are encouraged."

YOUNG RIDER, The Magazine for Horse and Pony Lovers

Fancy Publications, P.O. Box 8237, Lexington KY 40533. (859)260-9800. Fax: (859)260-9814. Web site: www.yo ungrider.com. **Editor:** Lesley Ward. Bimonthly magazine. Estab. 1994. "*Young Rider* magazine teaches young people, in an easy-to-read and entertaining way, how to look after their horses properly, and how to improve their riding skills safely."

Fiction Young adults: adventure, animal, horses, horse celebrities, famous equestrians. Buys 10 mss/year. Average word length: 1,500 maximum. Byline given.

Nonfiction Young adults: animal, careers, health (horse), sports, riding. Buys 20-30 mss/year. Average word length: 1,000 maximum. Byline given.

How to Contact/Writers Fiction/nonfiction: Query with published clips. Responds to queries in 2 weeks. Publishes ms 6-12 months after acceptance. Will consider simultaneous submissions, electronic submissions via disk or modem, previously published work.

Illustration Buys 2 illustrations/issue; 10 illustrations/year. Works on assignment only. Reviews ms/illustration packages from artists. Query. Contact: Lesley Ward, editor. Illustrations only: Query with samples. Contact: Lesley Ward, editor. Responds in 2 weeks. Samples returned with SASE. Credit line given.

Photography Buys photos with accompanying ms only. Uses color, slides, photos—in focus, good light. Model/property release required; captions required. Uses color 4 × 6 prints, 35mm transparencies. Query with samples. Responds in 2 weeks. Digital images must be high-res.

Terms Pays on publication. Buys first North American serial rights for mss, artwork, photos. Original artwork returned at job's completion. Pays $150 maximum for stories; $250 maximum for articles. Additional payment for ms/illustration packages and for photos accompanying articles. Pays $70-140 for color inside. Pays photographers per photo (range: $65-155). Sample copies for $3.50. Writer's/illustrator's/photo guidelines for SASE.

Young Writer's & Illustrator's Markets

The listings in this section are special because they publish work of young writers and artists (under age 18). Some of the magazines listed exclusively feature the work of young people. Others are adult magazines with special sections for the work of young writers. There are also a few book publishers listed that exclusively publish the work of young writers and artists. Many of the magazines and publishers listed here pay only in copies, meaning authors and illustrators receive one or more free copies of the magazine or book to which they contributed.

As with adult markets, markets for children expect writers to be familiar with their editorial needs before submitting. Many of the markets listed will send guidelines to writers. Guidelines state exactly what a publisher accepts and how to submit it. You can often get these by sending a request with a self-addressed, stamped envelope (SASE) to the magazine or publisher, or by checking a publication's Web site (a number of listings include Web addresses). In addition to obtaining guidelines, read through a few copies of any magazines you'd like to submit to—this is the best way to determine if your work is right for them.

A number of kids' magazines are available on newsstands or in libraries. Others are distributed only through schools, churches or home subscriptions. If you can't find a magazine you'd like to see, most editors will send sample copies for a small fee.

Before you submit your material to editors, take a few minutes to read Before Your First Sale on page 8 for more information on proper submission procedures. You may also want to check out two other sections—Contests, Awards & Grants and Conferences & Workshops. Some listings in these sections are open to students (some exclusively)—look for the phrase **Open to students** in bold. Additional opportunities and advice for young writers can be found in *The Young Writers Guide to Getting Published* (Writer's Digest Books) and *A Teen's Guide to Getting Published: the only writer's guide written by teens for teens*, by Danielle and Jessica Dunn (Prufrock Press). More information on these books are given in the Helpful Books & Publications section in the back of this book.

Information on companies listed in the previous edition but not included in this edition of *Children's Writer's & Illustrator's Market* may be found in the General Index.

CHIXLIT, the literary 'zine by and for chicks ages 7 to 17

P.O. Box 12051, Orange CA 92859. E-mail: submit@chixlit.com. Web site: www.chixlit.com. Bimonthly 'zine is a place for girls ages 7-17 to express themselves. "We cultivate talent and confidence; share writing techniques; communicate ideas and feelings; and let each other know we are not alone. Writers must be female and age 7-17, from anywhere in the world as long as writing in English; parent or guardian OK requested. Writer's guidelines on request and on Web site. Audience is also teachers, librarians, parents and others who want to encourage writing and confidence-building, as well as children's book authors who want to know what's going on in our heads!"

Magazine 95% written by young people. "We publish poems, short stories, reviews, rants, raves, love letters, song lyrics, journal entries and more. Always looking for regular contributors, critics, editors." Pays 1 free copy of the 'zine. Prizes for contests. Submit complete ms by e-mail (no attachments). Will accept typewritten form but prefer e-mail. Must be in English. "We plan a bilingual-Spanish-language edition for late 2008." Responds in 4 weeks, usually faster; "include your contact info!"

Artwork Publishes artwork and photography by girls ages 7-17 or of girls in that age range. Looks for "iconic images of chix, things chix like, or whatever makes you think of chix. Must be flat and scannable and look decent in b&w." No originals. Pays 1 free issue for artwork used and a small gift if chosen for the cover. "We prefer submission of work (original or a good color or b&w copy) in a flat envelope (not rolled) and sent to our P.O. box (so not too big)."

Tips "We dare you to dare. Our motto is, 'Words are powerful, and they can make you powerful too.' Buy a subscription or back issues to see what we're up to."

CICADA

Carus Publishing Company, 70 East Lake Street, Suite 200, Chicago IL 60001. (312)701-1720. Fax: (312)701-1728. Submissions address: 70 East Lake Street, Suite 300, Chicago IL 60601. E-mail: cicada@caruspub.com. Web site: www.cricketmag.com. **Editor-in-Chief:** Marianne Carus. **Executive Editor:** Deborah Vetter. **Editorial Assistant:** Pete Coco. **Art Director:** John Sandford. Bimonthly magazine.

- *Cicada* publishes work of writers and artists of high-school age and older (must be at least 14 years old). See the *Cicada* listing in the Magazines section for more information, or check their Web site or copies of the magazine.

🔲 THE CLAREMONT REVIEW

4980 Wesley Rd., Victoria BC V8Y 1Y9 Canada. (250)658-5221. Fax: (250)658-5387. E-mail: editor@theClaremontReview.ca. Web site: www.theClaremontReview.ca. Magazine. Publishes 2 books/year by young adults. Publishes poetry and fiction with literary value by students aged 13-19 anywhere in English-speaking world. Purpose in publishing work by young people: to provide a literary venue. Sponsors annual writing contest with March 15 deadline.

Magazines Uses 10-12 fiction stories (200-2,500 words); 30-40 poems. Pays in copies. Submit mss to editors. Submit complete ms. Will accept typewritten mss. SASE. Responds in 6 weeks (except during the summer).

Artwork Publishes artwork by young adults. Looks for b&w copies of imaginative art. Pays in copies. Send picture for review. Negative may be requested. Submit art and photographs to editors. SASE. Responds in 6 weeks.

Tips "Read us first—it saves disappointment. Know who we are and what we publish. We're closed July and August. SASE a must. American students send IRCs as American stamps *do not* work in Canada."

CREATIVE KIDS

P.O. Box 8813, Waco TX 76714-8813. (800)998-2208. Fax: (254)756-3339. E-mail: ck@prufrock.com. Web site: www.prufrock.com. **Editor:** Lacy Elwood. Magazine published 4 times/year. Estab. 1979. "Material is by children, for children." Purpose in publishing works by children: "to create a product that provides children with an authentic experience and to offer an opportunity for children to see their work in print. *Creative Kids* contains the best stories, poetry, opinion, artwork, games and photography by kids ages 8-16." Writers ages 8-16 must have statement by teacher or parent verifying originality. Writer's guidelines available on request with SASE. No adult submissions please.

Magazines Uses fiction and nonfiction stories (800-900 words), poetry, plays, ideas to share (200-750 words) per issue. Pays "free magazine." Submit mss to submissions editor. Will accept typewritten mss. Include SASE. Responds in 1 month.

Artwork/Photography Publishes artwork and photos by children. Looks for "any kind of drawing, cartoon, or painting." Pays "free magazine." Send color copy of the work to submissions editor. Include SASE. Responds in 1 month.

Tips "*Creative Kids* is a magazine by kids, for kids. The work represents children's ideas, questions, fears, concerns and pleasures. The material never contains racist, sexist, or violent expression. A person may submit one piece of work per envelope. Each piece must be labeled with the student's name, birth date, grade, school, home address and school address. Material submitted to *Creative Kids* must not be under consideration by any other publication. Items should be carefully prepared, proofread and double checked (perhaps also by a parent or teacher). All activities requiring solutions must be accompanied by the correct answers. Young writers and artists should always write for guidelines and then follow them. We only publish work created by children. Adult submissions will not be considered.''

CREATIVE WITH WORDS, Thematic anthologies
Creative with Words Publications, P.O. Box 223226, Carmel CA 93922. Fax: (831)655-8627. E-mail: geltrich@mbay.net.
Books Considers all categories except those dealing with sensationalism, death, violence, pornography/erotic expressions and overtly religious themes. Uses fairy tales, folklore items (up to 800 words) and poetry (not to exceed 20 lines, 46 characters across). Published Folklore and Nature Series: Seasons, Nature, School, Love and Relationships (all children and adults). Offers 20% discount on each copy of publication in which fiction or poetry by children appears. Submit mss to editor. Query; child, teacher or parent can submit; teacher and/or parents must verify originality of writing. Will accept typewritten and/or legibly handwritten mss sent with SASE. ''Will not go through agents or over-protective 'stage mothers.' '' Responds in 1 month after deadline of any theme.
Artwork/Photography Publishes b&w artwork, b&w photos and computer artwork created by children (language art work). No already existing computer artwork. Offers 20% discount on every copy of publication in which work by children appears. Submit artwork to editor, and request info on payment.
Tips ''Enjoy the English language, life and the world around you. Look at everything from a different perspective. Look at the greatness inside all of us. Be less descriptive and use words wisely. Let the reader experience a story through a viewpoint character, don't be overly dramatic. Match illustrations/photos to the meaning of the story or poem.''

FREE SPIRIT PUBLISHING
217 Fifth Ave. North, Suite 200, Minneapolis MN 55401-1299. (612)338-2068. Fax: (866)419-5199. E-mail: acquisitions@freespirit.com. Web site: www.freespirit.com. **Acquisitions:** Acquisitions Editor. Publishes 16-22 titles/year for children and teens, teachers, and parents. ''Free Spirit Publishing is the home of SELF-HELP FOR KIDS® and SELF-HELP FOR TEENS®, nonfiction, issue-driven, solution-focused books and materials for children and teens and the parents and teachers who care for them.''
• Free Spirit no longer accepts fiction or storybook submissions.
Books Publishes nonfiction. ''Submissions are accepted from prospective authors, including youth ages 16 and up, or through agents. Please review our catalog and author guidelines (both available online) before submitting proposal.'' Responds to queries/mss in 4 months. ''If you'd like materials returned, enclose a SASE with sufficient postage.'' Write, call, or e-mail for catalog and submission guidelines before sending submission. Accepts queries only by e-mail. Submission guidelines available online.
Tips ''We do not publish fiction or picture storybooks, books with animal or mythical characters, books with religious or New Age content, or single biographies, autobiographies, or memoirs. We prefer books written in a natural, friendly style.''

HIGH SCHOOL WRITER
P.O. Box 718, Grand Rapids MN 55744-0718. (218)326-8025. Fax: (218)326-8025. E-mail: writer@mx3.com. **Editor:** Emily Benes. Magazine published 6 times during the school year. ''The *High School Writer* is a magazine written *by* students *for* students. All submissions must exceed contemporary standards of decency.'' Purpose in publishing works by young people: to provide a real audience for student writers—and text for study. Submissions by junior high and middle school students accepted for our junior edition. Senior high students' works are accepted for our senior high edition. ''Students attending schools that subscribe to our publication are eligible to submit their work.'' Writer's guidelines available on request.
Magazines Uses fiction, nonfiction (2,000 words maximum) and poetry. Submit mss to editor. Submit complete ms (teacher must submit). Will accept typewritten, computer-generated (good quality) mss.
Tips ''Submissions should not be sent without first obtaining a copy of our guidelines (see page 2 of every issue). Also, submissions will not be considered unless student's school subscribes.''

HIGHLIGHTS FOR CHILDREN
803 Church St., Honesdale PA 18431. (570)253-1080. Magazine. Published monthly. ''We strive to provide wholesome, stimulating, entertaining material that will encourage children to read. Our audience is children ages 2-12.'' Purpose in publishing works by young people: to encourage children's creative expression.

● See *Highlights'* listing in the Magazines section.

Magazines 15-20% of magazine written by children. Uses stories and poems. Also uses jokes, riddles, tongue twisters. Features that occur occasionally: ''What Are Your Favorite Books?'' (8-10/year), Recipes (8-10/year), ''Science Letters'' (15-20/year). Special features that invite children's submissions on a specific topic occur several times per year. Recent examples include ''Amusement Park Rides,'' ''Funniest Dreams,'' ''Your Dream Vacation,'' and ''Help the Cartoonists.'' Pays in copies. Submit complete ms to the editor. Will accept typewritten, legibly handwritten and computer printout mss. Responds in 6 weeks.

Artwork Publishes artwork by children. Pays in copies. No cartoon or comic book characters. No commercial products. Submit b&w or color artwork on unlined paper for ''Your Own Pages.'' Features include ''Creatures Nobody Has Ever Seen'' (5-8/year) and ''You Illustrate the Story'' (18-20/year). Responds in 6 weeks.

Tips ''Remember to keep a photocopy of your work because we cannot return it. When submitting your work, please include your name, age, and full address.''

KWIL KIDS PUBLISHING, The Little Publishing Company That Kwil Built

Kwilville, P.O. Box 29556, Maple Ridge BC V2X 2V0 Canada. E-mail: kwilville@shaw.ca. Publishes weekly column in local paper, four quarterly newsletters. ''*Kwil Kids* come in all ages, shapes and sizes—from 4-64 and a whole lot more! Kwil does not pay for the creative work of children but provides opportunity/encouragement. We promote literacy, creativity and creative 'connections' through written and artistic expression and publish autobiographical, inspirational, stories of gentleness, compassion, truth and beauty. Our purpose is to foster a sense of pride and enthusiasm in young writers and artists, to celebrate the voice of youth and to encourage growth through joy-filled practice and cheerleading, not criticism.'' Must include name, age, address and parent signature (if a minor). Will send guidelines upon request.

Books Publishes autobiographical, inspirational, creative stories (alliterative, rhyming refrains, juicy words), short rhyming and nonrhyming poems (creative, fun, original, expressive) and creative nonfiction. Length: 500 words for fiction; 8-16 lines for poetry. No payments; self-published and sold ''at cost'' only (1 free copy). Submit mss to Kwil or Mr. Marquis. Submit complete ms. Send copy only; expect a reply but will not return ms. Will accept typewritten and legibly handwritten mss and e-mail. Include SASE or enclose IRC or $1 for postage, as US stamps may not be used from Canada. Responds in April, August and December.

Newsletter 95% of newsletter written by young people. Uses 15 short stories, poems (20-100 words). No payment; free newsletters only. Submit complete ms. Will accept typewritten and legibly handwritten mss and e-mail. Kwil answers every letter in verse. Responds in 4 weeks.

Artwork Publishes artwork and photography by children with writing. Looks for black ink sketches to go with writing and photos to go with writing. Submit by postal mail only; white background for sketches. Submit artwork/photos to Kwil publisher. Submit holiday/seasonal work 4 months in advance. Include SASE. Responds in 3 months.

Tips ''We love stories that teach a lesson or encourage peace, love and a fresh, new understanding. Just be who you are and do what you do. Then all of life's treasures will come to you.''

NEW MOON: The Magazine for Girls & Their Dreams

New Moon Publishing, Inc., 2 W. First St., #101, Duluth MN 55802. (218)728-5507. Fax: (218)728-0314. E-mail: girl@newmoon.org. Web site: www.newmoon.org. **Executive Editor:** Kate Freeborn. Bimonthly magazine. *New Moon*'s primary audience is girls ages 8-14. ''We publish a magazine that listens to girls.'' More than 70% of *New Moon* is written by girls. Purpose in publishing work by children/teens: ''We want girls' voices to be heard. *New Moon* wants girls to see that their opinions, dreams, thoughts and ideas count.'' Writer's guidelines available for SASE or online.

● See *New Moon*'s listing in the Magazines section.

Magazine Buys 6 fiction mss/year (1,200-1,600 words); 30 nonfiction mss/year (600 words). Submit to Editorial Department. Submit query or complete mss for nonfiction; complete ms only for fiction. ''We do not return or acknowledge unsolicited material. Do not send originals—we will not return any materials.'' Responds in 6 months if interested.

Artwork/Photography Publishes artwork and photography by girls. ''We do not return unsolicited material.''

Tips ''Read *New Moon* to completely understand our needs.''

POTLUCK CHILDREN'S LITERARY MAGAZINE

P.O. Box 546, Deerfield IL 60015. (847)948-1139. Fax: (847)317-9492. E-mail: submissions@potluckmagazine.org. Web site: www.potluckmagazine.org. A not-for-profit quarterly magazine for and by writers/artists ages 8-16. ''We look for works with imagery, humor and human truths. Editors are available to answer any questions the writer may have concerning his or her work. The purpose of *Potluck* is to educate today's young writers, to encourage creative expression and to provide a professional forum in which their voices can be heard. *Potluck* includes educational articles to help expand writing skills and the 'business' of writing. *Potluck* wants each writer's experience to be full of new accomplishments and new understandings." Writer's guidelines available on request with a SASE, within the magazine, or online.

● *Potluck* is celebrating its 10th anniversary.

Magazines 99% of magazine written by young people. Uses fiction (1,500 words); nonfiction (1,500 words); poetry (30 lines); book reviews (250 words). Pays with copy. Submit mss to Susan Napoli Picchietti, editor-in-chief. Submit complete ms; teacher may send en masse, but must review all work to ensure it complies with guidelines. Include a SASE for reply. Will accept typewritten and e-mailed mss (no attachments—place work within body of e-mail). Include SASE. Responds 6 weeks after deadline.

Artwork/Photography Publishes artwork by young artists. Looks for all types of artwork—no textured works. 8½×11 preferred. Pays in copies. Do not fold submissions. Include proper postage and envelope for return of original artwork. Color photo copy accepted. Submit artwork to Susan Napoli Picchietti, editor-in-chief. Include SASE. Responds in 6 weeks after deadline.

Tips "Relax, observe and acknowledge all that is around you. Life gives us a lot to draw on. Don't get carried away with, 'style'—let your words speak for themselves. If you want to be taken seriously as a writer, you must take yourself seriously. The rest will follow. Enjoy yourself and take pride in every piece, even the bad ones, because they keep you humble."

SKIPPING STONES

Multicultural Children's Magazine, P.O. Box 3939, Eugene OR 97403-0939. (541)342-4956. E-mail: editor@SkippingStones.org. Web site: www.SkippingStones.org. **Articles/Poems/Fiction Editor:** Arun N. Toke. 5 issues a year. Estab. 1988. Circulation 2,500. "*Skipping Stones* is a multicultural, nonprofit, children's magazine to encourage cooperation, creativity and celebration of cultural and environmental richness. It offers itself as a creative forum for communication among children from different lands and backgrounds. We prefer work by children under 18 years old. International, minorities and under-represented populations receive priority, multilingual submissions are encouraged." Guidelines for children's work available on request with SASE.

● *Skipping Stones*' theme for the Youth Honor Awards is multicultural/international understanding and nature awareness. Send SASE for guidelines and more information on the awards. *Skipping Stones*, now in it's 19th year, is winner of the N.A.M.E., Parents' Choice, and EDPRESS awards.

Magazines 70% written by children and teenagers. Uses 5-10 fiction short stories and plays (500-750 words); 5-10 nonfiction articles, interviews, letters, history, descriptions of celebrations (500-750 words); 15-20 poems, jokes, riddles, proverbs (250 words or less) per issue. Pays in contributor's copies. Submit mss to editor. Submit complete ms for fiction or nonfiction work; teachers and parents can also submit their contributions. Submissions should include "cover letter with name, age, address, school, cultural background, inspiration piece, dreams for future." Will accept typewritten, legibly handwritten and computer/word processor mss. Include SASE. Responds in 4 months. Accepts simultaneous submissions.

Artwork/Photography Publishes artwork and photography for children. Will review all varieties of ms/illustration packages. Wants comics, cartoons, b&w photos, color paintings, drawings (preferably ink & pen or pencil), 8×10, color photos OK. Prints 4-color cover/back cover and b&w inside. Subjects include children, people, celebrations, nature, ecology, multicultural. Pays in contributor's copies.

Terms "*Skipping Stones* is a labor of love. You'll receive complimentary contributor's (up to 4) copies depending on the extent/length of your contribution. 25% discount on additional copies. We may allow others to reprint (including by electronic means) articles and art or photographs." Responds to artists in 4 months. Sample copy for $5 and 4 first-class stamps.

Tips "Let the 'inner child' within you speak out—naturally, uninhibited." Wants "material that gives insight on cultural celebrations, lifestyle, custom and tradition, glimpse of daily life in other countries and cultures. Please, no mystery for the sake of mystery! Photos, songs, artwork are most welcome if they illustrate/highlight the points. Upcoming features: Living abroad, turning points, inspirations and magical moments in life, cultural celebrations around the world, folktales, caring for the earth, endangered species, your dreams and visions, heroes, kid-friendly analysis of current events, resolving conficts, summer experiences, poetry, and minority experiences."

STONE SOUP, The Magazine by Young Writers and Artists

Children's Art Foundation, P.O. Box 83, Santa Cruz CA 95063-0083. (831)426-5557. Fax: (831)426-1161. E-mail: editor@stonesoup.com. Web site: www.stonesoup.com. **Articles/Fiction Editor, Art Director:** Ms. Gerry Mandel. Magazine published 6 times/year. Circ. 20,000. "We publish fiction, poetry and artwork by children through age 13. Our preference is for work based on personal experiences and close observation of the world. Our audience is young people through age 13, as well as parents, teachers, librarians." Purpose in publishing works by young people: to encourage children to read and to express themselves through writing and art. Writer's guidelines available upon request with a SASE.

Magazines Uses animal, contemporary, fantasy, history, problem-solving, science fiction, sports, spy/mystery/

adventure fiction stories. Uses 5-10 fiction stories (150-2,500 words); 5-10 nonfiction stories (150-2,500 words); 2-4 poems per issue. Does not want to see classroom assignments and formula writing. Buys 65 mss/year. Byline given. Pays on publication. Buys all rights. Pays $40 each for stories and poems, $40 for book reviews. Contributors also receive 2 copies. Sample copy $4. Free writer's guidelines. "We don't publish straight nonfiction, but we do publish stories based on real events and experiences." Send complete ms to editor. Will accept typewritten and legibly handwritten mss. Do not include SASE. Send copies, not originals. "If we are interested in publishing your work, you will hear from us in 6 weeks. If you don't hear from us, it means we could not use your work. Don't be discouraged. Try again."

Artwork/Photography Does not publish artwork other than illustrations. Pays $25 for color illustrations. Contributors receive 2 copies. Sample copy $5. Free illustrator's guidelines. Send color copies, not originals. If you would like to illustrate for *Stone Soup*, send us 2 or 3 samples (color copies) of your work, along with a letter telling us what kinds of stories you would like to illustrate. We are looking for artists who can draw complete scenes, including the background. Send submissions to editor. Include SASE. Responds in 6 weeks. All artwork must be by children through age 13.

Tips "Only work by young people through age 13 is considered. Whether your work is about imaginary situations or real ones, use your own experiences and observations to give your work depth and a sense of reality. Read a few issues of our magazine to get an idea of what we like."

WHOLE NOTES

2305 Turrentine Drive, Las Cruces NM 88005. (505)541-5744. E-mail: rnhastings@zianet.com. **Editor:** Nancy Peters Hastings. Magazine published twice yearly. "We encourage interest in contemporary poetry by showcasing outstanding creative writing. We look for original, fresh perceptions in poems that demonstrate skill in using language effectively, with carefully chosen images and clear ideas. Our audience (general) loves poetry. We try to recognize excellence in creative writing by children as a way to encourage and promote imaginative thinking." Writer's guidelines available for SASE.

Magazines Every fourth issue is 100% by children. Writers should be 21 years old or younger. Uses 30 poems/issue (length open). Pays complimentary copy. Submit mss to editor. Submit complete ms. "No multiple submissions, please." Will accept typewritten and legibly handwritten mss. SASE. Responds in 2 months.

Artwork/Photography Publishes artwork and photographs by children. Looks for b&w line drawings which can easily be reproduced; b&w photos. Pays complimentary copy. Send clear photocopies. Submit artwork to Nancy Peters Hastings, editor. SASE. Responds in 2 months.

Tips Sample issue is $3. "We welcome translations. Send your best work. Don't send your only copy of your poem. Keep a photocopy."

THE WRITERS' SLATE

The Writing Conference, Inc., P.O. Box 664, Ottawa KS 66067. Phone/fax: (785)242-1995. E-mail: jbushman@writingconference.com. Web site: www.writingconference.com. Magazine. Publishes 3 issues/year online. *The Writers' Slate* accepts original poetry and prose from students enrolled in kindergarten-12th grade. The audience is students, teachers and librarians. Purpose in publishing works by young people: to give students the opportunity to publish and to give students the opportunity *to read* quality literature written by other students. Writer's guidelines are available on Web Site.

Magazines 90% of magazine written by young people. Uses 10-15 fiction, 1-2 nonfiction, 10-15 other mss per issue. Submit mss to Shelley McNerney, editor, 7619 Hemlock St., Overland Park KS 66204. Submit complete ms. Will accept typewritten mss. Responds in 1 month. Include SASE with ms if reply is desired.

Artwork Publishes artwork by young people. Bold, b&w, student artwork may accompany a piece of writing. Submit to Shelley McNerney, editor. Responds in 1 month.

Tips "Always accompany submission with a letter indicating name, home address, school, grade level and teacher's name. If you want a reply, include a SASE."

Agents & Art Reps

This section features listings of literary agents and art reps who either specialize in, or represent a good percentage of, children's writers and/or illustrators. While there are a number of children's publishers who are open to non-agented material, using the services of an agent or rep can be beneficial to a writer or artist. Agents and reps can get your work seen by editors and art directors more quickly. They are familiar with the market and have insights into which editors and art directors would be most interested in your work. Also, they negotiate contracts and will likely be able to get you a better deal than you could get on your own.

Agents and reps make their income by taking a percentage of what writers and illustrators receive from publishers. The standard percentage for agents is 10 to 15 percent; art reps generally take 25 to 30 percent. We have not included any agencies in this section that charge reading fees.

WHAT TO SEND

When putting together a package for an agent or rep, follow the guidelines given in their listings. Most agents open to submissions prefer initially to receive a query letter describing your work. For novels and longer works, some agents ask for an outline and a number of sample chapters, but you should send these only if you're asked to do so. Never fax or e-mail query letters or sample chapters to agents without their permission. Just as with publishers, agents receive a large volume of submissions. It may take them a long time to reply, so you may want to query several agents at one time. It's best, however, to have a complete manuscript considered by only one agent at a time. Always include a self-addressed, stamped envelope (SASE).

For initial contact with art reps, send a brief query letter and self-promo pieces, following the guidelines given in the listings. If you don't have a flier or brochure, send photocopies. Always include a SASE.

For those who both write and illustrate, some agents listed will consider the work of author/illustrators. Read through the listings for details.

As you consider approaching agents and reps with your work, keep in mind that they are very choosy about who they take on to represent. Your work must be high quality and presented professionally to make an impression on them. For more information on approaching agents and additional listings, see *Guide to Literary Agents* (Writer's Digest Books). For additional listings of art reps see *Artist's & Graphic Designer's Market* (Writer's Digest Books).

Information on agents and art reps listed in the previous edition but not included in this edition of *Children's Writer's & Illustrator's Market* may be found in the General Index.

An Organization for Agents

In some listings of agents you'll see references to AAR (The Association of Authors' Representatives). This organization requires its members to meet an established list of professional standards and code of ethics.

The objectives of AAR include keeping agents informed about conditions in publishing and related fields; encouraging cooperation among literary organizations; and assisting agents in representing their author-clients' interests. Officially, members are prohibited from directly or indirectly charging reading fees. They offer writers a list of member agents on their Web site. They also offer a list of recommended questions an author should ask an agent and other FAQs, all found on their Web site. They can be contacted at AAR, 676A 9th Ave., New York NY 10036. (212)840-5777. E-mail: aarinc@aar-online.org. Web site: www.aar-online.org.

AGENTS

ADAMS LITERARY
7845 Colony Rd., #215, Charlotte NC 28226. (212)786-9140. Fax: (212)786-9170. E-mail: info@adamsliterary.com. Web site: www.adamsliterary.com. **Contact:** Tracey Adams, Josh Adams. Estab. 2004. Member of AAR and SCBWI. 20% of clients are new/previously unpublished writers. 100% of material handled is books for young readers.
- Prior to becoming an agent, Tracey Adams worked in the editorial and marketing departments at several children's publishing houses.

Represents Considers fiction, picture books, middle grade, young adult. "We place authors' work based on insight and experience. Adams Literary offers editorial guidance and marketing knowledge."
How to Contact Adams Literary is closed to unsolicited e-mails, queries and submissions. See Web site for updates on submission policy.
Terms Agent receives 15% commission on domestic sales; 20% on foreign sales. Offers written contract.
Writers' Conferences Attends Bologna Book Fair in Bologna, Italy. Other conferences listed on Web site.
Tips "We represent authors, not books, so we enjoy forming long-term relationships with our clients. We work hard to be sure we are submitting work which is ready to be considered, but we respect the role of editors and don't over-edit manuscripts ourselves. Our style is assertive yet collaborative."

BOOKSTOP LITERARY AGENCY
67 Meadow View Rd., Orinda CA 94563. Web site: www.bookstopliterary.com. Seeking both new and established writers. Estab. 1983. 100% of material handled is books of young readers.
Represents Considers fiction, nonfiction, picture books, middle grade, young adult. "Special interest in Hispanic writers and illustrators for children."
How to Contact Query only with nonfiction; all others send entire ms with SASE. Considers simultaneous submissions. Responds in 6 weeks. Responds and returns material only with SASE.
Terms Agent receives 15% commission on domestic sales. Offers written contract, binding for 1 year.

ANDREA BROWN LITERARY AGENCY, INC.
1076 Eagle Dr., Salinas CA 93905. (831)422-5925. Web site: www.andreabrownlit.com. **President:** Andrea Brown. Estab. 1981. Member of SCBWI and WNBA. 20% of clients are new/previously unpublished writers. Specializes in "all kinds of children's books—illustrators and authors."
- Prior to opening her agency, Andrea Brown served as an editorial assistant at Random House and Dell Publishing and as an editor with Alfred A. Knopf.

Member Agents Andrea Brown, president; Laura Rennert, senior agent; Caryn Wiseman, agent; Jennifer Jaeger and Michelle Andelman, associate agents. Offices in California and New York City.
Represents 98% juvenile books. Considers: nonfiction (animals, anthropology/archaeology, art/architecture/

design, biography/autobiography, current affairs, ethnic/cultural interests, history, how-to, nature/environment, photography, popular culture, science/technology, sociology, sports); fiction (historical, science fiction); picture books, young adult.

How to Contact Query. Responds in 3 months to queries and mss. E-mail queries only.

Needs Mostly obtains new clients through recommendations, editors, clients and agents.

Recent Sales *Fire on Ice*, autobiography of Sasha Cohen (HarperCollins); three book series, by Ellen Hopkins (S&S); *Downside Up*, by Neal Shusterman (Simon & Schuster).

Terms Agent receives 15% commission on domestic sales; 20% on foreign sales. Written contract.

Writers' Conferences Agents at Andrea Brown Literary Agency attend Austin Writers League; SCBWI; Columbus Writers Conference; Willamette Writers Conference; Orange County Conferences; Mills College Childrens Literature Conference (Oakland CA); Asilomar (Pacific Grove CA); Maui Writers Conference; Southwest Writers Conference; San Diego State University Writer's Conference; Big Sur Children's Writing Workshop (Director); BookExpo America/Writer's Digest Books Writing Conference.

Tips Query first. "Taking on very few picture books. Must be unique—no rhyme, no anthropomorphism. Do not call or fax queries or manuscripts. E-mail queries first. Check Web site for details."

CURTIS BROWN, LTD.

Ten Astor Place, New York NY 10003. (212)473-5400. Fax: (212)598-0917. Seeking both new and established writers. Estab. 1914. Members of AAR and SCBWI. Signatory of WGA. SCBWI. **Staff includes:** Ginger Clark, Elizabeth Harding and Ginger Knowlton.

Represents Authors and illustrators of fiction, nonfiction, picture books, middle grade, young adult.

How to Contact Query with SASE. If a picture book, send only one picture book ms. Considers simultaneous queries, "but please tell us." Returns material only with SASE. Obtains clients through recommendations from others, queries/solicitations, conferences.

Terms Agent receives 15% commission on domestic sales; 20% on foreign sales. Offers written contract. 75 days notice must be given to terminate contract.

BROWNE & MILLER LITERARY ASSOCIATES, LLC

410 S. Michigan Ave., Suite 460, Chicago IL 60605. (312)922-3063. Fax: (312)922-1905. E-mail: mail@browneandmiller.com. Web site: www.browneandmiller.com. **Contact:** Danielle Egan-Miller, president. Prefers to work with established writers. Handles only certain types of work. Estab. 1971. Member of AAR, RWA, MWA. Represents 85+ clients. 5% of clients are new/previously unpublished writers. 15% of material handled is books for young readers.

● Prior to opening the agency, Danielle Egan-Miller worked as an editor.

Represents Considers primarily YA fiction, fiction, young adult. "We love great writing and have a wonderful list of authors writing YA in particular." Not looking for picture books, middle grade.

How to Contact Query with SASE. Accepts queries by e-mail. Considers simultaneous queries. Responds in 2-4 weeks to queries; 4-6 months to mss. Returns material only with SASE. Obtains clients through recommendations from others.

Recent Sales Sold 10 books for young readers in the last year.

Terms Agent receives 15% commission on domestic sales; 20% on foreign sales. Offers written contract, binding for 2 years. 30 days notice must be given to terminate contract.

Tips "We are very hands-on and do much editorial work with our clients. We are passionate about the books we represent and work hard to help clients reach their publishing goals."

N PEMA BROWNE LTD.

11 Tena Place, Valley Cottage NY 10989. (845)268-0029. **Contact:** Pema Browne. Estab. 1966. Represents 2 illustrators. 10% of artwork handled is children's book illustration. Specializes in general commercial. Markets include: all publishing areas; children's picture books. Clients include HarperCollins, Holiday House, Bantam Doubleday Dell, Nelson/Word, Hyperion, Putnam. Client list available upon request.

Handles Fiction, nonfiction, picture books, middle grade, young adult, manuscript/illustration packages. Looking for "professional and unique" talent.

Recent Sales *The Daring Ms. Quimby*, by Suzanne Whitaker (Holiday House).

Terms Rep receives 30% illustration commission; 15% author commission. Exclusive area representation is required. For promotional purposes, talent must provide color mailers to distribute. Representative pays mailing costs on promotion mailings.

How to Contact For first contact, send query letter, direct mail flier/brochure and SASE. If interested will ask to mail appropriate materials for review. Portfolios should include tearsheets and transparencies or good color photocopies, plus SASE. Accepts queries by mail only. Obtains new talent through recommendations and interviews (portfolio review).

Tips "We are doing more publishing—all types—less advertising." Looks for "continuity of illustration and dedication to work."

LIZA DAWSON ASSOCIATES

240 W. 35th Street, Suite 500, New York NY 10001. (201)791-4699. E-mail: anna@olswanger.com. Web site: www.olswanger.com. Member of SCBWI, WNBA, Authors Guild. Represents 10 clients. 30% of clients are new/unpublished writers. 50% of material handled is books for young readers.

  • Anna Olswanger coordinates the Jewish Children's Book Writers' Conference each fall at the 92nd Street Y in New York City and is a children's book author.

Represents Fiction, nonfiction; author-illustrator picture books.

How to Contact Query with first 5 pages. Must include e-mail address for response. Considers simultaneous queries. Responds in 3 weeks to queries; 6 weeks to mss. Obtains most new clients through recommendations and queries.

Terms Agent receives 15% commission on domestic sales; 20% commission on foreign sales. Offers written contract. Charges client for color photocopying and overseas postage.

DUNHAM LITERARY, INC.

156 Fifth Ave., Suite 625, New York NY 10010-7002. Web site: www.dunhamlit.com. **Contact:** Jennie Dunham. Seeking both new and established writers but prefers to work with established writers. Estab. 2000. Member of AAR, signatory of SCBWI. Represents 50 clients. 15% of clients are new/previously unpublished writers. 50% of material handled is books for young readers.

Represents Considers fiction, picture books, middle grade, young adult. Most agents represent children's books or adult books, and this agency represents both. Actively seeking mss with great story and voice. Not looking for activity books, workbooks, educational books, poetry.

How to Contact Query with SASE. Consider simultaneous queries and submissions. Responds in 2 weeks to queries; 2 months to mss. Returns material only with SASE. Obtains clients through recommendations from others.

Recent Sales Sold 30 books for young readers in the last year. *Winter's Tale*, by Robert Sabuda (Little Simon); *Clever Beatrice Christmas*, by Margaret Willey, illustrated by Heather Solomon (Atheneum); *Adele and Simon*, by Barbara McClintock (Farrar, Straus & Giroux); *Sweetgrass Basket*, by Marlene Carvell (Dutton); *How I Found the Strong*, by Margaret McMullan (Houghton Mifflin).

Terms Agent receives 15% commission on domestic sales; 20-25% on foreign sales. Offers written contract. 60 days notice must be given to terminate contract.

Fees The agency takes expenses from the clients' earnings for specific expenses documented during the marketing of a client's work in accordance with the AAR (Association of Authors' Representatives) Canon of Ethics. For example, photocopying, messenger, express mail, UPS, etc. The client is not asked to pay for these fees up front.

DWYER & O'GRADY, INC.

P.O. Box 790, Cedar Key FL 32625. (352)543-9307. Fax: (603)375-5373. E-mail: jdwyer@dwyerogrady.com. Web site: www.dwyerogrady.com. **Contact:** Jeff Dwyer. Estab. 1990. Member of Society of Illustrators, Graphic Artist's Guild, SCBWI, ABA. Represents 15 illustrators. Staff includes Elizabeth O'Grady, Jeff Dwyer. Specializes in children's books (picture books, middle grade and young adult). Markets include: publishing/books, audio/film.

  • Dwyer & O'Grady is currently not accepting new clients.

Handles Illustrators and writers of children's books.

Terms Agent receives 15% commission on domestic sales; 20% on foreign sales. Additional fees are negotiable. Exclusive representation is required (world rights). Advertising costs are paid by representative.

How to Contact For first contact, send query letter by postal mail only.

🖂 EDUCATIONAL DESIGN SERVICES INC.

7238 Treviso Lane, Boynton Beach FL 33437. E-mail: blinder@educationaldesignservices.com. Web site: www.educationaldesignservices.com. **Contact:** B. Linder. Handles only certain types of work. Estab. 1981. 80% of clients are new/previously unpublished writers.

Represents Considers text materials for K-12 market. "We specialize in educational materials to be used in classrooms (in class sets) or in teacher education classes." Actively seeking educational, text materials. Not looking for picture books, story books, fiction; no illustrators.

How to Contact Query with SASE or send outline and 1 sample chapter. Considers simultaneous queries and submissions if so indicated. Responds in 6-8 weeks to queries/mss. Returns material only with SASE. Obtains clients through recommendations from others, queries/solicitations, or through conferences.

Recent Sales *How to Solve Word Problems in Mathematics,* by Wayne (McGraw-Hill); *Reviewing U.S. & New York State History,* by Farran-Paci (Amsco); *Minority Report,* by Gunn-Singh (Scarecrow Education); *No Parent Left Behind,* by Petrosino & Spiegel (Rowman & Littlefield); *The Human Factor in Change,* by Zimbalist (Scarecrow Education).

Terms Agent receives 15% commission on domestic sales; 25% on foreign sales. Offers written contract, binding until any party opts out. Terminate contract through certified letter.

ETHAN ELLENBERG LITERARY AGENCY

548 Broadway, #5-E, New York NY 10012. (212)431-4554. Fax: (212)941-4652. E-mail: agent@ethanellenberg.com. Web site: EthanEllenberg.com. **Contact:** Ethan Ellenberg. Estab. 1983. Represents 80 clients. 10% of clients are new/previously unpublished writers. ''Children's books are an important area for us.''

• Prior to opening his agency, Ethan Ellenberg was contracts manager of Berkley/Jove and associate contracts manager for Bantam. Represents 2002 Cladecott Medal winner Eric Rohmann, for *My Friend Rabbit,* adapted by Nelvana and running in an animated series fall 2007 on NBC.

Represents ''We do a lot of children's books.'' Considers: picture books, middle grade, YA and selected.

How to Contact Picture books—send full ms with SASE. Young adults—send outline plus 3 sample chapters with SASE. Accepts queries by e-mail; does not accept attachments to e-mail queries or fax queries. Considers simultaneous queries and submissions. Responds in 10 days to queries; 1 month to mss. Returns materials only with SASE. ''See Web site for detailed instructions, please follow them carefully.''

Terms Agent receives 15% on domestic sales; 20% on foreign sales. Offers written contract, ''flexible.'' Charges for ''direct expenses only: photocopying for manuscript submissions, postage for submission and foreign rights sales.''

Tips ''We do consider new material from unsolicited authors. Write a clear letter with a succinct description of your book. We prefer the first three chapters when we consider fiction, but for children's book submissions, we prefer the full manuscript. For all submissions you must include SASE for return or the material is discarded. It's always hard to break in, but talent will find a home. We continue to seek natural storytellers and nonfiction writers with important books.'' This agency sold over 100 titles per year in the last 4 years (combining adult and children's books).

FLANNERY LITERARY

1155 South Washington St., Suite 202, Naperville IL 60540-3300. (630)428-2682. Fax: (630)428-2683. **Contact:** Jennifer Flannery. Estab. 1992. Represents 40 clients. 95% of clients are new/previously unpublished writers. Specializes in children's and young adult, juvenile fiction and nonfiction.

• Prior to opening her agency, Jennifer Flannery was an editorial assistant.

Represents 100% juvenile books. Considers: nonfiction, fiction, picture books, middle grade, young adult.

How to Contact Query. ''No e-mail or fax queries, please.'' Responds in 2 weeks to queries; 5 weeks to mss.

Needs Obtains new clients through referrals and queries.

Terms Agent receives 15% commission on domestic sales; 20% on foreign sales. Offers written contract, binding for life of book in print, with 30-day cancellation clause. 100% of business is derived from commissions on sales.

Tips ''Write an engrossing succinct query describing your work.'' Flannery Literary sold 20 titles in the last year.

BARRY GOLDBLATT LITERARY LLC

320 Seventh Ave., #266, Brooklyn NY 11215. (718)832-8787. Fax: (718)832-5558. E-mail: bgliterary@earthlink.net. Web site: www.bgliterary.com. **Contact:** Barry Goldblatt. Estab. 2000. Member of AAR, SCBWI. Represents 45 clients. 15% of clients are new/previously unpublished writers. 100% of material handled is books for young readers. Staff includes Barry Goldblatt (picture books, middle grade, and young adult novels).

Represents Considers picture books, fiction, middle grade, young adult.

How to Contact Send queries only; no longer accepting unsolicited manuscript submissions. Prefers to read material exclusively. Responds in 3 weeks to queries; 2 months to mss. Returns material only with SASE. Obtains clients through recommendations from others.

Recent Sales *River Palace,* by Tracie Vaughn Zimmer; *Something Wicked,* by Alan Gratz; *Odd Duck,* by Cecil Castellucci.

Terms Agent receives 15% commission on domestic sales; 20% on foreign and dramatic sales.

Tips ''I structure my relationship with each client differently, according to their wants and needs. I'm mostly hands-on, but some want more editorial input, others less. I'm pretty aggressive in selling work, but I'm fairly laid back in how I deal with clients. I'd say I'm quite friendly with most of my clients, and I like it that way. To me this is more than just a simple business relationship.''

ASHLEY GRAYSON LITERARY AGENCY

1342 18th St., San Pedro CA 90732. (310)514-0267. Fax: (310)514-1148. Seeking both new and established writers. Estab. 1976. Agency is member of AAR, SCBWI, SFWA, RWA. Represents 75 clients. 5-10% new writers. 25% books for young readers. Staff includes Ashley Grayson, young adult and middle grade; Carolyn Grayson, young adult, middle grade, some picture books; Denise Dumars, young adult.

Represents Handles fiction, middle grade, young adult. ''We represent top authors in the field and we market their books to publishers worldwide.'' Actively seeking fiction of high commercial potential.

How to Contact Query with SASE. Include first 3 pages of manuscript; if querying about a picture books, include entire text. Accepts queries by mail and e-mail. Considers simultaneous queries. Responds 1 month after query, 2-3 months after ms. Returns mss only with SASE. Obtains new clients through recommendations from others, queries/solicitations, conferences.

Recent Sales Sold 25+ books last year. *Juliet Dove, Queen of Love*, by Bruce Coville (Harcourt); *Alosha*, by Christopher Pike (TOR); *Sleeping Freshmen Never Lie*, by David Lubar (Dutton); *Ball Don't Lie*, by Matt de la Peña (Delacorte); *Wiley & Grampa's Creature Features*, by Kirk Scroggs (6-book series, Little Brown); *Street Pharm*, by Allison van Diepen (Simon Pulse). Also represents: J.B. Cheaney (Knopf), Bruce Wetter (Atheneum).

Terms Agent receives 15% on domestic sales, 20% on foreign sales. Offers written contract. Contract binding for 1 year. 30 days notice must be given for termination of contract.

Tips ''We do request revisions as they are required. We are long-time agents, professional and known in the business. We perform professionally for our clients and we ask the same of them.''

BARBARA S. KOUTS, LITERARY AGENT

P.O. Box 560, Bellport NY 11713. (631)286-1278. **Contact:** Barbara Kouts. Currently accepting new clients. Estab. 1980. Member of AAR. Represent 50 clients. 10% of clients are new/previously unpublished writers. Specializes in children's books.

Represents 100% juvenile books. Considers: nonfiction, fiction, picture books, ms/illustration packages, middle grade, young adult.

How to Contact Accepts queries by mail only. Responds in 1 week to queries; 6 weeks to mss.

Needs Obtains new clients through recommendations from others, solicitation, at conferences, etc.

Recent Sales *Code Talker*, by Joseph Bruchac (Dial); *The Penderwicks*, by Jeanne Birdsall (Knopf); *Frogg's Baby Sister*, by Jonathan London (Viking).

Terms Agent receives 10% commission on domestic sales; 20% on foreign sales. Charges for photocopying.

Tips ''Write, do not call. Be professional in your writing.''

MCINTOSH & OTIS, INC.

353 Lexington Ave., New York NY 10016. (212)687-7400. Fax: (212)687-6894. **Contact:** Edward Necarsulmer IV. Seeking both new and established writers. Estab. 1927. Member of AAR and SCBWI. 20% of clients are new/previously unpublished writers. 100% of material handled is books for young readers.

Represents Considers fiction, middle grade, young adult. ''McIntosh & Otis has a long history of representing authors of adult and children's books. The children's department is a separate division.'' Actively seeking ''books with memorable characters, distinctive voice, and a great plot.'' Not looking for educational, activity books, coloring books.

How to Contact Query with SASE. Exclusive submission only. Responds in 6 weeks. Returns material only with SASE. Obtains clients through recommendations from others or through conferences.

Terms Agent receives 15% commission on domestic sales; 20% on foreign sales.

Writers' Conferences Attends Bologna Book Fair in Bologna Italy in April, SCBWI Conference in New York in February, and regularly attends other conferences and industry conventions.

Tips ''No e-mail or phone calls!''

MEWS BOOKS

20 Bluewater Hill, Westport CT 06880. (203)227-1836. Fax: (203)227-1144. E-mail: mewsbooks@aol.com. **Contact:** Sidney B. Kramer. Seeking both new and established writers. Estab. 1974. 50% of material handled is books for young readers. Staff includes Sidney B. Kramer and Fran Pollak.

- Previously Sidney Kramer was Senior Vice President and founder of Bantam Books, President of New American Library, Director and Manager of Corgi Books in London, and an attorney.

Represents Considers adult nonfiction, fiction; picture books, middle grade, young adult with outstanding characters and stories. Actively seeking books that have continuity of character and story. Not looking for unedited, poorly written mss by authors seeking learning experience.

How to Contact Query with SASE, send outline and 2 sample chapters. Accepts short e-mail specific queries but not sumbissions or attachments. Prefers to read material exclusively. Responds in a few weeks to queries.

Returns material only with SASE. Obtains clients through recommendations from others, and through conferences.

Recent Sales Sold 10 books for young readers in the last year.

Terms Agent receives 15% commission on domestic sales; 20% on foreign sales. Offers written contract, binding for 1-2 years. "We never retain an unhappy author, but we cannot terminate in the middle of activity. If submission is accepted, we ask for $100 against all expenses. We occasionally make referrals to editing services."

ERIN MURPHY LITERARY AGENCY

2700 Woodlands Village, #300-458, Flagstaff AZ 86001-7127. (928)525-2056. Closed to unsolicited queries and submissions. Considers both new and established writers, by referral or personal contact (such as conferences) only. Estab. 1999. Member of SCBWI and AAR. Represents 50 clients. 40% of clients are new/previously unpublished writers. 100% of material handled is books of young readers.

● Prior to opening her agency, Erin Murphy was editor-in-chief at Northland Publishing/Rising Moon. Agency is not currently accepting unsolicited queries or submissions.

Represents Picture books, middle grade, young adult.

Terms Agent receives 15% commission on domestic sales; 20% on foreign sales. Offers written contract. 30 days notice must be given to terminate contract.

Recent sales Sold 25 books for young readers in the last year. Recent releases: *Ellie McDoodle: Have Pen, Will Travel,* by Ruth McNally Barshaw (Bloomsbury); *Honk If You Hate Me,* by Deborah Halverson (Delacorte); *I could Eat You Up,* by Jo Harper (Holiday House); *The One Where the Kid Nearly Jumps to His Death and Lands in California,* by Mary Hershey (Razorbill); *Theodosia and the Serpents of Chaos,* by R.L. LaFevers (Houghton); *How to Take the Ex Out of Ex-Boyfriend,* by Janette Rallison (Putnam).

N JEAN V. NAGGAR LITERARY AGENCY, INC.

216 E. 75th Street, Suite 1E, New York NY 10021.(212)794-1082. Fax: (212)794-3605. E-mail: jregel@jvnla.com. (all first initial last name@jvnla.com). Web site: www.jvnla.com. Seeking both new and established writers. Estab. 1978. Member of AAR, SCBWI. Represents 150 clients. Large percentage of clients are new/previously unpublished writers. 25% material handled is books for young readers.

Member Agents Jennifer Weltz (subrights, children's, adults); Jessica Regel (young adult, adult, subrights); Jean Naggar (adult, children's); Alice Tasman (adult, children's); Mollie Glick (adult, fiction and nonfiction, contracts).

Represents Handles nonfiction, fiction, picture books, middle grade, young adult.

How to Contact Query with SASE. Accepts queries by e-mail, mail. Prefers to read materials exclusively. Responds in 2 weeks to queries; response time for ms depends on the agent. Returns mss only with SASE. Obtains new clients through recommendations from others, queries/solicitations, conferences.

Recent Sales See Web site for information.

ALISON PICARD, LITERARY AGENT

P.O. Box 2000, Cotuit MA 02635. Phone/fax: (508)477-7192. E-mail: ajpicard@aol.com. **Contact:** Alison Picard. Seeking both new and established writers. Estab. 1985. Represents 50 clients. 40% of clients are new/previously unpublished writers. 20% of material handled is books for young readers.

● Prior to opening her agency, Alison Picard was an assistant at a large New York agency before co-founding Kidde, Hoyt & Picard in 1982. She became an independent agent in 1985.

Represents Considers nonfiction, fiction, a very few picture books, middle grade, young adult. "I represent juvenile and YA books. I do not handle short stories, articles, poetry or plays. I am especially interested in commercial nonfiction, romances and mysteries/suspense/thrillers. I work with agencies in Europe and Los Angeles to sell foreign and TV/film rights." Actively seeking middle grade fiction. Not looking for poetry or plays.

How to Contact Query with SASE. Accepts queries by e-mail with no attachments. Considers simultaneous queries and submissions. Responds in 2 weeks to queries; 4 months to mss. Returns material only with SASE. Obtains clients through queries/solicitations.

Recent Sales *Funerals and Fly Fishing,* by Mary Bartek (Henry Holt & Co.), *Stage Fright,* by Dina Friedman (Farrar Straus & Giroux), *Escaping into the Night,* by Dina Friedman (Simon & Schuster), *Celebritrees* and *The Peace Bell,* by Margi Preus (Henry Holt & Co.)

Terms Receives 15% commission on domestic sales; 20-25% on foreign sales. Offers written contract, binding for 1 year. 1-week notice must be given to terminate contract.

Tips "We currently have a backlog of submissions."

[N] PROSPECT AGENCY

285 5th Ave., PMB 445, Brooklyn NY 11215. (718)788-3217. Fax: (718)788-3217. E-mail: esk@prospectagency.com. Web site: www.prospectagency.com. **Contact:** Emily Sylvan Kim. Seeking both new and established writers. Estab. 2005. Agent is member of SCBWI and RWA. Represents 25 clients. 75% of clients are new/previously unpublished writers. 50% of material handled is books for young readers.

Represents Handles nonfiction, fiction, picture books, middle grade, young adult. "Prospect Agency is a small, personal agency that focuses on helping each client reach maximum success through hands-on editorial assistance and professional contract negitiations. We also strive to be on the cutting edge technologically." Actively seeking middle grade and YA books.

How to Contact Send outline and 3 sample chapters. Accepts queries through Web site. Considers sumultaneous queries, submissions. Responds in 6 weeks to query and mss. Discards unaccepted mss. Obtains new clients through recommendations from others, queries/solicitations, conferences.

Recent Sales Sold 2 books for young readers in the last year. (Also represents adult fiction.) Recent sales include: *God's Own Drunk*, by Tim Tharp (Knopf); Bewitching Season, by Marissa Doyle (Holt); *Debbie Harry Sings in French*, by Meagan Brothers (Holt); *Knights of the Hill Country*, by Tim Tharp (Knopf). Clients include: Rose Kent, Meagan Brothers, Catherine Stine.

Terms Agent receives 15% on domestic sales, 20% on foreign sales. Offers written contract.

Writer's Conferences Attends SCBWI Annual Winter Conference in New York (February annually); South Carolina Writers Workshop, Myrtle Beach, SC (October 2007); RWA (Romance Writers of America), location vaires (July annually).

Tips "I am a very hands-on agent who spends a lot of time forming personal relationships both with the work and the author him or herself. I try to balance the goals of selling individual product and managing a career."

WENDY SCHMALZ AGENCY

P.O. Box 831, Hudson NY 12534. (518)672-7697. Fax: (518)672-7662. E-mail: wendy@schmalzagency.com. **Contact:** Wendy Schmalz. Seeking both new and established writers. Estab. 2002. Member of AAR. Represents 30 clients. 10% of clients are new/previously unpublished writers. 50% of material handled is books for young readers.

● Prior to opening her agency, Wendy Schmalz was an agent for 23 years at Harold Ober Associates.

Represents Considers nonfiction, fiction, middle grade, young adult. Actively seeking young adult novels, middle grade novels. Not looking for picture books, science fiction or fantasy.

How to Contact Query with SASE. Accepts queries by e-mail. Considers simultaneous queries. Responds in 2 weeks to queries; 4-6 weeks to mss. Returns material only with SASE. Obtains clients through recommendations from others.

Recent Sales Sold 30 books for young readers in the last year.

Terms Agent receives 15% commission on domestic sales; 20% on foreign sales. Fees for photocopying and FedEx.

SUSAN SCHULMAN LITERARY AGENCY

454 W. 44th, New York NY 10036. (212)713-1633. Fax: (212)581-8830. E-mail: schulman@aol.com. Web site: www.schulmanagency.com. Seeking both new and established writers. Estab. 1980. Member of AAR, WGA, SCBWI, Dramatists Guild. 15% of material handled is books for young readers. Staff includes Emily Uhry, YA; Linda Megalti, picture books.

Represents Handles nonfiction, fiction, picture books, middle grade, young adult. Actively seeking well-written, original stories for any age group.

How to Contact Query with SASE. Accepts queries by e-mail, mail. Considers sumultaneous queries and submissions. Returns mss only with SASE. Obtains new clients through recommendations from others, queries/solicitations, conferences.

Recent Sales Of total agency sales, approximately 20% is children's literature. Recent sales include: 10-book deal to Scholastic for Jim Arnosky; *Remarkable Girl*, by Pamela Lowell (Marshall Cavendish); *I Get All Better*, by Vickie Cobb (4-book series with Lerner); film rights to *Geography Club*, by Brent Hartinger (East of Doheny); television rights to Louis Sachar's *Sideways Stories from Wayside School* (Nickelodeon).

Terms Agent receives 15% on domestic sales, 20% on foreign sales.

Writers' Conferences Attending IWWG in Geneva, Switzerland and New York and Columbus Writer's Conference.

Tips Schulman describes her agency as "professional boutique, long-standing, eclectic."

[N] SERENDIPITY LITERARY AGENCY

305 Gates Ave., Brooklyn NY 11216. (718)230-7689. Fax: (718)230-7829. E-mail: rbrooks@serendipitylit.com. Web site: www.serendipitylit.com. Contact: Regina Brooks. Estab. 2000. Represents 50 clients. 65% of clients are new/unpublished writers. 50% of material handled is books for young readers.

● Prior to becoming an agent, Regina Brooks was an acquisitions editor for John Wiley & Sons and McGraw-Hill Companies.

Represents Handles all children's books areas from picture books to young adult, both fiction and nonfiction. Actively seeking young adult novels with an urban flair and juvenile books.

How to Contact Prefers to read material exclusively. For nonfiction, submit outline, 1 sample chapter and SASE. Accepts e-mail queries. Responds to queries in 4 weeks; mss in 1 month. Obtains new clients through writer's conferences and referrals.

Recent Sales *A Wreath for Emmitt Till*, by Marilyn Nelson (Houghton Mifflin); *A Song for Present Existence*, by Marilyn Nelson and Tonya Hegamin (Scholastic); *Ruby and the Booker Boys*, by Derrick Barnes (Scholastic); *Brenda Buckley's Universe and Everything In It*, by Sundee Frazier (Delacorte Books for Young Readers); *Wait Until the Black Girl Sings*, by Bil Wright (Scholastic); *First Semester*, by Cecil R. Cross II (KimaniTru/Harlequin).

Terms Agent receives 15% commission on domestic sales; 20% on foreign sales. Offers written contract. Terminations notice—2 months.

Tips "I adore working with first-time authors whose books challenge the readers emotionally; tears and laughter. I also represent award-winning illustrators."

STIMOLA LITERARY STUDIO, LLC

308 Chase Court, Edgewater NJ 07020. Phone/fax: (201)945-9353. E-mail: LtryStudio@aol.com. **Contact:** Rosemary B. Stimola. Seeking both new and established writers. Estab. 1997. Member of AAR, SCBWI, ALA. Represents 45+ clients. 25% of clients are new/previously unpublished writers. 85% of material handled is books for young readers.

● Prior to opening her agency Rosemary Stimola was an independent children's bookseller.

Represents Preschool through young adult, fiction and nonfiction. Agency is owned and operated by a former educator and children's bookseller with a Ph.D. in Linguistics. Actively seeking remarkable young adult fiction and debut picture book author/illustrators. No institutional books.

How to Contact Query with SASE or e-mail. No attachments, please! Considers simultaneous queries. Responds in 3 weeks to queries; 4-6 weeks to mss. Returns material only with SASE. While unsolicited queries are welcome, most clients come through editor, agent, client referrals.

Recent Sales Sold 40 books for young readers in the last year. *The Hunger Games Trilogy*, by Suzanne Collins (Scholastic); *Hurricane Song*, by Paul Volponi (Viking/Penguin); *Be Gentle with the Dog Dear*, by Matthew Baek (Dial/Penguin); *Almost Astronauts*, by Tanya Lee Stone (Candlewick Press); *The Red Blazer Girls and the Ring of Rocamadour*, by Michael Beil (Knopf/ RandomHouse); *Nighty Night, Sleepy Sleep*, by Brian Anderson (Roaring Brook Press); *Carpe Diem!*, by Autumn Cornwell (Feiwel & Friends); *A Little Friendly Advice*, by Siobhan Vivian (Scholastic); *Scoot*, by Catherine Falwell (Greenwillow/Harper); *Big Chickens Fly the Coop*, by Leslie Helakoski (Dutton/Penguin).

Terms Agent receives 15% commission on domestic sales; 20% on foreign sales (if subagents used). Offers written contract, binding for all children's projects. 60 days notice must be given to terminate contract. Charges $85 one-time fee per project to cover expenses. Client provides all copies of submission. "Fee is taken from first advance payment and is payable *only* if manuscript is sold."

Writers' Conferences Will attend: ALA Midwinter, BEA, Bologna Book Fair, SCBWI-Illinois regional conference; SCBWI Annual Winter Conference in New York, SCBWI-New York Metro.

Tips Agent is hands-on, no-nonsense. May request revisions. Does not edit but may offer suggestions for improvement. Well-respected by clients and editors. "A firm but reasonable deal negotiator."

ANN TOBIAS—A LITERARY AGENCY FOR CHILDREN'S BOOKS

520 E. 84th St., Apt. 4L, New York NY 10028. **Contact:** Ann Tobias. Seeking both new and established writers. Handles only certain types of work. Estab. 1988. Represents 25 clients. 10% of clients are new/previously unpublished writers. 100% of material handled is books for children.

● Prior to opening her agency, Ann Tobias worked as a children's book editor at Harper, William Morrow, Scholastic.

Represents Fiction, nonfiction, middle grade, picture books, poetry, young adult, young readers.

How to Contact Send a one-page letter of inquiry accompanied by a one-page writing sample, double-spaced. No e-mail, fax or phone queries. Cannot sign for receipt of ms. Accepts simultaneous submissions for queries only. Must have 1 month exclusive basis for considering an entire ms after inviting author to submit. Responds to all queries accompanied by SASE; 2 months to mss. Returns material only with SASE. Obtains clients through recommendations from editors.

Recent Sales Sold 12 titles in the last year.

Terms Agent receives 15% commission on domestic sales; 20% on foreign sales.

Tips "Read at least 200 children's books in the age group and genre in which you hope to be published.

Follow this by reading another 100 children's books in other age groups and genres so you will have a feel for the field as a whole.''

S©OTT TREIMEL NY

434 Lafayette St., New York NY 10003. (212)505-8353. Fax: (212)505-0664. E-mail: st.ny@verizon.net. **Contact:** Scott Treimel. Estab. 1995. Represents 40 clients. 10% of clients are new/unpublished writers. Specializes in children's books, all genres: tightly focused segments of the trade and institutional markets. Member AAR, Author's Guild, SCBWI.

- Prior to opening his agency, Scott Treimel was an assistant to Marilyn E. Marlow of Curtis Brown; a rights agent for Scholastic, Inc.; a book packager and rights agent for United Feature Syndicate; the founding director of Warner Bros. Worldwide Publishing; a freelance editor; and a rights consultant for HarperCollins Children's Books.

Represents 100% juvenile books. Actively seeking career clients.

How to Contact Send query/ouline, SASE, sample chapters of no more than 50 pages. No multiple submissions. Queries without SASE will be recycled. No fax queries.

Recent Sales Sold 23 titles in the last year. *What Happened to Cass McBride?*, by Gail Gailes (Little, Brown); *Fragments*, by Jeff Johnston (Simon & Schuster); *The Ugliest Beast*, by Pat Hughes (Farrar, Straus & Giroux); *But That's Another Story*, by Mary Hanson (Random House/Schwartz & Wade); *Megido's Shadow*, by Art Slade (Random House/Wendy Lamb Books); *Death & Me*, by Richard Scrimger (Tundra Books).

Terms Agent receives 15-20% commission on domestic sales; 20-25% on foreign sales. Offers verbal or written contract, binding on a ''contract-by-contract basis.'' Charges for photocopying, overnight/express postage, messengers and books ordered for subsidiary rights sales. Offers editorial guidance, if extensive charges higher commission.

Writers' Conferences Speaks at Society of Children's Book Writers and Illustrators Conference; The New School; Southwest Writers Conference; Pikes Peak Writers Conference

Tips ''Keep cover letters short and do not pitch.''

WRITERS HOUSE

21 W. 26th St., New York NY 10010. (212)685-2400. Fax: (212)685-1781. Web site: www.writershouse.com. Estab. 1974. Member of AAR. Represents 280 clients. Specializes in all types of popular fiction and nonfiction. No scholarly, professional, poetry or screenplays.

Member Agents Amy Berkower; Merrilee Heifetz (middle grade and YA); Susan Cohen (picture book illustrators as well as children's authors); Jodi Reamer; Steven Malk (middle-grade, YA, and picture book illustrators and authors); Robin Rue; Kenneth Wright; Rebecca Sherman (picture book author/illustrators, middle grade & YA); Daniel Lazar (middle grade & YA).

Represents 35% juvenile books. Considers: nonfiction, fiction, picture books, middle grade, young adult.

How to Contact Query. Please check our Web site for more specific submission guidelines and info about our agents.

Needs Obtains new clients through referrals and query letters.

Terms Agent receives 15% commission on domestic sales; 20% on foreign sales. Offers written contract, binding for 1 year.

Tips ''Do not send manuscripts. Write a compelling letter. If you do, we'll ask to see your work.''

WRITERS HOUSE

(West Coast Office), 3368 Governor Dr., Suite 224F, San Diego CA 92122. (858)678-8767. Fax: (858)678-8530. **Contact:** Steven Malk.

- See Writers House listing above for more information.

Represents Nonfiction, fiction, picture books, middle-grade novels, young adult, illustrators.

WYLIE-MERRICK LITERARY AGENCY

1138 S. Webster St., Kokomo IN 46902. (765)459-8258. E-mail: See Web site. Web site: www.wylie-merrick.com. **Contact:** Sharene Martin-Brown or Robert Brown. Works with both new and established writers. Estab. 1999. Member of AAR, SCBWI. Represents 22 clients. 20% of clients are new/previously unpublished writers. 5% of material handled is books for young readers. Staff includes Sharene Martin-Brown (children's and adult fiction and selected commercial nonfiction), Robert Brown (adult fiction and nonfiction), and Ann Boyle (adult fiction).

- Always visit Web site before querying.

Represents Considers mainstream and genre fiction, nonfiction, selected commercial children's projects.

How to Contact ''See our Web site for detailed contact information; no phone queries please.''

Recent Sales *Windless Summer*, by Heather Sharfeddin (Bantam Dell); *Last Kiss*, by Jon Ripslinger; *Epoch*, by Tim Carter (Flux).

Terms Agent receives 15% commission on domestic sales; 20% on foreign sales. Offers written contract. Charges no fees prior to sale.

Writers' Conferences Recenlty attend BookExpo America (May 31-June 3, 2007); Willamette Writers Conference (August 3-5, 2007).

Tips "If you have to ask what constitutes being a professional writer, then you aren't ready to seek an agent. You should prepare yourself for a writing career in the same way you prepare for any other career—education and experience."

ART REPS

ART FACTORY

925 Elm Grove Rd., Elm Grove WI 53122. (262)785-1940. Fax: (262)785-1611. E-mail: tstocki@artfactoryltd.com. Web site: www.artfactoryltd.com. **Contact:** Tom Stocki. Commercial illustration representative. Estab. 1978. Represents 9 illustrators including: Tom Buchs, Tom Nachreiner, Todd Dakins, Linda Godfrey, Larry Mikec, Bill Scott, Gary Shea, Terry Herman, Troy Allen. 10% of artwork handled is children's book illustration. Currently open to illustrators seeking representation. Open to both new and established illustrators.

Handles Illustration.

Terms Receives 25-30% commission. Offers written contract. Advertising costs are split: 75% paid by illustrators; 25% paid by rep. "We try to mail samples of all our illustrators at one time and we try to update our Web site; so we ask the illustrators to keep up with new samples." Advertises in *Picturebook*, *Workbook*.

How to Contact For first contact, send query letter, tearsheets. Responds only if interested. Call to schedule an appointment. Portfolio should include tearsheets. Finds illustrators through queries/solicitations.

Tips "Have a unique style."

ASCIUTTO ART REPS., INC.

1712 E. Butler Circle, Chandler AZ 85225. (480)899-0600. Fax: (480)899-3636. E-mail: Aartreps@cox.net. **Contact:** Mary Anne Asciutto, art agent. Children's illustration representative since 1980. Specializing in children's illustrations for children's educational text books, grades K thru 8, children's trade books, children's magazines, posters, packaging, etc.

Recent Sales *Bats, Sharks, Whales, Snakes, Penguins, Alligators and Crocodiles*, illustrated by Meryl Henderson (Boyds Mills Press).

Terms Agency receives 25% commission. No geographic restrictions. Advertising and promotion costs are split: 75% paid by talent; 25% paid by representative.

How to Contact Send samples via email with a cover letter résumé. Submit sample portfolio for review with an SASE for it's return. Responds in 2 to 4 weeks. Portfolio should include at least 12 samples of original art, printed tearsheets, photocopies or color prints of most recent work.

Tips In obtaining representation, "be sure to connect with an agent who handles the kind of work, you (the artist) *want*."

CAROL BANCROFT & FRIENDS

4 Old Mill Plain Road., Danbury CT 06811. (203)730-8270 or (800)720-7020. Fax: (203)730-8275. E-mail: artists @carolbancroft.com. Web site: www.carolbancroft.com. **Owner:** Joy Elton Tricario. **Founder:** Carol Bancroft. Illustration representative for children's publishing. Estab. 1972. Member of SPAR, Society of Illustrators, Graphic Artists Guild, National Art Education Association, SCBWI. Represents 40 illustrators. Specializes in illustration for children's publishing-text and trade; any children's-related material. Clients include, but not limited to, Scholastic, Houghton Mifflin, HarperCollins, Dutton, Harcourt.

Handles Illustration for children of all ages.

Terms Rep receives 25-30% commission. Advertising costs are split: 75% paid by talent; 25% paid by representative. For promotional purposes, talent must provide "laser copies (not slides), tearsheets, promo pieces, good color photocopies, etc.; 6 pieces or more is best; narrative scenes and children interacting." Advertises in RSVP, Picture Book, Directory of Illustration.

How to Contact "Send either 2-3 samples with your Web site address to the e-mail address above or mail 6-10 samples, along with a self-addressed, stamped envelope (SASE) to the street address provided."

PEMA BROWNE LTD.

11 Tena Place, Valley Cottage NY 10989. (845)268-0029. **Contact:** Pema Browne. Estab. 1966. Represents 2 illustrators. 10% of artwork handled is children's book illustration. Specializes in general commercial. Markets

include: all publishing areas; children's picture books. Clients include HarperCollins, Holiday House, Bantam Doubleday Dell, Nelson/Word, Hyperion, Putnam. Client list available upon request.

Handles Fiction, nonfiction, picture books, middle grade, young adult, manuscript/illustration packages. Looking for "professional and unique" talent.

Recent Sales *The Daring Ms. Quimby*, by Suzanne Whitaker (Holiday House).

Terms Rep receives 30% illustration commission; 15% author commission. Exclusive area representation is required. For promotional purposes, talent must provide color mailers to distribute. Representative pays mailing costs on promotion mailings.

How to Contact For first contact, send query letter, direct mail flier/brochure and SASE. If interested will ask to mail appropriate materials for review. Portfolios should include tearsheets and transparencies or good color photocopies, plus SASE. Accepts queries by mail only. Obtains new talent through recommendations and interviews (portfolio review).

Tips "We are doing more publishing—all types—less advertising." Looks for "continuity of illustration and dedication to work."

CATUGEAU: ARTIST AGENT, LLC

3009 Margaret Jones Lane, Williamsburg VA 23185. (757)221-0666. Fax: (757)221-6669. E-mail: chris@catugeau.com. Web site: www.CATugeau.com. **Owner/Agent:** Chris Tugeau. Children's publishing trade book, mass market, educational. Estab. 1994. Member of SPAR, SCBWI, Graphic Artists Guild. Represents 35 illustrators. 95% of artwork handled is children's book illustration.
- Accepting limited new artists.

Handles Illustration ONL Y.

Terms Receives 25% commission. "Artists responsible for providing samples for portfolios, promotional books and mailings." Exclusive representation required in educational. Trade "house accounts" acceptable. Offers written contract. Advertises in *Picturebook*.

How to Contact For first contact, e-mail samples with note. No CDs. Responds ASAP. Finds illustrators through recommendations from others, conferences, personal search.

Tips "Do research, read articles on CAT Web site, study picture books at bookstores, promote yourself a bit to learn the industry. Be professional. Know what you do best, and be prepared to give rep what they need to present you! Do have e-mail and scanning capabilities, too."

CORNELL & McCARTHY, LLC

2-D Cross Hwy., Westport CT 06880. (203)454-4210. Fax: (203)454-4258. E-mail: contact@cmartreps.com. Web site: www.cmartreps.com. **Contact:** Merial Cornell. Children's book illustration representatives. Estab. 1989. Member of SCBWI and Graphic Artists Guild. Represents 30 illustrators. Specializes in children's books: trade, mass market, educational.

Handles Illustration.

Terms Agent receives 25% commission. Advertising costs are split: 75% paid by talent; 25% paid by representative. For promotional purposes, talent must provide 10-12 strong portfolio pieces relating to children's publishing.

How to Contact For first contact, send query letter, direct mail flier/brochure, tearsheets, photocopies and SASE or e-mail. Responds in 1 month. Obtains new talent through recommendations, solicitation, conferences.

Tips "Work hard on your portfolio."

CREATIVE FREELANCERS, INC.

4 Greenwich Hills Drive, Greenwich CT 06831 (800)398-9544. Web site: www.illustratorsonline.com; www.freelancers.com. **Contact:** Marilyn Howard. Commercial illustration representative. Estab. 1988. Represents over 30 illustrators. "Our staff members have art direction, art buying or illustration backgrounds." Specializes in children's books, advertising, architectural, conceptual. Markets include: advertising agencies; corporations/client direct; design firms; editorial/magazines; paper products/greeting cards; publishing/books; sales/promotion firms.

Handles Illustration. Artists must have published work.

Terms Rep receives 30% commission. Exclusive area representation is preferred. Advertising costs are split: 75% paid by talent; 25% paid by representative. For promotional purposes, talent must provide scans of artwork. Advertises in *American Showcase*, *Workbook*.

How to Contact For first contact, send tearsheets, low res jpegs or "whatever best shows work." Responds back only if interested.

Tips Looks for experience, professionalism and consistency of style. Obtains new talent through "word of mouth and Web site."

DIMENSION

13420 Morgan Ave. S., Burnsville MN 55337. (952)201-3981. Fax: (952)895-9315. E-mail: jkoltes@dimensioncreative.com. Web site: www.dimensioncreative.com. **Contact:** Joanne Koltes. Commercial illustration representative. Estab. 1982. Member of MN Book Builder. Represents 12 illustrators. 45% of artwork handled is children's book illustration. Staff includes Joanne Koltes.
Terms Advertises in *Picturebook* and *Minnesota Creative*.
How to Contact Contact via phone or e-mail. Responds only if interested.

DWYER & O'GRADY, INC.

P.O. Box 790, Cedar Key FL 32625-0790. (352)543-9307. Fax: (603)375-5373. E-mail: eogrady@dwyerogrady.com. Web site: www.dwyerogrady.com. **Contact:** Elizabeth O'Grady. Agents for children's artists and writers. Estab. 1990. Member of Society of Illustrators, Author's Guild, SCBWI, ABA. Represents 18 illustrators and 7 writers. Staff includes Elizabeth O'Grady, Jeffrey Dwyer. Specializes in children's books (picture books, middle grade and young adult). Markets include: publishing/books, audio/film.
  ● Dwyer & O'Grady is currently not accepting new clients.
Handles Illustrators and writers of children's books.
Recent Sales *Cheelin*, by James Rumford (Houghton); *Silent Music*, by James Rumford (Roaring Brook); *Hogwood Steps Out* and *The Longest Bark*, both written by Howard Mansfield, illustrated by Barry Moser (Roaring Brook); *Jewish Alphabet*, by Rich Michelson (Sleeping Bear); *Yatandou*, illustrated by Peter Sylvada (Sleeping Bear); *Ellen's Broom*, by Kelly Starling-Lyons (Putnam); *Stars on the Ceiling*, by Geoffrey Norman (Putnam); *Mogo*, illustrated by Lita Judge (Hyperion), *Halloween on Monster Street*, by Danny Schnitzlein, illustrated by Matt Faulkner (Peachtree); *Legend of the Cape May Diamond*, illustrated by E.B. Lewis (Sleeping Bear).
Terms Receives 15% commission domestic, 20% foreign. Additional fees are negotiable. Exclusive representation is required (world rights). Advertising costs are paid by representative.
How to Contact For first contact, send query letter by postal mail only.

PAT HACKETT/ARTIST REP

7014 N. Mercer Way, Mercer Island WA 98040-2130. (206)447-1600. Fax: (206)447-0739. Web site: www.pathackett.com. **Contact:** Pat Hackett. Commercial illustration representative. Estab. 1979. Member of Graphic Artists Guild. Represents 12 illustrators. 10% of artwork handled is children's book illustration. Currently open to illustrators seeking representation. Open to both new and established illustrators.
Handles Illustration. Looking for illustrators with unique, strong, salable style.
Represents Bryan Ballinger, Kooch Campbell, Jonathan Combs, Eldon Doty.
Terms Receives 25-33% commission. Advertising costs are split: 75% paid by illustrators; 25% paid by rep. Illustrator must provide portfolios (2-3) and promotional pieces. Advertises in *Picturebook*, *Workbook*.
How to Contact For first contact, send query letter, tearsheets, SASE, direct mail flier/brochure. Responds only if interested. Wait for response. Portfolio should include tearsheets. Lasers OK. Finds illustrators through recommendations from others, queries/solicitations.
Tips "Send query plus one or two samples, either by regular mail or e-mail."

HANNAH REPRESENTS

14431 Ventura Blvd., #108, Sherman Oaks CA 91423. (818)378-1644. E-mail: hannahrepresents@yahoo.com. **Contact:** Hannah Robinson. Literary representative for illustrators. Estab. 1997. 100% of artwork handled is children's book illustration. Looking for established illustrators only.
Handles Manuscript/illustration packages. Looking for illustrators with picture book story and illustration proposal.
Terms Receives 15% commission. Offers written contract.
How to Contact For first contact, send SASE and tearsheets. Responds only if interested. Call to schedule an appointment. Portfolio should include photocopies. Finds illustrators through recommendations from others, conferences, queries/solicitations, international.
Tips "Present a carefully developed range of characterization illustrations that are world-class enough to equal those in the best children's books."

HERMAN AGENCY

350 Central Park West, New York NY 10025. (212)749-4907. Fax: (212)662-5151. E-mail: ronnie@hermanagencyinc.com. Web site: www.hermanagencyinc.com. **Contact:** Ronnie Ann Herman. Literary and artistic agency. Estab. 1999. Member of SCBWI and Graphic Artists Guild. Illustrators include: Joy Allen, Tom Arma, Durga Bernhard, Ann Catherine Blake, Mary Bono, Jason Chapman, Seymour Chwast, Pascale Constantin, Kathy Couri, Doreen Gay-Kassel, Jan Spivey Gilchrist, Barry Gott, Steve Haskamp, Aleksey Ivanov, Jago, Gideon Kendall, Ana Martin Larranaga, Mike Lester, Bob McMahon, Margie Moore, Alexi Natchev, Jill Newton, John

Nez, Betina Ogden, Tamara Petrosino, Michael Rex, Pete Whitehead, Wendy Rouillard, David Sheldon, Richard Torrey, Mark Weber, Candace Whitman, Deborah Zemke. Authors include: Deloris Jordan. 90% of artwork handled is children's book illustration and related markets. Currently not accepting new clients unless they have been successfully published by major trade publishing houses.

Handles Illustration, manuscript/illustration packages and mss.

Terms Receives 25% commission for illustration assignments; 15% for ms assignments. Artists pay 75% of costs for promotional material, about $300 a year. Exclusive representation usually required. Offers written contract. Advertising costs are split: 75% paid by illustrator; 25% paid by rep. Advertises in *Picturebook*, *Directory of Illustration*, *Promo Pages*.

How to Contact For first contact, send samples, SASE, direct mail flier/brochure, tearsheets, photocopies. Authors should e-mail with a query. Responds in 1 month or less. "I will contact you if I like your samples." Portfolio should include tearsheets, photocopies, books, dummies. Finds illustrators and authors through recommendations from others, conferences, queries/solicitations.

HK PORTFOLIO

10 E. 29th St., 40G, New York NY 10016. (212)689-7830. E-mail: mela@hkportfolio.com. Web site: www.hkportfolio.com. **Contact:** Mela Bolinao. Illustration representative. Estab. 1986. Member of SPAR, Society of Illustrators and Graphic Artists Guild. Represents 44 illustrators. Specializes in illustration for juvenile markets. Markets include: advertising agencies; editorial/magazines; publishing/books.

Handles Illustration.

Recent Sales *Sweet Tooth*, illustrated by Jack E. Davis (Simon & Schuster); *The Perfect Nest*, illustrated by John Manders (Candlewick); *The Goodnight Train*, illustrated by by Laura Huliska Beith (Harcourt); *Ducks Dunk*, illustrated by Hiroe Nakata (Henry Holt); *Here Comes T. Rex Cottontail*, illustrated by Jack E. Davis (HarperCollins).

Terms Rep receives 25% commission. No geographic restrictions. Advertising costs are split: 75% paid by talent; 25% paid by representative. Advertises in *Picturebook*, *Directory of Illustration* and *Workbook*.

How to Contact No geographic restrictions. For first contact, send query letter, direct mail flier/brochure, Web site address, tearsheets, slides, photographs or color copies and SASE or send Web site link to mela@hkportfolio.com. Responds in 1 week. Portfolio should include at least 12 images appropriate for the juvenile market.

LEVY CREATIVE MANAGEMENT

300 E. 46th St., Suite 8E, New York NY 10017. (212)687-6465. Fax: (212)661-4839. E-mail: info@levycreative.com. Web site: www.levycreative.com. **Contact:** Sari Levy. Estab. 1998. Member of Society of Illustrators, Graphic Artists Guild, Art Directors Club. Represents 13 illustrators including: Alan Dingman, Marcos Chin, Thomas Fluharty, Max Gafe, Liz Lomax, Oren Sherman, Jason Tharp. 30% of artwork handled is children's book illustration. Currently open to illustrators seeking representation. Open to both new and established illustrators. Submission guidelines available on Web site.

Handles Illustration, manuscript/illustration packages.

Terms Exclusive representation required. Offers written contract. Advertising costs are split: 75% paid by illustrators; 25% paid by rep. Advertises in *Picturebook*, *American Showcase*, *Workbook*, *Alternative Pick*, *Contact*.

How to Contact For first contact, send tearsheets, photocopies, SASE. "See Web site for submission guidelines." Responds only if interested. Portfolio should include professionally presented materials. Finds illustrators through recommendations from others, word of mouth, competitions.

LINDGREN & SMITH

630 Ninth Ave., New York NY 10036. (212)397-7330. E-mail: representation@lsillustration.com. Web site: www.lindgrensmith.com/kids. **Contact:** Pat Lindgren, Piper Smith. Illustration representative. Estab. 1984. Member of SCBWI. Markets include children's books, advertising agencies; corporations; design firms; editorial; publishing.

Handles Illustration.

Terms Exclusive representation is required. Advertises in *The Workbook*.

How to Contact For first contact, send postcard or e-mail a link to a Web site or send one JPEG file. Responds only if interested via e-mail or phone.

Tips "Check to see if your work seems appropriate for the group."

MARLENA AGENCY, INC.

322 Ewing St., Princeton NJ 08540. (609)252-9405. Fax: (609)252-1949. E-mail: marlena@marlenaagency.com. Web site: www.marlenaagency.com. Commercial illustration representative. Estab. 1990. Member of Society of Illustrators. Represents 30 international illustrators including: Marc Mongeau, Gerard Dubois, Linda Helton, Paul Zwolak, Martin Jarrie, Serge Bloch, Hadley Hooper and Carmen Segovia. Staff includes Marlena Torzecka,

Simone Stark, Ella Lupo. Currently open to illustrators seeking representation. Open to both new and established illustrators. Submission guidelines available for #10 SASE.
Handles Illustration.
Recent Sales *Pebble Soup*, by Marc Mongeau (Rigby); *Sees Behind Trees*, by Linda Helton (Harcourt); *New Orleans Band*, by Marc Mongeau (Scott Foresman); *My Cat*, by Linda Helton (Scholastic).
Terms Exclusive representation required. Offers written contract. Requires printed portfolios, transparencies, direct mail piece (such as postcards), printed samples. Advertises in *Creative Blackbook, Workbook*.
How to Contact For first contact, send tearsheets, photocopies. Responds only if interested. Drop off or mail portfolio, photocopies. Portfolio should include tearsheets, photocopies. Finds illustrators through queries/solicitations, magazines and graphic design.
Tips ''Be creative and persistent.''

THE NEIS GROUP
152 Silver Hawk Ct, Dripping Springs TX 78620. (269)672-5756. Fax: (269)672-5756. E-mail: neisgroup@wmis.n et. Web site: www.neisgroup.com. **Contact:** Judy Neis. Commercial illustration representative. Estab. 1982. Represents 45 illustrators including: Lyn Boyer, Pam Thomson, Dan Sharp, Terry Workman, Liz Conrad, Garry Colby, Clint Hansen, Don McLean, Julie Borden, Johnna Bandle, Jack Pennington, Gary Ferster, Erika LeBarre, Joel Spector, John White, Neverne Covington, Ruth Pettis, Matt LeBarre. 60% of artwork handled is children's book illustration. Currently open to illustrators seeking representation. Looking for established illustrators only.
Handles Illustration, photography and calligraphy/manuscript packages.
Terms Receives 25% commission. Advertising costs are split: 75% paid by illustrator; 25% paid by rep. ''I prefer porfolios on CD, color printouts and e-mail capabilities whenever possible.'' Advertises in *Picturebook, American Showcase, Creative Black Book*.
How to Contact For first contact, send bio, tearsheets, direct mail flier/brochure. Responds only if interested. After initial contact, drop off portfolio of nonreturnables. Portfolio should include tearsheets, photocopies. Obtains new talent through recommendations from others and queries/solicitations.

WANDA NOWAK/CREATIVE ILLUSTRATORS AGENCY
231 E. 76th St., 5D, New York NY 10021. (212)535-0438, ext. 1624. Fax: (212)535-1629. E-mail: wanda@wandan ow.com. Web site: www.wandanow.com. **Contact:** Wanda Nowak. Commercial illustration representative. Estab. 1996. Represents 20 illustrators including: Emilie Chollat, Thea Kliros, Pierre Pratt, Frederique Bertrand, Ilja Bereznickas, Boris Kulikov, Yayo, Laurence Cleyet-Merle, E. Kerner, Ellen Usdin, Marie Lafrance, Stephane Jorisch. 50% of artwork handled is children's book illustration. Staff includes Wanda Nowak. Open to both new and established illustrators.
Handles Illustration. Looking for ''unique, individual style.''
Terms Receives 30% commission. Exclusive representation required. Offers written contract. Advertising costs are split: 70% paid by illustrators; 30% paid by rep. Advertises in *Picturebook, Workbook, The Alternative Pick, Black Book*.
How to Contact For first contact, send SASE. Responds only if interested. Drop off portfolio. Portfolio should include tearsheets. Finds illustrators through recommendations from others, sourcebooks like *CA, Picture Book, Creative Black Book*, exhibitions.
Tips ''Develop your own style. Send a little illustrated story, which will prove you can carry a character in different situations with facial expressions, etc.''

REMEN-WILLIS DESIGN GROUP—ANN REMEN-WILLIS
2964 Colton Rd., Pebble Beach CA 93953. (831)655-1407. Fax: (831)655-1408. E-mail: remenwillis@comcast.n et. Web sites:www.annremenwillis.com. or www.picture-book.com. Specializes in childrens' book illustration trade/education. Estab. 1984. Member of SCBWI. Represents 18 illustrators including: Dominic Catalano, Siri Weber Feeney, Doug Roy, Susan Jaekel, Dennis Hockerman, Rosiland Solomon, Meredith Johnson, Renate Lohmann, Robin Kerr, Len Ebert, Gary Undercuffler, Sheila Bailey, John Goodell. 100% of artwork handled is children's book illustration.
Terms Offers written contract. Advertising costs are split: 50% paid by illustrators; 50% paid by rep. Illustrator must provide small precise portfolio for promotion. Advertises in *Picturebook, Workbook*.
How to Contact For first contact, send tearsheets, photocopies or e-mail. Responds in 1 week.
Tips ''Send samples of only the type of work you are interested in receiving. Check out rep's forte first.''

RENAISSANCE HOUSE
9400 Lloydcrest Dr., Beverly Hills CA 90210. (800)547-5113. Fax: (310)860-9902. E-mail: info@renaissancehous e.net. Web site: www.renaissancehouse.net. or www.laredopublishing.com. **Contact:** Raquel Benatar. Children's, educational, multicultural, and textbooks, advertising rep. Estab. 1991. Represents 80 illustrators. 95%

of artwork handled is children's book illustration and photography. Currently open to illustrators and photographers seeking representation. Open to both new and established illustrators.

Handles Illustration and photography.

Recent Sales Maribel Suarez (Little Brown, Hyperion); Gabriel Pacheco (MacMillan); Ana Lopez (Scholastic); Ruth Araceli (Houghton Mifflin); Vivi Escriva (Albert Whitman); Marie Jara (Sparknotes); Sheli Petersen (McGraw-Hill).

Terms Exclusive and non-exclusive representation. Illustrators must provide scans of illustrations. Advertises in *Picturebook*, *Directory of Illustration*, own Web site and *Catalog of Illustrators*.

How to Contact For first contact send tearsheets. Responds in 2 weeks. Finds illustrators through recommendations from others, conferences, direct contact.

S.I. INTERNATIONAL

43 E. 19th St., New York NY 10003. (212)254-4996. Fax: (212)995-0911. E-mail: information@si-i.com. Web site: www.si-i.com. Commercial illustration representative. Estab. 1983. Member of SPAR, Graphic Artists Guild. Represents 50 illustrators. Specializes in license characters, educational publishing and children's illustration, digital art and design, mass market paperbacks. Markets include design firms; publishing/books; sales/promotion firms; licensing firms; digital art and design firms.

Handles Illustration. Looking for artists "who have the ability to do children's illustration and to do license characters either digitally or reflectively."

Terms Rep receives 25-30% commission. Advertising costs are split: 70% paid by talent; 30% paid by representative. "Contact agency for details. Must have mailer." Advertises in *Picturebook*.

How to Contact For first contact, send query letter, tearsheets. Responds in 3 weeks. After initial contact, write for appointment to show portfolio of tearsheets, slides.

SALZMAN INTERNATIONAL

1751 Charles Ave., Arcate CA 95521. (415)285-8267, (212)997-0115. Fax: (707)822-5500. E-mail: rs@salzint.com. Web site: www.salzint.com. Commercial illustration representative. Estab. 1982. Represents 20 illustrators. 20% of artwork is children's book illustration. Staff includes Richard Salzman. Open to illustrators seeking representation. Accepting both new and established illustrators.

Handles Accepts illustration.

Terms Receives 25% commission. Offers written contract. 100% of advertising costs paid by illustrator. Advertises in *Workbook*, ispot.com, altpick.com.

How to Contact For first contact, send link to Web site or printed samples. Portfolio should include tearsheets, photocopies; "best to post samples on Web site and send link." Finds illustrators through queries/solicitations.

LIZ SANDERS AGENCY

2415 E. Hangman Creek Lane, Spokane WA USA 99224-8514. E-mail: liz@lizsanders.com. Web site: www.lizsanders.com. Commercial illustration representative. Estab. 1985. Represents Craig Orback, Amy Ning, Tom Pansini, Chris Lensch, Kate Endle, Susan Synarski, Sudi McCollum, Sue Rama, Suzanne Beaky and more. Currently open to illustrators seeking representation. Open to both new and established illustrators.

Handles Illustration. Markets include publishing, entertainment, giftware and advertising.

Terms Receives 30% commission against pro bono mailing program. Offers written contract. Advertises in *Picturebook* and picture-book.com, *Workbook* and workbook.com, theispot.com, folioplanet.com. No geographic restrictions.

How to Contact For first contact, send tearsheets, direct mail flier/brochure, color copies, non-returnables or e-mail. Responds only if interested. After initial contact, submit portfolio. Portfolio should include tearsheets, photocopies. Obtains new talent through recommendations from others, conferences and queries/solicitations, Literary Market Place.

🌐 THOROGOOD KIDS

5 Dryden Street, Covent Garden, London WC2E 9NW United Kingdom. (44)(207)829-8468. Fax: (44)(208)8597507. E-mail: kids@thorogood.net. Web site: www.thorogood.net/kids. Commercial illustration representative. Estab. 1978. Represents 30 illustrators including: Nicola Slater, Anne Yvonne Gilbert, Olivier Latyk, Sophie Allsopp, Carol Morley, Philip Nicholson, Dan Hambe, Bill Dare, Christiane Engel, Robin Heighway-Bury, Leo Timmers, Kanako & Yuzuru, Shaunna Peterson, Daniel Egneus, Al Sacui, John Woodcock. Staff includes Doreen Thorogood, Steve Thorogood, Tom Thorogood. Open to illustrators seeking representation. Accepting both new and established illustrators. Guidelines not available.

Handles Accepts illustration, illustration/manuscript packages.

How to Contact For first contact, send tearsheets, photocopies, SASE, direct mail flyer/brochure. After initial contact, we will contact the illustrator if we want to see the portfolio. Portfolio should include tearsheets, photocopies. Finds illustrators through queries/solicitations, conferences.

Tips "Be unique and research your market. Talent will win out!"

TUGEAU 2, INC.

2231 Grandview Ave., Cleveland Heights OH 44106. (216)707-0854. Fax: (216)795-8404. E-mail: nicole@tugeau 2.com. Web site: www.tugeau2.com. Children's publishing art/illustration representative. Estab. 2003. Member of SCBWI. Represents 30 illustrators. Staff includes Nicole Tugeau, Jeremy Tugeau and assistant Margaret Bell. Open to illustrators seeking representation. Accepting both new and established illustrators.

Handles Accepts illustration.

Terms Receives 25% commission. Exclusive representation in the children's industry required. Offers written contract. Illustrator must provide digital portfolio (for Web and e-mail proposals) as well as 50-100 tearsheets (postcards or otherwise) with agency name and logo—to be kept inhouse for promotion. Advertises in *Picturebook*.

How to Contact For first contact, e-mail with 4 or 5 digital files of artwork. Responds immediately. Agency will request full portfolio with SASE if interested. Finds illustrators through recommendations from others, queries/solicitations.

Tips "Do not look for representation until you have a portfolio (12-15 pieces) geared toward the children's market. Hone in on your personal style, consistency, and diversity of scenes and characters. Be ready to articulate your ambitions in the industry and the time you will be able to commit to those ambitions."

GWEN WALTERS ARTIST REPRESENTATIVE

1801 S. Flagler Dr., #1202, W. Palm Beach FL 33401. (561)805-7739. E-mail: artincgw@aol.com. Web site: www.gwenWaltersartrep.com. Commercial illustration representative. Estab. 1976. Represents 18 illustrators. 90% of artwork handled is children's book illustration. Currently open to illustrators seeking representation. Looking for established illustrators only.

Handles Illustration.

Recent Sales Sells to "All major book publishers."

Terms Receives 30% commission. Artist needs to supply all promo material. Offers written contract. Advertising costs are split: 70% paid by illustrator; 30% paid by rep. Advertises in *Picturebook*, *RSVP*, *Directory of Illustration*.

How to Contact For first contact, send tearsheets. Responds only if interested. Finds illustrators through recommendations from others.

Tips "Go out and get some first-hand experience. Learn to tell yourself to understand the way the market works."

WENDYLYNN & CO.

504 Wilson Rd., Annapolis MD 21401. (401)224-2729. Fax: (410)224-2183. E-mail: wendy@wendylynn.com. Web site: www.wendylynn.com. **Contact:** Wendy Mays. Children's illustration representative. Estab. 2002. Member of SCBWI. Represents 24 illustrators. 100% of artwork handled is children's illustration. Staff includes Wendy Mays, Janice Onken. Currently open to illustrators seeking representation. Open to both new and established illustrators. Submission guidelines available on Web site.

Handles Illustration.

Terms Receives 25% commission. Exclusive representation required. Offers written contract. Requires 15-20 images submitted on disk. Advertises in *Picturebook* or *Creative Black Book*.

How to Contact For first contact, e-mail or send color photocopies or tearsheets with bio; e-mail is preferred. Responds ASAP. After initial contact mail artwork on CD and send tearsheets. Portfolio should include a minimum of 15 images. Finds illustrators through recommendations from others and from portfolio reviews.

Tips "In this day and age, you should be able to scan your own artwork and send files digitally to publishers. Also, having your own Web site is important, and knowing how to use Photoshop is a plus."

DEBORAH WOLFE LTD.

731 N. 24th St., Philadelphia PA 19130. (215)232-6666. Fax: (215)232-6585. E-mail: inquiry@illustrationonline.com. Web site: www.illustrationOnline.com. **Contact:** Deborah Wolfe. Commercial illustration representative. Estab. 1978. Member of Graphic Artist Guild. Represents 30 illustrators. Currently open to illustrators seeking representation.

Handles Illustration.

Terms Receives 25% commission. Exclusive representation required. Offers written contract. Advertising costs are split: 75% paid by illustrators; 25% paid by rep. Advertises in *Picturebook*, *Directory of Illustration*, *The Workbook*, *The Black Book*.

How to Contact Responds in 2 weeks. Portfolio should include "anything except originals." Finds illustrators through queries/solicitations.

Clubs & Organizations

Contacts made through organizations such as the ones listed in this section can be quite beneficial for children's writers and illustrators. Professional organizations provide numerous educational, business, and legal services in the form of newsletters, workshops, or seminars. Organizations can provide tips about how to be a more successful writer or artist, as well as what types of business records to keep, health and life insurance coverage to carry, and competitions to consider.

An added benefit of belonging to an organization is the opportunity to network with those who have similar interests, creating a support system. As in any business, knowing the right people can often help your career, and important contacts can be made through your peers. Membership in a writer's or artist's organization also shows publishers you're serious about your craft. This provides no guarantee your work will be published, but it gives you an added dimension of credibility and professionalism.

Some of the organizations listed here welcome anyone with an interest, while others are only open to published writers and professional artists. Organizations such as the Society of Children's Book Writers and Illustrators (SCBWI, www.scbwi.org) have varying levels of membership. SCBWI offers associate membership to those with no publishing credits, and full membership to those who have had work for children published. International organizations such as SCBWI also have regional chapters throughout the U.S. and the world. Write or call for more information regarding any group that interests you, or check the Web sites of the many organizations that list them. Be sure to get information about local chapters, membership qualifications, and services offered.

Information on organizations listed in the previous edition but not included in this edition of Children's Writer's & Illustrator's Market may be found in the General Index.

AMERICAN ALLIANCE FOR THEATRE & EDUCATION

7475 Wisconsin Avenue, Suite 300A Bethesda, MD 20814. (301)951-7977. E-mail: info@aate.com. Web site: www.aate.com. Purpose of organization: to promote standards of excellence in theatre and drama education. "We achieve this by assimilating quality practices in theatre and theatre education, connecting artists, educators, researchers and scholars with each other, and by providing opportunities for our members to learn, exchange and diversify their work, their audiences and their perspectives." Membership cost: $110 annually for individual in U.S. and Canada, $220 annually for organization, $60 annually for students, $70 annually for retired people; add $30 outside Canada and U.S. Holds annual conference (July). Newsletter published quarterly. Contests held for unpublished play reading project and annual awards in various categories. Awards plaque and stickers for published playbooks. Publishes list of unpublished plays deemed worthy of performance and stages readings at conference. Contact national office at number above or see Web site for contact information for Playwriting Network Chairpersons.

AMERICAN SOCIETY OF JOURNALISTS AND AUTHORS

1501 Broadway, Suite 302, New York NY 10036. Web site: www.asja.org. **Executive Director:** Anne Peace. Qualifications for membership: "Need to be a professional nonfiction writer. Refer to Web site for further qualifications." Membership cost: Application fee—$25; annual dues—$195. Group sponsors national conferences; monthly workshops in New York City. Workshops/conferences open to nonmembers. Publishes a newsletter for members that provides confidential information for nonfiction writers.

ARIZONA AUTHORS ASSOCIATION

P.O. Box 87857, Phoenix AZ 85080-7857. E-mail: info@azauthors.com. Web site: www.azauthors.com. **President:** Toby Heathcotte. Purpose of organization: to offer professional, educational and social opportunities to writers and authors, and serve as a network. Members must be authors, writers working toward publication, agents, publishers, publicists, printers, illustrators, etc. Membership cost: $45/year writers; $30/year students; $60/year other professionals in publishing industry. Holds regular workshops and meetings. Publishes bimonthly newsletter and Arizona Literary Magazine. Sponsors Annual Literary Contest in poetry, essays, short stories, novels, and published books with cash prizes and awards bestowed at a public banquet in Phoenix. Winning entries are also published or advertised in the *Arizona Literary Magazine.* First and second place winners in poetry, essay and short story categories are entered in the Pushcart Prize. Send SASE or view Web site for guidelines.

ASSITEJ/USA

1602 Belle View Blvd #810, Alexandria VA 22307. E-mail: info@assitej-usa.org. Web site: www.assitej-usa.org. Purpose of organization: to promote theater for children and young people by linking professional theaters and artists together; sponsoring national, international and regional conferences and providing publications and information. Also serves as US Center for International Association of Theatre for Children and Young People. Different levels of membership include: organizations, individuals, students, retirees, libraries. *TYA Today* includes original articles, reviews and works of criticism and theory, all of interest to theater practitioners (included with membership). Publishes journal that focuses on information on field in U.S. and abroad.

THE AUTHORS GUILD

31 East 32nd Street; New York, NY 10016. (212)563-5904. Fax: (212)564-5363. E-mail: staff@authorsguild.org. Web site: www.authorsguild.org. **Executive Director:** Paul Aiken. Purpose of organization: to offer services and materials intended to help authors with the business and legal aspects of their work, including contract problems, copyright matters, freedom of expression and taxation. Guild has 8,000 members. Qualifications for membership: Must be book author published by an established American publisher within 7 years or any author who has had 3 works (fiction or nonfiction) published by a magazine or magazines of general circulation in the last 18 months. Associate membership also available. Annual dues: $90. Different levels of membership include: associate membership with all rights except voting available to an author who has a firm contract offer or is currently negotiating a royalty contract from an established American publisher. "The Guild offers free contract reviews to its members. The Guild conducts several symposia each year at which experts provide information, offer advice and answer questions on subjects of interest and concern to authors. Typical subjects have been the rights of privacy and publicity, libel, wills and estates, taxation, copyright, editors and editing, the art of interviewing, standards of criticism and book reviewing. Transcripts of these symposia are published and circulated to members. The Authors Guild Bulletin, a quarterly journal, contains articles on matters of interest to writers, reports of Guild activities, contract surveys, advice on problem clauses in contracts, transcripts of Guild and League symposia and information on a variety of professional topics. Subscription included in the cost of the annual dues."

Resources

◪ CANADIAN SOCIETY OF CHILDREN'S AUTHORS, ILLUSTRATORS AND PERFORMERS, (CANSCAIP)

104-40 Orchard View Blvd., Toronto ON M4R 1B9 Canada. (416)515-1559. E-mail: office@canscaip.org. Web site: www.cansaip.org. **Office Manager:** Lena Coakley. Purpose of organization: development of Canadian children's culture and support for authors, illustrators and performers working in this field. Qualifications for membership: Members—professionals who have been published (not self-published) or have paid public performances/records/tapes to their credit. Friends—share interest in field of children's culture. Membership cost: $75 (Members dues), $35 (Friends dues), $45 (Institution dues). Sponsors workshops/conferences. Publishes newsletter: includes profiles of members; news round-up of members' activities countrywide; market news; news on awards, grants, etc; columns related to professional concerns.

LEWIS CARROLL SOCIETY OF NORTH AMERICA

P.O. Box 204, Napa CA 94559. E-mail: hedgehog@napanet.net. Web site: www.lewiscarroll.org/lcsna.html. **Secretary:** Cindy Watter. ''We are an organization of Carroll admirers of all ages and interests and a center for Carroll studies.'' Qualifications for membership: ''An interest in Lewis Carroll and a simple love for Alice (or the Snark for that matter).'' Membership cost: $25 (regular membership), $50 (contributing membership). The Society meets twice a year—in spring and in fall; locations vary. Publishes a quarterly newsletter, *Knight Letter*, and maintains an active publishing program.

THE CHILDREN'S BOOK COUNCIL, INC.

12 W. 37th St., 2nd Floor, New York NY 10018. (212)966-1990. Fax: (212)966-2073. E-mail: info@cbcbooks.org. Web site: www.cbcbooks.org. **Executive Director:** Robin Adelson. Purpose of organization: A nonprofit trade association of children's and young adult publishers and packagers, CBC promotes the enjoyment of books for children and young adults and works with national and international organizations to that end. The CBC has sponsored Children's Book Week since 1945 and Young People's Poetry Week since 1999. Qualifications for membership: trade publishers and packagers of children's and young adult books and related literary materials are eligible for membership. Publishers wishing to join should contact the CBC for dues information. Sponsors workshops and seminars for publishing company personnel. Individuals wishing to receive the CBC semi-annual journal, *CBC Features* with articles of interest to people working with children and books and materials brochures, may be placed on CBC's mailing list for a one-time-only fee of $60. Sells reading encouragement posters and graphics and informational materials suitable for libraries, teachers, booksellers, parents, and others working with children.

FLORIDA FREELANCE WRITERS ASSOCIATION

Cassell Network of Writers, P.O. Box A, North Stratford NH 03590. (603)922-8338. E-mail: FFWA@Writers-Editors.com. Web sites:www.ffwamembers.com. and www.writers-editors.com. **Executive Director:** Dana K. Cassell. Purpose of organization: To provide a link between Florida writers and buyers of the written word; to help writers run more effective editorial businesses. Qualifications for membership: ''None. We provide a variety of services and information, some for beginners and some for established pros.'' Membership cost: $90/year. Publishes a newsletter focusing on market news, business news, how-to tips for the serious writer. Annual *Directory of Florida Markets* included in FFWA newsletter section and electronic download. Publishes annual *Guide to CNW/Florida Writers*, which is distributed to editors around the country. Sponsors contest: annual deadline March 15. Guidelines on Web site. Categories: juvenile, adult nonfiction, adult fiction and poetry. Awards include cash for top prizes, certificate for others. Contest open to nonmembers.

GRAPHIC ARTISTS GUILD

32 Broadway, Suite 1114, New York NY 10004. (212)791-3400. Fax: (212) 791-0333. E-mail: membership@gag.org. Web site: www.gag.org. **President:** John P. Schmelzer. Purpose of organization: ''To promote and protect the economic interests of member artists. It is committed to improving conditions for all creators of graphic arts and raising standards for the entire industry.'' Qualification for full membership: 50% of income derived from the creation of artwork. Associate members include those in allied fields, students and retirees. Initiation fee: $30. Full memberships: $200; student membership: $75/year. Associate membership: $170/year. Publishes *Graphic Artists Guild Handbook, Pricing and Ethical Guidelines* (free to members, $34.95 retail). ''The Graphic Artists Guild is a national union that embraces all creators of graphic arts intended for presentation as originals or reproductions at all levels of skill and expertise. The long-range goals of the Guild are: to educate graphic artists and their clients about ethical and fair business practices; to educate graphic artists about emerging trends and technologies impacting the industry; to offer programs and services that anticipate and respond to the needs of our members, helping them prosper and enhancing their health and security; to advocate for the interests of our members in the legislative, judicial and regulatory arenas; to assure that our members are

recognized financially and professionally for the value they provide; to be responsible stewards for our members by building an organization that works efficiently on their behalf."

HORROR WRITERS ASSOCIATION

244 5th Avenue, suite 2767, New York, NY 10001. E-mail: hwa@horror.org. Web site: www.horror.org. **Office Manager:** Lisa Morton. Purpose of organization: To encourage public interest in horror and dark fantasy and to provide networking and career tools for members. Qualifications for membership: Complete membership rules online atwww.horror.org/memrule.htm. At least one low-level sale is required to join as an affiliate. Non-writing professionals who can show income from a horror-related field may join as an associate (booksellers, editors, agents, librarians, etc.) To qualify for full active membership, you must be a published, professional writer of horror. Membership cost: $65 annually. Holds annual Stoker Awards Weekend and HWA Business Meeting. Publishes monthly newsletter focusing on market news, industry news, HWA business for members. Sponsors awards. We give the Bram Stoker Awards for superior achievement in horror annually. Awards include a handmade Stoker trophy designed by sculptor Stephen Kirk. Awards open to nonmembers.

INTERNATIONAL READING ASSOCIATION

800 Barksdale Rd., P.O. Box 8139, Newark DE 19714-8139. (302)731-1600, ext. 293. Fax: (302)731-1057. E-mail: pubinfo@reading.org. Web site: www.reading.org. **Public Information Associate:** Beth Cady. Purpose of organization: "Formed in 1956, the International Reading Association seeks to promote high levels of literacy for all by improving the quality of reading instruction through studying the reading process and teaching techniques; serving as a clearinghouse for the dissemination of reading research through conferences, journals, and other publications; and actively encouraging the lifetime reading habit. Its goals include professional development, advocacy, partnerships, research, and global literacy development." **Open to students.** Basic membership: $36. Sponsors annual convention. Publishes a newsletter called "Reading Today." Sponsors a number of awards and fellowships. Visit the IRA Web site for more information on membership, conventions and awards.

THE INTERNATIONAL WOMEN'S WRITING GUILD

P.O. Box 810, Gracie Station, New York NY 10028. (212)737-7536. Fax: (212) 737-9469. E-mail: dirhahn@iwwg.org. Web site: www.iwwg.org. **Executive Director and Founder:** Hannelore Hahn. IWWG is "a network for the personal and professional empowerment of women through writing." Qualifications: open to any woman connected to the written word regardless of professional portfolio. Membership cost: $45 annually. "IWWG sponsors several annual conferences a year in all areas of the U.S. The major conference is held in June of each year at Skidmore College in Saratoga Springs, NY. It is a week-long conference attracting over 500 women internationally." Also publishes a 32-page newsletter, *Network*, 6 times/year; offers dental and vision insurance at group rates, referrals to literary agents.

⬛ LEAGUE OF CANADIAN POETS

920 Yonge St., Suite 608, Toronto ON M4W 3C7 Canada. (416)504-1657. Fax: (416)504-0096. Web site: www.poets.ca. **Acting Executive Director:** Joanna Poblocka. **President:** Mary Ellen Csamer. Inquiries to **Program Manager:** Joanna Poblocka. The L.C.P. is a national organization of published Canadian poets. Our constitutional objectives are to advance poetry in Canada and to promote the professional interests of the members. Qualifications for membership: full—publication of at least 1 book of poetry by a professional publisher; associate membership—an active interest in poetry, demonstrated by several magazine/periodical publication credits; student—an active interest in poetry, 12 sample poems required; supporting—any friend of poetry. Membership fees: full—$175/year, associate—$60, student—$20, supporting—$100. Holds an Annual General Meeting every spring; some events open to nonmembers. "We also organize reading programs in schools and public venues. We publish a newsletter which includes information on poetry/poetics in Canada and beyond. Also publish the books *Poetry Markets for Canadians*; *Who's Who in the League of Canadian Poets*; *Poets in the Classroom* (teaching guide), and online publications. The Gerald Lampert Memorial Award for the best first book of poetry published in Canada in the preceding year and The Pat Lowther Memorial Award for the best book of poetry by a Canadian woman published in the preceding year." Deadline for awards: November 1. Visitwww.poets.ca for more details. Sponsors youth poetry competition. Visitwww.youngpoets.ca for details.

LITERARY MANAGERS AND DRAMATURGS OF THE AMERICAS

P.O. Box 728 Villiage Station, New York NY 10014. E-mail: lmda@lmda.org. or lmdanyc@hotmail.com. Web site: www.lmda.org. LMDA is a not-for-profit service organization for the professions of literary management and dramaturgy. Student Membership: $25/year. Open to students in dramaturgy, performing arts and literature programs, or related disciplines. Proof of student status required. Includes national conference, New Dramaturg activities, local symposia, job phone and select membership meetings. Active Membership: $60/year. Open to full-time and part-time professionals working in the fields of literary management and dramaturgy. All privileges and services including voting rights and eligibility for office. Institutional Membership: $130/year. Open to theaters, universities, and other organizations. Includes all privileges and services except voting rights and eligibility for office. Publishes a newsletter featuring articles on literary management, dramaturgy, LMDA program updates and other articles of interest.

THE NATIONAL LEAGUE OF AMERICAN PEN WOMEN

1300 17th St. N.W., Washington DC 20036-1973. (202)785-1997. E-mail: nlapw1@verizon.net. Web site: www.a mericanpenwomen.org. **President:** Elaine Waidelich. Purpose of organization: to promote professional work in art, letters, and music since 1897. Qualifications for membership: An applicant must show ''proof of sale'' in each chosen category—art, letters, and music. Membership cost: $40 ($10 processing fee and $30 National dues); Annual fees—$30 plus Branch/State dues. Different levels of membership include: Active, Associate, International Affiliate, Members-at-Large, Honorary Members (in one or more of the following classifications: Art, Letters, and Music). Holds workshops/conferences. Publishes magazine 6 times/year titled *The Pen Woman*. Sponsors various contests in areas of Art, Letters, and Music. Awards made at Biennial Convention. Biannual scholarships awarded to non-Pen Women for mature women. Awards include cash prizes—up to $1,000. Specialized contests open to nonmembers.

NATIONAL WRITERS ASSOCIATION

10940 S. Parker Rd., #508, Parker CO 80138. (303)841-0246. Fax: (303)841-2607. E-mail: anitaedits@aol.com. Web site: www.nationalwriters.com. **Executive Director:** Sandy Whelchel. Purpose of organization: association for freelance writers. Qualifications for membership: associate membership—must be serious about writing; professional membership—must be published and paid writer (cite credentials). Membership cost: $65 associate; $85 professional; $35 student. Sponsors workshops/conferences: TV/screenwriting workshops, NWAF Annual Conferences, Literary Clearinghouse, editing and critiquing services, local chapters, National Writer's School. Open to non-members. Publishes industry news of interest to freelance writers; how-to articles; market information; member news and networking opportunities. Nonmember subscription: $20. Sponsors poetry contest; short story contest; article contest; novel contest. Awards cash for top 3 winners; books and/or certificates for other winners; honorable mention certificate places 5-10. Contests open to nonmembers.

NATIONAL WRITERS UNION

113 University Place, 6th Floor, New York NY 10003. (212)254-0279. E-mail: nwu@nwu.org. Web site: www.nw u.org. Students welcome. Purpose of organization: Advocacy for freelance writers. Qualifications for membership: ''Membership in the NWU is open to all qualified writers, and no one shall be barred or in any manner prejudiced within the Union on account of race, age, sex, sexual orientation, disability, national origin, religion or ideology. You are eligible for membership if you have published a book, a play, three articles, five poems, one short story or an equivalent amount of newsletter, publicity, technical, commercial, government or institutional copy. You are also eligible for membership if you have written an equal amount of unpublished material and you are actively writing and attempting to publish your work.'' Membership cost: annual writing income less than $4,500—$120/year or $67.50 1/2 year; $4,500-15,000—$195/year or $105 ½ year; $15,001-30,000— $265/year or $140 ½ year; $30,001-$45,000—$315 a year or $165 1/2 year; $45,001-$60,000—$340/year or $177.50 ½ year. Holds workshops throughout the country. Members only section on web site offers rich resources for freelance writers. Skilled contract advice and grievance help for memebers.

PEN AMERICAN CENTER

588 Broadway, Suite 303, New York NY 10012. (212)334-1660. Fax: (212)334-2181. E-mail: pen@pen.org. Web site: www.pen.org. Purpose of organization: ''An associate of writers working to advance literature, to defend free expression, and to foster international literary fellowship.'' Qualifications for membership: ''The standard qualification for a writer to become a member of PEN is publication of two or more books of a literary character, or one book generally acclaimed to be of exceptional distinction. Also eligible for membership: editors who have demonstrated commitment to excellence in their profession (usually construed as five years' service in book editing); translators who have published at least two book-length literary translations; playwrights whose works have been produced professionally; and literary essayists whose publications are extensive even if they have not yet been issued as a book. Candidates for membership may be nominated by a PEN member or they may nominate themselves with the support of two references from the literary community or from a current PEN member. Membership dues are $75 per year and many PEN members contribute their time by serving on committees, conducting campaigns and writing letters in connection with freedom-of-expression cases, contributing to the PEN journal, participating in PEN public events, helping to bring literature into underserved communities, and judging PEN literary awards. PEN members receive a subscription to the PEN journal, the PEN Annual Report, and have access to medical insurance at group rates. Members living in the New York metropolitan and tri-state area, or near the Branches, are invited to PEN events throughout the year. Membership

in PEN American Center includes reciprocal privileges in PEN American Center branches and in foreign PEN Centers for those traveling abroad. Application forms are available on the Web at www.pen.org. Associate Membership is open to everyone who supports PEN's mission, and your annual dues ($40; $20 for students) provides crucial support to PEN's programs. When you join as an Associate Member, not only will you receive a subscription to the PEN Journal (http://pen.org/page.php/prmID/150) and notices of all PEN events but you are also invited to participate in the work of PEN. PEN American Center is the largest of the 141 centers of International PEN, the world's oldest human rights organization and the oldest international literary organization. International PEN was founded in 1921 to dispel national, ethnic, and racial hatreds and to promote understanding among all countries. PEN American Center, founded a year later, works to advance literature, to defend free expression, and to foster international literary fellowship. The Center has a membership of 2,900 distinguished writers, editors, and translators. In addition to defending writers in prison or in danger of imprisonment for their work, PEN American Center sponsors public literary programs and forums on current issues, sends prominent authors to inner-city schools to encourage reading and writing, administers literary prizes, promotes international literature that might otherwise go unread in the United States, and offers grants and loans to writers facing financial or medical emergencies. In carrying out this work, PEN American Center builds upon the achievements of such dedicated past members as W.H. Auden, James Baldwin, Willa Cather, Robert Frost, Langston Hughes, Thomas Mann, Arthur Miller, Marianne Moore, Susan Sontag, and John Steinbeck. The Children's Book Authors' Committee sponsors annual public events focusing on the art of writing for children and young adults and on the diversity of literature for juvenile readers. The PEN/Phyllis Naylor Working Writer Fellowship was established in 2001 to assist a North American author of fiction for children or young adults (E-mail: awards@pen.org). Visit www.pen.org. for complete information. Sponsors several competitions per year. Monetary awards range from $2,000-35,000.

🌐 PLAYMARKET

P.O. Box 9767, Te Aro Wellington New Zealand. (64)4 3828462. Fax: (64)4 3828461. E-mail: info@playmarket.org.nz. Web site: www.playmarket.org.nz. **Director:** Mark Amery. **Script Development**: Jean Betts & Janie Walker. **Administrator:** Michael Daly. **Agency Coordinator:** Katrina Chandra. Purpose of organization: funded by Creative New Zealand, Playmarket serves as New Zealand's script advisory service and playwrights' agency. Playmarket offers script assessment, development and agency services to help New Zealand playwrights secure professional production for their plays. Playmarket runs the NZ Young Playwrights Competition, The Aotearoa Playwrights Conference and the Adam Playreading Series and administers the annual Bruce Mason Playwriting Award. The organization's magazine, *Playmarket News*, is published biannually. Inquiries e-mail info@playmarket.org.nz.

PUPPETEERS OF AMERICA, INC.

Membership Office: 26 Howard Ave, New Haven, CT 06519-2809. (888)568-6235. E-mail: membership@puppeteers.org. Web site: www.puppeteers.org. **Membership Officer:** Fred Thompson. Purpose of organization: to promote the art and appreciation of puppetry as a means of communications and as a performing art. The Pupeteers of America boasts an international membership. Qualifications for membership: interest in the art form. Membership cost: single adult, $50; seniors (65+) and youth members, $30 (6-17 years of age); full-time college student, $30; family, $70; couple, $60; senior couple, $50. Membership includes a bimonthly newsletter (*Playboard*). Discounts for workshops/conferences, access to the Audio Visual Library & Consultants in many areas of Puppetry. *The Puppetry Journal*, a quarterly periodical, provides a color photo gallery, news about puppeteers, puppet theaters, exhibitions, touring companies, technical tips, new products, new books, films, television, and events sponsored by the Chartered Guilds in each of the 8 P of A regions. Subscription: *Puppetry Journal* only, $40 (libraries only). The Puppeteers of America sponsors an annual National Day of Puppetry the last Saturday in April.

SCIENCE-FICTION AND FANTASY WRITERS OF AMERICA, INC.

P.O. Box 877, Chestertown MD 21620. E-mail: execdir@sfwa.org. Web site: www.sfwa.org. **Executive Director:** Jane Jewell. Purpose of organization: to encourage public interest in science fiction literature and provide organization format for writers/editors/artists within the genre. Qualifications for membership: at least 1 professional sale or other professional involvement within the field. Membership cost: annual active dues—$70; affiliate—$55; one-time installation fee of $10; dues year begins July 1. Different levels of membership include: active—requires 3 professional short stories or 1 novel published; associate—requires 1 professional sale; or affiliate—which requires some other professional involvement such as artist, editor, librarian, bookseller, teacher, etc. Workshops/conferences: annual awards banquet, usually in April or May. Open to nonmembers. Publishes quarterly journal, the SFWA *Bulletin*. Nonmember subscription: $18/year in U.S. Sponsors Nebula Awards for best published science fiction or fantasy in the categories of novel, novella, novelette and short story. Awards trophy. Also presents the Damon Knight Memorial Grand Master Award for Lifetime Achievement, and, beginning in 2006, the Andre Norton Award for Outstanding Young Adult Science Fiction or Fantasy Book of the Year.

SOCIETY OF CHILDREN'S BOOK WRITERS AND ILLUSTRATORS

8271 Beverly Blvd., Los Angeles CA 90048. (323)782-1010. E-mail: info@scbwi.org (autoresponse). Web site: www.scbwi.org. **President:** Stephen Mooser. **Executive Director:** Lin Oliver. **Chairperson, Board of Advisors:** Sue Alexander. Purpose of organization: to assist writers and illustrators working or interested in the field. Qualifications for membership: an interest in children's literature and illustration. Membership cost: $60/year. Plus one time $15 initiation fee. Different levels of membership include: full membership—published authors/illustrators; associate membership—unpublished writers/illustrators. Holds 100 events (workshops/conferences) worldwide each year. National Conference open to nonmembers. Publishes a newsletter focusing on writing and illustrating children's books. Sponsors grants for writers and illustrators who are members.

SOCIETY OF ILLUSTRATORS

128 E. 63rd St., New York NY 10021-7303. (212)838-2560. Fax: (212)838-2561. E-mail: info@societyillustrators. org. Web site: www.societyillustrators.org. **Contact:** Terrence Brown, director. "Purpose is to promote interest in the art of illustration for working professional illustrators and those in associated fields." Cost of membership: Initiation fee is $250. Annual dues for nonresident members (those living more than 125 air miles from SI's headquarters): $287. Dues for Resident Artist Members: $475 per year; Resident Associate Members: $552. "Artist Members shall include those who make illustration their profession and earn at least 60% of their income from their illustration. Associate Members are those who earn their living in the arts or who have made a substantial contribution to the art of illustration. This includes art directors, art buyers, creative supervisors, instructors, publishers and like categories. The candidate must complete and sign the application form which requires a brief biography, a listing of schools attended, other training and a résumé of his or her professional career. Candidates for Artist membership, in addition to the above requirements, must submit examples of their work." Sponsors contest. Sponsors "The Annual of American Illustration," which awards gold and silver medals. Open to nonmembers. Deadline: October 1. Also sponsors "The Original Art: The Best of Children's Book Illustration." Deadline: mid-August. Call for details.

SOCIETY OF MIDLAND AUTHORS

P.O. 10419, Chicago IL 60610-0419. Web site: www.midlandauthors.com. **President:** Thomas Frisbie. Purpose of organization: create closer association among writers of the Middle West; stimulate creative literary effort; maintain collection of members' works; encourage interest in reading and literature by cooperating with other educational and cultural agencies. Qualifications for membership: membership by invitation only. Must be author or co-author of a book demonstrating literary style and published by a recognized publisher and be identified through residence with Illinois, Indiana, Iowa, Kansas, Michigan, Minnesota, Missouri, Nebraska, North Dakota, Ohio, South Dakota or Wisconsin. **Open to students** (if authors). Membership cost: $35/year dues. Different levels of membership include: regular—published book authors; associate, nonvoting—not published as above but having some connection with literature, such as librarians, teachers, publishers and editors. Program meetings held 5 times a year, featuring authors, publishers, editors or the like individually or on panels. Usually second Tuesday of October, November, February, March and April. Also holds annual awards dinner in May. Publishes a newsletter focusing on news of members and general items of interest to writers. Sponsors contests. "Annual awards in six categories, given at annual dinner in May. Monetary awards for books published which premiered professionally in previous calendar year. Send SASE to contact person for details." Categories include adult fiction, adult nonfiction, juvenile fiction, juvenile nonfiction, poetry, biography. No picture books. Contest open to nonmembers. Deadline for contest: January 30.

SOCIETY OF SOUTHWESTERN AUTHORS

P.O. Box 30355, Tucson AZ 85751-0355. Fax: (520)751-7877. E-mail: Information: Penny Porter wporter202@aol.com. Web site: www.ssa-az/org. Purpose of organization: to promote fellowship among professional and associate members of the writing profession, to recognize members' achievements, to stimulate further achievement, and to assist persons seeking to become professional writers. Qualifications for membership: Professional Membership: proof of publication of a book, articles, TV screenplay, etc. Associate Membership: proof of desire to write, and/or become a professional. Self-published authors may receive status of Professional Membership at the discretion of the board of directors. Membership cost: $25 initiation plus $25/year dues. The Society of Southwestern Authors sponsors an annual 2-day Writers' Conference (all genres) held September 15-16, 2007 (check Web site for updated information). SSA publishes a bimonthly newsletter, *The Write Word*, promoting members' published works, advice to fellow writers, and up-to-the-minute trends in publishing and marketing. Yearly writing contest open to all writers; short story, memoir, poetry, children's stories. Applications available in February—write Mary Ann Hutchinson douglashutchinson@comcast.net; Subject Line: SSA Writer's Contest.

SOUTHWEST WRITERS

3721 Morris NE, Suite A, Albuquerque NM 87111. (505)265-9485. Fax: (505)265-9483. E-mail: swwriters@juno. com. Web site: www.southwestwriters.org. Non-profit organization dedicated to helping members of all levels in their writing. Members enjoy perks such as networking with professional and aspiring writers; substantial discounts on mini-conferences, workshops, writing classes, and annual and monthly SWW writing contest; monthly newsletter; two writing programs per month; critique groups, critique service (also for nonmembers); discounts at bookstores and other businesses; and Web site linking. Cost of membership: Individual, $60/year, $100/2 years; Two People, $50 each/year; Student, $40/year; Student under 18, $25/year; Outside U.S., $65/year; Lifetime, $750. See Web site for information.

TEXT AND ACADEMIC AUTHORS ASSOCIATION
P.O. Box 76477, St. Petersburg FL 33734-6477. (727)563-0020. Fax: (727)563-2409. E-mail: TEXT@tampabay.rr.com. Web site: www.taaonline.net. **President:** John Wakefield. Purpose of organization: to address the professional concerns of text and academic authors, to protect the interests of creators of intellectual property at all levels, and support efforts to enforce copyright protection. Qualifications for membership: all authors and prospective authors are welcome. Membership cost: $30 first year; $75 per year following years. Workshops/conferences: June each year. Newsletter focuses on all areas of interest to text authors.

VOLUNTEER LAWYERS FOR THE ARTS
1 E. 53rd St., 6th Floor, New York NY 10022-4201. (212)319-ARTS, ext. 1 (the Art Law Line). Fax: (212)752-6575. E-mail: askvla@vlany.org. Web site: www.vlany.org. **Executive Director:** Elena M. Paul. Purpose of organization: Volunteer Lawyers for the Arts is dedicated to providing free arts-related legal assistance to low-income artists and not-for-profit arts organizations in all creative fields. Over 800 attorneys in the New York area donate their time through VLA to artists and arts organizations unable to afford legal counsel. There is no membership required for our services. Everyone is welcome to use VLA's Art Law Line, a legal hotline for any artist or arts organization needing quick answers to arts-related questions. VLA also provides clinics, seminars and publications designed to educate artists on legal issues which affect their careers. Membership is through donations and is not required to use our services. Members receive discounts on publications and seminars as well as other benefits. Some of the many publications we carry are *All You Need to Know About the Music Business*; *Business and Legal Forms for Fine Artists, Photographers & Authors & Self-Publishers*; *Contracts for the Film & TV Industry*, plus many more.

WESTERN WRITERS OF AMERICA, INC.
1012 Mesa Vista Hall, MSCO6 3770, 1 University of New Mexico, Albuquerque NM 87131-0001. (505)277-5234. E-mail: wwa@unm.edu; candywwa@aol.com. Web site: www.westernwriters.org. **Executive Director:** Paul Andrew Hutton. **Open to students.** Purpose of organization: to further all types of literature that pertains to the American West. Membership requirements: must be a published author of Western material. Membership cost: $75/year ($90 foreign). Different levels of membership include: Active and Associate-the two vary upon number of books published. Holds annual conference. The 2007 conference held in Springfield, MO; 2008 in Scottsdale AZ, and 2009 in New Mexico. Publishes bimonthly magazine focusing on western literature, market trends, bookreviews, news of members, etc. Nonmembers may subscribe for $30 ($50 foreign). Sponsors youth writing contests. Spur Awards given annually for a variety of types of writing. Awards include plaque, certificate, publicity. Contest and Spur Awards open to nonmembers.

WOMEN WRITING THE WEST
8547 E. Arapahoe Rd., #J-541, Greenwood Village CO 80112. (303)773-8349. E-mail: WWWAdmin@lohseworks.com. Web site: www.womenwritingthewest.org. **Contact:** Joyce Lohse, administrator. Purpose of organization: "To gather and unite writers and other literature professionals writing and promoting the Women's West. The heart of this organization's interest is in the written record of women fo the American West." Qualifications for membership: Open to all interested persons worldwide. **Open to students.** Cost of membership: annual membership dues $50. Along with the annual dues there is an option to become a sustaining member for $100. Publisher dues are $50. "Sustaining members receive a WWW enamal logo pin, prominent listing in WWW publications, and the knowledge that they are assiting the organization. Members actively exchange ideas on a listserv e-bulletin board. Note: WWW membership also allows the choice of participation in our marketing marvel, the annual *WWW Catalog of Author's Books*." Holds an annual conference the third weekend in October. Publishes newsletter. "The focus of the WWW newsletter is current WWW activities; feature market, research, and experience articles of interest pertaining to American West literature; and member news." Sponsors annual WILLA Literary Award. "The WILLA Award is given in several catagories for outstanding literature featuring women's stories set in the West." The winner of a WILLA Literary Award receives $100 and a plaque at the annual conference luncheon. Contest open to non-members.

WRITERS GUILD OF ALBERTA
11759 Groat Rd., Edmonton AB T5M 3K6 Canada. (780)422-8174. Fax: (780)422-2663. E-mail: mail@writersguild.ab.ca. Web site: www.writersguild.ab.ca. Purpose of organization: to provide meeting ground and collective

voice for the writers in Alberta. Membership cost: $60/year; $30 for seniors/students. Holds workshops/conferences. Publishes a newsletter focusing on markets, competitions, contemporary issues related to the literary arts (writing, publishing, censorship, royalties etc.). Nonmembers may subscribe to newsletter. Subscription cost: $60/year. Sponsors annual Literary Awards in 7 categories (novel, nonfiction, short fiction, children's literature, poetry, drama, best first book). Awards include $1,000, leather-bound book, promotion and publicity. Open to nonmembers.

WRITERS OF KERN

P.O. Box 6694, Bakersfield CA 93386-6694. (661)399-0423. E-mail: sm@sandymoffett.com. Web site: http://home.bak.rr.com/writersofkern/. **Membership:** Sandy Moffett. Open to published writers and any person interested in writing. Dues: $45/year, $20 for students; $20 initiation fee. Types of memberships: Active—writers with published work; associate—writers working toward publication, affiliate—beginners and students. Monthly meetings held on the third Saturday of every month. Bi- or tri-annual writers' workshops, with speakers who are authors, agents, etc., on topics pertaining to writing; critique groups for several fiction genres, poetry, children's, nonfiction, journalism and screenwriting which meet bimonthly. Members receive a monthly newsletter with marketing tips, conferences and contests; access to club library; discount to annual CWC conference.

WRITERS' FEDERATION OF NEW BRUNSWICK

Box 37, Station A, Fredericton E3B 4Y2 Canada. (506)459-7228. E-mail: wfnb@nb.aibn.com. Web site: www.umce.ca/wfnb. **Executive Director:** Mary Hutchman. Purpose of organization: "to promote New Brunswick writing and to help writers at all stages of their development." Qualifications for membership: interest in writing. Membership cost: $40, basic annual membership; $20, high school students; $45, family membership; $50, institutional membership; $100, sustaining member; $250, patron; and $1,000, lifetime member. Holds workshops/conferences. Publishes a newsletter with articles concerning the craft of writing, member news, contests, markets, workshops and conference listings. Sponsors annual literary competition, $15 entry fee for members, $20 for nonmembers. Categories: fiction, nonfiction, poetry, children's literature—3 prizes per category of $150, $75, $50; Alfred Bailey Prize of $400 for poetry ms; The Richards Prize of $400 for short novel, collection of short stories or section of long novel; The Sheree Fitch Prize for writing by young people (14-18 years of age). Contest open to nonmembers (residents of Canada only).

Conferences & Workshops

Writers and illustrators eager to expand their knowledge of the children's publishing industry should consider attending one of the many conferences and workshops held each year. Whether you're a novice or seasoned professional, conferences and workshops are great places to pick up information on a variety of topics and network with experts in the publishing industry, as well as with your peers.

Listings in this section provide details about what conference and workshop courses are offered, where and when they are held, and the costs. Some of the national writing and art organizations also offer regional workshops throughout the year. Write, call or visit Web sites for information.

Writers can find listings of more than 1,000 conferences (searchable by type, location, and date) at The Writer's Digest/Shaw Guides Directory to Writers' Conferences, Seminars, and Workshop—www.writersdigest.com/conferences.

Members of the Society of Children's Book Writers and Illustrators can find information on conferences in national and local SCBWI newsletters. Nonmembers may attend SCBWI events as well. SCBWI conferences are listed in the beginning of this section under a separate subheading. For information on SCBWI's annual national conferences, contact them at (323)782-1010 or check their Web site for a complete calendar of national and regional events (www.scbwi.org). And read the Insider Report with author **Deborah Ruddell**—who was "discovered" at an SCBWI event—on page 310.

CONFERENCES & WORKSHOPS CALENDAR

To help you plan your conference travel, here is a month-by-month calendar of all the conferences, workshops and retreats included in this section. The calendar lists conferences alphabetically by the month in which they occur.

January
Butler University Children's Literature Conference (Indianapolis IN)
Kindling Words (Burlington VT)
San Diego State University Writers' Conference (San Diego CA)
SCBWI—Florida Regional Conference (Miami FL)
South Coast Writers Conference (Gold Beach OR)

February
San Francisco Writers Conference (San Francisco CA)
SCBWI; Annual Conference on Writing and Illustrating for Children (New York NY)

SCBWI—Norca (San Francisco/South); Retreat at Asilomar (Pacific Grove CA)
SCBWI—Southern Breeze; Spring Mingle (Atlanta GA)

March
AEC Conference on Southern Literature (Chattanooga TN)
Florida Christian Writers Conference (Bradenton FL)
Kentucky Writer's Workshop (Pineville KY)
SCBWI—Utah; Forum on Children's Literature (Orem UT)
Virginia Festival of the Book (Charlottesville VA)
Whidbey Island Writers' Conference (Langley WA)
Tennessee Williams/New Orleans Literary Festival (New Orleans LA)

April
Central Ohio Writers of Literature for Children (Columbus OH)
Children's Literature Conference (Hempstead NY)
Festival of Children's Literature (Minneapolis MN)
Festival of Faith and Writing (Grand Rapids MI)
Missouri Writers' Guild Annual State Conference (St. Charles MO)
Mount Hermon Christian Writers Conference (Mount Hermon CA)
Perspectives in Children's Literature Conference (Amherst MA)
SCBWI; Before-Bologna Conference (Bologna, Italy)
SCBWI—New England; Annual Conference (Nashua NH)
SCBWI—New York; Conference for Children's Book Illustrators & Author/Illustrators (New
     York NY)
SCBWI New Mexico Handsprings: A Conference for Children's Writers and Illustrators (Albu-
     querque NM)
SCBWI—Pocono Mountains Retreat (South Sterling PA)
Texas Mountain Trail Writers' Winter Retreat (Alpine TX)

May
Annual Spring Poetry Festival (New York NY)
BookExpo America/Writer's Digest Books Writers Conference (Los Angeles CA)
Oklahoma Writers' Federation, Inc. Annual Conference (Oklahoma City OK)
Pima Writers' Workshop (Tucson AZ)

June
East Texas Christian Writers Conference (Marshall TX)
The Environmental Writers' Conference and Workshop in Honor of Rachel Carson (Boothbay
     Harbor ME)
Great Lakes Writers Conference (Milwaukee WI)
Highland Summer Conference (Radford VA)
International Creative Writing Camp (Minot ND)
International Women's Writing Guild ''Remember the Magic'' Annual Summer Conference
     (Saratoga Spring NY)
Iowa Summer Writing Festival (Iowa City IA)
Manhattanville Summer Writers' Week (Purchase NY)
Outdoor Writers Association of America Annual Conference (Lake Charles LA)
SCBWI—Florida Mid-Year Writing Workshop (Orlando FL)
SCBWI—New Jersey; Annual Spring Conference (Princeton NJ)
Southeastern Writer's Association—Annual Writer's Workshop (Athens GA)

UMKC/Writers Place Writers Workshops (Kansas City MO)
Wesleyan Writers Conference (Middleton CT)
Write! Canada (Markham ON Canada)
Write-by-the-Lake Writer's Workshop & Retreat (Madison WI)
Write-to-Publish Conference (Wheaton IL)
Writing and Illustrating for Young Readers Workshop (Provo UT)

July

Children's Book Workshop at Castle Hill (Truro MA)
Conference for Writers & Illustrators of Children's Books (Corte Madera CA)
Highlights Foundation Writers Workshop at Chautauqua (Chautaqua NY)
Hofstra University Summer Workshop (Hempstead NY)
Iowa Summer Writing Festival (Iowa City IA)
Ligonier Valley Writers Conference (Ligonier PA)
The Manuscript Workshop in Vermont (Londonderry VT)
Maritime Writers' Workshop (Fredericton NB Canada)
Midwest Writers Workshop (Muncie IN)
Montrose Christian Writer's Conference (Montrose PA)
Pacific Northwest Children's Book Conference (Portland OR)
Pacific Northwest Writer Assn. Summer Writer's Conference (Seattle WA)
Robert Quackenbush's Children's Book Writing and Illustrating Workshop (New York NY)
Saskatchewan Festival of Words and Workshops (Moose Jaw SK Canada)
Steamboat Springs Writers Conference (Steamboat Springs CO)
The Victoria School of Writing (Victoria BC Canada)

August

Cape Cod Writer's Conference (Osterville MA)
The Columbus Writers Conference (Columbus OH)
Green Lake Writers Conference (Green Lake WI)
The Manuscript Workshop in Vermont (Londonderry VT)
The Pacific Coast Children's Writer's Workshop (Aptos CA)
SCBWI; Annual Conference on Writing and Illustrating for Children (Los Angeles CA)
Willamette Writers Annual Writers Conference (Portland OR)

September

East of Eden Writers Conference (Santa Clara CA)
League of Utah Writers' Roundup (Provo UT)
Maui Writers Conference (Kihei HI)
Moondance International Film Festival (Hollywood CA)
SCBWI—Carolinas; Annual Fall Conference (Durham NC)
SCBWI—Eastern Pennsylvania; Fall Philly Conference (Exton PA)
SCBWI—Idaho; Editor Day (Boise ID)
SCBWI—Midsouth Fall Conference (Nashville TN)
SCBWI—Northern Ohio; Annual Conference (Cleveland OH)
SCBWI—Rocky Mountain; Annual Fall Conference (Golden CO)
Society of Southwestern Authors' Wrangling with Writing (Tucson AZ)
South Coast Writers Conference (Gold Beach CO)

October

Flathead River Writers Conference (Whitefish MT)
Ozark Creative Writers, Inc. Conference (Eureka Springs AR)
SCBWI—Iowa Conference (Iowa City IA)
SCBWI—Midatlantic; Annual Fall Conference (Arlington VA)
SCBWI—Oregon Conferences (Portland OR)
SCBWI—Southern Breeze; Writing and Illustrating for Kids (Birmingham AL)
SCBWI—Ventura/Santa Barbara; Fall Conference (Thousand Oaks CA)
SCBWI—Wisconsin; Fall Retreat for Working Writers (Milton WI)
Surrey International Writer's Conference (Surrey BC Canada)
Vancouver Internatinoal Writers Festival (Vancouver BC Canada)
Write on the Sound Writers Conference (Edmonds WA)

November

Jewish Children's Book Writers' Conference (New York NY)
LaJolla Writers Conference (LaJolla CA)
North Carolina Writers' Network Fall Conference (Durham NC)
SCBWI—Illinois; Prairie Writers Day
SCBWI—Missouri; Children's Writer's Conference (St. Peters MO)

December

Big Sur Writing Workshop (Big Sur CA)

Multiple Events

The conference listings below include information on multiple or year-round events. Please read the listings for more information on the dates and locations of these events and check the conferences' Web sites.

American Christian Writers Conference
Booming Ground Writer's Community
Cat Writers Association Annual Writers Conference
Children's Authors' Bootcamp
Peter Davidson's How to Write a Children's Picture Book Seminar
The DIY Book Festival
Duke University Youth Programs: Creative Writer's Workshop
Duke University Youth Programs: Young Writer's Camp
Gotham Writers' Workshop (New York NY)
Highlights Foundation Founders Workshops (Honesdale PA)
Publishinggame.com Workshop
Rocky Mountain Retreats for Writers & Artists (Lyons CO)
SCBWI—Arizona; Events
SCBWI—Eastern Canada; Annual Events
SCBWI—Dakotas
SCBWI—Iowa Conferences
SCBWI—Los Angeles; Events
SCBWI—Metro New York; Professional Series (New York NY)
SCBWI—New Jersey; Mentoring Workshops
SCBWI—Oregon Conferences
SCBWI—Taiwan; Events
SCBWI—Western Washington State; Retreats & Conference

Southwest Writers Conferences

Split Rock Arts Program (St. Paul MN)

Sydney Children's Writers and Illustrators Network (Woollahra, Australia)

UMKC/Writers Place Writers Workshops (Kansas City MO)

Writers' League of Texas Workshop Series (Austin TX)

Information on conferences listed in the previous edition but not this edition of Children's Writer's & Illustrator's Market may be found in the General Index.

SCBWI CONFERENCES

SCBWI; ANNUAL CONFERENCES ON WRITING AND ILLUSTRATING FOR CHILDREN

8271 Beverly Blvd., Los Angeles CA 90048. (323)782-1010. Fax: (323)782-1892. E-mail: scbwi@scbwi.org. Web site: www.scbwi.org. **Conference Director:** Lin Oliver. Writer and illustrator workshops geared toward all levels. **Open to students.** Covers all aspects of children's book and magazine publishing—the novel, illustration techniques, marketing, etc. Annual conferences held in August in Los Angeles and in New York in February. Cost of conference (LA): approximately $390; includes all 4 days and one banquet meal. Write for more information or visit web site.

SCBWI—ARIZONA; EVENTS

P.O. Box 26384, Scottsdale AZ 85255-0123. E-mail: rascbwiaz@aol.com. Web site: www.scbwi-az.org. **Regional Advisor:** Michelle Parker-Rock. SCBWI Arizona will offer a variety of workshops, retreats, conferences, meetings and other craft and industry-related events throughout 2007-2008. Open to members and nonmembers, published and nonpublished. Registration to major events is usually limited. Pre-registration always required. Visit Web site, write or e-mail for more information.

🌐 SCBWI; BEFORE-BOLOGNA CONFERENCE

(1-323)782-1010 (PST). E-mail: Bologna@scbwi.org. Web site: www.scbwi.org. **Contact:** Bologna@scbwi.org. Two-day writer and illustrator conference for children's book professionals held in the spring every two years in association with the largest international children's book rights fair in the world, the Bologna Children's Book Fair (www.bookfair.bolognafiere.it). Next conference date: March 29-30, 2008. A professional craft-based conference, with talks, panels, and hands-on workshops. A chance to meet editors, art directors and agents and children's book creators, before the rights fair gets going. Registration limited to 100 attendees. Cost of conference: Early-bird special before December 1, 2007: SCBWI members 125€; nonmembers 175€. After December 1, 2007: SCBWI members 250€; nonmembers 275€. Attendance fee covers presentations and workshops; lunch on Saturday & Sunday, coffee breaks, closing cocktail party with industry professionals. Manuscript and illustration critiques available by reservation for additional fee (deadline for manuscripts to be received is January 31, 2008). Register at www.scbwi.org/events.htm. PayPal payment accepted. "Register early and reserve affordable rooms at local bed & breakfast establishments as well as benefit from Early-bird Special. Illustrators attent the Book Fair for free, if they submit illustrations to the illustration contest; others: often discounts for early registration to the Book Fair." SCBWI Bologna Biennial Conference 2008 program features: Tracey Adams (agent); Val Brathwaite (design director, Bloomsbury UK); Pat Cummings (author/illustrator; recent book: *Squashed in the Middle*); Steven Chudney (agent); Susan Fletcher (writer; recent book: *Alphabet of Dreams*); Susanne Gervay (writer; recent book: *That's Why I Wrote This Song*); Katherine Halligan (editorial director picture books, novelty and gifts, Scholastic UK); Laura Harris (publisher, Penguin Australia); Susanne Koppe (agent); Nancy Miles (agent); Sarah Odedina (editorial director, Bloomsbury UK); Bridget Strevens-Marzo (author/illustrator; recent book *How Do You Make a Baby Smile?*); Cecilia Yung (art director and vice president, Penguin Putnam), and others.

SCBWI—CAROLINAS; ANNUAL FALL CONFERENCE

E-mail: scgbooks@aol.com; dahl1033@aol.com. **Regional Advisor:** Stephanie Green. Assistant Regional Advisor: Candy Dahl. Annual conference held Sept. 28-30, 2007 at the Sheraton Imperial Airport Hotel, Durham, NC. Speakers include Lin Oliver; Caitlyn Dloughy, editorial director, Atheneum Books for Young Readers; Julie Strauss-Gabel, editor, Dutton; Joy Neaves, senior editor, Front Street Books; Molly O'Neill, school and library marketing associate, HarperCollins Children's Book; Carole Boston Weatherford, author of *Moses*, a Caldecott Honor Book 2006; Frances

O'Roark Dowell, author of *Dovey Coe and the Secret Language of Girls*, plus workshops on Web Site design, Illustration, and Writing for Alternative Markets. Special Friday Editor's Evening, Saturday Night Crystal Ball, First Pages, manuscript and portfolio critiques, and more. E-mail for more information.

⃞ SCBWI—DAKOTAS; SPRING CONFERENCE

100 N. Sanborn Blvd. #210, Mitchell SD 57301.E-mail: jean@santel.net. Web site: www.scbwidakotas.org. **Regional Advisor:** Jean Patrick. Conference for writers of all levels. "In addition to providing the basics about picture books and novels, we strive to offer unique information about other avenues for publication, including magazine writing, craft writing, work-for-hire writing and more. Our 2007 conference included keynote speakers Marilyn Kratz and Rose Ross Zebiker." Annual event held every spring. Check Web site for details.

SCBWI—DAKOTAS; WRITERS CONFERENCE IN CHILDREN'S LITERATURE

Grand Forks ND 58202-7209. (701)777-3321. E-mail: jean@jeanpatrick.com. Web site: www.und.edu/dept/english/ChildrensLit.html. or www.scbwidakotas.org. **Regional Advisor:** Jean Patrick. Conference sessions geared toward all levels. "Although the conference attendees are mostly writers, we encourage & welcome illustrators of every level." Open to students. "Our conference offers 3-4 children's authors, editors, publishers, illustrators, or agents. Past conferences have included Kent Brown (publisher, Boyds Mills Press); Stephanie Lane (editor, Random House); Jane Kurtz (author); Anastasia Suen (author); and Karen Ritz (illustrator). Conference held each fall. "Please call or e-mail to confirm dates. Writers and illustrators come from throughout the northern plains, including North Dakota, South Dakota, Montana, Minnesota, Iowa, and Canada." Writing facilities available: campus of University of North Dakota. Local art exhibits and/or concerts may coincide with conference. Cost of conference includes Friday evening reception and sessions, Saturday's sessions, and lunch. A manuscript may be submitted 1 month in advance for critique (extra charge). E-mail for more information.

⃞ SCBWI—DAKOTAS/UND WRITERS CONFERENCE IN CHILDREN'S LITERATURE

Department. of English, Merrifield Hall, Room 110, 276 Centennial Drive, Stop 7209, Univeristy of North Dakota, Grand Forks ND 58202. (701)777-3321 or (701)777-3984. E-mail: jean@jeanpatrick.com. Web site: www.und.edu. or www.scbwidakotas.com. **Regional Advisor:** Jean Patrick. Conference for all levels. "Our conference offers 3-4 chlidren's authors, editors, publishers, illustrators or agents. Past conferences have included Elaine Marie Alphin (author), Jane Kurtz (author), Alexandra Penfold (editor), Kent Brown (publisher), and Karen Ritz (illustrator)." Annual conference held every fall. "Please call or e-mail to confirm dates." Cost of conference to be determined. Cost included Friday evening sessions, Saturday sessions, and Saturday lunch. "We welcome writers, illustrators, and others who are interested in children's literature."

⃞ SCBWI—EASTERN CANADA; ANNUAL EVENTS

E-mail: ara@scbwicanada.org; ra@scbwicanada.org. Web site: www.scbwicanada.org. **Regional Advisor:** Lizann Flatt. Writer and illustrator event geared toward all levels. Usually offers one event in spring and another in the fall. Check Web site Events pages for updated information.

SCBWI—EASTERN PENNSYLVANIA; FALL PHILLY CONFERENCE

Whitford Country Club, Exton PA. Web site: www.scbwiepa.org. Conference focuses on writing skills, the publishing market, and finding inspiration. Manuscript and Portfolio critiques with editors available for an additional fee. Conference held in September. Registration is limited to 150. Information will be posted on the Web site in July. Cost: $90. Registration includes buffet lunch.

SCBWI—FLORIDA; MID-YEAR WRITING WORKSHOP

(305)382-2677. E-mail: lindabernfeld@hotmail.com. Web site: www.scbwiflorida.com. **Regional Advisor:** Linda Rodriguez Bernfeld. Annual workshop held in June in Orlando. Workshop is geared toward helping everyone hone their writing skills. Attendees choose one track and spend the day with industry leaders who share valuable information about that area of children's book writing. There are a minimum of 3 tracks, picture book, middle grade and young adult. The 4th track is variable, covering subjects such as non-fiction, humor or writing for magazines. Speakers in 2006 included Sue Corbett, Nancy Mercado (editor, Dial), Lisa Yee, Gloria Rothstein, Bill Farnsworth, Alexandra Penfold (assistant editor at Paula Wiseman Books), Tara Weikum (executive editor, HarperCollins), Dorian Cirrone, Ed Bloor and Paula Morrow. E-mail for more information.

SCBWI—FLORIDA; REGIONAL CONFERENCE

(305)382-2677. E-mail: lindabernfeld@hotmail.com. Web site: www.scbwiflorida.com. **Regional Advisor:** Linda Rodriguez Bernfeld. Assistant Regional Advisor: Vivian Fernandez. Annual conference held in January in Miami. 2008 conference will be held January 18-20. 2007 speakers included Bruce Hale (Chet Gecko series) and Barbara Seuling (*How to Write a Children's Book and Get it Published*). Cost of conference: approximately

$175. The 3-day conference will have workshops Friday afternoon, open mic and informal critique groups Friday evening. There will be a general session all day Saturday covering all aspects of writing for children. There will be hands on workshops Sunday morning led by industry leaders. There is a Saturday only option. Past speakers have included Judy Blume, Paula Danziger, Bruce Coville, Arthur Levine, Libba Bray and Kate DiCamillo. For more information, contact e-mail Linda Rodriguez Bernfeld at lindabernfeld@hotmail.com.

N SCBWI—IDAHO; EDITOR DAY
Email: neysajensen@msn.com. **Regional Advisor:** Sydney Husseman; **Assistant Regional Advisor:** Neysa Jensen. One day workshop focuses on the craft of writing, as well as getting to know an editor. One-on-one critiques available for an additional fee. Event held in Boise ID every September.

SCBWI—ILLINOIS; PRAIRIE WRITERS DAY
Chicago IL 60614. E-mail: esthersh@aol.com. Web site: www.scbwi-illinois.org/events. **Regional Advisor:** Esther Hershenhorn. Workshop held in early November at Dominican University in River Forest. Highlights 3 newly-published members and their editors, along with agents, booksellers and reviewers. Ms critiques and First Page readings are on the program. 2007 speakers included Andrea Beaty and her Abrams Editor Susan Van Metre; Deborah Ruddell and her Margaret McElderry Editor Karen Woytyla; agents Sara Crowe and Rosemary Stimola; and Andersons Book Buyer Jan Dundon; among others. Visit Web site for more information on this and other SCBWI—Illinois events or contact Sara Shacter at sfshacter@gmail.com.

SCBWI—IOWA CONFERENCES
E-mail: hecklit@aol.com. Web site: www.scbwi-iowa.org. **Regional Advisor:** Connie Heckert. Writer and illustrator workshops geared toward all levels. The Iowa Region offers conferences of high quality. Recent speakers included Bruce Coville, SCBWI Board Member and Author; Michael Stearns, Editorial Director and Foreign Acquisitions Manager, HarperCollins Children's Books; Lin Oliver, Executive Director, SCBWI and Co-Author of the Hank Zipzer series. Holds spring and fall events. Individual critiques and portfolio review offerings vary with the program and presenters. For more information e-mail or visit Web site.

SCBWI—LOS ANGELES; EVENTS
P.O. Box 1728, Pacific Palisades CA 90272. (310)573-7318. Web site: www.scbwisocal.org. **Co-regional Advisors:** Claudia Harrington (claudiascbwi@earthlink.net). and Edie Pagliasotti (ediescbwi@sbcgloablnet). SCBWI—Los Angeles hosts 7 major events each year: **Writer's Workshop** (winter)—half-day workshop featuring speaker demonstrating nuts and bolts techniques on the craft of writing for childrens; **Writer's Day** (spring)—a one-day conference featuring speakers, a professional forum, writing contests and awards; **Critiquenic** (summer)—a free informal critiquing session for writers and illustrators facilitated by published authors/illustrators, held after a picnic lunch; **Writers & Illustrator's Sunday Field Trip** (summer)—hands-on creative field trip for writers and illustrators; **Illustrator's Workshops** (summer and fall)—Half-day workhops featuring an illustrator demonstrating hands-on art techniques. Art director and/or art editor to be announced (*new*). **Working Writer's Retreat** (winter)—a 3-day, 2-night retreat featuring an editor, speakers, and intensive critiquing. See calendar of events on Web site for more details and dates.

SCBWI—METRO NEW YORK; PROFESSIONAL SERIES
P.O. Box 1475, Cooper Station, New York NY 10276-1475. (212)545-3719. E-mail: scbwi_metrony@yahoo.com. Web site: www.home.nyc.rr.com/scbwimetrony. **Regional Advisor:** Nancy Lewis. Writer and illustrator workshops geared toward all levels. **Open to students.** The Metro New York Professional Series generally meets the second Tuesday of each month, from October to June, 7-9 p.m. Check Web site to confirm location, dates, times and speakers. Cost of workshop: $12 for SCBWI members; $15 for nonmembers. "We feature an informal, almost intimate evening with coffee, cookies, and top editors, art directors, agents, publicity and marketing people, librarians, reviewers and more."

SCBWI—MIDATLANTIC; ANNUAL FALL CONFERENCE
Mid-Atlantic SCBWI, P.O. Box 3215, Reston, VA 20195-1215. E-mail: sydney.dunlap@adelphia.net or midatlanticscbwi@tidalwave.net. Web site: www.scbwi-midatlantic.org. **Conference Chair:** Sydney Dunlap. Regional Advisor: Ellen Braaf. Conference takes place Saturday, October 25, 2008 in Arlington, VA from 8 to 5. Keynote speaker: TBD. For updates and details visit Web site. Registration limited to 200. Conference fills quickly. Cost: $85 for SCBWI members; $110 for nonmembers. Includes continental breakfast.

N SCBWI—MIDSOUTH FALL CONFERENCE
P.O. Box 120013, Nashville TN 37212.(615)297-1667. E-mail: expressdog@bellsouth.net or cmoonwriter@aol.com. Web site: www.scbwi-midsouth.org. **Conference Coordinators:** Genetta Adair and Candie Moonshower.

Conference for writers and illustrators of all levels. In the past, workshops were offered on Plotting You Novel, Understanding the Language of Editors, Landing an Agent, How to Prepare a Portfolio, Negotiating a Contract, The Basics for Beginners, and many others. Attendees are invited to bring a manuscript and/or art portfolio to share in the optional, no-charge critique group session. Illustrators are invited to bring color copies of their art (*not* originals) to be displayed in the bookstore. For an additional fee, attendees may schedule a 15-minute manuscript critique or portfolio critique by the editor, art director or other expert consultant. Annual conference held in September. Registration limited to 120 attendees. Cost to be determined. The 2007 Midsouth Conference included SCBWI co-founder/Executive Director and author Lin Oliver, Clarion Books Editor Jennifer Wingertzahn, Henry Holt Associate Art Director Laurent Linn, Literary Agent Ginger Clark (Curtis Brown, Ltd.), and author Jaime Adoff.

SCBWI—MISSOURI; CHILDREN'S WRITER'S CONFERENCE

St. Charles County Community College, P.O. Box 76975, 103 CEAC, St. Peters MO 63376-0975. (314)213-8000, ext. 4108. Web site: www.geocities.com/scbwimo. **Regional Advisor:** Lynnea Annette. Writer and illustrator conference geared toward all levels. **Open to students.** Speakers include editors, writers, and other professionals. Topics vary from year to year, but each conference offers sessions for both writers and illustrators as well as for newcomers and published writers. Previous topics included: "What Happens When Your Manuscript is Accepted" by Dawn Weinstock, editor; "Writing—Hobby or Vocation?" by Chris Kelleher; "Mother Time Gives Advice: Perspectives from a 25 Year Veteran" by Judith Mathews, editor; "Don't Be a Starving Writer" by Vicki Berger Erwin, author; and "Words & Pictures: History in the Making," by author-illustrator Cheryl Harness. Annual conference held in early November. For exact date, see SCBWI Web site: www.scbwi.org or the events page of the Missouri SCBWI Web site. Registration limited to 75-90. Cost of conference includes one-day workshop (8 a.m. to 5 p.m.) plus lunch. Write for more information.

[N] SCBWI—NEW ENGLAND; ANNUAL CONFERENCE

Nashua NH 03063.E-mail: northernnera@scbwi.org. Web site: www.nescbwi.org. **Regional Advisor:** Janet Arden. Conference all levels of writers and illustrators. **Open to students.** "We offer many workshops at each conference, and often there is a multi-day format. Examples of subjects addressed: manuscript development, revision, marketing your work, productive school visits, picture book dummy formatting, adding texture to your illustrations, etc." Annual conference held April 12, 2008 at the Crowne Plaza Hotel. Registration limited to 450. Cost: TBD; includes pre-conference social, great keynote speaker, many workshop options, lunch, snacks, etc. "Keynote speaker for 2008 conference is Laurie Halse Anderson. "Details (additional speakers, theme, number of workshop choices, etc.) will be posted to our Web site as they become available. Registration will not start until March 2008. Opportunities for one-on-one manuscript critiques and portfolio reviews will be available at the conference."

[N] SCBWI—NEW JERSEY; ANNUAL SPRING CONFERENCE

E-mail: njscbwi@newjerseyscbwi.com. Web site: www.newjerseyscbwi.com. **Regional Advisor:** Kathy Temean. This day-long conference brings in editors from top houses, an agent, art director and art rep to speak to small groups about timely topics. All writers will find workshops to fit their level of expertise with the workshops scheduled throughout the day. With various writer workshops running throughout the day, all writers will find workshops to fit their level of expertise. Illustrators can attend special sessions with an art director and art rep. Published authors attending the conference are invited to sign and sell their books in the afternoon. Illustrators have the opportunity to display their artwork during the day. Editors will do one-on-one manuscript critiques and portfolio critiques will be available for the illustrators who attend for an additional cost. Continental breakfast and lunch is included with the cost of admission. Conference is traditionally held during the beginning of June. This year's conference will be held in Princeton, New Jersey. Please visit for more information or seewww.scbwi.org/events.htm.

SCBWI—NEW JERSEY; MENTORING WORKSHOPS

E-mail: njscbwi@newjerseyscbwi.com. Web site: www.newjerseyscbwi.com. **Regional Advisor:** Kathy Temean. These workshops have become very popular and fill quickly. Workshops provide an inspiring environment for writers to work on their manuscript and have personal contact with their mentor/editor. Each workshop consists of 14 writers and two editors. Weekend workshops allow writers to spend 45 minutes, one-on-one, with their mentor to discuss their manuscript and career direction, first page critiques, pitch sessions and other fun writing activities. One day workshops consist of 20 minute one-on-one critiques, plus first page critiques. These workshops are held in the Spring and Fall each year at various locations in New Jersey. Please visitwww.newjerseyscbwi.com for more information.

SCBWI—NEW MEXICO; HANDSPRINGS: A CONFERENCE FOR CHILDREN'S WRITERS AND ILLUSTRATORS

P.O. Box 1084, Socorro NM. E-mail: lucyscbwi@earthlink.net. Web site: www.scbwi-nm.org. **Registrar:** Lucy Hampton. **Regional Advisor:** Chris Eboch. Conference for beginner and intermediate writers and illustrators. "Each conference features three keynote speakers—editors, agents, and/or art directors. 2007 speakers include Mark McVeigh, senior editor, Dutton Children's Books; Krista Marino, editor, Delacorte; and Laurent Linn, Senior Designer for Henry Holt. Writers and illustrators lead breakout sessions. Past workshop topics included: From Slushpile to Contact; How Publishers Work and Why; How to Snare and Editor; Plot Your Dream into Reality; Layout, Design, and Illustration on Your Picture Book; and Irresistible Queries and Cover Letters." Annual workshop held in April. Registration limited to 100. "Offers classroom-style workshops and large-group presentations." Cost: $90-100 for basic Saturday registration $15-20 for Friday evening party with edtior panel; $30-40 for private critiques (lowest prices are for SCBWI members). "The Friday evening party included social time, a First Page critique panel with our visiting editors, mini book launches and an illustrators' portfolio display. Saturday features a full day of keynote speeches by visiting editors, agents and/or art directors; breakout workshops on the craft and business of writing; and optional one-on-one critiques with the editors or portfolio review by the art director."

SCBWI—NEW YORK; CONFERENCE FOR CHILDREN'S BOOK ILLUSTRATORS & AUTHOR/ ILLUSTRATORS

Monsey NY 10952. (845)356-7273. Web site: www.societyillustrators.org. **Conference Chair:** Frieda Gates. Held in April in New York at the Society of Illustrators. Registration limited to 80 portfolios shown out of 125 conferees. Portfolios are not judged first come-first served. Cost of conference: with portfolio—$110, members, $120 others; without portfolio—$75 members, $85 others; $50 additional for 30-minute portfolio evaluation; $25 additional for 15-minute book dummy evaluation. Call to receive a flier. "In addition to an exciting program of speakers, this conference provides a unique opportunity for illustrators and author/illustrators to have their portfolios reviewed by scores of art buyers and agents from the publishing and allied industries. Art buyers admitted free. Our reputation for exhibiting high-quality work of both new and established children's book illustrators, plus the ease of examining such an abundance of portfolios, has resulted in a large number of productive contacts between buyers and illustrators."

SCBWI—NORCA (SAN FRANCISCO/SOUTH); GOLDEN GATE CONFERENCE AT ASILOMAR

Web site: www.scbwinorca.org. **Co-Regional Advisor:** Jim Averbeck and Shirley Klock. While we welcome "not-yet-published" writers and illustrators, lectures and workshops are geared toward professionals and those striving to become professional. Program topics cover aspects of writing or illustrating picture books to young adult novels. Past speakers include editors, art directors, Newbery Award-winning authors, and Caldecott Award-winning illustrators. Annual conference, generally held last weekend in February; Friday evening through Sunday lunch. Registration limited to 100. Most rooms shared with one other person. Additional charge for single when available. Desks available in most rooms. All rooms have private baths. Conference center is set in wooded campus on Asilomar Beach in Pacific Grove, California. Approximate cost: $395 for SCBWI members, $575 for nonmembers; includes shared room, 6 meals, ice breaker party and all conference activities. Vegetarian meals available. One full scholarship is available to SCBWI members. Registration opens at the end of September and the conference sells out within days. A waiting list is formed. "Coming together for shared meals and activities builds a strong feeling of community among the speakers and conferees. For more information, including exact costs and dates, visit our Web site in September."

SCBWI—NORTHERN OHIO; ANNUAL CONFERENCE

℅ Blossom Farm, 2946 Lampson Road, Austinburg, Ohio 44010, (440) 275-1638. Email: annettesheldon@alltel. net. Web site: www.nohscbwi.org. **Regional Advisor:** Annette Sheldon. Writer and illustrator conference for all levels. Open to students. "This conference is the premier marketing/networking event of the year for Northern Ohio SCBWI. The emphasis is on current market trends; what the market is publishing; getting manuscripts/ portfolios market-ready; staying alive in the market post-publication; and the nuts and bolts of writing and illustrating for children. Additional emphasis is on meeting/networking with peers." Annual event held in September at the Sheraton Cleveland Airport Hotel. Registration limited to 200. Conference costs will be posted on our Web site with registration information. SCBWI members receive a discount. Additional fees may apply for late registration, critiques, or portfolio reviews. Cost includes an optional Friday evening Opening Banquet from 6-10 p.m. with keynote speaker; Saturday event from 8:30 a.m. to 5 p.m. which includes breakfast snack, full-day conference with headliner presentations, general sessions, breakout sessions, lunch, panel discussion, bookstore, and autograph session. An Illustrator Showcase is open to all attendees at no additional cost. Grand door prize, drawn at the end of the day Saturday, is free admission to the following year's conference.

Deborah Ruddell

*A writer from Peoria discovered at
L.A. SCBWI conference*

A good poem can freeze an experience forever," says picture book poet Deborah Ruddell. "It can tell a story. It can make you laugh, make you cry, or make you think. It can help you to know yourself and to understand the world. A good poem can even stay with you for a lifetime."

An experience that will surely stay with Ruddell for a lifetime is her meeting with fellow poet Sonya Sones at the 2003 SCBWI Annual Summer Conference in Los Angeles. Attending this event and meeting with Sones resulted in Ruddell's first book contract for her poetry collection *Today at the Bluebird Café: A Branchful of Birds*, and her follow-up title *A Whiff of Pine, a Hint of Skunk* (both McElderry). Here's her story.

Your path to publication was rather unique—and pretty much every writer's dream—finding an agent and a getting a contract as the direct result of a conference critique. Can you recount your critique meeting with Sonya Sones?
After reading Sonya Sones's brilliant and moving, *Stop Pretending* (HarperCollins), I couldn't imagine what she would make of my poems. She writes important YA novels in verse and I had submitted a collection of rhyming poems about birds intended for younger children. I thought she would tell me to go back to Peoria and write about something that mattered.

Instead . . . Sonya started our meeting by telling me that she wanted to read something that she had come across recently—"something lovely." I prepared myself to hear a famous poet's perfect poem, aimed at giving me something to strive for. She proceeded to read my *own* poem about a cardinal. Believe me, it had never sounded better. I did what any professional would do under the circumstances: I cried.

As I blubbered, Sonya handed me several e-mails to read. The first one was from the acclaimed poet and anthologist, Lee Bennett Hopkins. Sonya had read some of my poems to him over the phone, and the e-mail was his response to that call. I *thought* I read the words "exquisite" and "publisher," but I couldn't be sure because whole paragraphs seemed to be swimming across the page.

After that, the room went all wobbly. I'm embarrassed to recall that I put my head down on the table and told Sonya that I was no longer capable of reading. So she told me that, on Mr. Hopkins's advice, she had e-mailed Emma Dryden at McElderry Books to ask if she would like to see my work. This being a psychedelic daydream, Emma naturally said *yes*.

Sonya went on to say that she wanted me to meet her agent. (At this point, I half-expected her to add, "And *then*, I'll introduce you to the real Santa Claus! What do you think of that?" I mean, hadn't she done *enough*?)

I nodded weakly and we held hands across the table the way you do when someone changes your life, and you both know it.

Tell me about your initial meeting with your agent, and how he came to represent both you and your twin sister.

Sonya introduced me to her agent, Steven Malk, shortly after the big critique, and we agreed to meet the next morning in the hotel lobby. He asked me to bring any work that I had with me (Hooray! I had brought it to L.A.!), so I took all of my poems and a picture book dummy illustrated by my twin sister, Robin Luebs. During our brief meeting, Steven looked over the

Today at the Bluebird Café has a fanciful publishing history to match its whimsical tone. Author Deborah Ruddell submitted her collection of bird poems to be critiqued by author Sonya Sones at an SCBWI conference. Sones liked the poems so much that she introduced Ruddell to her agent and to editors. Not too long after that fateful conference, children were reading about Ruddell's birds and laughing in sympathy for the wood-pecker who complains, ''I ask you just once to consider/the aftertaste/of bark.''

materials without too much comment, told me a bit about himself, and said he would call me the following week—which he did, with an offer of representation for *both* of us.

Are you and your sister working on any projects together?

As I write this, Robin is completing the illustrations for her first book *How Do You Say Goodnight?*, by Raina Moore (HarperCollins, Fall 2008). It's a lovely bedtime book, and Robin's paintings are charming and gorgeous. When she comes up for air, we hope to get back to work on the picture book we've been collaborating on for years. Someday, we want to see our names together on a book jacket.

Why did you decide to attend that "magical" SCBWI conference? Had you been to such events before? What kind of involvement did you have in SCBWI before the L.A. conference?

I went to my first SCBWI national conference in 2000 all by myself, which was an overwhelming experience. I had a very positive critique with a well-known editor, but nothing ever came of it—partly, I think, because I was inexperienced and dropped the ball. Then, in 2001, I found my fabulous critique partners through the Illinois SCBWI chapter. My work was improving, but I still had only one story in *Highlights* to my credit. By 2003, I thought I was ready to try L.A. one more time. My critique group helped me polish every poem, and I was off!

So do you recommend all aspiring children's writers and illustrators attend SCBWI conferences? What tips can you offer for making the most of your conference-going experience?

There's just no substitute for attending the L.A. conference. You learn about the industry firsthand from the experts, you make connections with other writers and illustrators, and you get inspired! But if you're shy (like me), it helps to have a friend along. Also, I'd recommend packing in as much as you possibly can: go to every session you can squeeze in, listen with an open mind, take notes, get autographs, sip wine on the terrace, and have fun. Take all of your best work along, because you never know who might want to see it. (And if Sonya Sones does your critique, be prepared for anything!)

On your Web site bio you mention thinking back to when you were a kid when the "world felt new." Describe your experience as a grown-up first-time author entering the "new world" of children's publishing.

I know I'll never get to experience my first book again, so I'm trying to savor it as much as I can. But there's still an element of disbelief about it: I'm 57 years old, embarking on this brand new adventure and fulfilling a long-held ambition. I'm working with smart, creative editors and a witty, brilliant artist. All of us are working toward the same thing: making a beautiful book. What's it like? It's unforgettable!

A starred review in *Publishers Weekly* for *Today at the Bluebird Café* describes your passion for winged friends as "palpable and infectious." Do you indeed have a passion for birds? How did your collection of bird-themed poetry come about?

I was writing poems on random topics, when someone I knew mentioned that her aunt kept a robin in her bathroom. That inspired my first effort at bird poetry, and I loved writing about that bathroom-hogging robin so much that I just kept going. As I researched birds, I found them to be endlessly fascinating and funny. So I became a bird-lover by accident, and I've never regretted it.

How long have you been writing poetry? Do you have an interest in publishing in other genres?

I wrote some terrible poems in high school, took a really long break to do other things, and started up again in 1998. Like a million other children's writers, I'd love to write a memorable picture book someday.

What advice would you offer aspiring writers of poetry for young readers? What's your best advice on writing rhyme?

My best advice is to go to your library's children's poetry department and just dig in! When I was starting out, that's where I discovered most of the wonderful writers who inspired me, and where I learned how terribly far I had to go. Trying to match the quality of the poems I read in the library forced me to ask more of myself, to try never to settle for the ordinary, and to be willing to revise with a ruthless eye.

Writing in rhyme can be tricky and deadly in so many ways: bad rhythm, forced rhyme, worn-out rhyme, etc. Reading your work out loud (especially into a tape recorder) can expose its flaws with brutal honesty. And of course, nothing beats a truth-telling critique group.

Do you have any favorite poets (children's or adults) or can you recommend any books of poetry every poet should check out?

A few of my favorite poets are Robert Frost, Emily Dickinson, Billy Collins, Ogden Nash, Constance Levy, Joyce Sidman, Lilian Moore, Kristine O'Connell George, and Karla Kuskin. Myra Cohn Livingston's *Poem-Making* (HarperCollins) is a wonderful place for poets to start; Kristine O'Connell George's Web site (www.kristinegeorge.com) is an incomparable resource; and I would *never* miss a book by Sonya Sones!

I see from your Web site that you are open to doing school visits. Have you done any yet? What do you do to engage young readers? How do they respond to poetry?

I'm just now planning my first school visits, which I hope will be lively and fun for everyone involved. I've been gathering props for my presentations, including a crow costume for a child to wear as we dramatize one of the poems, and a hand-held gizmo that plays bird song recordings. Since I was once a teacher myself, I feel comfortable in schools and I can't wait to see how kids respond to the book.

Although you've already gotten some glowing reviews, your first book is not yet released as of this interview. (It's a Spring 2007 release.) As a first-time author, do you have any fears or apprehension about its release? What are you doing to prepare yourself? What are you doing to help promote your book?

My book-related fantasies have always stopped at the point of publication—just getting here was my only goal. Now that it's about to happen, of course I dream of the book doing well. I'm doing what I can to help it along, including having postcards and bookmarks made, setting up a Web site (www.deborahruddell.com), hosting a book launch party for which I have baked hundreds of cardinal-shaped cookies (might as well think big!), and saying *yes* to every invitation to talk about the book (even though I get sweaty palms every time I think about it). But I really don't have any apprehension about the book release itself—*Today at the Bluebird Café* has led a charmed life from the beginning, so I'm just trusting its karma and enjoying the ride.

Tell me about your next book, *A Whiff of Pine, a Hint of Skunk* **and any other upcoming projects.**

A Whiff of Pine, A Hint of Skunk is my forthcoming collection of forest poems to be published by Margaret K. McElderry Books. Research for this book took an unfortunate turn in 2005, when I broke my leg while hiking in the nature preserve near my house, but the long recuperation gave me plenty of quiet time to write.

I've recently completed a collection of poems about butterflies and moths that involved no broken bones whatsoever.

—Alice Pope

SCBWI—OREGON CONFERENCES

E-mail: robink@scbwior.com. Web site: www.scbwior.com. **Regional Advisor:** Robin Koontz. Writer and illustrator workshops and presentations geared toward all levels. "We invite editors, teachers, agents, attorneys, authors, illustrators and others in the business of writing and illustrating for children. They present lectures, workshops, and on-site critiques on a first-registered basis." Critique group network for local group meetings and regional retreats; see Web site for details. Two main events per year: Writers and Illustrators Retreat: Retreat held near Portland Thursday-Sunday the 2nd weekend in October. Cost of retreat: $325 plus $35.00 critique fee includes double occupancy and all meals; Spring Conference: Held in the Portland area (1-1/2 day event the third Fri-Sat in May); cost for presentations and workshops: about $100 includes continental breakfast and lunch on Saturday, critique fee $35.00-attendees only; Friday sessions cost about $45 includes snacks and coffee. Registration limited to 300 for the conference and 55 for the retreat. SCBWI Oregon is a regional chapter of the SCBWI. SCBWI Members receive a discount for all events.

SCBWI—POCONO MOUNTAINS RETREAT

Web site: www.scbwiepa.org. **Regional Advisor:** Laurie Krauss Kiernan. Held in the spring at Sterling Inn, Sterling PA. Faculty addresses writing, illustration and publishing. Registration limited to 100. Cost of retreat: tuition $140, room and board averages $200. For information and registration form, visit Web site.

⟦N⟧ SCBWI—ROCKY MOUNTAIN; ANNUAL FALL CONFERENCE

Colorado School of Mines and The Golden Hotel, Golden CO. E-mail: becky@rmcscbwi.org. Web site: www.rmc scbwi.org. **Co-Regional Advisors:** Becky Clark Cornwell and Colin Mucray. Open to students, "but only if they're serious about their writing career." Annual event held in September. (September 8-9, 2007, September 5-7, 2008). "A variety of topics pertinent to beginning through published writers and illustrators are offered every year. Our 2007 conference presenters: agent Andrea Brown; editors Theresa Howell (Rising Moon), Martha Mihalick (Greenwillow), Meredith Mundy Wasinger (Sterling); authorrs Betsy James, Elizabeth Delessert and more. We always have hight calibur presenters, portfolio reviews, manuscript critiques, one-on-one appointments, and easy online registration." See Web site for details about manuscripts critiques and portfolio reivews. "Join us in 2007 and bookmark our Web site for upcoming information on an even bigger 2008 conference! Ask to be added to our free e-mail newsletter so you can get up-to-the-minute conference info. See you in Colorado in September!"

SCBWI—SOUTHERN BREEZE; SPRINGMINGLE

P.O. Box 26282, Birmingham AL 35260. E-mail: JSKittinger@bellsouth.net. Web site: www.southern-breeze.o rg. **Regional Advisors:** Jo Kittinger and Donna Bowman. Writer and illustrator workshops geared toward intermediate, advanced and professional levels. Speakers typically include agents, editors, authors, art directors, illustrators. **Open to SCBWI members, non-members and college students.** Annual conference held in Atlanta, Georgia. Usually held in late February. Registration limited. Cost of conference: approximately $225; includes Friday dinner, Saturday lunch and Saturday banquet. Manuscript critiques and portfolio reviews available for addtional fee. Pre-registration is necessary. Send a SASE to Southern Breeze, P.O. Box 26282, Birmingham AL 35260 for more information or visit Web site: www.southern-breeze.org.

SCBWI—SOUTHERN BREEZE; WRITING AND ILLUSTRATING FOR KIDS

P.O. Box 26282, Birmingham AL 35260. E-mail: jskittinger@bellsouth.net. Web site: www.southern-breeze.org. **Regional Advisors:** Jo Kittinger and Donna Bowman. Writer and illustrator workshops geared toward all levels.

Open to SCBWI members, non-members and college students. All sessions pertain specifically to the production and support of quality children's literature. This one-day conference offers about 30 workshops on craft and the business of writing. Picture books, chapter books, novels covered. Entry and professional level topics addressed by published writers and illustrators, editors and agents. Annual conference. Fall conference is held the third weekend in October in the Birmingham, AL metropolitan area. (Museums, shopping, zoo, gardens, universities and colleges are within a short driving distance.) All workshops are limited to 25 or fewer people. Pre-registration is necessary. Some workshops fill quickly. Cost of conference: approximately $110 for members, $135 for nonmembers, $120 for students; program includes keynote speaker, 4 workshops (selected from 30), lunch, and Friday night dessert party. Mss critiques and portfolio reviews are available for an additional fee; mss must be sent early. Registration is by mail ahead of time. Manuscript and portfolio reviews must be pre-paid and scheduled. Send a SASE to: Southern Breeze, P.O. Box 26282, Birmingham AL 35260 or visit Web site. Fall conference is always held in Birmingham, Alabama. Room block at a hotel near conference site (usually a school) is by individual reservation and offers a conference rate. Keynote speakers to be announced.

🌐 SCBWI—TAIWAN; EVENTS

Fax: (886)2363-5358. E-mail: scbwi_taiwan@yahoo.com. Web site: www.scbwi.tw. Mailing list: http://groups.yahoo.com/group/scbwi_taiwan. **Regional Advisor:** Kathleen Ahrens. **Assistant Regional Advisor:** Irene Chen. Writer and illustrator workshops geared toward intermediate level. Open to students. Topics emphasized: "We regularly hold critiques for writers and for illustrators, and invite authors and illustrators visiting Taipei to give talks. See our Web site for more information."

SCBWI—UTAH; FORUM ON CHILDREN'S LITERATURE

Email: u.i.scbwi@mindspring.com. Web site: www.uvsc.edu/conted/c&w. **Regional Advisor:** Sydney Husseman. Annual conference for writers, illustrators, teachers, and librarians. Held in March at Utah Valley State College in Orem, UT. Learn from award-winning authors, illustrators, and editors. Art display and one-on-one critiques available for an additional fee.

SCBWI—VENTURA/SANTA BARBARA; FALL CONFERENCE

Simi Valley CA 93094-1389. (805)581-1906. E-mail: alexisinca@aol.com. Web site: www.scbwisocal.org/calendar. Writers'conference geared toward all levels. Speakers include editors, authors, illustrators and agents. Fiction and nonfiction picture books, middle grade and YA novels, and magazine submissions addressed. Annual writing contest in all genres plus illustration display. Conference held October 27, 2007 at California Lutheran University in Thousand Oaks, CA in cooperation with the School of Education. For fees and other information e-mail or go to Web site.

SCBWI—VENTURA/SANTA BARBARA; RETREAT FOR CHILDREN'S AUTHORS AND ILLUSTRATORS

E-mail: alexisinca@aol.com. Web site: www.scbwisocal.org. The Winter Retreat, usually held in Santa Barbara, focuses on craft or business issues. Go to Web site or e-mail for current theme and fee.

SCBWI—WESTERN WASHINGTON STATE; RETREATS & CONFERENCE

P.O. Box 1907, Port Townsend WA 98368. (206)340-4543. E-mail: scbwiwa@scbwi-washington.org. Web site: www.scbwi-washington.org. **Co-Regional Advisors:** Jolie Stekly and Sara Easterly. "Our 4th annual professional retreat for writers and illustrators will be held April 27, 2007 at Overlake Country Club in Medina, WA. It will be an intimate day of critiquing and workshopping. Writers will have work critiqued by two editors and an agent and workshop with Bruce Coville. Illustrators will be critiqued by an art director and agent and workshop with Paul O. Zelinsky." SCBWI WWA's 15th annual writing and illustrating for children conference will be held April 28, 2007 at Meydenbauer Center in Bellevue, WA. This one-day event will be packed full of opportunity for craft and professional growth. We will offer 5 different topic- and skill-oriented tracks for beginning, intermediate, and proffessional writers and illustrators. The conference will feature keynotes from Bruce Coville and Paul O. Zelinsky, sessions with 4 editors, 4 agents, and an art director, plus many more talented faculty members. New this year will be a networking lunch, wine-and-cheese reception celebrating published attendees and a juried art show. Registration will begin January 15 via our web site. Our first annual fall retreat will take place at the beautiful Mountain River Lodge in the Cascade Mountains October 19-21, 2007. This will be an intimate working retreat focused on novel revisions and picture book writing and illustrating. Please visit our Web site for even more event information."

SCBWI—WISCONSIN; FALL RETREAT FOR WORKING WRITERS

3446 Hazelnut Lane, Milton WI 53563. E-mail: pjberes@centurytel.net. Web site: www.scbwi-wi-com. **Regional Advisor:** Pam Beres. Writer and illustrator conference geared toward all levels. All our sessions pertain to children's writing/illustration. Faculty addresses writing/illustrating/publishing. Annual conference held October. Registration limited to 70. Conference center has retreat-style bedrooms with desks that can be used to draw/write. Cost of conference: $375 for SBCWI member; $450 for non-members; includes program, meals, lodging, ms critique. Write or go to our Web site for more information:www.scbwi-wi.com.

OTHER CONFERENCES

Many conferences and workshops included here focus on children's writing or illustrating and related business issues. Others appeal to a broader base of writers or artists, but still provide information that can be useful in creating material for children. Illustrators may be interested in painting and drawing workshops, for example, while writers can learn about techniques and meet editors and agents at general writing conferences. For more information vist the Web sites listed or contact conference coordinator.

AEC CONFERENCE ON SOUTHERN LITERATURE
3069 South Broad Street, Suite 2, Chattanooga TN 37408-3056. (423)267-1218. Fax: (423)267-1018. E-mail: info@artsedcouncil.org. Web site: www.artsedcouncil.org. **Executive Director:** Susan Robinson. **Open to students.** Conference is geared toward readers. Biennial conference held in late March. Cost of conference: $110 for 3 days. Visit Web site for more information. Features panel discussions, readings and commentaries for adults and students by today's foremost Southern writers.

AMERICAN CHRISTIAN WRITERS CONFERENCE
P.O. Box 110390, Nashville TN 37222-0390. 1(800)21-WRITE or (615)834-0450. Fax: (615)834-7736. E-mail: detroitwriters@aol.com. Web site: www.ACWriters.com. **Director:** Reg Forder. Writer and illustrator workshops geared toward beginner, intermediate and advanced levels. Classes offered include: fiction, nonfiction, poetry, photography, music, etc. Workshops held in 3 dozen U.S. cities. Call or write for a complete schedule of conferences. 75 minutes. Maximum class size: 30 (approximate). Cost of conference: $99, 1-day session; $169, 2-day session (discount given if paid 30 days in advance) includes tuition only.

ANNUAL SPRING POETRY FESTIVAL
City College, New York NY 10031. (212)650-6343. E-mail: barrywal23@aol.com. **Director, Poetry Outreach Center:** Pam Laskin. Writer workshops geared to all levels. **Open to students.** Annual poetry festival. Festival held May 1-8, 2007. Registration limited to 325. Cost of workshops and festival: free. Write for more information.

BIG SUR WRITING WORKSHOP
Henry Miller Library, Highway One, Big Sur CA 93920. Phone/fax: (831)667-2574. E-mail: magnus@henrymiller .org. Web site: www.henrymiller.org/CWW.html. **Contact:** Magnus Toren, executive director. Annual workshop held in December focusing on children's and young adult writing. Workshop held in Big Sur Lodge in Pfeiffer State Park. Cost of workshop: $595; included meals, lodging, workshop, Saturday evening reception; $385 if lodging not needed.

N BOOKEXPO AMERICA/WRITER'S DIGEST BOOKS WRITERS CONFERENCE
4700 East Galbraith Rd., Cincinnati OH 45236. (513) 531-2690. Fax: (513) 891-7185. E-mail: publicity@fwpu bs.com. Web site: www.writersdigest.com/bea. or www.bookexpoamerica.com/writersconference. **Contact:** Greg Hatfield, publicity manager. Estab. 2003. Annual. Conference duration: one day, May 30, 2007. Average attendance: 600. "The purpose of the conference is to prepare writers hoping to get their work published. We offer instruction on the craft of writing, as well as advice for submitting their work to publications, publishing houses and agents. We provide breakout sessions on these topics, including expert advice from industry professionals, and offer workshops on fiction and nonfiction, in the various genres (literary, children's, mystery, romance, etc.). We also provide attendees the opportunity to actually pitch their work to agents." Site: The conference facility varies from year to year, as we are part of the BookExpo America trade show. The 2007 conference took place in New York City; the 2008 conference will be held in Los Angeles. Themes and panels have included Writing Genre Fiction, Children's Writing, Brutal Truths About the Book Publishing Industry, Crafting a Strong Nonfiction Book Proposal, Crafting Your Novel Pitch, and Secrets to Irresistible Magazine Queries. Past speakers included Jodi Picoult, K.L. Going, Jerry B. Jenkins, Jonathan Karp, Steve Almond, John Warner, Heather Sellers, Donald Maass and Michael Cader. The price in 2007 was $199, which included a 6-month subscription to WritersMarket.com. Information available in February. For brochure, visit Web site. Agents and editors participate in conference.

BOOMING GROUND WRITER'S COMMUNITY

Buch E-462, 1866 Main Mall, UBC, Vancouver BC VGT 1Z1 Canada. (604)822-2469. Fax: (604)648-8848. E-mail: bg@arts.ubc.ca. Web site: http://bg.arts.ubg.ca. **Director:** Andrew Gray. Writer mentroshios geared toward beginner and advanced levels. **Open to students.** Online mentorship program—students work for 4 months with a mentor by e-mail. Program cost: $780 Canadian. Apply online; send manuscript sample with application. No art classes offered. Visit Web site for more information.

BUTLER UNIVERSITY CHILDREN'S LITERATURE CONFERENCE

2060 E. 54th Street, Indianapolis IN 46220. (317)254-0830. E-mail: kidsink@indy.net. Web site: www.butler. edu/childlit/about.htm. **Contact:** Shirley Mullin. Writer and illustrator conference geared toward all levels. **Open to college students.** Annual conference held the last Saturday of the month of January each year featuring top writers in the field of children's literature. Includes sessions such as Nuts and Bolts for Beginning Writers. Registration limited to 350. Cost of conference: $85; includes SCBWI Networking Luncheon, registration, 3 plenary addresses, 2 workshops, book signing, reception and conference bookstore. Write for more information. ''The conference is geared toward three groups: teachers, librarians and writers/illustrators.''

CAPE COD WRITER'S CONFERENCE

Cape Cod Writer's Center, P.O. Box 408, Osterville MA 02655. (508)420-0200. Fax: (508)420-0212. E-mail: writers@capecodwriterscenter.org. Web site: www.capecodwriterscenter.org. Courses and workshops geared toward beginner, intermediate and professional levels. Courses include: fiction, nonfiction, poetry, journalism, screenwriting, and writing for the young reader. Evening programs include speakers, a master class, panels, poetry, and prose reading. Manuscript evaluations and personal conferences with faculty, the agent and editor, are available. The Young Writers' Workshop for students interested in prose and poetry is held concurrent with the conference for 12- to 16-year-olds. Annual conference held third week in August on Cape Cod; 45th annual conference held August 19-20, 2007. Cost of conference: $70 to register; $100 for courses. See Web site for details.

CAT WRITERS' ASSOCIATION ANNUAL WRITERS CONFERENCE

President Nancy Peterson, 3603 Dundee Driveway, Chevy Chase MD 20815. (304) 951-9511. E-mail: cwa-Nancy@starpower.ne. Web site: www.catwriters.org. The Cat Writers' Association holds an annual conference at varying locations around the US. The agenda for the conference is filled with seminars, editor appointments, an autograph party, networking breakfast, reception and annual awards banquet, as well as the annual meeting of the association. See Web site for details.

CENTRAL OHIO WRITERS OF LITERATURE FOR CHILDREN, A Conference for Writers, Illustrators, Librarians, Parents, and Teachers

933 Hamlet St., Columbus OH 43201-3595. (614)291-8644. E-mail: cowriters@mail.com. Web site: www.sjms. net/conf. **Director:** Hari Ruiz. Writer and illustrator conference geared toward beginner, intermediate and advanced levels. **Also open to full-time high school and college students.** Annual conference. Held in April. Registration limited to 180. Cost of conference: students and seniors $75; all others early-bird $115; regular $125 (approximately); late $140. $40 additional charge for workshops for writers and illustrators led by published authors and illustrators, and 15-minute ms or portfolio evaluations. $55 for 20-minute ms and portfolio evaluations. $30 additional charge for ''pitch sessions'' with literary agent. ''Event is an all-day affair with one keynote speaker.''

CHILDREN'S AUTHORS' BOOTCAMP

P.O. Box 231, Allenspark CO 80510. (303)747-1014. E-mail: CABootcamp@msnl.com. Web site: www.WeMake Writers.com. **Contact:** Linda Arms White. Writer workshops geared toward beginner and intermediate levels. ''Children Authors' Bootcamp provides two full, information-packed days on the fundamentals of writing fiction for children. The workshop covers developing strong, unique characters; well-constructed plots; believable dialogue; seamless description and pacing; point of view; editing your own work; marketing your manuscripts to publishers, and more. Each day also includes in-class writing exercises and small group activities.'' Workshop held 4 times/year at various locations throughout the United States. Bootcamps are generally held in March, April, June, September, October and November. Please check our Web site for upcoming dates and locations. Maximum size is 55; average workshop has 40-50 participants. Cost of workshop varies; see Web site for details. Cost includes tuition for both Saturday and Sunday (9:00 a.m. to 4:30 p.m.); morning and afternoon snacks; lunch; handout packet.

N **CHILDREN'S BOOK WORKSHOP AT CASTLE HILL**
1 Depot Road, P.O. Box 756, Truro MA 02666-0756. (508)349-7511. Fax: (508)349-7513. E-mail: castlehill@gis.n et. Web site: www.castlehill.org. **Director:** Cherie Mittenthal. Writer workshops geared toward intermediate and advanced levels. **Open to students.** Annual workshop. Workshop held July 9-13. Registration limited to 10-12. Writing/art facilities available: classroom space. Cost of workshop: $310; includes week long workshop and one-on-one conference with teacher. Write for more information.

CHILDREN'S LITERATURE CONFERENCE
250 Hofstra University, U.C.C.E., Hempstead NY 11549. (516)463-5172. Fax: (516)463-4833. E-mail: uccelibarts @hofstra.edu. Web site: www.hofstra.edu. **Contact:** Judith Reed, Program Director, Personal Enrichment. Writer and illustrator workshops geared toward all levels. Emphasizes: fiction, nonfiction, poetry, submission procedures, picture books. Workshops will be held April 28, 2007. Cost of workshop: approximately $89; includes 2 workshops, morning coffee and lunch, 2 general sessions, and panel discussion with guest speakers and critiquing of randomly selected first-manuscript pages submitted by registrants. Write for more information. Co-sponsored by Society of Children's Book Writers and Illustrators.

THE COLUMBUS WRITERS CONFERENCE
P.O. Box 20548, Columbus OH 43220-0176. (614)451-3075. Fax: (614)451-0174. E-mail: angelaPL28@aol.com. Web site: www.creativevista.com. **Director:** Angela Palazzolo. "In addition to consultations with agents and editor, this two-day conference offers a wide variety of topics and has included writing in the following markets: children's, young adult, novel, short story, science fiction, fantasy, humor, mystery, finding and working with a literary agent, book proposals, working with an editor, query writing, screenwriting, magazine writing, travel, humor, and freelance writing. Specific sessions that have pertained to children: fiction, nonfiction, children's writing, children's markets, young adult, pitching children's books to agents and editors, and publishing children's poetry and stories. Annual conference. Conference held in August. Cost of conference is TBA. E-mail or call to request brochure or visit the Web site.

CONFERENCE FOR WRITERS & ILLUSTRATORS OF CHILDREN'S BOOKS
Book Passages, 51 Tamal Vista Blvd., Corte Madera CA 94925. (415)927-0960, ext. 234. Fax: (415)927-3069. E-mail: kathryn@bookpassage.com. Web site: www.bookpassage.com. **Conference Coordinators:** Kathryn Petrocelli and Reese Lakota. Writer and illustrator conference geared toward beginner and intermediate levels. Sessions cover such topics as the nuts and bolts of writing and illustrating, publisher's spotlight, market trends, developing characters/finding voice in your writing. Four-day conference held each July. Includes 3 lunches and a closing reception.

PETER DAVIDSON'S HOW TO WRITE A CHILDREN'S PICTURE BOOK SEMINAR
982 S. Emerald Hills Dr., Arnolds Park IA 51331-0497. E-mail: Peterdavidson@mchsi.com. **Seminar Presenter:** Peter Davidson. "This seminar is for anyone interested in writing and/or illustrating children's picture books. Beginners and experienced writers alike are welcome." **Open to students.** How to Write a Children's Picture Book is a one-day seminar devoted to principles and techniques of writing and illustrating children's picture books. Topics include Definition of a Picture Book, Picture Book Sizes, Developing an Idea, Plotting the Book, Writing the Book, Illustrating the Book, Formatting Your Manuscript, Copyrighting Your Work, Marketing Your Manuscript and Contract Terms. Seminars are presented year-round at community colleges. Even-numbered years, presents seminars in Minnesota, Iowa, Nebraska, Kansas, Colorado and Wyoming. Odd-numbered years, presents seminars in Illinois, Minnesota, Iowa, South Dakota, Missouri, Arkansas and Tennessee (write for a schedule). One day, 9 a.m.-4 p.m. Cost of workshop: varies from $40-59, depending on location; includes approximately 35 pages of handouts. Write for more information.

THE DIY BOOK FESTIVAL
7095 Hollywood Blvd., Suite 864, Los Angeles CA 90028-0893. (323)665-8080. Fax: (323)660-1776. E-mail: diyconvention@aol.com. Web site: www.diyconvention.com. **Managing Director:** Bruce Haring. Writer and illustrator workshops geared toward beginner and intermediate levels. **Open to students.** Festival focus on getting your book into print, book marketing and promotion. Annual workshop. Workshop held February-October, various cities. Cost of workshop: $50; includes admission to event, entry to prize competition, lunch for some events. Check out our Web site for current dates and locations:www.diyconvention.com.

DUKE UNIVERSITY YOUTH PROGRAMS: CREATIVE WRITERS' WORKSHOP
P.O. Box 90702, Durham NC 27708. (919)684-6259. Fax: (919)681-8235. E-mail: youth@duke.edu. Web site: www.learnmore.duke.edu/youth. **Contact:** Duke Youth Programs. Writer workshops geared toward intermediate to advanced levels. **Open to students.** The Creative Writers' Workshop provides an intensive creative

writing experience for advanced high school age writers who want to improve their skills in a community of writers. "The interactive format gives participants the opportunity to share their work in small groups, one-on-one with instructors, and receive feedback in a supportive environment. The review and critique process helps writers sharpen critical thinking skills and learn how to revise their work." Annual workshop. Every summer there is one 2-week residential session. Costs for 2007—$1,655 for residential campers; $1,055 for extended day campers; $825 for day campers. Visit Web site for more information.

DUKE UNIVERSITY YOUTH PROGRAMS: YOUNG WRITERS' CAMP

P.O. Box 90702, Durham NC 27708. (919)684-2827. Fax: (919)681-8235. E-mail: youth@duke.edu. Web site: www.learnmore.duke.edu/youth. **Contact:** Duke Youth Programs (919)684-6259. Beginner and intermediate levels writing workshops for middle and high school students. **Open to students** (grades 6-11). Summer Camp. The Young Writers' Camp offers courses to enhance participants skills in creative and expository writing. "Through a core curriculum of short fiction, poetry, journalism and playwriting students choose two courses for study to develop creative and analytical processes of writing. Students work on assignments and projects in and out of class, such as newspaper features, short stories, character studies, and journals." Annual workshop. Every summer there are three 2-week sessions with residential and day options. Costs for 2007—$1,655 for residential campers; $1,055 for extended day campers; $825 for day campers. Visit Web site or call for more information.

EAST OF EDEN WRITERS CONFERENCE

California Writers Club, P.O. Box 3254, Santa Clara, CA 95055. (408)247-1286. Fax: (408)927-5224. E-mail: eastofeden@southbaywriters.com. Web site: www.southbaywriters.com . Writer workshops geared toward beginner, intermediate and advanced levels. Open to students. Bi-annual conference. Next held September 5-7, 2008, in Salinas, CA (at the National Steinbeck Center and the Salinas Community Center.) Registration limited to 400. Cost of conference: around $300, depending on options chosen; includes Friday night dinner and program; Saturday breakfast, lunch, and full day of workshops and panels; "Night Owl" sessions; Saturday dinner program and Sunday brunch at John Steinbeck's family home are available for a small additional fee. "This conference, run by the nonprofit California Writers Club, will include many top-notch seminars on the art and business of writing. We'll have panels where writers can meet literary agents and editors and an Ask-A-Pro program, where writers can sign up to speak individually with faculty members of their choice."

EAST TEXAS CHRISTIAN WRITERS CONFERENCE

East Texas Baptist University, 1209 North Grove Street, Marshall TX 75670. (903)923-2083. Fax: (903)923-2077. E-mail: jcornish@etbu.edu or jhopkins@etbu.edu. Web site: www.etbu.edu/cwc2007. **Humanities Secretary:** Joy Cornish. Writer workshops geared toward beginner, intermediate and advanced levels. **Open to students.** Children's literature, books, stories, plays, art, and general literature. Annual conference. Workshop held first Friday and Saturday in June each year. Cost of workshop: $60/individual; $40/student; includes 5 writing workshops, materials, Friday evening dinner and luncheon; pre-conference workshops extra. Write, e-mail or call for more information.

THE ENVIROMENTAL WRITERS' CONFERENCE AND WORKSHOP IN HONOR OF RACHEL CARSON

(Formally the NEW-CUE Writer's Conference) The Spruce Point Inn, Boothbay Harbor ME. (845)398-4247. Fax: (845)398-4224. E-mail: info@new-cue.org. Web site: www.new-cue.org. **President:** Barbara Ward Klein. Writer and illustrator workshops geared toward beginner, intermediate, advanced and professional levels. "Our conference emphasizes environmental and nature writing for juvenile fiction and non-fiction." Workshop held in June every 2 years on the even numbered year. Registration limited to 100 participants. Writing/art facilities available: Large meeting rooms for featured authors/speakers. Smaller break-out rooms for concurrent sessions. Cost of workshop: $395/returning participants; $445/new—before May 1, 2008. Includes all featured and key-note addresses, concurrent sessions, workshops, guided outdoor activities and almost all meals. Submit writing sample, no longer than 3 pages. Write for more information. Additional information about featured speakers, The Spruce Point Inn, and the Boothbay Harbor Area is available on-line atwww.new-cue.org.

FESTIVAL OF CHILDREN'S LITERATURE

The Loft Literary Center, Suite 200, Open Book, 1011 Washington Avenue South, Minneapolis MN 55415. (612)379-8999. E-mail: loft@loft.org. Web site: www.loft.org. Writer workshops geared toward all levels. Workshops have included: "Nuts and Bolts of Publishing Nonfiction for Children"; Annual conference held in the Spring; speakers for 2007 included Caitlyn Dlouhy, executive editor, Atheneum Books for Young Readers along with many more writers, editors, publishers, and illustrators of children's literature. Registration limited to 185 people; smaller groups for breakout sessions. Writing facilities available with a performance hall, classrooms and writers studios. Cost of conference: approximately $153 for Friday and Saturday; $142 for Loft members;

includes admission to full and break-out sessions, Saturday lunch. Write for more information ,www.loft.org. "We also have a new program for advanced children's writer's called "Loft Master Track," a two-year apprentice ship with writers, editors and agents."

FESTIVAL OF FAITH AND WRITING

Department of English, Calvin College 1795 Knollcrest Circle SE, Grand Rapids MI 49546. (616)526-6770. E-mail: ffw@calvin.edu. Web site: www.calvin.edu/festival. E-mail all inquiries about attendance (for registration brochures, program information, etc.). Geared toward all levels of readers and writers. Open to students. "The Festival of Faith and Writing has talks, panel discussions, and workshops by nearly 100 individuals, many of whom compose, write, illustrate, and publish children's books and books for young adults. Each break-out session will have a session on children's books/young adult books. Please see Web site for list of authors and illustrators joining us for 2008." Conference held every other year. Held April 17-19, 2008. Registration limited to approximately 1,900 people. Cost of conference in 2006: $160 ($80 for students); includes all sessions, workshops, evening speakers. Cost subject to change in 2008. E-mail for more information. "This conference is geared towards a variety of writers and readers. The Festival brings together writers and readers who wonder about the intersections of faith with words on a page, lyrics in a melody, or images on a screen. Novelists, publishers, musicians, academics, poets, playwrights, editors, screenwriters, agents, journalists, preachers, students, and readers of every sort sit down together for three days of conversation and celebration."

FLATHEAD RIVER WRITERS CONFERENCE

P.O. Box 7711, Kalispell MT 59904. E-mail: conference@authorsoftheflathead.org. Web site: http://authorsofth eflathead.org. **Director:** Val Smith. Writer workshops geared toward beginner, intermediate, advanced and professional levels. **Open to students.** Along with our presenters, we periodically feature a children's writer workshop. Annual conference held mid-October. Registration limited to 100. Cost of workshop: $150; includes all lectures and a choice of weekend workshops plus breakfast and lunch. Write for more information.

FLORIDA CHRISTIAN WRITERS CONFERENCE

2344 Armour Ct., Titusville FL 32780. (321)269-5831. Fax: (321)747-0046. E-mail: billiewilson@cfl.rr.com. Web site: www.flwriters.org. **Conference Director:** Billie Wilson. Writer workshops geared toward all levels. **Open to students.**" We offer 53 one-hour workshops and 7 six-hour classes. Approximately 15 of these are for the children's genre." Annual workshop held in March. "We have 30 publishers and publications represented by editors teaching workshops and reading manuscripts from the conferees. The conference is limited to 200 people. Advanced or professional workshops are by invitation only via submitted application. Cost of workshop: $350; includes tuition and ms critiques and editor review of your ms plus personal appointments with editors. Write or e-mail for more information.

GOTHAM WRITERS' WORKSHOP

New York NY 10023. (877)974-8377. (212)307-6325. E-mail: dana@write.org. Web site: www.WritingClasses.c om. **Director, Student Affairs:** Dana Miller. Creative writing workshops taught by professional writers are geared toward beginner, intermediate and advanced levels. **Open to students.** " Workshops cover the fundamentals of plot, structure, voice, description, characterization, and dialogue appropriate to all forms of fiction and nonfiction for pre-schoolers through young adults. Students can work on picture books or begin middle-readers or young adult novels." Annual workshops held 4 times/year (10-week and 1-day workshops). Workshops held January, April, July, September/October. Registration limited to 14 students/in-person (NYC) class; 18 students/online class; 40 students for in-person (NYC) one-day workshops. Cost of workshop: $420 for 10-week workshops; $150 for 1-day workshops; 10-week NYC classes meet once a week for 3 hours; 10-week online classes include 10 week-long, asynchronous "meetings"; 1-day workshops are 7 hours and are held 8 times/year. E-mail for more information.

GREAT LAKES WRITER'S WORKSHOP

Milwaukee WI 53234-3922. (414)382-6176. Fax: (414)382-6332. E-mail: nancy.krase@alverno.edu. Web site: www.alverno.edu. **Coordinator:** Nancy Krase. Writing workshops geared toward beginner and intermediate levels; subjects include publishing, short story writing, novel writing, poetry, writing techniques/focus in character development, techniques for overcoming writers block. Annual workshop. Workshop held 3rd or 4th weekend in June, Friday evening and all day Saturday. Lauren Fox was featured author on Friday night of 2007 conference. Average length of each session: 2 hours. Cost of workshop: $115/entire workshop; $99 if you register before June 8. 2007 conference offered continental breakfast and keynote author Sheila Robinson on Saturday followed by choice of 2 workshops. See online brochure. Lunch is included in Saturday program with a featured author as keynote speaker. See online brochure or or call for more information.

GREEN LAKE WRITERS CONFERENCE

Green Lake Conference Center, W2511 State Hwy 23, Green Lake WI 54941. (920)294-3323. Fax: (920)294-3848. E-mail: program@glcc.org. Web site: www.glcc.org. **Program Coordinator:** Pat Zimmer. Writing workshops for beginning through advanced levels. Workshops: Nonfiction (short); Nonfiction (long); Fiction; Poetry; Inspiration/Devotional. Workshop held early August. Cost of program: $150; meals and lodging extra. E-mail or visit Web site for more information. Evening critique groups, editors on-hand for lecture and information.

HIGHLAND SUMMER CONFERENCE

P.O. Box 7014, Radford University, Radford VA 24142-7014. (540)831-5366. Fax: (540)831-5951. E-mail: jasbury @radford.edu. Web site: www.radford.edu/~arsc. **Director:** Grace Toney Edwards. **Assistant to the Director:** Jo Ann Asbury. **Open to students.** Writer workshops geared toward beginner, intermediate and advanced levels. Emphasizes Appalachian literature, culture and heritage. Annual workshop. Workshop held first 2 weeks in June annually. Registration limited to 20. Writing facilities available: computer center. Cost of workshop: Regular tuition (housing/meals extra). Must be registered student or special status student. E-mail, fax or call for more information. Past visiting authors include: Wilma Dykeman, Sue Ellen Bridgers, George Ella Lyon, Lou Kassem.

HIGHLIGHTS FOUNDATION FOUNDERS WORKSHOPS

Dept. CWF, 814 Court St., Honesdale PA 18431. (570)253-1192. Fax: (570)253-0179. E-mail: contact@highlightsf oundation.org. Web site: www.highlightsfoundation.org. **Contact:** Kent Brown, director. Workshops geared toward those interested in writing and illustrating for children, intermediate and advanced levels. Classes offered include: Writing Novels for Young Adults, Biography, Nonfiction Magazine Writing, Writing Historical Fiction, Wordplay: Writing Poetry for Children, Heart of the Novel, Nature Writing for Kids, Visual Art of the Picture Book, The Whole Novel Workshop, and more (see Web site for updated list). Workshops held in March, April, May, June, July, September, October and November near Honesdale, PA. Workshops limited to between 8 and 14 people. Cost of workshops range from $545 and up. Cost of workshop includes tuition, meals, conference supplies and housing. Call for application and more information.

HIGHLIGHTS FOUNDATION WRITERS WORKSHOP AT CHAUTAUQUA

Dept. CWL, 814 Court St., Honesdale PA 18431. (570) 253-1192. Fax: (570) 253-0179. E-mail: contact@highlight sfoundation.org. Web site: www.highlightsfoundation.org. **Contact:** Kent Brown, Director. Writer Workshops geared toward those interested in writing for children; beginner, intermediate and advanced levels. Classes include: Writing Poetry, Book Promotion, Characterization, Developing a Plot, How to Promote Your Book, and many many more. Annual workshop held: July 14-21, 2007, at Chautauqua Institution, Chautauqua, NY. Registration limited to 100. Cost of workshop: $2,200; $1,785 if registered by February 27, 2007. Includes tuition, meals, conference supplies. Cost does not include housing. Call for availability and pricing. Scholarships are available for first-time attendees. Call for more information or visit the Web site.

HOFSTRA UNIVERSITY SUMMER WRITERS' WORKSHOP

250 Hofstra University, UCCE, Hempstead NY 11549. (516) 463-7600. Fax: (516)463-4833. E-mail: uccelibarts@ hofstra.edu. Web site: www.hofstra.edu/ucce/summerwriting. **Contact:** Richard Pioreck, director or summer writing workshops; or Judith Reed, administrator. Writer workshops geared toward all levels. Classes offered include fiction, nonfiction, poetry, children's literature, stage/screenwriting and other genres. Annual workshop. Workshops held for 2 weeks in mid-July. Each workshop meets for $2\frac{1}{2}$ hours daily for a total of 25 hours. Students can register for 2 workshops, schedule an individual conference with the writer/instructor and submit a short ms (less than 10 pages) for critique. Enrollees may register as noncredit students or credit students. Cost of workshop: noncredit students' enrollment fee is approximately $425; 2-credit student enrollment fee is approximately $1,100/workshop undergraduate and graduate (2 credits); $2,100 undergraduate and graduate (4 credits). On-campus accommodations for the sessions are available for approximately $350/person for the 2-week conference. Students may attend any of the ancillary activities, a private conference, special programs and social events. All workshops include critiquing. Each participant is given one-on-one time for a half hour with workshop leader. Accepts inquiries by fax or e-mail. Web site includes details on dates, faculty, general description and tuition.

INTERNATIONAL CREATIVE WRITING CAMP

1930 23rd Ave., SE, Minot ND 58701-6081. (701)838-8472. Fax: (701)838-8472. E-mail: info@internationalmusic camp.com. Web site: www.internationalmusiccamp.com. **Camp Director:** Dr. Timothy Wollenzien. Writer and illustrator workshops geared toward beginner, intermediate and advanced levels. **Open to students.** Sessions offered include those covering poems, plays, mystery stories, essays. Workshop held June 24-30, 2007. Registration limited to 40. The summer camp location at the International Peace Garden on the Border between Manitoba and North Dakota is an ideal site for creative thinking. Excellent food, housing and recreation facilities are available. Cost of workshop: Before May 15th—$295; after May 15th—$320. Write for more information.

INTERNATIONAL WOMEN'S WRITING GUILD "REMEMBER THE MAGIC" ANNUAL SUMMER CONFERENCE

P.O. Box 810, Gracie Station, New York NY 10028-0082. (212)737-7536. Fax: (212) 737-9469. E-mail: iwwg@iwwg.org. Web site: www.iwwg.org. **Executive Director:** Hannelore Hahn. Writer and illustrator workshops geared toward all levels. Offers 65 different workshops—some are for children's book writers and illustrators. Also sponsors 13 other events throughout the U.S. Annual workshops. "Remember the Magic" workshops held 2nd or 3rd week in June. Length of each session: 1 hour-15 minutes; sessions take place for an entire week. Registration limited to 500. Cost of workshop: $1,004/single, $896/double (includes complete program, room and board). Write for more information. "This workshop always takes place at Skidmore College in Saratoga Springs NY."

IOWA SUMMER WRITING FESTIVAL

C215 Seashore Hall, Iowa City IA 52242. (319)335-4160. Fax: (319)335-4743. E-mail: iswfestival@uiowa.edu. Web site: www.uiowa.edu/~iswfest. **Director:** Amy Margolis. Writer workshops geared toward beginner, intermediate and advanced levels. Open to writers age 21 and over." We offer writing workshops across the genres, including workshops for children's writers in picture books, structuring writing for children, the young adult novel, and nonfiction." Annual workshop. Workshop held June and July. Registration limited to 12/workshop. Workshops meet in university classrooms. Cost of workshop: $500-525/week-long session; $250/weekend. Housing is separate and varies by facility. Write or call for more information.

JEWISH CHILDREN'S BOOK WRITERS' CONFERENCE

New York NY. E-mail: anna@olswanger.com. **Contact:** Anna Olswanger, conference coordinator. The 2006 conference faculty included executive editor Deborah Brodie of Roaring Brook Press/Holtzbrinck Publishing, executive editor Jill Davis of Bloomsbury Children's Books, publisher Joni Sussman of Kar-Ben Publishing, marketing vice president Terry M. Borzumato-Greenberg of Holiday House, literary agent Michele Beno of Curtis Brown Ltd., and artist and author representative Ronnie Ann Herman of the Herman Agency. Norman H. Finkelstein, winner of two National Jewish Book Awards, gave opening remarks. And the day included First Pages and Query Letter Clinic with the editors; talks on the Association of Jewish Libraries' Sydney Taylor Manuscript Competition and Israel's Multicultural Mix; and door prizes. Held in November, the Sunday before Thanksgiving. Cost of workshop: includes Kosher breakfast and lunch. E-mail for more information.

KENTUCKY WRITER'S WORKSHOP

1050 State Park Road, Pineville KY 40977. (606)337-3066 or (800)325-1712. Fax: (606)337-7250. E-mail: Dean.Henson@ky.gov. Web site: http://parks.ky.gov/resortparks/pm. **Event Coordinator:** Dean Henson. Writer workshops geared toward beginner and intermediate levels. **Open to students.** Annual workshop held in March. Writing facilities available: classroom setup. A special all-inclusive package is available and includes two nights accommodations, two evening buffet meals, and admission to all sessions. Write or call for more information.

KINDLING WORDS

Web site (for registration and information): www.kindlingwords.org. Annual retreat held in late-January near Burlington, Vermont. A retreat with three strands: writer, illustrator and editor; professional level. Intensive workshops for each strand, and an open schedule for conversations and networking. Registration limited to approximately 60. Tuition: $195. Hosted by the 4-star Inn at Essex (room and board extra). Participants must be published by a CCBC listed publisher, or if in publishing, occupy a professional position. Registration opens August 1 or as posted on the Web site, and fills quickly. Check Web site to see if spaces are available, to sign up to be notified when registration opens each year, or for more information.

LAJOLLA WRITERS CONFERENCE

P.O. Box 178122, San Diego CA 92177. (858)467-1978. E-mail: jkuritz@san.rr.com. Web site: www.lajollawritersconference.com. Founder: Antoinette Kuritz. Writer workshop geared toward beginner through advanced levels. "We offer sessions with children's book agents and editors; read-and-critique sessions with young adult authors, editors, agents and publishers, including children's book agent, Caryn Wiseman of the Andrea Brown Agency; IRA Award winner, John H. Ritter; Harcourt Children's Book Editor, Deborah Halverson. Annual workshop. 2007 conference dates: November 2-4. Registration limited to 200. Cost of workshop: $325; early bird, $265; includes classes Friday-Sunday, lunch and dinner Saturday. Write for more information.

LEAGUE OF UTAH WRITERS' ANNUAL ROUNDUP

P.O. Box 18430, Kearns UT 84118. (435) 313-4459. E-mail: jayrich@infowest.com. Web site: www.luwrite.com. **President Elect**: Marilyn Richardson. **Membership Chairman:** Dorothy Crofts. Writer workshops geared toward beginner, intermediate or advanced. Annual workshop. Roundup usually held 3rd weekend of September. 2007 conference held at Courtyard Marriot, St. George UT, September 14-15, 2007. Registration limited to 300. Cost is $99 for members/$129 for nonmembers registering before August 19; $120 for members; $150 non-members after August 19. Cost includes 3 meals, all workshops, general sessions, a syllabus, handouts and conference packet. Contact Marilyn Richardson with questions at (435)674-9792 or above e-mail address. Send registration to Dorothy Crofts, Membership Chairman, P.O. Box 18430, Kearns, UT 84118. Check Web site for updates and specifics.

LIGONIER VALLEY WRITERS CONFERENCE

P.O. Box B, Ligonier PA 15658-1602. (724)593-7294. E-mail: jgallagher@lhtc.net. Web site: www.ligoniervalley writers.org. **Contact:** Judith Gallagher. Writer programs geared toward all levels. **Open to students.** Annual conference features fiction, nonfiction, poetry and other genres. Annual conference held last weekend in July. Cost of workshop: $200; includes full weekend, some meals, all social events. Write or call for more information.

MANHATTANVILLE SUMMER WRITERS' WEEK

2900 Purchase Street, Purchase NY 10577-2103. (914)694-3425. Fax: (914)694-3488. E-mail: dowdr@mville.edu. Web site: www.manhattanville.edu. **Dean, School of Graduate & Professional Studies:** Ruth Dowd. Writer workshops geared toward writers and aspiring writers. **Open to students.** Writers' week offers a special workshop for writers interested in children's/young adult writing. We have featured such workshop leaders as: Patricia Gauch, Richard Peck, Elizabeth Winthrop and Janet Lisle. In 2007, Elizabeth-Ann Sachs will lead the workshop. Annual workshop held last week in June. Length of each session: one week. Cost of workshop: $695 (non-credit); includes a full week of writing activities, 5-day workshop on children's literature; lectures; readings; sessions with editors and agents; keynote speaker, Francine Prose; etc. Workshop may be taken for 2 graduate credits. Write or e-mail for more information.

⃞ THE MANUSCRIPT WORKSHOP IN VERMONT

P.O. Box 529, Londonderry VA 05148.(802)824-3968 or (212)877-4457. E-mail: aplbrk@earthlink.net. Web site: www.themanuscriptworkshop.com. **Director:** Barbara Seuling. Writer workshop for all levels. Annual workshop estab. 1992. Generally held mid to late July and August and sometimes early September. Intensive workshop spans 5 days, from dinner on Monday evening to lunch on Friday, and is primarily for writers of children's books, but open to illustrators who write. The time is divided among instructive hands-on sessions in the mornings, writing time in the afternoons, and critiquing in the evenings. A guest speaker from the world of children's books appears at each workshop. Registration is limited to 8; smaller workshops are considered for specialized workshops. Cost of workshop: $845 per person; includes a shared room and all meals. Private room available for additional cost. Inquire about smaller, specialized workshops in novel writing and picture books.

⃞ MARITIME WRITERS' WORKSHOP

UNB College of Extended Learning, P.O. Box 4400, Fredericton NB E3B 5A3 Canada. E-mail: extend@unb.ca. Web site: unb.ca/extend/writers/. **Coordinator:** Andrew Titus. Week-long workshop on writing for children, general approach, dealing with submitted material, geared to all levels and held in July. Annual workshop. 3 hours/day. Group workshop plus individual conferences, public readings, etc. Registration limited to 10/class. Cost of workshop: $395 tuition; meals and accommodations extra. Room and board on campus is approximately $320 for meals and a single room for the week. 10-20 ms pages due before conference (deadline announced). Limited scholarships available.

MAUI WRITERS CONFERENCE

P.O. Box 1118, Kihei HI 96753. (888)974-8373 or (808)879-0061. Fax: (808)879-6233. E-mail: writers@maui.net. Web site: www.mauiwriters.com. **Director:** Shannon Tullius. Writer workshops geared toward beginner, intermediate, advanced. **Open to students.** "We offer a small children's writing section covering picture books, middle grade and young adult. We invite one *New York Times* Bestselling Author and agents and editors, who give consultations." Annual workshop. Workshop held Labor Day weekend. Cost includes admittance to all conference sessions and classes only—no airfare, food or consultations.

MIDWEST WRITERS WORKSHOP

Department of Journalism, Ball State University, Muncie IN 47306. (765)282-1055. Fax: (765)285-7997. Web site: www.midwestwriters.org. **Director:** Earl L. Conn. Writer workshops geared toward intermediate level.

Topics include most genres. Past workshop presenters include Joyce Carol Oates, Jeffrey Deaver, James Alexander Thom, Bill Brashler and Richard Lederer. Workshop also includes ms evaluation and a writing contest. Annual workshop. Workshop will be held in late July. Registration tentatively limited to 125. Most meals included. Offers scholarships. Write for more information.

MISSOURI WRITERS' GUILD ANNUAL STATE CONFERENCE

(816)361-1281. E-mail: conferenceinfo@missouriwritersguild.org. Web site: www.missouriwritersguild.org. **Contact:** Karen Heywood, vice president and conference chairman. Writer and illustrator workshops geared to all levels. **Open to students.** Annual conference held late April or early May each year. 2007 conference held April 20-22 in St. Charles Convention Center in St. Charles MO. Cost of conference: $125-175.

MONTROSE CHRISTIAN WRITER'S CONFERENCE

Montrose PA 18801-1112. (570)278-1001. Fax: (570)278-3061. E-mail: mbc@montrosebible.org. Web site: www .montrosebible.org. **Executive Director:** Jim Fahringer. **Secretary-Registrar:** Donna Kosik. **Open to adults and students.** Writer workshops geared toward beginner, intermediate and advanced levels. Annual workshop held in July. Cost of workshop: $145 tuition, 2006 rate. Brochure available in April.

MOONDANCE INTERNATIONAL FILM FESTIVAL

970 Ninth St., Boulder CO 80302. (303)545-0202. E-mail: info@moondancefilmfestival.com (with MIFF or MOO NDANCE in the subject line). Web site: www.moondancefilmfestival.com. **Executive Director:** Elizabeth English. Moondance Film Festival Workshop Sessions include screenwriting, playwriting, short stories, filmmaking (feature, documentary, short, animation), TV and video filmmaking, writing for TV (MOW, sitcoms, drama), writing for animation, adaptation to screenplays (novels and short stories), how to get an agent, what agents want to see, and pitch panels. 2007 Festival held September 7-9 at Universal Studios City Walk in Hollywood. Cost of workshops, seminars, panels, pitch session: $50 each. Check Web site for more information and registration forms. The 2007 competition deadline for entries was May 1. See Web site for current deadlines and information. "The Moondance competition includes special categories for writers and filmmakers who create work for the children's market!" Entry forms and guidelines are on the Web site.

MOUNT HERMON CHRISTIAN WRITERS CONFERENCE

Mount Hermon Christian Conference Center, Mount Hermon CA 95041-0413. (831)335-4466. Fax: (831)335-9413. E-mail: rachelw@mhcamps.org. Web site: www.mounthermon.org/writers. **Director of Adult Ministries:** David R. Talbott. Writer workshops geared toward all levels. **Open to students over 16 years** with special teen track. Emphasizes religious writing for children via books, articles; Sunday school curriculum; marketing. 70 workshops offered include: Suitable Style for Children; Everything You Need to Know to Write and Market Your Children's Book; Take-Home Papers for Children. Workshops held annually over Palm Sunday weekend: March 14-18, 2008 and April 3-7, 2009. Length of each session: 5-day residential conferences held annually. Registration limited 45/class, but most are 20-30. Conference center with hotel-style accommodations. Cost of workshop: $660-990 variable; includes tuition, resource notebook, refreshment breaks, full room and board for 13 meals and 4 nights. Conference information posted annually on Web site by December 1. Write or e-mail for more information or call toll-free to 1-888-MH-CAMPS.

NORTH CAROLINA WRITERS' NETWORK FALL CONFERENCE

P.O. Box 954, Carrboro NC 27510-0954. (919)967.9540. Fax: (919)929.0535. E-mail: mail@ncwriters.org. Web site: www.ncwriters.org. Writing workshops and services geared toward beginner, intermediate and advanced or published levels. **Open to students.** We offer workshops, keynote, presentations and critique sessions in a variety of genres: fiction, poetry, creative nonfiction, children, youth, etc. Past youth and children writing faculty include Louise Hawes, Jackie Ogburn, Clay Carmichael, Carole Boston Weatherford, Susie Wilde, Stephanie Greene, Joy Neaves, and Frances O'Roark Dowell. Annual Conference to be held next at the Marriott Winston-Salem Twin City Quarter. Date: Nov. 16-18 (Most recent was in RTP, November 10-12). Cost of conference usually $250/members, $350/nonmembers, including all workshops, panels, roundtables, social activities and four meals. Extra costs for accommodations, master classes and critique sessions.

OKLAHOMA WRITERS' FEDERATION, INC. ANNUAL CONFERENCE

P.O. Box 2654, Stillwater OK 74076-2654. (405)762-6238. Fax: (405)377-0992. Web site: www.owfi.org. **President:** Moira Wiley. Writer workshops geared toward all levels. Illustrator workshops geared toward beginner level. **Open to students.** "During 2003 event, Emily Mitchell, assistant editor with Charlesbridge Publishing, presented a session titled The Basics of Children's Book Contracts (Law Degree Not Required). Other noteworthy topics cover the basics of writing, publishing and marketing in any genre." Annual conference. Held first Friday and Saturday in May each year. Registration limited to 420. Writing facilities available: book room, autograph party, free information room. Cost of workshop: $125 (early bird); $150 after (early bird date); $60 for single days; full tuition includes 2-day conference—all events including 2 banquets and one 10-minute appointment with an attending editor or agent of your choice (must be reserved in advance). "If writers would like to participate in the annual writing contest, they must become members of OWFI. You don't have to be a member to attend the conference." Write or e-mail for more information.

OUTDOOR WRITERS ASSOCIATION OF AMERICA ANNUAL CONFERENCE

158 Lower Georges Valley Rd., Spring Mills PA 16875. (406)728-7434. Fax: (406)728-7445. E-mail: owaa@monta na.com. **Meeting Planner:** Gail Brockbank. Writer workshops geared toward all levels. Annual 5-day conference. Craft Improvement seminars; newsmaker sessions. Workshop held in June. 2007 conference to be held in Roanoke, Virginia. Cost of workshop: $325; includes attendance at all workshops and most meals. Attendees must have prior approval from Executive Director before attendance is permitted. Write for more information.

OZARK CREATIVE WRITERS, INC. CONFERENCE

400 E. Chilhowie Ave., Johnson City TN, (423)439-6024. E-mail: ozarkcreativewriters@earthlink.net. Web site: www.ozarkcreativewriters.org. **Program Chair:** Chrissy Willis. **Open to students.** Writer's workshops geared to all levels. "All forms of the creative process dealing with the literary arts. We sometimes include songwriting. We invite best selling authors, editors and agents. We also promote writing by providing competitions in all genres." Always the second full weekend in October at Inn of the Ozarks in Eureka Springs AR, a resort town in the Ozark Mountains. "Approximately 200 attend the conference yearly. Many others enter the creative writing competition." Cost of registration/contest entry fee approximately $80-100. Includes entrance to all sessions, contest entry fees and continental breakfast. This does not include banquet meals or lodging.

THE PACIFIC COAST CHILDREN'S WRITERS WORKSHOP, for Middle Grade and Young Adult Novelists

P.O. Box 244, Aptos CA 95001. (831)684-2042. Web site: www.childrenswritersworkshop.com. **Founding Director:** Nancy Sondel. This 6th annual workshop is geared toward intermediate and professional levels; beginners may attend with some limits in participation. **Open to students.** "As with all enrollees, students must demonstrate competence in story-crafting and/or come prepared to learn from highly skilled writers. (Discount for students age 16-24.) Our keynotes, master class clinics, and hands-on focus sessions explore topics such as 'How to Craft Scenes Integrating Character, Plot and Theme in MG and YA Novels.' We focus on less-commonly discussed (but crucial) aspects of these topics." Annual conference held August 15-17, 2008. Registration limited to 40. Venue offers free use of the Hilton Hotel copier, printer, and more; sleeping rooms have DSL Internet access. "We have private veranda/conference rooms available day and night." Cost of workshop: $299-599, which covers Early Bird tuition, most meals, up to 3 faculty critiques per enrollee (written and/or in person), and optional academic/CEU credits. Various discounts available. "Our e-application includes essay questions about each writer's manuscript; sample chapters and synopsis must be submitted with the application, by mid-April for best critique options. Content: We focus on literary, character-driven, realistic novels with protagonists ages 11 and older. Our seminar-style, master-class format is 90 percent hands-on—highly interactive, with continuous dialogues between seasoned faculty and savvy, congenial peers. Saturday's intensive 9-hour program includes agent-editor, team-taught manuscript clinics; more. Sunday's critique clinics, led by an award-winning faculty author, feature 'Beyond Chapters One Through Three.' Our pre-workshop prep (personalized manuscript worksheets, peer critiques) maximizes learning and networking with the pros. For more information, please reach us via our Web site's contact form."

PACIFIC NORTHWEST CHILDREN'S BOOK CONFERENCE

Portland State University School of Extended Studies, P.O. Box 1491, Portland OR 97207. (503)725-4832 or (800)547-8887, ext. 4832. Fax: (503)725-9734. E-mail: ceed@pdx.edu. Web site: www.ceed.pdx.edu/children. Focus on the craft of writing and illustrating for children while working with an outstanding faculty of acclaimed editors, authors, and illustrators. Daily afternoon faculty-led writing and illustration workshops. Acquire specific information on how to become a professional in the field of children's literature. Annual workshop for all levels. Conference held July 9-13 on the campus of Reed College, Portland, Oregon. Cost of conference: $625 noncredit; $895 for 3 graduate credits; individual ms/portfolio reviews and room and board at Reed for an additional fee. Call for more information. Linda Zuckerman, editor, coordinates conference and collects knowledgeable and engaging presenters every year.

PACIFIC NORTHWEST WRITER ASSN. SUMMER WRITER'S CONFERENCE

PMB 2717, 1420 NW Gilman Blvd, Suite 2, Issaquah, WA 98027. (425) 673-BOOK (2665). E-mail: staff@pnwa.o rg. Web site: www.pnwa.org. Writer conference geared toward beginner, intermediate, advanced and professional levels. Meet agents and editors. Learn craft from renowned authors. Uncover new marketing secrets.

PNWA's 52nd Anniversary Conference was held July 26-29, 2007 at the Seattle Airport Hilton, Seattle, WA 98188. Annual conference held in July.

PERSPECTIVES IN CHILDREN'S LITERATURE CONFERENCE

School of Education, 226 Furcolo Hall, Amherst MA 01003-3035. (413)545-4190 or (413)545-1116. Fax: (413)545-2879. E-mail: childlit@educ.umass.edu. Web site: www.umass.edu/childlit. **Conference Coordinator:** Katelyn McLaughlin. Writer and illustrator workshops geared to all levels. Presenters talk about what inspires them, how they bring their stories to life and what their visions are for the future. Annual conference held in late March/early April. For more information contact coordinator by phone, fax or e-mail.''

PIMA WRITERS' WORKSHOP

Pima College, 2202 W. Anklam Rd., Tucson AZ 85709-0170. (520)206-6084. Fax: (520)206-6020. E-mail: mfiles @pima.edu. **Director:** Meg Files. Writer conference geared toward beginner, intermediate and advanced levels. **Open to students.** The conference features presentations and writing exercises on writing and publishing stories for children and young adults, among other genres. Annual conference. Workshop held in May. Cost of workshop: $75; includes tuition, manuscript consultation. Write for more information.

PUBLISHINGGAME.COM WORKSHOP

Newton MA 02459. (617)630-0945. E-mail: Alyza@publishinggame.com. Web site: www.publishinggame.com. **Coordinator:** Alyza Harris. Fern Reiss, author of the popular ''Publishing Game'' book series and CEO of Expertizing.com, will teach this one-day workshop. Writer workshops geared toward beginner, intermediate and advanced levels. **Open to students.** Sessions will include: Find A Literary Agent, Self-Publish Your Children's Book, Book Promotion For Children's Books. September—New York; October—Boston; November—New York; December—Philadelphia; January—Washington, DC; February—New York; March—New York; April—New York; May—Boston; June—Los Angeles, CA; July—San Francisco; August—Boston. Registration limited to 18. Fills quickly! Cost of workshop: $195; included information-packed course binder and light refreshments. E-mail for more information. Workshop now available as a 5-CD audio workshop. For information on getting more media attention for your children's book, see Fern Reiss' complemetary Expertizing workshop atwww.expertizingc.om.

ROBERT QUACKENBUSH'S CHILDREN'S BOOK WRITING AND ILLUSTRATING WORKSHOP

Studio address: 223 East 79th St., New York, NY 10021. Mailing address: 460 East 79th St., New York, NY 10021. (212)744-3822. Fax: (212)861-2761. E-mail: Rqstudios@aol.com. Web site: www.rquackenbush.com. **Contact:** Robert Quackenbush. A four-day extensive workshop on writing and illustrating books for young readers held annually the second week in July at author/artist Robert Quackenbush's Manhattan studio. The focus of this workshop is on creating manuscripts and/or illustrated book dummies from start to finish for picture books and beginning reader chapter books ready to submit to publishers. Also covered is writing fiction and nonfiction for middle grades and young adults, if that is the attendee's interest. In addition, attention is given to review of illustrator's portfolios and new trends in illustration, including animation for films, are explored. During the four days, the workshop meets from 9 a.m-4 p.m. including one hour for lunch. Registration is limited to 10. Some writing and/or art supplies are available at the studio and there is an art store nearby, if needed. There are also electrical outlets for attendee's laptop computers. Cost of workshop is $650. Attendees are responsible for arranging for their own hotel and meals. On request, suggestions are given for economical places to stay and eat. Recommended by Foder's *Great American Learning Vacations*, which says, ''This unique workshop, held annually since 1982, provides the opportunity to work with Robert Quackenbush, a prolific author and illustrator of children's books with more than 185 fiction and nonfiction books for young readers to his credit, including mysteries, biographies and songbooks. The workshop attracts both professional and beginning writers and artists of different ages from all over the world.'' Brochure available. Also inquire about fall, winter and spring workshops that meet once a week for ten weeks each that are offered to artists and writers in the New York area.

ROCKY MOUNTAIN RETREATS FOR WRITERS & ARTISTS

81 Cree Court, Lyons CO 80540. (303)823-0530. E-mail: ddebord@indra.com. Web site: www.expressionretreats .com. **Director:** Deborah DeBord. Writers and illustrator workshops geared to all levels. **Open to students.** Includes information on releasing creative energy, identifying strengths and interests, balancing busy lives, marketing creative works. Monthly conference. Registration limited to 4/session. Writing studio, weaving studio, private facilities available. Cost of workshop: $1,234/week; includes room, meals, materials, instruction.'' Treat yourself to a week of mountain air, sun, and personal expression. Flourish with the opportunity for sustained work punctuated by structured experiences designed to release the artist's creative energies. Relax

over candlelit gourmet meals followed by fireside discussions of the day's efforts. Discover the rhythm of filling the artistic well and drawing on its abundant resources.''

SAN DIEGO STATE UNIVERSITY WRITERS' CONFERENCE
The College of Extended Studies, San Diego CA 92182-1920. (619)594-2517. Fax: (619)594-8566. E-mail: extende d.std@sdsu.edu. Web site: www.neverstoplearning.net. **Conference Facilitator:** Jim Greene. Writer workshops geared toward beginner, intermediate and advanced levels. Emphasizes nonfiction, fiction, screenwriting, advanced novel writing; includes sessions specific to writing and illustrating for children. Workshops offered by children's editors, agents and writers. Annual workshops. Workshops held January 26-28, 2007. Registration limited. Cost of workshops: approximately $300. Call for more information or visit Web site.

SAN FRANCISCO WRITERS CONFERENCE
1029 Jones St., San Francisco CA 94109 (415)673-0939. Web site: www.sfwriters.org. **Co-founders:** Michael Larsen & Elizabeth Pomada. Writer workshops and panels geared toward beginner, intermediate, advanced and professional levels on the business of publishing, craft, and marketing. Annual conference held President's Day Weekend in mid-February. Registration limited to 300. Cost of conference: $425—$695 depending on time of registration; includes party, 2 breakfasts, and 3 lunches. Visit Web site for more information. The preliminary program for the following year's conference will be on the Web site by June.

⚁ SASKATCHEWAN FESTIVAL OF WORDS AND WORKSHOPS
217 Main Street, Moose Jaw SK S6H 0W1 Canada. (306)691-0557. Fax: (306)693-2994. E-mail: word.festival@sa sktel.net. Web site: www.festivalofwords.com. **Artistic Coordinator:** Gary Hyland. Writer workshops geared toward beginner and intermediate levels. **Open to students.** Readings that include a wide spectrum of genres— fiction, creative non-fiction, poetry, songwriting, screenwriting, playwriting, children's writing, panels, interviews and performances. Annual festival. Workshop held third weekend in July. Cost of workshop: $8/session— $125 for full festival pass. Write, e-mail, or visit Web site for more information.

SOCIETY OF SOUTHWESTERN AUTHORS' WRANGLING WITH WRITING
P.O. Box 30355, Tucson AZ 85751-0355. (520)546-9382. Fax: (520)296-0409. E-mail: wporter202@aol.com. Web site: www.ssa-az.org. **Conference Director:** Penny Porter. 32 Writer workshops geared toward all genres. ''Limited scholarships available.'' Sessions include Writing and Publishing the Young Adult Novel, What Agents Want to See in a Children's Book, Writing Books for Young Children, Writing the Children's Story. One-on-one interviews with agents/editors scheduled prior to conference at an additional cost of $20 for a 15-minute meeting. ''We always have several children's book editors and agents interested in meeting with children's writers.'' Annual workshop held September 15-16, 2007. Registration limited to 400. Hotel rooms have dataports for internet access. Tentative cost: $300 nonmembers, $225 for SSA members; includes 3 meals and 2 continental breakfasts, all workshop sessions—individual appointments with keynoters, author/teachers. Hotel accommodations are not included. Write for more information. ''SSA has put on this conference for over 25 years now. It's hands-on, it's friendly, and every year writers sell their manuscripts.''

SOUTH COAST WRITERS CONFERENCE
P.O. Box 590, 29392 Ellensburg Ave., Gold Beach OR 97444. (541)247-2741. E-mail: scwc@socc.edu. **Coordinator:** Janet Pretti. Writer workshops geared toward beginner, intermediate levels. **Open to students.** Includes fiction, nonfiction, nuts and bolts, poetry, feature writing, children's writing, publishing. Annual workshop. Workshop held Friday and Saturday of President's day weekend in February. Registration limited to 25-30 students/workshop. Cost of workshop: $55 before January 31, $65 after; includes Friday night author's reading and book signing, Saturday conference, choice of 4 workshop sessions, Saturday evening writers' circle (networking and critique). Write for more information. ''We also have two six-hour workshops Friday for more intensive writing exercises. The cost is an additional $40.''

SOUTHEASTERN WRITERS ASSOCIATION—ANNUAL WRITERS WORKSHOP
161 Woodstone, Athens GA 30605. E-mail: purple@southeasternwriters.com. Web site: www.southeasternwrit ers.com. **CFO:** Tim Hudson. **Open to all writers and students.** Students must be in high school or college. Scholarships available for college and high school students. See Web site. Classes offered in fiction, nonfiction, juvenile, humor, inspirational writing, and poetry. Intensive workshop in screenwriting offered in 2006. Annual workshop held in June. Cost of workshop: $359 before April 15; $399 after April 15; $125 daily tuition. Accommodations: Offers overnight accommodations on workshop site. Visit Web site for more information and cost of overnight accommodations. E-mail or send SASE for brochure.

SOUTHWEST WRITERS CONFERENCES

3721 Morris NE, Suite A, Albuquerque NM 87111. (505)265-9485. Fax: (505)265-9483. E-mail: swwriters@juno. com. Web site: www.southwestwriters.org. **Open to adults and students.** Writer workshops geared toward all genres at all levels of writing. Various aspects of writing covered, including children's. Quarterly mini-conference, monthly workshops, and writing classes. Examples from mini-conferences: Suzy Capozzi and Delacorte Press Editor Claudia Gable; Pitch, Publish and Promote conference with Literary Agent Katherine Sands, Mundania Press Publisher Bob Sanders and Literary Agent Jerry D. Simmons. Cracking the Code: Secrets of Writing and Selling Compelling Nonfiction conference featured literary agents Michael Larsen, Elizabeth Pomoda and Jeff Herman; Lee Gutkind, publisher; David Fryxell, editor; Lucinda Schroeder, criminologist/writer; and a panel of New Mexico publishers. Making a Good Script Great: All-day seminar with Dr. Linda Seger and other speakers. Dimension in Fiction and Non-fiction: All-day workshop with Sean Murphy. Prices vary, but usually $79-$179. Also offers annual and monthly contests, two monthly programs, monthly newsletter, critique service, Web site linking, e-mail forwarding and various discount perks. See Web site for information.

SPLIT ROCK ARTS PROGRAM

University of Minnesota, Twin Cities Campus, 360 Coffey Hall, 1420 Eckles Ave., St. Paul MN 55108-6084. (612)625-8100. Fax: (612)624-6210. E-mail: srap@cce.umn.edu. Web site: www.cce.umn.edu/splitrockarts. Workshop topics, including poetry, short fiction, memoir, novel, personal essay, young-adult literature, and children's picture books, among others, are taught by renowned writers, and geared toward students of intermediate, advanced, and professional levels. Weeklong and three-day workshops run June through August. Registration limited to 16/workshop. Graduate/Undergraduate credit and scholarships available. Cost of workshop: $365-545 and up. On-campus apartment-style housing available. Printed and online catalogs available in February.

N: STEAMBOAT SPRINGS WRITERS CONFERENCE

P.O. Box 774284, Steamboat Springs CO 80477. (970)879-8079. E-mail: sswriters@cs.com. Web site: www.stea mboatwriters.com. **Conference Director:** Harriet Freiberger. Writers' workshops geared toward intermediate levels. **Open to students.** Some years offer topics specific to children's writing. Annual conference since 1982. Workshops will be held in July. Registration limited to 35. Cost of workshop: $45; includes 4 seminars and luncheon. Write, e-mail or see Web site for more information.

SURREY INTERNATIONAL WRITER'S CONFERENCE

Guildford Continuing Education, 10707 146th St., Surrey BC U3R IT5 Canada. (604)589-2221. Fax: (604)588-9286. E-mail: contest@siwc.ca. Web site: www.siwc.ca. **Coordinator:** KC Dyer. Writer and illustrator workshops geared toward beginners, intermediate and advanced levels. Topics include marketing, children's agents and editors. Annual Conference. Conference held in October. Cost of conference includes all events for 3 days and most meals. Check our Web site for more information.

SYDNEY CHILDREN'S WRITERS AND ILLUSTRATORS NETWORK

The Hughenden Boutique Hotel, Woollahra NSW 2025 Australia. (61)(2)363-4863. Fax: (61)(2) 93620398. E-mail: admin@hughendenhotel.com.au. Web site: www.hughendenhotel.com.au. **Contact:** Susanne Gervay. Writer and illustrator workshops geared toward professionals. Topics emphasized include networking, information and expertise about Australian children's publishing industry. Workshop held the first Wednesday of every month, except for January, commencing at 10:30 a.m. Registration limited to 30. Writing facilities available: internet and conference facilities. Cost of workshop: $150 AUS; includes accommodation for one night at The Hughenden Boutique Hotel, breakfast. As a prerequisite must be published in a magazine of have a book contract. E-mail for more information. "This is a professional meeting which aims at an interchange of ideas and information between professional children's authors and illustrators. Editors and other invited guests speak from time to time."

N: TEXAS MOUNTAIN TRAIL WRITERS' WINTER RETREAT

HC 65 Box 20P, Alpine TX 79830. (432)364-2399. E-mail: bakedalaska@wfisp.com. **President:** Jackie Siglin. Writer and illustrator workshops geared toward beginner, intermediate and advanced levels. **Open to students.** Topics emphasized include: inside information from editors of children's magazines; children's illustrator hints on collaboration; children's writer tips toward publication. Other genres are also covered. Conference held in April. Registration limited to 30-35. Writing facilities available: large comfortable conference room, nearby dining, mountain tourist attractions. Cost of workshop: $120; includes casual, friendly entertainment, weekend conference and 4 meals, one-on-one visits with authors, illustrators, etc. Write for more information. "Nearby attractions include McDonald Observatory, Ft. Davis and Big Bend National Park."

UMKC/WRITERS PLACE WRITERS WORKSHOPS

5300 Rockhill Rd., Kansas City MO 64110-2450. (816)235-2736. Fax: (816)235-5279. E-mail: seatons@umkc.e du. **Contact:** Kathi Wittfeld. New Letters Writer's Conference and Mark Twain Writer's Workshop geared toward intermediate, advanced and professional levels. Workshops open to students and community. Annual workshops. Workshops held in Summer. Cost of workshop varies. Write for more information.

🖫 VANCOUVER INTERNATIONAL WRITERS FESTIVAL

1398 Cartwright St., Vancouver BC V6H 3R8 Canada. (604)681-6330. Fax: (604)681-8400. E-mail: viwf@writersf est.bc.ca. Web site: www.writersfest.bc.ca. **Artistic Director:** Hal Wake. Annual literary festival. The Vancouver International Writers Festival strives to encourage an appreciation of literature and to promote literacy by providing a forum where writers and readers can interact. This is accomplished by the production of special events and an annual Festival that feature writers from around the world. The Festival attracts over 12,000 readers of all ages to 60+ events on Granville Island, located in the heart of Vancouver. Held in late October (6-day festival). All writers who participate are invited by the A.D. The events are open to anyone who wishes to purchase tickets. Cost of events ranges from $10-22.

🖫 THE VICTORIA SCHOOL OF WRITING

306-620 View St., Victoria BC V8W 1J6 Canada. (250)595-3000. E-mail: info@victoriaschoolofwriting.org. Web site: www.victoriaschoolofwriting.org. **Director:** Jill Margo. Annual 5-day intensive session geared toward intermediate level. The 2007 conference included 1 workshop that covered writing for young adults. Workshop held in July. Registration limited to 12/workshop. Session includes close mentoring from established writers. Cost of session: $5 95 (Canadian); includes tuition and some meals. Please see Web site, e-mail or call for details.

VIRGINIA FESTIVAL OF THE BOOK

145 Ednam Dr., Charlottesville VA 22903. (434)924-6890. Fax: (434)296-4714. E-mail: vabook@virginia.edu. Web site: www.vabook.org. **Program Director:** Nancy Damon. **Open to Students.** Readings, panel discussions, presentations and workshops by author, and book-related professionals for children and adults. Most programs are free and open to the public. Held March 26-30, 2008. See Web site for more information.

WESLEYAN WRITERS CONFERENCE

Wesleyan University, Middletown CT 06459. (860)685-3604. Fax: (860)685-2441. E-mail: agreene@wesleyan.e du. Web site: www.wesleyan.edu/writers. **Director:** Anne Greene. Seminars, workshops, readings, ms advice; geared toward all levels. "This conference is useful for writers interested in how to structure a story, poem or nonfiction piece. Although we don't always offer classes in writing for children, the advice about structuring a piece is useful for writers of any sort, no matter who their audience is." One of the nation's best-selling children's authors was a student here. Classes in the novel, short story, fiction techniques, poetry, journalism and literary nonfiction. Guest speakers and panels offer discussion of fiction, poetry, reviewing, editing and publishing. Individual ms consultations available. Conference held annually the third week in June. Length of each session: 5 days. Usually, there are 100 participants at the Conference. Classrooms, meals, lodging and word processing facilities available on campus. Cost of conference 2007: tuition—$830, room—$175, meals (required of all participants)—$240. "Anyone may register; people who want financial aid must submit their work and be selected by scholarship judges." Call for a brochure or check Web site.

WHIDBEY ISLAND WRITERS' CONFERENCE

P.O. Box 1289, Langley WA 98260. (360)331-6714. E-mail: writers@whidbey.com. Web site: www.writeonwhid bey.org . **Writers Contact:** Elizabeth Guss, conference director. Three days focused on the tools you need to become a great writer. Learn from a variety of award-winning children's book authors and very experienced literary agents. Topics include: "Putting the character back in character" and "Contemporary and Historical Fiction for Children." Conference held February 29-March 2, 2008. Registration limited to 275. Cost: $395; early bird and member discounts available. Registration includes workshops, fireside chats, high tea book-signing reception, various activities, and daily luncheons. The conference offers consultation appointments with editors and agents. Preconference workshops available on February 28. Registrants may reduce the cost of their conference by volunteering. See the Web site for more information. "The uniquely personal and friendly weekend is designed to be highly interactive."

WILLAMETTE WRITERS ANNUAL WRITERS CONFERENCE

9045 SW Barbur Blvd., Suite 5A, Portland OR 97219. (503)452-1592. Fax: (503)452-0372. E-mail: wilwrite@willa mettewriters.com. Web site: www.willamettewriters.com. **Office Manager:** Bill Johnson. Writer workshops geared toward all levels. Emphasizes all areas of writing, including children's and young adult. Opportunities to meet one-on-one with leading literary agents and editors. Workshops held in August. Cost of conference: $230-$430; includes membership.

TENNESSEE WILLIAMS/NEW ORLEANS LITERARY FESTIVAL

938 Lafayette St., Suite 514, New Orleans LA 70113. (504)581-1144. Fax: (504)523-3680. E-mail: info@tennessee williams.net. Web site: www.tennesseewilliams.net. **Executive Director:** Paul J. Willis. Writer workshops geared toward beginner, intermediate, advanced, and professional levels. **Open to students.** Annual workshop. Workshop held around the third week in March (March 26-30, 2008). Master classes are limited in size to 100— all other panels offered have no cap. Cost of workshop: prices range from $15-35. Visit Web site for more information. "We are a literary festival and may occasionally offer panels/classes on children's writing and/ or illustration, but this is not done every year."

WRITE ON THE SOUND WRITERS CONFERENCE

700 Main St., Edmonds WA 98020-3032. (425)771-0228. Fax: (425)771-0253. E-mail: wots@ci.edmonds.wa.us. Web site: www.ci.edmonds.wa.us/ArtsCommission/index.stm. **Conference Coordinator:** Kris Gillespie. Writer workshops geared toward beginner, intermediate, advanced and professional levels with some sessions on writing for children. Annual conference held in Edmonds, on Puget Sound, on the first weekend in October with 2 full days of workshops. Registration limited to 200. Cost of conference: approximately $104 for early registration, $125 for late registration; includes two days of workshops plus one ticket to keynote lecture. Brochures are mailed in August. Attendees must pre-register. Write, e-mail or call for brochure. Writing contest and critiques for conference participants.

WRITE! CANADA

P.O. Box 34, Port Perry ON L9L 1A2 Canada. (905)294-6482. Fax: (905)471-6912. E-mail: info@thewordguild.c om. Web site: www.thewordguild.com. Estab. 1984. Annual conference for writers who are Christian. Hosted by The Word Guild, an association of Canadian writers and editors who are Christian. The Word Guild seeks to connect, develop, and promote its members. Keynote speaker, continuing classes, workshops, panels, editor appointments, reading times, critiques, and more. For all levels of writers from beginner to professional. Held at a retreat center in Guelph, Ontario in mid-June.

WRITE-BY-THE-LAKE WRITER'S WORKSHOP & RETREAT

610 Langdon St., Room 621, Madison WI 53703. (608)262-3447. E-mail: cdesmet@dcs.wisc.edu. Web site: www.dcs.wisc.edu/lsa/writing. **Coordinator:** Christine DeSmet. Writer workshops geared toward beginner and intermediate levels. **Open to students** (1-3 graduate credits available in English). "One week-long session is devoted to juvenile fiction." Annual workshop. Workshop held the third week of June. Registration limited to 15. Writing facilities available: computer labs. Cost of workshop: $325 before May 2 1; $355 after May 2 1. Cost includes instruction, reception, and continental breakfast each day. Write for more information. "Brochure goes online every January for the following June."

WRITE-TO-PUBLISH CONFERENCE

9118 W. Elmwood Dr., #1G, Niles IL 60714-5820. (847)296-3964. Fax: (847)296-0754. E-mail: lin@writetopublish.c om. Web site: www.writetopublish.com. **Director:** Lin Johnson. Writer workshops geared toward all levels. **Open to students.** Conference is focused for the Christian market and includes classes on writing for children. Annual conference held in June. Cost of conference approximately: $425; includes conference and banquet. For information e-mail brochure@writetopublish.com. Conference takes place at Wheaton College in the Chicago area.

WRITERS RETREAT WORKSHOP

(formerly Gary Provost's Writers Retreat Workshop), (800)642-2494 (for brochure). E-mail: jssitzes@aol.com. Web site: www.writersretreatworkshop.com. **Director:** Jason Sitzes. Intensive workshops geared toward beginner, intermediate and advanced levels. Workshops are appropriate for writers of full length novels for children/ YA. Also, for writers of all novels or narrative nonfiction. Annual workshop. Registration limited to 32: beginners and advanced. Writing facilities available: private rooms with desks. Cost includes tuition, food and lodging for nine nights, daily classes, writing space, time and assignments, consultation and instruction. One annual scholarship available: Feb deadline. Requirements: short synopsis required to determine appropriateness of novel for our nuts and bolts approach to getting the work in shape for publication. Write for more information. For complete updated details, visit www.writersretreatworkshop.com.

WRITERS' LEAGUE OF TEXAS WORKSHOP SERIES

1501 W. Fifth St., Suite E-2, Austin TX 78703. (512)499-8914. Fax: (512)499-0441. E-mail: wlt@writersleague.o rg. Web site: www.writersleague.org. **Contact:** Kristy Bordine. Writer workshops and conferences geared toward adults. Annual agents and editors conferences. Classes are held during weekend, and retreats/workshops are held throughout the year. Annual Teddy Children's Book Award of $1,000 presented each fall to book published the previous year.

◨ ◪ THE WRITERS' RETREAT

15 Canusa St., Stanstead QC J0B 3E5 Canada. (819)876-2065. E-mail: info@writersretreat.com. Web site: www. writersretreat.com. **Contact:** Micheline Cote. Workshops for beginners to advanced. **Open to students.** See our schedule at writersretreat.com/workshop.htm. Registration limited to 10-12 participants. Writing facilities available: Every participant has their own private studio. Cost of workshop vary from $190-$695 (lodging not included) depending on the length and format. Write for more information. The Writer's Retreat offers year-round lodging and literary services to its residents in Canada, Costa Rica, Mexico and the United States at www.WritersRetreat.com.

WRITING AND ILLUSTRATING FOR YOUNG READERS WORKSHOP

Brigham Young University, 348 Harman Continuing Education Bldg., Provo UT 84602-1532. (801)442-2568. Fax: (801)422-0745. E-mail: cw348@byu.edu. Web site: http://wifyr.byu.edu. Annual workshop held in June. Five-day workshop designed for people who want to write for children or teenagers. Participants focus on a single market during daily four-hour morning writing workshops: picture books, book-length fiction (novels), fantasy/science fiction, nonfiction, mystery, beginning writing or illustration. Afternoon workshop sessions feature a variety of topics of interest to writers for all youth ages. Workshop cost: $439—includes all workshop and breakout sessions plus a banquet on Thursday evening. Afternoon-only registration available; participants may attend these sessions all five days for a fee of $109. Attendance at the Thursday evening banquet is included in addition to the afternoon mingle, plenary, and breakout sessions.

Contests, Awards & Grants

P ublication is not the only way to get your work recognized. Contests and awards can also be great ways to gain recognition in the industry. Grants, offered by organizations like SCBWI, offer monetary recognition to writers, giving them more financial freedom as they work on projects.

When considering contests or applying for grants, be sure to study guidelines and requirements. Regard entry deadlines as gospel and follow the rules to the letter.

Note that some contests require nominations. For published authors and illustrators, competitions provide an excellent way to promote your work. Your publisher may not be aware of local competitions such as state-sponsored awards—if your book is eligible, have the appropriate person at your publishing company nominate or enter your work for consideration.

To select potential contests and grants, read through the listings that interest you, then send for more information about the types of written or illustrated material considered and other important details. A number of contests offer information through Web sites given in their listings.

If you are interested in knowing who has received certain awards in the past, check your local library or bookstores or consult *Children's Books: Awards & Honors*, compiled and edited by the Children's Book Council (www.cbcbooks.org). Many bookstores have special sections for books that are Caldecott and Newbery Medal winners. Visit the American Library Association Web site, www.ala.org, for information on the Caldecott, Newbery, Coretta Scott King and Printz Awards. Visit www.hbook.com for information on The Boston Globe-Horn Book Award. Visit www.scbwi.org/awards.htm for information on The Golden Kite Award.

For a contest success story see the Insider Report with **Jo Knowles**, author and award and grant recipient, on page 352.

Information on contests listed in the previous edition but not included in this edition of *Children's Writer's & Illustrator's Market* may be found in the General Index.

🌐 ACADEMY OF CHILDREN'S WRITERS' WRITING FOR CHILDREN COMPETITION

Academy of Children's Writers, P.O. Box 95, Huntington Cambridgeshire PE28 5RL England. 01487 832752. Fax: 01487 832752. E-mail: per_ardua@lycos.co.uk. **Contact:** Roger Dewar, contest director. Annual contest for the best unpublished short story writer for children. **Deadline:** March 31. Guidelines for SASE. **Charges $5 (US); £ (UK).** Prize: 1st Prize: £1,000; 2nd Prize: £300; 3rd Prize: £100. Judged by a panel appointed by the Academy of Children's Writers. Open to any writer.

JANE ADDAMS CHILDREN'S BOOK AWARDS

Jane Addams Peace Association, Inc./Women's International League for Peace and Freedom, 777 United Nations Plaza, New York NY 10017. (212)682-8830. Fax: (212)286-8211. E-mail: japa@igc.org. Web site: www.janeadda mspeace.org. **Contact:** Linda Belle. "Two copies of published books the previous year only." Annual award. Estab. 1953. Previously published submissions only. Submissions made by author, author's agent, person, group or publisher, submitted by the publisher. Must be published January 1-December 31 of preceding year. Deadline for entries: December 31. Check Web site for all submission information. Cash awards and certificate, $1,000 to winners (winning book) and $500 each to Honor Book winners (split between author and illustrator, if necessary). Judging by national committee from various N.S. regions (all are members of W.I.L.P.F.). The award ceremony is held in New York the third Friday October annually.

AIM MAGAZINE SHORT STORY CONTEST

P.O. Box 1174, Maywood IL 60153-8174. (773)874-6184. **Contest Director:** Ruth Apilado, associate editor. Annual contest. **Open to students.** Estab. 1983. Purpose of contest: "We solicit stories with lasting social significance proving that people from different racial/ethnic backgrounds are more alike than they are different." Unpublished submissions only. Deadline for entries: August 15. SASE for contest rules and entry forms. SASE for return of work. No entry fee. Awards $100. Judging by editors. Contest open to everyone. Winning entry published in fall issue of *AIM*. Subscription rate: $20/year. Single copy: $5.

⬛ ALCUIN CITATION AWARD

The Alcuin Society, P.O. Box 3216, Vancouver BC V6B 3X8 Canada. (604)732-5403. E-mail: leahgordon@shaw. ca. Web site: www.alcuinsociety.com /awards. Annual award. Estab. 1981. Purpose of contest: Alcuin Citations are awarded annually for excellence in Canadian book design. Previously published submissions from the year prior to the Award's Call for Entries (i.e., 2007 awards went to books published in 2006). Submissions made by the publisher, author or designer. Deadline for entries: mid-March. Entry fee is $25/book; include cheque and entry form with book; downloadable entry form available at web site. Awards certificate. Winning books are exhibited nationally, and internationally at the Frankfurt and Leipzig Book Fairs, and are Canada's entries in the international competition in Leipzig, "Book Design from all over the World" in the following Spring. Judging by professionals and those experienced in the field of book design. Requirements for entrants: Winners are selected from books designed and published in Canada. Awards are presented annually at an appropriate ceremony held in early June each year.

AMERICA & ME ESSAY CONTEST

Farm Bureau Insurance, P.O. Box 30400, 7373 W. Saginaw, Lansing MI 48909-7900. (517)323-7000. Fax: (517)323-6615. E-mail: lfedewa@fbinsmi.com. Web site: www.farmbureauinsurance-mi.co. **Contest Coordinator:** Lisa Fedewa. Annual contest. **Open to students only.** Estab. 1968. Purpose of the contest: to give Michigan 8th graders the opportunity to express their thoughts/feelings on America and their roles in America. Unpublished submissions only. Deadline for entries: mid-November. SASE for contest rules and entry forms. "We have a school mailing list. Any school located in Michigan is eligible to participate." Entries not returned. No entry fee. Awards savings bonds and plaques for state top ten ($500-1,000), certificates and plaques for top 3 winners from each school. Each school may submit up to 10 essays for judging. Judging by home office employee volunteers. Requirements for entrants: "Participants must work through their schools or our agents' sponsoring schools. No individual submissions will be accepted. Top ten essays and excerpts from other essays are published in booklet form following the contest. State capitol/schools receive copies."

AMERICAN ASSOCIATION OF UNIVERSITY WOMEN, NORTH CAROLINA DIVISION, AWARD IN JUVENILE LITERATURE

North Carolina Literary and Historical Association, 4610 Mail Service Center, Raleigh NC 27699-4610. (919)807-7290. Fax: (919)733-8807. E-mail: michael.hill@ncmail.net. **Award Coordinator:** Mr. Michael Hill. Annual award. Purpose of award: to recognize the year's best work of juvenile literature by a North Carolina resident. Book must be published during the year ending June 30. Submissions made by author, author's agent or publisher. Deadline for entries: July 15. SASE for contest rules. Awards a cup to the winner and winner's name inscribed on a plaque displayed within the North Carolina Office of Archives and History. Judging by Board of Award selected by sponsoring organization. Requirements for entrants: Author must have maintained either legal residence or actual physical residence, or a combination of both, in the state of North Carolina for three years immediately preceding the close of the contest period. Only published work (books) eligible.

AMERICAS AWARD

CLASP Committee on Teaching and Outreach, c/o Center for Latin American and Caribbean Studies, P.O. Box 413, Milwaukee WI 53201. (414)229-5986. Fax: (414)229-2879. E-mail: jkline@uwm.edu. Web site: www.uwm.edu/Dept/CLACS/outreach/americas.html. **Coordinator:** Julie Kline. Annual award. Estab. 1993. Purpose of contest: Up to two awards are given each spring in recognition of U.S. published works (from the previous year) of fiction, poetry, folklore or selected nonfiction (from picture books to works for young adults) in English or Spanish which authentically and engagingly relate to Latin America, the Caribbean, or to Latinos in the United States. By combining both and linking the "Americas," the intent is to reach beyond geographic borders, as well as multicultural-international boundaries, focusing instead upon cultural heritages within the hemisphere. Previously published submissions only. Submissions open to anyone with an interest in the theme of the award. Deadline for entries: January 15. Visit Web site or send SASE for contest rules and any committee changes. Awards $500 cash prize, plaque and a formal presentation at the Library of Congress, Washington DC. Judging by a review committee consisting of individuals in teaching, library work, outreach and children's literature specialists.

HANS CHRISTIAN ANDERSEN AWARD

IBBY International Board on Books for Young People, Nonnenweg 12, Postfach CH-4003 Basel Switzerland. (004161)272 29 17. Fax: (004161)272 27 57. E-mail: ibby@ibby.org. Web site: www.ibby.org. **Director:** Estelle Roth; Director Member Services, Communications and New Projects: Liz Page. Award offered every two years. Purpose of award: A Hans Christian Andersen Medal shall be awarded every two years by the International Board on Books for Young People (IBBY) to an author and to an illustrator, living at the time of the nomination, who by the outstanding value of their work are judged to have made a lasting contribution to literature for children and young people. The complete works of the author and of the illustrator will be taken into consideration in awarding the medal, which will be accompanied by a diploma. Published work only. Submissions are nominated by National Sections of IBBY in good standing. The National Sections select the candidates. The Hans Christian Andersen Award, named after Denmark's famous storyteller, is the highest international recognition given to an author and an illustrator of children's books. The Author's Award has been given since 1956, the Illustrator's Award since 1966. Her Majesty Queen Margrethe of Denmark is the Patron of the Hans Christian Andersen Awards. The Hans Christian Andersen Jury judges the books submitted for medals according to literary and artistic criteria. The awards are presented at the biennial congresses of IBBY.

THE ASPCA HENRY BERGH CHILDREN'S BOOK AWARD

The American Society For the Prevention of Cruelty to Animals, 424 E. 92nd St., New York NY 10128-6804. (212)876-7700, ext. 4409. Fax: (212)860-3435. E-mail: education@aspca.org. Web site: www.aspca.org/bookaward. **Award Manager:** Miriam Ramos, Director, Humane Education. Competition open to authors, illustrators, and publishers. Annual award. Estab. 2000. Purpose of contest: To honor outstanding children's literature that fosters empathy and compassion for all living things. Awards presented to authors. Previously published submissions only. Submissions made by author or author's agent. Must be published between January 2006-December 2006. Deadline for entries: October 31, 2006. Awards foil seals and plaque. Judging by professionals in animal welfare and children's literature. Requirements for entrants: Open to children's literature about animals and/or the environment published in 2006. Includes fiction, nonfiction and poetry in 5 categories: Companion Animals, Ecology and Environment, Humane Heroes, Illustration, and Young Adult.

ASTED/GRAND PRIX DE LITTERATURE JEUNESSE DU QUEBEC-ALVINE-BELISLE

Association pour l'avancement des sciences et des techniques de la documentation, 3414 Avenue du Parc, Bureau 202, Montreal QC H2X 2H5 Canada. (514)281-5012. Fax: (514)281-8219. E-mail: info@asted.org. Web site: www.asted.org. **Contact:** Olivia Marleau or Brigitte Moreay, co-presidents. "Prize granted for the best work in youth literature edited in French in the Quebec Province. Authors and editors can participate in the contest." Offered annually for books published during the preceding year. Deadline: June 1. Prize: $1,000.

ATLANTIC WRITING COMPETITION

Writer's Federation of Nova Scotia, 1113 Marginal Rd., Halifax NS B3H 4P7 Canada. (902)423-8116. Fax: (902)422-0881. E-mail: talk@writers.ns.ca. Web site: www.writers.ns.ca/competitions.html. Annual contest. Purpose is to encourage emerging writers in Atlantic Canada to explore their talents by sending unpublished work to any of five categories: novel, short story, poetry, writing for younger children, writing for juvenile/

young adult or essay/magazine article. Unpublished submissions only. Only open to residents of Atlantic Canada who are unpublished in category they enter. Visit Web site for more information.

BAKER'S PLAYS HIGH SCHOOL PLAYWRITING CONTEST

Baker's Plays, 45 W. 25th St., New York NY 10010. E-mail: publications@bakersplays.com Web site: www.bake rsplays.com. **Contest Director:** Deirdre Shaw. **Open to any high school students.** Annual contest. Estab. 1990. Purpose of the contest: to encourage playwrights at the high school level and to ensure the future of American theater. Unpublished submissions only. Postmark deadline: January 31. Notification: May. SASE for contest rules and entry forms. No entry fee. Awards $500 to the first place playwright with publication by Baker's Plays; $250 to the second place playwright with an honorable mention; and $100 to the third place playwright with an honorable mention in the series. Judged anonymously. Plays must be accompanied by the signature of a sponsoring high school drama or English teacher, and it is recommended that the play receive a production or a public reading prior to the submission. "To ensure return of manuscripts, please include SASE, otherwise the script paper will be recycled." Teachers must not submit student's work. The winning work will be listed in the Baker's Plays Catalogue, which is distributed to 50,000 prospective producing organizations.

● Baker's Plays is now encouraging submission via e-mail at publications@bakersplay.com.

JOHN AND PATRICIA BEATTY AWARD

California Library Association, 717 20th Street, Suite 200, Sacramento CA 95814. (916)447-8541. Fax: (916)447-8394. E-mail: info@cla-net.org. Web site: www.cla-net.org. **Executive Director:** Susan Negreen. Annual award. Estab. 1987. Purpose of award: "The purpose of the John and Patricia Beatty Award is to encourage the writing of quality children's books highlighting California, its culture, heritage and/or future." Previously published submissions only. Submissions made by the author, author's agent or review copies sent by publisher. The award is given to the author of a children's book published the preceding year. Deadline for entries: Submissions may be made January-December. Contact CLA Executive Director who will liaison with Beatty Award Committee. Awards cash prize of $500 and an engraved plaque. Judging by a 5-member selection committee appointed by the president of the California Library Association. Requirements for entrants: "Any children's or young adult book set in California and published in the U.S. during the calendar year preceding the presentation of the award is eligible for consideration. This includes works of fiction as well as nonfiction for children and young people of all ages. Reprints and compilations are not eligible. The California setting must be depicted authentically and must serve as an integral focus for the book." Winning selection is announced through press release during National Library Week in April. Author is presented with award at annual California Library Association Conference in November.

🔲 THE GEOFFREY BILSON AWARD FOR HISTORICAL FICTION FOR YOUNG PEOPLE

The Canadian Children's Book Centre, 40 Orchard View Blvd., Suite 101, Toronto ON M4R 1B9 Canada. (416)975-0010. Fax: (416)975-8970. E-mail: naseem@bookcentre.ca. Web site: www.bookcentre.ca. **Contact:** Naseem Hrab, librarian. Created in Geoffrey Bilson's memory in 1988. Offered annually for a previously published "outstanding work of historical fiction for young people by a Canadian author." Open to Canadian citizens and residents of Canada for at least 2 years. Deadline: January 15. Prize: $1,000. Judged by a jury selected by the Canadian Children's Book Centre.

THE IRMA S. AND JAMES H. BLACK BOOK AWARD

Bank Street College of Education, New York NY 10025-1898. (212)875-4450. Fax: (212)875-4558. E-mail: lindag @bnkst.edu. Web site: http://streetcat.bnkst.edu/html/isb.html. **Contact:** Linda Greengrass. Annual award. Estab. 1972. Purpose of award: "The award is given each spring for a book for young children, published in the previous year, for excellence of both text and illustrations." Entries must have been published during the previous calendar year (between January '06 and December '06 for 2007 award). Deadline for entries: mid-December. "Publishers submit books to us by sending them here to me at the Bank Street Library. Authors may ask their publishers to submit their books. Out of these, three to five books are chosen by a committee of older children and children's literature professionals. These books are then presented to children in selected first, second, and third grade classes here and at a number of other cooperating schools. These children are the final judges who pick the actual award winner. A scroll (one each for the author and illustrator, if they're different) with the recipient's name and a gold seal designed by Maurice Sendak are awarded in May."

WALDO M. AND GRACE C. BONDERMAN/IUPUI NATIONAL YOUTH THEATRE PLAYWRITING COMPETITION AND DEVELOPMENT WORKSHOP AND SYMPOSIUM

Bonderman Youth Theatre Playwriting Workshop, 1114 Red Oak Drive, Avon, IN 46123. E-mail: bonderma@iup ui.edu. Web site: www.liberalarts.iupui.edu/bonderman. **Director:** Dorothy Webb. **Open to students.** Chairperson, Canadian Association of Children's Librarians. Annual award. Estab. 1947. "The main purpose of the award is to encourage writing and publishing in Canada of good books for children up to and including age 14. If, in any year, no book is deemed to be of award calibe r, the award shall not be given that year. To merit consideration, the book must have been published in Canada and its author must be a Canadian citizen or a permanent resident of Canada." Previously published submissions only; must be published between January 1 and December 1 of the previous year. Deadline for entries: January 1. SASE for award rules. Entries not returned. No entry fee. Judging by committee of members of the Canadian Association of Children's Librarians. Requirements for entrants: Contest open only to Canadian authors or residents of Canada.

🌐 BOOKTRUST EARLY YEARS AWARDS

Booktrust, Book House, 45 E. Hill, Wandsworth, London SW18 2QZ United Kingdom. Fax: (00 44)20 8516 2978. E-mail: tarryn@booktrust.org.uk. Web site: www.booktrust.org.uk. **Contact:** Tarryn McKay. The Booktrust Early Years Awards were initially established in 1999 and are awarded annually. The awards are given to the best books, published between September 1 and the following August 31, in the opinion of the judges in each category. The categories are: Baby Book Award, Pre-School Award, and Best New Illustrator Award. Authors and illustrators must be of British nationality, or other nationals who have been residents in the British Isles for at least 10 years. Books can be any format. Deadline: June. Prize: £2,000 and a crystal award to each winner (to be split between author/illustrator if necessary). In addition, the publisher receives a crystal award naming them as "The Booktrust Early Years Awards Publisher of the Year."

THE BOSTON GLOBE-HORN BOOK AWARDS

The Boston Globe & The Horn Book, Inc., The Horn Book, 56 Roland St., Suite 200, Boston MA 02129. (617)628-0225. Fax: (617)628-0882. E-mail: info@hbook.com. Web site: www.hbook.com/awards/bghb/submissions_b ghb.asp. Annual award. Estab. 1967. Purpose of award: To reward literary excellence in children's and young adult books. Awards are for picture books, nonfiction, fiction and poetry. Up to two honor books may be chosen for each category. Books must be published between June 1, 2005 and May 31, 2006. Deadline for entries: May 2005. Textbks, e-books, and audiobooks will not be considered, nor will manuscripts. Books should be submitted by publishers, although the judges reserve the right to honor any eligible book. Award winners receive $500 and silver engraved bowl, honor book winners receive a silver engraved plate. Judging by 3 judges involved in children's book field. *The Horn Book Magazine* publishes speeches given at awards ceremonies. The book must have been published in the U.S.

ANN ARLYS BOWLER POETRY CONTEST

Bowler Poetry Contest, Weekly Reader Corporation, 200 First Stamford Place, P.O. Box 120023 Stamford, CT 06912-0023. Web site: http://www.weeklyreader.com/teachers/read/RDContests. **Open to students.** Annual contest. Estab. 1988. Purpose of the contest: to reward young-adult poets (grades 6-12). Unpublished submissions only. Submissions made by the author or nominated by a person or group of people. Entry form must include signature of teacher, parent or guardian, and student verifying originality. Maximum number of submissions per student: 3 poems. Deadline for entries: mid-January. SASE for contest rules and entry forms. No entry fee. Awards 6 winners $100 each, medal of honor and publication in *Read*. Semifinalists receive $50 each. Judging by *Read* and *Weekly Reader* editors and teachers. Requirements for entrants: the material must be original. Winning entries will be published in an issue of *Read*.

⚂ ANN CONNOR BRIMER AWARD

Nova Scotia Library Association, P.O. Box 36036, Halifax NS B3J 3S9 Canada. (902)490-5875. Fax: (902)490-5893. Web site: http://nsla.ns.ca/aboutnsla/brimeraward.html. **Award Director:** Heather MacKenzie. Annual award. Estab. 1991. Purpose of the contest: to recognize excellence in writing. Given to an author of a children's book who resides in Atlantic Canada. Previously published submissions only. Submissions made by the author's agent or nominated by a person or group of people. Must be published in previous year. Deadline for entries: October 15. SASE for contest rules and entry forms. No entry fee. Awards $1,000 and framed certificate. Judging by a selection committee. Requirements for entrants: Book must be intended for use up to age 15; in print and readily available; fiction or nonfiction except textbooks.

BUCKEYE CHILDREN'S BOOK AWARD

Ada Kent c/o Ohio School for the Deaf, 500 Morse Rd., Columbus OH 43214. (614)728-1414. E-mail: ddebened@ kent.edu. Web site: www.bcbookaward.info. **President:** Deb DeBenedictis. Correspondence should be sent to Ada Kent at the above address. **Open to students.** Award offered every 2 years. Estab. 1981. Purpose of the award: "The Buckeye Children's Book Award Program was designed to encourage children to read literature critically, to promote teacher and librarian involvement in children's literature programs, and to commend authors of such literature, as well as to promote the use of libraries. Awards are presented in the following three categories: grades K-2, grades 3-5, grades 6-8 and grades 9-12 (Teen Buckeye)." Previously published submissions only. Deadline for entries: February 1. "The nominees are submitted by the students by this date during the even year and the votes are submitted by this date during the odd year. This award is nominated and voted upon by children in Ohio. It is based upon criteria established in our bylaws. The winning authors are awarded a special plaque honoring them at a banquet given by one of the sponsoring organizations. The BCBA Board oversees the tallying of the votes and announces the winners in March of the voting year atwww.bc bookaward.info and in a number of national journals. The book must have been written by an author, a citizen of the United States and originally copyrighted in the U.S. within the last three years preceding the nomination year. The award-winning books are displayed in a historical display housed at the Reinberger Children's Library at Kent State Library School."

BYLINE MAGAZINE CONTESTS
P.O. Box 111, Albion, NY 14411. E-mail: robbi@bylinemag.com. Web site: www.bylinemag.com. **Contest Director:** Robbi Hess. Purpose of contest: *ByLine* runs 4 contests a month on many topics to encourage and motivate writers. Past topics include first chapter of a novel, children's fiction, children's poem, nonfiction for children, personal essay, general short stories, valentine or love poem, etc. Send SASE for contest flier with topic list and rules, or see Web site. Unpublished submissions only. Submissions made by the author. "We do not publish the contests' winning entries, just the names of the winners." Entry fee is $3-5. Awards cash prizes for first, second and third place. Amounts vary. Judging by qualified writers or editors. List of winners will appear in magazine.

BYLINE MAGAZINE STUDENT PAGE
P.O. Box 5240, Edmond OK 73083-5240. (405)348-5591. E-mail: mpreston@bylinemag.com. Web site: www.byl inemag.com. **Contest Director:** Marcia Preston, publisher. **Open to students.** Estab. 1981. "We offer writing contests for students in grades 1-12 on a monthly basis, September through May, with cash prizes and publica-tion of top entries." Previously unpublished submissions only. "This is not a market for illustration." Deadline for entries varies. "Entry fee usually $1." Awards cash and publication. Judging by qualified editors and writers. "We publish top entries in student contests. Winners' list published in magazine dated 2 months past deadline." Send SASE for details.

RANDOLPH CALDECOTT MEDAL
Association for Library Service to Children, Division of the American Library Association, 50 E. Huron, Chicago IL 60611. (312)280-2163. E-mail: alsc@ala.org. Web site: www.ala.org. **Executive Director:** Diane Foote. An-nual award. Estab. 1938. Purpose of the award: to honor the artist of the most outstanding picture book for children published in the U.S. (Illustrator must be U.S. citizen or resident.) Must be published year preceding award. Deadline for entries: December 31. SASE for award rules. Entries not returned. No entry fee. "Medal given at ALA Annual Conference during the Newbery/Caldecott Banquet."

CALIFORNIA YOUNG PLAYWRIGHTS CONTEST
Playwrights Project, 2356 Moore Street, #204, San Diego CA 92110. (619)239-8222. Fax: (619)239-8225. E-mail: write@playwrightsproject.org. Web site: www.playwrightsproject.org. **Director:** Deborah Salzer. **Open to Californians under age 19.** Annual contest. Estab. 1985. "Our organization and the contest is designed to nurture promising young writers. We hope to develop playwrights and audiences for live theater. We also teach playwriting." Submissions required to be unpublished and not produced professionally. Submissions made by the author. Deadline for entries: June 1. SASE for contest rules and entry form. No entry fee. Award is profes-sional productions of 3-5 short plays each year, participation of the writers in the entire production process, with a royalty awarded. Judging by professionals in the theater community, a committee of 5-7; changes somewhat each year. Works performed in San Diego at a professional theatre. Writers submitting scripts of 10 or more pages receive a detailed script evaluation letter upon request.

CALLIOPE FICTION CONTEST
Writers' Specialized Interest Group (SIG) of American Mensa, Ltd., 2506 SE Bitterbrush Dr., Madras, OR 97741. E-mail: cynthia@theriver.com. Web site: www.us.mensa.org. **Fiction Editor:** Sandy Raschke. **Open to stu-dents.** Annual contest. Estab. 1991. Purpose of contest: "To promote good writing and opportunities for getting published. To give our member/subscribers and others an entertaining and fun exercise in writing." Unpub-lished submissions only (all genres, no violence, profanity or extreme horror). Submissions made by author. Deadline for entries: changes annually but usually around September 15. Entry fee is $2 for nonsubscribers; subscribers get first entry fee. Awards small amount of cash (up to $75 for 1st place, to $10 for 3rd), certificates, full or mini-subscriptions to *Calliope* and various premiums and books, depending on donations. All winners are published in subsequent issues of *Calliope*. Judging by fiction editor, with concurrence of other editors, if needed. Requirements for entrants: winners must retain sufficient rights to have their stories published in the

January/February issue, or their entries will be disqualified; one-time rights. Open to all writers. No special considerations—other than following the guidelines. Contest theme, due dates and sometimes entry fees change annually. Always send SASE for complete rules; available after April 15 each year. Sample copies with prior winners are available for $3.

CANADA COUNCIL GOVERNOR GENERAL'S LITERARY AWARDS

350 Albert St., Ottawa ON K1P 5V8 Canada. (613)566-4410, ext. 4582. Fax: (613)566-4410. E-mail: joanne.laroc que-poirier@canadacouncil.ca. **Program Officer, Writing and Publishing Section:** TBA. Annual award. Estab. 1937. Purpose of award: given to the best English-language and the best French-language work in each of the seven categories of Fiction, Literary Nonfiction, Poetry, Drama, Children's Literature (text), Children's Literature (illustration) and Translation. Books must be first-edition trade books that have been written, translated or illustrated by Canadian citizens or permanent residents of Canada. In the case of Translation, the original work written in English or French, must also be a Canadian-authored title. English titles must be published between September 1, 2006 and September 30, 2007. Books must be submitted by publishers. Books must reach the Canada Council for the Arts no later than August 7, 2007. The deadlines are final; no bound proofs or books that miss the applicable deadlines will be given to the peer assessment committees. The awards ceremony is scheduled mid-November. Amount of award: $15,000 to winning authors; $1,000 to nonwinning finalists.

SANDRA CARON YOUNG ADULT POETRY PRIZE

National League of American Pen Women, Nob Hill, San Francisco Branch, 1544 Sweetwood Dr., Colma CA 94015-2029. E-mail: pennobhill@aol.com. Web site: www.soulmakingcontest.us. **Contact:** Eileen Malone. **Open to students.** Three poems/entry; one poem/page; one-page poems only from poets in grades 9-12. Annually. Deadline: November 30. Guidelines for SASE. Charges $5/entry (make checks payable to NLAPW, Nob Hill Branch). Prize: 1st Place: $100; 2nd Place: $50; 3rd Place: $25. Open to any writer in grade 9-12.

CHILDREN'S AFRICANA BOOK AWARD

Outreach Council of the African Studies Association, %Rutgers University, 132 George St., New Brunswick NJ 08901. (732)932-8173. Fax: (732)932-3394. Web site: www.africanstudies.org. Administered by Africa Access, P.O. Box 8028, Silver Springs MD 20910. (301)587-3040. Fax: (301)562-5244. E-mail: africaaccess@a ol.com. Web site: www.africaaccessreview.org. **Chairperson:** Brenda Randolph. Annually. Estab. 1991. Purpose of contest: "The Children's Africana Book Awards are presented annually to the authors and illustrators of the best books on Africa for children and young people published or republished in the U.S. The awards were created by the Outreach Council of the African Studies Association (ASA) to dispell stereotypes and encourage the publication and use of accurate, balanced children's materials about Africa. The awards are presented in 2 categories: Young Children and Older Readers. Since 1991, 48 books have been recognized." Entries must have been published in the calendar year previous to the award. No entry fee. Awards plaque, announcement each spring, reviews published at H-AFRTEACH and Africa Access Review, and in *Sankofa: Journal of African Children's & Young Adult Literature*. Judging by Outreach Council of ASA and children's literature scholars. "Work submitted for awards must be suitable for children ages 4-18; a significant portion of books' content must be about Africa; must by copyrighted in the calendar year prior to award year; must be published or republished in the US."

CHILDREN'S WRITER WRITING CONTESTS

93 Long Ridge Rd., West Redding CT 06896-1124. (203)792-8600. Fax: (203)792-8406. Web site: www.childrens writer.com. Contest offered twice per year by *Children's Writer*, the monthly newsletter of writing and publishing trends. Purpose of the award: To promote higher quality children's literature. "Each contest has its own theme. Any original unpublished piece, not accepted by any publisher at the time of submission, is eligible." Submissions made by the author. Deadline for entries: Last weekday in February and October. "We charge a $10 entry fee for nonsubscribers only, which is applicable against a subscription to *Children's Writer* Awards: 1st place—$250 or $500, a certificate and publication in *Children's Writer*; 2nd place—$100 or $250, and certificate; 3rd-5th places—$50 or $100 and certificates. To obtain the rules and theme for the current contest go to the Web site and click on "Writing Contests," or send a SASE to *Children's Writer* at the above address. Put "Contest Request" in the lower left of your envelope. Judging by a panel of 4 selected from the staff of the Institute of Children's Literature. "We acquire First North American Serial Rights (to print the winner in *Children's Writer*), after which all rights revert to author." Open to any writer. Entries are judged on age targeting, originality, quality of writing and, for nonfiction, how well the information is conveyed and accuracy. "Submit clear photocopies only, not originals; submission will *not* be returned. Manuscripts should be typed double-spaced. No pieces containing violence or derogatory, racist or sexist language or situations will be accepted, at the sole discretion of the judges."

CHILDREN'S WRITERS FICTION CONTEST

Stepping Stones, P.O. Box 601721, Miami Beach FL 33160. (305)944-6491. E-mail: williams872@earthlink.net. **Director:** V.R. Williams. Annual contest. Estab. 1993. Purpose of contest: to promote writing for children by giving children's writers an opportunity to submit work in competition. Unpublished submissions only. Submissions made by the author. Deadline for entries: August 31. SASE for contest rules and entry forms. Entry fee is $10. Awards cash prize, certificate; certificates for Honorable Mention. Judging by Williams, Walters & Associates. First rights to winning material acquired or purchased. Requirements for entrants: Work must be suitable for children and no longer than 1,500 words. Send SASE for list of winners. "Stories should have believable characters. Work submitted on colored paper, in book format, illustrated, or with photograph attached is not acceptable."

🅝 CHRISTIAN BOOK AWARDS

Evangelical Christian Publishers Assocation, 9633 South 48th Street, Suite 140, Phoenix, AZ 85044. (480)966-3998. Fax: (480)966-1944. E-mail: info@ecpa.org. Web site: www.ecpa.org. **President:** Mark W. Kuyper. Annual award. Established 1978. Categories include Children & Youth. "All entries must be evangelical in nature and cannot be contrary to ECPA's Statement of Faith (stated in official rules)." Deadline for entry: January (see Web site for specific date). Guidelines available on Web site in October. "The work must be submitted by an ECPA member publisher." Awards a Christian Book Award plaque.

COLORADO BOOK AWARDS

1490 Lafayette Street, Suite 101, Denver CO 80218. (303)894-7951, ext. 21. Fax: (303) 864-9361, E-mail: bookawardinfo@coloradohumanities.org. Web site: www.coloradocenterforthebook.org. Annual award established 1993. Previously published submissions only. Submissions are made by the author, author's agent, nominated by a person or group of people. Requires Colorado residency by author, illustrator, photographer, editor, or other major contributor. Deadline for entries: March 15. Entry fee is $50. Awards $250 and plaque. Judging by a panel of literary agents, booksellers and librarians. See Web site for complete contest guidelines and entry form.

THE COMMONWEALTH CLUB'S BOOK AWARDS CONTEST

The Commonwealth Club of California, 595 Market St., San Francisco CA 94105. (415)597-4846. Fax: (415)597-6729. E-mail: blane@commonwealthclub.org. Web site: www.commonwealthclub.org/bookawards. **Contact:** Barbara Lane. Chief Executive Officer: Gloria Duffy. Annual contest. Estab. 1932. Purpose of contest: the encouragement and production of literature in California. Juvenile categories included. Previously published submissions; must be published from January 1 to December 31, previous to contest year. Deadline for entries: January 31. SASE for contest rules and entry forms. No entry fee. Awards gold and silver medals. Judging by the Book Awards Jury. The contest is only open to California writers/illustrators (must have been resident of California when ms was accepted for publication). "The award winners will be honored at the Annual Book Awards Program." Winning entries are displayed at awards program and advertised in newsletter.

CRICKET LEAGUE

Cricket magazine, P.O. Box 300, 315 Fifth St., Peru IL 61354. (815)224-5803 ext 633. Web site: www.cricketmag.com/cricketleague.htm. Address entries to: Cricket League. **Open to students.** Monthly contest. Estab. 1973. "The purpose of Cricket League contests is to encourage creativity and give young people an opportunity to express themselves in writing, drawing, painting or photography. There is a contest each month. Possible categories include story, poetry, or art. Each contest relates to a *specific theme* described on each *Cricket* issue's Cricket League page. Signature verifying originality, age and address of entrant and permission to publish required. Entries which do not relate to the current month's theme cannot be considered." Unpublished submissions only. Deadline for entries: the 25th of each month. Cricket League rules, contest theme, and submission deadline information can be found in the current issue of *Cricket* and via Web site. "We prefer that children who enter the contests subscribe to the magazine or that they read *Cricket* in their school or library." No entry fee. Awards certificate suitable for framing and children's books or art/writing supplies. Judging by *Cricket* editors. Obtains right to print prizewinning entries in magazine. Refer to contest rules in current *Cricket* issue. Winning entries are published on the Cricket League pages in the *Cricket* magazine 3 months subsequent to the issue in which the contest was announced. Current theme, rules, and prizewinning entries also posted on the Web site.

DELACORTE DELL YEARLING CONTEST FOR A FIRST MIDDLE-GRADE NOVEL

Delacorte Press, Random House, Inc., 1745 Broadway, 9th Floor, New York NY 10019. Estab. 1992. Web site: www.randomhouse.com/kids/writingcontests/#middlegrade. Annual award. Purpose of the award: to encourage the writing of fiction for children ages 9-12, either contemporary or historical; to encourage unpublished writers in the field of middle grade fiction. Unpublished submissions only. No simultaneous submissions. Length: between 96-160 pages. Submissions made by author only. Must not be out with an agent. Entries should be postmarked between April 1 and June 30. Letter sized SASE for notification. Because of new postal regulations no manuscripts can be returned. No entry fee. Awards a $1,500 cash prize plus a hardcover and paperback book contract with a $7,500 advance against a royalties to be negotiated. Judging by Delacorte Press Books for Young Readers editorial staff. Open to U.S. and Canadian writers who have not previously published a novel for middle-grade readers (ages 9-12).

DELACORTE PRESS CONTEST FOR A FIRST YOUNG ADULT NOVEL

Delacorte Press, Books for Young Readers Department, 1745 Broadway, 9th Floor, New York NY 10019. Web site: www.randomhouse.com/kids/writingcontests. Annual award. Estab. 1982. Purpose of award: to encourage the writing of contemporary young adult fiction (for readers ages 12-18). Previously unpublished submissions only. Manuscripts sent to Delacorte Press may not be submitted to other publishers while under consideration for the prize. Entries must be submitted between October 1 and December 31. Length: between 100-224 pages. No entry fee. Awards a $1,500 cash prize and a $7,500 advance against royalties for world rights on a hardcover and paperback book contract. Works published in an upcoming Delacorte Press, an imprint of Random House, Inc., Books for Young Readers list. Judged by the editors of the Books for Young Readers Department of Delacorte Press. Requirements for entrants: The writer must be American or Canadian and must not have previously published a young adult novel but may have published anything else. Foreign-language mss and translations and mss submitted to a previous Delacorte Press are not eligible. Send SASE for notification. Guidelines are also available on our Web site.

MARGARET A. EDWARDS AWARD

50 East Huron St., Chicago IL 60611-2795. (312)280-4390 or (800)545-2433. Fax: (312)280-5276. E-mail: yalsa@ ala.org. Web site: www.ala.org/yalsa/edwards. Annual award administered by the Young Adult Library Services Association (YALSA) of the American Library Association (ALA) and sponsored by *School Library Journal* magazine. Purpose of award: ''ALA's Young Adult Library Services Association (YALSA), on behalf of librarians who work with young adults in all types of libraries, will give recognition to those authors whose book or books have provided young adults with a window through which they can view their world and which will help them to grow and to understand themselves and their role in relationships, society and the world.'' Previously published submissions only. Nomination form is available on the YALSA Web site. No entry fee. Judging by members of the Young Adult Library Services Association. Deadline for entry: December 1. ''The award will be given annually to an author whose book or books, over a period of time, have been accepted by young adults as an authentic voice that continues to illuminate their experiences and emotions, giving insight into their lives. The book or books should enable them to understand themselves, the world in which they live, and their relationship with others and with society. The book or books must be in print at the time of the nomination.''

DOROTHY CANFIELD FISHER CHILDREN'S BOOK AWARD

Vermont Department of Libraries, Northeast Regional Library, 23 Tilton Rd., St. Johnsbury VT 05819. (802)828-6954. Fax: (802)828-2199. E-mail: grace.greene@dol.state.vt.us. Web site: www.dcfaward.org. **Chair:** Steve Madden. Annual award. Estab. 1957. Purpose of the award: to encourage Vermont children to become enthusiastic and discriminating readers by providing them with books of good quality by living American or Canadian authors published in the current year. Deadline for entries: December of year book was published. SASE for award rules and entry forms or e-mail. No entry fee. Awards a scroll presented to the winning author at an award ceremony. Judging is by the children grades 4-8. They vote for their favorite book. Requirements for entrants: ''Titles must be original work, published in the United States, and be appropriate to children in grades 4 through 8. The book must be copyrighted in the current year. It must be written by an American author living in the U.S. or Canda, or a Canadian author living in Canada or the U.S.''

🔲 THE NORMA FLECK AWARD FOR CANADIAN CHILDREN'S NONFICTION

The Canadian Children's Book Centre, 40 Orchard View Blvd., Suite 101, Toronto ON M4R 1B9 Canada. (416)975-0010. Fax: (416)975-8970. E-mail: info@bookcentre.ca. Web site: www.bookcentre.ca. **Contact:** Shannon Howe, program coordinator. The Norma Fleck Award was established by the Fleck Family Foundation in May 1999 to honor the life of Norma Marie Fleck, and to recognize exceptional Canadian nonfiction books for young people. Publishers are welcome to nominate books using the online form. Offered annually for books published between May 1, 2006, and April 30, 2007. Open to Canadian citizens or landed immigrants. The jury will always include at least 3 of the following: a teacher, a librarian, a bookseller, and a reviewer. A juror will have a deep understanding of, and some involvement with, Canadian children's books. The Canadian Children's Book Centre will select the jury members. **Deadline: March 31 (annually).** Prize: $10,000 goes to the author (unless 40% or more of the text area is composed of original illustrations, in which case the award will be divided equally between the author and the artist).

FLICKER TALE CHILDREN'S BOOK AWARD

Flicker Tale Award Committee, North Dakota Library Association, Mandan Public Library, 609 West Main St., Mandan ND 58554. Web site: www.ndla.info/ftaward.htm. **Contact:** Kelly Loftis. Estab. 1979. Purpose of award: to give children across the state of North Dakota a chance to vote for their book of choice from a nominated list of 20: 4 in the picture book category; 4 in the intermediate category; 4 in the juvenile category (for more advanced readers); 4 in the upper grage level non-fiction category. Also, to promote awareness of quality literature for children. Previously published submissions only. Submissions nominated by librarians and teachers across the state of North Dakota. Awards a plaque from North Dakota Library Association and banquet dinner. Judging by children in North Dakota. Entry deadline in June.

FLORIDA STATE WRITING COMPETITION

Florida Freelance Writers Association, P.O. Box A, North Stratford NH 03590. (603)922-8338. Fax: (603)922-8339. E-mail: contest@writers-editors.com. Web site: www.writers-editors.com. **Executive Director:** Dana K. Cassell. Annual contest. Estab. 1984. Categories include children's literature (length appropriate to age category). Entry fee is $5 (members), $10 (nonmembers) or $10-20 for entries longer than 3,000 words. Awards $100 first prize, $75 second prize, $50 third prize, certificates for honorable mentions. Judging by teachers, editors and published authors. Judging criteria: interest and readability within age group, writing style and mechanics, originality, salability. Deadline: March 15. For copy of official entry form, send #10 SASE or visit Web site. List of winners on Web site.

DON FREEMAN MEMORIAL GRANT-IN-AID

Society of Children's Book Writers and Illustrators, 8271 Beverly Blvd., Los Angeles CA 90048. E-mail: scbwi@scbwi.org. Web site: www.scbwi.org. Estab. 1974. Purpose of award: to "enable picture book artists to further their understanding, training and work in the picture book genre." Applications and prepared materials are available in October and must be postmarked between February 1 and March 1. Grant awarded and announced in August. SASE for award rules and entry forms. SASE for return of entries. No entry fee. Annually awards one grant of $1,500 and one runner-up grant of $500. "The grant-in-aid is available to both full and associate members of the SCBWI who, as artists, seriously intend to make picture books their chief contribution to the field of children's literature."

FRIENDS OF THE AUSTIN PUBLIC LIBRARY AWARD FOR BEST CHILDREN'S AND BEST YOUNG ADULT'S BOOK

Web site: www.smu.edu/english/creativewriting/The_Texas_Institute_of_Letters.htm. Offered annually for work published January 1-December 31 of previous year to recognize the best book for children and young people. Writer must have been born in Texas or have lived in the state for at least 2 consecutive years at one time, or the subject matter must be associated with the state. See Web site for information on eligibility, deadlines, and the judges names and addresses to whom the books should be sent. Prize: $500 for each award winner.

THEODOR SEUSS GEISEL AWARD

Association for Library Service to Children, Division of the American Library Association, 50 E. Huron, Chicago IL 60611.(312)280-2163. E-mail: alsc@ala.org. Web site: www.ala.org. The Theodor Seuss Geisel Award, established in 2004, is given annually beginning in 2006 to the author(s) and illustrator(s) of the most distinguished contribution to the body of American children's literature known as beginning reader books published in the United States during the preceding year. The award is to recognize the author(s) and illustrator(s) of a beginning reader book who demonstrate great creativity and imagination in his/her/their literary and artistic achievements to engage children in reading. The award is named for the world-renowned children's author, Theodor Geisel. "A person's a person no matter how small," Theodor Geisel, a.k.a. Dr. Seuss, would say. "Children want the same things we want: to laugh, to be challenged, to be entertained and delighted." Brilliant, playful and always respectful of children, Dr. Seuss charmed his way into the consciousness of four generations of youngsters and parents. In the process, he helped them to read.

◪ AMELIA FRANCES HOWARD GIBBON AWARD FOR ILLUSTRATION

Canadian Library Association, 328 Frank St., Ottawa ON K2P 0X8 Canada. (613)232-9625. Web site: www.cla.ca. **Contact:** Chairperson, Canadian Association of Children's Librarians. Annual award. Estab. 1971. Purpose of the award: "to honor excellence in the illustration of children's book(s) in Canada. To merit consideration the book must have been published in Canada and its illustrator must be a Canadian citizen or a permanent resident of Canada." Previously published submissions only; must be published between January 1 and December 31 of the previous year. Deadline for entries: December 31. SASE for award rules. Entries not returned. No entry fee. Judging by selection committee of members of Canadian Association of Children's Librarians. Requirements for entrants: illustrator must be Canadian or Canadian resident.

GOLDEN KITE AWARDS

Society of Children's Book Writers and Illustrators, 8271 Beverly Blvd., Los Angeles CA 90048. (323)782-1010. E-mail: scbwi@scbwi.org. Web site: www.scbwi.org. **Contact:** SCBWI Golden Kite Coordinator. Annual award. Estab. 1973. "The works chosen will be those that the judges feel exhibit excellence in writing, and in the case of the picture-illustrated books—in illustration, and genuinely appeal to the interests and concerns of children. For the fiction and nonfiction awards, original works and single-author collections of stories or poems of which at least half are new and never before published in book form are eligible—anthologies and translations are not. For the picture-illustration awards, the art or photographs must be original works (the texts—which may be fiction or nonfiction—may be original, public domain or previously published). Deadline for entries: December 15. SASE for award rules. No entry fee. Awards, in addition to statuettes and plaques, the four winners receive $2,500 cash award plus trip to LA SCBWI Conference. Editors of four winning books receive $1,000 cash award. The panel of judges will consist of professional authors, illustrators, editors or agents." Requirements for entrants: "must be a member of SCBWI and books must be published in that year." Winning books will be displayed at national conference in August. Books to be entered, as well as further inquiries, should be submitted to: The Society of Children's Book Writers and Illustrators, above address.

GOVERNOR GENERAL'S LITERARY AWARD FOR CHILDREN'S LITERATURE

Canada Council for the Arts, 350 Albert St., P.O. Box 1047, Ottawa ON K1P 5V8 Canada. (613)566-4414, ext. 5576. Fax: (613)566-4410. E-mail: caroline.lecours@canadacouncil.ca. Web site: www.canadacouncil.ca/prizes/ggla. Offered for work published September 1-September 30. Submissions in English must be published between September 1, 2005 and September 30, 2006; submissions in French between July 1, 2005 and June 30, 2006. Publishers submit titles for consideration. Deadline: March 15, June 1 and August 7, depending on the book's publication date. Prize: Each laureate receives $15,000; nonwinning finalists receive $1,000.

GUIDEPOSTS YOUNG WRITERS CONTEST

Guideposts, 16 E. 34th St., New York NY 10016. (212)251-8100. E-mail: ywcontest@guideposts.org. Web site: gp4teens.com. Offered annually for unpublished high school juniors and seniors. Stories "needn't be about a highly dramatic situation, but it should record an experience that affected you and deeply changed you. Remember, *Guideposts* stories are true, not fiction, and they show how faith in God has made a specific difference in a person's life. We accept submissions after announcement is placed in the October issue each year. If the manuscript is place, we require all rights to the story in that version." Open only to high school juniors or seniors. Deadline: November 24. Prize: 1st Place: $10,000; 2nd Place: $8,000; 3rd Place: $6,000; 4th Place: $4,000; 5th Place: $3,000; 6th-10th Place: $1,000; 11th-20th Place: $250 gift certificate for college supplies.

THE MARILYN HALL AWARDS FOR YOUTH THEATRE

Beverly Hills Theatre Guild, P.O. Box 39729, Los Angeles CA 90039-0729. Web site: www.beverlyhillstheatreguild.org. **Contact:** Dick Dotterer. **Open to students.** Annual contest. Estab. 1998/99. Purpose of contest: "To encourage the creation and development of new plays for youth theatre." Unpublished submissions only. Authors must be U.S. citizens or legal residents and must sign entry form personally. Deadline for entries: between January 15 and last day of February each year (postmark accepted). Playwrights may submit up to two scripts. One nonprofessional production acceptable for eligibility. SASE for contest rules and entry forms. No entry fee. Awards: $500, 1st prize; $300, 2nd prize; $200, 3rd prize. Judging by theatre professionals cognizant of youth theatre and writing/producing.

HIGHLIGHTS FOR CHILDREN FICTION CONTEST

803 Church St., Honesdale PA 18431-1895. (570)253-1080. Fax: (570)251-7847. Web site: www.highlights.com. **Fiction Contest Editor:** Christine French Clark. Annual contest. Estab. 1980. Purpose of the contest: to stimulate interest in writing for children and reward and recognize excellence. Unpublished submissions only. Deadline for entries: February 28; entries accepted after January 1 only. SASE for contest rules and return of entries. No entry fee. Awards 3 prizes of $1,000 each in cash and a pewter bowl (or, at the winner's election, attendance at the Highlights Foundation Writers Workshop at Chautauqua) and a pewter bowl. Judging by a panel of *Highlights* editors and outside judges. Winning pieces are purchased for the cash prize of $1,000 and published in *Highlights*; other entries are considered for purchase at regular rates. Requirements for entrants: open to any writer 16 years of age or older. Winners announced in June. Length up to 800 words. Stories for beginning

readers should not exceed 500 words. Stories should be consistent with *Highlights* editorial requirements. No violence, crime or derogatory humor. Send SASE or visit Web site for guidelines and current theme.

ⓃN THE MARILYN HOLINSHEAD VISITING SCHOLARS FELLOWSHIP

Kerlan Grant-in-Aid, University of Minnesota, 113 Anderson Library, 222 21st Ave. South, Minneapolis MN 55455. E-mail: circ@umn.edu. Web site: http://special.lib.umn.edu/clrc/kerlan/index.php. This fellowship provides grants-in-aid for travel to the Kerlan Collection. These grants will be available for research study in 2007. The Kerlan Collection is one of the world's finest research collections in children's literature and contains over 100,000 books and original art and manuscript material for approximately 16,000 titles. For more information about our holdings, please visit the Kerlan Collection's Web site. Applicants may request up to $1,500. Send a letter with the proposed purpose, a plan to use specific research materials (manuscripts and art), dates, and budget (including airfare and per diem) to above address. The deadline for receipt of all materials is December 30, 2007. Travel and a written report on the project must be completed and submitted in 2008.

HRC SHOWCASE THEATRE

Hudson River Classics, Inc., P.O. Box 940, Hudson NY 12534. "(518)851 7244." Fax: "none" . E-mail: jangrice20 02@yahoo.com. **President:** Jan M. Grice. Annual contest. Estab. 1992. HRCs Showcase Theatre is a not-for-profit professional theater company dedicated to the advancement of performing in the Hudson River Valley area through reading of plays and providing opportunities for new playwrights. Unpublished submissions only. Submissions made by author and by the author's agent. Deadlines for entries: May 1st. SASE for contest rules and entry forms. Entry fee is $5. Awards $500 cash plus concert reading by professional actors. Judging by panel selected by Board of Directors. Requirements for entrants: Entrants must live in the northeastern U.S.

IMPRINT OF MIDLAND COMMUNITY THEATRE

Midland Community Theatre, 2000 W. Wadley, Midland TX 79705. (432)682-2544. Fax: (432)682-6136. E-mail: mclaren@mctmidland.org. Web site: www.mctmidland.org. **Chair :** William Payne. Estab. 1989. Open to students. Annual contest. Purpose of conference: "The McLaren Memorial Comedy Play Writing Competition was established in 1989 to honor long-time MCT volunteer Mike McLaren who loved a good comedy, whether he was on stage or in the front row." Unpublished submissions only. Submissions made by author. Deadline for entries: January 31st (scripts are accepted from December 1st through January 31st each year). SASE for contest rules and entry forms. Entry fee is $10 per script. Awards $400 for full-length winner and $200 for one-act winner as well as staged readings for 3 finalists in each category. Judging by the audience present at the McLaren festival when the staged readings are performed. Rights to winning material acquired or purchased. 1st right of production or refusal is acquired by MCT. Requirements for entrants: "Yes, the contest is open to *any* playwright, but the play submitted must be unpublished and never produced in a for-profit setting. One previous production in a *nonprofit* theatre is acceptable. 'Readings' do not count as productions."

INSIGHT WRITING CONTEST

Insight Magazine, 55 W. Oak Ridge Dr., Hagerstown MD 21740-7390. Web site: www.insightmagazine.org. **Open to students.** Annual contest. Unpublished submissions only. Submissions made by author. Deadline for entries: June. SASE for contest rules and entry forms. Awards first prizes, $ 100-250; second prizes, $75-200; third prizes, $50-150. Winning entries will be published in *Insight*. Contest includes three catagories: Student Short Story, General Short Story and Student Poetry. You must be age 22 or under to enter the student catagories. Entries must include cover sheet form available with SASE or on Web site.

IRA CHILDREN'S BOOK AWARDS

International Reading Association, 800 Barksdale Rd., P.O. Box 8139, Newark DE 19714-8139. (302)731-1600. Fax: (302)731-1057. E-mail: exec@reading.org. Web site: www.reading.org. Annual award. Awards are given for an author's first or second published book for fiction and nonfiction in three categories: primary (ages preschool-8), intermediate (ages 9-13), and young adult (ages 14-17). This award is intended for newly published authors who show unusual promise in the children's book field. Deadline for entries: November 1. Awards $500. For guidelines write or e-mail exec@reading.org.

JOSEPH HENRY JACKSON AND JAMES D. PHELAN LITERARY AWARDS

Sponsored by The San Francisco Foundation. Administered by Intersection for the Arts, 446 Valencia St., San Francisco CA 94103. (415)626-2787. Fax: (415)626-1636. Web site: www.theintersection.org/resource_awards. php. Submit entries to Awards Coordinator. **Open to Students.** Annual award. Estab. 1937. Purpose of award: to encourage young writers for an unpublished manuscript-in-progress. Submissions must be unpublished. Submissions made by author. Deadline for entry: March 31. SASE for contest rules and entry forms. Judging by established peers. All applicants must be 20-35 years of age. Applicants for the Henry Jackson Award must be residents of northern California or Nevada for 3 consecutive years immediately prior to the January 31 deadline. Applicants for the James D. Phelan awards must have been born in California but need not be current residents.

THE EZRA JACK KEATS NEW WRITER AND NEW ILLUSTRATOR AWARDS

Ezra Jack Keats Foundation/Administered by The Office of Children's Services, The New York Public Library, 455 Fifth Ave., New York NY 10016. (212)340-0906. Fax: (612)626-0377. E-mail: mtice@nypl.org. Web site: www.ezra-jack-keats.org. **Program Coordinator:** Margaret Tice. Annual awards. Purpose of the awards: ''The awards will be given to a promising new writer of picture books for children and a promising new illustrator of picture books for children. Selection criteria include books for children (ages 9 and under) that reflect the tradition of Ezra Jack Keats. These books portray: the universal qualities of childhood, strong and supportive family and adult relationships, the multicultural nature of our world.'' Submissions made by the publisher. Must be published in the preceding year. Deadline for entries: mid-December. SASE for contest rules and entry forms or email Margaret Tice at mtice@nypl.org. No entry fee. Awards $1,000 coupled with Ezra Jack Keats Bronze Medal. Judging by a panel of experts. ''The author or illustrator should have published no more than 3 children's books. Entries are judged on the outstanding features of the text, complemented by illustrations. Candidates need not be both author and illustrator. Entries should carry a 2006 copyright (for the 2007 award).'' Winning books and authors to be presented at reception at The New York Public Library.

EZRA JACK KEATS/KERLAN COLLECTION MEMORIAL FELLOWSHIP

Ezra Jack Keats/Kerlan Collection, Memorial Fellowship Committee, 113 Andersen Library, 222 21st Avenue South, University of Minnesota, Minneapolis, MN 55455. Web site: http://special.lib.umn.edu/clrc/kerlan/awards.php. This fellowship from the Ezra Jack Keats Foundation will provide $1,500 to a ''talented writer and/or illustrator of children's books who wishes to use the Kerlan Collection for the furtherance of his or her artistic development.'' Special consideration will be given to someone who would find it difficult to finance a visit to the Kerlan Collection. The Ezra Jack Keats Fellowship recipient will receive transportation costs and a per diem allotment. Applications for 2007 must be postmarked by December 30, 2006. For digital application materials, please visit Web site. For paper copies of the application send a large (6×9 or 9×12) self- addressed envelope with 87¢; postage envelope to above address.

KENTUCKY BLUEGRASS AWARD

Kentucky Reading Association, %Melissa Schutt, Eastern Kentucky University Libraries, Richmond KY 40475. (859)622- 6595. Fax: (859)622-1174. E-mail: melissa.schutt@eku.edu. Web site: www.kyreading.org. **Award Director:** Melissa Schutt. Submit entries to: Melissa Schutt. Annual award. Estab. 1983. Purpose of award: to promote readership among young children and young adolescents. Also to recognize exceptional creative efforts of authors and illustrators. Previously published submissions only. Submissions made by author, made by author's agent, nominated by teachers or librarians. Must be published no more than 3 years prior to the award year. Deadline for entries: March 15. Contest rules and entry forms are available from the Web site. No entry fee. Awards a framed certificate and invitation to be recognized at the annual luncheon of the Kentucky Bluegrass Award. Judging by children who participate through their schools or libraries. ''Books are reviewed by a panel of teachers and librarians before they are placed on a Master List for the year. These books must have been published within a three year period prior to the review. Winners are chosen from this list of preselected books. Books are divided into four divisions, K-2, 3-5, 6-8, 9-12 grades. Winners are chosen by children who either read the books or have the books read to them. Children from the entire state of Kentucky are involved in the selection of the annual winners for each of the divisions.''

CORETTA SCOTT KING AWARD

Coretta Scott King Committee, Ethnic and Multicultural Information Exchange Round Table, American Library Association, 50 E. Huron St., Chicago IL 60611. (312)280-4297. Fax: (312)280-3256. E-mail: olos@ala.org. Web site: www.ala.org/csk. The Coretta Scott King Award is an annual award for books (1 for text and 1 for illustration) that convey the spirit of brotherhood espoused by Martin Luther King, Jr.—and also speak to the Black experience—for young people. There is an award jury of children's librarians that judges the books— reviewing over the year—and making a decision in January. A copy of an entry must be sent to each juror by December 1 of the juried year. A copy of the jury list can be found on Web site. Call or e-mail ALA Office for Literary Services for jury list. Awards breakfast held on Tuesday morning during A.L.A. Annual Conference. See schedule at Web site.

N LA BELLE LETTRE SHORT STORY CONTEST

La Belle Lettre, P.O. Box 2009, Longview WA 98632. E-mail: admin@labellelettre.com. Web site: www.labellelettre.com. **Executive Director:** Jennifer Hill. Contest offered seasonally—spring, summer, fall and winter. ''La

Resources

Bell Lettre's mission in sponsoring these contests is to provide encouragement and support to writers. We aim to be a bridge to authors' literary accomplishments. Therefore (in addition to monetary awards for 1st, 2nd, and 3rd place) The 1st, 2nd, and 3rd place entries, three Honorable Mentions, and three submssions drawn at random will all receive critiques." Unpublished submissions only. Deadlines remain the same from year to year: May 1, August 1, November 1, February 1. Themes changes yearly. 2007 themes were: May1—Children's Short Story; August 1—Memoir/Personal Essay; November 1—Holiday Fiction/Nonfiction; February 1—Romance. Guidelines available on Web site. "Writers may also contact us vis "Contact Us" on our Web site." Entry fee is $6. Awards (in 2007): 1st place—$150 plus critique; 2nd place—$75 plus critique; 3rd place—$50 plus critique. Judging by Jennifer Hill, executive director and Mary Stone, assistant director. "Future judges may include other published authors. Writers retain all rights to submitted material. Contest are open to any/all writers. International writers may entry fees via PayPal, although entries must be submitted by mail."

LONGMEADOW JOURNAL LITERARY COMPETITION

c/o Rita and Robert Morton, 6750 N. Longmeadow, Lincolnwood IL 60712. (312)726-9789. Fax: (312)726-9772. **Contest Directors:** Rita and Robert Morton. Competition **open to students** (anyone age 10-19). Held annually and published every year. Estab. 1986. Purpose of contest: to encourage the young to write. Submissions are made by the author, nominated by a person or group of people, by teachers, librarians or parents. Deadline for entries: June 30. SASE. No entry fee. Awards first place, $175; second place, $100; and five prizes of $50. Judging by Rita Morton and Robert Morton. Works are published every year and are distributed to teachers and librarians and interested parties at no charge.

LOUISE LOUIS/EMILY F. BOURNE STUDENT POETRY AWARD

Poetry Society of America, 15 Gramercy Park South, New York NY 10003-1705. (212)254-9628. Fax: (212)673-2352. E-mail: eve@poetrysociety.org. Web site: www.poetrysociety.org. **Contact:** Program Director. **Open to students.** Annual award. Purpose of the award: award is for the best unpublished poem by a high or preparatory school student (grades 9-12) from the U.S. and its territories. Unpublished submissions only. Deadline for entries: Oct. 1 to Dec. 22. SASE for award rules and entry forms. Entries not returned. "High schools can send an unlimited number of submissions with one entry per individual student for a flat fee of $20. (High school students may send a single entry for $5.)" Award: $250. Judging by a professional poet. Requirements for entrants: Award open to all high school and preparatory students from the U.S. and its territories. School attended, as well as name and address, should be noted. PSA submission guidelines must be followed. These are printed in our fall calendar on our Web site and are readily available if those interested send us a SASE. Line limit: none. "The award-winning poem will be included in a sheaf of poems that will be part of the program at the award ceremony and sent to all PSA members."

MCLAREN MEMORIAL COMEDY PLAY WRITING COMPETITION

Midland Community Theatre, Inc., 2000 W. Wadley, Midland TX 79705.(432)682-2554. Web site: www.mctmidl and.org. **Contact:** William Payne. Annual competition. Accepts submissions in 2 division: one-act and full-length. Accepts submissions January 1, through the last day of Februrary for 2008 competition. Entries must be comedies for adults, teens or children; musical comedies not accepted. Work must never have been produced professionally or published. See Web site for competitions guidelines and required brochure with entry form. Entry fee: $15/script. Awards $400 for winning full-length play; $200 for winning one-act play; staged reading for full-length finalists. Winning one-act play will be presented in workshop format.

THE VICKY METCALF AWARD FOR CHILDREN'S LITERATURE

The Writers' Trust of Canada, 90 Richmond St. E., Suite 200, Toronto ON M5C 1P1 Canada. (416)504-8222. Fax: (416)504-9090. E-mail: info@writerstrust.com. Web site: www.writerstrust.com. **Contact:** James Davies. The Vicky Metcalf Award is presented each spring to a Canadian writer for a body of work in children's literature at The Writers' Trust Awards event in Toronto. Prize: $15,000. Open to Canadian residents only.

MILKWEED PRIZE FOR CHILDREN'S LITERATURE

Milkweed Editions, 1011 Washington Ave. S., Suite 300, Minneapolis MN 55415-1246. (612)332-3192. Fax: (612)215-2550. E-mail: editor@milkweed.org. Web site: www.milkweed.org. **Award Director:** Daniel Slager, editor-in-chief. Annual award. Estab. 1993. Purpose of the award: to recognize an outstanding literary novel for readers ages 8-13 and encourage writers to turn their attention to readers in this age group. Unpublished submissions only "in book form." Please send SASE or visit Web site for award guidelines. The prize is awarded to the best work for children ages 8-13 that Milkweed agrees to publish in a calendar year by a writer not previously published by Milkweed. The Prize consists of a $10,000 advance against royalties agreed to at the time of acceptance. Submissions must follow our usual children's guidelines.

MINNESOTA BOOK AWARDS

The Friends of the Saint Paul Public Library, 325 Cedar Street, Suite 555, Saint Paul, MN 55101. (651)222-3242. Fax: (651)222-1988. E-mail: mnbookawards@thefriends.org; friends@thefriends.org. Web site: www.thefriends.org. **Contact:** Stu Wilson or Ann Nelson. Annual award, established 1988. Purpose of contest: To recognize and honor achievement by members of Minnesota's book community. To be eligible for a Minnesota Book Award, a book must be the work of a Minnesota writer, or primary artistic creator such as an illustrator, anthology editor or photographer whose work is integral to the project. Current Minnesota residents are eligible, as are individuals engaged in ongoing literary work in the state and authors whose personal history, identity, or literary work reflect a strong Minnesota influence. Books may be submitted by anyone willing to pay the entry fee and provide the reading copies requested. This includes but is not limited to a book's author, illustrator, publisher, or agent. An entry fee of $30 per title is required. Each entry must include five non-returnable copies of the entered book, and must be professionally published and assigned an ISBN (Fine Press excepted). Work must hold copyright from the year previous to that in which award is given (2007 copyright for 2008 award). Deadline for entries: December. Cash and fine art trophy awards to winners. Judging is done by members of Minnesota's book community: librarians, booksellers, teachers and scholars, writers, reviewers and publishers. The Minnesota Book Awards includes 8 categories-Autobiography, Memoir & Creative Nonfiction; Children's Literature; Fine Press; General Nonfiction; Genre Fiction; Novel & Short Story; Poetry; Young Adult Literature; and a Readers' Choice Award. For complete guidelines, visit the Web site.

NATIONAL CHILDREN'S THEATRE FESTIVAL

Actors' Playhouse at the Miracle Theatre, 280 Miracle Mile, Coral Gables FL 33134. (305)444-9293, ext. 615. Fax: (305)444-4181. E-mail: maulding@actorsplayhouse.org. Web site: www.actorsplayhouse.org. **Director:** Earl Maulding. **Open to students.** Annual contest. Estab. 1994. Purpose of contest: to bring together the excitement of the theater arts and the magic of young audiences through the creation of new musical works and to create a venue for playwrights/composers to showcase their artistic products. Submissions must be unpublished. Submissions are made by author or author's agent. Deadline for entries: May 1 annually. Visit Web site or send SASE for contest rules and entry forms. Entry fee is $10. Awards: first prize of $500, full production, and transportation to Festival weekend based on availability. Final judges are of national reputation. Past judges include Joseph Robinette, Moses Goldberg and Luis Santeiro.

NATIONAL FOUNDATION FOR ADVANCEMENT IN THE ARTS

youngARTS, 444 Brickell Ave., P-14, Miami FL 33131. (305)377-1140. Fax: (305)377-1149. E-mail: info@nfaa.org. Web site: www.youngARTS.org. **Contact:** Carla Hill. **Open to students/high school seniors or other 17- and 18-year-olds.** Created to recognize and reward outstanding accomplishment in *cinematic arts, dance, jazz, music, photography, theater, voice, visual arts and/or writing.* youngARTS is an innovative national program of the National Foundation for Advancement in the Arts (NFAA). Established in 1981, youngARTS touches the lives of gifted young people across the country, providing financial support, scholarships and goal-oriented artistic, educational and career opportunities. Each year, from a pool of more than 8,000 applicants, an average of 800 youngARTS winners are chosen for NFAA support by panels of distinguished artists and educators. Deadline for registration: June 1 (early) and October 1. Deadline for submission of work: Nov. 5. Entry fee is $35(online)/40(paper). Fee waivers available based on need. Awards $100-10,000—unrestricted cash grants. Judging by a panel of artists and educators recognized in the field. Rights to submitted/winning material: NFAA/ARTS retains the right to duplicate work in an anthology or in Foundation literature unless otherwise specified by the artist. Requirements for entrants: Artists must be high school seniors or, if not enrolled in high school, must be 17 or 18 years old. Applicants must be U.S. citizens or residents, unless applying in jazz. Literary and Visual works will be published in an anthology distributed during youngARTS Week in Miami when the final adjudication takes place. NFAA invites up to 150 finalists to participate in youngARTS Week in January in Miami-Dade County, Florida. youngARTS Week is a once-in-a-lifetime experience consisting of performances, master classes, workshops, readings, exhibits, and enrichment activities with renowned artists and arts educators. All expenses are paid by NFAA, including airfare, hotel, meals and ground transportation.

NATIONAL PEACE ESSAY CONTEST

United States Institute of Peace, 1200 17th St. NW, Washington DC 20036. (202)429-3854. Fax: (202)429-6063. E-mail: education@usip.org. Web site: www.usip.org. **Open to high school students.** Annual contest. Estab. 1987. "The contest gives students the opportunity to do valuable research, writing and thinking on a topic of importance to international peace and conflict resolution. Teaching guides are available for teachers who allow the contest to be used as a classroom assignment." Deadline for entries is February 1, 2007. "Interested students, teachers and others may write or call to receive free contest kits. Please do not include SASE." Guidelines and rules on Web site. No entry fee. State Level Awards are $1,000 college scholarships. National winners are selected from among the 1st place state winners. National winners receive scholarships in the following amounts: first place $10,000; second $5,000; third $2,500. National amount includes State Award. First place state winners invited to an expenses-paid awards program in Washington, DC in June. Judging is conducted by education professionals from across the country and by the Board of Directors of the United States Institute of Peace. "All submissions become property of the U.S. Institute of Peace to use at its discretion and without royalty or any limitation. Students grades 9-12 in the U.S., its territories and overseas schools may submit essays for review by completing the application process. U.S. citizenship required for students attending overseas schools. National winning essays will be published by the U.S. Institute of Peace."

NATIONAL WRITERS ASSOCIATION NONFICTION CONTEST

10940 S. Parker Rd., #508, Parker CO 80134. (303)841-0246. **Executive Director:** Sandy Whelchel. Annual contest. Estab. 1971. Purpose of contest: "to encourage and recognize those who excel in nonfiction writing." Submissions made by author. Deadline for entries: December 31. SASE for contest rules and entry forms. Entry fee is $18. Awards 3 cash prizes; choice of books; Honorable Mention Certificate. "Two people read each entry; third party picks three top winners from top five." Judging sheets sent if entry accompanied by SASE. Condensed version of 1st place published in *Authorship*.

NATIONAL WRITERS ASSOCIATION SHORT STORY CONTEST

10940 S. Parker Rd., #508, Parker CO 80134. (303)841-0246. **Executive Director:** Sandy Whelchel. Annual contest. Estab. 1971. Purpose of contest: "To encourage writers in this creative form and to recognize those who excel in fiction writing." Submissions made by the author. Deadline for entries: July 1. SASE for contest rules and entry forms. Entry fee is $15. Awards 3 cash prizes, choice of books and certificates for Honorable Mentions. Judging by "two people read each entry; third person picks top three winners." Judging sheet copies available for SASE.

THE NENE AWARD

Hawaii State Library, Honolulu HI 96813. (808)586-3510. Fax: (808)586-3584. E-mail: hslear@netra.lib.state.hi. us. Estab. 1964. "The Nene Award was designed to help the children of Hawaii become acquainted with the best contemporary writers of fiction, become aware of the qualities that make a good book and choose the best rather than the mediocre." Previously published submissions only. Books must have been copyrighted not more than 6 years prior to presentation of award. Work is nominated by students, teachers and librarians in Hawaii. Nominations by publishers or authors are not accepted. Ballots are usually due around the middle of March. Awards plaque to the winning author who is invited to an awards ceremony in Honolulu. Judging by the children of Hawaii in grades 4-6. Requirements for entrants: books must be fiction, written by a living author, copyrighted not more than 6 years ago and suitable for children in grades 4, 5 and 6. Current and past winners are displayed in all participating school and public libraries. The award winner is announced in May.

▦ NESTLÉ CHILDREN'S BOOK PRIZE

Booktrust, Book House, 45 East Hill, Wandsworth London SW18 2QZ United Kingdom. Fax: (00 44)20 8516 2978. E-mail: hannah@booktrust.org.uk. Web site: www.booktrusted.com. **Contact:** Rosa Anderson. "The Nestlé Children's Book Prize was established in 1985 to encourage high standards and stimulate interest in children's books. The prize is split into 3 age categories: 5 and under, 6-8, 9-11. The books are judged by our adult panel, who shortlist 3 outstanding books in each category, and the final decision of who gets Gold, Silver and Bronze is left to the young judges. The young judges are chosen from classes of school children who complete a task for their age category; the best 50 from each category go on to judge the 3 books in their age category. From the 150 classes who judge the books, 1 class from each category is invited to present the award at the ceremony in London. The children are chosen from projects they submit with their votes." Open to works of fiction or poetry for children written in English by a citizen of the UK, or an author residing in the UK. All work must be submitted by a UK publisher. Deadline: June. Prize: Gold Award winners in each age category: £2,500; Silver Award winners in each age category: £1,500; Bronze Award winners in each age category: £500.

NEW ENGLAND BOOK AWARDS

New England Booksellers Association, 1700 Massachusetts Ave., Suite 332, Cambridge MA 02140. (617)576-3070. Fax: (617)576-3091. E-mail: nan@neba.org. Web site: www.newenglandbooks.org/NE_awards.html. **Assistant Executive Director:** Nan Sorenson. Annual award. Estab. 1990. Purpose of award: "to promote New England authors who have produced a body of work that stands as a significant contribution to New England's culture and is deserving of wider recognition." Previously published submissions only. Submissions made by New England booksellers; publishers. "Award given to authors 'body of work' not a specific book." Entries must be still in print and available. No entry fee. Judging by NEBA membership. Requirements for entrants: Author/illustrator must live in New England. Submit written nominations only; actual books should not be sent. Member bookstores receive materials to display winners' books.

NEW VOICES AWARD

Lee & Low Books, 95 Madison Ave., New York NY 10016. (212)779-4400. Fax: (212)532-6035. E-mail: general@l eeandlow.com. Web site: www.leeandlow.com/editorial/voices.html. **Editor-in-chief:** Louise May. **Open to students.** Annual award. Estab. 2000. Purpose of contest: Lee & Low Books is one of the few publishing companies owned by people of color. We have published more than 75 first-time writers and illustrators. Titles include *In Daddy's Arms I Am Tall: African Americans Celebrating Fathers*, winner of the Coretta Scott King Illustrator Award; *Passage to Freedom: The Sugihara Story*, an American Library Association Notable Book; and *Crazy Horse's Vision*, a Bank Street College Children's Book of the Year. Submissions made by author. Deadline for entries: October 31. SASE for contest rules or visit Web site. No entry fee. Awards New Voices Award—$1,000 prize and standard publication contract (regardless of whether or not writer has an agent) along with an advance on royalties; New Voices Honor Award—$500 prize. Judging by Lee & Low editors. Restrictions of media for illustrators: The author must be a writer of color who is a resident of the U.S. and who has not previously published a children's picture book. For additional information, send SASE or visit Lee & Low's Web site, (www.leeandlow.com/editorial/voices8.html).

JOHN NEWBERY MEDAL

Association for Library Service to Children, Division of the American Library Association, 50 E. Huron, Chicago IL 60611. E-mail: alsc@ala.org. Web site: www.ala.org. **Executive Director, ALSC:** Diane Foote. Annual award. Estab. 1922. Purpose of award: to recognize the most distinguished contribution to American children's literature published in the U.S. Previously published submissions only; must be published prior to year award is given. Deadline for entries: December 31. SASE for award rules. Entries not returned. No entry fee. Medal awarded at Caldecott/Newbery banquet during ALA annual conference. Judging by Newbery Award Selection Committee.

NORTH AMERICAN INTERNATIONAL AUTO SHOW HIGH SCHOOL POSTER CONTEST

Detroit Auto Dealers Association, 1900 W. Big Beaver Rd., Troy MI 48084-3531. (248)643-0250. Fax: (248)283-5148. E-mail: sherp@dada.org. Web site: www.naias.com. **Contact:** Sandy Herp. **Open to students.** Annual contest. Submissions made by the author and illustrator. Contact D.A.D.A. for contest rules and entry forms or retrieve rules from Web site. No entry fee. Awards in the High School Poster Contest are as follows: Chairman's Award—$1,000; Designer's Best of Show (Digital and Traditional)—$500; Best Theme—$250; Best Use of Color—$250; Most Creative—$250. A winner will be chosen in each category from grades 10, 11 and 12. Prizes: 1st place in 10, 11, 12—$500; 2nd place—$250; 3rd place—$100. The winners of the Designer's Best of Show Digital and Traditional will each receive $500. The winner of the Chairman's Award will receive $1,000. Entries will be judged by an independent panel of recognized representatives of the art community. Entrants must be Michigan high school students enrolled in grades 10-12. Winning posters may be displayed at the NAIAS 2006 and reproduced in the official NAIAI program, which is available to the public, international media, corporate executives and automotive suppliers. Winning posters may also be displayed on the official NAIAS Web site at the sole discretion of the NAIAS.

OHIOANA BOOK AWARDS

Ohioana Library Association, 274 E. First Ave., Suite 300, Columbus OH 43201. (614)466-3831. Fax: (614)728-6974. E-mail: ohioana@sloma.state.oh.us. Web site: www.OHIOANA.org. **Director:** Linda R. Hengst. Annual award. "The Ohioana Book Awards are given to books of outstanding literary quality. Purpose of contest: to provide recognition and encouragement to Ohio writers and to promote the work of Ohio writers. Up to six are given each year. Awards may be given in the following categories: fiction, nonfiction, children's/juvenile, poetry and books about Ohio or an Ohioan. Books must be received by the Ohioana Library during the calendar year prior to the year the award is given and must have a copyright date within the last two calendar years." Deadline for entries: December 31. SASE for award rules and entry forms (or downloaded from Ohioana's Web site at www.ohioana.org/awards/books.asp). No entry fee. Winners receive citation and glass sculpture. "Any book that has been written or edited by a person born in Ohio or who has lived in Ohio for at least five years is eligible."

OKLAHOMA BOOK AWARDS

Oklahoma Center for the Book, 200 NE 18th, Oklahoma City OK 73105. (405)521-2502. Fax: (405)525-7804. E-mail: gcarlile@oltn.odl.state.ok.us. Web site: www.odl.state.ok.us/ocb. **Executive Director:** Glenda Carlile. Annual award. Estab. 1989. Purpose of award: "to honor Oklahoma writers and books about our state." Previously published submissions only. Submissions made by the author, author's agent, or entered by a person or group of people, including the publisher. Must be published during the calendar year preceding the award. Awards are presented to best books in fiction, nonfiction, children/young adult, poetry, design/illustration for books about Oklahoma or books written by an author who was born, is living or has lived in Oklahoma.

Deadline for entries: early January. SASE for award rules and entry forms. No entry fee. Awards a medal—no cash prize. Judging by a panel of 5 people for each category—a librarian, a working writer in the genre, booksellers, editors, etc. Requirements for entrants: author must be an Oklahoma native, resident, former resident or have written a book with Oklahoma theme. Winner will be announced at banquet in Oklahoma City. The Arrell Gibson Lifetime Achievement Award is also presented each year for a body of work.

ONCE UPON A WORLD CHILDREN'S BOOK AWARD

Simon Wiesenthal Center's Museum of Tolerance Library and Archives, 1399 S. Roxbury Dr., Los Angeles CA 90035-4709. (310)772-7605. Fax: (310)772-7628. E-mail: bookaward@wiesenthal.net. Web site: www.wiesenthal.com/library. **Award Director:** Adaire J. Klein. Submit 4 copies of each entry to: Adaire J. Klein, Director of Library and Archival Services. Annual award. Estab. 1996. Submissions made by publishers, author or by author's agent. Suggestions from educators, libraries, and others accepted. Must be published January-December of previous year. Deadline for entries: March 30. SASE for contest rules and entry forms. Awards $1,000 and recognition of Honor Books. Judging by 3 independent judges familiar with children's literature. Award open to any writer with work in English language on subjects of tolerance, diversity, human understanding, and social justice for children 6-10 years old. The next award will be presented on October 28, 2007. Book Seals available from the Library.

ORBIS PICTUS AWARD FOR OUTSTANDING NONFICTION FOR CHILDREN

The National Council of Teachers of English, 1111 W. Kenyon Rd., Urbana IL 61801-1096. (217)328-3870. Fax: (217)328-0977. E-mail: dzagorski@ncte.org. Web site: www.ncte.org/elem/awards/orbispictus. **Chair, NCTE Committee on the Orbis Pictus Award for Outstanding Nonfiction for Children:** Sandip Wilson, Husson College, Bangor ME. Annual award. Estab. 1989. Purpose of award: To promote and recognize excellence in the writing of nonfiction for children. Previously published submissions only. Submissions made by author, author's agent, by a person or group of people. Must be published January 1-December 31 of contest year. Deadline for entries: November 30. Call for award information. No entry fee. Awards a plaque given at the NCTE Elementary Section Luncheon at the NCTE Annual Convention in November. Judging by a committee. "The name Orbis Pictus commemorates the work of Johannes Amos Comenius, 'Orbis Pictus—The World in Pictures' (1657), considered to be the first book actually planned for children."

N THE ORIGINAL ART

Museum of American Illustration at the Society of Illustrators, 128 E. 63rd St., New York NY 10021-7303. (212)838-2560. Fax: (212)838-2561. E-mail: dir@societyillustrators.org. Web site: www.societyillustrators.org. **Publicity and Awards Coordinator:** Kim Sall. Annual contest. Estab. 1981. Purpose of contest: to celebrate the fine art of children's book illustration. Previously published submissions only. Deadline for entries: August 20. Request "call for entries" to receive contest rules and entry forms. Entry fee is $20/book. Judging by seven professional artists and editors. Works will be displayed at the Society of Illustrators Museum of American Illustration in New York City October-November annually. Medals awarded; catalog published.

HELEN KEATING OTT AWARD FOR OUTSTANDING CONTRIBUTION TO CHILDREN'S LITERATURE

Church and Synagogue Library Association, 2920 SW Dolph Ct Ste 3A, Portland OR 97219. (503)244-6919. Fax: (503)977-3734. E-mail: csla@worldaccessnet.com. Web site: www.cslainfo.org. **Chair of Committee:** Kay Mowery. Annual award. Estab. 1980. "This award is given to a person or organization that has made a significant contribution to promoting high moral and ethical values through children's literature." Deadline for entries: April 1. "Recipient is honored in July during the conference." Awards certificate of recognition and a conference package consisting of all meals, day of awards banquet, two nights' housing and a complimentary 1 year membership. "A nomination for an award may be made by anyone. It should include the name, address and telephone number of the nominee, plus the church or synagogue relationship where appropriate. Nominations of an organization should include the name of a contact person. A detailed description of the reasons for the nomination should be given, accompanied by documentary evidence of accomplishment. The person(s) making the nomination should give his/her name, address and telephone number and a brief explanation of his/her knowledge of the nominee's accomplishments. Elements of creativity and innovation will be given high priority by the judges."

PATERSON PRIZE FOR BOOKS FOR YOUNG PEOPLE

Poetry Center at Passaic County Community College, One College Blvd., Paterson NJ 07505-1179. (973)684-6555. Fax: (973)523-6085. E-mail: mgillan@pccc.edu. Web site: www.pccc.edu/poetry. **Director:** Maria Mazziotti Gillan. Estab. 1996. Part of the Poetry Center's mission is "to recognize excellence in books for young people." Published submissions only. Submissions made by author, author's agent or publisher. Must be published between January 1-December 31 of year previous to award year. Deadline for entries: March 15.

SASE for contest rules and entry forms or visit Web site. Awards $500 for the author in either of 3 categories: PreK-Grade 3; Grades 4-6, Grades 7-12. Judging by a professional writer selected by the Poetry Center. Contest is open to any writer/illustrator.

PEN/PHYLLIS NAYLOR WORKING WRITER FELLOWSHIP

PEN, 588 Broadway, New York NY 10012. (212)334-1660, ext. 108. Fax: (212)334-2181. E-mail: awards@pen.org. Web site: www.pen.org. Submit entries to: awards coordinator. Must have published 2 books to be eligible. Annual contest. Estab. 2001. To support writers with a financial need and recognize work of high literary caliber. Unpublished submissions only. Submissions nominated. Deadline for entries: mid-January. Awards $5,000. Upon nomination by an editor or fellow writer, a panel of judges will select the winning book. Open to a writer of children's or young adult fiction in financial need, who has published at least two books, and no more than five during the past ten years. Please visit our Web site for full guidelines.

PENNSYLVANIA YOUNG READERS' CHOICE AWARDS PROGRAM

Pennsylvania School Librarians Association, 148 S. Bethelehem Pike, Ambler PA 19002-5822. (215)643-5048. Fax: (215)646-7250. E-mail: bellavance@verizon.net. Web site: www.psla.org. **Coordinator:** Jean B. Bellavance. Annual award. Estab. 1991. Submissions nominated by a person or group. Must be published within 5 years of the award for example, books published in 2003 to present are eligible for the 2007-2008 award. Deadline for entries: September 1. SASE for contest rules and entry forms. No entry fee. Framed certificate to winning authors. Judging by children of Pennsylvania (they vote). Requirements for entrants: currently living in North America. Reader's Choice Award is to promote reading of quality books by young people in the Commonwealth of Pennsylvania, to promote teacher and librarian involvement in children's literature, and to honor authors whose work has been recognized by the children of Pennsylvania. Four awards are given, one for each of the following grade level divisions: K-3, 3-6, 6-8, YA. View information at the Pennsylvania School Librarians Web site.

JAMES D. PHELAN AWARD

Intersection for the Arts, 446 Valencia Street, San Francisco CA 94103. (415)626-2787. Fax: (415)626-1636. E-mail: info@theintersection.org. Web site: www.theintersection.org. **Contest Director:** Kevin B. Chen. Submit entries to: Awards Coordinator. Annual contest. Estab. 1935. Purpose of contest: "To support unpublished manuscripts in progress." Unpublished submissions only. Submissions made by author. Deadline for entries: March 31. SASE for contest rules and entry forms. No entry fee. Awards: $2,000. Judging by 3 independent judges to be determined. "Must be born in California and must be between ages 20-35."

PLEASE TOUCH MUSEUM® BOOK AWARD

Please Touch Museum, 210 N. 21st St., Philadelphia PA 19103-1001. (215)963-0667. Fax: (215)963-0424. E-mail: kmiller@pleasetouchmuseum.org. Web site: www.pleasetouchmuseum.org. **Contact:** Frank Luzi. Annual award. Estab. 1985. Purpose of the award: "to recognize and encourage the publication of high-quality books for young children. The award is given to books that are imaginative, exceptionally illustrated and help foster a child's life-long love of reading. Each year we select one winner in two age categories—ages 3 and under and ages 4 to 7. These age categories reflect the age of the children Please Touch Museum serves. To be eligible for consideration, a book must: (1) Be distinguished in text, illustration, and ability to explore and clarify an idea for young children (ages 7 and under). (2) Be published within the last year by an American publisher. (3) Be by an American author and/or illustrator." SASE for award rules and entry forms. No entry fee. Publishing date deadlines apply. Judging by selected jury of children's literature experts, librarians and early childhood educators. Education store purchases books for selling at Book Award Ceremony and throughout the year. Autographing sessions may be held at Please Touch Museum, and at Philadelphia's Early Childhood Education Conference.

PNWA ANNUAL LITERARY CONTEST

Pacific Northwest Writers Association, PMB 2717-1420 NW Gilman Blvd, Ste 2, Issaquah, WA 98027. (425)673-2665. E-mail: staff@pnwa.org. Web site: www.pnwa.org. **Open to students.** Annual contest. Purpose of contest: "Valuable tool for writers as contest submissions are critiqued (2 critiques)." Unpublished submissions only. Submissions made by author. Deadline for entries: February 20, 2007. SASE for contest rules and entry forms. Entry fee is $35/entry for members, $50/entry for nonmembers. Awards $600—1st; $300—2nd; $150—3rd. Awards in all 12 categories.

POCKETS MAGAZINE FICTION CONTEST

Pockets Magazine, The Upper Room, P.O. Box 340004, Nashville TN 37203-0004. (615)340-7333. Fax: (615)340-7267. E-mail: pockets@upperroom.org. Web site: www.pockets.org. **Contact:** Lynn W. Gilliam, senior editor.

The purpose of the contest is to "find new freelance writers for the magazine." Annual competition for short stories. Award: $1,000 and publication in *Pockets*. Competition receives 400 submissions. Judged by *Pockets* editors and editors of other Upper Room publications. Guidelines available on Web site or upon request and SASE. No entry fee. No entry form. Note on envelope and first sheet: Fiction Contest. Submissions must be postmarked between March 1 and August 15 of the current year. Former winners are not eligible. **Unpublished submissions only.** Word length: 1,000-1,600 words. Winner notified November 1. Submissions returned after November 1 if accompanied by SASE.

EDGAR ALLAN POE AWARD

Mystery Writers of America, Inc., 6th Floor, 17 E. 47th St., New York NY 10017. (212)888-8171. Fax: (212)888-8107. E-mail: mwa@mysterywriters.org. Web site: www.mysterywriters.org. **Administrative Manager:** Margery Flax. Annual award. Estab. 1945. Purpose of the award: to honor authors of distinguished works in the mystery field. Previously published submissions only. Submissions made by the author, author's agent; "normally by the publisher." Work must be published/produced the year of the contest. Deadline for entries: November 30 "except for works only available in the month of December." SASE for award rules and entry forms. No entry fee. Awards ceramic bust of "Edgar" for winner; scrolls for all nominees. Judging by professional members of Mystery Writers of America (writers). Nominee press release sent after first Wednesday in February. Winner announced at the Edgar® Banquet, held in late April/early May.

MICHAEL L. PRINTZ AWARD

Young Adult Library Services Association, Division of the American Library Association, 50 E. Huron, Chicago IL 60611. Fax: (312)664-7459. E-mail: yalsa@ala.org. Web site: www.ala.org/yalsa. Annual award. The Michael L. Printz Award is an award for a book that exemplifies literary excellence in young adult literature. It is named for a Topeka, Kansas school librarian who was a long-time active member of the Young Adult Library Services Association. It will be selected annually by an award committee that can also name as many as 4 honor books. The award-winning book can be fiction, nonfiction, poetry or an anthology, and can be a work of joint authorship or editorship. The books must be published between January 1 and December 31 of the preceding year and be designated by its publisher as being either a young adult book or one published for the age range that YALSA defines as young adult, e.g. ages 12 through 18. The deadline for both committee and field nominations will be December 1.

PRIX ALVINE-BELISLE

Association pour l'avancement des sciences et des techniques de la documentation (ASTED) Inc., 3414 Avenue Du Parc, Bureau 202, Montreal QC H2X 2H5 Canada. (514)281-5012. Fax: (514)281-8219. E-mail: info@asted.org. **Executive Director:** Louis Cabral. Award open to children's book editors. Annual award. Estab. 1974. Purpose of contest: To recognize the best children's book published in French in Canada. Previously published submissions only. Submissions made by publishing house. Must be published the year before award. Deadline for entries: June 1. Awards $1,000. Judging by librarians jury.

QUILL AND SCROLL INTERNATIONAL WRITING/PHOTO CONTEST

Quill and Scroll, School of Journalism and Mass Communication, University of Iowa, Iowa City IA 52242-1528. (319)335-3457. Fax: (319)335-3989. E-mail: quill-scroll@uiowa.edu. Web site: www.uiowa.edu/~quill-sc. **Contest Director:** Vanessa Shelton. **Open to students.** Annual contest. Previously published submissions only. Submissions made by the author or school newspaper adviser. Must be published within the last year. Deadline for entries: February 5. SASE for contest rules and entry forms. Entry fee is $2/entry. Awards engraved plaque to junior high level sweepstakes winners. Judging by various judges. *Quill and Scroll* acquires the right to publish submitted material in the magazine if it is chosen as a winning entry. Requirements for entrants: must be students in grades 9-12 for high school division. Entry form available on Web site.

REDHOUSE CHILDREN'S BOOK AWARD

Federation of Children's Book Groups, 2 Bridge Wood View, Horsforth, Leeds LS18 5PE England. (44)(113)258-8910. E-mail: marianneadey@aol.com. Web site: www.redhousechildrensbookawards.co.uk. **Coordinator:** Marianne Adey. Purpose of the award: "The R.H.B.A. is an annual prize for the best children's book of the year judged by the children themselves." Categories: (I) books for younger children, (II) books for younger readers, (III) books for older readers. Estab. 1980. Works must be published in the United Kingdom. Deadline for entries: December 31. SASE for rules and entry forms. Entries not returned. Awards "a magnificent silver and oak trophy worth over $6,000 and a portfolio of children's work." Silver dishes to each category winner. Judging by children. Requirements for entrants: Work must be fiction and published in the UK during the current year (poetry is ineligible). Work will be published in current "Pick of the Year" publication.

Jo Knowles

*Awards & grants lead to agent,
publisher & first novel*

Jo Knowles says that it was Robert Cormier's *The Chocolate War* that turned her into a reader. "There is something about the raw truth of that book that showed me how powerful words can be," she says. It was college courses in children's literature and children's writing that got her started writing for young readers. And it was contests and grants that allowed her to make the transition from aspiring writer to published author.

Knowles won a Robert Cormier Scholarship for Most Promising Young Adult Writer, Simmons College in 2001. She received an SCBWI Work-in-Progress Grant for a Young Adult Novel in 2002, which attracted the attention of her agent Barry Goldblatt. And she won a PEN New England Children's Book Caucus Discovery Award in 2005, which lead to a contract with Candlewick for *Lessons from a Dead Girl* (2007).

In her debut novel, Knowles offers readers a powerful, often uncomfortable journey into the world of abuse and healing, chronicling the complex relationship between main character Laine and her best friend/tormentor Leah, who, Laine learns at the book's opening, has died. Here the author talks about tackling difficult topics in *Lessons from a Dead Girl*; offers advice on entering competitions; and discusses Cormier—who reviewed her work during her grad student days. "He told me I had talent, and that he hoped one day my book would be published with a blurb from him on the back. I have that letter framed in my office," she says. For more on Knowles and her work, visit www.joknowles.com.

You've referred to your path to publication as "long and winding." Applying for an SCBWI grant led you to find your agent, and winning the PEN New England Discovery Award led you to your publisher. Had you tried other avenues?

In the beginning I was submitting directly to editors. I was lucky enough to get revision requests right from the start, but I was very naive about the process. I didn't realize how common it was for editors to ask for a revision and still reject you in the end. So I'd head down one avenue, thinking, *This is it!* And then I'd wait, sometimes six months, and in one case I revised back and forth with an editor for two years, only to receive a rejection in the end. (This was all before I had an agent.) There's a lot of heartbreak in those "close calls," but in retrospect I'm grateful for all the twists and turns my path took. I grew as a writer with each revision request—and rejection, believe it or not.

Would you recommend contests and grants to other writers pursuing publication?

Absolutely! There are so many good things that come out of applying for a grant. First of all, you have to write a synopsis, which is very hard but really forces you to think about your manuscript and what it's about. I guess that sounds pretty obvious but when you do it for the first time, it's like a revelation!

Second, I think submitting a sample of your work, say 10 pages, makes you look at those pages in a really intense way, through the eyes of the most critical reader you can imagine. Every sentence counts! Since doing this I now revise my manuscripts in roughly 10-page chunks, which usually translates to two chapters for me. I look at those chapters and work on how they stand on their own. It's a great exercise.

Third, getting that call is the biggest thrill! At the time I got the call about the SCBWI grant I had been through some tough times in my personal life and was feeling pretty hopeless. I remember hanging up the phone and sitting on the floor and crying. It was wonderful! And then soon after that I received a letter from Barry Goldblatt (he'd read the notice about the grant in the SCBWI Bulletin) asking if I'd be interested in submitting my work to him. He'd only been in the [agenting] business for about a year or so at that point, so I was really lucky! And then when I applied for the PEN award I'd sort of sunk to that hopeless place again. I'd had some close calls with revision requests, but I was beginning to feel like maybe I just didn't have what it takes. A good friend of mine, Cynthia Lord (author of the Newbery Honor-winning *Rules*), encouraged me to give it a shot so I decided to take a chance on *Lessons from a Dead Girl,* a manuscript Barry hadn't actually shopped around yet because I had nearly given up on it. I was totally shocked and thrilled when I got the call and found out I won.

Any tips on catching the eye of judges?

Hand in your best work. I know that sounds a bit simple, but really I think you have to make those first pages sing, just like the first pages of any book. How can your first sentence hook the reader? What would make the judge keep going? Read the pages out loud, have someone else read them to you, read all the first chapters from your favorite books and think about what it is that makes those resonate with you. Don't just hand in any old thing for the sake of submitting. Respect the judges' time and only submit if you have something you've put your all into. Also, follow the rules to a T. Don't hand in more pages than requested. Follow the formatting guidelines. If the submissions say the excerpt should come from a completed work, don't hand in something you've only written the first chapter of. Be professional.

I didn't read your Web site until after I read your book. I wasn't surprised to see your references to Robert Cormier on your site. As I read *Lessons from a Dead Girl*, I kept thinking about *The Chocolate War*—your book evoked the same kind of emotions in me as his did. What appeals to you about Cormier's work?

Oh, thank you so much! Robert Cormier is my literary hero for so many reasons. When I was in high school *The Chocolate War* was required reading. I devoured that book. There was a raw truth to the story that shocked me. The complexity of each character just blew me away. They were all suffering—the victims *and* the tormentors. That was really the key. I love how Cormier switched points of view to show us the full complexity of the story. To show us how each character suffered in his unique way. With *Lessons from a Dead Girl,* I knew the only way to understand Laine's journey was to show Leah as victim as well as tormentor.

Lessons underscores the fact that often abuse leads to abuse. What led you to take readers on this difficult journey with Laine?

Well, ironically enough, I'm sure it stems back to _The Chocolate War_. Jerry's journey was intense, yes, but what resonated for me was his absolute isolation even as he was the focus of attention. I think anyone suffering abuse lives in a parallel world of isolation all the time, because of the secrets and shame they carry. I knew Laine's experience was not unique, and I wanted to expose it, to explore all the complex feelings a young person might have as she questions why the abuse happened, and why she "let" it happen.

Was it ever tough for you to make Laine endure so much in order to grow and move on? Were you ever tempted to go easier on her?

I don't think I ever wanted to back down from the scenes I saw unfolding in my head as I wrote them, but I did a lot of wincing. To tell the whole truth as I saw it was very hard, but I knew the only way for Laine to survive was to tell it all, to face _all_ of her memories, good and hard. From the moment I began writing, I knew that whatever Laine went through, she was going to make it. I didn't always know how, but I could see the ghost of her at the other side, waiting to become whole again.

In a blog post, you said, "I think when you work at home, alone, all day, you sort of start to wonder whether you actually exist." You've also described yourself as a "conference junkie." What's your advice to full-time writers as far as staying connected with peers in the writing world?

Oh, that was a hard day! I was feeling so incredibly isolated. I'm a freelance writer by day so I'm home alone in a very quiet setting. Having a blog really helps me stay connected to people. Listservs are a great way to stay connected with peers and meet new people, too. But of course these things are rather addictive and you need to set strict time limits or your day will disappear before you know it. Conferences are great because they give me something to look forward to—I actually get to see the people I've been talking with on my blog in person! It's such a treat to connect with friends who love to talk shop as much as I do.

Are you currently in a writers group?

Yes, but it's very small. My schedule has become kind of insane lately so I had to give up my in-person group. I currently share work with two close friends, Cindy Faughnan and Debbi Michiko Florence. I'm not sure how we got started but we have a system in place which I _love_. Every night (or almost every night), we log on to SKYPE at a scheduled time. We chat for a few minutes, and then say what we're going to work on for the night. Then, we all get to work, checking in every 15-20 minutes to report our progress. I can't tell you how many nights I thought I'd throw in the towel and turn on the TV but Cindy and Debbi are always there, and I feel like I can't let them down. Together we've developed a very sound and supportive writing routine. We also share work for feedback.

You teach writing to women in a prison. How did this come about? How does this work enrich your writing life?

An acquaintance asked if I'd help an inmate at a local women's prison write an article about a garden project he'd helped start there. I said yes, and met with the woman a few times. When she finished her article, she asked me if I would look at other writing. I said yes, and we continued meeting. Soon she asked to bring a friend and this trend continued so that we now have six women in the group. The editor of a local paper that publishes the women's essays in a weekly column called The Glass House accompanies me to the meetings. It's been an amazing learning experience, working with the women and developing a writing workshop that meets their needs. I guess you could say this is my new in-person writing group. Each week we start our group with a writing warm-up (I often post these on my blog and on my Web site), and all of us do these exercises. I'd forgotten how much buried emotion can come up out of these writing prompts, and I've enjoyed being surprised by my own writing, as well as the women's.

As a first-time author, were there any surprises during the publishing process? What has your relationship with your editor been like? With your agent?

It's funny but I don't think there have been too many surprises. The biggest surprise was getting an offer! My editor, Joan Powers, is wonderful. She is very straightforward, asks lots of questions, and trusts me to answer them in my revisions. I certainly don't think she ever shied away from asking tough questions, and I really appreciate that. My agent, Barry Goldblatt, is terrific. He's become a good friend who knows and cares about my career and

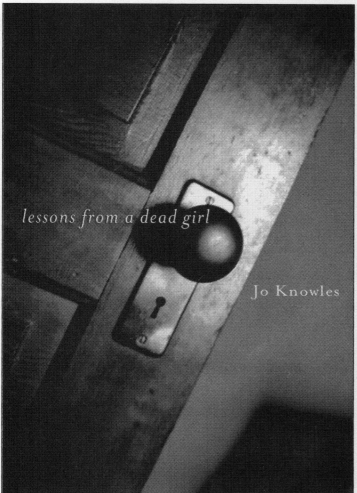

lessons from a dead girl

Jo Knowles

In *Lessons from a Dead Girl*, Jo Knowles introduces readers to Laine as she tries to deal with the death of her best friend Leah—who also happens to be Laine's tormenter. Knowles' debut novel deals with abuse, and while the author understands how difficult that can be, she "knew the only way for Laine to survive was to tell it all, to face *all* of her memories, good and hard." As Knowles took Laine through that process, she "could see the ghost of her at the other side, waiting to become whole again."

me. Barry has a reputation for being "brutally honest" but I think I should set the record straight right now and say he also has a huge heart. You have to be honest in this business. That may sound harsh but dishonesty will only lead to disappointment later. Barry knows that, and I think by being honest up front he is giving aspiring writers a huge gift. Writing is hard, hard work. But if you keep at it, if you keep revising, keep listening to the feedback rather than feeling it, you will get better, and you will succeed.

You're in the class of 2k7 collective. Why did you decide to join this group? How have you benefited from your membership thus far?

When Greg Fishbone put the original call out for 2007 debut authors, I thought it was a brilliant idea, especially since it seemed like many of the first people to sign up were from New England and we could do signings and events together. The writing community is so generous with information, and I thought what better way to pool our resources and talents so that we all help one another. It's a true co-op and I've learned a ton already by watching the first class members enter the world as "author." It's really exciting to go through this experience with friends.

You've admitted that you were a little nervous after sending me your manuscript to read. Are you apprehensive about your book arriving in stores?

Well, I'm a natural worrier but of course this is the biggie! I know that the subject matter of *Lessons from a Dead Girl* is a tough one, so there could be strong reactions to it one way or the other. This is a story that I felt had to be told though, and told with honesty, however painful or uncomfortable it might be. Again, I look back to Cormier and how brave he was to cut right to the truth in *The Chocolate War* and really in all of his books. He's not afraid to write about ugly things. Ugly things exist. I think that's the beauty of his work: he knows how to draw that curtain open and do it in a way that isn't sensational, but real.

You try to read at least one novel a week. What have you read lately? How do you choose?

Recent great reads are *Beige*, by Cecil Castellucci, and *Saint Iggy*, by K.L. Going. I usually choose titles that are getting buzz on blogs and forums, or via recommendations from friends. I also have quite a few writer friends so of course I try to read their books as soon as they hit the stands or if I can get my hands on an ARC.

Are there any upcoming projects you can tell me about?

I recently submitted a YA manuscript to my editor so I'm waiting to hear her reaction on that, and I'm currently revising an early draft of another YA novel, which I hope to submit to my agent soon for feedback.

If there is anything you'd like to offer aspiring writers, please feel free.

Hope. That would be the best thing I can offer. The road to publication can be a long one, but if you keep working at your craft, listening to feedback and applying it to your work, you can succeed. Believe it!

—Alice Pope

TOMAS RIVERA MEXICAN AMERICAN CHILDREN'S BOOK AWARD

Texas State University-San Marcos, EDU, 601 University Dr., San Marcos TX 78666-4613. (512)245-3839. Fax: (512)245-7911. E-mail: jb23@txstate.edu. **Award Director:** Dr. Jennifer Battle. Competition open to adults. Annual contest. Estab. 1995. Purpose of award: "To encourage authors, illustrators and publishers to produce books that authentically reflect the lives of Mexican American appropriate for children and young adults in the United States." Unpublished mss not accepted. Submissions made by "any interested individual or publishing company." Must be published the year prior to the year of consideration. Deadline for entries: November 1 of publication year. Contact Dr. Jennifer Battle for nomination forms, or send copy of book. No entry fee. Awards $3,000 per book. Judging of nominations by a regional committee, national committee judges finalists. Annual ceremony honoring the book and author/illustrator is held during Hispanic Heritage Month at Texas State University-San Marcos and a selected city.

◪ ROCKY MOUNTAIN BOOK AWARD: ALBERTA CHILDREN'S CHOICE BOOK AWARD

Rocky Mountain Book Award Committee, Box 42, Lethbridge AB T1J 3Y3 Canada. (403)381-0855. E-mail: rockymountainbookaward@shaw.ca. Web site: http://rmba.lethsd.ab.ca. **Contest Director:** Michelle Dimnik. Submit entries to: Richard Chase, board member. Open to students. Annual contest. Estab. 2001. Purpose of contest: "Reading motivation for students, promotion of Canadian authors, illustrators and publishers." Previously unpublished submissions only. Submissions made by author's agent or nominated by a person or group. Must be published between 2005-2007. Deadline for entries: January 17, 2008. SASE for contest rules and entry forms. No entry fee. Awards: Gold medal and author tour of selected Alberta schools. Judging by students. Requirements for entrants: Canadian authors and illustrators only.

◪ SASKATCHEWAN BOOK AWARDS: CHILDREN'S LITERATURE

Saskatchewan Book Awards, 205B-2314 11th Avenue, Regina SK S4P 0K1 Canada. (306)569-1585. Fax: (306)569-4187. E-mail: director@bookawards.sk.ca. Web site: www.bookawards.sk.ca. **Award Director:** Glenda James. Open to Saskatchewan authors only. Annual award. Estab. 1995. Purpose of contest: to celebrate Saskatchewan books and authors and to promote their work. Previously published submissions only. Submissions made by author, author's agent or publisher by September 15. SASE for contest rules and entry forms. Entry fee is $20 (Canadian). Awards $2,000 (Canadian). Judging by two children's literature authors outside of Saskatchewan. Requirements for entrants: Must be Saskatchewan resident; book must have ISBN number; book must have been published within the last year. Award-winning book will appear on TV talk shows and be pictured on bookmarks distributed to libraries, schools and bookstores in Saskatchewan.

SCBWI MAGAZINE MERIT AWARDS

Society of Children's Book Writers and Illustrators, 8271 Beverly Blvd., Los Angeles CA 90048. Fax: (323)782-1010. E-mail: scbwi@scbwi.org. Web site: www.scbwi.org. **Award Coordinator:** Dorothy Leon. Annual award. Estab. 1988. Purpose of the award: "to recognize outstanding original magazine work for young people published during that year and having been written or illustrated by members of SCBWI." Previously published submissions only. Entries must be submitted between January 1 and December 15 of the year of publication. For rules and procedures see Web site. No entry fee. Must be a SCBWI member. Awards plaques and honor certificates for each of 4 categories (fiction, nonfiction, illustration, poetry). Judging by a magazine editor and two "full" SCBWI members. "All magazine work for young people by an SCBWI member—writer, artist or photographer—is eligible during the year of original publication. In the case of co-authored work, both authors must be SCBWI members. Members must submit their own work." Requirements for entrants: 4 copies each of the published work and proof of publication (may be contents page) showing the name of the magazine and the date of issue. The SCBWI is a professional organization of writers and illustrators and others interested in children's literature. Membership is open to the general public at large.

SCBWI WORK-IN-PROGRESS GRANTS

Society of Children's Book Writers and Illustrators, 8271 Beverly Blvd., Los Angeles CA 90048. (323)782-1010. Fax: (323)782-1892. E-mail: scbwi@scbwi.org. Web site: www.scbwi.org. Annual award. "The SCBWI Work-in-Progress Grants have been established to assist children's book writers in the completion of a specific project." Four categories: (1) General Work-in-Progress Grant. (2) Grant for a Contemporary Novel for Young People. (3) Nonfiction Research Grant. (4) Grant for a Work Whose Author Has Never Had a Book Published. Requests for applications may be made beginning October 1. Completed applications accepted February 1-April 1 of each year. SASE for applications for grants. In any year, an applicant may apply for any of the grants except the one awarded for a work whose author has never had a book published. (The recipient of this grant will be chosen from entries in all categories.) Five grants of $1,500 will be awarded annually. Runner-up grants of $500 (one in each category) will also be awarded. "The grants are available to both full and associate members of the SCBWI. They are not available for projects on which there are already contracts." Previous recipients not eligible to apply.

SHUBERT FENDRICH MEMORIAL PLAYWRITING CONTEST

Pioneer Drama Service, Inc., P.O. Box 4267, Englewood CO 80155-4267. Fax: (303)779-4315. E-mail: submission s@pioneerdrama.com. Web site: www.pioneerdrama.com. **Director:** Lori Conary. Annual contest. Estab. 1990. Purpose of the contest: ''To encourage the development of quality theatrical material for educational and family theater.'' Previously unpublished submissions only. Open to all writers not currently published by Pioneer Drama Service. Deadline for entries: December 31. SASE for contest rules and guidelines. No entry fee. Cover letter, SASE for return of ms, and proof of production or staged reading must accompany all submissions. Awards $1,000 royalty advance and publication. Upon receipt of signed contracts, plays will be published and made available in our next catalog. Judging by editors. All rights acquired with acceptance of contract for publication. Restrictions for entrants: Any writers currently published by Pioneer Drama Service are not eligible.

SKIPPING STONES BOOK AWARDS

Skipping Stones, P.O. Box 3939, Eugene OR 97403-0939. (541)342-4956. E-mail: editor@skippingstones.org. Web site: www.skippingstones.org. Open to published books, magazines, educational videos, and DVDs. Annual awards. Purpose of contest: To recognize contributions to children's literature, teaching resources and educational audio/video resources in the areas of multicultural awareness, nature and ecology, social issues, peace and nonviolence. Submissions made by the author or publishers and/or producers. Deadline for entries: February 1. Send request for contest rules and entry forms or visit Web site. Entry fee is $50; 50% discount for small/nonprofit publishers. Each year, about 15-20 books and A/V resources are selected by a multicultural selection committee of editors, students, parents, teachers and librarians. Winners receive gold honor award seals, certificates and publicity via multiple outlets. Many educational publications announce the winners of our book awards. The reviews of winning books and educational videos/DVDs are published in the May-August issue of *Skipping Stones*, now in 19th year.

SKIPPING STONES YOUTH HONOR AWARDS

Skipping Stones, P.O. Box 3939, Eugene OR 97403-0939. (541)342-4956. E-mail: editor@SkippingStones.org. Web site: www.SkippingStones.org. **Open to students.** Annual awards. Purpose of contest: ''to recognize youth, 7 to 17, for their contributions to multicultural awareness, nature and ecology, social issues, peace and nonviolence. Also to promote creativity, self-esteem and writing skills and to recognize important work being done by youth organizations.'' Submissions made by the author. Deadline for entries: June 25. SASE for contest rules. Entries must include certificate of originality by a parent and/or teacher and a cover letter that included cultural background information on the authorr. Entry fee is $3. Everyone who enters the contest receives the September-October issue featuring Youth Awards. Judging by *Skipping Stones*' staff. ''Up to ten awards are given in three categories: (1) Compositions—(essays, poems, short stories, songs, travelogues, etc.) should be typed (double-spaced) or neatly handwritten. Fiction or nonfiction should be limited to 1,000 words; poems to 30 lines. Non-English writings are also welcome. (2) Artwork—(drawings, cartoons, paintings or photo essays with captions) should have the artist's name, age and address on the back of each page. Send the originals with SASE. Black & white photos are especially welcome. Limit: 8 pieces. (3) Youth Organizations—Tell us how your club or group works to: (a) preserve the nature and ecology in your area, (b) enhance the quality of life for low-income, minority or disabled or (c) improve racial or cultural harmony in your school or community. Use the same format as for compositions.'' The winners are published in the September-October issue of *Skipping Stones*. Now in it's 1 9th year, *Skipping Stones*, is a winner of N.A.M.E., EDPRESS and Parent's Choice Awards.

KAY SNOW WRITERS' CONTEST

Williamette Writers, 9045 SW Barbur Blvd. #5A, Portland OR 97219-4027. (503)452-1592. Fax: (503)452-0372. E-mail: wilwrite@willamettewriters.com. Web site: www.willamettewriters.com. **Contest Director:** Patricia MacAodha. Annual contest. **Open to students.** Purpose of contest: ''to encourage beginning and established writers to continue the craft.'' Unpublished, original submissions only. Submissions made by the author. Deadline for entries: May 15. SASE for contest rules and entry forms. Entry fee is $10, Williamette Writers' members; $15, nonmembers; free for student writers grades 1-12. Awards cash prize of $300 per category (fiction, nonfiction, juvenile, poetry, script writing), $50 for students in three divisions: 1-5, 6-8, 9-12. Judges are anonymous.

SOCIETY OF MIDLAND AUTHORS AWARDS

Society of Midland Authors, P.O. Box 10419, Chicago IL 60610-0419. E-mail: writercc@aol.com. Web site: www.midlandauthors.com. Annual award. Society estab. 1915. Purpose of award: ''to stimulate creative literary effort,'' one of the goals of the Society. There are six categories, including children's fiction and nonfiction, adult fiction and nonfiction, biography and poetry. Previously published submissions only. Submissions made by the author or publisher. Must be published during calendar year previous to deadline. Deadline for entries: February 15th. SASE for award rules and entry forms or check Web site. No entry fee. Awards plaque given at annual dinner, cash ($300). Judging by panel (reviewers, university faculty, writers, librarians) of 3 per category. Author must be currently residing in, born in, or have strong connections to the Midlands, i.e., Illinois, Indiana, Iowa, Kansas, Michigan, Minnesota, Missouri, Nebraska, North Dakota, South Dakota, Ohio or Wisconsin.

SOUTHWEST WRITERS ANNUAL CONTEST
SouthWest Writers, 3721 Morris NE, Suite A, Albuquerque NM 87111. (505)265-9485. Fax: (505)265-9483. E-mail: swwriters@juno.com. Web site: www.southwestwriters.org. Submit entries to: Contest Chair. **Open to adults and students.** Annual contest. Estab. 1982. Purpose of contest: to encourage writers of all genres. Also offers quarterly mini-conferences, critique groups (for $60/year, offers 2 monthly programs, monthly newsletter, annual writing and monthly writing contests, other workshops, various discount perks, Web site linking, e-mail forwarding and critique service (open to nonmembers). See Web site for more information or call or write.

GEORGE G. STONE CENTER FOR CHILDREN'S BOOKS RECOGNITION OF MERIT AWARD
George G. Stone Center for Children's Books, Claremont Graduate University, 740 N. College Ave., Claremont CA 91711-6188. (909)607-3670. **Award Director:** Carolyn Angus. Annual award. Estab. 1965. Purpose of the award: to recognize an author or illustrator of a children's book or a body of work exhibiting the "power to please and expand the awareness of children and teachers as they have shared the book in their classrooms." Previously published submissions only. SASE for award rules and entry forms. Entries not returned. No entry fee. Awards a scroll. Judging by a committee of teachers, professors of children's literature and librarians. Requirements for entrants: Nominations are made by students, teachers, professors and librarians. Award given in April.

THE JOAN G. SUGARMAN CHILDREN'S BOOK AWARD
Washington Independent Writers Legal and Educational Fund, Inc., P.O. Box 70437, Washington DC 20024-8437. (202)466-1344. E-mail: sugarman@Lefund.org. Web site: www.Lefund.org/sugarman.html. **Award Director:** Rob Anderson. Submit entries to: Rob Anderson. Award offered annually. Estab. 1987. Previously published submissions only during the two-year time frame specified for each award. Submissions made by author. No entry fee. Awards $1,000 cash prize for book judged best overall. Three honorable mentions in the categories of early readers, middle readers, and young adult readers are also recognized. Judging by a committee drawn from selected fields of children's literature, such as library science, editing, teaching, and psychology. Books eligible for the award must be written by an author residing in Virginia, Maryland or the District of Columbia and be published works with the copyright of 2002 or 2003. The books must be geared for children 15 years or younger, be original and have universal appeal. Since the books are judged on the basis of their written content, picture books without text are not eligible.

SYDNEY TAYLOR BOOK AWARD
Association of Jewish Libraries, c/o NFJC, 330 7th Ave., 21st Floor, New York NY 10001. (212)725-5359. E-mail: rkamin@temple-israel.org or ajllibs@osu.edu. Web site: www.jewishlibraries.org. **Contact:** Rachel Kamin, chair. Offered annually for work published during the current year. "Given to distinguished contributions to Jewish literature for children. One award for younder readers, one for older readers, and one for teens." Publishers submit books. Deadline: December 31. Guidelines on Web site. Awards certificate, cash award, and gold or silver seals for cover of winning book.

SYDNEY TAYLOR MANUSCRIPT COMPETITION
Association of Jewish Libraries, 204 Park St., Montclair NJ 07042. E-mail: aidonna@aol.com. Web site: www.jewishlibraries.org. **Coordinator:** Aileen Grossberg. **Open to students** and any unpublished writer of fiction. Annual contest. Estab. 1985. Purpose of the contest: "This competition is for unpublished writers of fiction. Material should be for readers ages 8-11, with universal appeal that will serve to deepen the understanding of Judaism for all children, revealing positive aspects of Jewish life." Unpublished submissions only. Deadline for entries: December 30. Download rules and forms from Web site or send SASE for contest rules and entry forms must be enclosed. No entry fee. Awards $1,000. Award winner will be notified in April, and the award will be presented at the convention in June. Judging by qualified judges from within the Association of Jewish Libraries. Requirements for entrants: must be an unpublished fiction writer; also, books must range from 64-200 pages in length. "AJL assumes no responsibility for publication, but hopes this cash incentive will serve to encourage new writers of children's stories with Jewish themes for all children."

TEDDY AWARD FOR BEST CHILDREN'S BOOK
Writers' League of Texas, 1501 W. Fifth St., Suite E-2, Austin TX 78703. (512)499-8914. Fax: (512)499-0441. E-mail: wlt@writersleague.org. Web site: www.writersleague.org. **Contact:** Kristy Bordine, membership administrator. Offered annually for work published June 1-May 31 in the previous year. Honors 2 outstanding books

for children published by members of the Writers' League of Texas. Awards and recognition presented at the Texas Book Festival in Austin, Texas. Writer's League of Texas dues may accompany entry fee. Deadline: May 31. Charges $25 fee. Prize: Two prizes of $1,000, and teddy bears.

THE TORONTO BOOK AWARDS

City of Toronto, 100 Queen St. W, 2nd Floor, West Tower, Toronto ON M5H 2N2 Canada. (416)392-8191. Fax: (416)392-1247. E-mail: bkurmey@toronto.ca. **Submit entries to:** Bev Kurmey, Protocol Officer. Annual award. Estab. 1974. Recognizes books of literary or artistic merit that are evocative of Toronto. Submissions made by author, author's agent or nominated by a person or group. Must be published the calendar year prior to the award year. Deadline for entries: last week day of February annually. Awards $15,000 in prize money. Judging by committee.

MUNICIPAL CHAPTER OF TORONTO IODE JEAN THROOP BOOK AWARD

Toronto Municipal IODE, 40 St. Clair Ave. E., Suite 205, Toronto ON M4T 1M9 Canada. (416)925-5078. Fax: (416)925-5127. E-mail: iodetoronto@bellnet.ca. **Contest Director:** Jennifer Werry. Submit entries to: Theo Heras, Lillian Smith Library, 239 College St., Toronto. Annual contest. Estab. 1974. Previously published submissions only. Submissions made by author. Deadline for entries: November 1. No entry fee. Awards: $1,000. If the illustrator is different from the author, the prize money is divided. Judging by Book Award Committee comprised of members of Toronto Municipal Chapter IODE. Requirements for entrants: Authors and illustrators must be Canadian and live within the GTA.

VEGETARIAN ESSAY CONTEST

The Vegetarian Resource Group, P.O. Box 1463, Baltimore MD 21203. (410)366-VEGE. Fax: (410)366-8804. E-mail: vrg@vrg.org. Web site: www.vrg.org. Annual contest. **Open to students.** Estab. 1985. Purpose of contest: to promote vegetarianism in young people. Unpublished submissions only. Deadline for entries: May 1 of each year. SASE for contest rules and entry forms. No entry fee. Awards $50 savings bond. Judging by awards committee. Acquires right for The Vegetarian Resource Group to reprint essays. Requirements for entrants: age 18 and under. Winning works may be published in *Vegetarian Journal*, instructional materials for students. "Submit 2-3 page essay on any aspect of vegetarianism, which is the abstinence of meat, fish and fowl. Entrants can base paper on interviewing, research or personal opinion. Need not be vegetarian to enter."

VFW VOICE OF DEMOCRACY

Veterans of Foreign Wars of the U.S., 406 W. 34th St., Kansas City MO 64111. (816)968-1117. Fax: (816)968-1149. Web site: www.vfw.org. **Open to high school students.** Annual contest. Estab. 1960. Purpose of contest: to give high school students the opportunity to voice their opinions about their responsibility to our country and to convey those opinions via the broadcast media to all of America. Deadline for entries: November 1. No entry fee. Winners receive awards ranging from $1,000-25,000. Requirements for entrants: "Ninth-twelfth grade students in public, parochial, private and home schools are eligible to compete. Former first place state winners are not eligible to compete again. Contact your participating high school teacher, counselor, our Web sitewww.vfw.org or your local VFW Post to enter."

VIRGINIA LIBRARY ASSOCIATION/JEFFERSON CUP

Virginia Library Association, P.O. Box 8277, Norfolk, VA 23503-0277 E-Mail lhahne@coastalnet.com. Web site: www.vla.org. **Executive Director:** Linda Hahne. Award director changes year to year. 2007 Jefferson Cup Director: Audrey Mitchell, e-mail amitchell@kwcps.k12.va.us. Annual award. Estab. 1983. Purpose of award "The Jefferson Cup honors a distinguished biography, historical fiction or American history book for young people. Presented since 1983, the Jefferson Cup Committee's goal is to promote reading about America's past; to encourage the quality writing of United States history, biography and historical fiction for young people and to recognize authors in these disciplines." Entries must be published in the year prior to selection. Deadline for entries, January 31. Additional information on the Jefferson Cup and criteria on making submissions is available on the VLA Web site at http://www.vla.org/demo/Youth-Serv/JC-How-To.html. Judging by committee. The book must be about US history or an American person, 1492 to present, or fiction that highlights the US past; author must reside in the US. The book must be published especially for young people.

WASHINGTON CHILDREN'S CHOICE PICTURE BOOK AWARD

Washington Library Media Association, P.O. Box 50194, Mukilteo WA 98275. E-mail: sonnend@edmonds.wednet.edu or khuebsch@@edmonds.wednet.edu. Web site: www.wlma.org/wccpba.htm. **Award Directors:** Dave Sonnen and Karen Heubschman. Submit nominations to: Kristin Galante, chairman; mail to Kristin Galante, WCCPBA, Lynndale Elementary School, 7200 191st SW, Lynnwood WA 98036. Annual award. Estab. 1982. Previously published submissions only. Submissions nominated by a person or group. Must be published within

2-3 years prior to year of award. Deadline for entries: January 15. SASE for contest rules and entry forms. Awards pewter plate, recognition. Judging by WCCPBA committee.

WASHINGTON POST/CHILDREN'S BOOK GUILD AWARD FOR NONFICTION
E-mail: theguild@childrensbookguild.org. Web site: www.childrensbookguild.org. **President:** changes yearly. Annual award. Estab. 1977. Purpose of award: "to honor an author or illustrator whose total work has contributed significantly to the quality of nonfiction for children." Award includes a cash prize and an engraved crystal paperweight. Judging by a jury of Children's Book Guild specialists, authors, illustrators and a *Washington Post* book critic. "One doesn't enter. One is selected. Our jury annually selects one author for the award."

WE ARE WRITERS, TOO!
Creative With Words Publications, Carmel CA 93922. Fax: (831)655-8627. E-mail: cwwpub@usa.net. Web site: members.tripod.com/CreativeWithWords. **Contest Director:** Brigitta Geltrich. **Open to students** (up to 19 years of age). Twice a year (January, August). Estab. 1975. Purpose of award: to further creative writing in children. Unpublished submissions only. Can submit year round on any theme (theme list available upon request and SASE). Deadlines for entries: year round. SASE for contest rules and entry forms. SASE for return of entries "if not accepted." No entry fee. Awards publication in an anthology. Judging by selected guest editors and educators. Contest open to children only (up to and including 19 years old). Writer should request contest rules. Include SASE with all correspondence. Age of child and home address must be stated and ms must be verified of its authenticity. Each story or poem must have a title. Creative with Words Publications (CWW) publishes the top 100-120 mss submitted to the contest. CWW also publishes anthologies on various themes throughout the year to which writers of all ages may submit.

WESTERN HERITAGE AWARDS
National Cowboy & Western Heritage Museum, 1700 NE 63rd St., Oklahoma City OK 73111-7997. (405)478-2250. Fax: (405)478-4714. E-mail: editor@nationalcowboymuseum.org. Web site: www.nationalcowboymuseum.org. **Director of Publications:** M.J. Van deventer. Annual award. Estab. 1961. Purpose of award: The WHA are presented annually to encourage the accurate and artistic telling of great stories of the West through 13 categories of western literature, television, film and music; including fiction, nonfiction, children's books and poetry. Previously published submissions only; must be published the calendar year before the awards are presented. Deadline for literary entries: November 30. Deadline for film, music and television entries: December 31. Entries not returned. Entry fee is $45/entry. Awards a Wrangler bronze sculpture designed by famed western artist, John Free. Judging by a panel of judges selected each year with distinction in various fields of western art and heritage. Requirements for entrants: The material must pertain to the development or preservation of the West, either from a historical or contemporary viewpoint. Literary entries must have been published between December 1 and November 30 of calendar year. Film, music or television entries must have been released or aired between January 1 and December 31 of calendar year of entry. Works recognized during special awards ceremonies held annually at the museum. There is an autograph party preceding the awards. Awards ceremonies are sometimes broadcast.

JACKIE WHITE MEMORIAL NATIONAL CHILDREN'S PLAY WRITING CONTEST
Columbia Entertainment Company, 309 Parkade Blvd., Columbia MO 65202-1447. (573)874-5628. E-mail: bybetsy@yahoo.com. Web site: www.cectheatre.org. **Contest Director:** Betsy Phillips. Annual contest. Estab. 1988. Purpose of contest: "To encourage writing of family-friendly scripts." Previously unpublished submissions only. Submissions made by author. Deadline for entries: June 1. SASE for contest rules and entry forms. Entry fee is $10. Awards $500 with production possible. Judging by current and past board members of CEC and at least one theater school parent. Play may be performed during the following season. 2006 winner may be presented during CEC's 2006-07 season. We reserve the right to award 1st place and prize monies without a production. All submissions will be read by at least three readers. Author will receive a written evaluation of the script.

LAURA INGALLS WILDER METAL
Association for Library Service to Children, Division of the American Library Association, 50 E. Huron, Chicago IL 60611. (312)280-2163. E-mail: alsc@ala.org. Web site: www.ala.org/ala/alsc/awardsscholarships/literaryawds/wildermedal/wildermedal.htm. **Executive Director:** Diane Foote. Award offered every 2 years. Purpose of the award: to recognize an author or illustrator whose books, published in the U.S., have over a period of years made a substantial and lasting contribution to children's literature. The candidates must be nominated by ALSC members. Medal presented at Newbery/Caldecott banquet during annual conference. Judging by Wilder Award Selection Committee.

RITA WILLIAMS YOUNG ADULT PROSE PRIZE

National League of American Pen Women, Nob Hill, San Francisco Branch, 1544 Sweetwood Dr., Colma CA 94015-2029. E-mail: pennobhill@aol.com. Web site: www.soulmakingcontest.us. **Contact:** Eileen Malone. **Open to students.** Up to 3,000 words in story, essay, journal entry, creative nonfiction, or memoir by writers in grades 9-12. Annual prize. Deadline: November 30. Guidelines for SASE. Charges $5/entry (make checks payable to NLAPW, Nob Hill Branch). Prize: 1st Place: $100; 2nd Place: $50; 3rd Place: $25. Open to any writer in grade 9-12.

PAUL A. WITTY OUTSTANDING LITERATURE AWARD

International Reading Association, Special Interest Group, Reading for Gifted and Creative Learning, School of Education, P.O. Box 297900, Fort Worth TX 76129. (817)257-6938. Fax: (817)257-7480. Web site: www.reading. org/association/awards/sig_witty.html. **Award Director:** Dr. Cathy Collins Block. **Open to students.** Annual award. Estab. 1979. Categories of entries: poetry/prose at elementary, junior high and senior high levels. Unpublished submissions only. Deadline for entries: February 1. SASE for award rules and entry forms. SASE for return of entries. No entry fee. Awards $25 and plaque, also certificates of merit. Judging by 2 committees for screening and awarding. Works will be published in International Reading Association publications. ''The elementary students' entries must be legible and may not exceed 1,000 words. Secondary students' prose entries should be typed and may exceed 1,000 words if necessary. At both elementary and secondary levels, if poetry is entered, a set of five poems must be submitted. All entries and requests for applications must include a self-addressed, stamped envelope.''

PAUL A. WITTY SHORT STORY AWARD

International Reading Association, P.O. Box 8139, 800 Barksdale Rd., Newark DE 19714-8139. (302)731-1600. E-mail: exec@reading.org. Web site: www.reading.org. ''The entry must be an original short story appearing in a young children's periodical for the first time. The short story should serve as a literary standard that encourages young readers to read periodicals.'' Deadline for entries: The entry must have been published for the first time in the eligibility year; the short story must be submitted during the calendar year of publication. Anyone wishing to nominate a short story should send it to the designated Paul A. Witty Short Award Subcommittee Chair by December 1. Award is $1,000 and recognition at the annual IRA Convention.

JOHN WOOD COMMUNITY COLLEGE CREATIVE WRITING CONTEST

Business Office—Writing Conference, John Wood Community College, 1301 S. 48th Street, Quincy IL 62305. (217)641-4940. Fax: (217)641-4900. E-mail: jmcgovern@jwcc.edu. Web site: www.jwcc.edu. **Contact:** Janet McGovern, education specialist. The college sponsors a writing contest for poetry, fiction and nonfiction. Entries for the contest are accpeted March-April of each year. Please see the JWCC Web site for more details or e-mail. jmcgovern@jwcc.edu for more information. In addition, the college sponsors writing workshops, readings, speakers, a humanities series, a photography show in spring, and an art competition in the fall.

ALICE WOOD MEMORIAL OHIOANA AWARD FOR CHILDREN'S LITERATURE

Ohioana Library Association, 274 E. First Ave., Suite 300, Columbus OH 43201. (614)466-3831. Fax: (614)728-6974. E-mail: ohioana@sloma.state.oh.us. Web site: www.ohioana.org. **Contact:** Linda R. Hengst. Offered to an author whose body of work has made, and continues to make, a significant contribution to literature for children or young adults and through their work as a writer, teacher, administrator, and community member, interest in children's literature has been encouraged and children have become involved with reading. Nomination forms for SASE. Recipient must have been born in Ohio or lived in Ohio at least 5 years. Deadline: December 31. Awards $1,000 cash prize.

WRITE IT NOW!

SmartWriters.com, 10823 Worthing Ave., San Diego CA 92126-2665. (858)689-2665. E-mail: editor@smartwrite rs.com. Web site: www.SmartWriters.com. **Editorial Director:** Roxyanne Young. Estab. 1994. Annual contest. ''Our purpose is to encourage new writers and help get their manuscripts into the hands of people who can help further their careers.'' Unpublished submissions only. Submissions made by author. Deadline for entries: February 1. SASE for contest rules and entry forms; also see Web site. Entry fee is $10. Awards a cash prize, books about writing, and an editorial review of the winning manuscripts. 2006's cash prize was $500, plus $100 cash prizes for category winners. Judging by published writers and editors. Requirement for entrants: ''This contest is open to all writers age 18 and older. There are 7 categories: Young Adult, Mid-grade, Chapter Book, Picture Book, Poetry, Nonfiction, and Illustration.'' See Web site for more details.

WRITING CONFERENCE WRITING CONTESTS

The Writing Conference, Inc., P.O. Box 664, Ottawa KS 66067. Phone/fax: (785)242-1995. E-mail: jbushman@w ritingconference.com. Web site: www.writingconference.com. **Contest Director:** John H. Bushman. **Open to**

students. Annual contest. Estab. 1988. Purpose of contest: to further writing by students with awards for narration, exposition and poetry at the elementary, middle school and high school levels. Unpublished submissions only. Submissions made by the author or teacher. Deadline for entries: January 8. SASE for contest rules and entry form or consult Web site. No entry fee. Awards plaque and publication of winning entry in *The Writers' Slate* online, April issue. Judging by a panel of teachers. Requirements for entrants: must be enrolled in school—K-12th grade.

✂ WRITING FOR CHILDREN COMPETITION

90 Richmond St. E, Suite 200, Toronto ON M5C 1P1 Canada. (416)703-8982, ext. 223. Fax: (416)504-9090. E-mail: projects@writersunion.ca. Web site: www.writersunion.ca. **Open to students** and Canadian citizens or landed immigrants who have not had a book published. Annual contest. Estab. 1997. Purpose of contest: to discover, encourage and promote new writers of children's literature. Unpublished submissions only. Submissions made by author. Deadline for entries: April 24. Entry fee is $15. Awards $1,500 and submission of winner and finalists to 3 publishers of children's books. Word limit: 1,500. Judging by members of the Writers Union of Canada (published book authors). Requirements for entrants: Open only to unpublished writers. Please do not send illustrations.

YEARBOOK EXCELLENCE CONTEST

Quill and Scroll Society, School of Journalism and Mass Communication, 100 Adler Building, Room E346, Iowa City IA 52242- 2004. (319)335-3457. Fax: (319)335-3989. E-mail: quill-scroll@uiowa.edu. Web site: www.uiowa .edu/~quill-sc. **Executive Director:** Vanessa Shelton. **Open to students whose schools have Quill and Scroll charters.** Annual contest. Estab. 1987. Purpose of contest: to recognize and reward student journalists for their work in yearbooks and to provide student winners an opportunity to apply for a scholarship to be used freshman year in college for students planning to major in journalism. Previously published submissions only. Submissions made by the author or school yearbook adviser. Must be published between in the 12-month span prior to contest deadline. Deadline for entries: November 1. SASE for contest rules and entry form. Entry fee is $2 per entry. Awards National Gold Key; sweepstakes winners receive plaque; seniors eligible for scholarships. Judging by various judges. Winning entries may be published in *Quill and Scroll* magazine.

✂ YOUNG ADULT CANADIAN BOOK AWARD

The Canadian Library Association, 328 Frank St., Ottawa ON K2P 0X8 Canada. (613)232-9625. Fax: (613)563-9895. Web site: www.cla.ca. **Contact:** Committee Chair. Annual award. Estab. 1981. Purpose of award: "to recognize the author of an outstanding English-language Canadian book which appeals to young adults between the ages of 13 and 18 that was published the preceding calendar year. Information is available upon request. We approach publishers. Entries are not returned. No entry fee. Awards a leather-bound book. Requirement for entrants: must be a work of fiction (novel or short stories), the title must be a Canadian publication in either hardcover or paperback, and the author must be a Canadian citizen or landed immigrant. Award given at the Canadian Library Association Conference.

THE YOUTH HONOR AWARD PROGRAM

Skipping Stones, P.O. Box 3939, Eugene OR 97403. (514)342-4956. E-mail: editor@skippingstones.org. Web site: www.skippingstones.org. **Director of Public Relations:** Arun N. Toke. **Open to students.** Annual contest. Estab. 1994. Purpose of contest: "To recognize creative and artistic works by young people that promote multicultural awareness and nature appreciation." Unpublished submissions only. Submissions made by author. Deadline for entries: June 25. SASE for contest rules and entry forms. Entry fee is $3; low-income entrants, free. "Ten winners will be published in our fall issue. Winners will also receive an Honor Award Certificate, a subscription to *Skipping Stones* and five nature and/or multicultural books."

THE ANNA ZORNIO MEMORIAL CHILDREN'S THEATRE PLAYWRITING AWARD

University of New Hampshire, Department of Theatre and Dance, Paul Creative Arts Center, 30 College Rd., Durham NH 03824-3538. (603)862-3538. Fax: (603)862-0298. E-mail: mike.wood@unh.edu. Web site: www.un h.edu/theatre-dance/zornio.html. **Contact:** Michael Wood. Contest every 4 years; next contest is November 2008 for 2009-2010 season. Estab. 1979. Purpose of the award: "to honor the late Anna Zornio, an alumna of The University of New Hampshire, for dedication to and inspiration of playwriting for young people, K-12th grade. Open to playwrights who are residents of the U.S. and Canada. Plays or musicals should run about 45 minutes." Unpublished submissions only. Submissions made by the author. Deadline for entries: March 3, 2008. SASE for award rules and entry forms. No entry fee. Awards $1,000 plus guaranteed production. Judging by faculty committee. Acquires rights to campus production. For more information visit Web site.

Helpful Books
& Publications

The editors of *Children's Writer's & Illustrator's Market* suggest the following books and periodicals to keep you informed on writing and illustrating techniques, trends in the field, business issues, industry news and changes, and additional markets.

BOOKS

An Author's Guide to Children's Book Promotion, Ninth edition, by Susan Salzman Raab, 345 Millwood Rd., Chappaqua NY 10514. (914)241-2117. E-mail: info@raabassociates.com. Web site: www.raabassociates.com/authors.htm.

The Business of Writing for Children, by Aaron Shepard, Shepard Publications. Web site: www.aaronshep.com/kidwriter/Business.html. Available on www.amazon.com.

Children's Writer Guide, (annual), The Institute of Children's Literature, 93 Long Ridge Rd., West Redding CT 06896-0811. (800)443-6078. Web site: www.writersbookstore.com.

The Children's Writer's Reference, by Berthe Amoss and Eric Suben, Writer's Digest Books, 4700 E. Galbraith Rd., Cincinnati OH 45236. (800)448-0915. Web site: www.writersdigest.com.

Children's Writer's Word Book, Second edition, by Alijandra Mogilner & Tayopa Mogilner, Writer's Digest Books, 4700 E. Galbraith Rd., Cincinnati OH 45236. (800)448-0915. Web site: www.writersdigest.com.

The Complete Idiot's Guide® to Publishing Children's Books, Second Edition, by Harold D. Underdown, Alpha Books, 201 W. 103rd St., Indianapolis IN 46290. Web site: www.underdown.org/cig.htm.

Creating Characters Kids Will Love, by Elaine Marie Alphin, Writer's Digest Books, 4700 E. Galbraith Rd., Cincinnati OH 45236. (800)448-0915. Web site: www.writersdigest.com.

Formatting & Submitting Your Manuscript, Second Edition, by Cynthia Laufenberg and the editors of Writer's Market, Writer's Digest Books, 4700 E. Galbraith Rd., Cincinnati OH 45236. (800)448-0915. Web site: www.writersdigest.com.

Guide to Literary Agents, edited by Chuck Sambuchino, Writer's Digest Books, 4700 E. Galbraith Rd., Cincinnati OH 45236. (800)448-0915. Web site: www.writersdigest.com.

How to Write a Children's Book and Get It Published, Third Edition, by Barbara Seuling, John Wiley & Sons, 111 River St., Hoboken NJ 07030. (201)748-6000. Web site: www.wiley.com.

How to Write and Illustrate Children's Books and Get Them Published, edited by Treld Pelkey Bicknell and Felicity Trottman, Writer's Digest Books, 4700 E. Galbraith Rd., Cincinnati OH 45236. (800)448-0915. Web site: www.writersdigest.com.

How to Write Attention-Grabbing Query & Cover Letters, by John Wood, Writer's Digest Books, 4700 E. Galbraith Rd., Cincinnati OH 45236. (800)448-0915. Web site: www.writers digest.com.

Illustrating Children's Books: Creating Pictures for Publication, by Martin Salisbury, Barron's Educational Series, 250 Wireless Blvd., Hauppauge NY 11788. (800)645-3476. Web site: www.barronseduc.com.

It's a Bunny-Eat-Bunny World: A Writer's Guide to Surviving and Thriving in Today's Competitive Children's Book Market, by Olga Litowinsky, Walker & Company, 104 Fifth Ave., New York NY 10011. (212)727-8300. Web site: www.walkerbooks.com.

Page After Page: discover the confidence & passion you need to start writing & keep writing (no matter what), by Heather Sellers, Writer's Digest Books, 4700 E. Galbraith Rd., Cincinnati OH 45236. (800)448-0915. Web site: www.writersdigest.com.

Picture Writing: A New Approach to Writing for Kids and Teens, by Anastasia Suen, Writer's Digest Books, 4700 E. Galbraith Rd., Cincinnati OH 45236. (800)448-0915. Web site: www.writersdigest.com.

Story Sparkers: A Creativity Guide for Children's Writers, by Marcia Thornton Jones and Debbie Dadey, Writer's Digest Books, 4700 E. Galbraith Rd., Cincinnati OH 45236. (800)448-0915. Web site: www.writersdigest.com.

Take Joy: A Writer's Guide to Loving the Craft, by Jane Yolen, Writer's Digest Books, 4700 E. Galbraith Rd., Cincinnati OH 45236. (800)448-0915. Web site: www.writersdigest.com.

A Teen's Guide to Getting Published; Publishing for Profit, Recognition and Academic Success, Second edition, by Jessica Dunn & Danielle Dunn, Prufrock Press, P.O. Box 8813, Waco TX 76714-8813. (800)998-2208. Web site: www.prufrock.com.

The Writer's Guide to Crafting Stories for Children, by Nancy Lamb, Writer's Digest Books, 4700 E. Galbraith Rd., Cincinnati OH 45236. (800)448-0915. Web site: www.writers digest.com.

Writing and Illustrating Children's Books for Publication: Two Perspectives, Revised Edition, by Berthe Amoss and Eric Suben, Writer's Digest Books, 4700 E. Galbraith Rd., Cincinnati OH 45236. (800)448-0915. Web site: www.writersdigest.com.

Writing for Children & Teenagers, Third Edition, by Lee Wyndham, revised by Arnold Madison, Writer's Digest Books, 4700 E. Galbraith Rd., Cincinnati OH 45236. (800)448-0915. Web site: www.writersdigest.com.

Writing for Young Adults, by Sherry Garland, Writer's Digest Books, 4700 E. Galbraith Rd., Cincinnati OH 45236. (800)448-0915. Web site: www.writersdigest.com.

Writing With Pictures: How to Write and Illustrate Children's Books, by Uri Shulevitz, Watson-Guptill Publications, 770 Broadway, New York NY 10003. (800)278-8477. Web site: www.watsonguptill.com/products.html.

You Can Write Children's Books, by Tracey E. Dils, Writer's Digest Books, 4700 E. Galbraith Rd., Cincinnati OH 45236. (800)448-0915. Web site: www.writersdigest.com.

You Can Write Children's Books Workbook, by Tracey E. Dils, Writer's Digest Books, 4700 E. Galbraith Rd., Cincinnati OH 45236. (800)448-0915. Web site: www.writersdigest.com.

Resources

The Young Writer's Guide to Getting Published, by Kathy Henderson, Writer's Digest Books, 4700 E. Galbraith Rd., Cincinnati OH 45236. (800)448-0915. Web site: www.writers digest.com.

PUBLICATIONS

Book Links: Connecting Books, Libraries and Classrooms, editor Laura Tillotson, American Library Association, 50 E. Huron St., Chicago IL 60611. (800)545-2433. Web site: www. ala.org/BookLinks. *Magazine published 6 times a year (September-July) for the purpose of connecting books, libraries and classrooms. Features articles on specific topics followed by bibliographies recommending books for further information. Subscription: $39.95/year.*

Children's Book Insider, editor Laura Backes, 901 Columbia Rd., Ft. Collins CO 80525-1838. (970)495-0056 or (800)807-1916. E-mail: mail@write4kids.com. Web site: www.write4ki ds.com. *Monthly newsletter covering markets, techniques and trends in children's publishing. Subscription: $29.95/year; electronic version $26.95/year.*

Children's Writer, editor Susan Tierney, The Institute of Children's Literature, 93 Long Ridge Rd., West Redding CT 06896-0811. (800)443-6078. Web site: www.childrenswriter.com. *Monthly newsletter of writing and publishing trends in the children's field. Subscription: $24/year; special introductory rate: $19.*

The Five Owls, editor Dr. Mark West, P.O. Box 235, Marathon TX 79842. (432)386-4257. Web site: www.fiveowls.com. *Quarterly online newsletter for readers personally and professionally involved in children's literature. Subscription: $35/year.*

The Horn Book Magazine, editor-in-chief Roger Sutton, The Horn Book Inc., 56 Roland St., Suite 200, Boston MA 02129. (800)325-1170. E-mail: info@hbook.com or cgross@hbook.c om. Web site: www.hbook.com. *Bimonthly guide to the children's book world including views on the industry and reviews of the latest books. Subscription: $34.95/year for new subscriptions; $49/year for renewals.*

The Lion and the Unicorn: A Critical Journal of Children's Literature, editors George Bodmer, Lisa Paul and Sandra Beckett, The Johns Hopkins University Press, P.O. Box 19966, Baltimore MD 21211-0966. (800)548-1784 or (410)516-6987 (outside the U.S. and Canada). E-mail: jrlncirc@press.jhu.edu. Web site: www.press.jhu.edu/journals/lion_an d_the_unicorn/. *Magazine published 3 times a year serving as a forum for discussion of children's literature featuring interviews with authors, editors and experts in the field. Subscription: $33/year.*

Once Upon a Time, editor Audrey Baird, 553 Winston Court, St. Paul MN 55118. (651)457-6223. E-mail: audreyouat@comcast.net. Web site: www.onceuponatimemag.com. *Quarterly support magazine for children's writers and illustrators and those interested in children's literature. Subscription: $27/year.*

Publishers Weekly, editor-in-chief Sara Nelson, Reed Business Information, a division of Reed Elsevier Inc., 360 Park Ave. S., New York NY 10010. (800)278-2991. Web site: www.publishersweekly.com. *Weekly trade publication covering all aspects of the publishing industry; includes coverage of the children's field and spring and fall issues devoted solely to children's books. Subscription: $239.99/year. Available on newsstands for $8/ issue. (Special issues are higher in price.)*

Society of Children's Book Writers and Illustrators Bulletin, editors Stephen Mooser and Lin Oliver, SCBWI, 8271 Beverly Blvd., Los Angeles CA 90048. (323)782-1010. E-mail: bulletin@scbwi.org. Web site: www.scbwi.org/pubs.htm. *Bimonthly newsletter of SCBWI covering news of interest to members. Subscription with $60/year membership.*

Resources

Useful Online Resources

The editors of *Children's Writer's & Illustrator's Market* suggest the following Web sites to keep you informed on writing and illustrating techniques, trends in the field, business issues, industry news and changes, and additional markets.

Amazon.com: www.amazon.com
Calling itself "A bookstore too big for the physical world," Amazon.com has more than 3 million books available on their Web site at discounted prices, plus a personal notification service of new releases, reader reviews, bestseller and suggested book information.

America Writes for Kids: http://usawrites4kids.drury.edu
Lists book authors by state along with interviews, profiles and writing tips.

Artlex Art Dictionary: www.artlex.com
Art dictionary with more than 3,200 terms

Association for Library Service to Children: www.ala.org
This site provides links to information about Newbery, Caldecott, Coretta Scott King, Michael L. Printz and Theodor Seuss Geisel Awards as well as a host of other awards for notable children's books.

Association of Authors' Representatives: www.aar.online.org
The Web site of the AAR offers a list of agent members, links, and frequently asked questions including useful advice for authors seeking representation.

Association of Illustrators: www.theaoi.com
This U.K.-based organization has been working since 1973 to promote illustration, illustrators' rights and standards. The Web site has discussion boards, artists' directories, events, links to agents and much more.

Authors and Illustrators for Children Webring: http://t.webring.com/hub?ring=aicwebring
Here you'll find a list of links of sites of interest to children's writers and illustrators or created by them.

The Authors Guild Online: www.authorsguild.org
The Web site of The Authors Guild offers articles and columns dealing with contract issues, copyright, electronic rights and other legal issues of concern to writers.

Barnes & Noble Online: www.barnesandnoble.com
The world's largest bookstore chain's Web site contains 600,000 in-stock titles at discount

Resources

prices as well as personalized recommendations, online events with authors and book forum access for members.

The Book Report Network: includes www.bookreporter.com; www.readinggroupguides.com; www.authorsontheweb.com; www.teenreads.com and www.kidsreads.com.
All the sites feature giveaways, book reviews, author and editor interviews, and recommended reads. A great way to stay connected.

Bookwire: www.bookwire.com
A gateway to finding information about publishers, booksellers, libraries, authors, reviews and awards. Also offers frequently asked publishing questions and answers, a calendar of events, a mailing list and other helpful resources.

Canadian Children's Book Centre: www.bookcentre.ca
The site for the CCBC includes profiles of illustrators and authors, information on recent books, a calendar of upcoming events, information on CCBC publications, and tips from Canadian children's authors.

Canadian Society of Children's Authors, Illustrators and Performers: www.canscaip.org
This organization promotes all aspects of children's writing, illustration and performance.

The Children's Book Council: www.cbcbooks.org
This site includes a complete list of CBC members with addresses, names and descriptions of what each publishes, and links to publishers' Web sites. Also offers previews of upcoming titles from members; articles from *CBC Features*, the Council's newsletter; and their catalog.

Children's Literature: www.childrenslit.com
Offers book reviews, lists of conferences, searchable database, links to over 1,000 author/illustrator Web sites and much more.

Children's Literature Web Guide: www.ucalgary.ca/~dkbrown
This site includes stories, poetry, resource lists, lists of conferences, links to book reviews, lists of awards (international), and information on books from classic to contemporary.

Children's Writer's & Illustrator's Market Web Page: www.cwim.com
Visit the new web page for market updates and sign up for a free e-newsletter.

Children's Writing Supersite: www.write4kids.com
This site (formerly Children's Writers Resource Center) includes highlights from the newsletter *Children's Book Insider*; definitions of publishing terms; answers to frequently asked questions; information on trends; information on small presses; a research center for Web information; and a catalog of material available from *CBI*.

The Colossal Directory of Children's Publishers Online: www.signaleader.com/childrenswriters
This site features links to Web sites of children's publishers and magazines and includes information on which publishers offer submission guidelines online.

Cynthia Leitich Smith's Web site: www.cynthialeitichsmith.com
In addition to information about her books and appearances and a blog, Cynthia Leitich Smith has assembled a site chock full of great useful and inspiring information including interviews with writers and illustrators, favorite reads, awards, bibliographies, and tons of helpful links, many to help writers explore diversity.

Database of Award-Winning Children's Literature: www.dawcl.com
A compilation of over 4,000 records of award-winning books throughout the U.S., Canada,

Australia, New Zealand and the U.K. You can search by age level, format, genre, setting, historical period, ethnicity or nationality of the protagonist, gender of protagonist, publication year, award name, or even by keyword. Begin here to compile your reading list of award-winners.

The Drawing Board: http://members.aol.com/thedrawing
This site for illustrators features articles, interviews, links and resources for illustrators from all fields.

Editor & Publisher: www.editorandpublisher.com
The Internet source for *Editor & Publisher*, this site provides up-to-date industry news, with other opportunities such as a research area and bookstore, a calendar of events and classifieds.

Imaginary Lands: www.imaginarylands.org
A fun site with links to Web sites about picture books, learning tools and children's literature.

International Board on Books for Young People: www.ibby.org
Founded in Switzerland in 1953, IBBY is a nonprofit that seeks to encourage the creation and distribution of quality children's literature. They cooperate with children's organizations and children's book institutions around the world.

International Reading Association: www.reading.org
This Web site includes articles; book lists; event, conference and convention information; and an online bookstore.

Kid Magazine Writers: www.kidmagwriters.com
Writer Jan Fields created this site to offer support and information to the often-neglected children's magazine writer. The Web site features editor interviews, articles on technique, special reports, an A to Z magazine market guide, and archives of monthly features.

National Association for the Education of Young Children: www.naeyc.org.
This organization is comprised of over 100,000 early childhood educators and others interested in the development and education of young children. Their Web site makes a great introduction and research resource for authors and illustrators of picture books.

National Writers Union: www.nwu.org
The union for freelance writers in U.S. Markets. The NWU offers contract advice, greviance assistance, health and liability insurance and much more.

Once Upon a Time: www.onceuponatimemag.com
This companion site to *Once Upon A Time* magazine offers excerpts from recent articles, notes for prospective contributors, and information about *OUAT*'s 11 regular columnists.

Picturebook: www.picture-book.com
This site brought to you by *Picturebook* sourcebook offers tons of links for illustrators, portfolio searching, and news, and offers a listserv, bulletin board and chatroom.

Planet Esmé: A Wonderful World of Children's Literature: www.planetesme.com
This site run by author Esmé Raji Codell, offers extensive lists of children's book recommendations, including the latest titles of note for various age groups, a great list of links, and more. Be sure to click on "join the club" to receive Codell's delightful e-mail newsletter.

Publishers' Catalogues Home Page: www.lights.com/publisher/index.html
A mammoth link collection of more than 6,000 publishers around the world arranged geographically. This site is one of the most comprehensive directories of publishers on the Internet.

The Purple Crayon: www.underdown.org

Editor Harold Underdown's site includes articles on trends, business, and cover letters and queries as well as interviews with editors and answers to frequently asked questions. He also includes links to a number of other sites helpful to writers and excerpts from his book *The Complete Idiot's Guide to Publishing Children's Books.*

Slantville: www.slantville.com

An online artists community, this site includes a yellow pages for artists, frequently asked questions and a library offering information on a number of issues of interest to illustrators. This is a great site to visit to view artists' portfolios.

Smartwriters.com: www.smartwriters.com

Writer, novelist, photographer, graphic designer, and co-founder of 2-Tier Software, Inc., Roxyanne Young, runs this online magazine, which is absolutely stuffed with resources for children's writers, teachers and young writers. It's also got contests, interviews, free books, advice and well—you just have to go there.

Society of Children's Book Writers and Illustrators: www.scbwi.org

This site includes information on awards and grants available to SCBWI members, a calendar of events listed by date and region, a list of publications available to members, and a site map for easy navigation. Follow the Regional Chapters link to find the SCBWI chapter in your area.

The Society of Illustrators: www.societyillustrators.org

Since 1901, this organization has been working to promote the interest of professional illustrators. Information on exhibitions, career advice, and many other links provided.

U.K. Children's Books: www.ukchildrensbooks.co.uk

Filled with links to author sites, illustrator sites, publishers, booksellers, and organizations—not to mention help with Web site design and other technicalities—visit this site no matter which side of the Atlantic you rest your head.

United States Board on Books for Young People: www.usbby.org

Serves as the U.S. national section of the International Board on Books for Young People.

United States Postal Service: www.usps.com

Offers domestic and International postage rate calculator, stamp ordering, zip code look up, express mail tracking and more.

Verla Kay's Web site: www.verlakay.com

Author Verla Kay's Web site features writer's tips, articles, a schedules of online workshops (with transcripts of past workshops), a good news board and helpful links.

Writersdigest.com: www.writersdigest.com

Brought to you by *Writer's Digest* magazine, this site features articles, resources, links, writing prompts, a bookstore, and more.

Writersmarket.com: www.writersmarket.com

This gateway to the *Writer's Market* online edition offers market news, FAQs, tips, featured markets and web resources, a free newsletter, and more.

Writing-world.com: www.writing-world.com/children/index.shtml

Site features reams of advice, links and offers a free bi-weekly newsletter.

Glossary

AAR. Association of Authors' Representatives.

ABA. American Booksellers Association.

ABC. Association of Booksellers for Children.

Advance. A sum of money a publisher pays a writer or illustrator prior to the publication of a book. It is usually paid in installments, such as one half on signing the contract, one half on delivery of a complete and satisfactory manuscript. The advance is paid against the royalty money that will be earned by the book.

ALA. American Library Association.

All rights. The rights contracted to a publisher permitting the use of material anywhere and in any form, including movie and book club sales, without additional payment to the creator.

Anthology. A collection of selected writings by various authors or gatherings of works by one author.

Anthropomorphization. The act of attributing human form and personality to things not human (such as animals).

ASAP. As soon as possible.

Assignment. An editor or art director asks a writer, illustrator or photographer to produce a specific piece for an agreed-upon fee.

B&W. Black and white.

Backlist. A publisher's list of books not published during the current season but still in print.

Biennially. Occurring once every 2 years.

Bimonthly. Occurring once every 2 months.

Biweekly. Occurring once every 2 weeks.

Book packager. A company that draws all elements of a book together, from the initial concept to writing and marketing strategies, then sells the book package to a book publisher and/or movie producer. Also known as book producer or book developer.

Book proposal. Package submitted to a publisher for consideration usually consisting of a synopsis, outline and sample chapters. (See Before Your First Sale, page 8.)

Business-size envelope. Also known as a #10 envelope. The standard size used in sending business correspondence.

Camera-ready. Refers to art that is completely prepared for copy camera platemaking.

Caption. A description of the subject matter of an illustration or photograph; photo captions include persons' names where appropriate. Also called cutline.

Clean-copy. A manuscript free of errors and needing no editing; it is ready for typesetting.

Clips. Samples, usually from newspapers or magazines, of a writer's published work.

Concept books. Books that deal with ideas, concepts and large-scale problems, promoting an understanding of what's happening in a child's world. Most prevalent are alphabet and counting books, but also includes books dealing with specific concerns facing young people (such as divorce, birth of a sibling, friendship or moving).

Contract. A written agreement stating the rights to be purchased by an editor, art director or producer and the amount of payment the writer, illustrator or photographer will receive for that sale. (See Running Your Business, page 13.)

Contributor's copies. The magazine issues sent to an author, illustrator or photographer in which her work appears.

Co-op publisher. A publisher that shares production costs with an author, but, unlike subsidy publishers, handles all marketing and distribution. An author receives a high percentage of royalties until her initial investment is recouped, then standard royalties. (*Children's Writer's & Illustrator's Market* does not include co-op publishers.)

Copy. The actual written material of a manuscript.

Copyediting. Editing a manuscript for grammar usage, spelling, punctuation and general style.

Copyright. A means to legally protect an author's/illustrator's/photographer's work. This can be shown by writing ©, the creator's name, and year of work's creation. (See Running Your Business, page 13.)

Cover letter. A brief letter, accompanying a complete manuscript, especially useful if responding to an editor's request for a manuscript. May also accompany a book proposal. (See Before Your First Sale, page 8.)

Cutline. See caption.

Division. An unincorporated branch of a company.

Dummy. A loose mock-up of a book showing placement of text and artwork.

Electronic submission. A submission of material by modem or on computer disk.

Final draft. The last version of a polished manuscript ready for submission to an editor.

First North American serial rights. The right to publish material in a periodical for the first time, in the United States or Canada. (See Running Your Business, page 13.)

F&Gs. Folded and gathered sheets. An early, not-yet-bound copy of a picture book.

Flat fee. A one-time payment.

Galleys. The first typeset version of a manuscript that has not yet been divided into pages.

Genre. A formulaic type of fiction, such as horror, mystery, romance, science fiction or western.

Glossy. A photograph with a shiny surface as opposed to one with a non-shiny matte finish.

Gouache. Opaque watercolor with an appreciable film thickness and an actual paint layer.

Halftone. Reproduction of a continuous tone illustration with the image formed by dots produced by a camera lens screen.

Hard copy. The printed copy of a computer's output.

Hardware. All the mechanically-integrated components of a computer that are not software—circuit boards, transistors and the machines that are the actual computer.

Hi-Lo. High interest, low reading level.

Home page. The first page of a Web site.

IBBY. International Board on Books for Young People.

Imprint. Name applied to a publisher's specific line of books.

Internet. A worldwide network of computers that offers access to a wide variety of electronic resources.

IRA. International Reading Association.

IRC. International Reply Coupon. Sold at the post office to enclose with text or artwork sent to a recipient outside your own country to cover postage costs when replying or returning work.

Keyline. Identification of the positions of illustrations and copy for the printer.

Layout. Arrangement of illustrations, photographs, text and headlines for printed material.

Line drawing. Illustration done with pencil or ink using no wash or other shading.

Mass market books. Paperback books directed toward an extremely large audience sold in supermarkets, drugstores, airports, newsstands, online retailers, and bookstores.

Mechanicals. Paste-up or preparation of work for printing.

Middle grade or mid-grade. See middle reader.

Middle reader. The general classification of books written for readers approximately ages 9-11. Often called middle grade or mid-grade.

Ms (mss). Manuscript(s).

Multiple submissions. See simultaneous submissions.

NCTE. National Council of Teachers of English.

One-time rights. Permission to publish a story in periodical or book form one time only. (See Running Your Business, page 13.)

Outline. A summary of a book's contents; often in the form of chapter headings with a descriptive sentence or two under each heading to show the scope of the book.

Package sale. The sale of a manuscript and illustrations/photos as a "package" paid for with one check.

Payment on acceptance. The writer, artist or photographer is paid for her work at the time the editor or art director decides to buy it.

Payment on publication. The writer, artist or photographer is paid for her work when it is published.

Picture book. A type of book aimed at preschoolers to 8-year-olds that tells a story using a combination of text and artwork, or artwork only.

Print. An impression pulled from an original plate, stone, block, screen or negative; also a positive made from a photographic negative.

Proofreading. Reading text to correct typographical errors.

Query. A letter to an editor or agent designed to capture interest in an article or book you have written or propose to write. (See Before Your First Sale, page 8.)

Reading fee. Money charged by some agents and publishers to read a submitted manuscript. (*Children's Writer's & Illustrator's Market* does not include agencies that charge reading fees.)

Reprint rights. Permission to print an already published work whose first rights have been sold to another magazine or book publisher. (See Running Your Business, page 13.)

Response time. The average length of time it takes an editor or art director to accept or reject a query or submission and inform the creator of the decision.

Rights. The bundle of permissions offered to an editor or art director in exchange for printing a manuscript, artwork or photographs. (See Running Your Business, page 13.)

Rough draft. A manuscript that has not been checked for errors in grammar, punctuation, spelling or content.

Roughs. Preliminary sketches or drawings.

Royalty. An agreed percentage paid by a publisher to a writer, illustrator or photographer for each copy of her work sold.

SAE. Self-addressed envelope.

SASE. Self-addressed, stamped envelope.

SCBWI. The Society of Children's Book Writers and Illustrators. (See listing in Clubs & Organizations section.)

Second serial rights. Permission for the reprinting of a work in another periodical after its first publication in book or magazine form. (See Running Your Business, page 13.)

Semiannual. Occurring every 6 months or twice a year.

Semimonthly. Occurring twice a month.

Semiweekly. Occurring twice a week.

Serial rights. The rights given by an author to a publisher to print a piece in one or more periodicals. (See Running Your Business, page 13.)

Simultaneous submissions. Queries or proposals sent to several publishers at the same time. Also called multiple submissions. (See Before Your First Sale, page 8.)

Slant. The approach to a story or piece of artwork that will appeal to readers of a particular publication.

Slush pile. Editors' term for their collections of unsolicited manuscripts.

Software. Programs and related documentation for use with a computer.

Solicited manuscript. Material that an editor has asked for or agreed to consider before being sent by a writer.

SPAR. Society of Photographers and Artists Representatives.

Speculation (spec). Creating a piece with no assurance from an editor or art director that it will be purchased or any reimbursements for material or labor paid.

Subsidiary rights. All rights other than book publishing rights included in a book contract, such as paperback, book club and movie rights. (See Running Your Business, page 13.)

Subsidy publisher. A book publisher that charges the author for the cost of typesetting, printing and promoting a book. Also called a vanity publisher. (*Children's Writer's & Illustrator's Market* does not include subsidy publishers.)

Synopsis. A brief summary of a story or novel. Usually a page to a page and a half, single-spaced, if part of a book proposal.

Tabloid. Publication printed on an ordinary newspaper page turned sideways and folded in half.

Tearsheet. Page from a magazine or newspaper containing your printed art, story, article, poem or photo.

Thumbnail. A rough layout in miniature.

Trade books. Books sold in bookstores and through online retailers, aimed at a smaller audience than mass market books, and printed in smaller quantities by publishers.

Transparencies. Positive color slides; not color prints.

Unsolicited manuscript. Material sent without an editor's, art director's or agent's request.

Vanity publisher. See subsidy publisher.

Work-for-hire. An arrangement between a writer, illustrator or photographer and a company under which the company retains complete control of the work's copyright. (See Running Your Business, page 13.)

YA. See young adult.

Young adult. The general classification of books written for readers approximately ages 12-18. Often referred to as YA.

Young reader. The general classification of books written for readers approximately ages 5-8.

Names Index

This index lists the editors, art directors, agents and art reps listed in *Children's Writer's & Illustrator's Market*, along with the publisher, publication or company for which they work. Names were culled from Book Publishers, Canadian & International Books Publishers, Magazines, Young Writer's & Illustrator's Markets, and Agents & Art Reps.

Age-Level Index

This index lists book and magazine publishers by the age-groups for which they publish. Use it to locate appropriate markets for your work, then carefully read the listings and follow the guidelines of each publisher. Use this index in conjunction with the Subject Index to further narrow your list of markets. **Picture Books** and **Picture-Oriented Material** are for preschoolers to 8-year-olds; **Young Readers** are for 5- to 8-year-olds; **Middle Readers** are for 9- to 11-year-olds; and **Young Adults** are for ages 12 and up.

BOOK PUBLISHERS
Picture Books

Young Readers

MAGAZINES
Picture-Oriented Material

Young Readers

Middle Readers

Young Adult/Teen

Age-Level Index

Subject Index

This index lists book and magazine publishers by the fiction and nonfiction subject areas in which they publish. Use it to locate appropriate markets for your work, then carefully read the listings and follow the guidelines of each publisher. Use this index in conjunction with Age-Level Index to further narrow your list of markets.

Animal

Subject Index

Folktales

Health

Hi-Lo

History

Humor

Subject Index

Multicultural

Nature/Environment

Poetry

Problem Novels

BOOK PUBLISHERS: NONFICTION

Activity Books

Animal

Arts/Crafts

Biography

Careers

Concept

Writer's Digest

DISCOVER A WORLD OF WRITING SUCCESS!

Are you ready to be praised, published, and paid for your writing? It's time to invest in your future with *Writer's Digest!* Beginners and experienced writers alike have been relying on *Writer's Digest*, the world's leading magazine for writers, for more than 80 years — and it keeps getting better! Each issue is brimming with:

- technique articles geared toward specific genres, including fiction, nonfiction, business writing and more

- business information specifically for writers, such as organizational advice, tax tips, and setting fees

- tips and tricks for rekindling your creative fire

- the latest and greatest markets for print, online and e-publishing

- and much more!

Get a FREE ISSUE of *Writer's Digest!*

NO RISK!
Send No Money Now!

☐ **Yes!** Please rush me my FREE issue of *Writer's Digest* — the world's leading magazine for writers. If I like what I read, I'll get a full year's subscription (6 issues, including the free issue) for only $19.96. That's 44% off the newsstand rate! If I'm not completely satisfied, I'll write "cancel" on your invoice, return it and owe nothing. The FREE issue is mine to keep, no matter what!

_____
Name (please print)

_____
Address

_____
City   State   ZIP

_____
E-mail (to contact me regarding my subscription)

☐ YES! Also e-mail me *Writer's Digest*'s FREE e-newsletter and other information of interest. *(We will not sell your e-mail address to outside companies.)*

Subscribers in Canada will be charged an additional US$10 (includes GST/HST) and invoiced. Outside the U.S. and Canada, add US$10 and remit payment in U.S. funds with this order. Annual newsstand rate: $35.94. Please allow 4-6 weeks for first-issue delivery.

Writer's Digest   www.writersdigest.com

J7FCMK

Get a FREE TRIAL ISSUE of Writer's Digest

Packed with creative inspiration, advice, and tips to guide you on the road to success, *Writer's Digest* offers everything you need to take your writing to the next level! You'll discover how to:

- create dynamic characters and page-turning plots
- submit query letters that publishers won't be able to refuse
- find the right agent or editor
- make it out of the slush-pile and into the hands of publishers
- write award-winning contest entries
- and more!

See for yourself — order your FREE trial issue today!

Music/Dance

Nature/Environment

Subject Index

Reference

Religious

Science

Self Help

Textbooks

MAGAZINES: FICTION
Adventure

Animal

Subject Index

Horsepower 252
Humpty Dumpty's Magazine 252
Jack and Jill 253
Kid Zone 257
Nature Friend Magazine 258
Nick Jr. Family Magazine 259
Passport 260
Positive Teens 261
Seventeen Magazine 263
Sparkle 264
TC Magazine (Teenage Christian) 266
Teen Magazine 266
U*S* Kids 267

Humor
Advocate, PKA's Publication 235
ASK 238
BabagaNewz 238
Boys' Quest 239
Brilliant Star 240
Cadet Quest 240
Careers and Colleges 242
Faces 248
Friend Magazine, The 248
Fun for Kidz 249
Guide Magazine 249
Hopscotch 251
Horsepower 252
Humpty Dumpty's Magazine 252
Insight 253
Jack and Jill 253
Ladybug 257
New Moon 258
Nick Jr. Family Magazine 259
Ranger Rick 262
Read 262
Read America 262
Seventeen Magazine 263
Skipping Stones 264
TC Magazine (Teenage Christian) 266
U*S* Kids 267

Interview/Profile
Advocate, PKA's Publication 235
AIM Magazine 236
American Cheerleader 236

American Girl 236
Aquila 237
ASK 238
BabagaNewz 238
Boys' Life 238
Cadet Quest 240
Career World 242
Careers and Colleges 242
Dramatics Magazine 247
Faces 248
Girls' Life 249
Guideposts Sweet 16 250
Highlights for Children 250
Horsepower 252
Insight 253
Jack and Jill 253
Kids Hall of Fame News, The 257
Muse 258
National Geographic Kids 258
New Moon 258
On Course 260
Passport 260
Positive Teens 261
Rainbow Rumpus 261
Seventeen Magazine 263
Skipping Stones 264
Sparkle 264
TC Magazine (Teenage Christian) 266
Teen Magazine 266
U*S* Kids 267
Winner 267

Math
Aquila 237
ASK 238
Boys' Quest 239
Hopscotch 251
Ladybug 257
Muse 258
New Moon 258
Nick Jr. Family Magazine 259
Science Weekly 263
Sparkle 264
Spider 265
YES Mag 268

Photography Index

This index lists markets that buy photos from freelancers and is divided into Book Publishers and Magazines. It's important to carefully read the listings and follow the guidelines of each publisher to which you submit.

MAGAZINES

General Index

Market listings that appeared in the 2007 edition of *Children's Writer's & Illustrator's Market* but do not appear in this edition are identified with a two-letter code explaining why the listing was omitted: **(NR)**—no response to our requests for updated information; **(RR)**—removed by request; **(UC)**—unable to contact; **(OB)**—out of business; **(ED)**—editorial decision.